Endorsements for *Sustainable Management: A Complete Guide for Faculty and Students* (3rd edition)

This book is an authoritative introduction into sustainable management. Petra Molthan-Hill has put together thought leaders that will inspire future generations of students. It is a great contribution to advance the educational agenda on sustainability.

Dr Dirk Matten, Professor of Sustainability, Hewlett-Packard Chair in Corporate Social Responsibility, Schulich School of Business, York University, Toronto, Canada

A road map for integrating SDGs into the management curricula. . . . The best part of this new edition of *Sustainable Management: A Complete Guide for Faculty and Students* is twofold. First, it has wider coverage from accounting to human resources to corporate strategy, and second, it has included a new chapter on climate change education (CCE). The book is designed in a way to enable faculty to use the learning resources shared in the book and inspire young minds. Thank you, Petra, for guiding us towards responsible management education.

Dr Divya Singhal, Professor and Chairperson, Centre for Social Sensitivity and Action, Goa Institute of Management, Goa, India

This third edition of the *Sustainable Management: A Complete Guide for Faculty and Students* continues to be a readily accessible, enlightened, and pragmatic introduction to the responsibilities that business and management students, along with their educators, have for creating a more humane, prosperous, and equitable world. It does this by giving readers an integrated toolkit of concepts and perspectives so that progress can be made on some of the most daunting challenges the world faces: climate change, poverty eradication, peacemaking, and how to embrace a low-carbon future.

Dr Al Rosenbloom, Co-Chair, PRME Anti-Poverty Working Group, and Professor Emeritus, Marketing and International Business, Dominican University, River Forest, IL, USA

The third edition of *Sustainable Management: A Complete Guide for Faculty and Students* should be required reading for all business school students and faculty as well as current business leaders. The clock is ticking ever closer to 2030, with most of the 17 SDGs of Agenda 2030 not yet achieved. The diversity of materials provided in this handbook should appeal to all lifelong learners and guide future decision-making by businesses and HEIs alike.

Dr Ellen E. Touchstone, MBA, PhD, FHEA, Inaugural Associate Dean, Responsible and Sustainable Business Education, and President, RCE Suzhou (Regional Center of Expertise in Education for Sustainable Development), International Business School Suzhou, at XJTLU, China

Among many other outstanding characteristics of this publication, what impressed me the most was the collection of contributors: some of the most experienced and knowledgeable academics and practitioners worldwide!

Dr Oliver Laasch, Chaired Professor of Responsible Management at ESCP Berlin, Germany, and Author of *Principles of Management: Practicing Ethics, Responsibility, Sustainability*

Building on the impact of the first and second edition of **The Business Student's Guide to Sustainable Management**, this revised handbook is an invaluable resource for students and educators alike. It includes a wide array of learning resources – overview essays, case examples, curricular supplements (film and print), reference lists, instructional guides available to faculty – to empower the business practitioner who recognises the necessity for, and the opportunities of, sustainable management.

Dr Mary C. Gentile, PhD, Creator/Director of Giving Voice to Values, and formerly the Richard M. Waitzer Bicentennial Professor of Ethics, University of Virginia Darden School of Business, USA www.GivingVoiceToValuesTheBook.com and www.GivingVoiceToValues.org

We have reached a tipping point in human history in which our past and current behaviours have upset the delicate balance of a fragile world, and we are likely to bring about our own demise unless we change what we are doing. But changing what we are doing is fundamentally dependent on our ability to discover, learn, and act upon the ecological principles on which all life depends. Education is the only social technology we have to change how whole societies think and act, and this book, with sustainability as its core pedagogical value and abundant practical pedagogical advice, shows how we can educate for a more sustainable and regenerative future. Such education is no longer an add-on but a necessary foundation to which all other subjects must connect.

Dr Norman Jackson, Emeritus Professor at the University of Surrey, UK and Founder of Lifewide Education https://www.lifewideeducation.uk/, which supports lifelong, lifewide, and ecological approaches to learning and education for sustainable regenerative futures

Sustainable Management: A Complete Guide for Faculty and Students is a comprehensive handbook that strongly contributes to the current challenge of higher management education worldwide: the integration of sustainability issues into management education.

All major business disciplines are covered, allowing the reader to learn about current sustainability-related challenges in a business context, through definitions and key concepts. Most importantly, it provides the reader with advice, supporting frameworks, examples of pedagogical activities, as well as further readings.

This guide should be put in the hands of all faculty, practitioners, and management teams of business schools as it offers a method and concrete examples of how to integrate sustainability issues into the whole curriculum and, consequently, into business practices.

Evelyne Gross, International Accreditations and Sustainability Expert, Valorisation and Transfer Committee Co-Coordinator of COLIFRI France (Franco-Colombian Association of Researchers), Sulitest Task Force Member, PRME Working Group on Climate Change and Environment Member

The purpose of education must always lie within the realm of implementation. This is more relevant for climate-related learnings now than ever before. Uncomplicating concepts and developing capability of professionals across the spectrum, from students to professionals, is imperative. This book provides sound, practical, and implementable perspectives that are essential. The content carries depth and is well organised to simplify learning for all, starting from educators and students to practitioners. Highly recommended as a guide for students, educators, and professionals.

Capt. Tapas Majumdar (Rets.), Founder Director, The Sustainability Practitioners, Member Board of Studies (BOS), Visiting Professor of Corporate Governance and Corporate Sustainability, India, Independent Director www.thesustainabilitypractitioners.com

Disruptions in global supply chains, the energy crisis, geopolitical threats, climate change, and loss of biodiversity are posing completely new challenges for companies. Sustainable leaders are needed and must be educated. This book covers all areas of a supply chain, making it an excellent resource for professors to provide this much-needed knowledge. Each chapter covers the necessary theoretical basics, followed by concrete practical applications, additional resources, as well as interactive games and activities to reinforce what has been learned so far. A really great textbook that every university that has placed the field of sustainable management at the centre of its teaching and research activities should make use of.

Prof. Dr habil. Lisa Fröhlich, Professor of Strategic Supply Management, CBS International Business School, Germany, and Board Member, PRME

The chapter on stakeholder engagement and corporate peacemaking offers an essential introduction to the role of business in enhancing multi-dimensional peace. The exercises included in the chapter help the reader to concretely understand what that looks like in practice, which is vital to moving responsible business engagement in fragile and conflict-affected situations forward.

Dr Christina Bache, Chair, United Nations Principles for Responsible Management Education (PRME) Working Group on Business for Peace

The chapter on linking sustainability to graduates' employability makes an important and timely contribution. What is particularly valuable is their introduction to the 'sustainability competency matrix' and how this can be used to help students develop their sustainability awareness and employability. They also helpfully provide examples of a wide range of activities and interventions at Nottingham Trent University that enable students to gain their 'sustainability employability award'.

Dr Peter Sewell, CPsychol, former Postgraduate Careers Manager at Lancaster University Management School, UK and Co-Creator of the CareerEDGE model of graduate employability

This book is a valuable tool for developing sustainability literacy across all business disciplines. The book includes reference to global sustainability initiatives of the United Nations that are incorporated into each chapter: the Global Compact, Principles for Responsible Management Education (PRME), and the Sustainable Development Goals (SDG). Instructors will find this book useful for its teaching suggestions, activities, ready-made stand-alone teaching sessions, and integration with core business disciplines. Learners will find this book useful for its focus on how sustainability applies to their business major area of study and for the opportunity to adopt personal sustainability behaviours. Administrators will find this book useful for its guidance on integrating sustainability across the business school curriculum. Whether for faculty or student, *Sustainable Management: A Complete Guide for Faculty and Students* will provide a strong foundation to move forward on your sustainability journey.

Nancy E. Landrum, PhD, Sustainability Training Institute, Germany

The release of the third edition of *Sustainable Management: A Complete Guide for Faculty and Students* could not have come at a better time, as educators in business and management schools around the world intensify their efforts to contribute to the United Nations 'Decade of Action' and move beyond provision of individual modules and courses on sustainability to integration of sustainability and the UN sustainable development goals into all subjects in the business school curriculum. With this text, Petra Molthan-Hill and her impressive team of contributors are doing the business community a great favour by providing innovative practitioner-centric examples of how to integrate sustainability into a wide range of subjects, using engaging, student-led pedagogies. The step-by-step instructional guides that come with mini-cases, links to short videos, suggested reading, and assignments are ready to use as they are, or to adapt, and will shorten the time it takes to introduce sustainability-oriented pedagogic innovation into multiple learning environments. As accreditation bodies such as AACSB, EFMD, AMBA, and CEEMAN and business school rankings such as the Times Higher Education (THE) social impact rankings put increasing emphasis on integration of sustainability into the curriculum, business school deans might consider making this book freely available to faculty in every discipline.

Alec Wersun, Lead Author of the PRME Blueprint for Integration of the SDGs into the Curriculum, Research, and Partnerships, Glasgow School for Business and Society, GCU, UK, and Member of the PRME Global Chapter Council

Sustainable management is becoming increasingly important for our teaching. That is why *"The Business Student's Guide to Sustainable Management (2nd edition)"* also inspires our teaching in strategic management. We successfully use the approaches and recommendations, for example, on how to develop sustainably responsible strategies in our lectures. Students analyse and discuss the text and apply the methods on own selected cases.

Prof. Dr. Kerstin Pichl, Deputy Head of Institute for Organizational Viability, School of Management and Law at Zurich University of Applied Sciences (ZHAW), Winterthur, Switzerland

SUSTAINABLE MANAGEMENT

Sustainable Management: A Complete Guide for Faculty and Students is both a textbook for students, as well as a teaching guide for educators. With a full introduction to sustainable management, the book covers a wide range of subject areas relevant to business and management students. It enables faculty to incorporate sustainability and climate solutions into their modules, and is also very accessible for self-directed studies.

This third edition features fully updated chapters on how to integrate the Sustainable Development Goals into key disciplines in business, including economics, operations, marketing, HR, strategy, and financial reporting. We also cover topics such as corporate peacemaking, greenhouse gas management and crowdsourcing. The book offers a new chapter on integrating climate solutions and climate change mitigation education into business and management schools, as well as many ideas in each chapter on how to do so. The chapter on employability and sustainability was fully redesigned adding new resources, which can be used in any educational establishment.

Educators in business schools and trainers in organisations will find short readymade seminars/sessions/workshops and a wide array of learning resources supported by a companion website.

Dr Petra Molthan-Hill, PhD, is Professor of sustainable management and education for sustainable development at Nottingham Business School, Nottingham Trent University (NTU), UK, and Co-Chair of the United Nations Principles for

Responsible Management Education (PRME) working group on climate change and environment. Molthan-Hill is an international multi-award-winning expert for climate change mitigation tools and education, and leads the 'Climate Literacy Training for Educators, Communities, Organisations and Students' (CLT-ECOS) distributed worldwide. She is the editor of two earlier editions of *The Business Student's Guide to Sustainable Management* and of *Storytelling for Sustainability in Higher Education: An Educator's Handbook,* and lead author of *The Handbook of Carbon Management: A step-by-step guide to high-impact climate solutions for every manager in every function.* She co-created NTU's 'Future Thinking' framework in 2016, which includes reference to the global Sustainable Development Goals (SDGs), and supported colleagues in all faculties to integrate the SDGs as Lead of NTU's Green Academy until 2021. Among others, she won gold in the QS Reimagine Education Awards in Sustainability (CLT-ECOS) in 2021, 'The Guardian University Award 2015 for Business Partnership' (Greenhouse Gas Management Project) together with NetPositive, and the Green Gown Award in the Sustainability Professional Award Category in 2016.

The Principles for Responsible Management Education Series

Since the inception of the UN-supported Principles for Responsible Management Education (PRME) in 2007, there has been increased debate over how to adapt management education to best meet the demands of the 21st-century business environment. While consensus has been reached by the majority of globally focused management education institutions that sustainability must be incorporated into management education curricula, the relevant question is no longer why management education should change, but how.

Volumes within the Routledge/PRME book series aim to cultivate and inspire actively engaged participants by offering practical examples and case studies to support the implementation of the Six Principles of Responsible Management Education. Books in the series aim to enable participants to transition from a global learning community to an action community.

Books in the series:

Integrating Gender Equality into Business and Management Education: Lessons Learned and Challenges Remaining
Edited by Patricia M. Flynn, Kathryn Haynes and Maureen A. Kilgour

Responsible Management Education and the Challenge of Poverty:
A Teaching Perspective
Edited by Milenko Gudić, Carole Parkes and Al Rosenbloom

Indigenous Aspirations and Rights: The Case for Responsible Business and Management
Edited by Amy Klemm Verbos, Ella Henry and Ana Maria Peredo

The Future MBA: 100 Ideas for Making Sustainability the Business of Business Education
By Giselle Weybrecht

Socially Responsive Organizations & the Challenge of Poverty
Edited by Milenko Gudić, Al Rosenbloom and Carole Parkes

Responsible Business: The Textbook for Management Learning, Competence and Innovation
By Oliver Laasch and Roger Conaway

Overcoming Challenges to Gender Equality in the Workplace: Leadership and Innovation
Edited by Patricia M. Flynn, Kathryn Haynes and Maureen A. Kilgour

Learning to Read the Signs: Reclaiming Pragmatism for the Practice of Sustainable Management, 2nd Edition
By F. Byron (Ron) Nahser

Inspirational Guide for the Implementation of PRME: Placing Sustainability at the Heart of Management Education
Edited by the Principles for Responsible Management Education Community

Anti-Corruption: Implementing Curriculum Change in Management Education
By Wolfgang Amann, Ronald Berenbeim, Tay Keong Tan, Matthias Kleinhempel, Alfred Lewis, Ruth Nieffer, Agata Stachowicz-Stanusch and Shiv Tripathi

Inspirational Guide for the Implementation of PRME: Learning to Go Beyond, Third Edition
Edited by Alan Murray, Denise Baden, Paul Cashian, Alec Wersun and Kathryn Haynes

Redefining Success: Integrating Sustainability into Management Education
Edited by Patricia M. Flynn, Tay Keong Tan and Milenko Gudić

The Business Student's Guide to Sustainable Management: Principles and Practice, Second Edition
Edited by Petra Molthan-Hill

Educating for Responsible Management: Putting Theory into Practice
Edited by Roz Sunley and Jennifer Leigh

Developing a Sustainability Mindset in Management Education
Edited by Kerul Kassel and Isabel Rimanoczy

Unmasking Irresponsible Leadership: Curriculum Development in 21st Century Management Education
By Lola-Peach Martins and Maria Lazzarin

Global Champions of Sustainable Development
Edited by Patricia M. Flynn, Milenko Gudić and Tay Keong Tan

Struggles and Successes in the Pursuit of Sustainable Development
Edited by Tay Keong Tan, Milenko Gudić and Patricia M. Flynn

The Sustainability Mindset Principles: A Guide to Develop a Mindset for a Better World
Isabel Rimanoczy

Business Transformation for a Sustainable Future
Edited by Samuel Petros Sebhatu, Bo Enquist and Bo Edvardsson

Responsible Management Education: The PRME Global Movement
Edited by the Principles for Responsible Management Education Community

Revolutionizing Sustainability Education: Stories and Tools of Mindset Transformation
Edited by Ekaterina Ivanova and Isabel Rimanoczy

Principles of Sustainable Business: Frameworks for Corporate Action on the SDGs
Edited by Rob van Tulder and Eveline van Mil

Sustainable Management: A Complete Guide for Faculty and Students, Third Edition
Edited by Petra Molthan-Hill

SUSTAINABLE MANAGEMENT

A Complete Guide
for Faculty and Students

Third Edition

Edited by **Petra Molthan-Hill**

Routledge
Taylor & Francis Group

LONDON AND NEW YORK

Designed cover image: ©Clerkenwell

Third edition published 2023
by Routledge
4 Park Square, Milton Park, Abingdon, Oxon, OX14 4RN

and by Routledge
605 Third Avenue, New York, NY 10158

Routledge is an imprint of the Taylor & Francis Group, an informa business

First edition published by Routledge 2014
Second edition published by Routledge 2017

British Library Cataloguing-in-Publication Data
  A catalogue record for this book is available from the British Library

    ISBN: 978-1-032-27920-6 (hbk)
    ISBN: 978-1-032-25375-6 (pbk)
    ISBN: 978-1-003-29466-5 (ebk)

DOI: 10.4324/9781003294665

Typeset in Goudy
by Apex CoVantage, LLC

We do not inherit the Earth from our ancestors; we borrow it from our children.

– Anon.

In a finite world you cannot have infinite desires,
Money really does grow on trees!
Though we are tethered to the Earth from death to birth
We can fill the universe with our hopes and dreams.

– Jerome Baddley

Sustainability is about protecting our options. This requires a new economic paradigm that allows humans to live and work in ways that can be maintained for decades and generations without depleting or causing harm to our environmental, social and economic resources.

– Bob Doppelt, Leading Change toward
Sustainability, 2nd ed. (Sheffield, UK:
Greenleaf Publishing, 2010), p 40

Contents

Embedding sustainability into core subjects

Adding core topics to the curriculum

Bringing it all together

Foreword

Dr. Mette Morsing

During the past few years, the global world has realised the importance of responsible management and leadership that makes business decisions with regards to their societal impact. In the wake of a global pandemic, rising inequalities, and environmental disasters, it has become increasingly clear that leaders with ethical and innovative approaches are in urgent demand. Climate change and humanitarian catastrophes have surfaced 'wicked problems' where no predefined methods are offered and where novel innovative solutions, curiosity, and critical-constructive problem resolution is deeply in demand.

UN Secretary-General António Guterres is calling upon business leaders to help set the world on track. The world's problems cannot be managed by governments alone, and the UN is enabling its convening power to make important organisations come together and collectively rethink and re-invest in societal betterment for the world. The Sustainable Development Goals is one major successful outcome of a multi-stakeholder effort convened by the UN where governments, businesses, and civil society organisations collectively agreed on emphasising these 17 goals for future efforts to improve planetary and social conditions for humanity.

One of the most important organisations in contemporary society is 'the business'. Businesses and their leaders hold the expertise, the executive capacity, and the resources to address the global challenges. Imagine a world where business leaders will, by default, take into account the positive societal impact of all their decisions. This could dramatically transform the world and make it likely that we will reach the SDGs in 2030.

The business school has a central role to play to support such global transformation. According to UNESCO, one in four students every year who is granted a degree in the world has a degree from business, economics, law, and management. This means that business (and law) schools graduate 70 million students each year who are potentially the future business leaders, making decisions for business conduct. This is a huge responsibility for business (and law) schools. According to Harvard Professors Rakesh Khurana and Daniel Penrice,[1] business schools have one of the most important tasks in the world in ensuring that future managers are educated to be more than 'mere craftsmen'. Khurana and Penrice encourage the business school and its students to challenge the corporate-centric short-termism economic profit and the best possible salary as the ultimate goal. This is what the Humboldtian ideal of university education has formulated as a responsibility for 'Bildung' (i.e. technical skills) as well as 'Ausbildung' (i.e. citizen skills, such as how to engage with democratic societies).

Sustainable Management: A Complete Guide for Faculty and Students is a book with exactly that ambition. The book provides an essential introduction to business school students on how to integrate the Sustainable Development Goals into practical business decisions. It offers insights into the complexity when established disciplines are confronted with the quest to address the SDGs, and what I really appreciate about this book is how Petra Molthan-Hill as the editor has invited an excellent group of expert scholars to provide their expert experience on the topic and the sub-discipline while giving concrete, valuable insights and approaches and frameworks to make future business leaders understand how they can become those change agents that the world needs.

Dr Mette Morsing
Head of PRME, UN Global Compact, New York

Note

1   Khurana, R. and Penrice, D. (2010). Business Education: The American Trajectory. In: Morsing, M. and Rovira, A.S. (Eds) *Business Schools and their Contribution to Society*. London: Sage.

SETTING
THE SCENE

INTRODUCTION

1

The structure and purpose of this book

Petra Molthan-Hill

Sustainability issues are relevant to all organisations of all sizes and in all sectors. Increasingly, organisations themselves are demanding sustainability literacy skills for a wide range of roles and responsibilities. If learners can gain these skills, they are therefore improving both their own employability as well as their ability to contribute to making their future workplace and society more sustainable. Yet despite this, and an ever-growing emphasis on employability within the education sector, there are currently few examples of sustainability literacy being addressed across the curriculum in mainstream education.

(Robinson, 2009: 130)

An understanding of 'responsible leadership' will incorporate authentic, values-driven, inclusive, ethical, sustainable, systemic and transformative leadership which considers the interests and perspectives of different stakeholders, both now and for the future, while focusing on addressing climate change and other key challenges, for example, leading towards net zero in fair and inclusive ways.

(QAA, 2023: 4)

DOI: 10.4324/9781003294665-3

The first quote from Robinson (2009) is still valid as we are writing the third edition in 2022/2023. While there have been advancements worldwide in mainstreaming the Sustainable Development Goals (SDGs) into the curricula of business schools, we are far from their full integration. The vision in the previous editions of our book that we could make sustainable management and responsible leadership the focus and centre of our curricula in business schools and beyond is shared in the new QAA (2023: 7) benchmark statement for Business and Management, the source of the QAA quote above. In this context, the third edition of this book is again supporting lecturers, and anyone responsible for learning and teaching in a business school, on this journey to integrating sustainable management into every discipline.

This book is written for undergraduates who are studying for a business or management degree and want to know the part played by **sustainability in the specific subjects they are studying (e.g. marketing)**. It is also a **textbook for faculty and educators wishing to embed sustainability into their subjects**. Furthermore, a business school aiming to embed sustainability across its curriculum will find lots of inspiration for each subject, and in the next chapter, there is an overview of how to do it systematically. In the previous second edition of this book, we added guidance and updated this guidance further in the third edition on how to address three key frameworks from the United Nations, the Principles for Responsible Management Education (PRME 2022), the Sustainable Development Goals (Sustainable Development Goals 2022), and the Principles of Global Compact (2022), in the curriculum. The third edition also has an additional focus on how climate solutions can be addressed in every discipline. This ties in with the QAA (2023: 7) benchmark statement for Business and Management, which states

> [s]ustainable management is a requirement for planetary survival. ...
> It is therefore imperative that the future managers and business leaders are equipped to engage meaningfully with, and respond to, climate challenges in order to embed climate solutions in all business functions and processes.

Each chapter has therefore been rewritten with this aim in mind; additionally, we have added a chapter on **climate change education (CCE)**. This new chapter provides the business school community with (1) an overview of the CCE's three dimensions – science, mitigation, and adaptation – and (2) many examples from several disciplines and support on how to integrate CCE into teaching and assessment. Another update in the third edition is a newly designed chapter about employability, and a companion website, where you can find templates, quizzes, and other supporting materials.

The book covers **all the main subjects** taught in a business or management degree, from accounting to human resources to corporate strategy. It can be used in two different ways: either by selecting a chapter in one subject area, such as economics or operations, and adding it to an existing 'conventional' module, usually towards the end of the first year or whenever students have been introduced to the subject in question, or by using the whole book as a textbook for a core module or a final-year elective in order to include the sustainability dimension in all subjects of management studied up to that point. For this purpose, the book offers 45 ready-made teaching and learning sessions, three for each subject, or enough to cover a year-long module on sustainability in business.

As a student, you can also choose to read the matching chapters after you have finished your core modules or in order to find inspiration for a research project or your assessments. You might also decide to read it in your final year of study to fill the gaps and to increase your employability, or just because you want to be a responsible manager in the future. Whatever the approach is, it is important that you, as a student, have a basic understanding of the discipline, such as operations management, before you can make use of the sessions included in this book. So, you might want to read this book in addition to the core texts in your modules. If educators want to integrate more than the three fully developed sessions suggested per subject, there are, on average, five additional teaching ideas provided in each chapter to enrich their teaching. If you, as a student, want to learn more about sustainability in relation to your discipline, you will also find further readings in each chapter, interesting movies, TED Talks, and so on. Special attention has been given to offer a variety of teaching methods, from role-play to case studies to artwork.

Chapters 7–18 are divided into five parts:

- **Chapter brief:** this outlines the learning outcomes and content of the chapter.

- **Core text:** here you will find an introduction to the key definitions and concepts to be studied in the subject concerned, which are later applied in the sessions.

- **Three fully developed sessions (for sessions of approximately 50–60 minutes):** each of these sessions is ready to be delivered without further preparation required by the educator. They can also be studied independently by you as a student. We recommend, however, that they be used in a group, as an exchange of ideas and understanding would be beneficial. Most sessions can be broken down into different exercises so that shorter activities can also be chosen. The three sessions in any one subject area mostly use different learning methods, for example, an artwork, a game, or a case study.

- **Additional teaching/learning materials and ideas:** this section in each chapter offers short summaries of additional ideas for teaching/self-study, such as movies or websites. Most of them are designed for additional sessions of about 60 minutes in length, but some larger activities are also suggested, such as consultancy projects, which could cover a whole term/module. As an educator, you will also find here ideas on how to address principles 5 and 6 of PRME (for further information about the PRME principles, please see Chapter 6).

- **Further readings:** here you will find, on average, five recommendations for deepening your knowledge in this area. Each book or article recommended is summarised in a short paragraph outlining the key benefits for the reader.

- **Companion website:** this website offers further guidance for educators on how to embed sustainable management into their discipline, as well as additional teaching material, suggestions for assessment, and pedagogical advice on how to use the material offered in this book. Students can also find quizzes to test themselves against the learning outcomes of each chapter.

Overview of the book

In **Chapter 2**, some of the **key concepts** used in this book and in sustainable management are briefly introduced. As the QAA (2023: 7) benchmark statement for Business and Management stresses '[m]anagement for economic, social and environmental sustainability needs to be integrated systematically within the Business and Management curriculum and across functional areas'. Guidance and a **framework for how to do this** are therefore offered. Anyone tasked with embedding sustainability into the curriculum of a business school will therefore find ideas about the various approaches they can take, and how they can be combined. In the second edition, we added content from Carole Parkes, then Chair of the PRME Chapter UK and Ireland, who offered inspiration on how to adopt PRME as a business school. In this third edition, we have added a new self-guided activity for teaching staff on how to make a sustainability and climate action plan for their own teaching.

In **Chapter 3**, new in this third edition, we have focused on how **climate change mitigation education** and climate solutions can be embedded into every discipline, as also recommended by the QAA (2023: 7). With the help of two fictional characters, we run you through the thought processes of two individuals, one at the beginning of their career in a faculty role, one in a more strategic administrative position. Integrated into this chapter is more generic information, for example, the importance that accreditation bodies such as AACSB now place on sustainability or theoretical models underpinning learning and assessment, and how they could be used to shape the integration of climate-related teaching and assessment. This information is useful for the incorporation of any sustainability-related topic, such as the SDGs, and could be read in conjunction with Chapter 2 or any of the other chapters. Chapter 3 also ends with a self-guided activity, in this case, how to design a teaching unit with assessment.

Chapter 4 then turns to how **sustainability links to employability**, and it explores why being literate in sustainability and climate change is imperative for all business students. It seeks to demonstrate how this links to graduates' employability, taking in turn the perspective of students, businesses, and employers. The similarities between 'sustainability competences' and those routinely sought by graduate employers are explored, and from this analysis, a sustainability competency matrix is created. Guidance is provided on how to use the matrix, either independently or within a module or course, to support analysis, reflection, and career management.

The focus throughout is that employability should be viewed as lifelong and lifewide (Lifewide Education, 2022) and not just about skills development. The matrix can be tailored to suit local circumstances, and students are encouraged to undertake such analysis and reflection regularly. We also explore how engagement in sustainability-related extra-curricular activities can be encouraged, and provide an example of how Nottingham Trent University rewards its students who develop their sustainability literacy, through its **Sustainability Employability Award**.

It should be stressed that the focus of the chapter is not just on 'green jobs', as it is clear there is potential to view all roles and tasks through a sustainability lens. Having such literacy, therefore, not only potentially enhances a student's own profile, but can also add value to any role they perform (whether as a volunteer, an employee, a manager, or an entrepreneur).

The definition of *sustainable management* we have chosen to use throughout this book is based on the **triple bottom line** as conceptualised by Elkington (1997). He suggested a focus on **people, planet, and profit**, in that order of importance. These three dimensions are now commonly used in sustainable management and are often referred to as the social, environmental, and economic dimensions of sustainable management. **Chapter 5** is dedicated to the exploration of this concept, discussing each dimension in turn, and addressing the question of how these three dimensions of sustainability – social, environmental, and economic – can be balanced.

In **Chapter 6** the different initiatives of the United Nations in relation to business are introduced: **Global Compact, PRME, and the Sustainable Development Goals**. As every chapter refers to these initiatives, you might find it useful to read this chapter in addition to the disciplines in which you are specifically interested.

In the following chapters, the core subjects taught in a business or management course for undergraduates are covered and suggestions are made as to how sustainable management can be taught in **accounting, economics, human resources, marketing, innovation, operations, and supply chain management**, as well as **business models**.

In addition, two further topics have been chosen which could form part of a year-long module/course or could be added to an existing module. Both are considered by the editor to be two of the major sustainability challenges that are faced today. One relates to the area of environmental sustainability: **greenhouse gas management (Chapter 15)**. The other relates to the area of social sustainability: **corporate peacemaking (Chapter 16)**.

The two final chapters bring all the previous topics together. **Chapter 17** is dedicated to **systems thinking**. Here, the main questions are how future managers can handle a complex system, such as an organisation/business, and how to link together all the separate subjects introduced previously. **The final chapter** offers a framework on how sustainably-responsible strategies can be designed into the overall **corporate strategy**.

All chapters in this book offer ideas on how to implement the **six principles of PRME** in a business school context. You will find in Chapter 6 more information about each principle, its background and application. Some projects described in this book are especially suitable for addressing principles 5 and 6 of PRME, and they can be found in the additional teaching ideas in each chapter. We have also introduced the various **PRME working groups, Global Compact, and/or the Global Reporting Initiative (2022)** in different chapters.

The **Sustainable Development Goals (SDGs)** are also integrated into every chapter of this book. You will find three introductory sessions about all the SDGs in Chapter 5 (third session) and Chapter 6 (first and second sessions); you can use these sessions as a starting point in any of the disciplines. References to individual goals, such as SDG 1, 'No Poverty,' or SDG 12, 'Responsible Consumption and Production,' are made throughout the book.

All chapters in this third edition have undergone a major revision to include the SDGs, again with a special focus on **SDG 13 ('Climate Action')**, but also to update the content generally. Some authors have designed new sessions and added new teaching/learning material for this specific edition.

We hope that this book, and the chapters it contains, will inspire many to contribute further towards a more sustainable future and inspire others to do the same.

References

Elkington, J. (1997): *Cannibals with Forks: The Triple Bottom Line of 21st Century Business* (Oxford, UK: Capstone Publishing)

Global Compact (2022): www.unglobalcompact.org/

Global Reporting Initiative (2022): www.globalreporting.org/about-gri/

Lifewide Education (2022): www.lifewideeducation.uk/

PRME (2022): United Nation Principles for Responsible Management Education. www.unprme.org/

QAA (2023): Benchmark Statement for Business and Management. https://www.qaa.ac.uk/the-quality-code/subject-benchmark-statements/subject-benchmark-statement-business-and-management

Robinson, Z. (2009): 'Greening Business: The Ability to Drive Environmental and Sustainability Improvements in the Workplace', in A. Stibbe (ed.), *The Handbook of Sustainability Literacy: Skills for a Changing World* (Totnes, UK: Green Books): 130–6

Sustainable Development Goals (2022): https://sustainabledevelopment.un.org/sdgs

2

A new framework for embedding sustainability into the business school curriculum

Petra Molthan-Hill, Carole Parkes, and Rajul Singh

In this chapter, some of the **key concepts** used in this book and in sustainable management are briefly introduced. Students might find it useful if they want to understand some of the underlying concepts or deepen their knowledge. However, this chapter is mainly written for business and management schools as **guidance and a framework on how to embed sustainability into management/ business education**. Thus, the chapter sets out strategies and processes for embedding sustainability into the curriculum of a business school with ideas about the various approaches they can take and how it can be all combined together. The following questions will be addressed:

1. What structural approaches can be taken by business schools to embed sustainability into the curriculum? (More a question of *how* it is taught rather than *what* is taught.)

2. What should be taught/studied? What have been identified as core skills and knowledge in sustainable management?

DOI: 10.4324/9781003294665-4

3. What approaches can be used in developing strategies for both structural and process change at school and curricula level?

To address these questions, conceptual frameworks, including the **UN-backed Principles for Responsible Management Education (PRME) Transformational Model** for embedding sustainability and responsible management into the business and management curriculum, are discussed. These frameworks can be used to assess the current status of how well sustainability is embedded in a business school and how it could be developed further.

Embedding sustainability in the structure of a business school

The first question to be addressed is how sustainability can be embedded in the structure of a business school. Godemann *et al.* (2011b) developed a matrix to distinguish between the different approaches adopted by business schools (see Table 2.1).

In the first quadrant, the '**piggyback**' approach, the business school will add some sustainability-related material to an existing module, such as a case study

Table 2.1: Matrix to illustrate integration of sustainability

	Existing structures	**New structures**
Narrow curricular	*Quadrant 1* Piggyback Integration of sustainability within existing structures by adding sustainability to individual sessions of courses or modules	*Quadrant 2* Digging deep Integration of sustainability through new, stand-alone modules
Broad curricular	*Quadrant 3* Mainstreaming Integration of sustainability within existing structures, but with the emphasis on a broader cross-curricular perspective (entire curriculum)	*Quadrant 4* Focusing Integration of sustainability through new, cross-disciplinary offerings, such as sustainability-related courses, which are required for all business school students and new programmes

Source: Adapted from Godemann *et al.* (2011a), based on Rusinko (2010).

with a sustainable focus, a framework used in sustainable management, such as the life cycle assessment (see Chapter 12), or some suggestions for further readings. The material in this book can be used for such a 'piggyback' approach, as lecturers/ business schools can choose to add one or more of the suggested sessions to an existing module. However, in the long term, it would be better to embed sustainability throughout each module so that related concepts can be integrated where they belong in the 'core teaching'. For this purpose, the following chapters of this book offer additional teaching material and further readings.

The next approach, '**digging deep**', is also an easy way to implement sustainability, as it is normally easier to offer a new elective/option than to change the existing curriculum. The content in this book can be used in this way so that business schools can offer a 'sustainable management' option in addition to their existing portfolio. Or business schools can choose to offer, for example, a module on 'greenhouse gas management' using the material in Chapter 15 so that some students are 'digging deep' in this area and developing a special expertise that will help them in the jobs market.

As Brad Smith (Vice Chair and President of Microsoft) points out in his foreword to 'Closing the Sustainability Skills Gap: Helping businesses move from pledges to progress' (2022):

> Just as governments, NGOs and companies have worked to bring digital skilling and computer science into schools, we will need similar partnerships to bring sustainability fluency and science into primary and secondary schools. And higher education institutions will need to strengthen and expand their undergraduate and graduate sustainability programs.

Even though this approach has its benefits, students may still not choose this option and therefore will not develop sustainability literacy, a skill set each student should acquire, as shown in the following.

The preferred approach for the application of this book is the third approach, '**mainstreaming**'. Each core subject would add the appropriate sections of this book to its teaching so the sessions on sustainable marketing would be integrated into the marketing module, the one on environmental economics into the economics module, and so on. It is important that this mainstreaming approach be coordinated. For example, it would not be good for the 'triple bottom line' to be introduced several times, once in accounting, once in human resources, and so on. It might be beneficial, therefore, to have some general introductions to sustainability (our Chapters 4, 5, 6, and 17) at the beginning of the first year and then build on these in the following core modules. Some aspects of the sustainability literacy approach (Stibbe, 2009) and/or climate literacy could be included in this general introduction (more on this later).

The fourth quadrant, '**focusing**', also addresses the broad curriculum but requires new structures to be established. An example could be an online course offered to students from all disciplines, introducing them to the main principles of sustainability as applied to different disciplines, such as law, business, science, or psychology. At Nottingham Trent University we have been offering such a 'Sustainability in Practice' certificate in each academic year since 2013 (Molthan-Hill *et al.*, 2016; Dharmasasmita *et al.*, 2017; Willats *et al.*, 2018), first with a focus on sustainability and food; now we have three versions on offer: energy, clothing, and food. The same matrix has been applied to climate change education (Molthan-Hill *et al.*, 2019); in this chapter, several examples for each approach, such as 'piggybacking', have been given, which might inspire readers to do the same.

A new framework for embedding sustainability into the business school curriculum

Although the Godemann *et al.* (2011b) matrix is helpful for making decisions on *how* sustainability can be integrated into the curriculum, it is less so on *what* should be taught. Sustainability-related teaching **content** needs to differentiate further between general sustainability knowledge (such as climate change), specific sustainability action strategies in business (subject-specific knowledge), and sustainability literacy skills, which are transferable and competency-based.

These different categories have therefore been integrated into a new framework, shown in Table 2.2, suggesting how to embed different aspects of sustainability into the curriculum, how it could be taught, and what could/should be taught. These new dimensions are explained further in the remaining parts of this chapter.

Sustainability-related knowledge

According to Bodenstein *et al.*'s (1997) study about the relationship between environmental knowledge and consumer decisions, a good lexical environmental knowledge merely indicates a consumer's educational background (particularly in science subjects). Instead, they insisted that students/consumers need to have action-specific knowledge.

In another study about climate change, Kempton *et al.* (1996) illustrate clearly how important specific knowledge about appropriate alternative actions appears to be needed for environmentally friendly behaviour. In the study, interviewees were linking global warming to ozone depletion and claimed that energy efficiency and reduced energy consumption had no impact on the greenhouse effect. This study also suggested that action-oriented knowledge depended on specific knowledge of the causes of a particular environmental problem. Translated into our topic, for example, business students would need to have a basic understanding of climate change. They would also need to know what **causes** climate change and how to apply this to a business context. Furthermore, they would then need to know which **action strategies** they can employ as future managers and employees to address these issues.

The focus of most chapters of this book is to teach these action strategies in business so students will learn tools and techniques on how to integrate sustainability into marketing, for example. We call this **subject-specific knowledge**. If readers are interested in increasing their general (lexical) understanding of sustainability-related topics, such as the sustainability of food, a very good starting point is Robertson's (2014) *Sustainability Principles and Practice*. Recently, with the rise of global awareness that climate change is caused by humans, a focus on climate solutions can be taken in business schools with keeping climate change science to a minimum. Initiatives such as 'Project Drawdown' (2022) or our FutureLearn online course **Climate Literacy and Action for All** (www.futurelearn.com/courses/climate-literacy-and-action-for-all) have followed this approach. In the next chapter we will explore this further.

Subject-specific knowledge can be taught in various ways, as suggested in Godemann *et al.*'s (2011b) matrix: Do students learn about carbon accounting, for example, in an option or in a core module? If in the core module, will it come at the end, or will it be integrated throughout the module right from the beginning?

In addition, students need to understand topics such as GHG (greenhouse gas) management in a company. As Chapter 15 shows, GHG management covers corporate strategy, operations, accounting, and marketing, so it cuts across different subject areas. Students need to have a basic understanding of how this applies to their subject or to the profession they will choose for their career. A final-year module can bring all these subjects together while simultaneously introducing students to GHG management (Molthan-Hill *et al.*, 2020).

However, using the analogy of IT, everybody today needs to know the basics, but we also need specialists. This applies even more to sustainability. Everyone needs to understand the basics, but some need to have specialist knowledge. Therefore, a business school should teach the basics of GHG, for example, to each student but also offer some the chance to become specialists by offering a year-long module on GHG management. In our chapter about GHG management we have made different suggestions for lecturers/business schools who want to introduce GHG management as part of the core curriculum or as a specialised, stand-alone module.

Sustainable and carbon literacy

Several authors (Stibbe, 2009; Courtice and Van der Kamp, 2013) have indicated that subject-specific knowledge alone will not be sufficient to develop managers who can deal with sustainability challenges appropriately. In the first *Handbook of Sustainability Literacy*, Stibbe (2009: 10f) illustrated the different aspects of sustainability literacy and defined the term as follows:

> This book uses the term Sustainability Literacy to indicate the skills, attitudes, competencies, dispositions and values that are necessary for surviving and thriving in the declining conditions of the world in ways which slow down that decline as far as possible. Gaining practical skills requires a form of learning which goes beyond memorising and repeating facts.

Given the current challenges we are facing, a stronger focus needs to be placed on climate literacy or **carbon literacy**. The latter term was coined and first defined by The Carbon Literacy Project (2013: 4) as '[a]n awareness of the carbon costs and impacts of everyday activities, and the ability and motivation to reduce emissions, on an individual, community and organisational basis'. The project has pioneered carbon literacy training – an accredited 'days' worth of learning' worldwide. For further information, contact info@carbonliteracy.com. We cover this in more detail in the next chapter.

Several aspects of sustainability literacy have been included in this book; in this introduction, we will reflect on **three key sustainability literacy skills as applied to management and business: systems thinking, values reflection, and philosophical assumptions in business**. Other skills have been integrated in individual chapters without making them explicit; a whole list of these skills can be found in Stibbe's (2009) handbook and the chapter by Robinson and Molthan-Hill (2021), the latter linking competencies to learning outcomes and assessments.

One approach that has established a momentum is the Sustainability Literacy Test (Sustainability Literacy Test – Sulitest, 2022). This is a training and assessment tool for raising awareness about sustainable development and global challenges, including the Sustainable Development Goals (SDGs). Sulitest is a non-profit organisation supported by entities of the United Nations (UNEP and UNDESA and UNESCO). The Higher Education Sustainability Initiative (HESI) also supports Sulitest as a tangible and concreate implementation of its mission. It is designed by and for users and built by academics, corporations, and non-profit organisations.

It was initiated by the Kedge Business School. It takes the form of an online multiple-choice-question assessment that has been developed to assesses a minimum level of knowledge in economic, social, and environmental responsibility. It was launched in late 2013 and is now in 17 countries, with 8 languages. The current version of the test consists of a random selection of 50 questions (30 international and 20 regionally specific or other specialism) and takes, on average, 30 minutes to complete. There are also SDG-specific modules, subject-specific modules, and business-related offerings. Although developed as a 'test', Sulitest can be used in learning mode as a development tool for students. Developments for the test include expanding beyond knowledge-based questions to those addressing skills and competencies and then mindsets, values, and attitudes. Plans for the test to be certificated are currently being implemented (www. sulitest.org).

Furthermore, Robinson (2009: 131f) pointed out:

> It is essential that learners are introduced to 'real world' examples and case studies. This could involve, for example, engagement with local organisations and employers or their own institutions by conducting informal environmental audits for them, or researching the activities of larger organisations to expose environmentally damaging practices and to identify paths for improvements.

Our experience has also been that students benefit from solving problems in the 'real world', and society benefits from it too – **throughout the book you will find different projects as undertaken by our students**, normally in the 'additional teaching material' section.

Systems thinking

Systems thinking is seen as a fundamental concept in sustainability (Robertson, 2014; Stibbe, 2009; Clayton and Radcliffe, 1996), and a *system* is often defined as a 'coherently organised set of elements' (Meadows, 2008: 188). Robertson (2014: 4) defines it further:

> A property of every system is that its identity is always more than the sum of its parts. The Earth itself is a system, made of many other nested and interrelated systems; the biophysical world is an intricate and multi-layered web, a complex, three-dimensional network of interconnected systems.

Schoemaker (2008) criticises business schools/lecturers for opting to teach well-defined problems and frameworks without offering support in how to deal with the 'messy ambiguities of the real world'. Systems thinking encourages acceptance of the complexity of the world and suggests **ways of dealing with the massive amounts of information and interconnectedness**. As it is such an important concept in sustainable management, it is not only embedded in many of the chapters through this book but also further explored in its own right in Chapter 17.

Worth mentioning here as a way of integrating systems thinking into the curriculum is to offer a computer simulation game, such as *En-ROADS*, introduced in the next chapter, or Meadows's (2001) *Fish Banks Ltd.*, introduced here: During this three-hour game, students are asked to run fishing companies with the aim of maximising profit for their shareholders. In addition to the original game, we have added some features, such as 'press announcements' from Greenpeace highlighting fish decline and recommendations for fishing quotas from the European Union. In all games we have played so far, students were so focused on their profit that, first, they overfished the 'deep sea' (where the profit is higher) before then turning to the coastal area to overfish there. The eventual collapse of the whole fishing industry appears to be something of a revelation for students, as is the calculation of the reasonable amount of money the companies could potentially have made while still maintaining their industry by fishing at a sustainable level, as revealed in the debrief. At this point, concepts such as 'systems thinking' and 'sustainable management' are also explained in relation to the game.

Values reflection

Another skill students need to develop in business education is to reflect on their values or to even realise that values feature in all business-related models. Several authors (MacIntyre, 1981; Watson, 2003; Verhezen, 2010; Trapp, 2011) highlight the fact that managers are reluctant to talk about the moral dimensions of their work or might insist that they try to be objective when it comes to business decisions, separating business interest from their own or other people's values.

Bird and Waters (1989: 73) label this phenomenon the 'moral muteness of managers':

> Many managers exhibit a reluctance to describe their actions in moral terms even when they are acting for moral reasons. They talk as if their actions were guided exclusively by organizational interests, practicality, and economic good sense even when in practice they honour morally defined standards codified in law, professional conventions, and social mores.

Molthan-Hill (2014) proposes that there is no value-neutral way of doing business; rather, it is a conflict between established values, which are framed as objective, and new or different values, such as environmental protection, which are framed as ethics. Jones (1991: 380) points out that managers/business students need to be able to identify the moral aspects of any business decision they have to make: 'a person who fails to recognise a moral issue will fail to employ moral decision-making schemata and will make the decision according to other schemata, economic rationality, for example'.

This is especially true when it comes to considering environmental or social values in a business decision: here, often, a bureaucratic, resource-orientated approach will be chosen. As Crane and Matten (2010) point out, all stages, not only the first one in the ethical decision-making process, are influenced by the issue's moral framing, the most important aspect of moral framing being the language in which moral issues are presented. The problem, they observe, is 'that many people in business are reluctant to ascribe moral terms to their work, even if acting for moral reasons, or if their actions have obvious moral consequences' (p. 153). Therefore, business students need to be enabled to identify the moral dimensions of normal business activities and decisions. In our experience, students tend to highlight business problems but have difficulty defining the underlying values or even acknowledging them.

Therefore, students need to learn mature moral language as part of their sustainability skill set in order to participate in the moral business discourse. They need to learn the appropriate words and concepts, but they also need to learn how to apply these concepts in the business world. Finally, the 'moral neutrality' of the business world needs to be questioned in the classroom (and maybe not only there . . .).

A discussion about the morality of ends and the morality of means within the business world needs to become the centrepiece of any sustainability study so that students reflect on their own values and decide for themselves which of them they consider applicable to the business world. Any module could start with a reflection on the values to be integrated into this subject area: for example, for accounting this could mean that the first session would discuss what needs to be included in a report to give a 'true' picture of the company. Should we focus only on financial values? Why? Should we give a financial value for environmental impacts? And if yes, how and also how much?

What is Giving Voice to Values?

Giving Voice to Values (GVV) is an innovative approach to values-driven leadership development in business education and the workplace, pioneered by Dr Mary C. Gentile (GentileM@darden.virginia.edu) (Gentile, 2016). GVV is based at University of Virginia–Darden School of Business, having been launched by Aspen Institute as incubator and founding partner, with Yale School of Management, then supported at Babson College 2009–16. Drawing on actual experience and scholarship, GVV fills a long-standing critical gap in the development of values-centred leaders.

GVV is not about persuading people to be more ethical; rather, GVV starts from the premise that most of us already want to act on our values, but that we also want to feel that we have a reasonable chance of doing so effectively and successfully. This pedagogy and curriculum are about raising those odds.

Rather than a focus on ethical *analysis*, the GVV curriculum focuses on ethical *implementation* and asks the question: 'What if I were going to act on my values? What would I say and do? How could I be most effective?'

Where can you find the book and the curriculum?

The curriculum is available at http://store.darden.virginia.edu/giving-voice-to-values (or under the 'Curriculum' tab at www.GivingVoiceToValues.org). (Teaching notes and B cases are available to registered and approved faculty members. Register at https://store.darden.virginia.edu/login.)

Who is using GVV?

Designed for use in graduate business curriculum, the approach has also moved well beyond that. GVV has been shared and/or piloted in over 1,400 educational and business settings on all seven continents. Pilot sites have included the United

States, Europe, Africa, India, China, Australia, Canada, Israel, United Arab Emirates, etc.

On the education side, GVV has been used in undergraduate, MBA, and executive education in hundreds of business schools around the world. It has been a featured part of the United Nations Global Compact PRME (Principles for Responsible Management Education) programming, and PRME was a partner supporting a GVV curriculum development initiative on anti-corruption in India. There is a GVV book series from Routledge/Greenleaf publishing at www.routledge.com/Giving-Voice-to-Values/book-series/GVV and www.routledge.com/business/posts/12540, and there are numerous titles in the previous GVV book series from Business Expert Press at www.business expertpress.com/product-category/business-ethics-corporate-citizenship-formerly-giving-voice-to-values/

For More Information on GVV, Contact: Mary C. Gentile Ph.D., GentileM@darden.virginia.edu, 978–255–7523 and visit: www.MaryGentile.com and www.GivingVoiceToValues.org.

Philosophical assumptions in business

Values reflection is part of understanding philosophical assumptions. Often, lecturers and students are not aware that the different business concepts and tools being taught have different underlying philosophical assumptions. In order to include sustainability, we can either involve students in the philosophical discussion of what should form part of a sustainably designed business system, or lecturers can decide what the philosophical assumptions are, and whether to make it explicit to students or not – as in the current system.

In his article 'Behind Global System Collapse: The Life-Blind Structure of Economic Rationality', McMurtry (2012) complains that 'social life standards to rationally regulate choices to cohere with life support systems are blinkered out' of the common understanding of 'economic rationality' (p. 50). In his opinion, this so-called '"rationality" rules out everything required for a healthy and flourishing human life' (p. 52). He recommends instead a 'life-coherent rationality', which is judged by 'consistency with and satisfaction of organic, ecological and social life requirements' (p. 56).

Our proposed new framework on how to embed sustainability into a business school curriculum suggests an optional module in business philosophy (see Table 2.2). Here students might discuss the underlying philosophical assumptions

Table 2.2: Proposed new framework for embedding sustainability into the business school curriculum

	Integrated approach		Specialist approach			Transdisciplinary approach		
Narrow (modules)	Subject-specific knowledge	Sustainability literacy skills (e.g. systems thinking)	Subject-specific knowledge	Additional sustainability knowledge	Sustainability literacy skills	Subject- and transdisciplinary-specific knowledge	Sustainability literacy skills (e.g. systems thinking)	Practical application (e.g. to business)
Broad (whole curriculum)								
Required	General sustainability knowledge (needs to be offered whatever the approach, might build on previous education, for example, school)							
Optional (can be decided for students)	Philosophical assumptions and values reflection							
Required	Strategic decision-making: graduate attributes, learning outcomes, quality process, key decision-makers							

Source: Developed from Godemann *et al.* (2011b) and Rusinko (2010).

of an existing business system. The aim of such a module could not only be the analysis of existing frameworks and concepts but also to design new concepts and tools while 'structuring what is to be preserved' (Habermas, 1984: 398). With regard to environmental issues, it would also allow room for discussions on how environmental and social issues could become part of such new concepts and tools.

Philosophical questions are only discussed in some chapters of this book. If business schools/lecturers/students want to integrate philosophy and values reflection further in their teaching/learning, a good starting point would be Molthan-Hill, 2015; Crane *et al.*, 2019 or Fisher *et al.*, 2012.

Mission, strategy, and key decision-makers

Fundamentally, our proposed new framework requires a clear commitment from the senior management of business schools, especially deans, in order to offer or even embed sustainability into the curriculum. This should start at university level. For example, Nottingham Trent University has, since 2010, promoted graduate attributes in sustainability, which have been a key driver for change not only in the business school but also throughout the university. Ryan and Tilbury (2013) have also shown how the quality assurance and quality enhancement system could support and promote sustainability teaching throughout courses and modules.

The position of a **sustainability coordinator** could be created to work with course and module leaders on how to embed sustainability into their modules, as well as coordinating all such efforts so that students do not carry out the same case study over and over again. Finally, a study by the European Foundation of Management Development and the Academy of Business in Society, which interviewed 131 deans and 136 faculty respondents, suggests that key decision-makers, such as the head of undergraduate studies, can help (or hinder) the process if they provide leadership in shaping and implementing their institution's sustainability-related agenda and objectives (Painter-Morland *et al.*, 2016). Engaged staff can add to existing modules or courses, as in the 'piggyback' approach mentioned earlier. However, 'mainstreaming' can only be achieved if key decision-makers support the integration of sustainability in all modules and courses. This book offers enough material to achieve that, and our proposed new framework as presented in Table 2.2 will help the appropriate decisions to be made.

Developing strategies for both structural and process change at school and curricula level

The **UN-backed principles for Responsible Management Education (PRME) initiative** offers a framework for embedding sustainability into the curriculum. The principles of PRME were developed in 2007 as a United Nations Global Compact initiative supported (at that time) by five academic institutions: AACSB International (the Association to Advance Collegiate Schools of Business), EFMD (the European Foundation for Management Development, the Aspen Institute Business and Society Program), EABIS (the European Academy of Business in Society), GRLI (the Globally Responsible Leadership Initiative), and the student-led organisation Net Impact. UN Secretary-General Ban Ki-moon set out the potential benefits of the PRME at the inaugural meeting in 2008:

> The Principles for Responsible Management Education have the capacity to take the case for universal values and business into classrooms on every continent.

PRME is the first organised relationship between the United Nations and business schools, and the initiative has grown to more than 880 leading academic institutions from over 85 countries. Its vision is to realise the Sustainable Development Goals through responsible management education.

Its mission at the outset was to 'inspire and champion responsible management education, research and thought leadership globally' (PRME, 2007) by engaging business and management schools to ensure they provide future business leaders with the skills needed to balance economic and sustainability goals while drawing attention to the Sustainable Development Goals (SDGs) and aligning academic institutions with the work of the UN Global Compact (2015; PRME, 2016).

By framing PRME within internationally accepted values, such as those portrayed in the United Nations Global Compact (UN Global Compact, 2000), the initiative consolidates and gives new momentum to educational initiatives on responsible management. These universal values support the Universal Declaration of Human Rights (United Nations General Assembly, 1948), the International Labour Organization's (1998) Declaration on Fundamental Principles and Rights at Work, the Rio Declaration on Environment and Development (United Nations, 2012), and the United Nations Convention Against Corruption (UN General Assembly, 2003).

The PRME initiative is a collaborative, collegial learning community that enables continuous improvement through sharing good practice in a network of networks. These networks comprise PRME Regional Chapters; PRME working groups, on key issues (for example, poverty, gender, and climate change); and PRME Champion Schools (over 45 worldwide). The PRME working groups have developed initiatives, published books and guides to develop the agenda in relation to their missions. Examples of these include Climate Literacy Training, Teaching Guides for Poverty, and the Sustainability Mindset (www.unprme.org/prme-working-groups). For many PRME signatories, the Principles for Responsible Management Education are not necessarily something new; however, through their key pillars of commitment (to the six principles), planning (strategies and processes), implementing (embedding in systems and processes), and enhanced communication with and reporting to stakeholders, they offer a platform for recognition of existing achievements in the field of responsible management education.

This institution-driven process of continuous improvement starts with the organisation's strategic vision and accreditation standards and, by working with, and learning from, partner organisations and other stakeholders, provides a framework for gradual, systemic change, a strategic journey that evolves over time. As Alcaraz and Thiruvattal (2010: 548) explain:

> PRME acts as a framework for dialogue, a framework for direction, a framework for meeting with colleagues, a framework for curriculum change, a framework for research and orientation, and a framework for experimenting with new learning methods.

Importantly, PRME inspires not only curriculum change and new horizons for research but also the transformation of the organisational culture, aligning the values and concepts that are taught and researched with the actions of the institution itself. This high-level commitment to a set of six voluntary principles as presented in Table 2.3 enables business school innovation through refocusing of resources and integration of activities that are critical to the successful delivery of management education fit for tackling the sustainability challenges of the next century.

The book **Responsible Management Education: The PRME Global Movement** (PRME, 2022) provides the most recent, comprehensive presentation of where PRME has been and where it intends to go in the future; it is open access and introduces, for example, each of its chapters and each of its working groups in a dedicated chapter.

Table 2.3: The Six Principles for Responsible Management Education

Topic	Principle
Declaration	As institutions of higher education involved in the development of current and future managers, we declare our willingness to progress in the implementation, within our institution, of the following principles, starting with those that are more relevant to our capacities and mission. We will report on progress to all our stakeholders and exchange effective practices related to these principles with other academic institutions.
Purpose	1. We will develop the capabilities of students to be future generators of sustainable value for business and society at large and to work for an inclusive and sustainable global economy.
Values	2. We will incorporate into our academic activities, curricula, and organisational practices* the values of global social responsibility as portrayed in international initiatives such as the United Nations Global Compact.
Method	3. We will create educational frameworks, materials, processes, and environments that enable effective learning experiences for responsible leadership.
Research	4. We will engage in conceptual and empirical research that advances our understanding about the role, dynamics, and impact of corporations in the creation of sustainable social, environmental, and economic value.
Partnership	5. We will interact with managers of business corporations to extend our knowledge of their challenges in meeting social and environmental responsibilities and to explore jointly effective approaches to meeting these challenges.
Dialogue	6. We will facilitate and support dialogue and debate among educators, students, business, government, consumers, media, civil society organisations, and other interested groups and stakeholders on critical issues related to global social responsibility and sustainability.
Organisational practice	We understand that our own organisational practices should serve as an example of the values and attitudes we convey to our students.

*Organisational practices were included in the principles at the 10th anniversary in 2017 to confirm the importance of the institutional role in embedding responsible management education.
Source: Hill, adapted from PRME (2007: n.p.).

Transformational model of implementation

In addressing 'how' to embed sustainability into the curriculum, PRME has developed a '[t]ransformational model of implementation' as presented in Table 2.4. This model, based on five main characteristics, considers both the complexities and specificities of integrating sustainability values into management schools and programmes. The five characteristics provide general guidance on strategic change management, recognising the need for a dual process of top-down and bottom-up commitment to sustainability. Such commitment is essential in the development of a system of values and related institutional structures, in creating an institution that understands how businesses and other stakeholders are striving to create sustainable value.

The transformational model of implementation acknowledges that different institutions are at different stages in their strategic journey, with differing expectancies of accreditation bodies and other stakeholders. Furthermore, the model

Table 2.4: Transformational model of PRME implementation

Step	Activity
1. Top-down commitment	Ensure leadership commitment to implement and mainstream PRME at an organisational level.
2. Bottom-up commitment	Support and incentivise faculty and staff to implement PRME through teaching, research, and engagement.
3. Long-term planning	Develop a plan for PRME implementation over a given time frame.
4. Resources	Secure and make available necessary resources, both human and budgetary.
5. Implementation	Take action, in alignment with the long-term plan and given resources.
6. Assessing impact	Measure impacts and progress towards goals, qualitatively and/or quantitatively.
7. Reporting and communicating	Share progress and engage with key stakeholders for continuous improvement.
8. Strategy	PRME values become an important, explicit, and effective part of the organisational strategy.

Source: Hill, adapted from PRME (2015: 6).

accepts that institutions have differing capacity for rapid change. The implementation of PRME is seen as a gradual process, set within the context of the organisations' long-term strategic plan. Collier *et al.* (2022) evaluated a more short-term approach that yielded meaningful changes in student learning and understanding about sustainable development and responsible management.

Finally, given the breadth of potential projects, actions, policies, and structural changes, PRME (2015: 5) recommends that:

> Each school should define its own path of progress towards sustainability, according to its specific story, development, size, social, cultural, and economic context where it operates, preferences and expertise of its faculty members, its own strategic positioning, etc., undertaking those sustainability practices that are more meaningful and impactful for the school and its stakeholders, like students, business, and local communities and progressing over time towards new issues.

Inspired by the Global Compact Management Model (UN Global Compact, 2010) and framed within the strategic change management characteristics discussed earlier, the model provides eight explicit steps in the implementation of PRME as presented in Table 2.4.

1st step: top-down commitment from leadership

In signalling a commitment to transformational change, it is crucial that the highest executive embraces and supports the ongoing implementation of PRME. Without such commitment, the initiative 'will remain peripheral to the institution and its mission, resource allocation, and activities' (PRME, 2015: 7). Such commitment must be authentic; otherwise, there is the risk that the PRME becomes merely a *box-checking* activity considered as a matter of compliance rather than a strategic commitment to continuous improvement. There are several drivers that foster deep commitment.

Student demand

Business Insider magazine pronounced that '[m]illennials' demand for sustainable products, not just socially responsible companies, represents an important shift in consumer priorities' (Mahler, 2015). This is something that many student organisations have been aware of for many years and thus have sustainability as an important part of their agendas and strategies. This includes, for example, Net Impact – a global community of students and professionals who aspire to be effective drivers of social and environmental change and who have supported the setting up of PRME. Oikos is another example – an international student-driven organisation for sustainability in economics and management, founded in 1987 in Switzerland. Oikos aims to embed environmental and social perspectives in faculties for economics and management. In the UK, the National Union of Students (NUS) (now Students Organising for Sustainability – SOS) has developed a number of sustainability change projects, such as Green Impact, Student Switch Off, SDG and ESD curriculum mapping, Carbon Challenge Programme, Student Eats, Dissertations for Good (now For Good) and Responsible Futures (www.sos-uk.org). PRME Global Students (PGS, 2022) attempts to achieve the same.

Furthermore, student demand for responsible management education is increasingly becoming linked with graduate employability (see also Chapter 4 in this book). As Bone and Agombar (2011) note:

> Contemporary and future socio-economic and environmental challenges set an overarching context for higher education as a whole, not least, indicating the kind of aptitudes, understanding and competencies that may be needed by our graduates, both now and for an uncertain future.

In preparation for their employment, many students believe that sustainable development and corporate social responsibility should be taught more at universities. In a study undertaken in 2016 by Yale University in collaboration with the World Business Council for Sustainable Development (WBCSD) and the Global Network for Advanced Management (GNAM), 61% of students (based on 3,700 responses from 29 business schools across 25 countries and five continents) 'want more faculty and staff with expertise in environmental sustainability and 55% think business schools should offer concentrations or joint-degree programs in this field; nearly two-thirds of students believe sustainability demands a more central position in the core curriculum' (Yale *et al.*, 2016: 9). In 2021, over 8,500 students took part in the Sustainability Skills Survey in the UK; 88% of students said they agree their place of study should actively incorporate and promote sustainable development, and 79% want to see sustainable development actively incorporated and promoted through all courses (www.sos-uk.org/research/sustainability-skills-survey).

Business pressure

There is a long history of business engagement with social and, more recently, environmental challenges that predates the current sustainability debates (Asongu, 2007). In the post-2015 development agenda, Global Compact business organisations seek to align their business strategies with the SDGs through the Global Compact Compass Tool (United Nations Global Compact, Global Reporting Initiative (GRI) and World Business Council for Sustainable Development, 2016).

> Unlike their predecessor, the Millennium Development Goals, the SDGs explicitly call on all businesses to apply their creativity and innovation to solve sustainable development challenges. The SDGs have been agreed by all governments, yet their success relies heavily on action and collaboration by all actors.
>
> (United Nations Global Compact, 2015)

However, despite these external drivers, the business sector often fails to see the opportunities in collaborating with business schools around sustainability goals and targets, notwithstanding a strong desire from schools to develop mutually beneficial relationships (Weybrecht, 2015, 2021).

Institutional drivers in the sector

Business schools and other institutions operate in a global marketplace and international ranking, and external accreditation plays an important role in graduate and postgraduate recruitment. There are three main business school accreditation organisations: the Association to Advance Collegiate Schools of Business (AACSB International), the European Foundation for Management Development (EFMD), and the Association of MBAs (AMBA) – all three of which were members of the PRME Steering Committee until 2018. The rise in the number of UK business schools applying for AACSB accreditations reflects this constant pressure to increase revenues, rankings, and reputation through accreditations (Davies, 2016).

The accreditation standards consist of three sections: (1) strategic management and innovation, (2) learner success, and (3) thought leadership, engagement, and societal impact. Each section contains standards that lead a business school to make a positive individual impact. The overall vision is of transforming business education for positive societal impact and its belief that business is a force for good in society (AACSB International, 2020).

Similarly, EFMD (2016) already included an 11th dimension in the EQUIS accreditation standards, dealing explicitly with ethics, responsibility, and sustainability, furthermore, citing PRME as demonstration of a 'school's formal commitments to ethics, responsibility and sustainability' (EFMD, 2016: 68).

In the field of executive education, AMBA's accreditation scheme recognises the role of responsible and sustainable management education within the MBA curricula and the development of MBA graduate attributes. In particular, the curriculum should reflect 'an understanding of the impact of sustainability, ethics and risk management on business decisions and performance, and on society as a whole' (2016: 8).

2nd step: bottom-up commitment from faculty and staff

Ensuring that all faculty members are aware of and respond to PRME remains an important goal, within the context of the transformational model, since it is ultimately up to the individual practitioner to implement both the 'what' and 'how' of change:

> If faculty members are not engaged, it will be very difficult to change the curricula and syllabi across programmes, to orient research towards sustainability-related topics, to involve students in sustainability-related extracurricular activities, or to keep close links with responsible and sustainable companies.
>
> (PRME, 2015: 13)

Faculty engagement usually starts with a few *enlightened* colleagues who, through structural changes and informal change mechanisms, disseminate their knowledge of, and passion for, responsible management education within *concentric circles* (PRME, 2015: 13; Collier *et al.*, 2022), leading to both *horizontal* and *vertical* learning throughout the institution.

3rd step: long-term planning

PRME implementation is, at its essence, a process of continuous improvement, and its implementation must be thought of as a strategic journey, with the ultimate goal of PRME becoming an integral part of the strategy of the organisation, embedding the values of corporate sustainability and responsibility into the daily activities of management-related higher education institutions. Achievement of strategic aims requires long-term planning, with the identification of school priorities, resources, and timescales. The PRME (2015: 16) **long-term reference framework** provides a matrix of the relevant elements that integrate the six principles of PRME with the thematic issues identified by the Global Compact. The framework may inform not only structural changes envisioned by the school, reflecting purpose (principle 1) and values (principle 2), but also possible actions, including innovation in teaching and learning methodologies (principle 3), research (principle 4), partnerships with business (principle 5), and dialogue with stakeholders and society at large (principle 6). The framework also highlights daily operations, since the framing language of the principles of PRME explicitly states: 'We understand that our own organizational practices should serve as example of the values and attitudes we convey to our students' (see also Table 2.3).

4th step: resources

Feasibility is a crucial feature in the implementation of PRME; therefore, the appropriate human and budgetary resources must be made available at the appropriate time to achieve the institutions' strategic aims. It is important to note that consideration should not just be given to internal resources, such as administrative support and specialised expertise in sustainability and responsible management teaching and research, but also the wealth of external resources available through the PRME learning community (www.unprme.org/resources).

5th step: implementation

Implementation must be both clearly defined and achievable – what is being done by whom, when, and how. Typically, given that the PRME reporting time frame is every two years, it is recommended that at least three to four central actions and/or policies be undertaken during each reporting cycle. The PRME Long-Term Reference Framework may guide institutional priorities, which are then translated into actionable policies with SMART (specific, measurable, achievable, realistic, and time-bound) objectives and key performance indicators, to allow for monitoring and evaluation of PRME initiatives, including an assessment of impact.

6th step: assessing impact

It is important to understand the effectiveness of any strategic change process, and embedding sustainability and responsible management principles across the institution is no exception. Both qualitative and quantitative measurements should support the process of continuous improvement, through monitoring, evaluation, and assessment of impact. This impact assessment includes, but is not limited to, impact on students, the institution itself, the local business community, and society at large. Institutions are encouraged in their sharing information on progress (SIP) reports (see the following) to monitor progress on their initiatives and report on previously identified ways of measuring impact. The Global Reporting Initiative (GRI) indicators can also provide some guidance for campus operations (United Nations Global Compact, Global Reporting Initiative (GRI) and World Business Council for Sustainable Development, 2016). PRME's transformational model (2015) provides detailed guidance on suggested **key performance indicators for each of the six principles**.

7th step: reporting to stakeholders

A central pillar of participating in PRME is to regularly **share information on progress** (SIP) made in implementing the six principles with peers in the PRME community and other stakeholders. These SIP reports are a requirement to remain a participant of PRME and must be submitted at least every two years. Such sharing of information also facilitates further connection and collaboration with stakeholders by communicating the role that management education is taking on embedding sustainability and responsibility into curricula, research, and organisational practices (PRME 2022) (www.unprme.org/reporting-sharing-information-on-progress).

8th step: strategy

The purpose of PRME is to embed the values of corporate sustainability and responsibility into the daily activities of management-related higher education establishments, and with continuous improvement, the goal is that these values will become an important, explicit, and effective part of their strategy, permeating all aspects of the institution as it undertakes its strategic journey. Since the launch of PRME, there have been many examples of a diverse range of institutions embracing a successful strategic approach to implementing PRME.

Conclusion

To summarise, our proposed new framework includes all the dimensions discussed previously in addition to those suggested by Godemann *et al.* (2011a):

- General sustainability knowledge, such as climate change
- Subject-specific knowledge, such as tools for sustainable marketing

- Specialised knowledge, such as environmental management systems

- Sustainability literacy skills, such as systems thinking instead of a myopic view

- Understanding of values underpinning management so that the integration of values reflection forms the basis of management education

- Philosophical assumptions in business, which can be discussed with students or decided for them (optional), with, in either case, these underlying assumptions being made transparent for students

- Engagement with business so that students solve 'real-life' problems for business and society

- Strategic decision-making: mission, strategy, and quality assurance process all aligned and supported by key decision-makers

When developing an approach for a business school/course/module, our proposed new framework enables the following **core questions** to be addressed:

- *How* will it be embedded?

- *What* should be taught?

- Will it comprise subject-specific knowledge, general sustainability-related knowledge, and/or sustainability literacy skills?

- Will the students solve 'real-life' problems?

When considering the strategies for both structural and process change at school and curricula level, the UN-backed Principles for Responsible Management Education (PRME, 2015) transformational model, together with the Global Reporting Initiative, provide a balanced approach for curriculum reorientation towards sustainability and responsible management, refocusing of research activities, and transparent dialogue with key stakeholders, supporting the development of responsible management education globally.

Beginning on the sustainability journey is often a challenging idea for individuals, and this is usually the first barrier to overcome towards embedding sustainability and climate action. The following activity was designed to help individuals reflect on their sustainability ambition through the development of personal and professional goals in the form of a Sustainability and Climate Action Plan.

Activity: Developing your Sustainability and Climate Action Plan

To succeed in the climate action journey, we must realise that while small actions can seem trivial, individual actions are critical. The 'Sustainability and Climate Action Plan' activity will provide an opportunity to create and then demonstrate personal actions towards sustainability. The two documents (Sustainability and Climate Action Plan Template and Sustainability and Climate Action Sticker Book, both available on the companion website) should be used together to create your individual goals towards these objectives. Each one of us should individually develop a Sustainability and Climate Integration Plan, especially students who can create and demonstrate personal/professional actions towards sustainability.

Step 1: Identifying your definition for sustainability (15 minutes)

Sustainability means different things to different people. While the most prevalent definition was presented by the Brundtland Commission in 1987, the definition can be different from different perspectives. It's therefore important to select or create a sustainability definition that aligns with your personal values as an individual.

Step 2: Identifying the relevant Sustainable Development Goals (15 minutes)

The 17 Sustainable Development Goals have been created as a global roadmap for achieving sustainable development by 2030 (Sustainable Development Goals, 2020). It's important to select the SDGs relevant to your personal and/or professional role to outline actions that you'll be taking for a positive impact towards these goals.

Step 3: Identifying the relevant PRME principles for your role (15 minutes)

More than 850 institutions worldwide are embedding PRME principles in their organisational practices. From the student perspective, it is useful to spread awareness about these principles, whose goal is to promote responsible management education worldwide. You are expected to select a few of the PRME principles that you encourage your institution/organisation to adopt.

Step 4: Identifying the relevant Good Life Goals (15 minutes)

The Good Life Goals are a set of personal actions that people around the world can take to support the Sustainable Development Goals (SDGs). They are behavioural/lifestyle tasks for individuals that are aligned with the SDGs' 169 targets and indicators. Watch the Good Life Goals video at **https://youtu.be/bbrYODvkvGk**. You should select some of the Good Life Goals that will help you take personal actions towards sustainability and climate action.

Step 5: Measuring your Ecological Footprint (15 minutes)

The Ecological Footprint (2003) is a metric that measures how much nature we have and how much nature we use. The footprint calculator helps individuals understand their impact on the planet and explore ways of reducing this through day-to-day actions. Answer questions in the footprint calculator to estimate your Ecological Footprint, and then list some high-impact actions to reduce this in the template.

Further readings

Business and Management Subject Benchmark Statements (2023) Available online at: https://www.qaa.ac.uk/the-quality-code/subject-benchmark-statements/subject-benchmark-statement-business-and-management

The Subject Benchmark Statement for Business and Management, regularly issued in the UK, describe the nature of study and the academic standards expected of graduates in these specific subject areas. They show what graduates might reasonably be expected to know, do and understand at the end of their studies. Especially noteworthy is that the 2023 statement has detailed information on how to teach sustainable management and also climate solutions. There is a separate Statement for Master's Degrees.

The Good Life Goals (2018) *Personal Actions That Everyone Can Take to Support the SDGs*. Available online at: www.wbcsd.org/Archive/Sustainable-Lifestyles/News/Personal-actions-that-everyone-can-take-to-support-the-SDGs [Accessed on 20 October 2019].

The Good Life Goals highlight the vital role of individual actions in achieving the ambitious SDGs. From the business perspective, they provide companies with valuable insight into the ways the SDGs link to actions, activities, and lifestyles of customers. They were created by Futerra, the 10YFP SLE Programme, Stockholm

Environment Institute (SEI), Institute for Global Environmental Strategies (IGES), UNESCO, UN Environment and WBCSD.

Moosmayer, D., Laasch, O., Parkes, C., and Brown, K. (Eds). (2020) *The Sage Handbook of Responsible Management Learning and Education* (London: Sage).

This handbook follows a decade of quite substantial development in the field of responsible management learning and education (RMLE). It brings together a broad range of voices and thoughts in an in-depth research and practice coverage of the field with 34 chapters and corresponding authors. The handbook provides a review of the state of the world and highlights the need for RMLE in its various forms, critical reflections of the field, and its institutionalisation.

Parkes, C., Buono, A., and Ghada, H. (2017) PRME 10th Anniversary Special Issue. The Principles for Responsible Management Education (PRME): The First Decade – What Has Been Achieved? The Next Decade – Responsible Management Education's Challenge for the Sustainable Development Goals (SDGs). *International Journal of Management Education*, 15(2), 61–5.

Parkes, C., Kolb, M., Schlange, L., Gudic, M., and Schmidpeter, R. (2020) IJME Special Issue. Implementing the Sustainable Development Goals (SDGs). *International Journal of Management Education*, 18(2), Part B.

These two journal special issues include a mix of theoretical contributions, new models and frameworks, case histories, and a range of studies – qualitative, quantitative, and mixed methods – focused on teaching, learning, and practice in responsible management education. An additional feature of the issues is the inclusion of invited thought pieces and critiques, drawing on the insight and experience of people who have been actively involved with PRME (and associated initiatives) in a variety of capacities.

Principles for Responsible Management Education (2020) *Blueprint for SDG Integration – Practicalities, Steps, Frameworks and Actors.* Available online at: https://d30mzt1bxg5llt.cloudfront.net/public/uploads/PDFs/BlueprintForSDGIntegration.pdf [Accessed on 6 March 2020].

The *Blueprint for SDG Integration* provides guidance frameworks to support business schools in the journey of integrating the SDGs into their curricula, research, and partnerships. The *Blueprint* encourages business schools to create their own SDG pathways, based on their organisational capacity, needs, and prevailing context, and offers a roadmap for schools that are on different stages of their SDG journey.

References

AACSB International (2020) *AACSB Business Accreditation Standards.* Available online at: www.aacsb.edu/educators/accreditation/business-accreditation/aacsb-business-accreditation-standards

Alcaraz, J., and Thiruvattal, E. (2010) An Interview with Manuel Escudero: The United Nations Principles for Responsible Management Education: A Global Call for Sustainability. *Academy of Management Learning & Education*, 9, 542–50.

AMBA (2016) *MBA Accreditation Criteria*. Association of MBA's. Available online at: www.mbaworld.com/en/accreditation/become-an-accredited-business-school

Asongu, J.J. (2007) The History of Corporate Social Responsibility. *Journal of Business and Public Policy*, 1(2), 1–18.

Ban ki-Moon (2008) *A Global Initiative, a Global Agenda, Principles of Responsible Management Education* (United Nations Global Compact). Available online at: www.unprme.org/resource-docs/PRMEBrochureFINALlowres.pdf

Bird, F., and Waters, J. (1989) The Moral Muteness of Managers. *California Management Review*, 32(1), 73–88.

Bodenstein, G., Spiller, A., and Elbers, H. (1997) *Strategische Konsumentscheidungen: Langfristige Weichenstellungen fuer das Umwelthandeln: Ergebnisse einer empirischen Studie, Diskussionsbeitraege des Fachbereichs Wirtschaftswissenschaften*, 234 (Duisburg, Germany: Gerhard-Mercator-Universitaet).

Bone, E., and Agombar, J. (2011) *First Year Attitudes Towards, and Skills in Sustainable Development* (York: Higher Education Academy).

The Carbon Literacy Project (2013) *The Carbon Literacy Standard*. Available online at: www.carbonliteracy.com

Clayton, A.M.H., and Radcliffe, N.J. (1996) *Sustainability: A Systems Approach* (London: Earthscan).

Collier, E., Odell, K.E., and Rosenbloom, A. (2022) Teaching Sustainable Development: An Approach to Rapidly Introducing the UN Sustainable Development Goals into an Undergraduate Business Curriculum. *Journal of Global Responsibility*, 13(4), ahead-of-print.

Courtice, P., and Van der Kamp, M. (2013) *Developing Leaders for the Future: Integrating Sustainability into Mainstream Leadership Programmes*. Working Paper of the Cambridge Programme for Sustainability Leadership, Commissioned by the Academy of Business in Society, Cambridge.

Crane, A., and Matten, D. (2010) *Business Ethics: Managing Citizenship and Sustainability in the Age of Globalization* (Oxford, UK: Oxford University Press).

Crane, A., Matten, D., Spence, L.J., and Glozer, S. (2019) *Business Ethics Managing Corporate Citizenship and Sustainability in the Age of Globalization* (Oxford, UK: Oxford University Press): 5th edition.

Davies, J. (2016) *Reflections on the Role of the Business School Dean* (London: Chartered Association of Business Schools).

Dharmasasmita, A., Puntha, H., and Molthan-Hill, P. (2017) Practical Challenges and Digital Learning: Getting the Balance Right for Future-Thinking. *On the Horizon*, 25(1), 33–44. ISSN 1074–8121

Ecological Footprint (2003) *How Many Planets Does It Take to Sustain Your Lifestyle?* Available online at: https://www.footprintcalculator.org/home/en

European Foundation for Management Development (EFMD) (2016) *Quality Improvement System: The EFMD Accreditation for International Business Schools*. Available online at: www.efmd.org/equis [Accessed 3 September 2016]

Fisher, C., Lovell, A., and Valero-Silva, N. (2012) *Business Ethics and Values* (Harlow, UK: Financial Times Prentice Hall): 4th edition.

Gentile, M. (2016) *Giving Voice to Values*. Available online at: www.darden.virginia.edu/ibis/initiatives/giving-voice-to-vaues//?utm_source=Copy+of+GVV+is+moving&utm_campaign=4%2F29%2F16+Email&utm_medium=email

Godemann, J., Herzig, C., and Moon, J. (2011a) *Approaches to Changing the Curriculum*. Paper Presented at the ISIBS Workshop: Session II, University of Nottingham, Nottingham, 20–21 October.

Godemann, J., Herzig, C., Moon, J., and Powell, A. (2011b) *Integrating Sustainability into Business Schools – Analysis of 100 UN PRME Sharing Information on Progress (SIP) Reports*. ICCSR Research Paper Series No. 58. Available online at: https://researchportal.bath.ac.uk/en/publications/integrating-sustainability-into-business-schools-analysis-of-100

Good Life Goals (2018). Available online at: https://sdghub.com/goodlifegoals/

Habermas, J. (1984) *The Theory of Communicative Action. Volume 1: Reason and the Rationalization of Society* (London: Heinemann).

International Labour Organization (ILO) (1998) *Declaration on Fundamental Principles and Rights at Work*. Eighty-Sixth Session, Geneva, 18 June. Available online at: www.ilo.org/declaration/info/publications/WCMS_467653/lang-en/index.htm

Jones, T.M. (1991) Ethical Decision Making by Individuals in Organizations: An Issue-Contingent Model. *Academy of Management Review*, 16, 366–95.

Kempton, W., Boster, J.S., and Hartley, J.A. (1996) *Environmental Values in American Culture* (Cambridge, MA: The MIT Press).

MacIntyre, A. (1981) *After Virtue: A Study in Moral Theory* (London: Duckworth).

Mahler, D. (2015) How Important Is Sustainability to Millennials. *Business Insider*. Available online at: www.businessinsider.com/how-important-is-sustainability-to-millennials-2015-10?IR=T

McMurtry, J. (2012) Behind Global System Collapse: The Life-Blind Structure of Economic Rationality. *Journal of Business Ethics*, 108(1), 49–60.

Meadows, D.H. (2008) *Thinking in Systems: A Primer* (White River, VT: Chelsea Green).

Meadows, D.L. (2001) *Fish Banks, Ltd: Game Administrator's Manual* (Durham: University of New Hampshire). Available online at: https://forio.com/store/mit-fishbanks-renewable-resource-management-simulation/

Molthan-Hill, P. (2014) The Moral Muteness of Managers: An Anglo-American Phenomenon? German and British Managers and Their Moral Reasoning About Environmental Sustainability in Business. *International Journal of Cross-Cultural Management*, 14(3), 289–305.

Molthan-Hill, P. (2015) Making the Business Case: Intercultural Differences in Framing Economic Rationality Related to Environmental Issues. *Critical Perspectives on International Business*, 11(1), 72–91.

Molthan-Hill, P., Dharmasasmita, A., and Winfield, F. (2016) Academic Freedom, Bureaucracy and Procedures: The Challenge of Curriculum Development for Sustainability. In Leal Filho, W., and Davim, J.P. (Eds). *Challenges in Higher Education for Sustainability* (Cham, Switzerland: Springer): 199–215.

Molthan-Hill, P., Robinson, Z.P., Hope, A., Dharmasasmita, A., and McManus, E. (2020) Reducing Carbon Emissions in Business through Responsible Management Education: Influence at the Micro-, Meso- and Macro-Levels. *International Journal of Management Education*, 18(1), 100328. ISSN 1472–8117.

Molthan-Hill, P., Worsfold, N., Nagy, G.J., Leal Filho, W., and Mifsud, M. (2019) Climate Change Education for Universities: A Conceptual Framework from an International Study. *Journal of Cleaner Production*, 226, 1092–101. ISSN 0959–6526.

Painter-Morland, M., Sabet, E., Molthan-Hill, P., Goworek, H., and De Leeuw, S. (2016) Beyond the Curriculum: Integrating Sustainability into Business Schools. *Journal of Business Ethics*, 139(4), 737–54.

PGS (2022) *PRME Global Students*. Available online at: www.unprme.org/prme-global-students

Principles for Responsible Management Education (2007) *Six Principles*. Available online at: www.unprme.org/history-of-prme

Principles for Responsible Management Education (2015) *Transformational Model: For PRME Implementation*. Available online at: https://d30mzt1bxg5llt.cloudfront.net/public/uploads/PDFs/PRMETransformationalWeb.pdf

Principles for Responsible Management Education (2016) *Management Education and the Sustainable Development Goals: Transforming Education to Act Responsibly and Find Opportunities*. Available online at: www.unprme.org/resources [Accessed 3 September 2016].

Principles for Responsible Management Education (2020) *Blueprint for SDG Integration – Practicalities, Steps, Frameworks and Actors*. Available online at: https://d30mzt1bxg5llt.cloudfront.net/public/uploads/PDFs/BlueprintForSDGIntegration.pdf [Accessed on 6 March 2020].

PRME (2022) *Responsible Management Education: The PRME Global Movement*. Available online at: www.taylorfrancis.com/books/oa-edit/10.4324/9781003186311/responsible-management-education-principles-responsible-management-education

Project Drawdown (2022) *Table of Solutions*. Available online at: https://drawdown.org/solutions/table-of-solutions

Robertson, M. (2014) *Sustainability Principles and Practice* (Oxon, UK: Routledge).

Robinson, Z. (2009) Greening Business: The Ability to Drive Environmental and Sustainability Improvements in the Workplace. In Stibbe, A. (Ed). *The Handbook of Sustainability Literacy: Skills for a Changing World* (Totnes, UK: Green Books): 130–6.

Robinson, Z., and Molthan-Hill, P. (2021) Assessing Competencies for Future-Fit Graduates and Responsible Leaders. In Baughan, P. (Ed). *Assessment and Feedback in a Post-Pandemic Era: A Time for Learning and Inclusion* (York: Advance HE): 196–213. ISBN 9781916359352

Rusinko, C.A. (2010) Integrating Sustainability in Management and Business Education. *The Academy of Management Learning and Education*, 9(3), 507–19.

Ryan, A., and Tilbury, D. (2013) Uncharted Waters: Voyages for Education for Sustainable Development in the Higher Education Curriculum. *The Curriculum Journal*, 24(2) (special issue: Education for Sustainable Development as the DESD Approaches 2014: What Have We Achieved and Ways Forward?), 2–13.

Schoemaker, P.J.H. (2008) The Future Challenges of Business: Rethinking Management Education. *California Management Review*, 50(1), 119–39.

Smith, B. (2022) Closing the Sustainability Skills Gap: Helping Businesses Move from Pledges to Progress. *Microsoft*, 2 November. Available online at: https://blogs.microsoft.com/on-the-issues/2022/11/02/closing-sustainability-skills-gap/#:~:text=Today%20Microsoft%20is%20publishing%20a,move%20from%20pledges%20to%20progress

Stibbe, A. (Ed) (2009) *The Handbook of Sustainability Literacy: Skills for a Changing World* (Totnes, UK: Green Books).

Sustainability Literacy Test – Sulitest (2022) Available online at: http://sulitest.org

Sustainable Development Goals (2020) Available online at: www.un.org/sustainabledevelopment/sustainable-development-goals/

Trapp, N.L. (2011) Staff Attitudes to Talking Openly About Ethical Dilemmas: The Role of Business Ethics Conceptions and Trust. *Journal of Business Ethics*, 103(4), 543–52.

United Nations (2012) *The Future We Want. Outcome of the Conference* (Rio de Janeiro, Brazil: UNCSD).

United Nations General Assembly (1948) *Universal Declaration of Human Rights*, 10 December, 217 A (III). Available online at: www.un.org/en/universal-declaration-human-rights/index.html

United Nations General Assembly (2003) *United Nations Convention Against Corruption*, 31 October, A/58/422. Available online at: www.refworld.org/docid/3fdc4d3e7.html

United Nations Global Compact (2000) *Ten Principles of the UN Global Compact*. Available online at: www.unglobalcompact.org/what-is-gc/mission/principles

United Nations Global Compact (2010) *UN Global Compact Management Model: Framework for Implementation, Human Rights, Labour, Environement, Anti-Corruption*. Available online at: www.unglobalcompact.org/docs/news_events/9.1_news_archives/2010_06_17/UN_Global_Compact_Management_Model.pdf

United Nations Global Compact (2015) *Impact: Transforming Business, Changing the World*. Available online at: www.unglobalcompact.org/library/1331

United Nations Global Compact, Global Reporting Initiative (GRI) and World Business Council for Sustainable Development (2016) *SDG Compass: The Guide for Business Action on the SDGs, United Nations Global Compact, Global Reporting Initiative, and World Business Council for Sustainable Development*. Available online at: http://sdgcompass.org/wp-content/uploads/2015/12/019104_SDG_Compass_Guide_2015.pdf

Verhezen, P. (2010) Giving Voice in a Culture of Silence: From a Culture of Compliance to a Culture of Integrity. *Journal of Business Ethics*, 96(2), 187–206.

Watson, T.J. (2003) Ethical Choice in Managerial Work: The Scope for Moral Choices in an Ethically Irrational World. *Human Relations*, 56, 167–85.

Weybrecht, G. (2015) *Shaping the Future Business Leader: State of Sustainability Education Overview* (New York: United Nations Global Compact, Principles for Responsible Management Education).

Weybrecht, G. (2021). How Management Education Is Engaging Students in the Sustainable Development Goals. *International Journal of Sustainability in Higher Education.* https://doi.org/10.1108/IJSHE-10-2020-0419

Willats, J., Erlandsson, L., Molthan-Hill, P., Dharmasasmita, A., and Simmons, E. (2018). A University Wide Approach to Integrating the Sustainable Development Goals in the Curriculum – A Case Study from the Nottingham Trent University Green Academy. In Leal Filho, W. (Ed). *Implementing Sustainability in the Curriculum of Universities: Approaches, Methods and Projects, World Sustainability* (Berlin: Springer): 63–78. ISBN 9783319702803

Yale, CBE, GNAM, and WBCSD (2016) *Rising Leaders on Environmental Sustainability and Climate Change: A Global Survey of Business Students.* Available online at: https://cbey.yale.edu/search?redirected&search_term=files%20Rising%20Leaders%20on%20Environmental%20Sustainability%20Climate%20Change%20Nov%202015%20pdf

3

Climate change mitigation education in business schools: Now it is time to save the day!

Petra Molthan-Hill, Lia Blaj-Ward, Jennifer S. A. Leigh, and Florian Kapmeier

Climate change is one of the key challenges of this century due to its impact on society and the economy. Students are asking their business schools to scale up climate change education (CCE) across all disciplines, and employers are looking for graduates ready to work on solutions. This desire for solutions is shared by faculty; however, in a recent survey, many highlighted that they lack knowledge about climate change mitigation and how to integrate CCE into their disciplines.

This chapter supports lecturers, professors and senior management in their journey to get an overview of CCE and, more importantly, to find high-impact climate solutions to be integrated and assessed in their teaching units.

In this chapter:

- We will explain the pressing issue of cutting greenhouse gases and why business students need to understand the basic concept of climate change and how to mitigate it.

DOI: 10.4324/9781003294665-5

- We will explain the three dimensions of CCE and share various climate change mitigation education examples in several business disciplines.

- We will accompany two fictional characters at different career stages in their thought processes and pathways on how to integrate CCE.

- We will end this chapter with a self-guided activity on how you can integrate CCE in your own teaching unit with assessment.

Before we summarise the challenge humanity is facing with regard to climate change, we want to highlight that we already have all the solutions we need to reduce further global warming; for a detailed overview of climate solutions, please refer to *The Handbook of Carbon Management: A step-by-step guide to high-impact climate solutions for every manager in every function*, especially Chapters 1, 4–7, and 10. Sharing these climate solutions with our students is a key aim of CCE.

Background

The prosperity industrialised countries have built up over the last decades is also due to the generation and deployment of relatively inexpensive energy and electricity from burning fossil fuels such as coal, oil, and gas. Burning fossil fuels leads to carbon dioxide emissions that accumulate in the atmosphere as carbon dioxide concentration. Further, there are other greenhouse gas (GHG) emissions, such as methane, nitrous oxide, and fluorescent gases accumulating in the atmosphere. Ecosystem services remove GHGs from the atmosphere (IPCC, 2018). As long as emissions and uptakes are similar in size, GHG concentration is balanced. However, human-induced carbon dioxide emissions are currently about twice as high as the net uptake. As a consequence, atmospheric carbon dioxide concentration increases, and currently, it does so exponentially, as does the concentration of all GHGs (IPCC, 2018). These dynamics can be better understood using a bathtub analogy (Figure 3.1). The concentration of atmospheric GHGs reaches higher levels when the inflow to the tub (emissions) exceeds the outflow (net removal). It remains constant when inflow equals outflow and decreases when outflow exceeds inflow (Sterman, 2011).

Figure 3.1: Bathtub analogy of CO$_2$ emissions, concentration, and net removals.

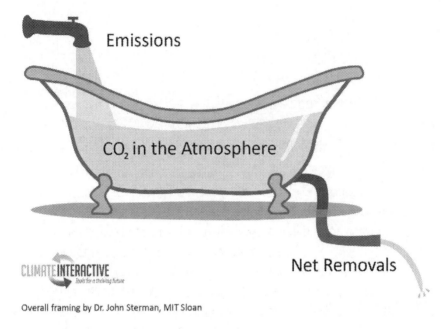

Overall framing by Dr. John Sterman, MIT Sloan

Source: Used with permission from Climate Interactive.

The increase in atmospheric GHG concentration comes with side effects, such as a rise in the average global temperature, which is referred to as global warming. Since the start of industrialisation, the Earth has already warmed by roughly 1.2 °C (IPCC, 2018). This warming has large impacts on our lives: unprecedented heatwaves in Europe, wildfires in the Arctic, extreme floods in Pakistan, and so on.

Reports from the Intergovernmental Panel on Climate Change (IPCC) state that if we continue to emit GHGs on this pathway, we will have warmed up Earth to levels with consequences that are not in line with our understanding of safety, health, and prosperity. The NGO Climate Interactive (2020) estimates that temperature in a baseline scenario will reach 3.6 °C (6.4 °F) above pre-industrial times by 2100. This will have dramatic consequences for all species on Earth, including humans in every country: until 2100, with this temperature rise, the expected additional deaths caused by extreme heat will increase dramatically (Vicedo-Cabrera et al., 2018); a large fraction of invertebrates, insects, and plants will lose more than half of their climatic range (Warren et al., 2018); the yield of the three major crops will drastically decrease (Zhao et al., 2017); and the effect on the economy (e.g. Stern et al., 2021; Dietz and Stern, 2015) will be at the order of magnitude compared to the impact of the Covid pandemic.

In the Paris Agreement, world leaders have agreed to limit global warming to 'well below 2 °C and as close to 1.5 °C as possible' (UNFCCC, 2015). The IPCC (2018) highlights that the global society can still achieve these goals. To do so, society will be required to cut GHGs emissions by half by the end of this decade and reach net zero GHG emissions by the middle of the century (UNFCCC, 2021). This requires a society-wide transformation across the globe. Corporate action plays a vital role in this transformation, as corporate activities contribute heavily to global GHG emissions (Krabbe et al., 2015). Doerr (2021) lays out an action plan for reducing current worldwide GHG emissions of 59 gigatons across all sectors.

Higher education needs to educate students, and thus future corporate and political leaders, as well as the general society to understand the basic physics of climate change, possible actions for how to mitigate and adapt to climate change, and the actions likely impacts on reducing global warming and related co-benefits.

Professional development of faculty who want to integrate CCE

Faculty in business schools will have different degrees of personal, experiential knowledge about how climate change impacts individual livelihoods, communities, and society and may be uncertain about:

- How to frame climate change (mitigation) as content for a university course;

- How their immediate subject area can make the most relevant contribution to mitigating climate change by reducing GHG emissions and increasing carbon sinks;

- How best to scaffold the engagement of stakeholders (students, other academics, and external businesses) with CCE;

- What pedagogic approaches would be most relevant to delivering impactful CCE;

- How to assess climate-relevant learning in ways that benefit both students and external communities;

- How to navigate the quality assurance processes within an institution that stipulate how changes to university curricula can be made; and/or

- How to respond to the requirements of professional accrediting bodies such as the Association to Advance Collegiate Schools of Business (AACSB).

The need for professional development is clearly highlighted in two recent studies. A study carried out by the Yale Centre for Business Education (2016) notes the salience of environmental concerns among students from 29 reputable business schools worldwide. It emphasises students' clear orientation towards organisations that show awareness of environmental challenges and commitment to addressing these. The student respondents asked for faculty with greater knowledge of climate change and for climate literacy to be given a more central place in business school curricula, reflecting more fully the ethos of responsible management education (RME). Attention to climate change is a core thread within RME as it ties in with equitable use and enjoyment of Earth's resources, with public health, and with building and living in sustainable cities and communities.

Maloni et al. (2021) sought out student views which reported that business schools do not necessarily 'walk their talk' in their opinion and asked for greater attention to be paid to accountability in RME. The authors formulate a decisive call to action:

> We must take a hard look at ourselves, including our values, commitment, and accountability, to accept ownership for forging future business leaders who are both motivated and trained to curtail the negative environmental and social impacts of business. Failure to do so challenges the legitimacy of our educational institutions.
>
> (p. 13)

This is echoed by Harvard University's (2022) initiative to scale up climate education across all disciplines and its plan to build a team of educators that includes, alongside faculty, the students being taught, other staff within the university, alumni, and external partners.

Learning about the climate, both for faculty and for students, requires a greater degree of interdisciplinarity and cross-functional working and a greater degree of empathy. Climate challenges are not only an academic topic but also a reality which affects students, faculty, and others personally and professionally (Harvard University, 2022). The approach required to facilitate this type of learning is oriented towards the whole person and the broader system to which a person belongs. This may necessitate a more substantial mindset shift. A coaching approach that acknowledges the inevitable permeability between academic, personal, and professional learning may be more relevant in this regard (e.g. Cox and Flynn, 2022).

Educational developers can play an important role in enabling faculty to address climate change. They do so most effectively by bringing together and sustaining communities of practice that share 'a sense of mutual commitment' (Chen et al., 2022: p. 125). These communities are a safe space for experimenting with new ideas and approaches, often cross-institutional, to counteract professional isolation with any given university where climate change is not an educational priority. They have the potential to generate transformative outcomes for students and faculty alike.

The remainder of this chapter takes a closer look at ways to leverage resources and build communities of practice to achieve transformational outcomes in business schools. Useful points of entry into the journey of learning about and acting on climate change within the context of business schools are internationally recognised development resources, such as the Climate Literacy Training (Molthan-Hill and Winfield, 2023), the free online course Climate Literacy and Action for All (2023), or the different modes of engagement with the climate simulators C-ROADS (Sterman et al., 2013; Rooney-Varga et al., 2018) and En-ROADS (Climate Interactive, 2022), as well as readings which unpack the why and how of confronting climate change from complementary perspectives, such as André's (2020) *Lead for the Planet*, building on her substantial experience of teaching climate change at her university, or Nicholas's (2021) *Under the Sky We Make*, drawing on her lived, personal experience to create a sense of purpose and urgency.

Climate change mitigation education

Each business school discipline can contribute in its unique way to confronting climate change. In order to understand climate change and empower faculty to teach, it is important to differentiate between three dimensions: climate change science, climate change mitigation education (CCME), and climate change adaptation education (CCAE) (Mochizuki and Bryan, 2015). In Table 3.1 we summarise the content that could be taught in each dimension and how we suggest applying them to business schools. First, climate change science addresses the underlying natural science of the carbon cycle, causes of global warming and climate (e.g. greenhouse gas concentration, temperature increase, etc.), and other impacts (e.g. on sea level

Table 3.1: The three dimensions of climate change education in business schools

Climate Change Education (CCE)	Content	Implications for business schools
Climate change science education	• Carbon cycle • Greenhouse gases and their global warming potential • Sources of greenhouse gases, such as the burning of fossil fuels or food waste • Impacts of climate change on nature, species, and countries • Carbon sinks and carbon storage	Business school students need to have a basic understanding of climate change science to inform the decisions they must take regarding impactful climate solutions and in response to risks for organisations and societies. One hour required in one of the core modules/courses.
Climate Change Mitigation Education (CCME)	• Climate solutions on the energy supply side, such as carbon price, fossil fuel phase outs, subsidies of renewable resources (solar, wind, water, tidal) • Climate solutions on the demand side to reduce energy consumption, such as insulating buildings and increasing energy efficiency in factories • Climate solutions to reduce other greenhouse gas emissions, such as methane or nitrous oxide, by changing diets, reducing food waste, or transforming to organic agriculture; or F-gases, for example, by changing the need for air-conditioning through better building design and the need for refrigeration through reduced transport of goods • Climate solutions to capture existing greenhouse gas emissions from the atmosphere, such as increasing natural carbon sinks, for example, greening cities with vertical farming or regrowing seagrass in coastal areas or climate solutions in development but not yet scalable, such as technological carbon dioxide removal	These climate solutions need to be taught in every discipline in a business school. In **operations**, every measurement to reduce energy consumption should be a priority in the decision-making process. In **economics or strategy**, students need to learn about policies to incentivise the transition to a low-carbon society and new models, such as 'doughnut economics' or 'Earth4All'. In **accounting**, students need to learn carbon accounting and how to integrate this into corporate reporting. In **HR**, this might include changes to recruitment processes (more virtual), integrating climate-related performance indicators, or hiring staff with distinct capabilities necessary for the organisation's sustainability transformation. And so on: students need to be equipped with tools and frameworks to transform **every** discipline.

| **Climate Change Adaptation Education (CCAE)** | • Concept of resilience
• Disaster risk reduction strategies
• Designing factories and storage facilities so that they can cope better with flooding and other problems caused by climate change
• Knowledge of how to swiftly restore facilities and supply chains after climate disasters | Some of these topics need to be taught in every business school, such as restoring and future-proofing supply chains. Others are especially important for business schools in the more vulnerable nations, which have to already react or be prepared for climate disasters, such as immense flooding. |

rise, crop yield, the economy, health, inequalities, etc.). While students might have a basic understanding of climate change science from their previous education or by keeping up to date with the news, students in the Yale (2016) study highlighted that they are far less knowledgeable about what business can actually do about climate change and that this was not covered in the curriculum of their business schools. In Tables 3.1 and 3.2, we provide ideas on how these issues can be addressed in different subject areas. More ideas on what business can do are laid out in the aforementioned *The Handbook of Carbon Management: A Step-By-Step Guide to High-Impact Climate Solutions for Every Manager in Every Function* (Molthan-Hill et al., 2023).

Second, climate change mitigation will prevent dangerous anthropogenic interference within the climate system (IPCC, 2022). According to the Earth Index,

> the G20 countries are responsible for about 80% of global GHG emissions. For the G20 in total, GHG emissions increased in 2019, resulting in an Earth Index score of −15%. The power sector had a score of 5%, indicating that while there was a slight decline in emissions, the pace of reductions would have to be 20 times higher than in 2019 to be on track for meeting the aggregate G20 target. Emissions increased in all the other sectors, yielding negative Earth Index scores and revealing the extent to which outcomes and aspirations are not yet aligned, at least at the level of the entire G20.
>
> (Corporate Knights, 2022: 12)

Therefore, closing the gap between GHG emissions pledges and current actions and policies to reduce GHG emissions requires ambitious climate change mitigation efforts to transform to an energy-efficient, low-carbon economy, globally (McKenzie, 2021; UNFCCC, 2015). Business schools must intensify joint efforts to (1) provide learning opportunities about and (2) take action on GHG emission reductions to avoid massive climate change adaptation in the future. In all chapters of this book, we highlight the importance of CCME within CCE and make recommendations on how CCME can be integrated into every business school discipline.

Third, CCAE addresses adapting to life in a changing climate by reducing risk from harmful climate change impacts. Climate mitigation and adaptation goals have synergies and trade-offs with efforts to achieve sustainable development (IPCC, 2022). Historically, most developing and low-emitting countries are more vulnerable and suffering the most from climate change. They are thus focusing on fast adaptation (Simmons, 2020). Business schools might want to put a stronger

Table 3.2: CCE by subject area within business schools

Subject area	Examples of curriculum topics and sources	CCE generated impact
Procurement, Supply, and Logistics	**Topics:** Mapping and measuring greenhouse gas (GHG) emissions in supply chain components and activities to identify the most substantial sources of GHG emissions (e.g. purchasing, transporting and processing raw materials; generating waste from the production process; packaging products; engaging customers in the identification of creative re-use solutions at the end of a product's intended life). **Sources:** Chartered Institute of Procurement and Supply (www.cips.org), see in particular Rowsell (2022); Lăzăroiu et al. (2020); Macfarlanes (2020)	• Raising the awareness of businesses with regard to their direct or indirect impact on the climate, especially in the supply chain. • Working with businesses to collate and interpret data about their contribution to GHG emissions. • Making recommendations to businesses on changes they can implement to reduce GHGs in the short, medium and long term (e.g., through direct practical steps or through developing processes and policies.) • Working with businesses to develop a strategic, organisation-wide approach to reducing GHG emissions.
Marketing	**Topics:** • Creating a climate-responsible product offer • Framing promotion messages for climate-conscious audiences as well as climate-unaware ones to ensure appropriate engagement with the product offer • Ensuring consistency of messages about the climate across channels (e.g. advertisements, product labeling and packaging, pricing strategies). **Sources:** Rashidi-Sabet and Madhavaram (2022); Townsend (2022)	Working with businesses to highlight the climate-responsible nature of their offer and to align communications with climate change mitigation actions.
Carbon Accounting	**Topics:** Generating a GHG emissions inventory for an organisation to underpin the organisation's strategy, objectives and KPI's towards Net Zero, in response to legal, regulatory requirements, and/or as a way of exercising corporate social responsibility. **Sources:** Bui et al. (2022); Kaplan and Ramanna (2022)	Working with businesses to establish • organisational and operational boundaries; • a base year to track performance over a period of time; • select and apply calculation tools in line with global standards and national regulations; and • make decisions about what information to report for maximum transparency.

focus on CCAE by teaching about resilience. We recommend that they ensure that their graduates are aware of how to reduce GHC emisssions and trade-offs. For instance, graduates might join companies that intend to increase fossil fuel extraction in more vulnerable countries to realize short-term economic benefits. Yet, these eventually lead to even more climate-related catastrophic events, such as floods, droughts, or storms. Also, graduates might belong to the more affluent part of the population that has a higher carbon footprint from excessive flying, high consumption, and air-conditioning the outdoors to have a comfortable life (Molthan-Hill et al., 2023).

Discipline-specific examples

The discipline-specific examples we have included in Table 3.2 are illustrative only. For a detailed discussion, please see Chapters 7, 11, and 14 in this book, as well as Chapters 8, 9, and 12 in Molthan-Hill et al.'s (2023) *Handbook of Carbon Management*. We chose procurement, marketing, and carbon accounting as examples of how to integrate CCME into teaching. Procurement decisions have the potential to impact almost three-quarters of a business's financial viability. Marketing is the business subject most directly linked to engaging customers in conversation and positive action about the climate, purchasing products and services aligned with their values. Carbon accounting generates data to underpin relevant, impactful decisions in a business about reducing its carbon footprint while maintaining financial viability and generating value not only for shareholders but also for the communities associated directly or indirectly with a business organisation. We emphasise, however, that all subject areas have a relevant contribution to make to CCME, and that the most impactful solutions are identified when collaboration across subject areas in business schools occurs.

In relation to each of the three selected areas, Table 3.2 offers examples of topics that are central to business students' understanding of climate change, as well as authentic, recent, and relevant scholarly and professional sources that faculty could engage with in order to develop their own and their students' awareness of how business activities and the climate are intertwined. We also identified ways in which CCE can generate immediate impact through tasks that students are set either for learning purposes or specifically for assessment, with emphasis on mitigation.

Prof. Alpha and Dr Omega: Taking on the challenge of learning and teaching strategy design

In the following section, we introduce the archetypal characters of Prof. Alpha and Dr Omega, two faculty from the same institution, to illustrate different and overlapping ways about integrating CCE into the business school curriculum using top-down and bottom-up approaches. CCE faculty development must cover numerous dimensions, such as course content revisions, disciplinary insights on mitigating climate change, scaffolding stakeholder engagement with CCE, and relevant pedagogic approaches for impactful CCE – all of which require appropriate CCE assessment for internal evaluators and external accreditors, as well as the fit with quality assurance processes within an institution. Through this next section, the two characters' story arcs engage with a variety of these topics. Prof. Alpha's story focuses on the strategic integration of CCE from an administrative perspective, or 'top-down'. In a complementary fashion, Dr Omega's story focuses on grassroots or 'bottom-up' orientation to adapting curriculum and integrating CCE. Our intent is to offer a realistic and perhaps non-linear way in which curriculum changes happen in response to external and internal drivers. Within the narrative we have integrated some of the relevant teaching and learning and assessment concepts involved in curricular changes, such as accreditation, student learning outcomes (SLO), and curriculum mapping. We recommend reading them together with the unfolding story, as they underpin the decisions being taken.

Prof. Alpha's strategic initiative for CCE

Prof. Alpha is a full, tenured professor in the accounting department at Thousand Oaks University. She has recently been promoted to an associate dean role in academic administration. The new dean has tasked her with leading the integration of explicit environmental and social impact throughout the business school curriculum and co-curricular programming to better align with the school's and university's recent mission statement updates. Specifically, the dean wants Alpha to champion a school-wide learning outcome related to climate change so that every single student in the business school has basic knowledge of climate-related science. The dean explicitly emphasised that important donors wanted their legacy to include support of sustainability priorities at their alma mater, and incorporating a school-wide learning outcome related to climate change was the starting point to pair with the recent mission statement updates. In fact, the donors had suggested to her and the dean a copy of a book by a US academic, Dr Rae André, titled *Lead for the Planet: Five Practices for Confronting Climate Change* as means to orient to the topic quickly.

Excited to prove herself in academic leadership, at the same time, Alpha is at a bit of a loss. The next AACSB accreditation reports are not due for three years, but it is hard to know where to start this process. 'Should I survey my colleagues to know what is happening already inside and outside the classroom? Is it better to talk to the senior professors to get them involved from the beginning? How will this impact existing quality reviews for course design and approvals, assessment practices for accreditation, instructor autonomy and freedom, and not add to the workload of the already-stressed faculty? I know that change takes a long time when integrating new experiential learning and potentially transformative pedagogies. Reading about PRME integration, I already feel a bit behind!' At Babson College in Massachusetts, USA, developing and implementing a tailored institutional framework for environmental and social responsibility was an eight-year change process (Greenberg et al., 2017). This made Alpha realise that integrating attention to climate change in the curriculum is going to take a while.

Alpha decided to start with some research on the accreditation standards. 'Perhaps these have mandates for sustainability-related topics? I'll ask our institutional assessment coordinator to see what they know'.

National accreditation agencies and assessment

Accreditation standards are strong external influences on higher education and business schools. In the UK, for example, the national accreditation standards are set by academics in collaboration with professional bodies and evaluated by the Quality Assurance Agency (QAA) until 2023 (QAA, 2019, 2022). In March 2023, QAA updated their Subject Benchmark for Business and Management to include education for sustainable development quoting: 'Sustainable management is a requirement for planetary survival' (2023: 7). In the United States, accreditation for higher education institutions happens through six regional associations: New England, Middle States, North Central, Southern, Western, and Northwest, all of which are recognised by the US Department of Education, 2022. These accrediting bodies examine institutions overall, in a holistic manner, rather than specific programs within institutions. Currently, these bodies neither mandate specific student learning outcomes nor climate change mandates in their accreditation standards. Alternatively, their holistic approach utilises a variety of direct and indirect measures from across the institution, including some from academic programs. In the United States all higher education institutions must have this regional accreditation to receive certain federal funding (CHEA, n.d.). Understanding the role and influence of these organisations is important to understand the influence of governmental stakeholders and standard setters in higher education.

Alpha had recently heard Dr Beck-Dudley, president and CEO of AACSB, speak about the updated 2020 standards at an academic conference and her emphasis on business schools' role in fostering positive societal impact (AACSB, 2022a). 'Surely, this was promising, especially the requirement updates in 2020 AACSB added Standard 9.1 on page 62: "The school demonstrates positive societal impact through internal and external initiatives and/or activities, consistent with the school's mission, strategies, and expected outcomes"'. Alpha spotted that AACSB even suggested institutions to use the UN's Sustainable Development Goals as a framework for documenting 'societal impact activities and initiatives across all areas of the standards', including Standard 4: curriculum. 'This certainly would help matters, since climate connects to several of the SDGs next to #13 Climate Action', she thought. She read about how the AACSB developed a framework to foster social impact leaders (AACSB, 2022b). Flipping over to the EQUIS website (n.d.), Alpha could see strong parallels since that organisation had already integrated ethics, responsibility, and sustainability (ERS) into all instructional programme levels, faculty, and research and development (EQUIS, 2022). 'Great!' Alpha thought. 'Now that the demands of accreditations are aligning more with our strategic direction and the goals of our donors, it looks like we can use assessment information for both agencies'.

Business school accreditation

Many business schools participate in various accreditation processes. Standards resulting from an accreditation have direct implications for teaching and learning assessment practices. The most popular business school accreditation organisations include:

- AACSB: www.aacsb.edu/
- ACBSP: https://acbsp.org/general/custom.asp?page=accreditation-types
- AMBA: www.associationofmbas.com/business-schools/accreditation/
- EQUIS: www.efmdglobal.org/accreditations/business-schools/equis/
- IACBE: https://iacbe.org/

These associations offer structure and guidance to members on how to align their curriculum to the various standards promoted at each institution. The AACSB refers to standards for accreditation as Assurance of Learning (AoL). AACSB has recently updated its standards (Borschbach and Mescon, 2021). These updates have implications for CCE. They now explicitly emphasise the various faculty roles beyond content delivery, such as mentoring, facilitating, and connecting. Specifically, Standard 9 states: 'The school demonstrates positive societal impact through internal and external initiatives and/or activities, consistent with the school's mission, strategies, and expected outcomes'. AACSB-accredited institutions are expected to document their positive societal impact across various standards, such as Standard 1 (strategic planning), Standard 4 (curriculum), Standard 8 (scholarship), and Standard 9 (external initiatives and/or activities) (AACSB, 2020). These Standard changes directly support curricular innovations, such as CCE, that create both social and ecological impacts.

'Since accreditors are now promoting social impact, it will certainly help me make the business case to my senior colleagues that creating climate-focused learning outcomes align with the accreditors' interests', reflected Alpha. Her mind raced ahead. 'This curricular revision and co-curricular development can be a means to partially address this standard and not add more work. Also, it seems that the pre-promotion faculty are more open to these types of changes'. Her mind moving backwards in time, she recalled that during a tea break, she had been talking with Omega, a recent hire, who seemed to mention something about GHG emissions, or climate change, or something similar. Surely, he would be onboard.

Alpha considered these insights further. 'Well, I now have a business-case argument for senior faculty and some coalition of younger faculty, but I still don't know what we have going on now. Maybe I'm making assumptions without data'. Thinking back to her days on the institutional assessment committee at the university, she remembered two key dimensions required for internal programme reviews – explicit learning outcomes and curriculum mapping. Completing a curriculum map in a chart or table would be a good visual to depict when and where in the curriculum the learning goals or outcomes are already addressed that relate to our mission updates. We can then pair this with the most recent EQUIS standards and AACSB updates. She played with this idea in her mind. 'We could start with a modified version of curriculum mapping with faculty identifying what learning outcomes are already being covered that relate to our mission updates. We could use the SDGs as a framework for charting out the mission-related learning outcomes. I could even use the template from Nottingham Business School in the UK, which I was given at the last PRME conference [see Template 1]'.

Template 1: Mapping the SDGs.

NOTTINGHAM
BUSINESS SCHOOL

Mapping the UN Sustainable Development Goals (SDGs)

Please complete form and email to muhammadusman.mazhar@ntu.ac.uk

Your name

List all the modules, which you teach and where you have integrated the SDGs:

Fill the section below for one module of your choice which you see as the most advanced with regards to the integration of the SDGs:

Context *(tick or highlight all that are relevant)*

Level of study
- Undergraduate year 1 (level 4)
- Undergraduate year 2 (level 5)
- Undergraduate year 3/4 (level 6)
- Postgraduate (level 7)

Type
- Case study used in teaching
- Module content
- Teaching method/s
- Module assessment
- Research or research-informed teaching (see back of page)
- Continuing Professional Development (CPD) activities
- Other _____

Which of the Sustainable Development Goals does this relate to?

Give a brief description of how you have integrated the SDGs in your module (if not highlighted above, please tell us which module):

We are looking for good practice case studies for the PRME report, can we use yours: Yes/No

Template 1: Continued

Research Focused

If you are doing research, please tick which of the SDGs your research relates to?

Give a brief description of your research.

Source: Copyright Nottingham Business School, UK.

Learning outcomes and curriculum mapping

The assessment cycle often begins with identifying **student learning outcomes** (SLOs) detailing what student learners should be able to demonstrate, represent, or produce upon completion of a programme of study (Maki, 2010). SLOs are typically linked to a module or experience (or a sequence of modules or experiences) designed to achieve that outcome. The most famous mode for developing SLOs is Bloom's

Taxonomy (1956), which covers three main domains of learning: cognitive, psychomotor, and affective. We note extensive critiques of Bloom's pyramid model based on advances in educational research over the last 50 years (see Kreitzer and Madaus, 1994) and offer other alternative SLO taxonomies later in the chapter.

These outcomes can be developed at the extra-institutional, institution, school/division, course (programme), module (class), or assignment levels. We will discuss these different types of SLO at the various levels in detail as the chapter progresses and provide climate-focused examples. These levels form a type of nested hierarchy of sorts, so when conducting assessments, it is important to determine which level of assessment you are targeting and understand how they are interconnected.

In an ideal world, any given level of assessment builds upon the preceding levels. A common practice of identifying these alignments is through the process of curriculum mapping. '**Curriculum mapping** is a procedure for documenting and visualising student learning at the programmatic level' (Archambault and Masunaga, 2015: 504). Often a chart or table, curriculum maps show educators and administrators when in the course certain learning goals or outcomes are addressed. Curriculum mapping is a dynamic and ongoing process in higher education as new institutional mandates are adopted, accreditation standards updated, and new programs added to the curriculum.

Thinking back to the conversation with the donors, Alpha recalled how at one point they were strongly concerned about integrating the basics of climate change science into the curriculum. Also, in the last advisory meeting with businesses, a couple of hiring managers mentioned the demands for employees who have training in climate-related issues. 'I'm pretty sure this isn't being taught, although the curriculum map would confirm this definitively. Hopefully, the mapping exercise will identify some potential modules to consider', reflected Alpha.

Racing ahead in her mind, she thought, 'What would a climate change curriculum map actually look like? Students would need to understand carbon accounting. I know that much from presentations at recent accounting conferences. That way, they could measure the reductions achieved. Businesses like to quantify outcomes'.

'Now that I think of it', she pondered further, 'operations and supply chain faculty could help with quantifying energy efficiency practices. We would need to help students understand the basic best practices of climate change communication. It can't be all "doom and gloom" anymore'. Taking another moment to think about other disciplines, she added, 'What should be integrated into marketing? Perhaps Omega has some ideas. By the end of the curriculum, our MBA students should be able to critique "business as usual" corporate strategy and identify how climate change dimensions could be integrated into the standard analysis tools like SWOT and perhaps even design a climate-focused SWOT. There's a lot to rethink, it turns out!'

Dr Omega's search for teaching climate solutions

Omega has recently completed his doctorate in marketing and has worked at the Thousand Oaks University for five years. He has been increasingly involved in course design and redesigns with the rapid shift towards digital marketing. This type of 'traditional top-down course design' emphasised the insights from external bodies, like professional marketing associations, informing how he might update courses and learning activities to address new digital marketing learning outcomes (Lund Dean et al., 2022: 8). These reworks went smoothly since he could make these decisions independently.

He has worked as faculty advisor for the student marketing club and built strong relationships with the leaders and many club members. After a recent event, he asked the students what they would like to see changed in their course degree. Nearly all students mentioned their desire for more focus on environmental topics, such as how marketing can avoid greenwashing and promote environmentally friendly products and services. Several students mentioned their concerns about climate change and participation in one of the numerous environmental clubs on campus or participation in protests as part of the Fridays For Future movement. He realised that in student-selected projects of this term, nearly each one focused on these areas, including teams that focused on the storytelling approaches used by organisers of the climate emergency protests. He wondered what it would take to introduce these changes and shift towards 'engaged learning [with] bottom up design' with students (Lund Dean et al., 2022: 8). After all, he had revised several courses recently. 'How can I make such changes to honour students' passion and interests?'

Even with motivated students in his classes, he knew that many young people felt discouragement and despair about climate change. Integrating these grand

Sample curriculum map:	Required module	I=Introduced R=Reinforced A=Assessed M=Mastery							
		Introduction to business	*Accounting*	*Economics*	*Organisational behavior*	*Operations management*	*Marketing*	*Human resources*	*Strategy capstone*
Climate change learning outcomes									
Designing systems to maximize energy efficiency for firms.		I	R	R		M			M, A
Implementing carbon reduction policies in organisations.					I			R	M, A
Generating climate change communication plans for SMEs.		I			I		A		M, A
Critiquing gaps in standard business analysis tools in regards to climate change.		I	R	R		R		R	M, A

challenge topics rife with emotional and political dimensions would require more active learning and attention to the psychological issues facing Generation Z students. 'How can I craft learning experiences that blend marketing with today's topics and prioritise positive experiences that activate motivation, hope, and positivity vs reinforcing anxiety?' he mused.

Emotions and experiential learning

Key findings in sustainability pedagogy and experiential learning point to the need for active learning and attention to positive and negative emotions in learning when covering content like climate change and other polarising topics. Based on the institutional instruction norms, personal teaching philosophy, and individual skill sets, instructors need to make thoughtful instructional design decisions to achieve learning outcomes. Following is a selection of resources that offer guidance on these important facets of facilitating experiential learning.

Course Design:

- Lund Dean, K., Niemi, N., and Fornaciari, C. (2022). *Course Design and Assessment*. Edward Elgar.

Active Learning:

- Creutzig, F., and Kapmeier, F. (2020). 'Engage, don't preach: Active learning triggers climate action.' *Energy Research & Social Science*, *70*, 101779, ISSN 2214–6296. https://doi.org/10.1016/j.erss.2020.101779.
- Molthan-Hill, P., Robinson, Z. P., Hope, A., Dharmasasmita, A., and McManus, E. (2020). 'Reducing carbon emissions in business through responsible management education: influence at the micro-, meso- and macro-levels.' *International Journal of Management Education*, *18* (1), 100328. ISSN 1472–8117

Academic Emotions:

- Pekrun, R., and Linnenbrink-Garcia, L. (2012). 'Academic emotions and student engagement', in S. L. Christenson, A. L. Reschley, and C. Wylie (eds.), *Handbook of Research on Student Engagement* (pp. 259–82). New York: Springer.

A few days later, Omega was thinking back to past experiences that didn't go so well, when he just threw in new case studies and exercises and didn't really think about their intention. The students were confused, the simulations ran over time in the tutorials, and the students complained that the activities didn't match the module assessment. 'I do have control of readings and could add something small in an upcoming unit, like fast fashion or coffee production. This type of small change won't violate our approval process for quality control if it's not extensive'. He'd learned the hard way in another marketing course by making too many changes to module content and adding in the digital marketing end-of-module assessments that weren't pre-approved by the committee. While they were more engaging for the students and more interesting to mark, it had not made the quality committee members happy when they found out.

The idea from the workshop

A recent faculty development workshop had offered a session on course planning. What was it again? Looking around his desk, he pulled out the worksheet he reflected on the 'backward design' model (Wiggins and McTighe, 2005). 'Instead of focusing on the learning activities, I need to start further upstream with the bigger picture: What should my students know about climate literacy and digital marketing at the end of the module? How will I know whether the students know the specific climate literacy and marketing learning outcome I develop? What activities and materials will best contribute to this learning outcome?'

'In terms of module outcomes, there should be something like, "Students will evaluate different climate change mitigation tools in marketing." In order to evaluate and compare tools, I need to provide them with the foundational concepts on the topic – heck, I need to learn some of this, too!' he reflected. 'So, I'd need another learning outcome focused on knowledge: "Students will understand evidence-based consumer education campaign strategies for textiles." While this is a little specific, it fits with students' interests in sustainable fashion. It wouldn't hurt to have a learning outcome for packaging, since this is such an important dimension of marketing. Something to the effect that "students will be able to explain the top green packaging strategies for UK retailers". However, there's more to it than that'. He paused. 'I'd like students to be able to apply these ideas and determine which packaging strategies fit with any given brand. Ultimately, it would be more analytical and to the effect students will be able to distinguish between green packaging strategies that align with brand image and those that do not'.

'I know I can't do all these immediately, but I can add readings and support knowledge-focused learning outcomes. I could add a mitigation-focused reading on garment washing instructions and carbon reduction'.

Student learning outcomes (SLO)

What do we want our students to know, do, feel, or be as a result of their educational experiences? Our answer to these questions in assessment terms is student learning outcomes. While simple on the surface, this question is like a layered dessert or potentially a horrible concoction. With multiple actors invested in the assessment process, there are many answers to this question. If it's complementary between the various interests, then learning can become a delicious trifle. If there are contradictions between the assessment layers, the contrasting interest 'flavours' can clash, making learning a mouthful of oddly composed tastes and textures. First, we need to begin with a taxonomy or framework, whether it's Bloom (1956) or updated versions of cognitive, psychomotor, or affective (Krathwohl et al., 1964; Anderson and Krathwohl, 2000), SOLO (Biggs and Collis, 1982; Biggs, 1999), constructive alignment (Biggs, 2014), or Fink's non-hierarchical model (2003, 2009).

'It's energizing to think about the learning activities I can do with the students. If I take the SLO, "students will understand evidence-based consumer education campaign strategies for textiles", I need to provide students with the big picture about energy sources and their impact on climate at the macro-societal level, so they understand options for companies and consumers. I could use a simulation for this'. He remembered the environmental club had a challenge using the En-ROADS[1] climate solutions simulation model, co-developed by Climate Interactive and the MIT Sloan Sustainability Initiative. En-ROADS is embedded in current scientific understanding, is fully documented, and calculates a scenario in less than a second. 'My students definitely like interactive simulations like this.

1   www.climateinteractive.org/en-roads.

Climate Interactive offers different modes of interactions that can be helpful, depending on the setting and learning outcomes, from an interactive workshop over a role-playing game to a student assignment. Since I don't want to incorporate this into a formal module assessment just yet, I could just do some informal discussion about how En-ROADS helps enhance their understanding of energy and climate, by talking to them after the final exams. It will help me understand what students are getting from the activity'.

Direct and indirect assessment

To date, there are a limited number of studies on climate-related assessment within business and higher education more broadly, although some research exists on sustainability-related assessment (Molthan-Hill and Blaj-Ward, 2022).

Given this state of affairs, returning to assessment basics can be helpful. Once formal SLOs are developed, educators need to determine whether the students are meeting these SLOs or not. For each SLO, criteria need to be established to evaluate performance. Broadly speaking, **criteria** '[i]n the higher education context . . . are specifications of the quality of inputs, processes or outputs and/or standards (academic, competence, service or organisational) against which provision or performance can be evaluated. More specifically, in a learning context, they may be the articulation of the judgments of student learning against which students are (summatively) assessed' (Harvey, 2023).

Once criteria are established, evidence needs to be collected. We can think about evidence in two different ways: direct and indirect (Suskie, 2018). **Direct evidence** of student learning is data where students demonstrate (or do not demonstrate) specific knowledge, skills, and/or behaviours and it needs to be tangible, visible, and measurable. For instance, summative assessment assignment from the end of the term. Direct evidence is compelling because you are directly reviewing students' work performances and evaluating what they've learned from the assignment, module, or programme. The second type of evidence is **indirect evidence**. This is data that requires reflection about student learning and is more of a proxy that students are likely learning (i.e. grades). Indirect measures are not as strong as direct measures since we need to make assumptions about what exactly the proxy signs mean.

Engaging with En-ROADS

Based on his prior experience with En-ROADS and assessing the different modes of interaction with it, Omega found that the role-playing game Climate Action Simulation (Jones et al., 2019; Rooney-Varga et al., 2020) would be a good fit with his class outcomes. The Climate Action Simulation is a mock UN Summit game that embeds the simulation of the natural-technical climate-energy system (with En-ROADS) in a simulation of social interactions in a role-play. Participants take on the roles of world leaders in different delegations at a UN climate emergency summit, such as representatives of world governments; clean tech; conventional energy; industry and commerce; land, agriculture, and forestry; and climate justice hawks. They are charged with negotiating the policies and actions for an energy transition that meets international climate goals of limiting global warming to well below 2 °C, as agreed in the Paris Agreement.

He read that the role-playing game increases the sense of urgency, as well as the motivation of participants to act on climate, and may help build consensus towards ambitious climate action (Rooney-Varga et al., 2018, 2020, 2021a, 2021b). To learn more about the background, structure, and behaviour of the simulator and the best-practice tips to facilitate the simulation, Omega participated in the eight-week, free-of-charge En-ROADS training[2] and downloaded all game materials.[3] He decided to kick off the next course with the Climate Action Simulation, divided over two sessions of 90 minutes each. 'The simulation will enable my students to better understand why corporate environmental sustainability in marketing is crucial'.

For the simulation two months later, he assigned the students to six delegations. 'I prepared the delegation tables according to the delegations' social and financial

2   https://learn.climateinteractive.org/.
3   www.climateinteractive.org/climate-action-simulation/leading-the-climate-action-simulation/#materials.

status and resulting inequalities. I put a tablecloth on the table for the conventional energy delegation and provided snacks and drinks. The climate justice hawks simply had to sit on the floor'. He gave his students time to study their delegation-specific two-page briefings. In the role as the UN secretary-general, he then officially welcomed the delegations and formally called the summit to order. Using En-ROADS, he described the 'baseline emissions scenario' and the expected climate and non-climate impacts. 'Especially showing non-climate impacts such as "expected additional deaths due to extreme heat", "species losing more than 50% of their climatic range", or the "impact of climate change on the economy" turned out to be very helpful to underline the urgency for climate action'.

Omega then called the delegations to negotiate over the policies to mitigate climate change. After the negotiations, a representative of each delegation gave a one-minute plenary speech that included the proposed action. After each speech, he tested the proposed action with En-ROADS and explored its expected impacts on the climate-energy system together with the audience. 'This worked out great! En-ROADS is especially powerful when it challenges the participants' mental models: asking the students for their expectations on temperature impact before I entered the pledges into En-ROADS turned out to be a big learning opportunity'. At the end of the first class, all delegations had negotiated and delivered their speeches. The proposed actions decreased the expected temperature by 2100, but it was still way above the goal. Omega finished this class requesting the participants to become more ambitious for the upcoming rounds of negotiations in the next class.

Further, Omega asked his students to work on the En-ROADS student assignment[4] that he slightly adapted to his course's needs. In the roles of their delegation, the students developed a climate scenario in line with their delegation's position. They handed in a four-slide presentation of their scenarios and an analysis before the next class. 'This made them reflect deeper about their negotiation position and the effectiveness of the policies'.

Welcoming his students in the role of the UN secretary-general to the second class, Omega let the students negotiate two more rounds. The students presented their pledges in plenary speeches, and Omega tested them with En-ROADS until the temperature increase until 2100 was 1.8 °C. He then declared the summit as a success. 'It was very interesting to see how some of the delegations negotiated over specific actions. The conventional energy delegation and the world governments

4   www.climateinteractive.org/guided-assignment/.

Figure 3.2: The delegation of the climate justice hawks delivers a plenary speech during a Climate Action Simulation at the ESB Business School, Reutlingen University.

Source: Florian Kapmeier, ESB Business School.

negotiated hard about the carbon price. Students built coalitions to strengthen their negotiation position'. The role-play ended with a 30-minute debrief for students to reveal their feelings, express what they like about the future scenario, and what their next steps are towards making this scenario happen. Insights from these two non-graded kick-off sessions carried the conversations in the marketing class for the entire semester.

The students were inspired to contribute their own climate solutions and organised a weekly clothes swap shop to counteract the negative sides of fast fashion. Omega realised that he could go further with his marketing class and encourage his students to act as consultants to retailers and other organisations as part of Thousand Oaks' Student Consulting. A local government official had asked if his students could promote pro-environmental behaviour in the city with different campaigns engaging more citizens. 'This could be a fantastic piece of assessment', he thought and decided to make a bigger change to his course in the next academic year. Reading Robinson and Molthan-Hill's (2021) 'Assessing competencies for future-fit graduates and responsible leaders' inspired him to add impact assessment to his course.

Motivating strategic change with allies, inspiration, and less coercion

Back with Alpha, after a long day of meetings, she looked at her calendar and noticed this week's faculty meeting where she would introduce the idea of incorporating climate change formally into the curriculum. 'What's going to be the best way forward with this initiative? Faculty don't like being told what to do, but it's no use hiding that this is top-down. That said, if we work together, we could make a strong impact in our classrooms and the community'. She recalled a recent presentation on a course where student teams from Nottingham Business School partnered with local organisations to recommend measures to reduce greenhouse gas emissions. This type of consulting builds relationships with future employers, provides students with real-life application, and has direct positive benefits for the community by reducing emissions (Molthan-Hill et al., 2020). This type of learning would work for so many of our stakeholders – students, employers, donors, and top administrators.

'Who might be some allies here? Well, Prof. Foresight had sat on the university strategy committee. He might have some insights into sustainability at the institutional level. Then there's Prof. Examiner, who recently sat on the AACSB accreditation committee. Perhaps a chat with her would be savvy. Oh yeah, and there's that Omega, who was doing this En-ROADS simulation in his class last week when I was there auditing his afternoon section. The students were so engaged, amazing! Perhaps I can ask him to share his insights on students' interests'.

We end the journey here with Dr Omega and Prof. Alpha. Clearly, there's much more ahead for each of their initiatives. Alpha will need to think about her change management strategies and build a coalition to integrate systemic change in the business school. Omega will need to work closely with the quality committee to follow guidelines as he attempts to make adjustments to his courses in advance of broader institutional changes. He will also need to figure out the politics within the marketing department to make sure senior faculty members aren't opposed to these changes. After all, they sit on his annual review committee.

Conclusion

Embedded in the literature on climate change and CCE, in this chapter we offer a contextualised view of possible first steps about how to integrate CCE using a fictitious case study. We provide two lenses on curricular change management: one top-down (Prof. Alpha) and one bottom-up (Dr. Omega). We intend that these CCE approaches, disciplinary insights, best practice examples, and foundational learning and teaching assessment concepts help business school colleagues build the fundamentals to begin their own curricular revisions in their business schools towards scientifically based CCE.

Self-guided activity: designing a new teaching unit with assessment worksheet

In this activity, you will familiarise yourself with the steps you have to consider when designing a new teaching unit. It would be good to have some uninterrupted time where you can plan your new teaching unit. Redesigning teaching to incorporate climate change mitigation and solutions strategies can take many different forms. For some modules, it may require integrating a new learning outcomes, and for others, it may require a radical redesign of the entire module. This worksheet is designed to assist in both instances. A more detailed worksheet can be found on the companion website.

1. **Reflection:** What is your *why* for integrating climate change mitigation and solutions into your course?
   - Take some time to journal, doodle, or build a model about your reason and rationale for your changes.

2. **Starting small:** Is there an activity that you could easily integrate into your teaching?
   - What is the key message you want to communicate?

3. **Redesigning some of your teaching:** Decide which course, module, or other teaching unit you want to transform.
   - What do you want the students to learn? (See step 4.)
   - Do you need to inform yourself? (See step 5.)
   - Which learning activities do you want to use? (See step 6.)
   - How do you want to assess that the learning outcomes have been achieved? (See step 7.)
   - Do you need to get buy-in from someone? (See step 8.)
   - Are you walking the talk? (See step 9.)

Table 3.3: SLO review grid

Question	Yes	No
Does the outcome support the program goals?	☐	☐
Does the outcome describe what the program intends for students to know (cognitive), value (affective), or do (behavioural)?	☐	☐
Is the outcome detailed and specific?	☐	☐
Is the outcome measurable?*	☐	☐
Is the outcome a result of learning?	☐	☐
Do you have or can you create an activity to enable students to learn and demonstrate the desired outcome?	☐	☐
Can the results from assessing this outcome be used to make decisions on how to improve the program?	☐	☐

*Taken from Nazareth University Assessment Committee Resources.

- When will you teach this for the first time?
- Ready to go . . .

4. **Student learning outcomes (SLO):** What do you want students to learn about climate change?
   - Conduct a review of our SLO with the following tool.* Revise as necessary.

5. **Professional development and preparation:** What upskilling and updates do you need to make to integrate CCE into your modules?
   - What content areas do you need to expand? Is there a chapter in this book that could help you with this? Are there workshops or webinars in your discipline?

6. **Learning activities:** How can you provide teaching and learning opportunities that support your climate change SLOs?
   - What learning activities support each SLO?

7. **Assessment practices:** In what ways can you determine if students are learning what you intend?
   - Do you have self-determination with summative assessments? If so, are there opportunities to develop social impact assessments where students have action projects or consulting projects where they apply climate mitigation strategies using disciplinary knowledge?

8. **Administrative and colleague support:** How can you ensure your supervisors or line managers support course design changes?
   - Do you need permission to make changes to your course? If so, what are the procedures to follow for authorising changes (co-instructors, section supervisors, deans, rectors, quality review committees, accreditation committees, others)?

9. **Walking the talk (syllabus):** What policies and practices might you change or alter to integrate climate change concepts?

References

AACSB. (2020). *2020 Guiding Principles and Standards for AACSB Business Accreditation.* Available at www.aacsb.edu/-/media/documents/accreditation/2020-aacsb-business-accreditation-standards-july-2021.pdf?rev=7f4c2893dc1e47eb91c472d9fc59b238&hash=833E7A4A1E094BADDACDAAB60CF2CD69

AACSB. (2022a, July). *2020 Guiding Principles and Standards for AACSB Business Accreditation.* Available at www.aacsb.edu/-/media/documents/accreditation/2020-aacsb-business-accreditation-standards-jul-1-2022.pdf?rev=b40ee40b26a14d4185c504d00bade58f&hash=9B649E9B8413DFD660C6C2AFAAD10429

AACSB. (2022b, July). *Accelerating a Framework for Societal Impact Leadership: Insights from the 2021–22 Innovation Committee.* Available at www.aacsb.edu/-/media/publications/research-reports/accelerating-a-framework-for-societal-impact-leadership.pdf?rev=42d77bf6221e4769b80330e55eeb7d46&hash=F790E5E4D1904B833BF6AEBA5A154459

AACSB. (n.d.). *AACSB Accreditation.* Available at www.aacsb.edu/

ACBSP. (n.d.). *Types of Accreditation.* Available at https://acbsp.org/general/custom.asp?page=accreditation-types

AMBA. (n.d.). *What Is Association of MBAs Accreditation?* Available at www.associationofmbas.com/business-schools/accreditation/

Anderson, L.W., & Krathwohl, D.R. (2000). *A Taxonomy for Learning, Teaching, and Assessing: A Revision of Bloom's Taxonomy of Educational Objectives,* Complete ed. New York: Longman. Print.

André, R. (2020). *Lead for the Planet: Five Practices for Confronting Climate Change.* Toronto: University of Toronto Press.

Archambault, S.G., & Masunaga, J. (2015). Curriculum mapping as a strategic planning tool. *Journal of Library Administration,* 55(6), 503–19.

Biggs, J. (1999). What the student does: Teaching for enhanced learning. *Higher Education Research & Development,* 18(1), 57–75. https://doi.org/10.1080/0729436990180105

Biggs, J. (2014). Constructive alignment in university teaching. *HERDSA Review of Higher Education,* 1, 5–22. Available at www.herdsa.org.au/herdsa-review-higher-education-vol-1/5-22

Biggs, J., & Collis, K. (1982). *Evaluating the Quality of Learning: The SOLO Taxonomy.* New York: Academic Press.

Bloom, B.S. (1956). *Taxonomy of Educational Objectives, Handbook I: The Cognitive Domain.* New York: David McKay Co Inc.

Borschbach, A., & Mescon, T. (2021). *Transforming Assurance of Learning for Lasting Impact.* Available at www.aacsb.edu/insights/articles/2021/05/transforming-assurance-of-learning-for-lasting-impact

Bui, B., Houqe, M.N., & Zahir-ul-Hassan, M.K. (2022). Moderating effect of carbon accounting systems on strategy and carbon performance: A CDP analysis. *Journal of Management Control, 33,* 483–524. https://doi.org/10.1007/s00187-022-00346-7

CHEA. (n.d.). *Regional Accrediting Organizations.* Available at www.chea.org/regional-accrediting-organizations-accreditor-type

Chen, C.V.H.-H., Kearns, K., Eaton, L., Hoffmann, D.S., Leonard, D., & Samuels, M. (2022). Caring for our communities of practice in educational development. *To Improve the Academy: A Journal of Educational Development, 41*(1). https://doi.org/10.3998/tia.460

Climate Interactive. (2020). *En-ROADS Updated with New Baseline Scenario. Blog Post at Climate Interactive.* Available at https://www.climateinteractive.org/blog/en-roads-updated-with-new-baseline-scenario/

Climate Interactive. (2022). *Top Resources and Materials.* Available at https://support.climateinteractive.org/support/solutions/articles/47001152426-top-resources-materials

Climate Literacy and Action for All. (2023). Available at https://www.futurelearn.com/courses/climate-literacy-and-action-for-Climate Literacy and Action for all

Corporate Knights. (2022). *Earth Index: Tracking the G20 Response to the Climate Emergency.* Available at www.corporateknights.com/wp-content/uploads/2022/04/2022-Earth-Index-Report.pdf

Cox, C., & Flynn, S. (2022). *Climate Change Coaching: The Power of Connection to Create Climate Action.* London: Open University Press.

Creutzig, F., & Kapmeier, F. (2020). Engage, don't preach: Active learning triggers climate action. *Energy Research & Social Science, 70,* 101779. https://doi.org/10.1016/j.erss.2020.101779

Dietz, S., & Stern, N. (2015). Endogenous growth, convexity of damage and climate risk: How Nordhaus' framework supports deep cuts in carbon emissions. *The Economic Journal, 125*(583), 574–620.

Doerr, J. (2021). *Speed & Scale: A Global Action Plan for Solving our Climate Crisis Now.* London: Penguin.

EQUIS. (2022). *EFMD Accreditation for International Business Schools.* Available at www.efmdglobal.org/wp-content/uploads/2022_EQUIS_Standards_and_Criteria.pdf

EQUIS. (n.d.). *EQUIS.* Available at www.efmdglobal.org/accreditations/business-schools/equis/

Fink, L.D. (2003). *Creating Significant Learning Experiences: An Integrated Approach to Designing College Courses.* San Francisco: Jossey-Bass.

Fink, L.D. (2009). *A Self-Directed Guide to Designing Course for Significant Learning.* Available at www.bu.edu/sph/files/2014/03/www.deefinkandassociates.com_GuidetoCourseDesignAug05.pdf

Greenberg, D.N., Deets, S., Erzurumlu, S., Hunt, J., Manwaring, M., Rodgers, V., & Swanson, E. (2017). Signing to living PRME: Learning from a journey towards responsible management education. *The International Journal of Management Education, 15*(2), Part B, 205–18. https://doi.org/10.1016/j.ijme.2017.02.007

Harvard University. (2022). *The Future of Climate Education at Harvard University.* Available at www.harvard.edu/climate-and-sustainability/wp-content/uploads/sites/7/2022/09/Harvard-Climate-Edu-Report-Final-v2.pdf

Harvey, L. (2023). *Analytic Quality Glossary.* Available at www.qualityresearchinternational.com/glossary/

IACBE. (n.d.). *International Accreditation Council for Business Education.* Available at https://iacbe.org/

Intergovernmental Panel on Climate Change (IPCC). (2018). Summary for policymakers. In V. Masson-Delmotte, P. Zhai, H.O. Pörtner, D. Roberts, J. Skea, P.R. Shukla, A. Pirani, W. Moufouma-Okia, C. Péan, R. Pidcock, S. Connors, J.B.R. Matthews, Y. Chen, X. Zhou, M.I. Gomis, E. Lonnoy, T. Maycock, M. Tignor, & T. Waterfield (eds.), *Global Warming of 1.5 °C. An IPCC Special Report on the Impacts of Global Warming of 1.5 °C Above Pre-Industrial Levels and Related Global Greenhouse Gas Emission Pathways, in the Context of Strengthening the Global Response to the Threat of Climate Change* (p. 32). World Meteorological Organization Technical Document. Available at https://www.ipcc.ch/site/assets/uploads/sites/2/2022/06/SR15_Summary_Volume_HR.pdf

IPCC. (2022). *Climate Change 2022: Mitigation of Climate Change. Contribution of Working Group III to the Sixth Assessment Report of the Intergovernmental Panel on Climate Change. Chapter 1.* Cambridge, UK and New York, NY: Cambridge University Press. doi: 10.1017/9781009157926.003

Jones, A.P., Johnston, E., Cheung, L., Zahar, Y, Kapmeier, F., Bhandari, B., Sterman, J.D., Rooney-Varga, J.N., & Reed, C. (2019). *Climate Action Simulation: Facilitator's Guide.* Cambridge, MA: Climate Interactive and MIT Sloan Sustainability Initiative.

Kaplan, R.S., & Ramanna, K. (2022). We need better carbon accounting: Here's how to get there. *Harvard Business Review.* Available at https://hbr.org/2022/04/we-need-better-carbon-accounting-heres-how-to-get-there

Krabbe, O., Linthorst, G., Blok, K., Crijns-Graus, W., van Vuuren Detlef, P., Höhne, N., Faria, P., Aden, N., & Pineda Alberto, C. (2015). Aligning corporate greenhouse-gas emissions targets with climate goals. *Nature Climate Change, 5*(12), 1057–60.

Krathwohl, D.R., Bloom, B.S., & Masia, B.B. (1964). *Taxonomy of Educational Objectives: Handbook II: Affective Domain.* New York: David McKay Co.

Kreitzer, A.E., & Madaus, G.F. (1994). Empirical investigations of the hierarchical structure of the taxonomy. In L.W. Anderson & L.A. Sosniak (eds.), *Bloom's Taxonomy: A Forty-Year Retrospective: Ninety-Third Yearbook of the National Society for the Study of Education, Part II* (pp. 64–81). Chicago, IL: University of Chicago Press.

Lăzăroiu, G., Ionescu, L., Uţă, C., Hurloiu, I., Andronie, M., & Dijmărescu, I. (2020). Environmentally responsible behavior and sustainability policy adoption in green public procurement. *Sustainability, 12*(5), 2110. MDPI AG. http://dx.doi.org/10.3390/su12052110

Lund Dean, K., Niemi, N., & Fornaciari, C. (2022). *Course Design and Assessment*. Northampton, MA: Edward Elgar.

Macfarlanes. (2020). *Managing Climate Change in Supply Chain Contracts*. Available at www.macfarlanes.com/what-we-think/in-depth/2020/managing-climate-change-in-supply-chain-contracts/

Maki, P.L. (2010). *Assessing for Learning: Building a Sustainable Commitment Across the Institution*, 2nd ed. Sterling, VA: Stylus.

Maloni, M.J., Palmer, T.B., Cohen, M., Gligor, D.M., Grout, J.R., & Myers, R. (2021). Decoupling responsible management education: Do business schools walk their talk? *The International Journal of Management Education*, 19(1), 100456. https://doi.org/10.1016/j.ijme.2021.100456

McKenzie, M. (2021). Climate change education and communication in global review: Tracking progress through national submissions to the UNFCCC Secretariat. *Environmental Education Research*, 27, 631–651.

Mochizuki, Y., & Bryan, A. (2015). Climate change education in the context of education for sustainable development: Rationale and principles. *Research*, 9(1), 4–26. https://doi.org/10.1177/0973408215569109

Molthan-Hill, P., & Blaj-Ward, L. (2022). Assessing climate solutions and taking climate leadership: How can universities prepare their students for challenging times? *Teaching in Higher Education*, 27(7), 943–52. https://doi.org/10.1080/13562517.2022.2034782

Molthan-Hill, P., Robinson, Z.P., Hope, A., Dharmasasmita, A., & McManus, E. (2020). Reducing carbon emissions in business through responsible management education: Influence at the micro-, meso- and macro-levels. *International Journal of Management Education*, 18(1), 100328.

Molthan-Hill, P., & Winfield, F. (2023). Climate literacy training for all. In P. Molthan-Hill, F. Winfield, R. Howarth, & M. Mazhar (eds.), *The Handbook of Carbon Management: A Step-by-Step Guide to High-Impact Climate Solutions for Every Manager in Every Function*. New York: Routledge.

Molthan-Hill, P., Winfield, F., Howarth, R., & Mazhar, M. (2023). *The Handbook of Carbon Management: A Step-by-Step Guide to High-Impact Climate Solutions for Every Manager in Every Function*. New York: Routledge.

Nicholas, K. (2021). *Under the Sky We Make*. New York: Putnam.

Pekrun, R., & Linnenbrink-Garcia, L. (2012). Academic emotions and student engagement. In S.L. Christenson, A.L. Reschley, & C. Wylie (eds.), *Handbook of Research on Student Engagement* (pp. 259–82). New York: Springer.

Quality Assurance Agency. (2019). *Subject Benchmark Statement: Business and Management*. Available at www.qaa.ac.uk/docs/qaa/subject-benchmark-statements/subject-benchmark-statement-business-and-management.pdf?sfvrsn=db39c881_5

Quality Assurance Agency. (2022, July 22). *QAA Demits DQB Status to Focus on Sector and Students in England*. Available at www.qaa.ac.uk/news-events/news/qaa-demits-dqb-status-to-focus-on-sector-and-students-in-england

Quality Assurance Agency. (2023, March 8). *Subject Benchmark Statement: Business and Management*. Available at https://www.qaa.ac.uk/the-quality-code/subject-benchmark-statements/subject-benchmark-statement-business-and-management

Rashidi-Sabet, S., & Madhavaram, S. (2022). A strategic marketing framework for emerging out of the climate change social trap: The case of the fashion industry. *Journal of Macromarketing, 42*(2), 267–91. https://doi.org/10.1177/02761467211058083

Robinson, Z., & Molthan-Hill, P. (2021). Assessing competencies for future-fit graduates and responsible leaders. In P. Baughan (ed.), *Assessment and Feedback in a Post-Pandemic Era: A Time for Learning and Inclusion* (pp. 196–213). York: Advance HE.

Rooney-Varga, J.N., Fracassi, E., Franck, T., Kapmeier, F., McCarthy, C., McNeal, K.S., Norfles, N., Rath, K., & Sterman, J.D. (2021a). A simulation game that motivates people to act on climate. In J.W. Dash (ed.), *World Scientific Encyclopedia of Climate Change* (vol. 3, pp. 231–43). Singapore: World Scientific.

Rooney-Varga, J.N., Hensel, M., McCarthy, C., McNeal, K., Norfles, N., Rath, K., Schnell, A.H., & Sterman, J.D. (2021b). Building consensus for ambitious climate action through the world climate simulation. *Earth's Future, 9*. https://doi.org/10.1029/2021EF002283

Rooney-Varga, J.N., Kapmeier, F., Sterman, J.D., Jones, A.P., Putko, M., & Rath, K. (2020). The climate action simulation. *Simulation & Gaming, 51*(2), 114–40.

Rooney-Varga, J.N., Sterman, J.D., Fracassi, E., Franck, T., Kapmeier, F., Kurker, V., Johnston, E., Jones, A.P., & Rath, K. (2018). Combining role-play with interactive simulation to motivate informed climate action: Evidence from the world climate simulation. *PLoS One, 13*(8), e0202877. https://doi.org/10.1371/journal.pone.0202877

Rowsell, J. (2022). *Why Procurement Can't Tackle Climate Change Alone*. Available at www.cips.org/supply-management/news/2022/may/why-procurement-cant-tackle-climate-change-alone/

Simmons, D. (2020). *What Is 'Climate Justice'?* Available at https://yaleclimateconnections.org/2020/07/what-is-climate-justice/

Sterman, J.D. (2011). Communicating climate change risks in a skeptical world. *Climatic Change, 108*(4), 811–26.

Sterman, J.D., Fiddaman, T., Franck, T., Jones, A., McCauley, S., Rice, P., Sawin, E., & Siegel, L. (2013). Management flight simulators to support climate negotiations. *Environmental Modelling & Software, 44*, 122–35.

Stern, N., Patel, I., & Ward, B. (2021). Covid-19, climate change, and the environment: A sustainable, inclusive, and resilient global recovery. *BMJ, 375*, n2405. Available at www.bmj.com/content/bmj/375/bmj.n2405.full.pdf

Suskie, L. (2018). *Assessing Student Learning: A Common Sense Guide*, 3rd ed. San Francisco: Jossey-Bass.

Townsend, S. (2022). *43 People Changing Advertising for the Climate*. Available at www.forbes.com/sites/solitairetownsend/2022/06/23/43-people-changing-advertising-for-the-climate/?sh=5b11634a72b2

UNFCCC. (2015). *Decision 1/CP.21-Adoption of the Paris Agreement*. In Report of the Conference of the Parties on Its Twenty-First Session, Held in Paris from 30 November to 13

December 2015. Addendum. Part two: Action Taken by the Conference of the Parties at Its Twenty-First Session. Paris: UNFCCC.

UNFCCC. (2021). *Decision -/CP.26. Glasgow Climate Pact. Report, Glasgow.* In Glasgow Climate Pact, COP26. United Nations, Glasgow, Scotland, UK.

US Department of Education. (2022). *Accreditation in the United States.* Available at https://www2.ed.gov/admins/finaid/accred/accreditation_pg6.html#RegionalInstitutional

Vicedo-Cabrera, A.M., Guo, Y., Sera, F., Huber, V., Schleussner, C.-F., Mitchell, D., Tong, S., Coelho, Md.S.Z.S., Saldiva, P.H.N., Lavigne, E., Correa, P.M., Ortega, N.V., Kan, H., Osorio, S., Kyselý, J., Urban, A., Jaakkola, J.J.K., Ryti, N.R.I., Pascal, M., Goodman, P.G., Zeka, A., Michelozzi, P., Scortichini, M., Hashizume, M., Honda, Y., Hurtado-Diaz, M., Cruz, J., Seposo, X., Kim, H., Tobias, A., Íñiguez, C., Forsberg, B., Åström, D.O., Ragettli, M.S., Röösli, M., Guo, Y.L., Wu, C.-F., Zanobetti, A., Schwartz, J., Bell, M.L., Dang, T.N., Do Van, D., Heaviside, C., Vardoulakis, S., Hajat, S., Haines, A., Armstrong, B., Ebi, K.L., & Gasparrini, A. (2018). Temperature-related mortality impacts under and beyond Paris agreement climate change scenarios. *Climatic Change, 150*(3), 391–402.

Warren, R., Price, J., Graham, E., Forstenhaeusler, N., & VanDerWal, J. (2018). The projected effect on insects, vertebrates, and plants of limiting global warming to 1.5 °C rather than 2 °C. *Science, 360*(6390), 791–5.

Wiggins, G., & McTighe, J. (2005). *Understanding by Design,* 2nd ed. Alexandria, VA: Association for Supervision and Curriculum Development ASCD.

Yale, CBE, GNAM, & WBCSD. (2016). *Rising Leaders on Environmental Sustainability and Climate Change: A Global Survey of Business Students.* Available at https://cbey.yale.edu/research/rising-leaders-on-environmental-sustainability-and-climate-change

Zhao, C., Liu, B., Piao, S., Wang, X., Lobell, D.B., Huang, Y., Huang, M., Yao, Y., Bassu, S., Ciais, P., Durand, J.-L., Elliott, J., Ewert, F., Janssens, I.A., Li, T., Lin, E., Liu, Q., Martre, P., Müller, C., Peng, S., Peñuelas, J., Ruane, A.C., Wallach, D., Wang, T., Wu, D., Liu, Z., Zhu, Y., Zhu, Z., & Asseng, S. (2017). Temperature increase reduces global yields of major crops in four independent estimates. *Proceedings of the National Academy of Sciences, 114*(35), 9326–31.

4

Sustainable and employable graduates

Fiona Winfield and Richard Howarth

The aim of this chapter is to give business and management students and staff (including lecturers, mentors, tutors, and career professionals) a grounding in the relationship between students' employability and their sustainability literacy. This will provide a sense of direction in these important areas for staff and students alike. To support this, the chapter will define employability, address the overall demand for sustainability literacy, and work with some relevant core frameworks and taxonomies. We will therefore explore why every student can, and should, be a 'sustainability student' and a 'sustainability graduate'.

At the end of this chapter, you will be able to:

- Understand the connection between sustainability literacy and employability.

- Conceptualise the role and relationship of competences from selected frameworks and guidelines.

- Recognise the importance of this work being longitudinal, linked to regular competence development.

- Appreciate how to support planning and the development of competences over time.

DOI: 10.4324/9781003294665-6

To assist you, a Sustainability Competency Matrix is provided, which links to and supports:

- The undertaking of a 'personal gap analysis'.

- The identification of areas for personal development.

- The review of progress and developments over time, linked to the notion of employability being lifelong and lifewide, with ongoing development and transformation.

How are employability and sustainability connected?

As will be clear from the introductory chapter in this book and from its table of contents, most chapters relate to how sustainability, the SDGs, and climate change can be mainstreamed and integrated into taught business modules. In this chapter, by contrast, we focus on how sustainability and related topics are also firmly linked to learners' employability, how academic and careers colleagues can help learners understand the connections, and how value can be added in both these spaces, now and in the future.

Students do not only need to grasp the academic links and the relevance of sustainability to their discipline but also need to make the connection between what they study, the skills and competences they develop, and why these things matter. Having made these connections, they then need the ability and confidence to articulate what they can do to add value to a future employer, and establish how to effect change in their personal and working lives. This requires self-awareness, reflection, analysis, planning, and action. Whilst we include a mapping activity to provide a snapshot at a specific point in time, this work should be ongoing and could be supported through tutorials, for example. Reflection, personal development planning, and the assessment of progress are therefore key. In our experience, students usually need guidance to do this, so ideally any related activities will be embedded within suitable modules through the learner's journey. It is also a good idea for academic staff to collaborate with others, both inside and outside the institution. For example, working closely with internal departments, such as careers and employability, alumni services, and maybe sustainable development, as well as involving employers and other external organisations, such as professional bodies.

Why should every student be a 'sustainability student'?

Accenture stated in their 2021 report (p. 7), 'Shaping the sustainable organization', that '[o]perating sustainably and equitably is not an option – it's a business imperative', and it will have an impact on an organisation's 'talent strategy' (p. 4). Students, therefore, need to be prepared for this changing landscape. Also in 2021, James Coe of the University of Liverpool stated on the Wonkhe site that 'it would be a dereliction of our collective duties to not educate students in the economic, social, and political trade-offs they will be faced with if we are to avert climate disaster'. However, these topics should not just be an add-on or afterthought; the SOS website states: '[s]ustainability should be woven through every subject like a golden thread. Every student should be a sustainability student'. Likewise, according to Project Drawdown (2021), every job can be (and is) a 'sustainability job'.

Back in 2015, the Higher Education Academy (now Advance HE) surveyed UK employers to establish the confidence they had in their existing employees' sustainability skills. Approximately 20% of senior leaders surveyed believed there were significant gaps in both awareness and skills, preventing their organisation from effective participation in a sustainable economy (Drayson, 2015). Clearly, employers want and need employees with the right skills, attitudes, and 'sustainability literacy', to fill the gaps. With that survey having been conducted quite a while ago, one would hope the gaps would have narrowed by now.

In 2016, a report by UNGC-Accenture Strategy revealed their research into CEOs' attitudes to sustainability at that time. Many different organisations were surveyed, involving 1,000+ business leaders from more than 100 countries. Their report clearly identified the importance of sustainability to those leaders and their organisations, with:

- 97% of CEOs seeing sustainability as 'important to the future success of their business' and

- 89% saying 'commitment to sustainability is translating into real impact in their industry'.

Three years later, the equivalent 2019 survey (p. 14) found that *just a fifth* of the CEOs surveyed believed that business was, in fact, 'playing a critical role in contributing to the global sustainability goals and that fewer than half [were] integrating sustainability into their business operations'. In one of their more recent surveys published in November 2021 (featuring over 1,000 CEOs and in-depth interviews with more than 100 respondents), Accenture found that the situation had become even bleaker in terms of companies' preparedness vis-à-vis sustainability and achieving net zero.

One might assume that Covid contributed to the worsening of the situation. However, the 2021 GlobeScan report highlighted that, while in 2020 nearly half of those surveyed had predicted the pandemic would lead to sustainability being de-prioritised, by 2021 only 24% believed that to be true. In fact, just under a third suggested that 'one legacy of the pandemic will be more attention being given to the environment' (p. 5). Meanwhile, in the Accenture 2021 survey (p. 16), 'over half (57%) of CEOs [claimed they were] prioritizing climate action in their recovery from the COVID-19 pandemic'.

Sustainability and climate change appear now to be firmly on the agenda of many organisations, with a fair number issuing pledges to reduce carbon emissions and to reach net zero by a specific date. It is often unclear, however, exactly how these targets will be met (Doepel, 2022).

Graduates, therefore, need to be ready, both to support and meet the challenges ahead.

The demand from employers

With the need, and in some circumstances, the requirement, to reach net zero, it is evident there will be demand for more than just a few extra people with specialist knowledge and expertise. This goes beyond the recruitment of employees with the ability to perform what might be deemed 'green jobs' in specific sectors. In reality, such knowledge and expertise are needed within the core of *all* business, not just within more traditional areas, such as waste and energy management, conservation, and estates. This affects all types of sectors and industries as well.

A report published in 2022 by the SME Climate Hub found that 60% of UK SMEs surveyed had already developed a plan to reduce emissions, with over 80% aiming to reduce their waste and improve their energy efficiency. They stated, however, that almost two-thirds of respondents saw a 'lack of in-house skills and knowledge' as the main barrier to action (Edie, 2022). Deloitte (2022) also states that 'green skills' need developing across the workforce, with other research finding that three-quarters of professionals in senior sustainability roles believe that by 2050, all jobs will need 'green' or sustainability skills.

In 2018, the international professional services firm PwC published their report 'Workforce of the future: the green world in 2030', announcing they were seeking to recruit 100,000 employees worldwide to help business clients reach net zero (DiNapoli, 2021). In autumn 2021, PwC followed this up by launching the UK Green Jobs Barometer (PwC, 2021). The following year, EY announced that it was creating EY Carbon to support UK business to decarbonise and was hence seeking to recruit 1,300 employees over the following three years (EY, 2022). The European Union also monitors the development of the Environmental Goods and Services Sector, and the 'Switch to Green' initiative and associated website are useful resources for anyone operating in Europe (EU, 2022).

Between companies seeking to recruit employees with the appropriate skill set and consultancy firms seeking to take on people to work with their clients, it can be seen that sustainability literacy is in demand. For many roles, having technical knowledge is, however, not nearly as important as being persuasive, with the ability to analyse a situation well, and the capability of devising workable solutions that will be adopted by colleagues. This needs a good level of awareness of potential sustainability and climate change issues, while caring enough to want to act on the matter in hand. It needs the mindset and imagination to see opportunities, along with problem-solving skills to identify practical solutions. It also requires interpersonal skills to collaborate, persuade, and negotiate with people, so that solutions are agreed upon and practices evolve.

One example of where these aspects of learning (specifically in relation to sustainability) are being explored currently is through the work of the 'Inner Development Goals' (IDG), founded by the 29k Foundation, Ekskäret Foundation, and the New Division (Inner Development Goals, 2022). The IDG is a non-profit organisation and is a collaboration between the public and private sectors. At its heart is the belief that we all need to develop our 'inner abilities' to achieve the Sustainable Development Goals (SDGs).

This work, similar to that carried out by UNESCO and the QAA in the UK, for example, points specifically to the imperative of focusing on transformation and change within individuals and learners. In doing so, five dimensions are highlighted (see Figure 4.1), which the IDG believes should guide and frame the work being undertaken in this area.

This wider view and context is relevant, as Alex Hall-Chen (Senior Policy Advisor at the UK's Institute of Directors) identified that '[d]emand for graduate skills among employers remains strong – particularly in transferable employability skills such as critical thinking, communication, and leadership – and the higher

Figure 4.1: The five dimensions of the Inner Development Goals framework.

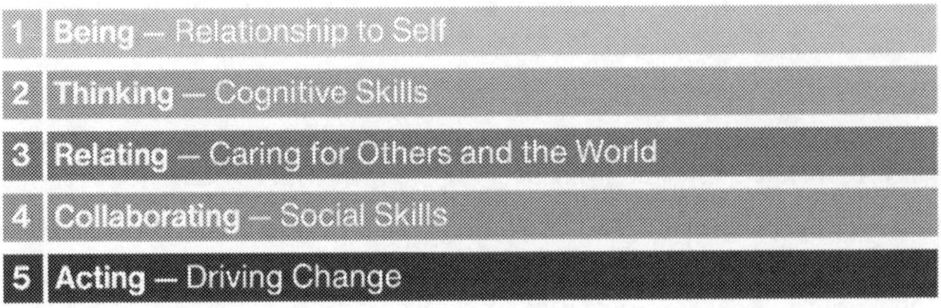

1	**Being** — Relationship to Self
2	**Thinking** — Cognitive Skills
3	**Relating** — Caring for Others and the World
4	**Collaborating** — Social Skills
5	**Acting** — Driving Change

Source: Growth that Matters AB (2021).

education sector will be an essential component in meeting the UK's rapidly changing skills needs' (see Universities UK, 2022). In many ways, *sustainability* skills and behaviours are no different from those routinely sought by graduate employers. They are very similar to the usual attitudes, behaviours, and personal capabilities stipulated (often referred to as a *soft* skills set), including also teamworking and cooperating with colleagues, exhibiting empathy with others, networking, enthusiasm, and problem-solving (see, for example, Prospects, 2021).

To meet the challenge of achieving net zero, business school graduates, as future managers and leaders, will require a grounding in many aspects of sustainability and climate change. They do not necessarily need detailed knowledge of the technical side, such as carbon emissions and carbon accounting, but they do need to understand how it is good business sense to view *all* decisions with a sustainability lens. Reflecting this, business school accreditation bodies, such as the EFMD and AACSB, are keen to see topics linked to ESG (environmental, social, and governance) and ERS (ethics, responsibility, and sustainability) embedded *throughout* the curriculum (see, for example, De Novellis, 2022; Jirova, 2022). Graduates ideally need to embrace sustainability and understand how they can contribute to the agenda and make a difference, whether they choose to work for themselves, for a local SME, or for a multinational. The Chartered Management Institute (CMI) also supports this view, as witnessed in a recent article on their website titled 'Why every manager is on the front line of ESG planning' (Rowland, 2022).

Although business school graduates are in high demand, there is strong competition, as many employers will accept applications from *any* graduate. This means that students need to stand out from the crowd and be able to offer an employer something extra, regardless of the discipline studied or the role sought. At Nottingham Business School (NBS), ensuring our students have sustainability and climate literacy is, we believe, vital for the planet and society. As a bonus, being able to articulate how this literacy adds value to an employer should mean that they will be viewed as more employable. For many roles, it is possible that 'sustainability literacy' will not be explicitly mentioned in the person specification or job description, but being able to demonstrate such literacy may mean that a candidate is more appealing at the application or interview stage.

To summarise, with countries around the world pledging to reach net zero by 2050 and the need to meet interim goals sooner, organisations of all types urgently require their employees to have the requisite knowledge, skills, and behaviours to enable appropriate decisions to be made. There will be a certain demand for specialised 'green' jobs, which require an in-depth knowledge of sustainability, climate change, and carbon management. However, in order for all organisations to ensure that global temperatures do not rise by more than 1.5 °C, sustainability-orientated skills and competences will be needed by *all* employees, in *all* lines of work, in *all* types of organisations, across *all* industries and sectors. All students from business schools should therefore be equipped, not only with relevant skills, competences, and behaviours, but also with the ability to recognise where changes can be made, and with the confidence to put forward appropriate suggestions and solutions.

The demand from students

According to research carried out in 2020 by SOS International (Students Organizing for Sustainability), 'most universities are not yet ensuring that all their graduates are equipped with the knowledge and competences needed to be leaders for a sustainable and just future' (SOS International, 2021: 4). With just under 7,000 student respondents from over 100 HEIs to SOS's 2020 global survey, it is revealing to note that half of the students said they were willing to accept a salary sacrifice of 15% to work in a role that contributed to positive environmental and social change. When asked, 'How important, if at all, are the following factors when considering your future career or type of job?' (SOS International, 2021: 27):

> 68% selected: 'If the company or organisation contributes to helping the environment'.

> 74% chose: 'If the job has or contributes to a social purpose'.

Results are available by continent, even by institution, where there are sufficient numbers. While the survey is global, some parts of the world are under-represented – less than 2% were from North America, for example. It is also worth noting that, in the more recent UK results, 54% of respondents stated they 'would accept a salary £3,000 [approximately $3,500] lower than average to work in a job that contributes to positive social and environmental change' (SOS, 2022: 7).

Although there is a lack of insight relating to North America in the SOS results, work undertaken in Canada noted the gap between students and industry, in relation to needs and business education. This was identified by an organisation founded in 2019 as the 'Canadian Business Youth Council for Sustainable Development'. Now known as Re_Generation, this youth-led non-profit organisation is advocating for change in business education and beyond (Re_Generation, 2022). They created a successful 'Our Future, Our Business' campaign that received the support of 65 youth organisations, 130 high-level business executives, and 100 civil society organisations, recognising the need for reform in business education with respect to 'sustainability'. As they further state on their website, their aim is to 're_imagine schools', 're_purpose careers', and 're_model companies' to align with regenerative principles. They provide resources for individuals to launch impact-driven careers, advocate for change within companies and schools, and advance public policies that promote regenerative and sustainable business practices (Re_Generation, 2022).

Meanwhile in Europe, it has been announced that students and staff at the University of Barcelona, Spain, will take a mandatory module on the climate crisis from 2024, following a week-long occupation of university buildings by student activists in November 2022 (Burgen, 2022). This is a good step forward, but in our opinion, it would be even better to embed sustainability and climate solutions *throughout the curriculum*, in all disciplines, as this book seeks to do in relation to the business curriculum.

From the above, it would appear that many students have an appetite to develop their sustainability literacy and to work for organisations that take the environment into account. This reinforces the need to embed environmental, social, and governance (ESG) issues, and specifically climate change, carbon management, and principles of the circular economy, into the curriculum. It is concerning to note that when asked in the SOS survey which word best describes how they feel about climate change and the future, three-quarters of respondents said they were 'worried'. It is therefore really important that universities and colleges try to help students understand that high-impact solutions exist already and are available to all organisations. This should mean that graduates *can* all make a difference, no matter what role they undertake. Covering topics as suggested in this book is a really good start, but that alone is not enough. It is important that students are enabled to:

- Make sense of sustainability-related issues

- Reflect on what they know

- Identify what they can do

- Understand how they can really add value and make a difference to the world around them.

Employability and sustainability – connecting what matters

There are many definitions of 'employability', but the one we use here is from Cole (2022: 2). 'It is shaped by the results of a combination of learning opportunities across multiple spaces in our lives, it is both lifelong and lifewide and in this respect is developed both in the classroom, and critically, in life more broadly.' Cole explains that it is not just about securing employment, it is about our identity and understanding who or what we wish to become in the future.

This is an approach that also goes beyond a focus on the acquisition of skills, and it encourages an offer to learners that can be personalised and tailored to the individual in their own context. As Cole (2022: 8) stresses, it is 'fluid, constantly needing to evolve as we go through life, therefore, reflective practice, self-efficacy and resilience are all crucial in order to help us thrive in an ever-changing and complex future world'.

Taking Cole's (2019) original 'Dimensions for Learning Taxonomy' (now further developed as the *Employability Redefined Taxonomy* and used as the foundation of our work in employability across Nottingham Trent University), Figure 4.2 demonstrates how we seek to link employability to sustainability at NTU.

As a further development, we have constructed Figure 4.3, where we seek to combine the elements of employability identified by Cole (2019) and the sustainability competence frameworks identified in various sources. These include UNESCO (2015/2022) and the European Commission's GreenComp (2022), along

Figure 4.2: Linking employability to sustainability at NTU.

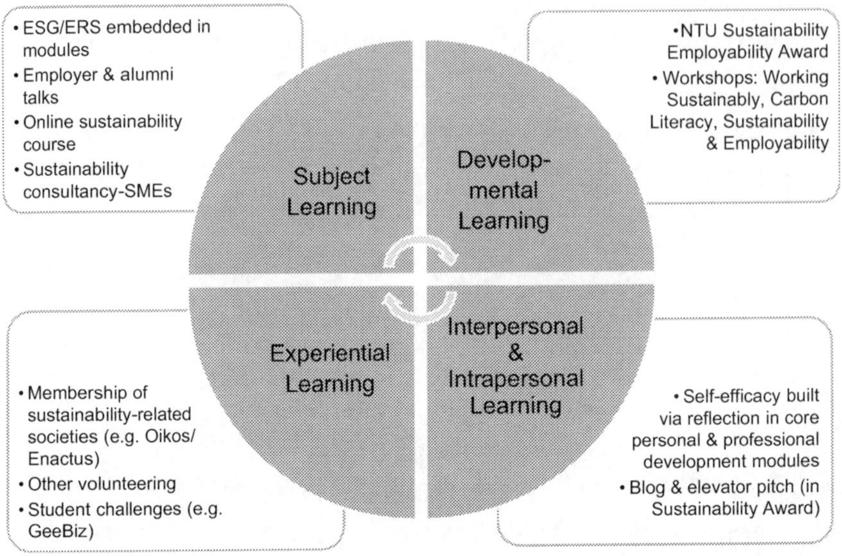

- ESG/ERS embedded in modules
- Employer & alumni talks
- Online sustainability course
- Sustainability consultancy-SMEs

Subject Learning

Developmental Learning

- NTU Sustainability Employability Award
- Workshops: Working Sustainably, Carbon Literacy, Sustainability & Employability

Experiential Learning

Interpersonal & Intrapersonal Learning

- Membership of sustainability-related societies (e.g. Oikos/ Enactus)
- Other volunteering
- Student challenges (e.g. GeeBiz)

- Self-efficacy built via reflection in core personal & professional development modules
- Blog & elevator pitch (in Sustainability Award)

Source: Cole (2019). Adapted with permission.

with the work published by Advance HE and the QAA (2021) in their Education for Sustainable Development Guidance, and finally, the World Economic Forum (WEF, 2021).

The mapping that underpins the framework in Figure 4.3 identifies overlaps between employability skills and competences in general, and specifically within the domain of sustainability/sustainable development. This further supports our claim that a focus on this area is vital to the work of business schools, the outcomes for degree programmes, and the outcomes for all our learners.

At the core of Figure 4.3's integrating framework is the individual and their sense of who they are. This is rooted in self-awareness and the individual's identity, and it connects to their values. Implicit is also an understanding of other people's values and the impact and influence of external factors (such as culture, friends, and family), especially in relation to sustainability. This leads to action taken by the individual (or not, as the case may be). In some frameworks, this will be classed as the 'normative' competence, with the role of emotional intelligence, adaptability, and reflection being of particular relevance here. The competences in our model also relate to future thinking, systems thinking and critical thinking, problem-solving, and strategic thinking.

Figure 4.3: Integrating employability with sustainability competences.

Source: Howarth and Winfield, based on work by the Advance HE/QAA (2021), Cole (2019), European Commission (2022), UNESCO (2015/2022), WEF (2021).

Learners need an understanding of their current situation, both in relation to these competences and to the development of their own employability. They will need to articulate what they want to achieve, supporting this with timelines and a roadmap of how they will get to their chosen destination. Regular progress reviews and reflection will be important, along with the development of resilience and self-efficacy, so learners believe they really *can* achieve their desired career goals.

Without this focus on the individual, sustainability can seem a rather abstract and potentially overwhelming concept, which may simply be about knowing more 'stuff', and with action seeming beyond the reach of an individual, which in reality it is not.

In Figure 4.3, there are three themes surrounding the individual, which pull together and connect the elements from the frameworks used as the basis. These are grouped as:

- **Facilitators** (bottom three hexagons): the ability to organise oneself and others, and create and deliver plans, supported by an ability to use digital technology appropriately, ensuring effective research and task completion, underpinned by a clear understanding of current affairs and implications.

- **Taking action** (top three hexagons): whether individually or collectively, the ability to communicate effectively with others in a responsible manner, within the wider context, and to bring about change.

- **Core sustainability knowledge and competences** (hexagons to the left): ensuring planning and action are rooted in a clear understanding of the challenges, barriers, and enablers.

The arrows in Figure 4.3 reflect that this is an **ongoing process** of development within the overall framework – not only starting with an emphasis on planning, but also stressing implementation and outcomes – leading to a focus on the future.

Starting point – personalising the journey and empowering learner success

As stressed earlier, there is a crucial role for academic members of staff and careers guidance colleagues to help students as learners recognise their current situation and the value they can add to an organisation in the future. Self-awareness will be at the heart of this process, and a useful exercise is a '**personal gap analysis**', to ascertain what needs addressing further. This activity could take place within a classroom setting (and we provide guidance later in the chapter), or it could be undertaken independently. Ideally, however, this personal analysis and reflection should be encouraged and preferably integrated into all business degrees. It should also be undertaken at the start and towards the end of each level, and definitely not treated as a one-off activity.

Having identified the ideal range of competences for a business student, we propose operationalising this by using our competency matrix (see Table 4.1). Please note, the version shown in this chapter is condensed and includes headlines only. Table 4.2 then shows the descriptors linked to each competence, and

Table 4.1: Condensed version of the Sustainability Competency Matrix (devised by Howarth and Winfield).

Sustainability Competency Matrix (personal gap analysis) condensed				
Competences *(In the template online, each shows the descriptors, to aid understanding)*	**Own rating** **1 = low** **5 = high**	**Evidence/ examples (where and how developed)**	**Your priorities (and why)**	**Linked to objective no.** *(on your personal development plan)*
Responsible leadership				
Collective action and teamworking				
Communications				
Commercial awareness				
Digital literacy				
Organisation				
Strategic and anticipatory thinking				
Climate and sustainability literacy				
Recognising and embracing complexity				
Add further competences of specific relevance to your subject area and/ or future aspirations				

on the book's companion website there will be a downloadable template, combining the two.

The matrix provided by us is not meant to be definitive, however, and you may wish to adapt it, depending on local circumstances and the extent to which related topics are covered in your curriculum. It is also worth checking against professional body requirements, as they will usually issue their own tailored list of what is needed for membership, accreditation, and possibly exemptions.

Table 4.2: Elements of the Sustainability Competency Matrix – with descriptors (Howarth and Winfield).

Sustainability Competency Matrix (personal gap analysis) descriptors

Responsible leadership

- Taking responsibility for the direction and outcomes of a team/group
- Motivating, supporting, coaching, influencing others
- Using anticipatory/strategic thinking in actions
- Using sustainability and climate literacy
- Proactively attending to issues of ethics
- Proactively attending to issues of equality and diversity

Collective action and teamworking

- Working with others to achieve a common goal
- Making a personal contribution to, and impact on, a team
- Demonstrating empathy, recognising others' contributions, and supporting them (e.g. when solving problems)
- Learning from others
- Recognising differences and dealing with conflict

Communications

- Ability to explain complex ideas
- Appropriately selecting methods and messages, ensuring clarity
- Adaptability to interact with others, using different approaches
- Appreciation of importance of dialogue and two-way communications
- Accepting and providing feedback as necessary
- Building a rapport in different settings (one-to-one and one-to-many)

Commercial awareness

- Comprehension of current affairs and trends related to the economy, business, markets, and organisations
- Understanding of key sources of information and their effective use
- Ability to provide insights to priorities and challenges related to success in selected settings (from a business and customer perspective)
- Awareness of relevant labour market conditions, job opportunities, and recruitment processes

Digital literacy

- Capacity to research and select information effectively using a variety of digital sources
- Recognition of the credibility and reliability of different sources
- Ability to use software effectively (e.g. MS Teams, Word, Outlook, PowerPoint, Excel, academic referencing aids, etc.)

Organisation

- Ability to prioritise, plan, and finish work
- Punctuality and attendance, underpinned by preparation (ensuring effective engagement and participation)
- Capacity to manage time, including adherence to deadlines and timeframes

- Ability to use industry-relevant software (e.g. Excel, SAGE, Google Analytics, databases, etc.)
- Effective use of social media (e.g. to aid professional development)
- Capacity to manage, store, and retrieve information, paying attention to data protection and related legal responsibilities

Strategic and anticipatory thinking

- Ability to identify one's own values and those of others (past, current, and future)
- Creating/articulating a vision of the future, recognising and embracing uncertainty
- Planning actions/outcomes and recognising implementation challenges and opportunities
- Recognising relationships and dependencies (and the impact of change)
- Agility of mind and action, alternative outcomes – benefits and challenges
- Capacity to analyse systems and spot problems, challenges/opportunities in context

Climate and sustainability literacy

- Recognising challenges and opportunities related to UN SDGs
- Understanding roles of stakeholders/key players (in business, society, government) as agents of change
- Identifying high-impact solutions and prioritising action(s) related to climate change
- Understanding the role and importance of communication and education in sustainability and climate action

- Ability to balance academic work alongside other commitments (e.g. employment, volunteering, extra-curricular activities, or other responsibilities)
- Awareness of risks and critical success factors, and the ability to identify and manage their impact

Recognising and embracing complexity

- Possessing an open mindset – willing to challenge and question norms and current practice
- Understanding problems in context, using tools/frameworks to support, as appropriate
- Demonstrating analysis and logic to solve problems with data/information
- Evidencing critical thinking, recognising and managing how ambiguity underpins proposals
- Selecting, using, analysing, and interpreting information/data (using reliable sources)
- Finding new solutions to complex problems and explaining their foundations

Add further competences of specific relevance to your subject area and/or future aspirations:

- …
- …
- …
- …

Follow-on – leading the journey, facilitating change and progress

To reiterate, the nature of a personal gap analysis, and the need to monitor progress, means this should not be a one-off exercise. It is beneficial to complete the matrix near the start of the degree course and revisit it later. From a tutor's perspective, if the exercise can be linked to learning outcomes and the assessment of one or more modules, engagement is more likely, and more benefits should be felt by the learners. Depending on the nature of the school or institute, this work may be supported or facilitated through personal tutoring or mentoring programmes. Recognising how progress, in relation to the competency matrix, can be achieved and facilitated is important to the student journey, as is progress within modules and the wider programme or degree.

The key thing is for learners to reflect on where they are at given points in their journey, and academic staff and careers guidance colleagues have an important role to play in signposting students to relevant opportunities and activities to help narrow identified gaps. It is also important that reflection takes place later on as well, to acknowledge which areas have been developed, to what extent, and where the gaps still exist. To gain maximum benefit, each learner should be able to articulate clearly which competences they possess, through strong examples. Practising this articulation, in front of others on their course (see suggested sessions in the following pages) or with friends and family (if there are no suitable modules in which to house these), will stand everyone in good stead for future job interviews.

Supporting development

Where and how competences are developed will be an important consideration. For many institutions, this will be through embedding and mainstreaming ESG and ERS topics reflecting subject 'benchmarks', the school or institution's own strategy, or linked to the requirements of external recognition. Depending on where your institution sits in the development and integration of sustainability and climate change in the curriculum, some competences will be developed through studying existing or new modules/courses. Other aspects might not be covered and may need to be developed through extra-curricular opportunities, an approach that reflects lifewide learning, featured in Cole's 2022 definition of employability (see also Lifewide Education, 2022).

If there are personal development–type modules in your institution's undergraduate and postgraduate degrees, they would be ideal to incorporate relevant exercises and activities, particularly when the employability and careers service is involved. Using some form of ePortfolio is also recommended, and, for an undergraduate, this could be revisited throughout the degree, and built upon at each level. To support the learners who have identified gaps and development areas, it is a good idea to have a menu of extra-curricular opportunities available linked to sustainability, ethics, responsible leadership, and the SDGs, and to promote these in a timely manner. Interestingly, in the report 'Future Graduate Skills: A Scoping Study', it was identified that '[e]xtra-curricular activities and work placements/ internships were also considered as particularly important by business leaders, but seemingly undervalued by graduates' (Change Agents UK *et al.*, 2020: 1). The value of extra-curricular activity may therefore need to be introduced, explained, and promoted regularly to learners.

In NBS, we embed sustainability (and other ESG/ERS topics) throughout our curricula. Additionally, within NTU, any student can work towards a bronze, silver, or gold Employability Award, by undertaking activities and gaining relevant experience. In 2021, to coincide with COP26 in Glasgow (Scotland), a new version of our award was launched – the Sustainability Employability Award – complementing the existing digital, enterprise, and global variants. This enables our students to select sustainability-related activities and undertake personal development, while reflecting on the progress achieved at each level. More information is provided in Table 4.3.

As can be seen, there is flexibility for personalisation within NTU's Sustainability Employability Award, and the contributing experiences can be tailored to suit the student's interests and future aspirations. The types of extra-curricular activities that can be selected for the Silver Award include:

- Optional NTU webinars or workshops, for example: the employability 'Working Sustainably' workshop, NTU's 'Introduction to Carbon Literacy', or NBS's 'Climate Literacy & Action for All' online course.

- NTU sustainability-focused roles, for example: eco champion or fair-trade auditor.

- NTSU (student union) official societies, for example: Sustainability or Conservation Society.

- Uni-wide activities, for example: student conference linked to COP26 (November 2021), NTU Green Week, NTU Global Week (all of which may involve activities in the community).

- NTU in collaboration with external organisations, for example: full Carbon Literacy Training (working with the Carbon Literacy Trust), membership in Enactus or oikos International, or working on a student challenge, such as GeeBiz or the University Business Challenge/Global Masters Challenge.

The NTU Employability team's work on the development of the Sustainability Employability Award is at the heart of NTU's achievement of being finalists in the 'Tomorrow's Employees' category of the 2022 Green Gown Awards (UK and Ireland). The award's introduction and success could not have been achieved without the collaboration of the NTU Green Academy, NTU Global, NTU Enterprise, and NTU Volunteering, plus, of course, the support of many external organisations that provide opportunities for our students. We also built on the experience of our well-established work within NBS of linking employability to sustainability and responsible management, which formed the basis of the winning submission to the EAUC's Green Gown Awards in 2017 (see Sustainability Exchange, 2017).

Table 4.3: NTU's Sustainability Employability Award structure

NTU's Sustainability Employability Award (launched during COP26, November 2021)
Bronze (total 50 points)
• One of the NTU Sustainability in Practice online courses (clothing/energy/food)
• LinkedIn Learning course: The employee guide to sustainability
• Sustainability reflection no. 1
Silver (total 50 points)
• A minimum of 45 points' worth of extra-curricular sustainability-related experience and/or skills development (workshops/webinars/activities/challenges/volunteering – local/national/international) – selected from a menu, or self-selected and submitted for validation
• Sustainability reflection no. 2
Gold – the 'Sustainable Graduate' showcase (total 50 points)
• Create a sustainability elevator pitch
• Create a PowerPoint slide or poster
• Answer sustainability-related interview questions or write a blog
• Sustainability reflection no. 3

Final thoughts

Through this chapter, we have explored the growing need for sustainability and climate literacy from all sides: business schools, students, employers, and implicitly, society at large. We have sought to highlight and demonstrate the link between sustainability literacy and employability, whether as an imperative or as an extra string to one's bow.

We have drawn on the work of a number of different organisations and experts to build our own sustainability competency framework. We have subsequently developed a matrix that can be used by any student or institution (either as provided or with further tailoring). When used by students, this should enable a better understanding of who they are and where there are gaps, in order to identify development needs, in relation to a whole range of competences.

We have also showcased an initiative, which could be replicated in any institution, to reward students for engagement with extra-curricular sustainability-related activities (many of which probably exist in your institution and community already).

We hope this approach is seen as useful, and we would welcome feedback from anyone who introduces our matrix or a similar sustainability award in their own institution.

Suggested activities

In this chapter, we discussed why we believe that having a good understanding of sustainability and being climate literate will allow graduates to be an effective employee, manager, or entrepreneur in the future. To understand whether certain competences require further development, everyone needs to think about their current situation and identify gaps that need filling. They also need to be aware of how to evidence those competences and their increasing sustainability literacy.

In the following, we provide the outline for two sessions. However, these activities can be carried out by anyone on their own or with fellow students – they do not have to be part of a taught session.

The first set of activities should take place early on in the degree or programme. Having said that, even if a student is partway through, it is never too late to do this. The sooner it is done, the sooner students can start to address any gaps and feel competent at being able to articulate their strengths and explain clearly what they can bring to a work environment. They will start by taking stock of their current situation, ideally within a personal and professional development type of module. If, however, this does not exist in your establishment, it could be undertaken as part of an employability or careers session, or even with a group of friends or like-minded students, as a means of taking control of their personal career management.

Before working through this, it is assumed that anyone participating in the following activities has read through this chapter or been made aware of its contents. When focusing on the competences, links and distinctions should be recognised; in examining the descriptors, overlaps might be noted. With a complex idea, for example, it is one thing to understand the issues, to have an open mind or the ability to solve problems. This is different from being able to communicate the idea effectively to others.

Session 1: Establishing a baseline

Preparation

- Download the full Sustainability Competency Matrix and read through each competency group, the accompanying descriptors and different elements. If you do not have access to the template, please copy out the headings in

Table 4.1 and use the information in Table 4.2 to help you understand each competence.

- Think about each one in turn, and make rough notes of any examples where you feel you are strong. It is particularly important that you can demonstrate your understanding.

- If any of the terms or headings are unfamiliar, read around the subject. There is a list of references at the end of the chapter, and you can refer to the various frameworks used to build the matrix, if you need further explanation.

- Make sure to add a date to your matrix (and keep a note of each time you update it).

Activity 1 (10 minutes)

Work individually.

Look at each competency group in turn. Refer to your rough preparatory notes regarding the experience you have or evidence you can provide. Under each heading in the full template, there are sub-headings to clarify what each might cover; you do not need to be able to demonstrate every one of the sub-headings.

Now you need to give each competency group a score from 1 to 5 (note it in the 'Own rating' column for each group). Use the following scoring system to support your ratings:

1. Little or no knowledge or understanding.

2. Good level of understanding and insight.

3. Understanding and insight are good, with occasional application.

4. Understanding and insights (and thus competence) are supported by regular application, and evidence can be shared.

5. Clear understanding and insight, frequent application, and multiple detailed examples can be shared.

If you feel you rate highly overall for a given group (a score of 3, 4, or 5), you should have a strong example or notes regarding evidence that you could easily pull together, to justify your rating. Evidence could be from a wide range of sources, both from the business school/university and/or externally. Examples could be academic or extra-curricular, linked to work experience or volunteering. Alternatively, they could be connected to membership of a club or society, or a student challenge or project. While it is fine to have one or two older examples, it would be preferable to have recent, up-to-date topical instances.

Activity 2 (20 minutes)

Work in pairs or threes. *(If working in threes, you might need more time, or you may have to focus on just one or two examples.)*

Quickly compare your scores with your fellow student(s). Then focus on those where you have given yourself a score of 3, 4, or 5.

Referring to your rough notes, where you have scored highly, explain what evidence or examples you would use to justify your rating. Try to be as succinct as possible, and use the STAR(R) technique to structure your example(s). If this is new to you, STAR(R) stands for:

- Situation/Task

- Action

- Result

- (Reflection)

For more guidance on the STAR(R) technique and competency-based interviews, refer to Prospects: www.prospects.ac.uk/careers-advice/interview-tips/competency-based-interviews.

- Listen *carefully* to your fellow students' examples.

- Maybe they have cited activities in which you have also taken part, but perhaps did not make the link.

- Their examples might also help you generate more ideas of where you could uncover evidence, or might provide information on initiatives in which you could participate.

Activity 3 (10 minutes)

Work individually.

You will need to decide how to fill any gaps, prioritising elements that seem most relevant/important to your personal circumstances (at any given time).

- Where you give yourself a score of 1 or 2, think about how you can develop your knowledge and understanding, and start to apply it.

- With a score of 3 or 4, think about how you can use the specific competence more frequently, or how you might be able to provide stronger evidence, and explain the benefits derived to others (keeping the STAR(R) framework in mind!).

- If you cannot see the relevance of a specific competence to your current or future circumstances, it is worth doing some research; you may be unaware that a particular element is in fact vital to the sort of industry or role you wish to enter.

Create a **personal development plan**, or update an existing plan: set yourself objectives depending on your priorities (number each objective and note where they tie into the matrix); regularly record and track relevant examples (experiential learning, work and volunteering, competitions, development and insights) so you can refer to them in the future when preparing for job applications, for example.

Activity 4 (20 minutes)

Work in pairs or threes.

Identify constructive ideas about how each of you can improve the score of at least one (or if there is enough time, preferably more) of the competency groups. This might come from earlier discussions or by checking your upcoming modules and their assessments, which could develop certain knowledge, behaviour, and skills.

Other ways of locating relevant personal development opportunities include:

- Events promoted by your careers and employability team, or via websites and resources available to you (in-house or externally). Check if your institution holds a 'Sustainability Action Week', 'Green Week', or participates in 'Fair-Trade fortnight', or similar.

- Stainability-related student challenges. For example, GeeBiz (Global Enterprise Challenge: www.geebiz.org/), which takes place around Easter time. Also, check out employers that are of potential interest, and follow them on social media – some use challenges as a way of identifying suitable talent.

- LinkedIn learning and other online platforms for short courses. Investigate online climate literacy-type short courses that might be open to you, free of charge.

- Clubs and societies offered as part of your student union or guild, or enterprise hub. They might have an Enactus society or be part of oikos International, for example. If none of these exists, why not research whether it would be something worth developing?

Follow-up work

You now need to complete the activity that you started in the session, so you have a full set of ratings and details of evidence you possess already, or need to collect together.

- Where you have identified gaps, you need to create a **personal development plan** or update your existing plan. This could be a simple 'to-do' list, but ideally, it will show clear priorities and timelines. Planned activities should also be explicitly linked to the development of specific competences. (A template will be provided on the companion website, but you may need to request access.)

- Do not be over-ambitious. It is better to target one or two competences at a time.

- Try to schedule a regular review when you can add notes of any new examples identified. If you have monthly or termly meetings with a mentor or personal tutor, that would be an ideal time to review and discuss progress.

Session 2, later in the year, will be a more formal chance for you to review your progress and make fresh plans.

Session 2: Reviewing progress and moving forward

Preparation

- Review your original matrix in full and, if necessary, return to Tables 4.1 and 4.2 to remind yourself of any of the key terms.

- Refer to your notes and the evidence assembled as the year has progressed.

- Look at each score and give yourself a new rating for each group (perhaps in a different colour). Your new rating may be:

  - Higher (where you have clearly demonstrated good progress and have stronger evidence than before).

  - Lower (where you realise that perhaps your understanding and development was not as far advanced as you previously believed).

  - The same as before (perhaps the right opportunities have not yet materialised).

- Hopefully, the categories that you prioritised will have moved up at least one rank, maybe more. If not, reflect on why that might be – try to be honest with yourself. If some scores were too high originally, again, reflect on why that might have been.

- Identify at least advert for a job that you can imagine applying for in the future. Not sure where to look for something suitable? Contact your university or business school's careers and employability team, or take a look at a job portal, such as Prospects: www.prospects.ac.uk/. If your business school is affiliated to the EFMD, check if you have access to Highered: https://highered.global/.

- Look closely at the job description or the profile of the ideal candidate mentioned in your selected advert. Note any skills or competences that are stipulated as essential.

- Take a copy of the advert and your notes to the session, as well as your updated matrix and details of additional evidence.

Activity 1 (20 minutes)

Work in pairs or threes (these can either be the same people as in the first session, or you could work with a different group to hear new ideas).

- Summarise your overall situation – explain how many scores have gone up, stayed the same, or even gone down.

- Give details of the activities you have undertaken to fill your identified priorities. Remember to structure your examples using the STAR(R) technique (see activity 2 in session 1 for further information).

- Again, listen carefully to the examples of the other group members; quite often we take things we do for granted, and it may be that you have more experiences you can draw on than you first thought.

Activity 2 (15 minutes)

Work individually.

- There will probably still be gaps, so identify what your *next priorities* are, then feed those into your **personal development plan** for the next stage of your life.

- If you only drew up a simple 'to-do' list the first time, now would be a good time to complete a fuller action plan.

Activity 3 (25 minutes)

Work in small groups.

- Have a look at the job adverts you each located in turn. Discuss your notes relating to what you believe the employer is seeking (this should be clear either in the advert, the job description, or the person specification).

- Are there any crossovers with your matrix? Are there any requirements that you would find hard to evidence? Are there any gaps (that is, attributes or skills the employer requires that do not feature on the matrix)?

Follow-up work

Use the activities in session 2 to further inform and update your own matrix and priority areas on your personal development plan.

The activity with the job adverts is intended to ensure that you see the relevance of acquiring and developing the competencies featured in the matrix. If you find that the attributes required for the sorts of roles you are seeking are not included in the matrix, remember you can tailor it by adding categories into the final group. Anything that comes up frequently should be a high priority for you.

Revisit your matrix and your plan regularly, and keep track of anything you do that might contribute to your bank of evidence. If your business school or college uses an ePortfolio, try collating all your examples in there. Otherwise, make sure you keep a file or folder with them (either electronically or as hard copy notes).

Additional teaching material and ideas

Sulitest can be used by educational institutions to map their learners' sustainability literacy. Its mission is 'to expand **sustainable knowledge, skills, and mindset** that motivates individuals to become deeply committed to build a sustainable future and to make informed and effective decisions'. The organisation makes available quizzes and tests to help institutions measure and improve their students' sustainability literacy. Further information: www.sulitest.org.

Climate Literacy and Action for All (free NTU online course available via FutureLearn, launched November 2022).

In this three-week course, you will learn how to become 'climate literate' to help you make climate-conscious decisions. Included are the calculations necessary to estimate the greenhouse gas emissions of various human activities and the tools to choose climate solutions with the highest impact, for the benefit of all: www.futurelearn.com/courses/climate-literacy-and-action-for-all.

The student society **Enactus** is available in 33 countries. It is 'a network of leaders committed to using business as a catalyst for positive social and environmental impact. We educate, inspire, and support young people to use innovation and entrepreneurship to solve the world's biggest problems'. Further information: https://enactus.org/.

The student society **oikos International** exists in over 20 countries. Its aim is to 'raise awareness for sustainability and transform our own education. As we work towards the change we want to see in the world in our particular contexts, we explore and practice the leadership our world needs in the 21st century'. Further information: https://oikos-international.org/.

IEMA (Institute of Environmental Management and Assessment). This is the professional body for those working in environmental roles. It provides a sustainability skills map for those who wish to take on more specialist roles. Further information: www.iema.net/sustainabiliy-skills-map.

EYCarbon: EY's website has some useful resources, even for those not looking to employ this management consultancy. There are links to related articles as well. Further information: www.ey.com/en_uk/sustainability/ey-carbon.

Further readings

Cole, D., and Pendry, V. (2020) *Redefining education for work, life and the future*, www.lifewideeducation. uk/blog/redefining-education-for-work-life-and-the-future (accessed 12 October 2022). This paper encourages a focus on education that is more human-centred and forward/ future-looking, to support success across multiple dimensions and disciplines. Lifewide Education, where the paper is located, is a not-for-profit, community-based, educational enterprise, which champions and supports a lifewide and ecological approach to lifelong learning, personal development, education, and achievement.

The **Education for Green Jobs** initiative focuses on supporting curricula updates to build the workforce needed for sustainability, improving education, placements, and careers, as well as enhancing communication between employers and educators. See their Global Guidance for Green Jobs, available at https://wedocs.unep.org/bitstream/handle/ 20.500.11822/35070/GGEGJ.pdf and the **Green Learning Network,** part of the Green Forum, https://thegreenforum.org/group/91/about.

Microsoft (2022) *Closing the sustainability skills gap* – this report seeks to help businesses move from pledges to progress.' It includes research from Microsoft and Boston Consulting Group (BCG). It identifies the need for both specialist sustainability roles and broader teams in organisations, which combine their business, project, and wider skills with sustainability knowledge: https://query.prod.cms.rt.microsoft.com/cms/api/am/binary/ RE5bhuF.

The **PwC** website also has various related articles and statistics: www.pwc.co.uk/who-we-are/our-purpose/building-trust-in-the-climate-transition/supporting-a-fair-transition/ green-jobs-barometer.html.

QAA (2023) Business & Management – Subject Benchmark Statement (March): https:// www.qaa.ac.uk/the-quality-code/subject-benchmark-statements/subject-benchmark-statement-business-and-management. The new benchmark statement has ESD (Educational for Sustainable Development) and related topics woven throughout, with lots of mentions of ERS/ESG, responsible management and employability.

Students Organizing for Sustainability International (SOS). This is a grouping of international student-led and student-focused organisations working on sustainability and social justice. SOS supports more and better action, the scaling of programmes and campaigns, strengthens capacity to empower student leadership, and amplifies the voice of students to influence systemic change(s). Further information: https://sos. earth/.

References

Advance HE/QAA (2021) *Education for sustainable development guidance, executive summary,* March, https://www.qaa.ac.uk/docs/qaa/guidance/education-for-sustainable-development-guidance-executive-summary.pdf (accessed 1 May 2023).

Burgen, S. (2022) Barcelona students to take mandatory climate crisis module from 2024, *The Guardian,* 12 November, www.theguardian.com/world/2022/nov/12/barcelona-students-to-take-mandatory-climate-crisis-module-from-2024 (accessed 14 November 2022).

Change Agents UK, EAUC & Cook, I. (2020) *Future graduate skills: A scoping study,* October, www.sustainabilityexchange.ac.uk/files/future_graduate_skills_report_change_agents_uk_eauc_october_2020.pdf (accessed 18 November 2022).

Coe, J. (2021) Universities set to push towards net-zero target, *Wonkhe,* 20 October, https://wonkhe.com/blogs/universities-set-to-push-towards-net-zero-target/ (accessed 23 November 2021).

Cole, D. (2019) *Defining and developing an approach to employability: A study of sports degree provision,* PhD thesis, London: Northumbria University.

Cole, D. (2022) *NTU employability redefined taxonomy narrative, Internal Briefing Paper,* NTU, https://www.ntu.ac.uk/staff-profiles/employability/doug-cole.

Deloitte (2022) *Deloitte and IEMA launch report to build green skills across the UK workforce,* 28 April, https://www2.deloitte.com/uk/en/pages/press-releases/articles/deloitte-and-iema-launch-report-to-build-green-skills-across-the-uk-workforce.html (accessed 3 August 2022).

De Novellis, M. (2022) *Integrated approaches to teaching sustainability,* www.aacsb.edu/insights/articles/2022/05/integrated-approaches-to-teaching-sustainability (accessed 25 October 2022).

DiNapoli, J. (2021) *PwC planning to hire 100,000 over five years in major ESG push,* 15 June, www.reuters.com/business/sustainable-business/pwc-planning-hire-100000-over-five-years-major-esg-push-2021-06-15/ (accessed 3 August 2022).

Doepel, R. (2022) *More than half of UK businesses have net-zero plans, but how can these targets be reached?* www.edie.net/more-than-half-of-uk-businesses-have-net-zero-plans-but-how-can-these-targets-be-reached/ (accessed 12 October 2022).

Drayson, R. (2015) Student attitudes towards, and skills for, sustainable development summary 4: sustainability, skills and employability, *Higher Education Academy,* September, https://www.advance-he.ac.uk/knowledge-hub/student-attitudes-towards-and-skills-sustainable-development-2015 (accessed 26 March 2023).

Edie (2022) *Survey: 2 in 3 SMEs don't think they have skills needed for net-zero transition,* 23 February, www.edie.net/survey-2-in-3-smes-dont-think-they-have-skills-needed-for-net-zero-transition/ (accessed 10 September 2022).

EU (2022) *Switch2Green,* www.switchtogreen.eu/the-green-employment-initiative/ (accessed 3 August 2022).

European Commission (2022) *GreenComp: The European sustainability competence framework*, https://joint-research-centre.ec.europa.eu/greencomp-european-sustainability-competence-framework_en (accessed 12 October 2022).

EY (2022) *EY carbon launched to support listed businesses preparing net zero plans ahead of looming 2023 deadline*, www.ey.com/en_uk/news/2022/02/ey-carbon-launched-to-support-listed-businesses-preparing-net-zero-plans-ahead-of-looming-2023-deadline (accessed 3 August 2022).

Globescan (2021) *The 2021 globescan/sustainability leaders survey*, https://globescan.com/2021/07/28/2021-sustainability-leaders-report/ (accessed 23 November 2021).

Growth That Matters AB (2021) *Inner development goals: Background, method and the IDG framework*, https://www.innerdevelopmentgoals.org/framework (accessed 1 May 2023).

Inner Development Goals (2022) *Transformational skills for sustainable development*, www.innerdevelopmentgoals.org/about (accessed 19 October 2022).

Jirova, A. (2022) *Mainstreaming the SDGs in business schools*, EFMD Global Blog, https://blog.efmdglobal.org/2022/08/30/mainstreaming-the-sdgs-in-business-schools/ (accessed 25 October 2022).

Lifewide Education (2022) www.lifewideeducation.uk/lifewide-learning.html (accessed 18 November 2022).

Project Drawdown (2021) *Climate solutions at work*, https://drawdown.org/publications/climate-solutions-at-work (accessed 23 November 2021).

Prospects (2021) *What skills do employers want?* www.prospects.ac.uk/careers-advice/applying-for-jobs/what-skills-do-employers-want (accessed 25 November 2021).

PWC (2021) *Green jobs barometer*, www.pwc.co.uk/who-we-are/purpose/green-jobs-barometer.pdf (accessed 3 August 2022).

QAA (2021) *Education for sustainable development guidance 2021*, https://www.qaa.ac.uk/the-quality-code/education-for-sustainable-development (accessed 26 March 2023).

Re_Generation (2022) *A new agenda for business*, www.re-generation.ca/our-manifesto/ (accessed 5 November 2022).

Rowland (2022) Why every manager is on the front line of ESG planning, *CMI*, 7 June, www.managers.org.uk/knowledge-and-insights/article/why-every-manager-is-on-the-front-line-of-esg-planning/ (accessed 12 October 2022).

SOS (2022) *Sustainability skills survey 2021–22*, https://uploads-ssl.webflow.com/6008334066c47be740656954/62de805cb0d9030a96c6e88a_20220125_SOS-UK%20Sustainability%20Skills%202021-22%20-%20HE%20only%20-%20FINAL.pdf (accessed 3 August 2022).

SOS International (2021) *Students, sustainability and education*, https://sos.earth/survey/ (accessed 3 August 2022).

Sustainability Exchange (2017) *Future-proof your career – green gown awards – Nottingham Trent University*, www.sustainabilityexchange.ac.uk/green_gown_awards_2017_nottingham_trent_univers (accessed 11 October 2022).

UNESCO (2015) *Skills are crucial to achieve the 2030 agenda for sustainable development*, updated 2022, www.unesco.org/en/articles/skills-are-crucial-achieve-2030-agenda-sustainable-development (accessed 12 October 2022).

UNGC – Accenture Strategy (2016) *Agenda 2030: A window of opportunity – Infographic*, https://d306pr3pise04h.cloudfront.net/docs/news_events%2F8.1%2FUNGC-Accenture-CEO-study-2016-infographic.pdf (accessed 25 November 2021).

Universities UK (2022) *Strong demand for graduates amid UK skills shortage*, 11 April, www.universitiesuk.ac.uk/latest/news/strong-demand-graduates-amid-uk-skills (accessed 15 September 2022).

WEF (2021) *These are the skills young people will need for the green jobs of the future*, 23 August, Available at: www.weforum.org/agenda/2021/08/these-are-the-skills-young-people-will-need-for-the-green-jobs-of-the-future/ (accessed 25 November 2021).

5
Integrating the three pillars of sustainability: Social, environmental, and economic

Al Dharmasasmita, Seraphina Brown, and Sigrun M. Wagner

This chapter introduces the idea of sustainability as being constructed from social, environmental, and economic elements. It also explores these elements as being fundamentally linked and why this is important for business. Approaching sustainable business from each of the three perspectives, this chapter provides two sessions detailing the importance of integrating sustainability and one on how this is all related to the Sustainable Development Goals.

In this chapter, you will learn to:

- Recognise the fundamental linkages between social, environmental, and economic pillars of sustainability in a business framework.

- Understand the **triple bottom line** and what it means for business.

- Appreciate the applied principles of sustainability and why they are fundamental to business.

- Link the triple bottom line (TBL) to the SDGs.

DOI: 10.4324/9781003294665-7

Hitchcock and Willard (2009: 3) contend that sustainability in business can be understood as 'a **framework** for making sense of what is happening in the world so that you can foresee changes and take action *before* they happen' [emphasis added]. Sustainability, therefore, encourages you to observe the relationships between social, economic, and environmental trends (Elkington, 1997) and be proactive instead of reactive to events. The three pillars of sustainability are often depicted as three circles of an overlapping Venn diagram (for example, Figure 5.1a), emphasising the importance of the links between social, environmental, and economic sustainability. Others prefer the 3-Nested-dependencies model (Figure 5.1b). The model

Figure 5.1: (a) The three pillars of sustainability. **(b)** The 3-Nested-dependencies model.

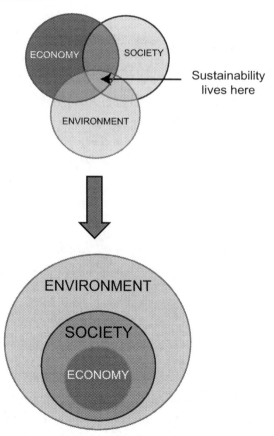

Source: Adapted from Willard (2010), http://sustainabilityadvantage.com/2010/07/20/3-sustainability-models/; (b) based on Bob Doppelt (2010), *The Power of Sustainable Thinking*, and Peter Senge *et al*. (2008), *The Necessary Revolution*.

depicts that without a thriving natural environment, it is impossible for society and economy to prosper. For the purpose of this chapter, we will adopt Figure 5.1b to illustrate the interdependencies between the three pillars of sustainability.

The use of '**sustainable business**' has seen a steady uptake across the literature (Michel *et al.*, 2011), and its further application looks set to increase into the future. In this context, students need to come to their own mutual understanding of what sustainability and sustainable business are. In sharing these thoughts and understanding each other's perspective, you will also be better placed to understand the different perceptions taken on sustainability in marketing or accounting later in this book.

It is important to underline that, in recent years, there has been a move away from dictionary definitions of *sustainability* to more *reflexive* understandings which link closely to personal values and observation of the world around you, as explained by Dermondy in a reference to a mutual comprehension of sustainability:

> Usually a shared broader understanding emerges that embraces notions of corporate and individual citizenship, changing consumption patterns, social capital, personal values-driven behaviour, politics and legislation, the fair distribution of economic, environmental and social assets, and proactive personal and collective responsibilities – wrapped within an organisational and individual behavioural context that includes fairly traded products and services, reduction in energy usage, increasing use of public transport and decreasing use of cars, local organic food, reducing food miles, ecotourism, and non-supermarket shopping.
>
> (2010: 12)

This 'mutual comprehension of sustainability' can be argued to be in line with most of the seventeen Sustainable Development Goals (SDGs) that have been agreed by the United Nations (2015).

Sustainability and the triple bottom line

The classic understanding of sustainability in a business context is expressed in Elkington's (1997) *Cannibals with Forks*, in which the idea of the **triple bottom line (TBL)** is introduced. This is the quintessential account of the importance of sustainability and business. Elkington expresses 'sustainability' for a new millennium, suggesting that, in the past, it has been understood as an attempt to harmonise the traditional financial bottom line with an environmental agenda. He suggests that it is essential for businesses to look towards a new horizon of a *triple bottom line*, involving *not only economic prosperity and environmental quality but also social justice*. Hence, Elkington asks that businesses look not only to their conventional 'bottom line', or the account of profit and loss of their business, but also measure, in some shape or form, the societal impacts of their operations and gauge the impact on the planet by how environmentally responsible it has been. In this way, the TBL scheme of thought illuminates the concept of three pillars of sustainability in a business context.

Following a similar train of thought to that shown here in the 3-Nested-dependencies model (Figure 5.1b), Elkington breaks down the three tenets of sustainability into **people, planet, and profit**. *Note the order*: Elkington is implicitly suggesting that businesses need to follow this mandate of importance, rather than the (almost) exclusive focus on profit seen to characterise much of business thought in popular imagination up until recently. Additionally, *Cannibals with Forks* represents a reversal in the way transparency of business is imagined: companies are now held accountable not just by industry and government regulators but just as often by environmentalists, the societies they operate in, and media campaigns. Business leaders need to look beyond their own shareholder interests to consider the importance of **stakeholders**, or those that can be argued to have some effect on, or be affected by, a business (Freeman, 1984). This can therefore include not only the shareholders but also the customers, suppliers, local communities, the natural environment, governments, and employees.

TBL has, since the publication of *Cannibals with Forks*, seen much traction in both the academic and business communities. Its philosophy and practice have been examined and promoted by many in the business community, such as Fisk (2010) and Willard (2012).

Various reports by Accenture, as commissioned by the **United Nations Global Compact (UNGC)**, have emphasised the importance of sustainability strategies, with 81% of CEOs surveyed stating their companies are already developing new sustainable products and services and transitioning to net zero business models whereby the SDGs 'provide an opportunity to rethink approaches to sustainable value creation' (Accenture, 2021, 2016, 2013).

Nevertheless, TBL is renowned enough to have also collected a wealth of criticism. The main critique levelled at TBL is that, despite its pretensions, sustainability does not fit neatly into the business case, as Elkington would suggest, and that there is no standard of measurement for the 'non-traditional' social and environmental elements. Robins (2006) contends that the difficulty of quantifying the people and planet elements casts doubt on whether TBL really is a bottom line. It is probably best seen as a 'framing device' to make sense of business relationships rather than underpinning a new kind of accounting (Blowfield, 2013: 229). Elkington himself has acknowledged in recent years that the concept was never meant to be 'just an accounting system' (2018: 3) but as a provocation for breakthrough system change and for disruption.

Despite these contentions, the fact remains that TBL has enjoyed a large and receptive audience in the business community. Elkington (1997: 73) notes that it is difficult to measure progress against TBL, as the pillars of society, environment, and economy are 'in constant flux, due to social, political, economic and environmental pressures, cycles, and conflicts. So, the sustainability challenge is tougher than any of the other challenges in isolation'. However, he also highlights that, while the path may not be easy and will be easily obscured, sustainability is well worth pursuing, and TBL is an excellent start to asking the questions of your business that sustainability demands, though as emphasised by Elkington in 2020, capitalism and companies need to go beyond the focus on bottom lines and become 'radically more economically more inclusive, socially just, and – crucially – environmentally restorative'.

Positive thought, positive action, and intertwining for growth

Business is uniquely positioned in the sustainability frontier in that it not only can be a powerful force of positive change in and of itself but can also influence consumers to change behaviour in positive ways (Fisk, 2010). Elkington (1997) suggests that, throughout the 21st century, businesses, much more than governments or NGOs (non-governmental organisations), will be in the driving seat of society and leading future change. Laughland and Bansal (2011) concur that the new business-as-society paradigm will require the efforts of organisations across sectors. Furthermore, Elkington (1997: 70) argues that 'some of the most interesting challenges are found *not within but between* the areas covered by economic, social and environmental, bottom lines'.

Thus, understanding the interactions between discernible pillars of sustainability, and the feedback to business, will be crucial in the next few decades as businesses seek to embed sustainability more thoroughly into operations and processes fit for the 21st century.

Approaching sustainability from each of the three elements, seeking to recognise the fundamental linkages between the sustainability pillars in order to develop a holistic understanding of business and sustainability, is a great way to comprehend sustainability overall.

Overemphasis on any of the elements of sustainability is detrimental to the achievement of strong sustainability. People, planet, and profit should not be viewed as separate entities in business but instead as being intimately intertwined (Elkington, 1997). Looking at the big picture, Hitchcock and Willard (2009) argue that without a healthy economy, unemployment may be high, creating a whole host of societal problems; and governments no longer have the revenues to handle increased social ills. If the provision of a healthy environment is ignored, the foundations of the economy are often undermined, and human health and well-being are negatively affected. Thus, '[h]olding the other realms hostage to one ultimately backfires' (Hitchcock and Willard, 2009: 9).

Figge *et al.* (2002) advocate the use of a BSC (balanced scorecard) as a tool to incorporate environmental and social management within the general management of a firm. The BSC methodology was developed in the early 1990s to counter ideological problems of short-termism in management accounting (Kaplan and Norton, 1992). The purpose of the BSC as a tool is to formulate a hierarchic system of strategic objectives (Figge *et al.*, 2002). BSC offers significant scope in terms of sustainability, as it allows the simultaneous incorporation of elements of environmental and social sustainability integrally into financial thought.

While conflicts between the three performance categories inevitably occur, practically businesses should seek to achieve improvements across the board. What differentiates the BSC as a corporate sustainability performance tool is the opportunity to incorporate environmental and social factors (as being notoriously difficult to quantify) into mainstream business thought and activity. This offers three major advantages: first, sustainability management that is economically sound is resilient and not deemed extraneous in times of economic crisis but fundamental. Second, Figge *et al.* (2002) argue that sustainability management that contributes to economic objectives helps a business orientate itself towards competitors and provides a positive example of success. Finally, the top-down integration of environmental and social factors ensures that corporate sustainability management considers all three facets of sustainability (ibid.), which is crucial for understanding the overlapping elements of sustainability and the ways they are important for a business's strategy.

In summary, for sustainability to be valuable to both the organisation and its stakeholders, it must be integrated into the way a company does business (Epstein, 2008). Not only is it damaging to view sustainability in terms of just one of its pillars, but it is also difficult to achieve strong sustainability in business without achieving the balanced success of social, environmental, and economic goals that are thoroughly understood as fundamentally linked. Without understanding this, the progress of sustainable businesses will likely stagnate.

Challenges of sustainable integration

Many have made good progress through reporting on sustainability, but it is unlikely that any company has fully integrated or achieved sustainability (KPMG, 2020; Epstein, 2008). Understanding the barriers to sustainability and its successful integration in a business context also deserves consideration.

One of the main detractions concerning the incorporation of social, environmental, and economic metrics in the path to sustainability is that sustainability does not fit neatly into 'the **business case**'. Sustainability improvements often demand that investments are made to ensure success, but these investments are often based on long-term and intangible rewards (Laughland and Bansal, 2011). Additionally, the payback period for sustainability-related investments often exceeds that required to approve projects, and initiatives are treated as standalone rather than integral (ibid.). This is complicated by the difficulty in directly comparing financial short-term gains to value-creating long-term impacts. However, the MIT Sloan Management Review (2016) report details that sustainability-related spending has survived the recession, with almost 60% of companies suggesting they have increased their investments since 2010. Thus, enthusiasm for sustainability is growing across all sectors, demonstrating that companies view sustainability as a necessary investment of capital rather than a medium of short-term returns.

Molthan-Hill (2014) highlights the Anglo-American bias in the use of the phrase 'the business case' to infer that environmental improvements or considerations are extraneous to the activity of business in British mangers. In comparison, their German counterparts are more likely to refer to the business rationality of 'survival' and thus more fluently integrate environmental and sustainability concepts into their business thought. It is important to consider these linguistic and cultural attributes in the attitudes to sustainability many possess.

CSR has been suggested to be the latest in a series of management fads, failing to convince customers of genuine motives but instead reminding them of ethical appeasement. It has been suggested also that 'social responsibility' was too flimsy a concept to generate any interest with business leaders (Elkington, 2014). Looking at sustainability as a new form of value demanded by society and effective businesses boosts the resilience and applicability of the term in corporate circles. Understanding sustainability in this way represents a new horizon for businesses, and demonstrating that the most effective and long-lasting sustainability solutions derive from all three parts of sustainability is important. This is supported in Devinney's (2009: 54) argument that the TBL is a 'template that should be applied more rigorously and consistently across . . . all studies'.

Finally, Laughland and Bansal (2011) detail that business leaders are hesitant about communicating about sustainability to their employees and colleagues in a genuine manner and managing expectations in terms of progress. Hitchcock and Willard (2009) suggest that many of today's employees want to work for a company that shares their values, citing the finding that 92% would be more inclined to work for a company that was known for being environmentally friendly (Mattioli, 2007), reflecting the central concern for the environment among Generation Z (AI, 2019). This can be a differentiating factor for companies from their competitors (Robertson, 2017). Sustainability is a broad-enough canvas to encompass most people's concerns, be they local or global, social or environmental, and thus can help infuse even the most mundane jobs with meaning (Hitchcock and Willard, 2009).

A framework that does this encompassing particularly well is the so-called doughnuts economics framework by Kate Raworth (2017). The environmental element of sustainability comes in the shape of planetary boundaries which form the outer ring of the doughnut as the ecological ceiling, whilst the social element forms the inner ring as a foundation ensuring people have access to the basics of life. The economic side can be found between these two as the safe and just space for a regenerative and distributive economy to flourish.

Figure 5.2: The doughnut of ecological ceiling and social foundation encompassing a safe and just space for humankind.

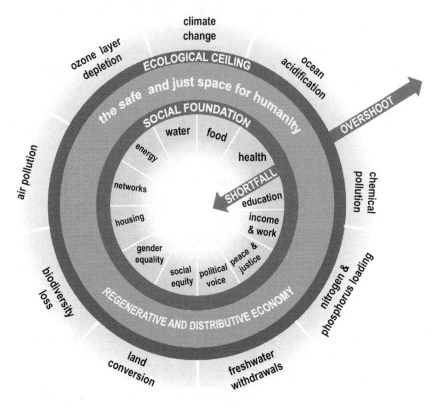

Source: https://doughnuteconomics.org/about-doughnut-economics. Permission for use of graph granted by Doughnut Economics Action Lab (DEAL) under Creative Commons Licence.

Whilst there is justified cause to be pessimistic whether businesses can be truly sustainable, given the seeming lack of progress, for example, on corporate climate action, there is also plenty of reason for optimism concerning the state of sustainability in business. Sustainability is also spurring collaborative management solutions, where business leaders are working within and between their sectors to share innovation. The potential for the successful fusion of business and sustainability goals remains great. This points to the crucial goal of SDG no. 17 – partnerships, though the sector has much to contribute when it comes to the achievement of each of the goals individually and as a whole. We will now turn to each element of the TBL in turn, stressing that whilst we cover them separately, the interconnections are evident.

Environmental sustainability and business

This section of the chapter will focus on the environmental dimension of sustainability. Incorporating environmental thinking into business considerations is perceived as notoriously difficult, despite the fact that improving environmental and social sustainability can often provide new value to a business. One way to make sense of this is to look at the value the environment and nature provide for business in the form of ecosystem goods and services. *Ecosystem services* (ES) can be defined as services provided by the natural environment that benefit people (HM Government, 2013). Figure 5.3 gives examples of the various types of ecosystem services that nature's capital – biodiversity – gifts humanity and how they interact with socioeconomic and well-being factors, emphasising the interdependencies of the TBL.

If businesses had to pay for the use of these services, taking into account their value contribution to the global economy, the price system we use would be very different, as Costanza *et al.* (1997) argue, estimating the value to be in the range of US$16–54 trillion annually. For example, the impact of pollinating insects is estimated to be worth £440 million to UK agriculture alone (Defra, 2015; BBC, 2010). Although criticisms have been raised against such thinking, putting a monetary value on to the planet's services aligns with the language of business we could argue.

PES (payments for ecosystem services) therefore offer a new opportunity to business, in that they bring economic thinking and a market mechanism into the provision of ES. PES are voluntary market transactions between buyers and sellers (beneficiaries and providers) of ES. In this way, PES involve a business paying another party to protect an area of land where it provides an obvious benefit to the company.

PES approaches in developing countries have demonstrated their capacity to help alleviate poverty and conserve natural resources as part of a single top-down scheme (RELU, 2012). One example of this in agricultural supply chains is the case of coffee. Coffee is one of the most valuable legally traded export commodities in the world and is grown across many of the world's most biodiverse regions (Ricketts *et al.*, 2004). Session 1 provides more detail on the linkages between ES and business, using a case study of Starbucks.

Two further guiding principles for the environmental element of the triple bottom line can be found in eco-efficiency and eco-effectiveness. *Eco-efficiency*

Figure 5.3: Linkages between ecosystem services and human well-being.

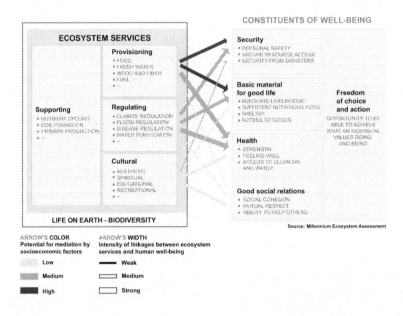

Source: Millennium Ecosystem Assessment, 2005, www.millenniumassessment.org/documents/document.356.aspx.pdf. Image credit Philippe Rekacewicz, Emmanuelle Bournay, UNEP/GRID-Arendal.

is generally defined as 'doing more with less' and was initially introduced by the World Business Council for Sustainable Development in 2006 as delivering

> competitively priced goods and services that satisfy human needs and bring quality of life, while progressively reducing ecological impacts and resource intensity throughout the life-cycle to a level at least in line with the Earth's estimated carrying capacity.

The concept therefore aims at environmental responsibility and economic efficiency – creating more value with less impact on the environment, which is measured through the ratio between a product and its impact, thus closely related to resource productivity. Despite the advantages of eco-efficiency for moving businesses towards environmental sustainability, it could be argued to be only a necessary condition for sustainable development, not a sufficient one (Elkington, 1997), as being 'less bad' does not reach very far or deep. This is where eco-effectiveness comes into the picture, which entails working on the right things rather than 'making the wrong things less bad' (McDonough and Braungart, 2002: 76). Eco-effectiveness encourages a cyclical cradle-to-cradle approach that can also be found in the circular economy.

To conclude, maybe businesses need to ask, 'What can we do for the environment?' rather than 'What can the environment do for us?' This is reflected throughout the targets of goal 12: responsible consumption and production. Particularly, target 12.6: 'Encourage companies, especially large and transnational companies, to adopt sustainable practices and to integrate sustainability information into their reporting cycle' (United Nations, 2015).

Social sustainability and business

This section of the chapter will focus on the social dimension of sustainability and the importance for business to recognise the significant role that society and business play in affecting and effecting one another. Magis and Shinn (2009: 1) state that 'sustainability is premised on *systems theory*, stipulating that society, the environment, and the economy are **interrelated constituents of a larger system**. The system can only remain viable to the extent that *each of the constituents functions properly*'. This highlights the notion that business and society do need each other for survival and prosperity.

Several academics have approached the social dimension from two different angles: **socio-efficiency** and **socio-effectiveness** (Hockerts, 1999; Figge and Hahn, 2001). Socio-efficiency can be termed as the relationship between a company's value added and impact on the society, and the impact can be both positive, for example, the creating of work, and negative, such as work accidents and human rights abuses. However, Dyllick and Hockerts (2002) argue that its concern is predominantly with increasing economic sustainability, and although valuable, it only leads to relative improvements of society which can be limited to a micro-scale. Socio-effectiveness, the authors further contend, is when '[b]usiness conduct should be judged not on a relative scale but rather in relation to the *absolute positive social impact a firm could reasonably have achieved*' (p. 138; our italics). Henceforth, what needs to be considered is the **overall impact** of business on its society, linking back to the 3-Nested-dependencies model (Figure 5.1b) earlier in this chapter.

Waage *et al.* (2005: 1149) contend that social sustainability 'span[s] from labour conditions and wages through access to natural resources-based needs (e.g. food, water), to socioeconomic resources (health, informational/educational, financial) etc.'. The authors further state that social aspects of sustainability relate to 'not only to what employees are paid, but also to how the product, and production process, affects the parameters of people's lives (e.g. access to the full range of resources – natural, informational/educational, health, financial, etc.)', and that businesses need to look beyond the company, that is, consider not just the employees but all stakeholders who can be affected, such as the community directly impacted and the society as a whole that can be indirectly affected by the company's processes. On both a macro- and micro-level, businesses need to ask themselves some of the questions listed in Figure 5.4 in order to help them address social sustainability in their processes. Businesses can have an immense impact not only on citizens in society but also on local politics and institutions.

Companies tend to address social sustainability issues, such as labour rights and human rights, in their CSR strategies. However, much more can be done in

Figure 5.4: A company's framework for social sustainability.

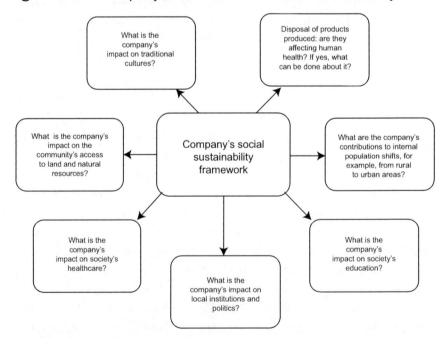

Source: Adapted from Waage *et al.* (2005).

this area. For example, an area that tends to be neglected in a company's CSR is anti-corruption, where strategies to address this are often not part of companies' CSR policies (Carr and Outhwaite, 2011).

More and more businesses are also starting to address social sustainability in their processes, and some of them have not only received positive attention but have also been labelled as 'pioneers' or 'champions' in their sector (see Flynn *et al.*, 2019, for examples of sustainability champions). Examples are Heineken leading the alcohol industry in the fight against alcohol abuse (Wills, 2013), and the Shared Interest Society helping farmers in developing countries through its ethical and cooperative micro-financing (Beavis, 2013).

Social sustainability concepts and practices are on the rise, and it makes business sense for companies to integrate social issues in their overall strategy, as this can not only improve the company's brand but also increase its legitimacy to operate (the so-called 'license to operate' proposed and defined by Donaldson and Dunfee, 1999). Furthermore, evidence has shown that if businesses address their impact on society, this can have a positive knock-on effect on the environment, which in turn can ultimately lead to a more progressive economic sustainability (Porter and Kramer, 2011).

Economic sustainability and business: what does it mean?

The economic element of sustainability arose from economic growth models that assessed the limits imposed by the carrying capacity of the Earth (Crane and Matten, 2015), which can also be thought of as planetary boundaries (Rockström *et al.*, 2009) – the ecological ceiling in the doughnut economics that introduced earlier the Brundtland definition of sustainability emerged from this line of thought: 'development that meets the needs of the present without compromising the ability of future generations to meet their own needs' (UNCED, 1987). The implications of economic sustainability on business activity and ethics occur on different levels. The first, narrow understanding of sustainability in business focuses on the economic performance of the company and the maintenance of a business model that secures the long-term economic performance of the company. This recognises the need to focus on strategies that lead to longer-term rise in share price, market share, or revenue, rather than short-term emphasis on profits (ibid.). A broader, more holistic understanding of economic sustainability, Crane and Matten (2015) argue, would be the company's ideological stance on the economic framework upon which it is embedded. Again, this links back to Figure 5.1b of the 3-Nested-dependencies model mentioned earlier in this chapter.

One way to interpret this could be a business engaging in **tax avoidance** or evasion. While the latter violates the law, the former is possible through subtle accounting tricks or the use of tax havens. Nevertheless, the reluctance of a business to pay into the political institutional environment upon which its success is based is economically unsustainable (ibid.).

Barford and Holt (2013) have written on the rise of **tax shaming**, with the recession making the public increasingly aware of what they perceive as **tax injustice**. This can have an unquantifiable and lasting effect on a brand's hard-won appeal. The public is also increasingly aware of the capabilities of multinational corporations to evade tax obligations, which has been promoted as 'sound business practice', while many companies without an international arm are not able to avoid paying large tax bills.

Linking this back to the stakeholder theory discussed earlier in this chapter, can you think of the effects on local communities and the government, or even your education, as a result of companies not paying tax in the country that they operate in? (You might also want to apply the 'systems theory' mentioned earlier.)

Crane and Matten (2015) suggest an important understanding for business is that sustainability is about systems maintenance, that is, ensuring that **our actions as humans do not interfere with the long-term viability of the biotic system** (see also Edwards *et al.*, 2021). Business sustainability therefore has strong links to systems theory, which seeks to understand 'problems' as being embedded in particular organisational structures, cultures, and business environments.

Nevertheless, the tripartite model of sustainability remains pre-eminent, as it arises from an understanding that not only is it impractical but also sometimes impossible to address the sustainability of the natural environment within a business framework without also considering social and economic aspects (Crane and Matten, 2015).

An important dimension of sustainability is that of **intergenerational equity**: *equality between one generation and another*. This also has important implications for geographically distant populations, and thus, the role of globalisation in business is important. Globalisation has accentuated the homogenisation of ethics across the globe. This means that business faces the same ethical questions worldwide, and it is in emerging economies and developing nations where questions of business ethics are most pertinent (Crane and Matten, 2015). It also makes a business's activities across the world much more transparent to the observant role and thus holds a business accountable. A consideration of social justice in the developing world is often deeply embedded in environmental justice.

Can you think of other practices by companies that can have an adverse effect on the natural environment and/or society? To give an example, what about the zero hours contract? How can this impact the local communities? What about its impact on the economy?

Sustainability cannot be managed exclusively as a **public relations** strategy, or it will be *greenwashing*. Reputational benefits are not the only advantages companies can derive from pursuing sustainability, and stakeholders expect any communication a company produces expressing its efforts towards sustainability to be consistent with results. No organisation has managed to become fully sustainable – this is perhaps an impossible task. Instead, a company's focus should be on conceiving a sustainability framework, modelling social, environmental, and economic performance, and using this as an opportunity to create real value for multiple stakeholders. Simultaneously, this model of corporate sustainability challenges managers to understand the complex interrelationships between economic, environmental, and social performance (Epstein, 2008).

Conclusion

Whilst it is important for business to think about growing (and developing) and the conventional 'bottom line' of profits, it has become imperative that the concepts of **people** and **planet** be integrated into business practices in order to achieve the **profit**. One way forward to summarise the contemporary landscape of sustainability and business is expressed by Porter and Kramer (2011), in the creation of 'shared value'. This focuses on the connections between societal and economic progress, expressing that businesses have the potential to create the next wave of global growth, reflecting the progress in corporate thinking on sustainability. Shared value is created through a company enhancing its competitiveness while simultaneously advancing the economic and social benefits of the community in which it is embedded. There is plenty of scope to include environmental thinking in business sustainability in the form of the doughnut economics model (Raworth, 2017). The purpose of a corporation needs to be redefined as creating shared value for the environment and society, rather than just creating monetary value, that is, profit. In this fashion, sustainability is and will be integral to businesses and reshape their relationships with society and the environment.

Suggested sessions

Session 1: Starbucks, impact investment and ecosystem services

Learning outcomes

- Explore the **triple bottom line** with reference to the case study, and understand how all three elements are inextricably linked.

- Relate the efficacy of **impact investment** to sustainability and encourage consideration in other areas of business.

- Understand the motivations of businesses in ensuring a scheme that covers all three pillars of sustainability.

Background

Across the globe, over 25 million people are directly dependent on growing coffee for a living. The frontier of coffee-growing is expanding into some of the most important and sensitive biodiverse regions. Also, the market for coffee is often volatile, with farmers suffering from the falling price of coffee. This damages the livelihoods of farmers who aim to cultivate high-quality coffee using traditional, shade-grown techniques that have proven biodiversity benefits (Prickett, 2005). Non-traditional production practices do not require the presence of trees and thus are detrimental to the surrounding tropical ecosystem, as well as requiring the regular application of pesticides, which have their own environmental impacts. Farmers who are priced out of the market are often tempted to convert to growing coca (for cocaine), exposing the community to violent and unstable cartels and contributing to the global problem of drug trafficking (Oxfam Coffee Game, 2005). This trend threatens not only the long-term availability of high-quality coffee but also the integrity of local and sensitive ecosystems, and the overall well-being of communities that depend on it for an income, thereby addressing all three pillars of sustainability.

The opportunity to address this was identified in 1998 with the cooperation of Starbucks and Conservation International, an NGO with a focus on international biodiversity conservation. This first collaboration involved a field project in the southern state of Chiapas, Mexico, as Starbucks sought to source shade-grown, ecologically sound, premium coffee (Prickett, 2005). Starbucks subsequently partnered with Verde Ventures, a programme founded in 2001 as a key component in the development of Conservation International's sustainable economies model (Conservation International, 2014). Verde Ventures represents an important change in that they seek to advance the role of SMEs (small- and medium-sized enterprises) in the coffee-growing trade. SMEs employ local people, giving communities a personal and economic stake in protecting their own natural resources. Despite their significant economic role in developing nations, many SMEs suffer from lack of access to financing, which not only means they are economically unstable but also that SMEs are increasingly unable to invest in their own growth or adopt sustainable business practices (ibid.). Considering the potential to contribute towards both improvements in ecosystem health as well as human well-being (while providing a high-quality product), access to finance is paramount.

This model also offers a hands-off approach, as opposed to direct intervention, which allows human well-being goals to be delivered and allows the community ownership of its sustainable growth. In addition to a focus on habitat conservation, Verde Ventures offers training and education programmes focusing on environmentally preferential agricultural practices, for example, in developing a community-run tree nursery adjacent to coffee crops. Verde Ventures also aims to promote the role of women in the community, furthering their education and facilitating their role in the business of both producing and marketing coffee and other native plants which offer health benefits (ibid.).

Starbucks made the decision to increase its farmer loans to $20 million by 2015 (ibid.). Based on the success of their investment with Verde Ventures, Starbucks also developed green coffee-sourcing guidelines to incorporate its environmental and social standards into worldwide purchasing criteria. In 2012, Starbucks ethically sourced 93% of its coffee and aims to increase this to 100% by 2015 (Starbucks, 2014). Starbucks has since consistently achieved a 99% figure on its ethical sourcing for coffee and focuses particularly on climate change.

Activity 1

You are asked to form groups of no more than five. Using the diagram that follows, each group will address one of two perspectives with reference to the Verde Ventures case study. List the benefits of Starbucks's impact investment programme either:

1.   From the point of view of the CEO of Starbucks, or

2.   From the point of view of the recipient farm managers.

Write on the diagram where you think a benefit would lie. For example, the farmer's ability to access funding, ensuring financial security, may be an economic benefit. Allow ten minutes to discuss and compare results. Ideas may be, for example, strictly social or socioeconomic or could address all three facets of sustainability.

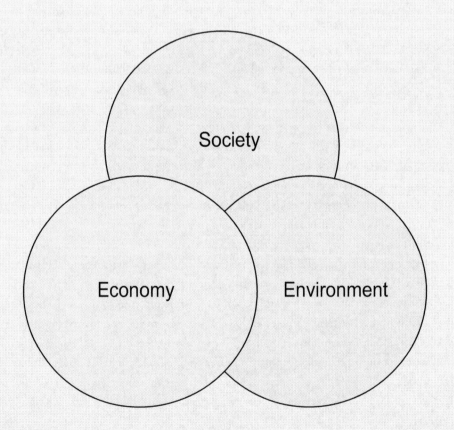

Activity 2

Remaining in groups, consider the following questions. Write down answers and then compare them as a class:

1. What could have happened without the investment? What driving market forces can be identified?

2. Starbucks is looking to invest $20 million with Verde Ventures by 2015. Is this a small amount, considering the size of the company? Is there need to invest more?

3. Can you assess that real change has occurred? And if so, how?

4. Is sustainability an effective mechanism to understand why and how change should occur with reference to the case study? Consider:

   a) Which side benefited more from the investment: Starbucks or the recipient community?

   b) Is sustainability a political tool?

Activity 3

On your own, write down examples of any other areas of business practice in which impact investment (also known as socially responsible investment) can be especially effective and why you think this is. Consider the sustainability advantages and disadvantages.

Session 2: Monsanto and social impact

Learning outcomes

- Differentiate between the concepts of 'socio-efficiency' and social sustainability.

- Be aware of the impacts that social issues can have on the environmental and economic aspects of business.

- Understand the role that social sustainability plays in the value chain of business's processes.

This session focuses on the social aspect of sustainability and the impact it can have on the environmental and economic dimension of a business.

Activity 1 (10 minutes)

1. As a collective session/tutorial group. Discuss some of the effects, which you may have read recently, that business has had on society, be it positive or negative. Divide your answers into a 'negative' category and a 'positive' category.

2. What are some of the areas that business has had influence on? For example, are they wages, healthcare, local politics, education, training?

3. Have any of these areas directly or indirectly impacted on the environment? What about the economy?

Activity 2 (20 minutes)

In groups of three, read the following case study individually:

Monsanto and India (adapted from Shiva, 2013)

Monsanto India's website uses phrases such as 'Improving farmers lives' [sic], 'apply innovation . . . help farmers', and 'innovative . . . agricultural company', alongside pictures of smiling, prosperous farmers from the state of Maharashtra, India. However, Monsanto has a part to play in the epidemic of farmers' suicides in India resulting from the company's growing control over cotton seed supply: **95% of India's cotton seed is now controlled by Monsanto**.

Control over seed is the first link in the food chain because seed is the source of life. When a corporation controls seed, it controls life, especially the life of farmers.

Monsanto's domineering control over the seed sector in India, and globally, can be a cause of alarm. This is what connects farmers' suicides in India to *Monsanto v. Percy Schmeiser* in Canada, to *Monsanto v. Bowman* in the United States, and to farmers in Brazil suing Monsanto for $2.2 billion for unfair collection of royalty.

Through patents on seed, Monsanto has become the 'life lord' of our planet, collecting rents for life's renewal from farmers, the original breeders.

Patents on seed are illegal because putting a toxic gene into a plant cell is neither 'creating' nor 'inventing' a plant. These are seeds of deception – the deception that Monsanto is the creator of seeds and life; the deception that while Monsanto sues farmers and traps them in debt, it pretends to be working for farmers' welfare; and the deception that GMOs (genetically modified organisms) feed the world. GMOs are failing to control pests and weeds and have instead led to the emergence of superpests and superweeds.

The entry of Monsanto into the Indian seed sector was made possible with a 1988 Seed Policy imposed by the World Bank, requiring the government of India to deregulate the seed sector. Five things changed with Monsanto's entry: First, Indian companies were locked into joint ventures and licensing arrangements, and concentration over the seed sector increased. Second, seed, which had been the farmers' common resource, became the 'intellectual property' of Monsanto, for which it started collecting royalties, thus raising the costs of seed. Third, open pollinated cotton seeds were displaced by hybrids, including GMO hybrids. A renewable resource became a non-renewable, patented commodity. Fourth, cotton, which had earlier been grown as a mixture with food crops, now had to be grown as a monoculture, with higher vulnerability to pests, disease, drought, and crop failure. Fifth, Monsanto started to subvert India's regulatory processes and, in fact, started to use public resources to push its non-renewable hybrids and GMOs through so-called public–private partnerships.

An internal advisory by the agricultural ministry of India in January 2012 had this to say to the cotton-growing states in India: 'Cotton farmers are in a deep crisis since shifting to Bt cotton. The spate of farmer suicides in 2011–12 has been particularly severe among Bt cotton farmers.'

The highest acreage of Bt cotton is in Maharashtra, and this is also where the highest farmer suicide rates are. Suicides increased after Bt cotton was introduced: Monsanto's royalty extraction and the high costs of seed and chemicals have created a debt trap. According to the government of India data, nearly 75% of rural debt is due to the purchase of raw materials, such as seeds. As Monsanto's profits grow, farmers' debt grows. It is in this systemic sense that Monsanto's seeds are seeds of suicide.

Now, as a group, fill in the diagram that follows with impacts that you think Monsanto can have on India, the farming sector in India, and the community in general.

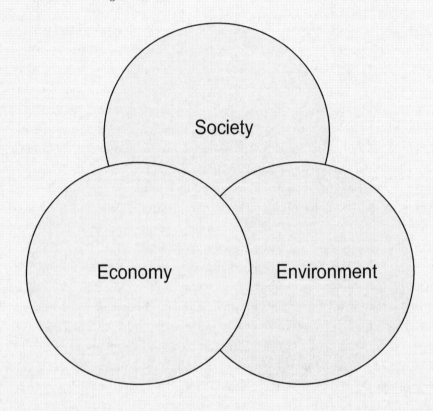

Activity 3 (20 minutes)

Still in your groups, complete the table that follows based on the Monsanto case study. Note that there can be more than one stakeholder in each group:

Social exposure of a business		
	Stakeholders	**Claim/issue**
Internal		
Along the value chain		
In the local community		
Society as a whole		

Session 3: The role of business in achieving the Sustainable Development Goals

Learning outcomes

- Having further knowledge of the Sustainable Development Goals.

- Reflect upon the student's own role in contributing to the goals and the UN Sustainable Development Agenda.

- Being able to link goal 17 (partnership for the goals) (SDGs, 2016) with business processes.

This activity focuses on the student's personal and professional contributions to the Sustainable Development Goals and the importance of partnership in reaching the goals. Students are asked to consider the various roles within a business and how they can have an impact and to reflect upon their own perceptions of the goals.

This is designed to be a practical activity whereby students will be physically moving to different areas of a room. This session describes the generic concept of the activity, but it can be picked up and adapted depending on the size of the group of students, and it can also be tailored to a specific discipline with the business school/university.

Setup

Begin by choosing a few of the Sustainable Development Goals. It is suggested that you pick approximately five of the goals for every 20 students. Try to select a variety of goals covering all three aspects of sustainability as discussed in this chapter. For example, you might choose goal 2: zero hunger; goal 5: gender equality; goal 9: industry, innovation, and infrastructure; goal 12: climate action; and goal 15: life on land.

Assign each goal to a separate area of the room, for example, the four corners and the centre of the room. It is advised that you label the area according to the assigned goal (printouts of the goals are available for download in the teaching materials); otherwise, you can simply use Post-it notes or scrap paper. Students will be prompted to move to the various areas of the room, depending on their answers to questions during the activities.

If you have time, the three activities can be repeated using a different selection of goals.

Activity 1 (15 minutes)

Considering your own personal values and interests, which one of the Sustainable Development Goals is most important to you? Move to the area of the room assigned to the goal you have chosen.

Discuss the following with the other students that have chosen the same SDG as you. If you are the only one by your SDG, join the person or group closest to you.

1. Why did you choose this SDG?

2. In what way can you contribute to fulfilling it?

3. To which element of the triple bottom line can you link this SDG?

You will be asked to feedback to the wider group following your discussion.

Activity 2 (15 minutes)

Considering your desired **future** professional role, which one of the Sustainable Development Goals do you feel you can contribute to in the most adequate way? Move to the area of the room assigned to the goal you have chosen.

For activity 2, an alternative would be to assign students a role within a business rather than asking them to identify their desired future role. This will ensure a variety of roles is covered.

Discuss the following with the other students that have chosen the same SDG as you. If you are the only one by your SDG, join the person or group closest to you.

1. What is your desired future professional role?

2. Why did you choose this SDG?

3. In what way can you contribute to fulfilling it?

4. To which element of the triple bottom line can you link this SDG?

You will be asked to feedback to the wider group following your discussion.

Activity 3 (20 minutes)

Following the various group discussions, have your answers changed? Considering your desired future professional role, which one of the Sustainable Development Goals do you *now* feel you can contribute to in the most adequate way? Move to the area of the room assigned to the goal you have chosen.

Discuss the following with the other students that have chosen the same SDG as you. If you are the only one by your SDG, join the person or group closest to you.

1. Has your answer changed, and why?

2. How can you overcome the possible obstacles in achieving the Sustainable Development Goals within your future role in business?

3. Draw a mind map or something similar signposting the way between now and the future role you want to have with the identified obstacles on the way as well as measures to overcome them.

You will be asked to show your drawings to the wider group following your discussion.

Additional teaching material and ideas

The Oxfam Coffee Chain Game.

www.readkong.com/page/the-coffee-chain-game-1545475.

This is an excellent group activity which highlights discrepancies in profit at both ends of the coffee supply chain. It details the market pressures felt by those in the coffee industry, and the trickle-down effect of low coffee prices on developing nations. This game helps players understand the different protagonists in the coffee supply chain and their influence on determining a fair price. It also develops negotiation skills. It can be played within an hour, including debriefing. We modified it slightly by giving the 'roasters' the power to lead the discussion and determine the price if there is disagreement. This makes the game more challenging and reflects real-life negotiation as depicted in the film *Black Gold*.

Black Gold

www.imdb.com/title/tt0492447/.

This film makes an excellent follow-up to either the coffee chain game earlier or to session 1. This feature-length documentary film focuses on the contrast between struggling African coffee farmers and successful multinational coffee companies. It is an astute insight into the daily reality of those in developing nations struggling to get a reasonable price for an excellent product and a hearty endorsement of Fairtrade.

The sustainability balanced scorecard

Session 3 is a good starting point for understanding how sustainability fits into the business case. However, it can be useful to go into more detail, and the use of a BSC (balanced scorecard) methodology is a good way to do this. Figge *et al.* (2002) detail the application of a sustainability balanced scorecard, an activity that can be extended across two or three sessions as a group project. Students can profile a business in detail using online resources, dividing the company's perspectives into the financial perspective, the customer perspective, and the internal process perspective. The purpose of the BSC is to formulate a hierarchic system of strategic objectives, derived from these perspectives. This is an excellent way to embed sustainability perspectives into business thought rather than as an extra activity.

Managing sustainability

This is a term-long module where students act as consultants to a given desk-based or real company. They have to assess their 'own' company on how they address social, environmental, and economic sustainability and give recommendations on how to improve these three areas. In every session, they are taught one of the concepts of sustainability as given in this book and have to apply it directly to their 'own' company. The exercises are so designed that they also understand how the different functions within a company relate to each other, so it is a good module to connect various core modules while simultaneously applying sustainability concepts. Further information can be obtained from petra.molthan-hill@ntu.ac.uk.

Climate change, companies, and individual behaviour

According to Wynes and Nicholas (2017), the four most effective actions that can be taken by individuals to reduce their impact on the climate are living car-free, avoiding air travel, adopting a plant-based diet, and having smaller families (fewer children). You can organise a discussion about the role companies could or should play to effect changes in individual behaviour. This could be organised around each area, or it could be structured as a formal debate where one group of students adopts the proposition ('This house believes that companies have a role . . .'), whereas another group adopts the role of opposition. A sub-question to discuss could include how this addresses the triple bottom line. If students need help, here's a short video that can help them in preparing for debating: www.youtube.com/watch?v=yi6Im-Sb6Vw.

Further readings

Crane, A., Matten, D., Glozer, S., and Spence, L. (2015) *Business Ethics: Managing Corporate Citizenship and Sustainability in the Age of Globalisation*, 5th ed. (Oxford, UK: Oxford University Press).

An excellent entry-level textbook about the world of business ethics, now in its 5th edition, with additional co-authors. The book covers the foundation of business ethics, applying understandings to each of a corporation's major stakeholders. It details the role of sustainability (in particular, social sustainability) in ethical business and why it is important.

Elkington, J. (1997) *Cannibals with Forks: The Triple Bottom Line of 21st Century Business* (Oxford, UK: Capstone Publishing).

> The quintessential read for understanding the importance of integrating all three elements of sustainability in business and why the triple bottom line is important in this. While some of the claims about lacklustre attitudes to sustainability may feel a little dated, Elkington's book remains a worthwhile read and provides a solid understanding of the business case for sustainability from the ground up. You can also check out his 2012 book *The Zeronauts: Breaking the Sustainability Barrier* and his webpage: https://johnelkington.com.

Raworth, K. (2017) *Doughnut Economics: Seven Ways to Think Like a 21st-Century Economist* (London, UK: Random House Business Books).

> Despite its economics title, a very useful book for business students to read as it very aptly illustrates the importance of the social foundations and the ecological ceiling (or planetary boundaries) of an economy that is regenerative and restorative and thus truly and fully sustainable across all three sustainability dimensions.

United Nations (2016) *The Lazy Persons Guide to Saving the World*. Available online at www.un.org/sustainabledevelopment/takeaction/, accessed 20 November 2022.

> This webpage from the United Nations shows how everyone has a role to play in creating a better world and reaching the SDGs. We are all part of the solution to sustainability issues, and *The Lazy Persons Guide to Saving the World* shows how you can contribute to a better future through small actions in your everyday life, at home and beyond.

Wagner, S.M. (2020) *Business and Environmental Sustainability: Foundations, Challenges and Corporate Functions* (Abingdon, UK: Routledge).

> A book specifically about the environmental element of the triple bottom line, with a thorough introduction to various tools, concepts, and frameworks before delving into specific environmental challenges and how various corporate functions and value chain activities can contribute to environmental sustainability.

Websites

https://corporate.marksandspencer.com/plan-a.

> 'We're calling it Plan A because we believe it's now the only way to do business.' Marks & Spencer are proud advocates of embedding sustainability top-down, throughout the whole business. The website provides information on how they are achieving this and their progress towards sustainable goals.

https://nbs.net/.

> The Network for Business Sustainability (NBS) is a non-profit venture that works towards advancing sustainable development to build a fairer and more environmentally sound future by improving business practice around six critical themes.

https://teebweb.org.

> The Economics of Ecosystems and Biodiversity introduces the concept of ecosystem services and their use in a business context. It draws attention to the global economic benefits of biodiversity and its increasing importance as a field of interest in the next few decades. TEEB highlights that businesses have a crucial role in halting biodiversity loss that can also have benefits for the company.

www.ethicalconsumer.org/.

> This offers comparisons of companies' ethical and environmental intentions and monitors the progress of a large number of companies, aiming to make global business more sustainable and transparent through consumer pressure.

www.youtube.com/user/learnsustainability/videos.

> Some great videos of varying lengths that describe different sustainability concepts in various languages.

References

Accenture (2013) *The UN Global Compact-Accenture CEO Study on Sustainability 2013: Architects of a Better World.* Available online at www.unglobalcompact.org/library/451, accessed 13 September 2022.

Accenture (2016) *The UN Global Compact-Accenture Strategy CEO Study 2016 Agenda 2030: A Window of Opportunity.* Available online at www.unglobalcompact.org/library/4331, accessed 13 September 2022.

Accenture (2021) *The UN Global Compact – Accenture CEO Study on Sustainability.* Available online at www.accenture.com/gb-en/insights/sustainability/ungc, accessed 21 November 2022.

AI (2019) *Amnesty International.* Available online at www.amnesty.org/en/latest/news/2019/12/climate-change-ranks-highest-as-vital-issue-of-our-time/, accessed 22 November 2022.

Barford, V., and G. Holt (2013) 'Google, Amazon, Starbucks: The Rise of Tax Shaming', *BBC News*, 21 May. Available online at www.bbc.co.uk/news/magazine-20560359, accessed 21 March 2014.

BBC (2010) 'Loss of Bees Could Be "a Blow to UK Economy"', *BBC News*. Available online at www.bbc.co.uk/news/10371300, accessed 21 November 2022.

Beavis, L. (2013) 'Shared Interest: Investing in a Fairer World', *The Guardian*. Available online at www.theguardian.com/sustainable-business/shared-interest-investing-fairer-world, accessed 30 March 2014.

Blowfield, M. (2013) *Business and Sustainability* (Oxford, UK: Oxford University Press).

Carr, I., and O. Outhwaite (2011) 'Controlling Corruption through Corporate Social Responsibility and Corporate Governance', *Journal of Corporate Law Studies*, 11(Part 2): 299–341.

Conservation International (2014) *Verde Ventures 2*. Available online at www.conservation. org/projects/conservation-international-ventures-llc, accessed 12 September 2022.

Costanza, R., R. d'Arge, R. De Groot, S. Farber, M. Grasso, B. Hannon, and M. van den Belt (1997) 'The Value of the World's Ecosystem Services and Natural Capital', *Ecological Economics*, 25(1): 3–15.

Crane, A., and D. Matten (2015) *Business Ethics: Managing Corporate Citizenship and Sustainability in the Age of Globalisation*, 4th ed. (Oxford, UK: Oxford University Press).

Defra (2015) *What Nature Can Do for You: A Practical Introduction to Making the Most of Natural Services, Assets and Resources in Policy and Decision Making*. Available online at https:// assets.publishing.service.gov.uk/government/uploads/system/uploads/attachment_data/ file/396840/pb13897-nature-do-for-you.pdf, accessed 13 September 2022.

Dermondy, J. (2010) 'Evaluating Greener Marketing', in C. Roberts, and J. Roberts (eds.), *Greener by Degrees: Exploring Sustainability through Higher Education Criteria* (Cheltenham, UK: University of Gloucester): 12–20.

Devinney, T.M. (2009) 'Is the Socially Responsible Corporation a Myth? The Good, the Bad, and the Ugly of Corporate Social Responsibility', *The Academy of Management Perspectives*, 23(2): 44–56.

Donaldson, T., and T.W. Dunfee (1999) *Ties That Bind: A Social Contracts Approach to Business Ethics* (Cambridge, MA: Harvard Business School Press).

Doppelt, B. (2010) *The Power of Sustainable Thinking, How to Create a Positive Future for the Climate, the Planet, Your Organization and Your Life* (Abingdon, UK: Routledge).

Dyllick, T., and K. Hockerts (2002) 'Beyond the Business Case for Corporate Sustainability', *Business Strategy and the Environment*, 11: 130–41.

Edwards, M.G., J.M. Alcaraz, and S.E. Cornell (2021) 'Management Education and Earth System Science: Transformation as if Planetary Boundaries Mattered', *Business & Society*, 60(1): 26–56.

Elkington, J. (1997) *Cannibals with Forks: The Triple Bottom Line of 21st Century Business* (Oxford, UK: Capstone Publishing).

Elkington, J. (2014) *From the Triple Bottom Line to Zero*. Available online at www.johnel kington.com/activities/ideas.asp, accessed 16 March 2014.

Elkington, J. (2018) '25 Years Ago I Coined the Phrase "Triple Bottom Line": Here's Why It's Time to Rethink It', *Harvard Business Review*, 25: 2–5.

Elkington, J. (2020) *Green Swans: The Coming Boom in Regenerative Capitalism* (Austin, TX: Greenleaf Book Group).

Epstein, M.J. (2008) *Making Sustainability Work: Best Practices in Managing and Measuring Corporate Social, Environmental and Economic Impacts* (Sheffield, UK: Greenleaf Publishing).

Figge, F., and T. Hahn (2001) 'Sustainable Value Added: Measuring Corporate Contributions to Sustainability', in *Conference Proceedings on the 2001 Business Strategy and the Environment Conference in Leeds* (Shipley, UK: ERP Environment): 83–92.

Figge, F., T. Hahn, S. Schaltegger, and M. Wagner (2002) 'The Sustainability Balanced Scorecard: Linking Sustainability Management to Business Strategy', *Business Strategy and the Environment*, 11: 269–84.

Fisk, P. (2010) *People, Planet, Profit: How to Embrace Sustainability for Innovation and Business Growth* (London, UK: Kogan Page).

Flynn, P., M. Gudić, and T.K. Tan (eds.) (2019) *Global Champions of Sustainable Development* (Abingdon, UK: Routledge).

Freeman, R.E. (1984). *Strategic Management: A Stakeholder Approach* (Boston: Pitman Publishing; Lisbon: Letras).

Hitchcock, D., and M. Willard (2009) *The Business Guide to Sustainability: Practical Strategies and Tools for Organisations*, 2nd ed. (London: Earthscan).

HM Government (2013) *Guidance: Ecosystem Services*. Available online at www.gov.uk/ecosystems-services, accessed 28 March 2014.

Hockerts, K. (1999) 'The Sustainability Radar: A Tool for the Innovation of Sustainable Products and Services', *Greener Management International*, 25: 29–49.

Kaplan, R., and D. Norton (1992) 'The Balanced Scorecard: Measures that Drive Performance', *Harvard Business Review* (January–February): 71–9.

KPMG (2020) *The KPMG Survey of Sustainability Reporting 2020*. Available online at https://home.kpmg/xx/en/home/insights/2020/11/the-time-has-come-survey-of-sustainability-reporting.html, accessed 20 November 2022.

Laughland, P., and M. Bansal (2011) 'The Top Ten Reasons Why Businesses aren't More Sustainable', *Ivey Business Journal*. Available online at http://iveybusinessjournal.com/publication/the-top-ten-reasons-why-businesses-arent-more-sustainable/, accessed 14 March 2014.

Magis, K., and C. Shinn (2009) 'Emergent Principles of Social Sustainability', in J. Dillard, V. Dujon, and M.C. King (eds.), *Understanding the Social Dimension of Sustainability* (New York: Routledge): 15–44.

Mattioli, D. (2007) 'How Going Green Draws Talent, Cuts Costs', *Wall Street Journal*. Available online at http://online.wsj.com/news/articles/SB119492843191791132, accessed 28 March 2014.

McDonough, W., and M. Braungart (2002) *Cradle to Cradle: Remaking the Way We Make Things* (New York: North Point Press).

Michel, J., Y. Shen, A. Aiden, A. Veres, M. Gray, J. Pickett, D. Hoiberg, D. Clancy, P. Norvig, J. Orwant, S. Pinker, M. Nowak, and E. Aiden (2011) 'Quantitative Analysis of Culture Using Millions of Digitised Books', *Science*, 14(331): 176–82.

Millennium Ecosystem Assessment (2005) *Ecosystems and Human Well-Being: Synthesis* (Washington, DC: Island Press). Available online at www.millenniumassessment.org/documents/document.356.aspx.pdf, accessed 8 September 2016.

MIT Sloan Management Review (2016) *Investing for a Sustainable Future: Investors Care More About the Future than Many Executives Believe*. Available online at http://sloanreview.mit.edu/projects/investing-for-a-sustainable-future/, accessed 9 September 2016.

Molthan-Hill, P. (2014) 'Making the Business Case: Intercultural Differences in Framing Economic Rationality Related to Environmental Issues', *Critical Perspectives on International Business*, 11(1): 72–91.

Oxfam Coffee Game (2005) *The Coffee Chain Game*. Available online at https://resources4 rethinking.ca/en/resource/the-coffee-chain-game, accessed 12 September 2022; www.read kong.com/page/the-coffee-chain-game-1545475, accessed 22 November 2022.

Porter, M.E., and M.R. Kramer (2011) 'Creating Shared Value', *Harvard Business Review*, (January–February): 62–77.

Prickett, G. (2005) *Business Industry Perspectives on the Findings of Millennium Ecosystem Assessment*. Available online at www.maweb.org/documents/document.706.aspx.pdf, accessed 19 March 2013.

Raworth, K. (2017) *Doughnut Economics: Seven Ways to Think Like a 21st-Century Economist* (London: Random House Business Books).

RELU (Rural Economy and Land Use Programme) (2012) *Enhancing the Environment through Payment for Ecosystem Services*. Available online at www.relu.ac.uk/news/policy%20and %20practice%20notes/39%20PES/PES.pdf, accessed 28 March 2014.

Ricketts, T.H., G.C. Daily, P.R. Ehrlich, and C.D. Michener (2004) 'Economic Value of Tropical Forests to Coffee Production', *PNAS*, 101(34): 12579–82.

Robertson, M. (2017) *Sustainability Principles and Practice*, 2nd ed. (Abingdon: Routledge).

Robins, F. (2006) 'The Challenge of TBL: A Responsibility to Whom?', *Business and Society Review*, 111(1): 1–14.

Rockström, J., W. Steffen, K. Noone, A. Persson, F. Chapin, E. Lambin, T. Lenton, M. Scheffer, C. Folke, H.J. Schellnhuber, and B. Nykvist (2009) 'Planetary Boundaries: Exploring the Safe Operating Space for Humanity', *Ecology and Society*, 14(2): 32.

SDGs (2016) *17 Goals to Transform Our World, United Nations Sustainable Development Goals*. Available online at www.un.org/sustainabledevelopment/sustainable-development-goals/, accessed 14 September 2016.

Senge, P.M., B. Smith, N. Kruschwitz, J. Laur, and S. Schley (2008) *The Necessary Revolution: How Individuals and Organizations Are Working Together to Create a Sustainable World* (London, UK: Nicholas Brealey).

Shiva, V. (2013) *The Seeds of Suicide: How Monsanto Destroys Farming*. Available online at www.globalresearch.ca/the-seeds-of-suicide-how-monsanto-destroys-farming/5329947, accessed 31 March 2014.

Starbucks (2014) *Responsibly Grown Coffee*. Available online at www.starbucks.com/responsibility/sourcing/coffee/, accessed 13 September 2022.

UNCED (United Nations Conference on Environment and Development) (1987) *Our Common Future* (Zurich, Switzerland: Conches).

United Nations (2015) *Sustainable Development Goals*. Available online at https://sustainable development.un.org/?menu=1300, accessed 9 September 2016.

Waage, S.A., K. Geiser, F. Irwin, A.B. Weissman, M.D. Bertolucci, P. Fisk, G. Basile, S. Cowan, H. Cauley, and A. McPherson (2005) 'Fitting Together the Building Blocks for Sustainability: A Revised Model for Integrating Ecological, Social and Financial Factors into Business Decision-Making', *Journal of Cleaner Production*, 13(12): 1145–63.

WBCSD (2006) *Eco-Efficiency Learning Module, World Business Council for Sustainable Development.* Available online at www.wbcsd.org/Projects/Education/Resources/Eco-efficiency-Learning-Module, accessed 21 November 2022.

Willard, B. (2010) *Three Sustainability Models.* Available online at https://sustainabilityadvantage.com/2010/07/20/3-sustainability-models/, accessed 21 November 2022.

Willard, B. (2012) *The Sustainability Advantage: 7 Business Case Benefits of the Triple Bottom Line* (Vancouver, Canada: New Society Publishers).

Wills, J. (2013) 'Heineken: Leading the Fight Against Alcohol Abuse', *The Guardian.* Available online at www.theguardian.com/sustainable-business/heineken-leading-fight-alcohol-abuse, accessed 30 March 2014.

Wynes, S., and K.A. Nicholas (2017) 'The Climate Mitigation Gap: Education and Government Recommendations Miss the Most Effective Individual Actions', *Environmental Research Letters*, 12(7): 074024.

6

PRME, the UN Global Compact, and the Sustainable Development Goals

Tabani Ndlovu and Sihle Ndlovu

This chapter seeks to:

- Give business students a comprehensive overview of the UN Global Compact, the Principles of Responsible Management Education (PRME), as well as the Sustainable Development Goals (SDGs).

- Facilitate a discussion among students on how issues relating to the UN Global Compact, PRME, and the SDGs are relevant to business students and the future of the world, as well as review current approaches to tackling these issues in the wake of global crises, such as the Covid-19 pandemic.

- Inspire business students to acknowledge their pivotal role as future business leaders, entrepreneurs, and/ or employees by giving them skills to translate the principles of PRME and SDGs into practical outputs.

DOI: 10.4324/9781003294665-8

Introduction

Discussions and debates on climate change tend to reference the United Nations Global Compact, the Principles of Responsible Management Education (PRME), and Sustainable Development Goals (SDGs). It is therefore important that these concepts are unpacked and made accessible if they are to be adopted and applied. This chapter offers an overview of these concepts and identifies the role of business in tackling environmental issues facing the world today. It singles out business students (in their capacity as global citizens and future players in the business domain) as a key cog capable of driving forward the sustainability agenda in general and responsible business management practices in particular. Business students are an integral part of future business decision-making. To this end, universities in general and business schools in particular play a unique role in equipping business graduates with skills to tackle the ethical and sustainability challenges facing the world today and in years to come (Godemann et al., 2011).

This chapter presents the UN Global Compact, PRME, as well as the SDGs, appraising each as a framework of solutions aimed at addressing sustainability and ethical issues facing the world, specifically those related to business. The chapter then discusses the role of business both as a contributor to and as well as a key stakeholder and part of possible solutions to today's challenges. Thereafter, the discussion considers how today's global challenges are relevant to business students. The chapter concludes by offering some proposals on how best to align today's business management education with the global sustainability and ethical challenges before giving some simulated sessions aimed at dealing with PRME in a business school context. The next section makes a personal link between individuals and the topical sustainability issues facing our world today. The sustainability issues trigger questions on what world every one of us would like to live in. The questions seek to stimulate thoughts on what each one of us can do to ensure that our ideal world becomes a reality.

What world do you want to live in?

There are fundamental questions facing all citizens of the world today regarding what world we want and how business students as future players in business can play a role in re-envisioning the role of business as a positive lever for change. The questions can be summarised as:

1. What world would you ideally want to live in?

2. How different is the world you live in now from the one you yearn for?

3. What could you do as an individual to help realise your ideal world?

4. What role can business play in ushering in your ideal world, and what role do you think you can play in business to bring about positive change?

The world we live in today is far from ideal. It is full of strife, economic and political upheavals, intolerance, natural disasters, and severe inequalities between those who have and those who have not (Solt, 2016). These issues have resulted in increased security and welfare concerns, have caused divisions and, at times, conflict. Many of these points have been exacerbated by the Covid-19 pandemic changes, which led to global shutdowns that isolated nations and communities worldwide (Murayama et al., 2021). The disenfranchisement of nations and communities exposed the divisions between nations, showing in particular how poor, vulnerable nations are really on their own in the face of global calamities (Birdsall et al., 2006; Clark, 2011). When faced with the choice to share Covid-19 vaccines with poor nations, many developed nations chose to hoard vaccines, undermining efforts to take a collaborative, global approach and stop the spread of the pandemic (Hassoun, 2021).

If nations showed such divisions and prioritised short-term nationalistic opportunities at a time when a global approach would have helped eradicate the Covid-19 pandemic, this raises questions about commitments made towards greening the planet, in particular, the propensity of rich nations to help their less-developed counterparts adjust to, and mitigate the effects of, climate change.

A significant part of the global population has been displaced as people move in search of safer havens and/or better economic prospects (Cattaneo et al., 2020; Black et al., 2013; Benson, 2011). The migration challenges witnessed between Africa, the Middle East, and Europe; those from South America towards the North (USA and Canada); those from African countries towards South Africa; etc. will continue to grow unless action is taken to address the causes of migration, which include increased adverse effects of climate change, such as famines, floods, and cyclones, among others (Adepoju et al., 2010; Black et al., 2011). Business activities have been fingered in fuelling issues such as pollution, corporate greed, materialism, and other acts which cause or fuel some of the ethical challenges facing the world. Notwithstanding this, business and, especially, business leaders present the biggest hope for positively shaping the world and mobilising resources to address some of the challenges facing the world (Elkington and Hartigan, 2008).

Business students hold the promise to take decisive actions both at an individual level as well as on behalf of their organisations. As future business entrepreneurs, employees, and/or managers, they have the potential to positively influence their world by ushering in a more compassionate and responsible corporate approach.

By equipping students with information on issues facing the world and on the difference they can make, they are better able to make informed and conscientious choices in their day-to-day lives (Haney et al., 2020). Recognising the need for coordinated global efforts to mobilise businesses to adopt sustainable business practices, the United Nations came up with the Global Compact, which is discussed in the following.

Overview of the UN Global Compact, its links to PRME and SDGs

Launched in 2000, the **UN Global Compact** is a cross-sectoral initiative of businesses, UN agencies, civil society, as well as labour organisations united by the desire to change the world through developing and disseminating more sustainable and responsible business practices broadly (Rasche et al., 2013). By August 2022, over 16,786 participating corporate stakeholders representing over 161 countries have published 95,541 reports showing a steady growth in performance towards the stated goals (UN Global Compact, 2022).

The UN Global Compact principles act as statements of intent for how businesses should conduct themselves for the benefit of all global stakeholders (both present and future). The UN Global Compact principles, however, remain high-level aspirational statements and require the active involvement and cooperation of business organisations globally for implementation. Such involvement has to be resilient, especially in the face of growing challenges, such as increased propensity for global pandemics, increased incidences of climate change disasters, such as the August 2022 floods in Pakistan, desertification leading to famines, and mass starvation, among other immediate concerns facing the global community. Climate change and its effects tend to be pushed back ostensibly because they are sometimes viewed as distant and long-term. Business schools need to re-orient curricula to highlight the impending challenges emanating from unsustainable human practices. Business students need sustainability education to proactively take a stand on what role they will and can play in sustainability discourse and practice.

Table 6.1: The UN Global Compact principles

Principles		Principal aims for business	Implications for business
Human rights	**Principle 1**	Support and respect the protection of internationally proclaimed human rights.	Businesses have a vast network of stakeholders whose rights can easily be infringed upon if due care is not taken. Such stakeholders include employees and contract workers, customers, supply chains and workers therein, communities around the business operations, as well as any other people who come into contact with the company or its products or services. Organisations ought to think carefully about their impact on all these people.
	Principle 2	Make sure that they are not complicit in human rights abuses.	Businesses should take a clear stand against human rights abuses, using their power to promote equality and, where necessary, condemn acts of human rights abuses.
Labour rights	**Principle 3**	Uphold the freedom of association and the effective recognition of the right to collective bargaining.	Employees should not be victimised for affiliating with particular unions or groupings and should be afforded the right to self-determination and rights to collective bargaining.
	Principle 4	Eliminate all forms of forced and compulsory labour.	Businesses should pay fair wages and shun sweatshops or any form of coerced labour that infringes or undermines employees' rights.
	Principle 5	Abolish child labour.	Businesses must take a stand against use of under-age labour of any kind.
	Principle 6	Eliminate discrimination in respect of employment and occupation.	Businesses must promote equality and fairness together with fair remuneration.
Environment	**Principle 7**	Support a precautionary approach to environmental challenges.	Businesses should minimise their effects on the environment and promote efforts for greener practices.
	Principle 8	Promote greater environmental responsibility.	Businesses should proactively combat climate change and minimise their ecological footprint.
	Principle 9	Develop and diffuse environmentally friendly technologies.	Efforts should be made to explore and propagate innovative and environmentally friendly technologies.
Anti-corruption	**Principle 10**	Work against corruption in all its forms, including extortion and bribery.	Corruption creates inequality of opportunities, and businesses need to enact policies and implement practices that forbid corruption, extortion, and bribery, to create a level playing field.

Source: Compiled by author based on UN Global Compact (2022).

At the heart of the United Nations' Global Compact is the belief that responsible business practices can deliver future competitiveness while also addressing social and environmental concerns (Nosratabadi, 2019). The UN Global Compact is the largest sustainability initiative which seeks the alignment of organisational strategies and operations with universally agreed principles of human rights, labour rights, environmental responsibility, as well as eradication of corruption for the betterment of mankind (Rasche et al., 2013). The UN Global Compact is premised on ten principles, as summarised in the following.

To ensure the UN Global Compact was deliverable in practical, meaningful. and measurable terms, there was need to ensure that the education of current and future business leaders had at its core the sustainability and responsible management agenda derived from the UN Global Compact (Sedlacek, 2013; Mousa et al., 2020). The principles of PRME were developed to ensure that business management curricula proactively sought to equip future business leaders with skills to grapple with increasing sustainability and responsible management issues facing the world. The next section discusses the principles of PRME.

The Principles of Responsible Management Education (PRME)

Launched in 2007 under the direction of the then UN secretary-general Ban Ki-Moon, Principles of Responsible Management Education (PRME) was developed to cultivate and embed the concepts of responsible management into business education.

There are six principles underpinning the Principles of Responsible Management Education (PRME), consisting of:

1. The overall **purpose** of equipping students who are poised to be future generators of sustainable value to benefit their businesses and society.

2. The adoption of internationally accepted **values** of global social responsibility as espoused in the United Nations Global Compact to act as a guide for the design of academic activities and curricula.

3. The adoption of appropriate **pedagogical frameworks** to facilitate teaching and learning of sustainability and responsible business leadership.

4. The pursuit of empirical and conceptual **research** to better capture and understand the role and/or impact of corporations in the global sustainability discourse.

5. The adoption of a collegiate approach to actively foster **collaboration** between business, academia, and other broader stakeholders as a way of collectively tackling the social and environmental challenges facing society.

6. The need to engender continuing **dialogue** between students, educators, business, government, consumers, the media, and civil society to get a holistic view of the evolving agenda of global social responsibility and sustainability management.

Source: PRME (2022)

In turn, the principles of PRME are themselves underpinned by three pillars:

1. Continuous improvement

2. A learning network

3. Reporting progress to stakeholders

(PRME, 2022)

At the heart of PRME is the idea of a collegiate and collaborative approach emphasising the transparent sharing of performance outputs. This is encapsulated in the seventh principle of PRME, known as 'sharing information on progress' (SIP), (PRME Reporting, 2022). The SIP is a reporting requirement which allows for the exchange of best practice performance outputs to foster a progressive and learning community. When different stakeholders can see what others have achieved, this spurs momentum and encourages more action to be taken to further build on the reported achievements. A total of 256 SIP reports was submitted for the period 1 May 2021 to 1 May 2022. Reports were reviewed/judged by a 22-member panel drawn from 13 countries to identify those considered to represent excellence in reporting (PRME Reporting, 2022).

PRME aims to develop future business leaders with the acumen to competently manage ethical and sustainability challenges facing the world in the 21st century. The rationale for PRME was that despite the recognition for the need to teach responsible business management education principles, the approach to date could do with more embedding of sustainability-related concepts into business and management curricula across universities and business schools around the world (Pearson et al., 2005).

PRME were, and still are, an attempt to help transform management education by embedding internationally accepted values aligned to the United

Nations' Global Compact. The ten principles are centred on the respect and protection of human rights, protection of labour rights and abolition of all forms of forced labour and any unfairness in employment, protection of the environment and adoption of environmentally friendly technologies, as well as efforts to combat corruption in all its forms. The principles represent a culture of continuous improvement towards better stewardship of the world's natural resources, more humane treatment of fellow human beings, and responsible corporate practices.

The principles of PRME offer coordinated approaches for the education of business students globally through the adoption of pedagogies and methodologies designed to align sustainability thinking with the business management curricula (Sedlacek, 2013). This highlights the role of universities and business schools in being the citadels of sustainability and responsible business practice knowledge for students who pass through their courses. Behind PRME are the PRME working groups, which are discussed in the following.

PRME working groups

PRME working groups develop and disseminate information and material on the different topics related to sustainability and the UN Global Compact. They seek to raise awareness of, and foster more collaboration in, advancing the objects of the UN Global Compact. The working groups are summarised in the table that follows.

Information from PRME working groups is particularly valuable for business students seeking to enhance their understanding of the UN Global Compact, PRME, and the SDGs. Teachers and business managers will find PRME working groups as valuable reservoirs of information on sustainability initiatives as well as progress on the delivery against defined sustainability agendas.

While PRME offers a clear agenda for the learning of responsible business management principles, there was still a need to develop a more universal delivery framework mobilising all stakeholders to work collaboratively towards tackling global issues. This owes to the fact that the key challenges facing the world today are broader than just ethics and sustainability, requiring a more holistic approach from around the world. To this end, the Sustainable Development Goals (SDGs) were developed. The SDGs are discussed in more detail in the following section.

Table 6.2: PRME working groups

No	PRME working group	Working group area of focus
1	PRME working group on anti-corruption in curriculum change	This working group seeks to embed the teaching of business ethics in business management curricula as a way of combating corruption. The group further seeks to promote research and dissemination of information related to initiatives to combat corruption as a way to promote transparency and accountability.
2	PRME working group on business and human rights	This working group's aim is to equip current and future managers with skills and information to combat human rights abuses. It fosters research and collaborations in highlighting problems associated with this as well as sharing information on progress.
3	PRME working group on business for peace	Global peace is an essential ingredient for business success, and businesses can play a pivotal role in connecting stakeholders and promoting peace initiatives. This working group acts as the conduit that facilitates discussions and collaborations in this area.
4	PRME working group on climate change and environment	This working group was incepted in New York at the Global Forum 2015 and focuses on the 13 'climate action' while also addressing several other SDGs, such as SDG 6, 'Clean Water and Sanitation'. The group seeks to 'help business schools and other organizational stakeholders to embed climate change and environmental education into their teaching and training' through the development and dissemination of frameworks around policy and strategy formulation, teaching approaches as well as fostering collaborative approaches between business schools and other stakeholders.
5	PRME working group on developing a sustainability mindset	Sustainability is as much a social issue as it is a personal one. To fully embrace this, individuals need a personal appreciation of the issues related to sustainability. This working group researches ways of further cultivating an appropriate attitude and mindset that recognises the challenges facing the world today to conjure steps that can be taken to mitigate such challenges.
6	PRME working group on gender equality	This working group seeks to address gender imbalances and effects thereof by promoting awareness and collaborative efforts to combat this.
7	PRME working group on poverty, a challenge for management education	This working group recognises the key role of business innovation in combating poverty and promotes a multi-stakeholder approach in seeking ways to eradicate poverty.

#	Working group	Description
8	PRME working group on sharing information on progress (SIPs)	Sharing of information on initiatives and progress is key in creating momentum for change. This working group seeks to encourage production of timely, regular, and good-quality information to create a learning culture driven by continuous improvement.
9	PRME working group on sustainable leadership in the era of climate change	This group seeks to foster innovative curriculum changes to address climate change issues facing the world. The working group is currently inactive.
10	PRME working group on the incorporation of the principles in executive degree programmes *(group no longer active)*	This working group sought to integrate principles of responsible management into executive education in a coordinated, systematic, and consistent way. It sought to facilitate research and innovation in inspiring responsible future leaders through tailored curricula.
11	Working 50+20 – management education for the world joint project	This working group came about as a result of the collaboration between the Globally Responsible Leadership Initiative (GRLI) and the World Business School Council for Sustainable Business and PRME, with the agenda to craft a futuristic management education agenda, envisaging challenges and opportunities in 20 years' time as well as 50 years' time.

Source: PRME (2022).

Sustainable Development Goals (SDGs)

The SDGs are a coordinated global attempt to eradicate global social and environmental issues, such as 'poverty, hunger, disease, unmet schooling, gender inequality, and environmental degradation' (Sachs, 2012: 2206). The SDGs are also commonly referred to as 'Transforming our world: the 2030 Agenda for Sustainable Development' and comprise 17 all-encompassing goals further split into 169 intergovernmental aspirational objectives aimed at ushering in a more equitable world by 2030.

Figure 6.1 summarises the 17 SDGs, which demonstrate a commitment by global leaders to ensure no one is left behind in the quest for a more equitable world.

The SDGs cover different forms of challenges facing the world, ranging from eradication of poverty and famine, health, education, equality, justice and peace, provision of clean water and sustainable energy, a clean and sustainable environment with positive efforts on climate change, sustainable flora and fauna, as well as collaborative efforts to provide education for all. Different stakeholders need to focus on those goals that they are better equipped to deliver.

Attempts to deliver all of them at once may result in mediocre outputs which may impact on progress. The next section discusses the relevance of SDGs to the business community.

Figure 6.1: The Sustainable Development Goals.

Source: PRME (2022).

Why business leaders need to concern themselves with SDGs

The SDGs represent an agreed list of global priorities to be delivered by 2030 if this world is to be made fair, tolerant, just, equitable, safe, prosperous, environmentally friendly, and enjoyable. The SDGs replace the Millennium Development Goals (MDGs), which were developed in 2000 but were criticised as lacking the voices of those meant to benefit from the initiatives (Larionova, 2020). The SDGs therefore represent the views of broader stakeholder groups, including those people perceived to be bearing the brunt of global injustices.

Challenging the status quo

Achieving the objectives encapsulated in the SDGs will require a significant shift from our current thinking and practices. To achieve this, we need to evaluate all aspects of our lives and ensure that we apply our skills, competences, and resources in making positive changes around us. We need to ensure that our use of natural resources does not deplete these to the detriment of future generations and compromise on the quality of life today. We need to keep the ecosystem in balance, fish responsibly, use land produce responsibly, and be innovative in the way we meet our needs.

This means that we ought to challenge some aspects of our lives, such as the 'throw-away' mentality that characterises today's fashion-driven consumption culture. Businesses will have to work closely with their supply chains, customers, and end users to innovatively think of new ways of meeting current needs without breaking the bank.

As business is a key stakeholder in the responsibility discussion, it follows that those businesses that embrace this in their operations and products or services as well as the treatment of people (*customers, employees, and other stakeholders*) can build better brands and enhance their competitiveness (Martínez, 2012). Taking a stand and focusing on chosen SDGs can position the business as a responsible, principled, and caring enterprise, helping to make the world better while eliminating waste and generating a fair return for investors.

Studies indicate that employees increasingly prefer more responsible employers (Alonso-Almeida and Llach, 2019; Obrad and Gherheş, 2018; Tamm et al., 2010; Nagori and Trivedi, 2015). The adoption of appropriate SDGs can help give tangible evidence of the organisation's outputs and enhance competitiveness. Challenges facing the world are of concern not only to the people around the world but also to organisations and the people who run and work for them as well as those served by the businesses. Table 6.3 lists the 17 SDGs with some brief explanatory notes on each. A column has been left blank for you to consider what different initiatives can be undertaken against each SDG either in the context of your personal life or in the context of your organisation. This underscores the point that sustainability and responsible practices are as much a personal priority as they are a business prerequisite. The current framing of the sustainability debate is such that it feels remote. This chapter argues that it is each and every person's priority to start in their locality, sharing with their neighbours until we have a global movement.

The following table summarises the 17 SDGs, their implications, and an opportunity for you to translate each one in the context of your personal life. This is meant to spur thoughts on what each one of us can do in our local contexts.

Table 6.3: SDGs, objectives, and possible examples of initiatives

SDGs	Implications	Examples Please think of initiatives that can be undertaken in your locality under each of these SDGs
1. No poverty	Eradicate all forms of poverty by 2030. Businesses and individuals can do a lot to open up opportunities and access to resources to close income gaps and reduce poverty.	
2. Zero hunger	All global citizens must have access to unrestricted, sustainable, and nutritious food.	
3. Good health and well-being	Well-being and better lifestyles should be promoted for a healthier global population.	
4. Quality education	Life-long learning opportunities through inclusive quality education.	
5. Gender equality	Address the gender equality gap especially by empowering women and girls.	

SDGs	Implications	Examples **Please think of initiatives that can be undertaken in your locality under each of these SDGs**
6. **Clean water and sanitation**	Ensure access to sustainable clean water and sanitation for all.	
7. **Affordable and clean energy**	Ensure sustainable, clean, and reliable energy is available to all.	
8. **Decent work and economic growth**	Avail opportunities for decent work to spur inclusive economic growth and productivity.	
9. **Industry, innovation, and infrastructure**	Use innovation to promote inclusive industrialisation through resilient infrastructure.	
10. **Reduced inequalities**	Close inequality between and within countries.	
11. **Sustainable cities and communities**	Build inclusive, resilient, sustainable, and safe human settlements.	
12. **Responsible consumption and production**	Produce sustainably and promote responsible consumption.	
13. **Climate action**	Prioritise and take immediate steps to combat climate change and its effects.	
14. **Life below water**	Promote sustainable use of seas, oceans, and marine life and other marine resources.	
15. **Life on land**	Protect, restore, and promote sustainable use of forests; promote biodiversity; reduce land degradation/desertification; preserve terrestrial ecosystems.	
16. **Peace, justice, and strong institutions**	Build effective, accountable, and inclusive institutions, and promote justice for all through fair-to-build peaceful and inclusive societies.	
17. **Partnerships for the goals**	Foster collaborative efforts to further push for the implementation of sustainable development globally.	

Source: SDGs (2023).

Joining the dots: relating the UN Global Compact, PRME, and SDGs

Despite its noble intentions, the UN Global Compact however remains a strategic commitment which needs a delivery plan that has the potential to tap into grassroots stakeholders to cultivate more interest and garner more support for the initiative. To this end, business management schools, in their role as the rite of passage for future business entrepreneurs, employees, and/or business leaders, remain an important reservoir in which to incorporate sustainable management and responsible management content (García-Feijoo et al., 2020). This helps equip future business leaders with requisite skills and competences to grapple with ethical and sustainability-related issues facing the business community as well as the world today (Sedlacek, 2013).

PRME remains a key vehicle for embedding sustainability and responsible management into business management content (Godemann et al., 2014). To ensure that the adoption of sustainable and responsible practices was endorsed by broader stakeholders, the Sustainable Development Goals were introduced (Sachs, 2012). The figure that follows summarises the link between the United Nations Global Compact, the principles of PRME, as well as the Sustainable Development Goals.

The preceding figure provides interconnectivity between the UN Global Compact, the PRME, and the SDGs, implying that certain initiatives could tick several boxes across these different concepts, complementing efforts in each. It starts with the UN Global Compact as the overarching central theme, anchored on four broad principles of fostering anti-corruption initiatives, upholding human rights, protecting the environment, and promoting fair labour practices. The six PRME principles form a further deployment pad while they hinge on the SDGs.

How global issues are of concern to you as business students

As highlighted earlier, the world around us is far from ideal – it is plagued with famines; political turmoil; social and economic upheaval; racial, religious, and political intolerances; migration, causing social tensions and xenophobic attacks; terrorism; economic imbalances; etc. (Nemetz, 2022; Solt, 2016; Kliot and Newman, 2013; Fuentes-Nieva and Galasso, 2014). Most of these issues are a result of

Figure 6.2: The link between the UN Global Compact, the PRME, and the SDGs.

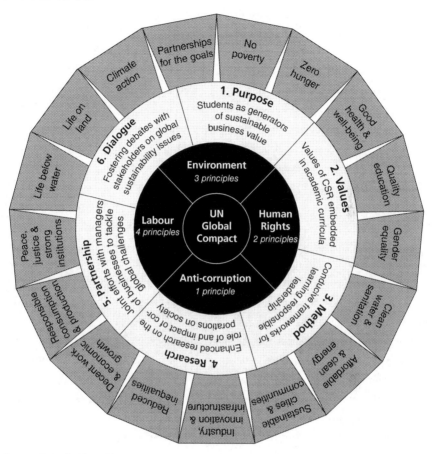

Source: Compiled by author.

human activities and can be changed by humans if they so will. The issues directly affect communities that form the customer base for businesses. The same communities are also the source of the labour force for businesses and provide the immediate external environment within which business operates. Since business operates within and actively interacts with its external environments, increased business unsustainability of any kind has direct impacts on both the business itself and the people who work therein and those who buy its products or services, not to mention investors and broader stakeholders. Unsustainable business practices therefore threaten the fabric of mankind (Nemetz, 2022; Coetzee, 2012). Unsustainable business practices erode the trust between the business and its stakeholders (society), making it unviable.

Corrupt business practices promote an unfair business landscape and compromise consumer choice (Holliday et al., 2002). According to Willard (2012), society gives businesses a license to operate by allowing such businesses to operate in their midst (Hutter and O'Mahony, 2009). Should businesses breach the trust with the communities within which they operate, this can result in the withdrawal of the license to operate. The withdrawal of the license to operate may manifest itself through protests, boycotts, and may see communities and other stakeholders disrupting business activities or even lobbying for the concerned businesses to close. Table 6.4 lists examples of organisations that faced reprisals following misdemeanours.

Payment of bribes or adoption of misleading business practices may see companies with inferior products winning contracts, exposing consumers and society to risks of poor or inferior products and shortcuts, all for the benefit of greedy businesspeople. As shown in the few examples that follow, when such vices are uncovered, the impact is widespread for consumers, businesses concerned, and society, often resulting in the concerned business paying out large fines or even collapsing, rendering workers jobless.

When businesses fail, productivity is affected, unemployment may set in, people's incomes and/or livelihoods suffer, poverty may set in, and distribution of resources may be compromised, possibly perpetuating further large-scale migration and contributing to social and economic strife. Unsustainable business practices are therefore against everyone's long-term interests and need to be eradicated. The responsibility lies with all of us and particularly those employed to work in and/or lead companies to ensure that they operate in a way that respects the interests of all stakeholders. This is where YOU as a business student come in. You have a role to play!

Table 6.4 Examples of consequences of unethical practices in business

No.	Company name	Example of incident	Impact on company
1	VW	VW allegedly installed devices that gave misleading emissions figures in over 482,000 vehicles sold in the United States. There is potential that over 800,000 sold in Europe could also be affected.	VW was fined 502 million euros by the European Commission and a further US$25 billion by the US government for the scandal. This does not take into account the cost of damage to the brand.
2	GlaxoSmithKline	The company sold its antidepressants (Paxil) for unapproved uses and failed to declare sensitive safety data relating to the drug tests.	Fined $3 billion by the FDA for misleading marketing. Damage to the brand and loss of brand value.
3	BAE Systems	BAE was alleged to have paid bribes to secure a £40 billion arms contract in the Saudi Al-Yamamah deal.	In 2010, BAE was fined £286 million for alleged bribery. Compromised brand and reputation.
4	Arthur Anderson	Was alleged to have been complicit in the Enron scandal.	Arthur Anderson folded up following revelations of its role in the Enron scandal.
5	Mattel	The doll maker outsourced manufacturing to China as a way to cut costs but ended up with unsafe products coated with toxic lead paint.	In addition to the loss of credibility and brand value, Mattel was fined $2.3 million for violating consumer safety laws.
6	Alstom	Allegedly paid over $75 million worth of bribes to governments around the world to win contracts.	The company was fined $772.3 million over the scandal. This is in addition to the impact on the brand.

Source: Compiled by author.

Suggested sessions

The subjects of sustainability and responsible management are not just theoretical; rather, they bring up practical and personal issues that affect each and every one of us, the world we live in, the businesses around us, the climate conditions around us, and implications for the future. To that end, the following sessions focus on relating the subjects of sustainability and responsible management to each and every participant/student.

Session 1: Understanding the status quo and mapping the current terrain

This chapter has given an overview of the UN Global Compact principles, the principles of PRME, as well as the SDGs as a delivery vehicle to usher in a more sustainable world. Rather than dictate to you what such a world would look like, the first activity will utilise Padlet to brainstorm and collect ideas on the state of the world today; current efforts to tackle global challenges as well as what additional actions can be taken to usher in a better world.

Activity 1 (15 minutes)

Think about the world you live in today, and using your devices – iPads, mobile phones, laptops – launch Padlet and post your views on:

- When it comes to global sustainability and responsible business management, what do you consider to be the five biggest achievements to date?

Activity 2 (15 minutes)

Using Padlet again, post ideas (words or phrases) that summarise what you consider to be the key threats/challenges affecting your generation (and future generations) in the world today. (Be broad and capture as many different things as possible.)

Activity 3 (30 minutes)

Split into two groups so that one group considers the positive list while the other considers the negative list.

In your group, collate the ideas and group them according to the SDGs using the following table as your template. Reflect on:

- Which issues pose the biggest threats? (You may want to think short-term vs long-term.)

- Which issues present the biggest opportunities?

No.	Proposed idea	SDG that idea fits into	Rank the ideas on the threats that they pose, with 1 as the highest threat, 2 as the next highest, etc.

Session 2: The Sustainable Development Goals applied to your community

Not everyone can deliver on all the Sustainable Development Goals. This session seeks to help you make sense of, and prioritise the needs within, your environment and context. Consider you and your organisation's resources and competences before choosing which SDGs to focus on.

Activity 1 (15 minutes)

Think of the top five needs or challenges most prevalent in your community. This can be at a local suburb/city/region or national level (you have to remember, though, that trying to deliver on too broad a scope may be a challenge). Have a discussion in your groups on the causes of each of the top five needs, that is, is it failure by government, natural disasters, famine, or other factors?

Activity 2 (15 minutes)

Using the priority list drawn up in activity 3 (session 1), situate the identified needs within a relevant SDG. Which are the top five SDGs for your community/ area? If unchecked, what could be the long-term impacts of each challenge to your community or area if left unchecked?

Use the following table for this task.

No.	Identified challenges or needs in your community	SDG that need/ challenge fits into	Possible impact of challenge	Rank the ideas on the threats that they pose, with 1 as the highest threat, 2 as the next highest, etc.

Activity 3 (15 minutes)

Considering the identified priority SDGs for your community in the preceding text, think about which community stakeholders could deliver each. Try to answer each of the following questions for each SDG:

1. How equipped are those stakeholders to deliver on the proposed SDG? Are they capable/ready?

2. What could businesses do to help?

3. Are they helping at the moment? If so, how?

4. What difference could the business make for the benefit of other stakeholders?

5. How could businesses benefit from such activities?

Activity 4 (15 minutes)

Draw a mind map for each of the SDGs you have identified as top priority, showing the relevant stakeholders and their actual and potential actions and outputs for the relevant SDG. Present these mind maps to your colleagues.

Session 3: Global Compact activity

The UN Global Compact is a cross-sectoral initiative bringing together businesses, UN agencies, civil society, as well as labour organisations, working together to foster more sustainable and responsible business practices (Rasche et al., 2013). As at end of August 2022, there were over 16,786 corporate stakeholders representing over 161 countries from around the world. If the vision of the founders of the UN Global Compact are to be realised, more stakeholders need to pick up the mantle and engage actively in promoting and upholding sustainable business practices.

Activity 1 (15 minutes)

Conduct online research to find out which companies in your local community/ province or country have signed up to the UN Global Compact. Did you know the identified companies were signatories to the UN Global Compact? How effective do you think they are as stakeholders?

Activity 2 (10 minutes)

Using the list of SDGs identified in session 2 earlier, which stakeholders can you identify in your local area/province or country positioned to help address the SDGs you identified?

Are the identified organisations signatories to the UN Global Compact?

Are the identified organisations active in the area of CSR/sustainability? If they are, how could their activities be better aligned with the identified SDGs?

Activity 3 (25 minutes)

You have been asked to convene a group of stakeholders in your local area with the aim of mobilising support for the UN Global Compact. As usual, engagement in sustainability initiatives by different stakeholders has to be mutually beneficial.

Split yourselves into two groups, one group representing advocates of the UN Global Compact, and one group representing groups of business stakeholders who need to be convinced that they need to sign up as stakeholders and signatories to the UN Global Compact.

> *Group 1* – Prepare a presentation with five key points on why businesses in your local area should sign up to the UN Global

Compact. In your presentations, highlight both the benefits and risks of not signing up to the UN Global Compact. The arguments must be tailored to suit the identified businesses in the local area.

Group 2 – Think of what your shareholders will need as information to agree to sign up to the UN Global Compact. Make a list. Critically analyse the proposed benefits of signing up and the risks of not signing up to the UN Global Compact presented by your counterparts. In your view, do you think the arguments make good business sense? Would you sign up based on the presented arguments. Would your shareholders agree?

Activity 4 (10 minutes)

Debrief (all). Reflect on the possible reasons businesses in your local area may not be actively engaged with the UN Global Compact and associated initiatives. What can you do as business students to change this? What will you do to change this? Is this enough?

Additional teaching material and ideas

Our place in the world

Based on where we are in the world, the impact of unsustainable decisions affects us differently. Some of our actions cause adverse effects on people in other parts of the world, especially those in developing countries. Those living in luxury sometimes forget that their lifestyles and consumption patterns directly affect poor countries, such as sources of raw materials and labour. Split yourselves into two groups, one group representing developed countries, and the other representing developing countries. In your groups, consider how the lifestyles of people in the other group directly or indirectly affect you. What would you advise them to do to mitigate the effects of their lifestyles on your well-being? What SDGs directly relate to the identified actions? Share your views and listen to what they have to say about your own lifestyles. Considering your views, could you solve the problems affecting you in isolation, or do you require a collaborative approach? How does this relate to the state of the world today?

The Green&Great sustainability game

https://greenandgreat.socialsimulations.org/#use-the-game (Green&Great, 2023).

In this simulation, students play the roles of managers in different organisations, managing resources and competing for contracts. Performance requires establishing balances between economics, environmental impacts, and employee well-being, so decisions have to be made considering the overall performance of the business. Players monitor the performance of the company via the sustainability monitor, allowing an on-time, real-time performance data and corrective action. The game brings to the fore the complex and intricate nature of business operations and requires players to first establish societal and organisational priorities so as to steer their businesses in a way that delivers maximum stakeholder benefits.

The UN Global Compact dilemma simulation

www.inexlibris.com/Articles/download/6050b434-be8c-4f8e-b01a-27da14dae215 (InexLibris, 2016).

The game was developed by KPMG and is useful for exploring different ways of managing dilemmas facing different stakeholders when it comes to sustainability.

This game captures the challenges around the UN Global Compact and requires four to six players representing different stakeholder groups, such as organisational managers, employees, consumers, regulators, among others. The game is aimed at developing awareness of UN Global Compact issues among those who are not familiar with this while, at the same time, challenging those who may have prior knowledge. As players take different roles, they bring into the game expectations of their adopted roles and analyse the implications of these against the ten principles of the UN Global Compact. Challenges and opportunities are then analysed and discussed with proposals on how best any such challenges can be managed and how opportunities can be maximised.

MyUK Prime Minister game

www.parliament.uk (UK Parliament, 2016).

Imagine you were at the very top of British politics, with the power to influence policy and design your own priorities! While this game is focused on political priorities, its concept can be applied to sustainability issues, which can be brought into the main political thrust of any country's politics. Starting on a fresh slate allows for original aspirations to be laid out, although this has to be balanced with other key priorities to ensure the country still performs competitively. Please use the link provided to access the original game, then infuse into the game sustainability priorities aligned to the UN Global Compact. What are the key barriers to integrating a UNGC perspective? How best can the identified barriers be managed? What would you need to build a broad consensus and advance sustainability priorities among the two houses in the UK?

Further readings

Gupta, J. and Vegelin, C. (2016). 'Sustainable Development Goals and Inclusive Development.' *International Environmental Agreements: Politics, Law and Economics*, 1–16.

This journal article discusses how achievement of the Sustainable Development Goals (SDGs) may have been hampered by the tensions posed by pursuit of sustainable development on one hand pitted against the need for economic growth, social progression, and environmental sustainability on the other. The paper proposes an alternative approach of inclusive development premised on social, ecological, and relational inclusiveness. The argument highlights complexity of the sustainability argument and raises questions on the framing of the 17 SDGs and their associated targets.

Niklasson, L. (2020). *Improving the Sustainable Development Goals (Routledge Focus on Environment and Sustainability)*. Routledge.

This book provides a succinct evaluation of the Sustainable Development Goals (SDGs), often referred to as Agenda 2030. The book chronicles the formulation as well as implementation of the SDGs, providing a crucial analysis that helps in evaluating the progress of the goals. It appraises both the drivers and barriers hampering achievement of the SDGs and provides a multi-faceted view facilitating a broader perspective on the goals and their place in achieving a sustainable planet.

Rasche, A. and Kell, G. (2010). *The United Nations Global Compact: Achievements, Trends and Challenges*. Cambridge University Press.

This book provides a succinct appraisal of the UN Global Compact, tracing its history and achievements to date, while giving a rationale for the UN Global Compact. The book explores areas related to the UN Global Compact that have not been extensively covered before, bringing new insights about this topical initiative. It highlights the importance of communication and networks. The book uses case studies to showcase the value of shared objectives in ushering in a new era of sustainable practices.

Steele, W. and Rickards, L. (2021). *The Sustainable Development Goals in Higher Education: A Transformative Agenda*. Palgrave Macmillan.

This book examines the need for higher education institutions to transform themselves and, by so doing, the world and inculcates a sense of social and environmental justice into higher education participants. The book argues that this transformation is necessary if Sustainable Development Goals are to be achieved. Higher education institutions are challenged to play the role of change enablers through the combination of deep institutional commitments, bold ethical commitments, and action underpinned by an embedding of SDGs into the curriculum.

Swilling, M. (2019). *The Age of Sustainability: Just Transitions in a Complex World (Routledge Studies in Sustainable Development)*. Routledge.

The book poses questions to readers on what it means to be human in the Anthropocene. It questions the demarcations and contours of a just 21st century that is poised to usher in poverty eradication, bridging inequality gaps and eradicating social injustices while maintaining a balance of the ecosystems that sustain life on Earth. The book adopts a combination of a personal narrative to dig deep to find the passion necessary to fuel sustainability activism.

References

Adepoju, A., Van Noorloos, F. and Zoomers, A. (2010). Europe's Migration Agreements with Migrant-Sending Countries in the Global South: A Critical Review. *International Migration*, 48(3), 42–75.

Alonso-Almeida, M.D.M. and Llach, J. (2019). Socially Responsible Companies: Are they the Best Workplace for Millennials? A Cross-National Analysis. *Corporate Social Responsibility and Environmental Management*, 26(1), 238–47.

Benson, M. (2011). The Movement Beyond (Lifestyle) Migration: Mobile Practices and the Constitution of a Better Way of Life. *Mobilities*, 6(2), 221–35.

Birdsall, N., Vanzetti, D. and de Córdoba, S.F. (2006). *The World Is Not Flat: Inequality and Injustice in Our Global Economy*. UNU-WIDER.

Black, R., Arnell, N.W., Adger, W.N., Thomas, D. and Geddes, A. (2013). Migration, Immobility and Displacement Outcomes Following Extreme Events. *Environmental Science & Policy*, 27, 32–43.

Black, R., Bennett, S.R., Thomas, S.M. and Beddington, J.R. (2011). Climate Change: Migration as Adaptation. *Nature*, 478(7370), 447–9.

Cattaneo, C., Beine, M., Fröhlich, C.J., Kniveton, D., Martinez-Zarzoso, I., Mastrorillo, M., Millock, K., Piguet, E. and Schraven, B. (2020). Human Migration in the Era of Climate Change. *Review of Environmental Economics and Policy*, 13(2), 189–206.

Clark, R. (2011). World Income Inequality in the Global Era: New Estimates, 1990–2008. *Social Problems*, 58(4), 565–92.

Coetzee, J. (2012). *The Social Contract with Business: Beyond the Quest for Global Sustainability*. Xlibris Corporation.

Elkington, J. and Hartigan, P. (2008). *The Power of Unreasonable People: How Social Entrepreneurs Create Markets that Change the World*. Harvard Business School Publishing.

Fuentes-Nieva, R. and Galasso, N. (2014). *Working for the Few: Political Capture and Economic Inequality* (Vol. 178). Oxfam.

García-Feijoo, M., Eizaguirre, A. and Rica-Aspiunza, A. (2020). Systematic Review of Sustainable-Development-Goal Deployment in Business Schools. *Sustainability*, 12(1), 440.

Godemann, J., Haertle, J., Herzig, C. and Moon, J. (2014). United Nations Supported Principles for Responsible Management Education: Purpose, Progress and Prospects. *Journal of Cleaner Production*, 62(1), 16–23.

Godemann, J., Herzig, C., Moon, J. and Powell, A. (2011). *Integrating Sustainability into Business Schools – Analysis of 100 UN PRME Sharing Information on Progress (SIP) Reports*. International Centre for Corporate Social Responsibility, 58–2011.

Green&Great (2023). Available at: https://greenandgreat.socialsimulations.org

Haney, A.B., Pope, J. and Arden, Z. (2020). Making It Personal: Developing Sustainability Leaders in Business. *Organization & Environment*, 33(2), 155–74.

Hassoun, N. (2021). Against Vaccine Nationalism. *Journal of Medical Ethics*, *47*(11), 773–4.

Holliday, C.O., Schmidheiny, S. and Watts, P. (2002). *Walking the Talk: The Business Case for Sustainable Development*. Berrett-Koehler Publishers.

Hutter, B.M. and O'Mahony, J. (2009). *The Role of Civil Society Organisations in Regulating Business*. Centre for the Analysis of Risk and Regulation, London School of Economics and Political Science.

InexLibris (2016). Available at: www.inexlibris.com/Articles/download/6050b434-be8c-4f8e-b01a-27da14dae215

Kliot, N. and Newman, D. (2013). *Geopolitics at the End of the Twentieth Century: The Changing World Political Map*. Routledge.

Larionova, M. (2020). The Challenges of Attaining the Millennium Development Goals (MDGs). *International Organisations Research Journal*, *15*(1), 155–76.

Martínez, R. (2012). Inequality and the New Human Development Index. *Applied Economics Letters*, *19*(6), 533–5.

Mousa, M., Massoud, H.K., Ayoubi, R.M. and Abdelgaffar, H.A. (2020). Should Responsible Management Education Become a Priority? A Qualitative Study of Academics in Egyptian Public Business Schools. *The International Journal of Management Education*, *18*(1), 100326.

Murayama, H., Okubo, R. and Tabuchi, T. (2021). Increase in Social Isolation During the COVID-19 Pandemic and Its Association with Mental Health: Findings from the JACSIS 2020 Study. *International Journal of Environmental Research and Public Health*, *18*(16), 8238.

Nagori, V. and Trivedi, B. (2015). DSS for Gap Analysis between the Motivational Preferences of Employees and Employers. *International Conference on Management and Information Systems September*, *18*(1), 20.

Nemetz, P.N. (2022). *Unsustainable World: Are We Losing the Battle to Save Our Planet?* Routledge.

Nosratabadi, S., Mosavi, A., Shamshirband, S., Zavadskas, E.K., Rakotonirainy, A. and Chau, K.W. (2019). Sustainable Business Models: A Review. *Sustainability*, *11*(6), 1663.

Obrad, C. and Gherheș, V. (2018). A Human Resources Perspective on Responsible Corporate Behavior. Case Study: The Multinational Companies in Western Romania. *Sustainability*, *10*(3), 726.

Pearson, S., Honeywood, S. and O'Toole, M. (2005). Not Yet Learning for Sustainability: The Challenge of Environmental Education in a University. *International Research in Geographical & Environmental Education*, *14*(3), 173–86.

PRME (2022). *Principles of Responsible Management Education*. Available at: www.unprme.org/

PRME Reporting (2022). Available at: www.unprme.org/exemplary-reporting-1

Rasche, A., Waddock, S. and McIntosh, M. (2013). The United Nations Global Compact Retrospect and Prospect. *Business & Society*, *52*(1), 6–30.

Sachs, J.D. (2012). From Millennium Development Goals to Sustainable Development Goals. *The Lancet*, *379*(9832), 2206–11.

SDGs (2023). *UN Sustainability Development Goals*. Available at: https://sdgs.un.org/goals

Sedlacek, S. (2013). The Role of Universities in Fostering Sustainable Development at the Regional Level. *Journal of Cleaner Production*, 48, 74–84.

Solt, F. (2016). The Standardized World Income Inequality Database. *Social Science Quarterly*, 97(5), 1267–1281.

Tamm, K., Eamets, R. and Mõtsmees, P. (2010). *Are Employees Better Off in Socially Responsible Firms?* (No. 5407). Institute for the Study of Labor (IZA).

UK Parliament (2016). Available at: www.parliament.uk

UN Global Compact (2022). Available at: www.unglobalcompact.org/www.unglobalcompact.org/what-is-gc/participants

Willard, B. (2012). *The New Sustainability Advantage: Seven Business Case Benefits of a Triple Bottom Line*. New Society Publishers.

EMBEDDING SUSTAINABILITY INTO CORE SUBJECTS

7
Sustainability reporting

Christian Herzig and Biswaraj Ghosh

This chapter is seeking to:

- Enhance appreciation of non- or extra-financial reporting and the forms it can take.

- Foster understanding of the content and design of sustainability reporting.

- Impart awareness of the key reasons companies develop sustainability reports and websites.

- Develop knowledge about recent developments (e.g. guidelines and regulatory frameworks) and the capability of evaluating their role in enhancing transparency and accountability.

- Impart awareness of some problems in sustainability reporting.

Introduction

This chapter introduces the evolution and advancement of corporate reporting beyond purely financial information as a way to communicate corporate policies, performances, and impacts regarding the environment and society to a broad range of stakeholders. The chapter begins with a historical perspective detailing the growth

DOI: 10.4324/9781003294665-10

of and drivers for different forms of non- or extra-financial reporting. This includes observations on sustainability reporting frameworks as well as regulations. Then, perspectives and reasons are outlined, which aim to explain the existence of sustainability reports and the use of the internet for sustainability reporting. The chapter concludes with a reflection on some problem areas associated with sustainability reporting.

Developments

In Europe, a number of companies started publishing **social reports** in the 1970s. With these reports, companies informed their stakeholders about the company's activities, products, and services and related positive and negative social impacts. This new type of report also included new social accounting techniques, such as the value-added statement, which presents the added value generated by an organisation and how it is appropriated to the contributors of the value, hence a way to show how the value was created and attributed to a larger number of stakeholders (e.g. employees, the state, creditors) rather than just the shareholders. The emergence of these new forms of accounting and reporting can be seen in the light of rising income levels at that time, which shifted the focus of society and politics to objectives such as quality of life while, at the same time, the negative effects of quantitative economic growth and a Tayloristic organisation of production processes were evaluated critically in society. The rise in social reporting in the 1970s is often seen to be the first development of non- or extra-financial corporate reporting, although it was preceded by the disclosure of employee and community issues within annual reports for many decades (Guthrie and Parker, 1989). However, by the end of the 1970s, social reporting was already in decline again. Among the reasons for this decline were an inadequate target group orientation; a mismatch between the information interests of most stakeholders and social reports that were often scientifically designed and remote from the reality of most people's lives; a misuse of social reporting as a public relations tool, which reduced its reliability and credibility; an insufficient integration of social and financial reporting; and the positive economic and political development of Europe, with job movements to the services sector and improved working conditions (Dierkes and Antal, 1985; Hemmer, 1996; Herzig and Schaltegger, 2011).

Various incidents of environmental catastrophe occurred in the late 1980s and 1990s (e.g. Schweizerhalle, Sandoz, Switzerland; Griesheim, Hoechst AG, Germany), and companies were scrutinised for being responsible for these environmental disasters. In response to the increased pressure for greater transparency and accountability, companies, in particular those operating within environmentally sensitive industries, started to publish **environmental reports** to explain to stakeholders how the organisational activities impacted on the natural environment (e.g. through air and water emissions, types and amounts of wastes, etc.) and how these impacts would be managed. The environmental reporting activities were partly forced by new laws (compulsory reporting) and partly voluntary. Overall, environmental reporting superseded to a large extent the early social reporting activities of companies. Until the end of the last millennium, the number of environmental reports and the attention they received in the media and society increased significantly, and their average quality improved – from initially being primarily green glossaries and one-off reports, to more comprehensive environmental reports published on a regular (e.g. annual) basis (Herzig and Schaltegger, 2011). An example of a voluntary approach to environmental reporting is the European Union Eco-Management and Audit Scheme (EMAS). The scheme, which became an internationally applicable standard in 2009, acknowledges companies that manage and improve their environmental performance and document their respective achievements through publicly available environmental statements, a specific form of an environmental report (www.emas.eu).

Succeeding years saw different attempts to integrate environmental and social issues within corporate reporting (e.g. safety, health, and the environment reports). Since the mid-1990s, and increasingly towards the end of that decade, the attention shifted towards **sustainability reports** (e.g. Kolk, 2004). Sustainability reports reflect companies' claims to depict an overall picture of their ecological, social, and economic sustainability activities and performance and to inform stakeholders as to how and to what extent these corporations contribute to sustainable development (Herzig and Schaltegger, 2011). One of the earliest examples is Shell's so-called 'three Ps' report (people, planet, and profits), published in 1999, the title of which already reflects a multidimensional reporting style. In certain industrial sectors, the number of stand-alone sustainability reports nowadays exceeds those of environmental reports – in particular, if one also considers that companies use various alternative titles for their reports, with which they endeavour to demonstrate their wider responsibility to society (e.g. 'corporate (social) responsibility report', 'corporate citizenship report', or 'report to society'). Similarly with environmental statements, there is a trend towards more integrated reporting (BMU, 2007). In practice, many of these reports are still published as stand-alone sustainability reports. Compared to social reporting in the 1970s (where emphasis was placed on employee-related issues and value creation for various stakeholders), social aspects within sustainability reports are nowadays often more globally and also more comprehensively dealt with, in terms of moral and ethical questions of sustainable development (e.g. child labour in the supply chain, human rights, poverty alleviation, gender issues, and trading relationships). In recent years, new laws have been enacted, for instance, the modern slavery act, that necessitate disclosure regarding supply chain practices. It is to be noted that based on a KPMG study, reporting was limited to only 12% of sample companies resorting to sustainability in 1993 compared to over 80% in 2020. This massive growth in sustainability reporting is not only due to legislations but also due to corporations understanding the link between sustainability performance and its impact on financial outcomes and enterprise value creation (KPMG, 2020).

A growing body of international and national guidance documents for sustainability reporting has evolved to support companies in developing reports and communicating externally their social, environmental, and economic performance and impacts in order to satisfy the information needs of interested stakeholder groups (UNEP *et al.*, 2010; Adams and Narayanan, 2007; Leipziger, 2010). The most generally accepted and universally applied **sustainability reporting framework** is probably that provided by the **Global Reporting Initiative** (GRI; www.globalreporting.org). It remains the most widely adopted sustainability standard according to the 2020 KPMG survey (KPMG, 2020) and was developed through an international multi-stakeholder consultation process (involving representations from businesses, civil societies, academia, and public institutions worldwide). It comprises reporting guidelines (the most recent, fourth version, called G4, has been subsequently developed into GRI Sustainability Reporting Standards, or GRI Standards for short), sector-specific guidance, and other resources, such as templates for a basic GRI report, checklists, or a GRI content index (GRI, 2021). The gradual advancements in the GRI guidelines since their first inception in 2000 are substantiated by a number of requirements, including to remove any ambiguity in the interpretation of concepts and principles, to better allow companies to improve their understanding of material issues to be included in sustainability reports, to include additional disclosure requirements as gathered from the stakeholder consultative method, and to reach harmonisation with other major published guidelines or initiatives, including integrated reporting (see further in the text that follows). GRI defines **reporting principles** that organisations must comply with to report in accordance with the GRI Standards. They serve the provision of information to inform decision-making and assessment of the organisational impact on and contributions to sustainable development (GRI, 2021). In essence, the GRI principles attempt to standardise sustainability reporting and ensure relevant, useful, and timely information that truly reflects the organisations' sustainability activities and supports stakeholder decision-making.

Besides stand-alone sustainability reports, **extended financial reports and integrated (business) reports** have received more attention in recent years. Mainly driven by the increasing interest of investors and analysts as well as regulatory requirements for sustainability disclosure, there has been more focus on selected environmental and social aspects of corporate performance in financial reports. According to a study by UNEP and others (UNEP *et al.*, 2010) as well as other surveys (e.g. KPMG, 2020), disclosure of sustainability issues has become the subject of a growing body of regulations. For a long time, however, most of these – largely voluntary – regulations have been limited to companies of a certain (usually large) size, state-owned or listed companies, or companies that are significant emitters of pollution. However, most recent developments show that this is going to change, that is, the scope will be extended and become mandatory. An important development at the European level was the implementation of the EU Accounting Modernisation Directive, in which the reformed law regulated the balance sheet (European Parliament and European Council, EU, 2003). This directive forced large, capital market–oriented public-interest companies with an average number of employees of more than 500 to include non-financial performance indicators, specifically environmental and labour-related indicators, in the prognosis reports included in their annual reports. Due to this Directive 2014/95/EU, also known as the Non-Financial Reporting Directive (NFRD), about 10,000 European companies have been obliged since 2017 to report in their annual reports on their corporate responsibility policies, related outcomes and risks, and risk management (European Parliament and European Council, EC, 2014).

With the current further development of the directive into the Corporate Sustainability Reporting Directive (CSRD), the reporting obligation will be extended in stages over the next few years to:

- All large companies which, on the balance sheet date, fulfil at least two of the three criteria, namely, a balance sheet total of at least 20 million euros, net sales of at least 40 million euros, and/or an average number of employees of at least 250 during the financial year.

- All companies listed on the stock exchange, with the exception of micro-enterprises. However, listed SMEs are also included within the scope.

- Around 50,000 European companies are expected to be affected by the updated CSRD. On 5 January 2023, the CSRD entered into force in line with the commitment made under the **European Green Deal.**

- Elsewhere, for example, the Securities Exchange Board of India made it mandatory for the top 1,000 companies by market capitalisation to report on their sustainability performance as part of the Business Responsibility and Sustainability Report from the financial year 2022–2023 (PWC, 2021).

Likewise, in October 2021, the Saudi Exchange issued an ESG disclosure guidelines document to encourage 200 listed companies to engage in voluntary ESG reporting. The guidelines do not provide a fixed set of criteria but rather explain the significance and benefits of ESG disclosure for local stakeholders, and present a benchmarking of the most common material themes and key issues for issuers to consider. Another voluntary initiative to enhance **IR (integrated reporting)** is the IIRC (International Integrated Reporting Council), which was co-founded by GRI and the Prince's Accounting for Sustainability Project (and other international partners) in 2010 (www.theiirc.org). This encompasses a multi-stakeholder approach that brings in the views of investors, civil society organisations, accountants, regulators, businesses, and standard-makers who share a common perspective on the importance of communicating to the users of reports how value is created. IIRC defines the framework as an instrument for companies to concisely communicate 'about how an organisation's strategy, governance, performance and prospects, in the context of its external environment, lead to the creation of value over the short, medium and long term' (IIRC, 2013: 7). The framework was updated in January 2021 to enable more decision-useful reporting. The framework's revision resulted in improved insight into the quality and integrity of the reporting process and a clearer distinction between outputs and outcomes. Another part of the revision was the simplification of the required responsibility statement for the integrated report and a stronger focus on balanced reporting of conservation of value and erosion scenarios (IIRC, 2021). Overall, the initiative can be seen as an attempt to enable companies to demonstrate to interested stakeholder groups the connections between corporate strategy; governance; financial, social, and environmental policies; and performances and, simultaneously, to establish the ability of such companies to create and sustain value over time along six different capital bases. In other words, organisations are required to demonstrate how their policies, strategies, and actions have resulted in value augmentation or otherwise pertaining to the natural capital, social, and human capitals, intellectual capital, manufactured capital, and financial capital. Such an integrated approach to reporting may enable stakeholders to better understand how an organisation's financial capital is affected by the performance in the five remaining capital bases. Recent years have seen a growth in IR adoption mainly fuelled by companies operating in France, India, Japan, Sri Lanka, Malaysia, and South Africa. The following videos introduce the initiative in a simple and easy-to-understand format.

- HRH the Prince of Wales introduces IR and its significance: www.youtube.com/watch?v=BIVWxmqGs9M.

- Susanne Stormer, Vice President, Corporate Sustainability, Novo Nordisk (a global healthcare company headquartered in Denmark), briefly explains Novo Nordisk's journey towards IR: www.youtube.com/watch?v=fUocAfqmm1o.

Furthermore, it should also be noted that apart from GRI and IR reporting standards, there are other frameworks, including the Sustainability Accounting Standards Board (SASB) framework, and the International Standards Organization (ISO) standards are also adopted by companies for sustainability reporting. Moreover, newer standards are being developed currently – for instance, the International Sustainability Standards Board (ISSB), developed through a multi-stakeholder collaboration involving IIRC, SASB, and TCFD, amongst other standard-setting bodies. ISSB aims to focus on sustainability-related enterprise value creation and climate-related disclosure (KPMG, 2022). The following video provides further information about the new standard.

https://players.brightcove.net/3755095886001/default_default/index.html?videoId=6287295090001

However, it should be noted that irrespective of the framework used, there are certain common topics that are usually found in extra-financial reports. These topics relate to different aspects of the environmental, societal, and governance (ESG) dimensions. The following table highlights the common topics included in external reports.

Table 7.1: Common topics in sustainability reports

Environment	Common topics
Energy use	Topic 1 – Renewable energy
	Topic 2 – Carbon neutrality
	Topic 3 – Energy savings
	Topic 4 – Total green building certified
	Topic 5 – Leverage technology
	Topic 6 – Pledge
	Topic 7 – Reduction in electricity consumption
	Topic 8 – EV fleet leased or purchased
	Topic 9 – Installation of EV charging stations
	Topic 10 – Supplier energy reduction programme
	Topic 11– Money invested
	Topic 12 – Short-, medium-, long-term target
Water use	Topic 1 – Water neutrality
	Topic 2 – Water saved and water efficiency programs
	Topic 3 – Rainwater harvested
	Topic 4 – Water conservation practice
	Topic 5 – Recycled water
	Topic 6 – Regenerative practice
	Topic 7 – Total freshwater procured
	Topic 8 – Water treatment
	Topic 9 – Money invested
	Topic 10 – Short-, medium-, long-term target
Waste	Topic 1 – Total waste generated
	Topic 2 – Total waste diverted away from landfill
	Topic 3 – Total organic/inorganic waste generated
	Topic 4 – Waste management strategy
	Topic 5 – Money invested
	Topic 6 – Short-, medium-, long-term target

Environment	Common topics
Biodiversity	Topic 1 – Afforestation
	Topic 2 – Certified FSC, certified palm oil procurement
	Topic 3 – Animal welfare
	Topic 4 – Short-, medium-, long-term target

Any other resources used

Social	Common topics
Employees	Topic 1 – Health and well-being
	Topic 2 – Satisfaction, experience
	Topic 3 – Training, upskilling
	Topic 4 – Diversity inclusion
	Topic 5 – Culture and work environment
	Topic 6 – Career and performance review
	Topic 7 – Talent attraction and retention
	Topic 8 – Maternity/paternity support
	Topic 9 – Employee engagement
	Topic 10 – Hiring and onboarding
	Topic 11 – HR/talent/compensation strategy/equal pay
	Topic 12 – Digital transformation
	Topic 13 – Short-, medium-, long-term target
	Topic 14 – Money invested
Customers	Topic 1 – Promoting sustainable living
	Topic 2 – Responsible marketing
	Topic 3 – Ease of use
	Topic 4 – Help reduce customer energy, water, waste, other footprint
	Topic 5 – Customer experience
	Topic 6 – Data protection, cybersecurity
	Topic 7 – Net promoter score
	Topic 8 – Short-, medium-, long-term target

(Continued...)

Social	Common topics
	Topic 9 – Extended producer liability
Suppliers	Topic 1 – Supplier training and upskilling
	Topic 2 – Supplier assessment/audit
	Topic 3 – Supplier diversity
	Topic 4 – Supplier ESG training
	Topic 5 – Short-, medium-, long-term target
	Topic 6 – Money invested
Government	Topic 1 – Liaise with local/national regulators
	Topic 2 – Contribute to policy advocacy
	Topic 3 – Responsible taxpayer
	Topic 4 – Short-, medium-, long-term target
NGOs	Topic 1 – Strategic partnerships
Community	Topic 1 – Training and skill development
	Topic 2 – Local talent
	Topic 3 – CSR programme
	Topic 4 – Philanthropic activities
	Topic 5 – Employee volunteering hours
	Topic 6 – Carbon offset projects
	Topic 7 – Short-, medium-, long-term target
	Topic 8 – Money invested
Governance	**Common topics**
Risk profile	Topic 1 – Climate-related risk (acute, chronic, transitional) and financial impact
	Topic 3 – Pandemic and international mobility risks
	Topic 4 – Chief risk officer
	Topic 5 – Other risks
Policies	Topic 1 – Environmental/natural capital policy
	Topic 2 – Procurement and supply chain policy
	Topic 3 – Tax policy
	Topic 4 – Business travel policy

Governance	Common topics
	Topic 5 – Electronic vehicle policy
	Topic 6 – Human rights/people policy
	Topic 7 – Business responsibility and code of
	conduct policy
	Topic 8 – Responsible marketing and promotions policy
	Topic 9 – Responsible business partner policy
	Topic 10 – Maternity/paternity policy
	Topic 11 – Waste management policy
Governance structure	Topic 1 – Board experience and expertise on sustainability
	Topic 2 – Sustainability board representation
	Topic 3 – ESG/sustainability committee/council/unit/ department
	Topic 4 – Number of meetings on sustainability
	Topic 5 – Grievance/feedback mechanism
	Topic 6 – Internal and external dialogue on sustainability matters
	Topic 7 – Internal and external reporting channels
Assurance	Topic 1 – External audit
	Topic 2 – Internal audit
Employee representation	Topic 1 – People with disabilities
	Topic 2 – LGBTQIA+
	Topic 3 – Women representation in top management and total workforce

Internet-based reporting

While there has been a constant increase in publishing sustainability reports (see, for example, what is probably the world's largest online database for sustainability reports at www.corporateregister.com), the limitations of printed reports have encouraged companies to turn to the more expansive possibilities provided by the internet. Greater use of the internet for sustainability reporting is often attributed to its advantages in **providing more sustainability information** and **increasing information accessibility and comprehensibility** (Adams and Frost, 2006; Herzig and Godemann, 2010). With the media-specific linking possibilities and the use of the HTML format, reporting is, for example, no longer limited by the number of printed pages. A large quantity of information, including historical company information and links to other information sources related to the company or to other organisations, can be offered online without necessarily overwhelming the reader. The internet allows a company to present an integrated view of different aspects of sustainability and allows interested stakeholders to select, from a large information database, that information which is of specific interest to them. Moreover, the internet offers possibilities, such as 24-hour accessibility, addressee-specific information tailoring and distribution, individual access for stakeholders, and a combination of different media elements, such as words, figures, images, or videos (Isenmann, 2005). Finally, the range of communication possibilities through stakeholder engagement and **dialogue in online sustainability reporting** extends much further than in printed sustainability reports (Unerman and Bennett, 2004; Unerman, 2007). While in printed reports stakeholder dialogue mainly takes place prior to production and the results of these stakeholder engagement processes can be documented in the reports, dialogue-based online relationships can include various forms of interaction (mutual asynchronous forms, such as mail-to functions or discussion forums, as well as mutual synchronous forms, such as chats, audio, or videoconferencing) (Herzig and Schaltegger, 2011).

However, there are also several disadvantages to using the internet. Some stakeholders tend to be excluded from the internet or hindered in their use of it. Information on websites can be changed without warning, and the assurance of web content is difficult. On the other hand, considerations to encourage a wider application of EMAS by reducing the costs of publishing environmental statements has raised a debate about the necessity of printed reports. In practice, more and more companies have abandoned printed reports completely and solely focus on internet-based sustainability reporting.

Perspectives

Why do companies engage in sustainability reporting? A widely recognised motive underlying sustainability reporting is the **business case for sustainability**. Perceived benefits and pressures of social and environmental reporting, as observed by Spence and Gray (2007) in their UK study, include business efficiency, market drivers, reputation and risk management, stakeholder management, internal champions, and mimetic motivations – each viewed as expressing ideas on the legitimate mores of business and yet forming a part of an overall business case (see also Bebbington et al., 2008; Burritt and Schaltegger, 2010).

Another widely accepted motive for sustainability reporting is that it is a way of assisting companies in **managing threats to organisational legitimacy** or the right to operate (Deegan, 2002). The link between sustainability reporting and the establishment, maintenance, or repair of legitimacy has been investigated in a large body of accounting research (e.g. Milne and Patten, 2002; Neu et al., 1998; O'Donovan, 2002).

Other rationale for reporting may be explained by the need to manage the expectations of diverse **stakeholder** groups. Reporting allows organisations to communicate their sustainability performance, targets, and plans and how social expectations on responsible conduct are met, thereby also **signalling** interested stakeholder groups of the importance attached to undertaking a sustainable business. Due to **information asymmetry**, organisations resort to reporting to credibly convey performance-related information to diverse **stakeholder groups** to secure **legitimacy**.

Further discussion on the motivations fuelling sustainability report is available at: https://medium.com/@livabl/business-case-for-sustainability-reporting-a-theoretical-perspective-2d68cd2a7013.

Several researchers (e.g. Milne et al., 2009; Adams and Frost, 2006; Deegan and Rankin, 1996; Neu et al., 1998; O'Donovan, 2002; Wiseman, 1982) have noted a potential lack of relationship between environmental and social disclosure and performance. The so-called '**performance–portrayal gap**' (Adams, 2004) reflects a way to measure the level of accountability of organisations by comparing a company's ethical, social, and environmental performance disclosures with information obtained on the company's performance from other sources. This concept has been used to demonstrate that reporting is likely to assist management both in controlling the perceptions of stakeholders and in seeking legitimacy and/or reputation rather than in enhancing stakeholder accountability for the real impact of companies' activities on society. Concern about the predominance of the business case perspective has thus been raised, deflecting attention from social change and current problems to be addressed in sustainability reports to the benefit of increased corporate reputation of powerful elites that steer society in a direction that reinforces their own dominance (Welford, 1998; see also Brown and Fraser, 2006; Cooper and Owen, 2007).

To confront managerial capture of the social and environmental agenda and to reveal possible contradictions between a company's self-presentation on the one hand and stakeholder perspectives on the other, the concept of **shadow reporting** has been put forward (Gray *et al.*, 1997; Dey, 2007). Shadow accounting can be viewed as a technology that collects and compiles, makes visible, represents, and communicates evidence from external sources, including newspaper articles, NGO (non-governmental organisation) reports, direct testaments from workers, ex-employees, trade unions, suppliers, public pollution registers, etc., in order to reveal contradictions between what companies disclose in their corporate reports and what they suppress; problematises companies' activities; and provides additional insights into environmental and social impacts associated with these activities (Dey *et al.*, 2011). It is important to note that such corporate shadow accounting can be understood as an attempt to challenge corporate reporting and move away from an organisation-centred perspective of sustainability reporting through the use of independent but not necessarily objective sources (Dey *et al.*, 2011).

Some problem areas

In addition to the rhetoric of sustainability and the performance–portrayal gap addressed in the previous section, reporting on sustainability is associated with further problems. First, sustainable development is a **contested concept**. Its meaning can vary according to the context in which business operates and is dynamic in that its meaning, application, and use have changed over time. This makes recording and reporting on sustainability difficult. The fact that it over-laps with other concepts (such as 'corporate social responsibility' or 'corporate citizenship') adds to this complexity, and the fairly fast and often-changing terminology applied to non- or extra-financial reporting initiatives is equally unhelpful. Owen and O'Dwyer (2008) saw a tendency for 'corporate respon-sibility' to displace 'sustainability' and 'social and environmental', while later, 'environmental, social and governance' seemed to have become the term of choice (UNEP *et al.*, 2010).

Another problem related to the concept of sustainable development is reflected in the observation that sustainability reports have tended to often focus on *perfor-mance* measurement (e.g. the amount of wastewater and air emissions) and leave out the *impacts* of corporate activities (e.g. information about the condition of the surrounding environment of the organisation), which can be more material to stake-holders than the usually more narrowly defined performance aspects (Herzig *et al.*, 2011). Is the legal corporation perhaps the **wrong entity** to report on sustainability and demonstrate accountability for material, social, and environmental impacts? As Gray (2006a: 73) states, 'precise, reliable statements of organisations' sustainability are oxymorons. Sustainability is a planetary, perhaps regional, certainly spatial concept and its application at the organisational level is difficult at best'. An interesting alternative approach in this regard is presented by the Italian reporting concept of 'bilanciosocialeterritoriale', which aims to integrate various protagonists within a region ('territoriale') and reflects a commitment to report on impacts more broadly.

In the past, sustainability reports were also criticised for being non-specific, because they aimed at a diffuse and excessively wide group of potential readers. A **lack of target group orientation** can create an information overload and result in extensive sustainability reports – noted by some, but in practice mostly read by only a few. In addition to that, if environmental, social, and economic aspects of organisational activities are considered in an additive rather than integrative manner, reports fail to recognise and mention possible and actual conflicts and challenges embodied in companies' approach to sustainability (Gray, 2006b; Herzig and Godemann, 2010).

Adams and Narayanan (2007) stressed that guidance documents on managing reporting and stakeholder engagement can differ in terms of the extent to which they are concerned with the interest of business and the views and needs of a broad range of stakeholders. There remains a **tension between using reporting guidelines as a legitimating exercise** (to report the minimum required in such guidelines) and demonstrating accountability for views and needs of a broad range of stakeholders. Given that some guidelines focus on the needs of business and prescribe report content at the expense of concern with processes of stakeholder engagement, they concluded that 'without mandatory reporting guidelines focusing on processes of reporting and governance structures, some companies will continue to produce reports which leave out impacts which are material to key stakeholder groups' (Adams and Narayanan, 2007: 83). In fact, for many years, there has been a lively debate about the role governments should play in sustainability reporting. Some researchers have called for governments to put in place at least a **minimal regulatory framework** in order to overcome the incompleteness of voluntary non-financial reporting and the reluctance of a vast majority of companies to make any kind of sustainability disclosure (among others, this includes a large number of medium-sized, non-listed enterprises). This would prevent companies from conveying a misleading view of their activities and seeking to manage public impressions in their own interest through the provision of false information (Adams and Narayanan, 2007; Gray, 2006b). In contrast, sceptics have often questioned whether regulations (alone) can have a significant impact on both corporate accountability and the quality of sustainability information published in reports (Owen *et al.*, 1997; Schaltegger, 1997) or stressed that command and control regulation may not only be costly but also stifle innovation (Buhr, 2007). Concern has been raised about a '**too simplistic view**, according to which the regulation of environmental reporting would prevent all the shortcomings of voluntary environmental disclosures' (Larrinaga *et al.*, 2002: 737). In their analysis of the Spanish environmental disclosure standard, Larrinaga *et al.* (2002) conclude that at a minimum more participation in the form of discursive dialogue is needed for the development of regulation and the effective enforcement of legislation (see also Owen and O'Dwyer, 2008).

Other concerns associated with sustainability reporting include the limited contribution that current assurance practices in sustainability reporting can make to promoting greater transparency and true accountability to the stakeholders (due to ambiguities and inconsistencies in current approaches to sustainability assurance, for example, independence and degree of thoroughness of audits) (see Owen and O'Dwyer, 2008; O'Dwyer, 2011), the limited comparability of ecological and social performance information published in sustainability reports (resulting from data collection and presentation practices, which can vary over time or between companies), and a sometimes low quality of data published in reports (e.g. due to a lack of measurement capability). It remains to be seen how, for example, the European Union's current attempts to address these challenges (by introducing external audit requirements, albeit starting with limited assurance, and shifting reporting to sustainability factors that affect the company and go beyond what is already recognised in financial reporting – double materiality) will improve the quality and comparability of sustainability reporting in the future.

Suggested sessions

The three sessions can be undertaken separately or as a series of sessions in the order presented. In the following sections, you will find general information about the role-play, activities, and a brief of the case company (relevant for all sessions) before more specific instructions for each session are given. While you can work on the activities of session 1 using the materials given in the textbook and the *Unilever Sustainable Living Plan: 2010 to 2020 Progress Report and Unilever Annual Report and Accounts 2010 highlighting progress made by Unilever under the Sustainable Living Plan (SLP) 2010*, activities in sessions 2 and 3 should be carried out in a computer laboratory or with the help of laptops/tablets.

Role-play and activities

Food Business Reform is a sustainability consulting company whose mission is to constructively engage with companies operating in the food sector with the aim of encouraging greater levels of social responsibility, transparency, and accountability. Your team has been retained to advise Unilever on their reporting aspects as part of their ongoing contract between Unilever and Food Business Reform.

Your team's task is to critically assess the extent to which **Unilever's SLP 2010–2020 progress report, Unilever Annual Report and Accounts 2020,** and the company's website succeed in fully demonstrating transparency and accountability for the company's impact in terms of promoting sustainable development.

Company background

A common household name in the 21st century, Unilever was formed in 1929 by the merger of its founding companies, which in turn had their origins in the late 18th century. Most of us recognise Unilever as a major player within the FMCG (fast-moving consumer goods) sector, with hundreds of different products ranging from soaps and hygiene products to food products. Familiar brands such as Dove, Pond's, Knorr, Pureit, and Axe are all part of a portfolio available to a wide range of customers globally.

During its 90-year journey, Unilever has witnessed several negative world events, including the Great Depression, the Second World War, and the hard economic environments of the 1970s marked by rising inflation. Nonetheless, with the expansion of the world economy and the rise in the standard of living in Western Europe during the late 1950s, alongside the emergence of new opportunities in other parts of the world slowly welcoming economic reforms, Unilever made steady progress through acquisitions and new market entries and continued to extend its product portfolios until the late 1970s. From the 1980s to the late 1990s, however, owing to a change in strategy and emphasis placed on core products in its portfolio, Unilever gradually withdrew most of its existing product ranges. With the advent of the 21st century, Unilever's priorities have been to focus on the uncertainties of the modern world that have become the 'new normal', in addition to meeting the needs of the modern world consumer base (Unilever, 2012: 4).

To account for the uncertainties and pressures emanating from social, environmental, and economic issues of the modern world, Unilever developed 'the Compass' in 2009 that shapes their business strategy and model supplemented by the SLP in 2010. In 2020, Unilever celebrated the tenth anniversary of the SLP and reflected on its successes, failures, and the lessons learnt (Unilever, 2020). The Compass and the SLP drive the activities shaped around Unilever's vision and purpose statements:

> **Unilever vision statement:** 'Our Vision is to be the global leader in sustainable business. We will demonstrate how our purpose-led, future-fit business model drives superior performance, consistently delivering financial results in the top third of our industry' (The Unilever Compass, 2009).

> **Unilever purpose statement:** 'OUR PURPOSE IS TO MAKE SUSTAINABLE LIVING COMMONPLACE' (The Unilever Compass, 2009).

Unilever uses both the web platform and printed reports to communicate their sustainability commitments to a wide range of stakeholders. Links to the *Unilever Sustainable Living Plan: 2010–2020 progress report*, *Unilever Annual Report and Accounts 2020*, and the corresponding online information are provided in the session material. The annual report is a stand-alone, annual document which provides sustainability information in accordance to the GRI Standards. Additionally,

Unilever is providing sustainability information through their Sustainability Reporting Centre (www.unilever.com/planet-and-society/sustainability-reporting-centre/). The centre contains reports about Unilever's Sustainable Living Plan or Unilever's performance regarding human rights (https://assets.unilever.com/files/92ui5egz/production/0ead3d5a36007724459bb1acbf437a190cfc2e42.pdf/unilever-human-rights-report-2020.pdf), as well as information about Unilever's general reporting principles and assurances. Furthermore, Unilever's Planet and Society Hub provides more information regarding their actions on sustainable living (www.unilever.com/planet-and-society/).

Session 1: Sustainability reporting principles

This chapter has introduced the GRI Standards as one of the most generally accepted and widely applied reporting frameworks. Using the principles on reporting presented in Table 7.1, students are asked to evaluate how Unilever addresses the reporting principles of the GRI.

Activity 1 (30 minutes)

Work in small groups and critically examine the content of the Unilever Sustainable Living Plan: 2010–2020 progress report and Unilever Annual Report and Accounts 2020 (printed copy or PDF from www.unilever.com/planet-and-society/sustainability-reporting-centre/reporting-archive/) according to the key concepts and principles in Table 7.1 and also described earlier. Each group concentrates on the key concepts and two or three of the principles and presents its results to the class. Discuss to what extent the report accommodates the key concepts and eight principles.

Activity 2 (15 minutes)

Did you encounter any challenges when evaluating the report according to the principles? Which principles, if at all, did you find more difficult to assess than others?

Activity 3 (10 minutes)

Can you imagine any tensions or challenges which companies such as Unilever might face when trying to follow all key concepts and principles?

Please refer to the companion website for further information on GRI reporting concepts and principles.

Session 2: Comparing external views with a company's self-presentation on sustainability

As part of your assessment of the report's transparency, your consulting team has conducted an online search for external media coverage about Unilever and how impacts associated with its activities are perceived by stakeholders. The coverage includes reports about the company and the sector published by critical stakeholder groups, such as NGOs, newspaper and magazine articles, and contributions on social media. Please refer to the companion website for further information and resources.

Activity 1 (25–30 minutes)

Compare and contrast the previous information with the environmental and social accounts provided by Unilever in the Unilever Sustainable Living Plan: 2010 to 2020 Progress Report and Unilever Annual Report and Accounts 2020. Discuss to what extent the company's self-presentation covers the issues raised by various stakeholders. How does your appraisal influence your evaluation of the extent to which Unilever succeeds in demonstrating transparency and accountability for the company's impact in terms of promoting sustainable development? How, if at all, does Unilever address these concerns? Can you identify any other shadow reports reporting against Unilever?

Activity 2 (20–25 minutes)

If you have discovered a divergence between Unilever's reporting practice and the views and statements of external stakeholders, what could be the reasons for this?

Additional activity for participants who have attended Session 1 (10 minutes)

Are the earlier materials helpful when evaluating the extent to which Unilever follows the GRI reporting principles? If yes, how?

Session 3: The use of the internet for reporting on sustainability issues (computer laboratory session)

You have advised Unilever on their sustainability reporting practice, and they have welcomed your critical evaluation of the *Unilever Sustainable Living Plan: 2010 to 2020 Progress Report and Unilever Annual Report and Accounts 2020*. They believe that they can benefit from further exploration of the strengths and weaknesses of their approach to reporting and have assigned a new task to you. Given the increased importance attributed to internet-based technologies for sustainability disclosure, Unilever wants to review the way in which they use the internet for improved (1) provision, (2) accessibility, and (3) comprehensibility of sustainability information, as well as for (4) more dialogue-orientated approaches to sustainability reporting.

Activity 1 (25 minutes)

Work in groups. Each group should critically examine the Unilever Sustainability Reporting Centre (www.unilever.com/planet-and-society/sustainability-reporting-centre/) in one of the four dimensions detailed earlier in the chapter – provision, accessibility, comprehensibility, and dialogue – by which the internet-based reporting system can stand out against the print-based reporting system. Use the list of criteria presented in Table 7.2, and share your findings with the class. Which areas are covered well, and which are not? Suggest the use of internet features that you think would aid one's understanding and evaluation of the sustainability performance of the company.

Please refer to the companion website for further information and resources on the criteria for evaluating Unilever's Sustainability website.

Activity 2 (10–15 minutes)

The list of criteria is not meant to be exclusive and comprehensive. Can you think of any additional criteria? Does Unilever use this feature that you have suggested, or have you encountered the use of this technology on any other (sustainability) website before?

Activity 3 (10–15 minutes)

Note that the reporting principles of the GRI are expected to help in defining what should be included in the sustainability report and attaining an appropriate level of reporting quality. How do you think the internet can complement or potentially compromise these objectives? Reflect on individual principles.

Additional activity for participants who have attended Session 2 (10 minutes)

In session 2, we discussed gaps between, on the one hand, Unilever's self-presentation on sustainability and, on the other, statements and viewpoints of external stakeholders. What role does or could the internet play in this regard?

Additional teaching material and ideas

1. By relying on sustainability reporting frameworks such as the GRI Standards and/or internet-based reporting framework, critically evaluate Unilever's reporting effectiveness on sustainability performance. (More info in teaching guide for lecturers, pdf to this book, more info, see Chapter 1).

2. Please refer to the comments made in the short video which can be found at: https://globalreportinginitiative.medium.com/transparency-offers-the-pathway-to-a-more-sustainable-earth-1cdd2529fe11. In what ways do you think sustainability reporting may enhance transparency both within the organisation and externally? Do you think the benefits derived from transparency suggested in the interview can be truly achieved by sustainability reporting? You may want to refer to the concept of shadow reporting and the critique of the performance–portrayal gap introduced in this chapter.

3. Small- and medium-sized enterprises (SMEs) constitute a large part of our economies and – in total – account for much of businesses' social and environmental effects. Please reflect on the specific characteristics of SMEs and what that might mean for the sustainability reporting practices of these types of organisations. As multinational companies operate within and across various national boundaries characterised by differences in cultural, socioeconomic, and political contexts requiring diverse approaches to engage in sustainability, how (if at all) is it possible to incorporate and consider such differences in a consolidated global sustainability report? Will such an attempt not result in leaving out national-level or even significant local-level issues concerning sustainability and stakeholder needs, that is, compromising accountability to local stakeholders?

4. This chapter has argued that the use of the internet for sustainability reporting will increase in relevance. In practice, reporting strategies of companies include various combinations of print and internet or exclusively focus on one of the two. Which strategy would work most effectively from your point of view?

5. The conflation of corporate governance, financial, and sustainability reporting
    has recently been reinforced by the move towards IR. Consider the following,
    and make notes on aspects that you believe are important:
    a. www.youtube.com/watch?v=gX86CiPxpK8
    b. www.youtube.com/watch?v=1edG79CHx84
    c. https://assets.kpmg/content/dam/kpmg/pdf/2014/10/bridging-the-gap-
        between-integrated-and-gri-g4-reporting.pdf
    d. www.cgma.org/resources/reports/integrated-reporting.html

Working in small groups, discuss the following: Is there a need for IR, or is it
just another reporting fad? Will IR enhance the value of reporting for both
internal and external stakeholder needs? If at all, do you find any merit of IR
in permitting stakeholders to better appraise how sustainable an organisation
is both financially and otherwise?

Further readings

Godemann, J., and G. Michelsen (eds.) (2011), *Sustainability Communication. Interdisciplinary Perspectives and Theoretical Foundations* (Dordrecht, Netherlands: Springer).

> This handbook gives a broad overview of theoretical frameworks and methods associated with the concepts of sustainability communication and reporting. These refer to, for example, sociological and psychological aspects, media, and communication theories, as well as constructivism. In the last part of the handbook, 'Practice of Sustainability Communication', links to climate change and biodiversity communication, sustainable consumption, and stakeholder participation are introduced and explained.

Gray, R. H., C. Adams, and D. Owen (eds.) (2014), *Accountability, Social Responsibility and Sustainability: Accounting for Society and the Environment* (Upper Saddle River, NJ: Pearson).

> This textbook is a must for students who want to gain comprehensive views on the developments in accountability, social responsibility, and sustainability theories and practices and their relevance for socio-environmental and financial issues. This in-depth and nuanced guide to the topic represents a critical account of the tensions between the way in which organisations are controlled and their greater responsibility and accountability to society.

Herzig, C. (2022), 'Corporate Sustainability Reporting and Materiality', in J. Moon, M. Morsing, A. Rasche, A. Kourula (eds.), *Corporate Sustainability* (Cambridge, UK: Cambridge University Press).

This book chapter provides an overview of sustainability reporting while, at the same time, presenting a critical evaluation of corporate reporting practice. The chapter also offers a critical account of the contribution regulation and assurance can make to enhanced transparency and true accountability to stakeholders of companies.

Hopwood, A., J. Unerman, and J. Fries (eds.) (2010), *Accounting for Sustainability: Practical Insights* (London: Routledge).

This book provides a great starting point for students who intend to gain rich insights on the different tools and techniques that companies use to advance their sustainability agenda and embed sustainability in their decision-making and reporting. The book features case studies from eight organisations, including HSBC, Sainsbury's, Novo Nordisk, and BT, providing practical guidance to professionals and students alike.

Laine, M., H. Tregidga, and J. Unerman (2021), *Sustainability Accounting and Accountability* (New York, NY: Routledge).

This authoritative textbook covers the key subject areas and issues currently under discussion in the field of sustainability accounting and reporting. Areas examined include, for example, the assurance of sustainability reports, silent and shadow reports, integrated reporting, and sustainability reporting in the public sector. This book provides probably one of the most comprehensive and contemporary accounts of the theory and practice of sustainability reporting.

Schaltegger, S., M. Bennett, and R. Burritt (eds.) (2006), *Sustainability Accounting and Reporting* (Dordrecht, Netherlands: Springer).

Songini, L., A. Pistoni, and C. Herzig (eds.) (2013), *Accounting and Control for Sustainability, Studies in Managerial and Financial Accounting* (Bingley, UK: Emerald Publishing).

The edited book explores challenges and prospects in sustainability accounting research. Topics include the disclosure practice of SMEs, determinants of corporate social responsibility disclosure, and water accounting and accountability.

Unerman, J., J. Bebbington, and B. O'Dwyer (eds.) (2014), *Sustainability Accounting and Accountability*, 2nd ed. (London: Routledge).

References

Adams, C. (2004) 'The Ethical, Social and Environmental Reporting – Performance Portrayal Gap', *Accounting, Auditing & Accountability Journal* 17.5: 731–57.

Adams, C., and G. Frost (2006) 'Accessibility and Functionality of the Corporate Web Site: Implications for Sustainability Reporting', *Business Strategy and the Environment* 15: 275–87.

Adams, C., and V. Narayanan (2007) 'The "Standardization" of Sustainability Reporting', in J. Unerman, J. Bebbington, and B. O'Dwyer (eds.), *Sustainability Accounting and Accountability* (London: Routledge): 70–85.

Bebbington, J., C. Larrinaga, and J.M. Moneva (2008) 'Corporate Social Reporting and Reputation Risk Management', *Accounting, Auditing and Accountability Journal* 21: 337–61.

BMU (Bundesumweltministerium) [German Federal Ministry for the Environment] (2007) *EMAS: Von der UmwelterklärungzumNachhaltigkeitsbericht* [EMAS: From the Environmental Statement to the Sustainability Report] (only available in German) (Berlin, Germany: BMU).

Brown, J., and M. Fraser (2006) 'Approaches and Perspectives in Social and Environmental Accounting: An Overview of the Conceptual Landscape', *Business Strategy and the Environment* 15.2: 103–17.

Buhr, N. (2007) 'Histories of and Rationales for Sustainability Reporting', in J. Unerman, J. Bebbington, and B. O'Dwyer (eds.), *Sustainability Accounting and Accountability* (London: Routledge): 57–69.

Burritt, R.L., and S. Schaltegger (2010) 'Sustainability Accounting and Reporting: Fad or Trend?', *Accounting, Auditing and Accountability Journal* 23.7: 829–46.

Cooper, S.M., and D.L. Owen (2007) 'Corporate Social Reporting and Stakeholder Accountability: The Missing Link', *Accounting, Organizations and Society* 32.7–8: 649–67.

Deegan, C. (2002) 'The Legitimising Effect of Social and Environmental Disclosures: A Theoretical Foundation', *Accounting, Auditing and Accountability Journal* 15: 282–311.

Deegan, C., and M. Rankin (1996) 'Do Australian Companies Report Environmental News Objectively? An Analysis of Environmental Disclosures by Firms Prosecuted Successfully by the Environmental Protection Authority', *Accounting, Auditing and Accountability Journal* 9.2: 50–67.

Dey, C. (2007) 'Developing Silent and Shadow Accounts', in J. Unerman, J. Bebbington, and B. O'Dwyer (eds.), *Sustainability Accounting and Accountability* (London: Routledge): 307–26.

Dey, C., S. Russell, and I. Thomson (2011) 'Exploring the Potential of Shadow Accounts in Problematising Institutional Conduct', in S. Osbourne, and A. Ball (eds.), *Social Accounting and Public Management: Accountability for the Common Good* (Abingdon, UK: Routledge): 64–75.

Dierkes, M., and B. Antal (1985) 'The Usefulness and Use of Social Reporting Information', *Accounting, Organizations and Society* 10: 29–34.

EC (European Commission) (2014) *Disclosure of Non-Financial Information by Certain Large Companies: European Parliament and Council Reach Agreement on Commission Proposal to Improve Transparency.* http://europa.eu/rapid/press-release_STATEMENT-14-29_en.htm, accessed 4 April 2014.

EU (European Union (2003) 'Directives 2003/51/EC of the European Parliament and of the Council of 18 June 2003 Amending Directives 78/660/EEC, 83/349/EEC, 86/635/EEC and 91/674/EEC on the Annual and Consolidated Accounts of Certain Types of Companies, Banks and Other Financial Institutions and Insurance Undertakings', *Official Journal of the European Union* 16–22.

Gray, R., C. Dey, D. Owen, and S. Zadek (1997) 'Struggling with the Praxis of Social Accounting: Stakeholders, Accountability, Audits and Procedures', *Accounting, Auditing and
Accountability Journal* 10.3: 325–64.

Gray, R.H. (2006a) 'Does Sustainability Reporting Improve Corporate Behaviour? Wrong
Question? Right Time?', *Accounting and Business Research* 36.1: 65–88.

Gray, R.H. (2006b) 'Social, Environmental and Sustainability Reporting and Organisational
Value Creation? Whose Value? Whose Creation?', *Accounting, Auditing and Accountability
Journal* 19: 793–819.

GRI (2021) *The GRI Standards Update 2021*. www.globalreporting.org/standards/download-
the-standards/

Guthrie, J., and L.D. Parker (1989) 'Corporate Social Reporting: Emerging Trends in Accountability and Theory', *Accounting and Business Research* 19: 343–52.

Hemmer, E. (1996) 'Sozialbilanzen. Das ScheiterneinergescheitertenIdee' [Social Reporting.
The Failure of a Failed Idea], *Arbeitgeber* 23: 796–800.

Herzig, C. (2022) 'Reporting, Materiality and Corporate Sustainability', in Rasche, A.,
Morsing, M., Moon, J., Kourula, A. (eds.), *Corporate Sustainability*: Managing Responsible Business in a Globalised World (Cambridge, UK: Cambridge University Press),
334–369.

Herzig, C., and J. Godemann (2010) 'Internet-Supported Sustainability Reporting: Developments in Germany', *Management Research Review* 33: 1064–82.

Herzig, C., J. Moon, M. Halme, and M. Kuisma (2011) 'Report of Company Self-Presentations',
FP7 CSR Impact Project.

Herzig, C., and S. Schaltegger (2011) 'Corporate Sustainability Reporting', in J. Godemann,
and G. Michelsen (eds.), *Sustainability Communication. Interdisciplinary Perspectives and
Theoretical Foundations* (Dordrecht, Netherlands: Springer): 151–69.

Hetze, K., P.M. Bögel, Y. Glock, S. Bekmeier-Feuerhahn, and A. Emde (2019) 'Online Stakeholder Dialogue – Quo vadis? An Empirical Analysis in German-Speaking Countries',
Corporate Communications: An International Journal 24(2): 248–68.

IIRC (International Integrated Reporting Council) (2013) *The International (IR) Framework*.
www.theiirc.org/wp-content/uploads/2013/12/13-12-08-THE-INTERNATIONAL-IR-
FRAMEWORK-2-1.pdf, accessed 5 April 2014.

IIRC (International Integrated Reporting Council) (2021) *The International (IR) Framework*.
https://www.integratedreporting.org/wp-content/uploads/2021/01/InternationalIntegrated
ReportingFramework.pdf.

Isenmann, R. (2005) 'Corporate Sustainability Reporting. A Case for the Internet', in L. Hilty,
E. Seifert, and R. Treibert (eds.), *Information Systems for Sustainable Development* (Hershey,
PA: Idea Group): 164–212.

Kolk, A. (2004) 'A Decade of Sustainability Reporting: Developments and Significance', *International Journal for Environmental and Sustainable Development* 3: 51–64.

KPMG (2020) *The KPMG Survey of Sustainability Reporting 2020*. https://kpmg.com/xx/en/home/insights/2020/11/the-time-has-come-survey-of-sustainability-reporting.html, accessed 20 June 2022.

KPMG (2022) *ISSB*. https://kpmg.com/xx/en/home/insights/2022/08/issb-proposals-discussions.html, accessed 30 March 2023.

Larrinaga, C., F. Carrasco, C. Correa, F. Llena, and J.M. Moneva (2002) 'Accountability and Accounting Regulation: The Case of the Spanish Environmental Disclosure Standard', *European Accounting Review* 11: 723–40.

Leipziger, D. (2010) *The Corporate Responsibility Code Book* (Sheffield, UK: Greenleaf Publishing).

Milne, M.J., and D.M. Patten (2002) 'Securing Organizational Legitimacy: An Experimental Decision Case Examining the Impact of Environmental Disclosures', *Accounting, Auditing and Accountability Journal* 15.3: 372–405.

Milne, M.J., H. Tregidga, and S. Walton (2009) 'Words Not Actions! The Ideological Role of Sustainable Development Reporting', *Accounting, Auditing and Accountability Journal* 22.8: 1211–57.

Neu, D., H. Warsame, and K. Pedwell (1998) 'Managing Public Impressions: Environmental Disclosures in Annual Reports', *Accounting, Organizations and Society* 23.3: 265–82.

O'Donovan, G. (2002) 'Environmental Disclosures in the Annual Report: Extending the Applicability and Predictive Power of Legitimacy Theory', *Accounting, Auditing and Accountability Journal* 15.3: 344–71.

O'Dwyer, B. (2011) 'The Case of Sustainability Assurance: Constructing a New Assurance Service', *Contemporary Accounting Research* 28.4: 1230–66.

Owen, D., R.H. Gray, and J. Bebbington (1997) 'Green Accounting: Cosmetic Irrelevance of Radical Agenda for Change', *Asia-Pacific Journal of Accounting* 4: 175–98.

Owen, D., and B. O'Dwyer (2008) 'Corporate Social Responsibility: The Reporting and Assurance Dimension', in A. Crane, D. Matten, A. McWiliams, J. Moon, and D. Siegel (eds.), *The Oxford Handbook of Corporate Social Responsibility* (Oxford, UK: Oxford University Press): 384–409.

PWC (2021) *Business Responsibility and Sustainability Report*. https://www.pwc.in/assets/pdfs/consulting/esg/business-responsibility-and-sustainability-report.pdf, accessed 20 June 2022.

Saudi Exchange (2021) *ESG Guidelines*. https://www.saudiexchange.sa/wps/portal/saudiexchange/listing/issuer-guides/esg-guidelines, accessed 30 March 2023.

Schaltegger, S. (1997) 'Information Costs, Quality of Information and Stakeholder Involvement', *Eco-Management and Auditing* (November): 87–97.

Shell (1999) *The Shell Report 1999: People, Planet & Profits – An Act of Commitment* (London: Royal Dutch/Shell Group of Companies).

Spence, C., and R.H. Gray (2007) *Social and Environmental Reporting and the Business Case Research Report 98* (London: Association of Chartered Certified Accountants).

UNEP (UN Environment Programme), KPMG Advisory NV, GRI (Global Reporting Initiative) and Unit for Corporate Governance in Africa (2010) *Carrots and Sticks: Promoting*

Transparency and Sustainability. An Update on Trends in Voluntary and Mandatory Approaches to Sustainability Reporting. www.globalreporting.org/resourcelibrary/Carrots-And-Sticks-Promoting-Transparency-And-Sustainbability.pdf, accessed 15 June 2014.

Unerman, J. (2007) 'Stakeholder Engagement and Dialogue', in J. Unerman, J. Bebbington, and B. O'Dwyer (eds.), *Sustainability Accounting and Accountability* (London: Routledge): 86–103.

Unerman, J., and M. Bennett (2004) 'Increased Stakeholder Dialogue and the Internet: Towards Greater Corporate Accountability or Reinforcing Capitalist Hegemony?', *Accounting, Organizations and Society* 29: 685–707.

Unilever (2009) *The Unilever Compass.* https://assets.unilever.com/files/92ui5egz/production/ebc4f41bd9e39901ea4ae5bec7519d1b606adf8b.pdf/Compass-Strategy.pdf.

Unilever (2012) *Unilever Sustainable Living Plan: Progress Report 2012.* www.unilever.com/Images/uslp-progress-report-2012-fi_tcm13-387367_tcm244-409862_en.pdf, accessed 15 June 2014.

Unilever (2020) *Unilever Sustainable Living Plan 2010 to 2020. Summary of 10 Years' Progress.* https://www.unilever.com/files/92ui5egz/production/16cb778e4d31b81509dc5937001559f1f5c863ab.pdf.

Welford, R. (1998) 'Corporate Environmental Management, Technology and Sustainable Development: Postmodern Perspectives and the Need for a Critical Research Agenda', *Business Strategy and the Environment* 7.1: 1–12.

Wiseman, J. (1982) 'An Evaluation of Environmental Disclosures Made in Corporate Annual Reports', *Accounting, Organizations and Society* 7.1: 53–63.

8

Designing sustainable business *with* the base of the pyramid

Angelo P. Bisignano, Patricia H. Werhane, and Michael Ehret

Traditional economic and financial approaches promoted profit orientation and the maximisation of shareholders' wealth as key goals of the firm (Friedman 1970). In this perspective, managers should primarily look after the interests of shareholders.

Stakeholder theory shifted the attention from shareholders' economic and financial goals to the complex interests of social stakeholders (Freeman 1984). More recently, the *shared values* framework invited firms to re-balance their economic and financial interests to create wider social and environmental impacts with their stakeholders (Porter and Kramer 2011).

Prahalad and Hart (2002) proposed that an enterprise-based approach to marginalised markets could reduce poverty, preserving the financial goals of the firm. By specifically serving poor customers (the so-called base of the pyramid) with dedicated products and services, firms can achieve sustainable financial performance while addressing poverty reduction.

Achieving superior stakeholder value is a suitable option, but collaboration is key. Motivating non-financial stakeholders

DOI: 10.4324/9781003294665-11

to contribute resources is a condition to generate profits and maintain the firm (Barney 2018). In the context of economic development, service scholars echo this proposition, identifying businesses operating under economic constraints as pioneers of service innovations (Flores Letelier *et al.* 2003).

This approach has enormous potential to *end poverty in all its forms everywhere* (UN Sustainable Development Goal 1). However, without responsible management, this approach presents the risk to re-create imperialistic dynamics on the poor of the world. Global managers hence require responsible frameworks to design sustainable business practices with the base of the pyramid (BoP).

On completion of this chapter, students should be able to:

- Understand the value(s) in designing sustainable business with the base of the pyramid.

- Evaluate the wider social and environmental impacts of enterprise-based approaches to poverty eradication.

- Redesign the strategic approach to the economic, relational, and innovative aspects of the business.

Introduction

Traditional economic and financial approaches consolidated the view that orientation to profit and maximisation of shareholder value are the key goals of the firm (Friedman 1970). Here, the manager is a mere agent of the shareholders, and its role is to protect their financial interests and to increase their wealth (Freeman *et al.* 2010). Not all shareholder approaches are as cynical as they appear. Assuming that political-legal systems ensure fair and evenly distributed development opportunities, shareholder approaches would ensure the most efficient use of the resource base for economic development. However, a growing range of research shows that pure regulatory to economic development fails (Pels *et al.* 2022). Building on the resource-based view, management theory is identifying the case for an activist approach of business management to stakeholder value. Economic development contexts offer strong cases. Financial innovations like micro-credit, digital payments, and electronic wallets are proving as disruptive innovations. Rather than a mere balance between financial and economic development goals, fintech innovators in emerging economies leapfrog incumbents of rich-world economies (Burlamaqui and Kattel 2016; Wenner *et al.* 2018). Digital business models aiming to 'bank the unbanked' out-compete established banking approaches. Service researchers hold that innovating in extreme environments renders competitive value propositions (Reynoso *et al.* 2015).

The *triple bottom line* (TBL) framework first proposed firms should keep separate accounts to record all their financial, social, and environmental costs (Elkington 1997). In doing so, organisations acknowledge that their activities and goals are not only economic but also social and environmental.

Drawing from public relations strategies, the *corporate social responsibility* (CSR) literature invited firms to consider philanthropy as a key aspect of every business (Carroll 1991). Despite the early success, the CSR movement failed to recognise social activities as more than just ancillary experiences to the firm's traditional goals. The *shared values* approach represented a turning point in organisation studies (Porter and Kramer 2011). This explicitly argued that the improvement of society is part of the firm's responsibility: social and environmental goals should be integral to the firm's mission. Firms must orient management practices outwardly to identify opportunities that create measurable business and social value.[1] They should reassess products and markets and redefine value chains to integrate solutions with social impact. Collaboration with social actors becomes critical to leverage the power of market-based competition in addressing social problems.

Stakeholder theory (ST) introduced eventually a multidisciplinary approach to rethink firms' goals (Freeman 1984). ST proposes an alternative to business strategies serving only the immediate financial interests of owners. ST advocates that firms should satisfy not only the interests of shareholders but also the ones of other social groups. The attention shifts from economic and financial goals to the wider interests in the attainments of the firm. ST implicitly introduced that the firm has a moral responsibility in pursuing the well-being of interlocutors in business and society (Freeman *et al.* 2010). This is not only a mere ethical mandate but also a precondition for the financial survival of the firm. Firms need to attract non-financial stakeholders for forming unique resources if the aim is to sustain financial profits (Barney 2018).

1   Recently, this view became a mainstream corporate governance approach for major corporations: www.businessroundtable.org/business-roundtable-redefines-the-purpose-of-a-corporation-to-promote-an-economy-that-serves-all-americans.

The UN Global Compact defines *social sustainability* as one of the cardinal points of corporate sustainability. Firms must manage business impacts on 'employees, workers in the value chain, customers and local communities' (UN 2022a). This expands the boundaries of an organisation's objectives to include sustainable social and development goals. The firm must adopt an osmotic approach to the management of resources. To create real value, managers must engage in conversations with social and institutional actors, as 'without non-shareholder stakeholders providing resources that have the potential to generate economic profits, there will be no profits' (Barney 2018: 3306). Building sustainable businesses ensures that multinational enterprises (MNEs) can still *do well by doing good* and balance commercially viable strategies with a responsibility to the UN Sustainable Development Goals (SDG).

This chapter focuses on how firms can make SDG 1 (i.e. *end poverty in all its forms everywhere*) one of their main corporate goals.

Ending poverty as a sustainable business goal

Poverty[2] has been steadily declining over the last two decades worldwide, giving hopes to achieve SDG 1 by 2030. The Covid-19 pandemic and climate change pushed millions back into a situation of vulnerability, even in high-income countries.[3] Despite the lack of accurate recent data, as many as 75 million more people might now live below the line of extreme poverty (World Bank 2022a). Other threats loom. Regional wars and a possible recession remind us of the fragility of the fight against poverty. More structural challenges also affect the global effort to achieve SDG 1. Surely, the long-term reduction trend of the total spending in government aid as part of GNI from development countries is affecting the fight on poverty in middle- and low-income countries (OECD 2022). However, the major structural threat is posed from climate change. Climate change creates human displacement, energy deprivation, job insecurity, and food shortages. Such impact risks to be particularly devastating in rural areas, where agriculture remains the main source of income and subsistence (World Bank 2021). Tackling climate change and poverty causes calls for united approaches to create sustainable solutions to

---

2 Further analysis on www.worldbank.org/en/topic/poverty.
3 www.poverty.ac.uk; www.weforum.org/agenda/2021/07/poverty-risk-covid19-eu.

emerging crises. The world needs activism and responsibility from wider social actors beyond policymakers. In this, firms and business schools must take a primary role.

For business students, understanding poverty is the first step to recalibrate the mindsets from financial-based approaches to inclusive models. Responsible management education should teach poverty 'as a multidimensional threshold concept that encompasses a person's freedoms and capabilities' (Mason and Rosenbloom 2022: 72). Business students must understand that although income remains a useful tool for measuring poverty trends, poverty is not only absolute but also relative to the human potential (Bradshaw 2007). Holistic conceptualisations of poverty must include what a person can achieve in developing its human potential (Sen 1999). Increased income is therefore a tool towards freedom and a more self-determined life (Mason and Rosenbloom 2022). Poverty is relative not just to what a person can do but to the values that the same person can hold over time (Sen 2011). The understanding and measurement of development must shift from income alone to a multidimensional approach that includes different types of deprivations (Alkire and Foster 2011). Access to education, health, safety, clean water, and opportunities for choice remain as important as income. Global managers can contribute to achieve true development by coupling income increase with the development of opportunities for individuals in their own context (Banerjee *et al.* 2011). Balancing goals as diverse as profit orientation, maximisation of shareholders' wealth, and poverty eradication can be challenging for modern firms. It is crucial to understand the faces of poverty and the associated social tensions (Grimm 2022).

Prahalad and Hart (2002) argued that firms can successfully address the multiple dimensions of poverty while achieving profitable financial results. Such enterprise-based approaches to poverty eradication advocate firms should consider the poor of the world as a consolidated global market and design specific products and services for improving their living standards (Prahalad 2004). Such perspectives work on the assumption that the poor will buy affordable solutions for basic needs. These, in turn, will increase sanitation, energy independency, education, and nutrition. Better living conditions will eventually take households out of poverty and will allow them to access future value-added products and services (Prahalad and Hammond 2002). As global firms focused traditionally on middle- or high-income customers in developed economies, they neglected the potential of low-income markets in emerging economies (Prahalad and Hart 2002).

The enterprise-based approach openly invites firms in addressing the needs of people at the *base of the pyramid*[4] (henceforth, BoP). This demographic term indicates the estimated 1.8 billion people that just before the Covid-19 pandemic were living with less than \$3.65 per day (at purchasing power parity in 2017 USD). Even more astounding, at least 648 million people struggle in conditions of extreme poverty, surviving with less than \$2.15 a day[5] (World Bank 2022a, 2022b).

For Prahalad and Hart (2002), lifting people out of poverty makes strategic sense. Three main arguments exist for adopting the enterprise-based approach to poverty as a viable sustainable business.

The *economic argument* suggests that markets at the base of the pyramid are strategic for competing at a global level. First, the current aggregated global size of the BoP represents a strategic opportunity for multinational enterprises (MNEs). Although the individual household's basic income[6] is limited, the potential of the BoP as a consolidated global market is high. Firms will achieve economies of scale more efficiently or find niches of a valuable size. Second, BoP markets tend to be in emerging economies. Their potential for further growth is high. For example, Cambodia averaged a growth of about 7.7% per annum in the period 1998–2019 and successfully coordinated programs that moved people out of poverty (World Bank 2022c). The Covid-19 pandemic suddenly halted growth trends in many emerging economies and pushed millions back into poverty. Rwanda, for example, grew at an annual average of 7.2% until 2019, before GDP fell by 3.4% in 2020 due to the Covid-19 pandemic (World Bank 2022d). Growth is again picking up momentum in these emerging economies despite some critical challenges, such as gaps in accessing education and the impact of climate change (World Bank 2022a).

The *strategic argument* builds on the assumption that the future demand at the BoP will change not only in terms of size but also in terms of its nature. BoP households often aspire and dream to improve their living standards (Dupas 2014).

---

4   The literature often uses interchangeably the terms 'base/bottom of the pyramid'. An argument exists to distinguish between the base (people living below the poverty line) and the bottom (people living in extreme poverty). In this chapter, we follow the suggestion of Calton *et al.* (2013), who propose to avoid the term 'bottom of the pyramid' because of its negative connotations.

5   The World Bank recently increased these values to include non-monetary elements of human development, such as access to education and health (World Bank 2022b).

6   With *household basic income* we indicate the amount of money a family must earn to cover needs such as food, energy, and shelter. Any remaining is classified as household disposable income.

When the UN SDG 1 is achieved, the future disposable income of households currently living in poverty will increase. BoP customers will demand more value-added products and services. They will likely show brand loyalty to firms with which they developed effective long-term relations. MNEs like Unilever or CEMEX deliberately targeted the BoP to establish themselves as market leaders in emerging markets while pursuing their original missions.

Emerging countries often have a volatile environment for business and poor infrastructures. The UN Global Compact argues how poverty and the associated lack of social development can hamper business development in emerging markets. Besides, 'actions to achieve social sustainability may unlock new markets, help retain and attract business partners, or be the source for innovation for new product or service lines' (UN 2022a).

Hart and Christensen (2002) argued that such challenges help MNEs foster organisational creativity, innovation, and problem-solving. BoP customers are normally more open to test alternative solutions to problems and to experiment new business models (Dupas 2014). Firms can reinvent their approach to business, introducing simple and ingenuous solutions that are effective in difficult environmental conditions. Not least, extreme environments frequently turn out as the vital context for competitive leapfrogging innovations (Flores Letelier *et al.* 2003; Burlamaqui and Kattel 2016).

Figure 8.1: The world income pyramid in 2019.

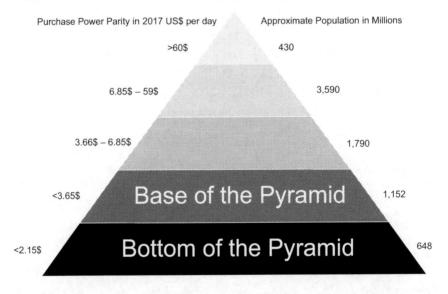

Source: Adapted and updated from Prahalad and Hart (2002); data 2021 from World Bank (2022).

The *social argument* advocates that, in designing enterprise-based solutions with the BoP, MNEs can engage constructively with the UN SDG 1 and contribute to poverty eradication. The PRME anti-poverty working group highlights how chartering human rights at the BoP contributes to a powerful dialogue amongst social interlocutors. Different than with environmental or labour issues, national legislators struggle to motivate firms to engage with poverty. Poverty alleviation remains a 'positive duty' for corporations (Van Tulder and Kolk 2007: 97). Responsible management plays a key role in ensuring firms develop an internal drive towards reducing income inequality. This facilitates the interface between business and society and strengthens the sense of purpose in management education (PRME principle 1).

The interdependence of the Sustainable Development Goals sees poverty as a cornerstone for action. For example, poor households inefficiently use water and energy resources. They often settle on riverbanks and burn kerosene with detrimental impacts on water pollution (SDG 6, SDG 14, SDG 15), on the air (SDG 13), and on sustainable sources of energy (SDG 7). Poverty forces families to prioritise basic needs, with negative effects on nutrition (SDG 2), health (SDG 3), and education (SDG 4). The poor often live and work in informal economies, increasing the risks of inequality and exploitation at work (SDG 8 and SDG 9), and women remain especially vulnerable in these contexts (SDG 5). Firms can tackle a variety of issues by empowering individuals and by creating robust partnerships across society. By tackling SDG 1, firms can build stronger bases towards the achievement of all the other goals.

Some issues exist with the enterprise-based approach to poverty eradication. First, empowering individuals to create more sustainable societies requires not only increasing incomes but also distributing them more equally. Since 2004 to 2019, the poverty rate at 3.65 US$ per day decreased from 32.82% to 9.59% in Peru, from 65.75% to 24.67% in Indonesia, and from 76.63% to 44.78% in India, three countries where this approach has widely taken place. However, over the same period, the Gini index[7] in the same countries did not show similar improvements in terms of income equality – Peru from 49.9 to 43.8, Indonesia from 32.7 to 37, and India 34.4 to 35.7 (World Bank 2022e). Higher income inequality can lead to social unrest, migration, and social displacement. These are all factors that eventually will re-perpetuate situations of poverty. Second, poverty eradication needs emerge as a set of actions that involve all social stakeholders.

---

7 The Gini index measures income inequalities within societies. It ranges from perfect equality (0, everyone has the same income) to perfect inequality (100, where one person has all the income). Lower figures indicate more equality.

PRME Anti-Poverty Working Group (poverty, a challenge for management education)

PRME established this working group following the 1st Global Forum for Management Education. Its vision is to integrate poverty-related discussions into all levels of management education worldwide. The working group wants to reshape the social environment of business management, by ensuring that dialogue with all stakeholders informs both managerial and educational solutions. The group shares a collection of best practices and inspirational solutions for integrating discussions on poverty in the curriculum.

Further info at: www.antipovertywg.com.

Join the LinkedIn group at: www.linkedin.com/groups/3792037/profile.

Solutions that are merely stewarded from corporations have proven effective in the short-term but have often failed to create a sustainable legacy. The UN Global Compact's principles focus on the social dimension of corporate sustainability. They invite firms to develop 'people-centered approaches to business impacts on sustainable development' to defend human rights and address poverty (UN 2015). Commercial approaches to poverty reduction attracted severe criticism for their lack of respect and understanding (Banerjee et al. 2011). Critics contend that the BoP discourse serves an ideological function for neoliberalism (Arora and Romijn 2011). And purely commercial approaches might mask new forms of corporate imperialism (Newell and Frynas 2007). After some initial success, the enterprise-based approach does not seem to have achieved the expected impact on poverty reduction (Simanis 2012). Calton et al. (2013: 721) indeed argue that this first approach to the BoP led, perhaps unintentionally, to a 'buccaneering style of business enterprise' in approaching BoP markets. MNEs overlooked the social complexities of operating at the BoP and mainly achieved commercial success in the form of short-term returns (Simanis 2012). Commercially focused MNEs failed to realise the importance of entwining commercial and social value (Rangan 2011). Without understanding the notions of poverty and success at the BoP, firms failed to entice local communities to join the BoP revolution in the long-term (Calton et al. 2013). It is hence important to redesign a sustainable approach to the BoP so that firms could do business 'with the BoP, rather than at the BoP' (London and Hart 2011: xi).

The literature has recently shifted from the mere commercial perspective typical of the first wave of strategies at the BoP to a more relational and inclusive approach. In what Simanis and Hart (2008) call BoP2, deep dialogue and involvement of all social actors play a critical part in strategic decision-making. Responsible managers will need to learn how to develop new human-centred models for interfacing with stakeholders.

Rethinking sustainable business at the BoP

Firms can experience different solutions for alleviating poverty. Examples include the transparency via labelling (e.g. fair trade), the widespread distribution of micro-credit, and the development of codes of conduct that can help firms create self-regulating standards (Van Tulder and Kolk 2007). Prahalad and Hart's (2002) enterprise-based approach proposes to engage commercially with the BoP to balance the economic and financial goals of the firm with poverty eradication. The next sections explore how firms can develop sustainable strategies in order to put SDG 1 at the centre of their corporate sustainability. In particular, responsible managers need to *rethink*:

- *Business models*. Managers must re-evaluate how the poor engage with products and services, to tailor effective, sustainable solutions against poverty. Life at the BoP must become the centre of sustainable business models.

- *Stakeholders relations*. Managers must propose new mental mapping that can help redesigning relations with stakeholders. Social interlocutors will move from a mere interest in the attainment of the goal of the company to an active involvement in the implementation of the firm's strategy.

Rethinking business models at the BoP

Despite recognising the economic argument, firms operating in traditional markets often shunned BoP customers. Prahalad and Hammond (2002) hold that firms struggle to design solutions that work because they fail to understand the different economic dynamics in BoP markets. This section explores how firms can rethink their business models to address the issue of poverty while offering products and services at the BoP.

The starting point of business model design is the insight that customers do not value resources or product per se but seek services that address their needs. Thus, anything a firm might offer (products, software, ideas, services) is a platform for value-creation activities and becomes effective only in the domain of the user's contexts (Macdonald *et al.* 2016). Business models need to bridge between unaddressed needs and idle resources to address poverty effectively with the BoP (Figure 8.2).

The **four pillars of value creation** show how firms activate resources to create business models that create value for individuals and communities (Ehret *et al.* 2013).

Such an outside-in approach has substantial implications for business model design at the BoP. By building on each value-creation pillar, managers can develop *adaptation* or *redefinition* strategies to rethink their business models. With the former, firms adapt their current model to the unique conditions of the BoP market. With redefinition strategies, firms reinvent their approach to the design and delivery of products and services.

Value propositions address the user's economic contexts, reflecting their value in use (Chesbrough *et al.* 2006). A common assumption holds that household products and toiletries might simply be too expensive for BoP customers. While such purchases have little impact on a family's budget at the top of the pyramid, they represent immobilised financial resources at the BoP. Such households often lack adequate storage capacity and immediate access to clean running water. Furthermore, their budgets are often dependent on unstable income streams from informal work. The lack of infrastructure also often represents a critical barrier. Infrastructure may be present but is unreliable, poorly maintained, and subject to blackouts. *Scaling down* is an adaptation strategy where the firm shapes its product/services to fit the infrastructure or income levels in the region. For example,

Figure 8.2: Business models at the BoP.

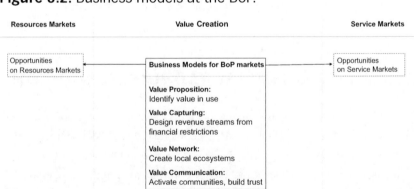

Procter & Gamble[8] focused on the value-in use of toiletries in emerging markets to reduce the costs associated with packaging by using recycled materials.

Case study: *scaling-down* in action

Safaricom, a mobile operator, launched its mPesa service in Kenya to offer a mobile money platform that provides basic banking services. The mobile network infrastructure in Kenya was mainly GSM, and the diffusion of smartphones was scarce. Safaricom focused on the available standards and introduced a banking service that would allow virtual transactions on the GSM network (i.e. text messaging). This innovation has since been introduced in Europe as well.
Sources: www.youtube.com/watch?v=i0dBWaen3aQ; www.youtube.com/watch?v=zQo4VoLyHe0.

Adaptation strategies can be ineffective in areas with difficult access to clean running water or energy. *Decoupling* is an effective redefinition strategy in these cases. The idea is to decouple the use of products and services from infrastructures. For example, Godrej launched the 'chotu kool', a portable refrigerator that does not require connection to the electric grid (McDonald *et al.* 2021). The firm focuses on the infrastructure available in the market to design innovative products to facilitate the access to the benefits of the products. Financial restrictions are common challenges at the BoP. By adjusting **value-capturing** mechanisms to the economic reality of users, firms can design business models that address financial restrictions. In traditional product markets, the dominant value-capturing mechanism used to be product price, varied by volume discounts or differentiation premiums. The business model considers a broader range of revenue streams besides the sales of goods and can therefore be a means to adapt business to economic development contexts (Ndubisi *et al.* 2016).

Miniaturisation is an adaptation strategy that synchronises the purchasing process with daily use and financial limitations. Procter & Gamble succeeded by offering its toiletries in single-use sachets. At the BoP, several $0.20 purchases in a month become suddenly more affordable than a single $10 one. Regular purchases promote regular usage and increase sanitation, contributing to fighting poverty. To succeed, firms must implement capillary distribution, maximise turnover to achieve scale, and promote

8 www.pginvestor.com/esg/environmental/plastic-packaging/default.aspx.

regular use over time (Simanis 2012). Nevertheless, firms should consider the unintended consequences of an increase in plastic pollution (Sy-Changco *et al*. 2011).

Radical redefinition strategies that build on value-capturing mechanisms include *non-ownership* concepts, where firms offer access, sharing, or renting options for a resource instead of selling the ownership rights of the product (Ndubisi *et al*. 2016). Sarvajal in India launched automated dispensers for accessing safe purified drinking water in underserved areas (Macomber and Sinha 2013). Similarly, Ecotact introduced pay-per-use toilets and showers to improve sanitation in urban slums in Kenya (Sydow *et al*. 2019). In doing so, the firm does not only provide a vital service but also restores dignity to the users of sanitation services (Ziegler *et al*. 2013).

Case study: new value propositions in rural healthcare

Offering healthcare services in rural areas is challenging. Villages are poorly connected, and there is a lack of professional medical staff and hospitals. LifeSpring, a network of low-cost maternity and children's hospitals, combined strategies such as *decoupling* and *scaling down* to overcome the critical lack of medical staff in rural India. The firm disaggregated its complex operations into discrete tasks that low-skilled individuals can perform. This allowed doctors to specialise only in tasks demanding their expertise, with other health workers performing simpler procedures.

General Electric (GE) redesigned its CT scans to address such issues in rural China. CT scans are costly to run and require specialised staff. Rural hospitals do not have the scale capacity and the trained technicians to afford them. GE not only simplified and miniaturised the scan technology but also focused on creating a device that was easy to use for non-specialists. This innovation not only proved to be a commercial success in rural China but also redefined GE's approach to innovation in developed markets. Sources: (Immelt *et al*. 2009; OECD 2015).

Multi-sided business models typically reside on the third pillar of business modelling: the **value network**. These approaches build explicitly on the ability of the firm to leverage external relations. The growth of ubiquitous computing enhances connectivity of business. Co-creation with a diverse set of stakeholders enhances the social dimension of value ecosystems. Because of their outside-in philosophy, collaborative approaches strive to develop networks for value creation, building on ecosystems consisting of supply chain and marketing channel-partners, complementing services, and non-business stakeholders (Ehret *et al.* 2013). The underlying rationale holds that firms cannot adapt resources to user needs in isolation. Therefore, networks increase both effectiveness and efficiency of value creation (London and Jäger 2019). Especially in BoP contexts, non-government organisations play vital roles in identifying the economic context and in closing resource loopholes (Chesbrough *et al.* 2006).

An effective adaptation strategy is *subsidisation*, where one side of the market may subsidise other sides. Well-known examples are the advertising sponsored services on internet search engines or platform-sponsored component markets, like razor blades or desktop printing. In these markets, the gains of selling in a market subsidise the losses of selling in another while building a presence over a long horizon. At the BoP, social and institutional partners (e.g. private donors, government, NGOs, and industry associations) normally subsidise the purchase.

Case study: *subsidisation* in action

Shoemaker Toms originally popularised the one-for-one giving model. In the scheme, a customer purchasing a pair of shoes in a 'top of the pyramid' market automatically became the donor of a matching pair to a person in need in a BoP market. However, the scheme had unintended consequences, such as undermining local shoemakers and offering unsuitable shoes to the BoP market. Ultimately, the scheme was not really tackling the root causes of poverty locally.

Eyeglasses.com tweaked the model by matching each eyewear purchase in a high-income country with a donation to a foundation paying for the surgery to restore one person's sight in India.

The approach allowed the firm to build awareness in the high-income market and to develop brand awareness in the BoP market. Plus, it empowered local associations to tackle the causes of poverty.

Sources: https://knowledge.wharton.upenn.edu/article/one-one-business-model-social-impact-avoiding-unintended-consequences/; www.eyeglasses.com/piwear/; https://sustainablebrands.com/read/product-service-design-innovation/ask-first-give-second-the-one-for-one-giving-model-gets-a-revamp.

Micro-enterprising is a partnership-centred redefinition strategy that builds on existing ecosystems and networks to engage local economic actors (Scott *et al.* 2012). Grameen Bank, awarded the Nobel Peace Prize in 2006, offered credit to poor women in rural contexts so they could create micro-enterprises selling services to local communities. The aim was to allow women in poverty-stricken rural contexts to achieve financial independence, escape poverty, and reshape their roles in local communities. Over the years, micro-enterprising surely contributed to shift the conversation on poor rural communities. Nevertheless, results have not always fulfilled its full potential (Banerjee and Jackson 2017).

Case study: *micro-enterprising* in action

The success of micro-enterprising is strongly linked to the understanding of how social relations interweave different stakeholders in local communities.

Avon successfully trained and financed women to develop independent micro-enterprises that sell its products across both shanty towns and rural areas in South Africa (Scott *et al.* 2012).

Hindustan Unilever (HUL), the Indian arm of the British conglomerate, relies on more than 160,000 shakti women entrepreneurs in 18 states, addressing poverty and marginalisation. These networks were crucial to sustain logistics when the Covid-19 pandemic disrupted the supply chain for fast-moving consumer goods. However, for both companies, replicating the success in other states/countries proved challenging (Rangan and Rohithari 2007).

Sources: www.avonworldwide.com/supporting-women/stand4her-report; www.hul.co.in/planet-and-society/case-studies/enhancing-livelihoods-through-project-shakti/.

The fourth essential pillar, **value communication**, resides strongly on social capital of communities and informal and interpersonal relationships (Ndubisi *et al.* 2016). Trust and commitment become as important as business relationships to nurture this outside-in approach to business modelling.

An adaptation strategy that activates communities and networks is the *supply chains redesign*. Firms collaborate with social and institutional partners to reorganise supply chain dynamics to make products more affordable to BoP customers (Heuer *et al.* 2020). Prosperity Initiative promoted the Mekong bamboo consortium to facilitate access to low-cost bamboo timber for huts in Vietnam (Nguyen 2011). Different private and public interlocutors shared expertise and integrated processes. BoP customers were included in the supply chain with roles as diverse as cultural consultants or manufacturers of bamboo artefacts. End customers traded their expertise for access to discounted products and services.

Community-based purchasing is a redefinition strategy that decouples the traditional buyer–seller relationship. The firm promotes purchasing groups and stewards the community in using the product.

Case study: *community-based purchasing* in action

CEMEX, a Mexican cement maker, launched a community-based scheme called 'Patrimonio Hoy', helping BoP customers upgrade their homes. BoP households must save for months, must purchase a single bag, and cannot afford to immobilise such a resource during the construction of their house. Bags can be misplaced, stolen, or dispersed because of lack of secure storage. 'Patrimonio Hoy' offered free storage, professional advice, and coordination of community-based purchases. Community members pooled their resources together to purchase materials for the first house and then moved to the construction of the next one. This made families safer, urban areas cleaner, and communities stronger.

Source: https://wdi.umich.edu/wp-content/uploads/Child-Impact-Case-Study-1-Improved-Housing-Patrimonio-Hoy.pdf.

Community-based models are also useful promotional tools. Success stories generate positive word-of-mouth and brand loyalty. Contrary to common assumptions, BoP customers are extremely brand-aware and associate higher value to known brands (Prahalad and Hart 2002). However, they might live in media-dark areas, where access to traditional media advertising is not readily available (e.g. billboards, TV). Customers who participated in the 'Patrimonio Hoy' project continued to purchase CEMEX products when they emerged from poverty, and also became ambassadors of the firm.

Table 8.1: A summary of the available strategies for business model design with the BoP

Focus on approach	Value proposition	Value capturing	Value network	Value communication
Adaptation	Scaling down	Miniaturisation	Subsidisation	Supply chains redesign
Redefinition	Decoupling	Non-ownership	Micro-enterprising	Community-based purchasing

Both adaptation and redefinition strategies show the importance for managers to understand the unique BoP economic dynamics for better designing suitable business models. Redefinition strategies especially invite responsible managers to review their approach to stakeholders' relations.

Case study: *d.light*

Today, almost 2 billion people live without complete access to reliable electricity (World Bank 2022f). Around 43% of the population of sub-Saharan Africa lacks access to electricity (IEA 2022). Many use charcoal as a source of lighting, with detrimental effects on emissions and health.

The d.light initiative shows that using a combination of different strategies can be a resourceful way to approach BoP markets. Families in rural areas frequently lack access to the grid for powering lights. The firm transformed the lives of more than 135 million people using human-centred design approaches and a combination of business models to engage *with* the BoP. The firm used *decoupling* to create off-grid solar-powered lanterns. *Scale-down* kept the cost of the unit low. *Subsidisation* helped coordinate donors and governments to pay for a portion of the lantern's costs, with the family paying only a residual and affordable price.

Source: www.dlight.com/; Chu *et al.* (2020).

Successful business models showed that the inclusion of a variety of stakeholders in the functioning of the firm's operations is fundamental to work with the BoP. By engaging in deep dialogue with users, a firm can anticipate

possible bottlenecks in future operations and prevent potential cultural rejec-
tions (Simanis 2012). Working with the BoP requires responsible managers to
invest in building trust, and this, in turn, calls for rethinking relations with all
stakeholders. Firms should rethink not only their economic approach to business but also their social one. BoP consumers must be treated with respect, and
their dignity assured (Santos and Laczniak 2009). This would help them create
change rather than wait for the markets to change.

Rethinking stakeholder relations

Enterprise-based approaches risk transforming the poor into mere consumers,
without addressing sustainable development (Simanis and Hart 2008). MNEs
must reinvent not only how they sell to the poor but also how they embed co-
invention and co-creation within local communities (Simanis 2012).

Stakeholder theory distinguishes between primary (e.g. employees, customers, suppliers) and secondary interlocutors (e.g. NGOs, local communities, and
governments). In working with the BoP, these differences fade. All interlocutors
represent key partners for facilitating constructive relationships between the firm
and BoP customers (Simanis and Hart 2008). Working *with* the BoP means stakeholder relations must become co-creators of value (London and Jäger 2019). This
will facilitate the emergence of bottom-up solutions, co-created with local communities. ST embeds a concern for moral conduct in value creation (Freeman *et
al.* 2010). To work responsibly with the BoP, 'it is attuned to work within or in
solidarity with value-based social networks where differences are respected and
community dialogue and engagement are encouraged' (Calton *et al.* 2013: 722).

Stakeholders engage in multiple webs of relationships that create complex networks that firms must learn to master. Calton *et al.* (2013) propose three frameworks that help responsible managers engage with local communities, build direct
and personal relationships, and keep ongoing dialogues.

The first framework proposes a mapping model based on 'decentred stakeholder
networks', which reframe stakeholder relationships as system-centred rather than
firm-centred (Werhane 2008, 2011). This perspective removes the firm as central
focus, and it recasts it 'as an equal participant in an unfolding, multilateral pattern
of firm/stakeholder interactions' (Calton *et al.* 2013: 725). The central focus is
now the system of nodes and relationships of the many participants in the process.

Figure 8.3: A decentred stakeholder network.

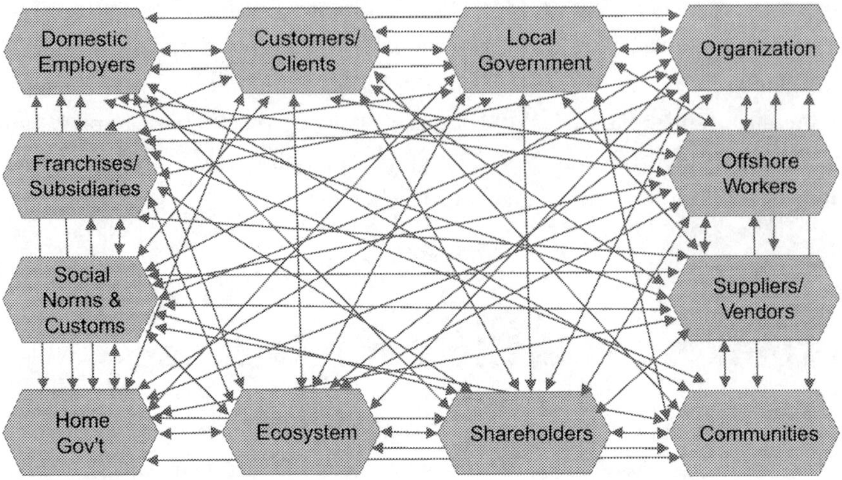

Source: Werhane (2011).

This shift in mindset accommodates the global complexity of interrelationships between the firm and all its interlocutors and considers the interactions between all stakeholders (Werhane 2011). While the firm remains important, responsible managers must monitor the subsystems created in the map. *Respectful listening* and *empathy* guide dialogue with multiple stakeholders (Santos and Laczniak 2009).

Dialogues identify tensions, individual agendas, and conflicting expectations (Grimm 2022). Responsible managers must propose solutions that consider the impact of the firm on the entire system. This approach is crucial for MNEs to understand local cultures and to gain knowledge across sectors and areas of operations.

The second framework is based on the notion of global action networks – GANs (Calton *et al.* 2013). GANs link firms with NGOs and governments in specific projects. Networks are built on social respect, trust, and sense of obligation. MNEs must identify the interests of all actors and offer complementary resources and competences to entice each partner into cooperation.

The interlocutors across the networks often speak different languages, present different cultural priorities, and have unique organisational identities. GANs facilitate the framing of the problem, address misconceptions, and minimise misunderstandings. Responsible managers can *institute multidisciplinary roles* with linguistic and cultural expertise. These will work across the network, facilitating the 'community conversation that brings together diverse voices caught up in the shared problem domain' (Calton *et al.* 2013: 727). In addition, responsible managers can *propose alternative forms of communication*. For example, artistic artefacts, games, and experiences proved successful to communicate effectively within diverse networks.

Networks generally work based on interactive exchanges and mutual recognition of interests. The goals and interests of all participants must be protected. Besides, peer pressure, losing face, and a diffuse sense of obligation can enforce social contracts and minimise moral hazard. Responsible managers can *define coordination processes and structures* that can support these often-informal functioning mechanisms. Useful examples are transparent platforms and forums where partners can scrutinise the behaviours of other network's participants. Similarly, responsible managers can *promote action learning opportunities* aimed at developing trust between participants. A successful strategy is for responsible managers to *identify the public good* that GANs must achieve. In the case of poverty eradication, MNEs and their partners must agree on the dimensions of poverty prioritised and share the reasons behind the choice.

Networks are great opportunities for learning and knowledge sharing. A key element of a functioning network is the shared understanding amongst partners that each is developing new competences and that the system as a whole will generate more knowledge than individually possible. Responsible managers need to design opportunities for learning for all participants. Individuals, firms, and NGOs that are able to integrate successfully the knowledge created in the network into their own portfolio of resources will increase their commitment to the future network activities. Responsible managers can also create opportunities for reflection within the organisation and the network. These are especially important for assessing the long-term impact of learning on sustainable business practices.

Finally, decision-making in problem-based networks is often informal and non-linear. A firm's direct leadership will not necessarily spur the active engagement of local actors. GANs require systems of governance that balance the power between all actors and allow the diverse voices to emerge. Responsible managers can *mobilise shared and participative leadership* to favour the partners' proactive engagement. Instruments such as round tables, action–learning experiences, network teams, and buddying schemes will allow people within the network's organisations to understand the other's perspective, to voice their views, and ultimately, to influence decision-making.

The third framework invites firms to develop human-centred solutions that address local contexts in specific ways. Responsible managers must rethink their conceptualisation of stakeholders. These are not mere aggregated groups (e.g. the BoP customers) but real, individual people (Werhane 2008). People have faces, stories, dreams. These inform how MNEs define their interaction with the different communities, helping responsible managers tailor solutions to each local context (McVea and Freeman 2005). Firms are entangled in a complex, adaptive system which assumes 'networks of relationships between individuals or groups of individuals, it affects and is affected by individuals, real people with names and faces' (Werhane 2011: 121). This framework proposes to use the names and faces of actual stakeholders to present mental map of stakeholders' relations. Replacing the box 'employee' with the actual photo and a short biography of one specific person not only visualises the category more vividly but also allows responsible managers to make sense of working and life conditions immediately.

A critical point of SDG 1 is to understand that poverty exists everywhere, yet in different forms. Targets 1.2 and 1.3 set by the UN remind us that the meaning of *poverty* varies according to national definitions and to the presence of nationally appropriate social protection systems. MNEs often fail to understand poverty and to comprehend its implications for families and communities. The 'names and faces' framework not only humanises the participants in partnership projects but also allows managers to make sense of the human sustainability of BoP strategies.

A common myth in working at the BoP is that solutions can be rapidly scaled and globalised to achieve profitable results (Simanis 2012). This framework considers that the experience of poverty is not the same in every context. The visualisation of people in stakeholders map facilitates the immediate understanding of what makes unique each situation (Calton *et al.* 2013). In the BoP approach, firms have often hoped that doing business at the BoP could be an incubator of global innovation. Surely, there is ingenuity at the BoP, and there is scope to replicate some successful practices in other contexts. However, SDG 1 stresses that to eliminate poverty everywhere, we need to understand how poverty manifests in the lives of individuals across nations and how it is experienced in each context. Socioeconomic, political, regulatory, and cultural conditions make each context unique. 'One-size-fits-all' solutions to alleviate poverty are not necessarily effective in diverse BoP situations (Werhane 2011).

Case study: collaborating to reduce emissions and poverty

Around 2.4 billion people worldwide use solid fuels for cooking. This is not only inefficient but also leads to an estimated 3.2 million deaths per year (WHO 2022). The Africa Biogas Partnership Program is a partnership between enterprises, NGOs, governments, research centres, and donor associations to promote clean cooking throughout Africa. The partnership shows that combining effective business models *with* the BoP and engaging frameworks of stakeholders management can help in launching and maintaining enterprising solutions that both reduce carbon emissions and help communities emerge from extreme poverty.

The firm trained almost 30,000 people in Uganda alone to use biogas as a solution for clean cooking. Users reduced carbon emissions, saved in energy costs, and improved their health. Clients also generate extra income from the sale of bio-slurry for agriculture purposes.

Source: Clemens *et al.* (2018); www.biogassolutions.co.ug/.

The adoption of a human-centred map allows NGOs, firms, local governments, and local opinion leaders to identify paths to tailored solutions. All stakeholders would work with the precise situation in mind and better comprehend each other's point of view. The UN Global Compact invites firms to engage in partnerships with stakeholders to 'create long-term value and achieve a positive impact on society' (UN 2022b). These three frameworks offer sophisticated instruments to responsible managers to rethink the firm's engagement with a plurality of social actors. Firms need to transform their business practices and proactively engage local communities.

Stakeholder relations within the BoP are normally multi-layered, dynamic, and long-term oriented. To develop the necessary competences, global firms need to *nurture relations* across and beyond their areas of operation and direct interest. Responsible managers must *educate* communities to share knowledge and to be, in turn, educated by them. Responsible managers need to remember that people in poverty work hard to preserve their dignity, value highly the opinion of leaders, consider the impacts on the local community, and are more likely to voice their concerns in engaged working groups. PRME principle 6 reminds us that dialogue is fundamental for inspiring responsible managers. If firms want to balance the achievement of economic and social goals, business educators need to promote *empathy*, *openness*, and *transparency* in responsible management. These are fundamental skills for global responsible managers to facilitate the emergence of trust and to promote continuous dialogue. The emergence of trust in relations that are dynamic and long-term oriented often benefits from testimonials. Firms working with the BoP need to show true commitment and belief. *Direct involvement* of personnel in local activities often inspires the stakeholders to comprehend, in turn, the human aspect of firms. This form of corporate outreach promotes alternative views on poverty within the firm. Employees will hence comprehend more easily the firm's role in the webs of social and political relations in the local context.

The three frameworks decentralise the role of the firm and focus on the learning processes stemming from open-system interactions. MNEs cannot lead the challenge to poverty by keeping their interests at the centre of the agenda. Turning people at the BoP into consumers might create market opportunities in the short term. However, to be truly effective, the enterprise-based approach needs to be human-centred and create interactions that produce continuous learning. Shared action–learning experiences will enact cooperation, unearth social tensions, and ultimately contribute to the eradication of poverty.

Suggested sessions

Session 1: Understanding poverty and the BoP

Activity 1 (20 minutes)

The World Bank defines *poverty* in income's *absolute terms*.

- What does $3.65 a day (at PPP) buy you? And $2.15?

- What are the implications of monetary thresholds for absolute poverty?

The EU measures poverty in *relative terms* as 'economic distance' from acceptable standards of living (calculated as the income at 60% of the median household income after taxes and benefits).

- What are the implications of calculating poverty in relative terms?

- How would you define *poverty* in your country?

Activity 2 (30 minutes)

Use the following resources to research poverty in an emerging country:

- http://hdr.undp.org/en/data

- http://povertydata.worldbank.org/poverty/home/

- http://stats.oecd.org/

And in a developed economy:

- www.poverty.ac.uk

- www.jrf.org.uk/data

- http://spotlightonpoverty.org/

- www.irp.wisc.edu/

- www.bls.gov/pir/spmhome.htm

1. Compare growth data, poverty data, and income inequality within a country and between two countries of your choice.

2. Identify infrastructural challenges to address poverty.

3. Elaborate on the social dimensions of poverty other than income.

4. What measures would you use?

Session 2: sustainable business models

Activity 1 (25 minutes)

Malnutrition, marginalisation, and lack of sanitation are associated with poverty in emerging economies. Sit down on the floor and watch this video from M. Viswanathan on www.subsistencemarketplaces.org/:

> 'Cooking A Meal In Rural Tanzania – Bottom-Up Virtual Immersion In Subsistence Marketplaces': https://vimeo.com/300511346.

1. Assess how these conditions affect people waiting for the food.

2. Apply one (or more) *adaptation* and *redefinition* strategies (see table 8.1) to introduce a product or service that can alleviate poverty.

3. What are the major challenges to serve the family in the video? How can we overcome them?

Activity 2 (25 minutes)

BoP solutions are rarely associated to situations of poverty in developed economies. Identify the same condition associated with poverty and social marginalisation from activity 1 in your city.

- Would you be able to use the same solution you proposed?

- Imagine launching a start-up in your city commercialising this product. Which stakeholders would you engage? How? Use the frameworks discussed in the chapter to visualise your stakeholder relations.

Session 3: understanding life at the BoP

Activity 1 (20 minutes)

Watch the talk 'A 20 second blood test without bleeding' (www.youtube.com/watch?v=RyeQt0GodsE).

- How did the start-up approach the issue by focusing on the users and on the social context of poverty?

- How did they accommodate the role of the ASHA worker?

- How critical was the understanding of the social and cultural aspects of rural India in shaping the design of the device?

Activity 2 (30 minutes)

Watch the talk 'Inventing is the easy part' (www.ted.com/talks/daniel_schnitzer_inventing_is_the_easy_part).

- What social aspects did the firm underestimate in its first approach?

- Which business model would you design for selling this device in Haiti? (See Table 8.1.)

- Draw and compare maps of stakeholder relations for both experiences, using the frameworks presented in the chapter.

Additional teaching material and ideas

Debate: *Should life-treatment drugs be free or sold for a price to motivate consumption?*

Prepare an argument and a rebuttal for each stance. Consider economic as well as social and systemic aspects in accessing medications (e.g. who takes the drug in the community; which organisation is selling/administering the drug?).

Mini poster presentations

Prepare a mini poster presentation introducing a business model to deliver life-saving drugs to BoP customers. Refer to the different *adaptation* and *redefinition* strategies (Table 8.1) to produce an alternative to selling or free distribution. Ensure you use a bottom-up approach that considers how the model will embrace all social interactions.

Role-play

Consider a global pharmaceutical firm and identify its stakeholders. Imagine introducing the business model you proposed in the poster within a BoP community. With others, act the role of the firm and of two other stakeholders using first the traditional stakeholder model and then the *decentred stakeholders network* and the *names and faces* models discussed in the chapter.

Reflective presentation

Prepare a reflective presentation (you may want to use alternative forms, such as a video, a dynamic photo collage, or an artistic artefact) that elaborates your understanding of the role of enterprises in *ending poverty in all its forms everywhere* (SDG 1). You can also reflect on how your interpretation of the fight to poverty has changed. See inspiring examples on the World's Largest Lesson website: https://worldslargestlesson.globalgoals.org/resources/.

Business plan competition

Join a business plan competition, such as the *Global Innovation Challenge* (www.socialshifters.co) or the *Enactus World Cup* (www.enactus.org).

Further readings

Casado Caneque, F., and S. L. Hart (2015), *Base of the Pyramid 3.0: Sustainable Development Through Innovation and Entrepreneurship* (Sheffield: Greenleaf).

> This book is an insightful collection of perspectives on the enterprise-based approach to poverty eradication. The lessons learnt from both success and failure stories help prospective responsible managers to anticipate challenges in working with the BoP.

Karnani, A. (2011) *Fighting Poverty Together: Rethinking Strategies for Business, Governments, and Civil Society to Reduce Poverty* (New York: Palgrave Macmillan).

> In a world where capitalism represents the dominant economic logic, this book highlights the central role of collaboration in the fight against poverty. The author offers a critical view of Prahalad's enterprise-based approach and calls for more pragmatic solutions based on empowering individuals through employment.

McGarvey, D. (2018), *Poverty Safari: Understanding the Anger of Britain's Underclass* (London: Picador).

> This passionate polemic on the causes of poverty offers an understanding of poverty in high-income countries. It brings to the surface lived experiences of poverty as a concept more socially systemic than purely economic.

Moellendorf, D. (2022), *Mobilizing Hope: Climate Change and Global Poverty* (New York: Oxford University Press).

> As climate change and poverty generate anxieties for the global world, this book offers innovative and accessible responses to the moral problems of growing social injustice. A vision to combine sustainability and prosperity bridging social activism and collective responsibility.

Werhane, P. H., L. Newton, and R. Wolfe (2020), *Alleviating Poverty Through Profitable Partnerships: Globalization, Markets, and Economic Well-Being*, 2nd ed. (New York and London: Routledge).

> This thought-provoking book questions the traditional assumptions on poverty as an economic condition and redefines it as a system. Each chapter presents a series of case studies from different angles, with the aim creating a win–win result for individuals, organisations, and communities.

Video resources

TED has an inspiring playlist on poverty and BoP approaches (www.ted.com/topics/poverty).

References

Alkire, S. and J. Foster (2011) 'Counting and Multidimensional Poverty Measurement'. *Journal of Public Economics* 95.7: 476–87.

Arora, S. and H. Romijn (2011) 'The Empty Rhetoric of Poverty Reduction at the Base of the Pyramid'. *Organization* 19.4: 481–505.

Banerjee, A.V., A. Banerjee and E. Duflo (2011) *Poor Economics: A Radical Rethinking of the Way to Fight Global Poverty* (New York: Public Affairs).

Banerjee, S.B. and L. Jackson (2017) 'Microfinance and the Business of Poverty Reduction: Critical Perspectives from Rural Bangladesh'. *Human Relations* 70.1: 63–91.

Barney, J.B. (2018) 'Why Resource-Based Theory's Model of Profit Appropriation must Incorporate a Stakeholder Perspective'. *Strategic Management Journal* 39.13: 3305–25.

Bradshaw, T.K. (2007) 'Theories of Poverty and Anti-Poverty Programs in Community Development'. *Community Development* 38.1: 7–25.

Burlamaqui, L. and R. Kattel (2016) 'Development as Leapfrogging, not Convergence, not Catch-Up: Towards Schumpeterian Theories of Finance and Development'. *Review of Political Economy* 28.2: 270–88.

Calton, J.M., P.H. Werhane, L.P. Hartman and D. Bevan (2013) 'Building Partnerships to Create Social and Economic Value at the Base of the Global Development Pyramid'. *Journal of Business Ethics* 117: 721–33.

Carroll, A.B. (1991) 'The Pyramid of Corporate Social Responsibility: Towards the Moral Management of Organizational Stakeholders'. *Business Horizons* (July–August): 39–48.

Chesbrough, H., S. Ahern, M. Finn and S. Guerraz (2006) 'Business Models for Technology in the Developing World: The Role of Non-Governmental Organizations'. *California Management Review* 48.3: 48–61.

Chu, M., K.G. Palepu and D. Karadzhova Botha (2020) 'D.Light'. *Harvard Business School Case* 321–69.

Clemens, H., R. Bailis, A. Nyambane and V. Ndung'u (2018) 'Africa Biogas Partnership Program: A Review of Clean Cooking Implementation Through Market Development in East Africa'. *Energy for Sustainable Development* 46: 23–31.

Dupas, P. (2014) 'Short-Run Subsidies and Long-Run Adoption of New Health Products: Experimental Evidence from Kenya'. *Econometrica* 82.1: 197–228.

Ehret, M., V. Kashyap and J. Wirtz (2013) 'Business Models: Impact on Business Markets and Opportunities for Marketing Research'. *Industrial Marketing Management* 42.5: 649–55.

Elkington, J. (1997) *Cannibals with Forks: The Triple Bottom Line of Twenty-First Century Business* (Oxford: Capstone).

Flores Letelier, M., F. Flores and C. Spinosa (2003) 'Developing Productive Customers in Emerging Markets'. *California Management Review* 45.4: 77–103.

Freeman, R.E. (1984) *Strategic Management: A Stakeholder Approach* (Boston, MA: Pittman).

Freeman, R.E., J.S. Harrison, A.C. Wicks, B.L. Parmar and S. DeColle (2010) *Stakeholder Theory: The State of the Art* (Cambridge, UK: Cambridge University Press).

Friedman, M. (1970) 'The Social Responsibility of Business Is to Increase Its Profits'. *New York Times* 32.13: 122–6.

Grimm, J. (2022) 'Cognitive Frames of Poverty and Tension Handling in Base-of-the-Pyramid Business Models'. *Business & Society* 61: 2070–214.

Hart, S.L. and C.M. Christensen (2002) 'The Great Leap: Driving Innovation from the Base of the Pyramid'. *Sloan Management Review* 44.1: 51–6.

Heuer, M.A., U. Khalid and S. Seuring (2020) 'Bottoms Up: Delivering Sustainable Value in the Base of the Pyramid'. *Business Strategy and the Environment* 29.3: 1605–16.

IEA (2022) *Africa Energy Outlook*. www.iea.org/reports/africa-energy-outlook-2022 7th December 2022.

Immelt, J.R., V. Govindarajan and C. Trimble (2009) 'How GE Is Disrupting Itself'. *Harvard Business Review* (October) 87.10: 3–11.

London, T. and S.L. Hart (2011) *Next Generation Business Strategies for the Base of the Pyramid: New Approaches for Building Mutual Value* (Upper Saddle River, NJ: FT).

London, T. and U. Jäger (2019) 'Cocreating with the Base of the Pyramid'. *Stanford Social Innovation Review* 16.3: 40–7.

Macdonald, E.K., M. Kleinaltenkamp and H.N. Wilson (2016) 'How Business Customers Judge Solutions: Solution Quality and Value in Use'. *Journal of Marketing* 80.3: 96–120.

Macomber, J.D. and M. Sinha (2013) 'Sarvajal: Water for All'. *Harvard Business School Case* 211–28.

Mason, G. and A. Rosenbloom (2022) 'Poverty, Vulnerability, and the Role of Responsible Management Education in a Post-COVID World'. *Journal of Global Responsibility* 13.1: 72–86.

McDonald, R., D. van Bever and E. Ojomo (2021) 'Chotukool: "Little Cool," Big Opportunity'. *Harvard Business School Case* 616–20.

McVea, J. and R.E. Freeman (2005) 'A Names-and-Faces Approach to Stakeholder Management'. *Journal of Management Inquiry* 14: 57–69.

Ndubisi, N.O., M. Ehret and J. Wirtz (2016) 'Relational Governance Mechanisms and Uncertainties in Nonownership'. *Services. Psychology & Marketing* 33.4: 250–66.

Newell, P. and J.G. Frynas (2007) 'Beyond CSR? Business, Poverty and Social Justice: An Introduction'. *Third World Quarterly* 28.4: 669–81.

Nguyen, M.H. (2011) *Mekong Bamboo: Doing Business with the Poor*. www.inclusivebusiness.net/node/1105 7th December 2022.

OECD (2015) *Innovation Policies for Inclusive Growth* (Paris: OECD).

OECD (2022) www.oecd.org/dac/financing-sustainable-development/development-finance-standards/official-development-assistance.htm 7th December 2022.

Pels, J., L. Araujo and T.A. Kidd (2022) 'Informal Sellers and Formal Markets: A Habitus Gap'. *Journal of Business & Industrial Marketing* 37.6, in printing.

Porter, M.E. and M.R. Kramer (2011) 'Creating Shared Value'. *Harvard Business Review* (January): 63–70.

Prahalad, C.K. (2004) *The Fortune at the Bottom of the Pyramid: Eradicating Poverty Through Profits* (Upper Saddle River, NJ: Wharton Publishing).

Prahalad, C.K. and S.L. Hammond (2002) 'Serving the World's Poor, Profitably'. *Harvard Business Review* (September) 80.9: 48–58.

Prahalad, C.K. and S.L. Hart (2002) 'The Fortune at the Bottom of the Pyramid'. *Strategy+Business* 26: 54–67.

Rangan, V.K., M. Chu and D. Petkoski (2011) 'The Globe: Segmenting the Base of the Pyramid'. *Harvard Business Review* (June) 89.6: 113–17.

Rangan, V.K. and R. Rohithari (2007) 'Unilever in India: Hindustan Lever's Project Shakti – Marketing FMCG to the Rural Consumer'. *Harvard Business School Case* 505-56.

Reynoso, J., J. Kandampully, X. Fan and H. Paulose (2015) 'Learning from Socially Driven Service Innovation in Emerging Economies'. *Journal of Service Management* 26.1: 156–76.

Santos, N.J. and G.R. Laczniak (2009) 'Marketing to the Poor: An Integrative Justice Model for Engaging Impoverished Market Segments'. *Journal of Public Policy & Marketing* 28.1: 3–15.

Scott, L., C. Dolan, M. Johnstone-Louis, K. Sugden and M. Wu (2012) 'Enterprise and Inequality: A Study of Avon in South Africa'. *Entrepreneurship Theory and Practice* 36: 543–68.

Sen, A. (1999) *Development as freedom* (New York: Anchor Books).

Sen, A. (2011) *The Idea of Justice* (Cambridge, MA: Belknap Press).

Simanis, E. (2012) 'Reality Check at the Bottom of the Pyramid'. *Harvard Business Review* (June): 2–6.

Simanis, E. and S.L. Hart (2008) *The Base of the Pyramid Protocol: Towards Next Generation BoP Strategy*, 2nd ed. (Ithaca, NY: Cornell University).

Sy-Changco, J.A., C. Pornpitakpan, R. Singh and C.M. Bonilla (2011) 'Managerial Insights into Sachet Marketing Strategies and Popularity in the Philippines'. *Asia Pacific Journal of Marketing and Logistics* 23.5: 18–27.

Sydow, A., G. Ciambotti, A. Sottini and A. Argiolas (2019) *Ecotact: Making Public Restrooms in Kenya Sustainable and Attractive* (Thousand Oaks, CA: Sage).

UN (2015) *Poverty Footprint*. www.unglobalcompact.org/docs/issues_doc/human_rights/Poverty Footprint.pdf 7th December 2022.

UN (2022a) www.unglobalcompact.org/what-is-gc/our-work/social 7th December 2022.

UN (2022b) www.unglobalcompact.org/take-action/partnerships/how-to-partner 7th December 2022.

Van Tulder, R. and A. Kolk (2007) 'Poverty Alleviation as a Corporate Issue'. In Wankel, C. (Ed.), *21st Century Management: A Reference Handbook* (Thousand Oaks, CA: Sage).

Wenner, G., J.T. Bram, M. Marino, E. Obeysekare and K. Mehta (2018) "Organizational Models of Mobile Payment Systems in Low-Resource Environments". *Information Technology for Development* 24.4: 681–705.

Werhane, P.H. (2008) 'Mental Models, Moral Imagination, and Systems Thinking in the Age of Globalization'. *Journal of Business Ethics* 78: 463–74.

Werhane, P.H. (2011) 'Globalization, Mental Models and Decentering Stakeholder Models'. In Phillips, R. (Ed.), *Stakeholder Theory: Impacts and Prospects* (Cheltenham, UK: Edward Elgar Publishing): 111–29.

WHO (2022) www.who.int/news-room/fact-sheets/detail/household-air-pollution-and-health 7th December 2022.

World Bank (2021) *Resilience Rating System: A Methodology for Building and Tracking Resilience to Climate Change.* https://openknowledge.worldbank.org/handle/10986/35039 7th December 2022.

World Bank (2022a) *Poverty and Shared Prosperity: Correcting Course.* https://openknowledge.worldbank.org/handle/10986/37739 7th December 2022.

World Bank (2022b) http://povertydata.worldbank.org/poverty/home/ 7th December 2022.

World Bank (2022c) www.worldbank.org/en/country/cambodia/overview 7th December 2022.

World Bank (2022d) www.worldbank.org/en/country/rwanda/overview 7th December 2022.

World Bank (2022e) https://databank.worldbank.org/source/world-development-indicators 7th December 2022.

World Bank (2022f) *Off-Grid Solar Market Trends.* https://openknowledge.worldbank.org/handle/10986/38163 7th December 2022.

Ziegler, R., H.K. Benson and C. Dietsche (2013) 'Toilet Monuments: An Investigation of Innovation for Human Development'. *Journal of Human Development and Capabilities* 14.3: 420–40.

9
Economics for a low-carbon future

Rosa Maria Fernandez

In this chapter you will learn about the interactions between economy and environment as well as how economists try to solve the puzzle of giving the right value to our environmental resources so that sustainable development can be achieved. In this context, the Sustainable Development Goals (SDG) agreed by the United Nations in September 2015 (UN 2015) and discussed in detail in another chapter of this book will be used as framework.

The aim of the chapter is to give business and management staff and students an overview of how economics concepts, approaches, and tools can be applied by companies in their decision-making process to make it more sustainable and aligned with Principles of Responsible Management Education (Global Compact 2014). Several sessions and other teaching units will help on this journey.

At the end of this chapter, you will be able to:

- Identify basic concepts related to environmental economics. Environmental economics focuses on the efficient allocation of natural resources and environmental goods and services while considering the requirements to achieve sustainable development.

DOI: 10.4324/9781003294665-12

- Gain a reasonable overview of some policies and instruments used to tackle environment-related issues as necessary incentives for producers and consumers to change their behaviour into a more sustainable one. These include, for instance, taxes and emissions trading as part of what is called carbon pricing.

- Distinguish the main methods used to give a monetary value to environmental goods and services, including an introduction to waste management as one of the policies for which these methods could be applied.

- Discuss in an informed way the influence of international trade on the environment.

Introduction to environmental economics

The classical study of economics did not use to pay attention to the interactions between economy and environmental resources, with environmental economics not appearing as a distinct field until the 1960s (CFI 2021). The focus, considered narrow by many (Pearce and Turner 1990), was on the balance between supply and demand for products and services to achieve equilibrium levels of production and their corresponding market prices.

The production process was conceived as a linear one: take–make–consume–dispose (European Environment Agency 2016). Goods and services were obtained for consumption, or capital assets were created to be part of the capital stock that ultimately would be used to produce more goods and services. From goods and services consumed we obtain different levels of utility or satisfaction, and that was the end of the chain.

Any production process requires the use of inputs, and many of those inputs are natural resources (fuels, raw materials, water, etc.) (World Economic Forum 2014). Additionally, both production and consumption generate some waste, and even natural systems generate their own waste, for instance, the leaves falling from trees. That waste goes back into our environment unless it is recycled and reintroduced into the system, so we can have waste in the form of CO_2 into the atmosphere, plastic bags on a landfill, or chemical products in a river. These are all polluting and health-threatening elements, contributors to climate change, now considered 'the biggest long-term threat to the global economy' (Swiss Re 2021). Additionally, as human beings, we also give positive value to the possibility of contemplating natural resources' beauty or visiting them for leisure, like a national park. So when we use the environment as a waste sink, the impact on society will be negative.

All these interactions suggest that the economy should be defined as a **circular process** instead of a linear one (see Figure 9.1), and we should be aware of the consequences of not being careful and exceeding the environment's assimilative capacity (Steffen et al. 2015). This *assimilative capacity* can be defined as the ability of the environment to adapt to changing conditions and keep performing the functions that it is supposed to perform to keep ecosystems in balance (Beder 1996).

The current climate crisis calls for changes in the economics discipline, with prominent names urging to recognise the importance of climate change and daring to question some of the basic assumptions used for decades (Acemoglu 2021). In this regard, the *Stern Review on the Economics of Climate Change* (Stern 2006) increased the awareness over climate change consequences by quantifying the cost of inaction in GDP terms. Environmental economics and ecological economics can provide some solutions but must also recognise the need for a socio-ecological

Figure 9.1: The circular economy.

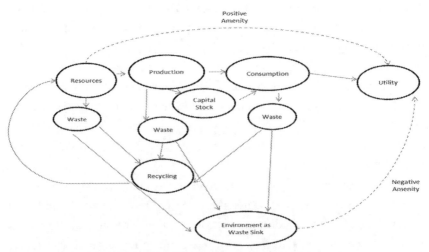

Source: Author's elaboration, adapted from Pearce and Turner (1990).

transformation, since there cannot be climate change mitigation without climate justice, as those most vulnerable to climate change are not the ones responsible for it (Laurent 2020).

To make economic agents (producers, consumers, and governments) behave in an environmentally friendly way, we should make them pay for the resources used and for the damage they impose on the environment and society. But to do that, we need to assign a monetary value to natural resources, to incorporate said value into the costs of production and into the market price of goods and services. This is not always possible, because property rights are not always well-defined for natural resources, and they have characteristics of public goods: they are non-rival (for instance, protection of biodiversity) and non-excludable (for instance, street lighting) (Hanley et al. 2013).

If our use of resources does not account for the negative consequences that we impose on others, then there is a divergence between the costs that society will suffer and the private costs that we are accountable for. This difference is called **externality**, which exists when 'the consumption or production choices of one person or firm enter the utility or production function of another entity without that entity's permission or compensation' (Kolstad 2009: 91).

This definition has a negative connotation and makes us think of greenhouse gas emissions, water contamination, the health risks of passive smoking, etc. But externalities can also be positive, and we can find ourselves enjoying the benefits of actions taken by someone else without paying for them. A typical example is vaccination against disease (Perman et al. 2011). If you receive a vaccination, you are protected against the disease, and so are the persons around you (they will not get it from you), and you will be contributing to cost savings on your community's health system.

We are more interested in the negative externalities because they lead to potentially threatening conditions for human life, and it is understandable that authorities try to prevent possible negative effects on large population groups.

In the next section, you will learn about the different policies and instruments used to correct externalities, focusing on the reduction of greenhouse gasses as one of the most concerning pollution problems. Environmental economics has investigated the links between economy and environment and has evolved into more specific areas, such as climate economics. The tools it uses provide insights of how environmental policies (for instance, taxes, subsidies, or feed-in tariffs) can affect companies' costs and influence markets. The markets can then contribute to help the environment instead of harming it (Hanley et al. 2013). Companies can use these tools to better account for the real costs that they impose on society and environment. They can then change behaviour and adopt strategies that contribute to the achievement of sustainable development instead of hindering it (Fernandez 2011). This requires a shift in the business paradigm so that climate change adaptation and mitigation become part of business strategies and leadership (Raynor and Pankratz 2020).

But a wider shift is also necessary for economics as a discipline, from the content we teach to how we teach it. The concept of 'doughnut economics' (Raworth 2022) is gaining momentum. It challenges the assumptions about the need for growth and the function of economic systems to be both distributive and regenerative. The centre of the doughnut replaces GDP as goal by the creation of an interconnected space for human well-being. This chapter aims to contribute to that shift by making you question what is being done, and how it's being done, to live in a more sustainable planet.

Instruments for controlling pollution and greenhouse gas emissions

Having mentioned some of the characteristics of environmental resources, the fact that we cannot assign them a market price creates what we call a **market failure**. Governments may try to intervene in the market to correct a market failure, but sometimes it is government behaviour (giving subsidies to polluting activities or not taxing them sufficiently) that creates the failure (Tietenberg and Lewis 2009). An example could be the subsidies to the coal industry in China (Parry et al. 2021).

The purpose of intervention is to make the polluter internalise the externality (US EPA 2010). If that purpose is achieved, the result will be a socially efficient level of production, with its equivalent socially efficient level of pollution. This point is reached when the benefits from one extra unit of production are equal to the damages that producing that extra unit will impose on society. This will be the point where the MNPB (marginal net private benefits) are equal to the MEC (marginal external costs) (US EPA 2010), as shown by point Qe in Figure 9.2.

Figure 9.2: Socially efficient production.

Notation: *MNPB* = marginal net private benefits; *MPC* = marginal private costs; *MEC* = marginal external costs; *Q* = excessive level of production; *Qe* = socially efficient level of production (equivalent to socially efficient level of pollution).

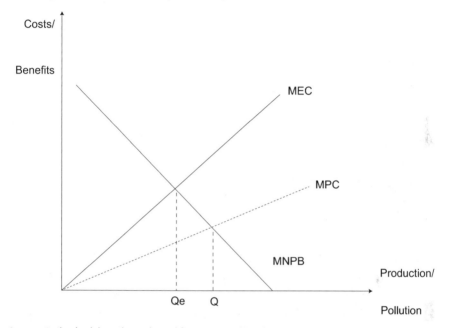

Source: Author's elaboration, adapted from US EPA (2010).

Government interventions can be grouped to obtain a country's set of environmental policies. These are not only concerned about pollution control, but the examples offered by this chapter focus on this specific area. We aim to cover the instruments used for the control of greenhouse gasses, prominent sources of pollution, and drivers of climate change. The relevance of these interventions for businesses is that policies usually translate into obligations they need to fulfil. Consequently, businesses are expected or may be forced to change behaviour. Some of those changes may involve the modification of production processes, which entail costs (unless fully subsidised).

We can distinguish two main approaches when implementing measures for pollution control. The most widely used until recently is called **command and control,** where government imposes a measure, usually a technological standard, and commands all the firms in the industry to adopt it (Perman et al. 2011). If the standard is not met, firms will have to pay a penalty or charge. This approach directly uses the regulatory power of governments and does not take into consideration that different firms have different cost structures. This means that what for one firm can be easily achievable may be totally unaffordable for another firm. This is one of the reasons this approach is not considered cost-efficient (see, for instance, US EPA 2010).

The other approach involves using market economic incentives (Kolstad 2009) through **market-based instruments**. We will explore here the ones acknowledged as most efficient.

Market-based instruments consider the different cost structures of each firm. Firms can make decisions about reducing their level of pollution or not, depending on what is more cost-effective for them. If their costs for reducing pollution, called **abatement costs** (Field and Field 2013), are higher than what they would have to pay to the government for excessive pollution (a tax per unit of pollution), or if their costs are higher than what they should pay under a regime of authorised limited pollution (a permits system), then they will pay. Otherwise, they will reduce pollution.

The first of the market-based instruments are **environmental taxes**. They can take several forms, but in general, we talk about a uniform tax per unit of pollution (Pearce and Turner 1990). If the tax is established correctly, it will be at a level where the costs of reducing one more unit of pollution (MAC: marginal abatement costs) equalise the damage imposed to society by that extra unit (MSD: marginal social damage), as shown by point Qe in Figure 9.3. This will be equivalent to the equilibrium point previously described (MNPB = MEC).

Alternatively, governments can approve the use of a system of **marketable permits**. Several countries have been using this system with relative success, though it is controversial as detractors question if it is ethical to buy the right to pollute (Tietenberg and Lewis 2009). But the European Union is using it through the ETS (European Emissions Trading Scheme), so its acceptance by authorities can be considered widespread (Perman et al. 2011).

The rationale behind a permit system relies on authorities establishing a maximum amount that can be emitted of one pollutant (for instance, CO_2), which is

Figure 9.3: Internalisation of externalities through taxation and permits.

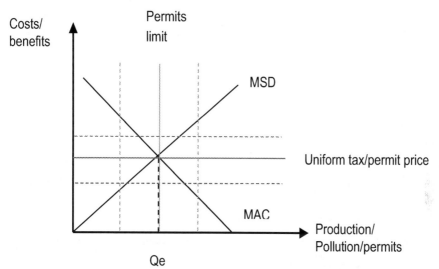

Source: Author's elaboration, adapted from Perman et al. (2011).

called a ceiling or cap (vertical line in Figure 9.3). Once this level is fixed, they distribute permits to firms according to their individual level of emissions, and then firms can trade the permits freely in the market. This means that if a firm does not use all its permits because it is reducing its level of emissions, it can go to the market and sell its surplus to those firms who are not so efficient in reducing pollution and need more permits than those initially allocated.

Carbon taxes and emissions permits are the main components of what is known today as 'carbon pricing'. They both have the aim of internalising the externality created by greenhouse gas emissions, mainly carbon dioxide (Aldy and Stavins, 2012). If designed correctly, emission costs would be too high, so polluters will need to act and find ways to emit less.

If the market is efficient, the price of the permits will be indicative of their scarcity and will incentivise firms to adopt cleaner technologies to reduce pollution. That should be cheaper than buying permits (US EPA 2010).

However, there are two issues associated with this system. The first one refers to how governments decide on the ceiling and how many permits to assign to each firm. This is usually based on the historical level of emissions, what is called grand-fathering (Hanley et al. 2007), which can lead to an over-allocation of permits. The second issue has to do with the way permits are distributed to each firm. It can be done for free or through an auction system (European Commission 2013). If permits are distributed for free and there is an excessive number in the market, the price is not high enough to incentivise firms to go greener. Bayer and Aklin (2020) argue, however, that even with a low price in the ETS, emissions would be reduced if the discourse of the legislator (the EU in this case) is credible enough regarding the approval of more stringent regulations in the future, which would make the affected sectors react.

Taxes also present issues. They are politically unpopular, and as shown by the dotted lines in Figure 9.3, it is difficult for the regulator to fix the tax at the right level as the information about the point of socially efficient pollution is usually unknown, and we may end up with too low or too high levels of taxes. If the latter case happens, some companies will end up with too onerous operating costs, which may end in their disappearance.

The last market-based instruments to be explored here are **subsidies**. Their use responds to the idea that industries should be paid to reduce pollution so that they can get enough resources to acquire more efficient equipment (US EPA 2010). The subsidy will be received only if the firm manages to reduce pollution to a certain threshold. But there are problems associated with the philosophy of subsidies. The main one relates to the fact that even if they can be effective at firm level, the reduction in costs that the subsidy would bring could create a 'call effect' and attract more firms into the market, causing the total emissions level to increase (Pearce and Turner 1990). This makes them less efficient than taxes for the purpose of reducing greenhouse gasses and other forms of pollution. Another criticism comes from the contradiction between this instrument and the 'polluter pays' principle, since with subsidies it is taxpayers who compensate firms for any pollution reduction in what would be a 'victim pays' principle (Bovenberg and Goulder 2002). Understandably, companies prefer subsidies as instrument for pollution control, though many consider it a burden and would prefer no environmental regulation at all. However, nowadays, it is common practice to increase government intervention on markets. All kinds of initiatives and regulations are being launched, aiming for decarbonisation and reduction of greenhouse gas emissions (Raynor and Pankratz 2020), which makes any expectation on the part of businesses to see a reduction on environmental requirements unrealistic.

Case study 1: US Water Pollution Control Act (WPCA, 1972) and Municipal Wastewater Treatment Plant Subsidy Program

The WPCA was primarily based on what we have defined as command-and-control approach, expecting firms to apply the 'best practicable technology'. The quality of waters improved compared to what would have happened without the regulation, but research (Keiser and Shapiro 2019) estimated that more cost-effective approaches could have been used.

In subsequent amendments, a programme of subsidies for secondary treatment of wastewaters requiring the construction of appropriate plants was established. Again, research (Field and Field 2013) showed that subsidies provided less incentives to implement the right control plant costs.

None of the instruments are perfect (as it is shown by case study 1), and there are many issues associated with information costs and administrative costs (Kolstad 2009). One of the problems is the type and amount of information that companies release. It can be argued, though, that market-based instruments are more efficient than command-and-control ones. They provide more incentives to change behaviour, particularly if they are well designed, which could result in firms revealing relevant information to the regulator. Good practice in this area could be the application of rules and principles of the Global Reporting Initiative, or GRI (GRI 2015). You will find out more about it in session 1.

We have mentioned the difficulties in giving environmental resources and environmental degradation a monetary value, so in our next section you will see some of the techniques used to try to overcome these difficulties.

Environmental valuation techniques

There are many methods that economists can use to try to assign economic value to environmental goods and services. Why is this necessary? One obvious reason is to calculate the damage cost of an environmental disaster so that those affected can be compensated. But it is equally important if a government needs to decide between undertaking an environmental project or not, or between allowing a mining activity in an area close to a natural park or not (Tietenberg and Lewis 2009). Companies also need to make these calculations when deciding if they begin a particular activity and where it is going to take place. A cost–benefit analysis needs to be applied, even if there is controversy with this approach. There is no agreement on which is the correct discount rate[1] to be used, or with regard to the appropriateness of cost–benefit analysis to value the environment (Perman et al. 2011). In general, a project will take place if its net present value (NPV) is positive, according to the formula:

$$NPV = \sum_{t=0}^{t=T} \frac{Bt - Ct}{(1+r)^t}$$

Notation: B is benefits; C, costs; r, discount rate; t, time period, from moment 0 to moment T, usually measured in years (Perman et al. 2011).

We can also calculate our willingness to pay (WTP) for improvements on environmental quality or our willingness to accept compensation (WTA) if we experience environmental quality decreases (Hanley et al. 2013). Those values, considered quite similar until recently, are now thought to differ significantly in some cases. Which of them is used for our calculations will have an influence on our decision-making process (Hanley et al. 2013). The information necessary for those calculations is gathered using the methods mentioned in the following pages and other similar techniques.

Our willingness to pay (WTP) is calculated by adding the values that we give to environmental goods and services. It is therefore necessary to identify which type of value will be part of the **total economic value** (TEV) of the said environmental goods and services. We have **use values** (derived mostly from utilisation on production processes) and **non-use values** (derived from the pleasure that the mere existence of the good or the option to use it in the future gives us). It is not certain that environmental goods and services will be used with an economic purpose. We may find satisfaction (value) from spending a relaxing day at a national park (recreational purpose) (Perman et al. 2011). But when no direct income is obtained or a price is paid, the other values tend to be ignored or underestimated (such as biodiversity conservation or carbon absorption), though all of them should be counted as part of the TEV.

---

1   *Discount rate* is the interest rate applied to make current and future costs and benefits comparable by converting future amounts into their equivalent value in the present. The low discount rate was a criticism to the Stern review at that time, as it supposedly made the future risks of climate change more costly and the need for action more urgent (Ackerman 2007).

Once we have these values clear, we could calculate our WTP as:

$$WTP = Use\,Value + Option\,Value + Nonuse\,Value$$

(Tietenberg and Lewis 2009)

These use and non-use values may play against each other when deciding between preservation or exploitation (for instance, when deciding whether to keep a forest untouched or start logging to sell the timber and get a profit). Managing forests sustainably (part of SDG 15) and using oceans, seas, and marine ecosystems for sustainable development (SDG 14) are among the SDGs setup for 2030 (UN 2015).

In this context, for businesses to contribute to the SDGs, particularly through the creation of strategies for climate change adaptation and mitigation (SDG 13), they need to change their perception of what constitutes 'value creation' and how to capture it, rethinking not only priorities but also time horizons and constraints (Raynor and Pankratz 2020). Environmental economics techniques, such as the calculations described earlier, can help different economic sectors in their climate adaptation and mitigation efforts. For instance, they can help estimate the cost of improving the provision of hydropower for businesses in areas subject to water shortages due to climate change (Niroomand and Perkins 2020).

One of the most common techniques for environmental valuation is the **contingent valuation method**. It uses surveys to ask people about their willingness to pay for the implementation of one particular environmental project (see case study 2). As it is based on people's stated preferences, it incorporates the non-use values of the environmental resources concerned (Hanley et al. 2013). Issues associated with this method derive from its reliance on people's answers, which may not be accurate or may be biased for different reasons (see Harrison 2006 for some of the issues).

Case study 2: Urban park in Thessaloniki (Greece)

The lack of green spaces in the largest urban areas of Greece has been a motive of concern for a long time. In Thessaloniki, the local government proposed plans to redevelop the city, including the increase of green areas around the Thessaloniki International Fair from 3% to 60%, through the creation of an urban park. Contingent valuation estimated that local residents would be willing to pay, on average, between €4 and €4.5 bi-monthly in the form of a 'green tax' to make the project happen (Latinopoulos et al. 2016).

Hedonic pricing, however, tries to extract the value of an environmental resource (for instance, air quality) from the influence that changes on the quality of that resource create on the value of related marketed goods, such as land prices or wages. This method is classified as a 'revealed preference' approach (since the changes on market will reflect the actual preferences of consumers). Statistically, the hedonic pricing regression equation will give us the demand curve for the environmental good, resource, or service under consideration. The type of question being answered is, for instance, how much would the price of a house change if it is close to a dirty river or a clean one (Kolstad 2009)?

$$P_i = f\left(E_{il} \ldots E_{im}, N_{il} \ldots N_{in}, S_{il} \ldots S_{iq}\right)$$

Notation: The price (P) of a house (i) is a function of its environmental attributes (E), like noise, scenic views (listed or counted from l to m); neighbourhood characteristics (N), like public transport, proximity to schools (from l to n); and site characteristics (S), like size of bedrooms, garage (from l to q) (Hanley et al. 2013).

This method is also used to indicate to employers how much they should pay in wage premiums or wage differentials to those employees who undertake riskier jobs. This will be conditioned by the levels of risk aversion of each person and by the cost to each employer of implementing safety measures that would reduce those risks (Kolstad 2009). A responsible employer will make these decisions by taking into consideration the principles of the UN Global Compact (Global Compact 2014) related to labour and human rights.

A more controversial application is to calculate what is called the **value of a statistical life (VSL)**, where the objective is to ascertain the amount that people are willing to pay to avoid a risk by the probability of death from that risk, in our case, an environmental risk (Tietenberg and Lewis 2009).

The equation in this case would have the form:

$$w = f\left(\pi, z\right) + \epsilon$$

Notation: w is the wage rate, as a function (f) of ϖ, the probability of death on the job, and z, other characteristics of the job, with ε being an error term.

The value of statistical life would be calculated as:

$$VSL = \frac{\Delta w}{\Delta \pi} = \frac{\Delta f\left(\pi, z\right)}{\Delta \pi}$$

(Kolstad 2009)

Notation: Δ signifies change or variation, so the equation would read that the VSL is calculated as the variation of the wage rate over/dependent on the variation on the probability to die on the job.

There are many other methods available, such as the **travel cost method,** another example of the revealed preferences approach. By finding out how many times people visit one site and for how long, as well as how much they spend on the trip, we estimate the demand for the site (Hanley et al. 2013).

The equation that can be used for the estimation would be of the form:

$$Ln(V_i) = a - bC_i + \varepsilon$$

Notation: $Ln(V_i)$ is the natural log of visits per year per person (i), C_i the costs of the trip, and ε the error term (Hanley et al. 2013).

Giving a monetary value to environmental goods or services is not easy, but an estimation will allow us to undertake, for instance, cost–benefit analysis to decide if it is worthwhile or not to implement a particular project, or to decide which are the best policy measures that can be taken to protect the environment, like the taxes, permits, or command-and-control measures discussed in the previous section. Valuing environmental goods and services should also be common practice for private firms, as they are responsible for the depletion and damage they cause when using them in their production processes, and hence, it would affect their possibilities of using them in the future. Utilising all these different approaches, environmental economics contributes to the achievement of SDG 7 (ensuring access to affordable, reliable, sustainable, and modern energy for all), SDG 8 (the promotion of sustained, inclusive, and sustainable economic growth), and SDG 9 (building resilient infrastructure, promoting inclusive and sustainable industrialisation, and fostering innovation) (UN 2015).

An example of policy decision-making: waste management policies

One of the policies for which environmental valuation techniques can be used is that of municipal waste management. Waste generation has been increasing over time in developed societies up until very recently (just see Eurostat data: http://ec.europa.eu/eurostat/waste). It occurs parallell to economic growth, and as such, the type of waste has evolved, so the way to treat it needs to be adapted.

Our environment has a large assimilative capacity. But the amounts of waste generated and accumulated and its nature, sometimes particularly damaging, make it necessary to adopt policies to ensure that behaviour becomes more sustainable. Surprisingly, most policies focus on how to dispose of the generated waste and on recycling instead of on how to reduce the amount that is initially generated (Turner 1995).

Once waste is generated, policies can only focus on its disposal. It makes sense, then, to have a group of policies dedicated to avoiding or minimising the risk of illegal disposal. Options within this group can include patrolling or surveillance to catch fly-tippers (for instance, the initiative of Oregon: Regional Illegal Dumping Patrol, at www.oregonmetro.gov/tools-living/garbage-and-recycling/rid-patrol). If they are caught, a severe penalty or fine is issued to those found guilty. This option may be expensive to implement, and it is difficult to determine the adequate level of penalty. Alternatively, the government could increase the number of places available for legal disposal. This would not be optimal, since the initial problem is the limited amount of land available for these purposes (OECD 2011).

When the issue relates to the consequences of legal disposal, we must consider the external effects of the different alternatives. Using a landfill site has environmental and health impacts. Landfill taxes try to prevent an excessive use of the sites (HMRC 2012). This would involve reducing the amount of waste generated or searching for alternatives to disposal, such as reuse, recycling, or incineration with energy production.

Subsidising the use of recycled materials or commanding their use in a minimum percentage could decrease the amount of waste arriving at landfill sites. However, subsidies can have negative consequences, as we saw in section 2 of this chapter, so its use is controversial (So 2014). Whichever option is chosen, policymakers will apply a cost–benefit analysis to the process to weigh the advantages and disadvantages of each alternative. Hedonic pricing or contingent valuation could be methods used for this cost–benefit analysis. If we consider the distance between the place where the waste is generated and the place where it is going to be disposed of, the travel cost method can be part of the analysis. You will work on these possibilities in session 2.

More recently, public outcry about the use (and abuse) of plastics has driven attention to policies both in production and consumption. An example are the charges that many countries impose on lightweight plastic shopping bags. Even if said charges confirm the influence they can have in changing people's behaviour, there is less evidence on their impact towards the environment (ScAAN 2019). At the same time, public scrutiny has encouraged (some would say pressured) companies to reduce the use of plastics, particularly in packaging, with more innovative solutions including fully compostable packaging (Sullivan and Chapman 2021).

International trade and the environment

The final section of this chapter tries to answer questions such as: Is international trade good for the environment? Do gains from trade liberalisation get outweighed by damage to the environment? What is the environmental impact of transporting goods internationally?

If we already know that production processes and transport cause negative externalities, why would it be desirable to get involved in international trade?

The consequences of trade over environment have been widely studied, and so have been the consequences of environmental regulation over competitiveness and international trade. This section will not look at all the relevant aspects in detail but will give an overview of the main ones so that discussion and further analysis can be achieved in future exercises (see session 3).

One of the main concerns of international trade regarding the environment relates to the suspicion that when developed countries adopt more stringent environmental regulations, polluting activities move to less-developed countries, where those regulations are very basic or do not exist. It could also happen that less-developed countries attract pollution-intensive firms with the promise of lower pollution-control standards to boost their economic growth rates (Field and Field 2013). The assumption is that regulation will increase production costs and will negatively affect industrial competitiveness. This is what we know as the **pollution haven hypothesis** (Kolstad 2009).

On the other hand, there are theories suggesting that countries will specialise in the production processes of those factors in which they are more abundant. If that is the case, countries more abundant in capital will focus on capital-intensive industries, and countries abundant in labour will focus on labour-intensive industries. The follow-up of that rationale, known as the **factor endowment hypothesis**, will lead us to think that capital-intensive industries are more pollutant than labour-intensive ones. This comes from the idea that heavily pollutant industries (paper, steel, chemicals, etc.) need large amounts of capital investment to start working (Perman et al. 2011). Evidence (Cole and Elliot 2005) seems to suggest that developed countries would be more abundant in capital, and developing countries more abundant in labour, so more pollutant activities would concentrate in developed countries.

The view that pollution havens exist or prevail gained popularity based on episodes such as the Bhopal disaster of 1984 (Field and Field 2013). That case made visible how the desire to attract foreign companies could have disastrous consequences. The loss of lives and persistent health problems, the pollution of water, and the contamination of underground soil are effects still felt today (Economic Times 2019). This is not a problem constrained to less-developed countries. Local pollution havens emerge in any country where long-term environmental damage is the accepted trade-off attached to the social short-term gains of job creation by polluting companies (Morrone and Basta 2013).

Existing studies analyse three main effects of trade on environment. These can be classified as follows (Grossman and Krueger 1991; Brock and Taylor 2005) and represented by the following equation:

$$z = S\sigma e$$

Notation: Emissions (z) are equal to the overall scale of activity (S), multiplied by the share of dirty goods in total output (σ), multiplied by the emissions per unit of the dirty good (e) (Perman et al. 2011).

1. **Scale effect.** With trade, there is better or easier access to markets, and this is supposed to contribute to economic growth. The scale effect measures the increase in pollution associated with the growth of the economy (scaled up) compared to the increase in levels of economic activity, while keeping constant the mix of goods and the production techniques used. This is supposed to have a negative effect on environment (Tietenberg and Lewis 2009).

2. **Composition effect.** When there is trade liberalisation, the mix of goods produced is likely to change, so the size and importance of the different economic sectors in the country or economy would be modified. Depending on which production factors the economy is more abundant in, and thus which type of industry it is specialised in, the effect on the environment can be positive or negative (if the country becomes more oriented towards dirtier industries) (Perman et al. 2011).

3. **Technique effect.** This refers to the change in production methods associated with trade liberalisation. One of the assumptions about trade is that it increases the levels of income per capita. If that is true, consumers will demand products of higher quality and less environmentally damaging. As a result of consumer demand, producers will need to change their production processes, and furthermore, if governments become responsive to such demand for better environmental quality, they will approve more stringent environmental regulations. This will encourage producers to innovate and offer less-polluting goods and services. Hence, the technique effect will have a positive effect on the environment (Jaffe et al. 1995).

Additionally, another theory also builds on the idea of the influence of environmental regulation, but in this case arguing that it will enhance innovation and increase companies' competitiveness, so it will contribute positively to economic growth. Under this idea, known as the **Porter hypothesis**, firms would not move from developed countries to developing ones just to save costs (Porter and Van der Linde 1995; Palmer et al. 1995).

In a world in which businesses consider the consequences of their activities at a global scale, acting according to principles of responsible management, the risk of pollution havens would be reduced and the Porter hypothesis should dominate.

What we have, however, is the influence of many factors on both trade and decision-making processes, so there is no fixed or easy answer to the questions that we previously formulated.

Environmental issues have, in many cases, an international dimension, and some international environmental agreements end up having effects on the way trade takes place. They effectively can change how production takes place, which type of inputs can be used for production, or what items can be traded internationally. Some examples of these agreements include the Montreal Protocol, the Basel Convention on Transboundary Movements of Hazardous Wastes, or the Convention on International Trade in Endangered Species of Wild Fauna and Flora (Field and Field 2013).

In any case, any policy or regulation, and any business decision, should account for the consequences over different segments of society. When tackling climate change, developed countries seem to expect a seamless transition from less-developed nations to more sustainable practices when they fail themselves to implement actions effectively (Jayaraman 2019). Climate change is happening in an unjust way, so action should endeavour to correct the inequalities created. However, evidence suggests (Joseph Rowntree Foundation 2014) that some adaptation and mitigation policies can worsen inequity, so there is a need to integrate social justice aspects into climate change policies and business behaviour.

The biggest proportion of carbon emissions caused by international trade, around 30%, comes from freight transport (OECD/ITF 2015) and is expected to grow. This is caused by the fragmentation of production processes across the globe. Suggestions to reduce this negative impact go from the creation of sustainable value chains (see the corresponding chapter on this volume) to trade more locally instead of more globally (to reduce transport distances). But some argue that regional trade agreements have actually contributed to increase emissions (Tian et al. 2022). This can only mean that to find the right balance and perhaps a final positive effect of trade on environment, action in multiple fronts is required: from the reduction of fossil fuels use in production and transport, to a full rethink of production and trade patterns worldwide. These are not easy tasks and will take time.

Suggested sessions

Session 1: How do companies report their societal and environmental impacts?

In this chapter we introduced you to the concept of marginal abatement costs, defined as the cost of reducing one additional unit of pollution. In this session we explore how companies report their progress on their efforts to deal with pollution. Do they identify which are their social and environmental impacts? Do they use the terminology we have seen in the chapter, such as externalities, abatement, market-based instruments? Or do they focus on something else? To help with reporting, the most famous initiative in place is the Global Reporting Initiative (GRI). It started producing guidelines that now have become standards. You can learn about its history here: www.globalreporting.org/about-gri/mission-history/.

In this session you will look at the Standards for Sustainable Reporting and will see real examples of reporting. At the end of the session, you will be able to identify opportunities for improvement in the way companies provide information related to sustainability. Based on the information you will see, you will attempt to find initiatives for them to improve their sustainability records in the three relevant areas: economic, social, and environmental.

Pre-session work

- Read the Universal Standards (or some of them at least) for sustainability reporting that you can find in the following website: www.globalreporting.org/standards/g4/Pages/default.aspx.

- Read the specific standards that apply to the oil and gas sector, which you can find here: www.globalreporting.org/standards/standards-development/sector-standard-for-oil-and-gas/.

- Look at how the company Galp reports about sustainability according to the GRI Standards: www.galp.com/corp/en/sustainability/reporting.

Activity 1

You can work individually or in groups, as decided by your tutor.

Having looked at the standards for reporting and those for the oil and gas sector, have you managed to find out how the oil companies deal with externalities in their reporting? Have you identified any of the concepts learnt through the chapter? Would you consider the reporting of the selected company as a good one, or can it be improved? Based on the tools learnt in the chapter, could you suggest a different way for companies to report about their externalities?

Is the report balanced in terms of the information provided for the economic, environmental, and social areas, or is it focusing on one or two of them?

Activity 2

Work in groups.

Choose another company belonging to the same sector from which you have access to its sustainability report; compare it to the company analysed in activity 1, and decide if its report is better or worse, and why.

Choose, if time allows it, a company from a different sector and make the same comparison.

At the end of the session, each group would share with the class the findings for each sector and together discuss to decide if there are sectors which report particularly well or bad (if that is the case, try to identify possible reasons for it).

Session 2: Waste management and environmental valuation

The aim of this session is twofold: On the one hand, to have a better understanding of the problems that waste generation can cause and, with that in mind, to try to formulate the best waste management policies possible. On the other hand, to try to apply the methodology of cost–benefit analysis and determine which are the pros and cons of each policy option, figuring out which would be the most appropriate environmental valuation technique to use in the calculations required.

When we described the interactions between economy and environment, we saw that one of the main roles that our environment plays is that of waste sink. But what if we generate so much waste that the environment cannot cope with it?

Pre-session work

Watch the video *Pyramids of Waste: The Light Bulb Conspiracy* (2010), 52 minutes' duration (www.youtube.com/watch?v=e9xmn228HM0). Based on the problems identified in the video, consider how to improve waste management policies and promote recycling to prevent problems associated with excessive waste generation. Those ideas will be discussed during the session.

Activity 1

Make a list of all the proposals, and try to identify the costs and benefits associated with each of them. Based on the different costs and benefits, work in groups to decide which would be the policy that as experts you would recommend to the government.

Activity 2

Assuming that at least five different options have been identified, again work in groups trying to determine which valuation technique, or combination of techniques, could be used to obtain those costs and benefits for each of the options.

Session 3: How can we regulate greenhouse gas emissions?

The aim of this session is to evaluate to which extent environmental regulations and instruments can affect trade in particular industries.

At the end of the session, you will be able to identify the difficulties on regulating environmental issues when agreement between several countries is required, by looking at one particular instrument, the European Emissions Trading Scheme, and propose your own solution to this conflict.

Pre-session activity

Review the basic concepts related to environmental regulations and trade:

- Scale, technique, and composition effects
- Pollution haven hypothesis
- Porter hypothesis

Activity 1a: Research and role-play

The European Emissions Trading Scheme (ETS) regulates the emissions of certain greenhouse gasses for particular sectors within the EU territory and some adjacent countries. You can find the most relevant information on this link: https://ec.europa.eu/clima/eu-action/eu-emissions-trading-system-eu-ets_en.

- Find out which sectors are the ones affected.
- Which countries consider themselves at risk of 'carbon leakage', and what does this mean?

Divide the class in two groups. One will be a group of EU countries supposedly affected by carbon leakage, and the other one a group of EU countries not affected. Each group will give reasons (pro and against) for the implementation of the ETS latest changes, and in the end, it will need to be decided if the changes are worthy or not. Which argument prevails?

Activity 1b: Research and role-play

In trying to prevent the 'carbon leakage' problem, the EU is planning to introduce a Carbon Border Adjustment Mechanism (CBAM) for imports coming from third countries with less-ambitious climate targets.

- Find out how it is planned to work and which sectors will be most affected.

Based on the conclusions of the previous activity and your research on the CBAM, reflect individually on both ETS and CBAM as policy instruments to reduce greenhouse gas emissions. Which one do you think is better to achieve the reduction of emissions? Are the two of them necessary? Would any other instrument be preferable?
   Then form groups, according to the different positions:

- ETS better than CBAM
- CBAM better than ETS
- Both instruments needed
- Different or additional instruments needed

Discuss the arguments, pro and con, for each position (taking into account EU and third countries' role in international trade), and see if you can reach a conclusion about what would be the ideal mix of policy instruments to regulate greenhouse gas emissions. Does your conclusion involve more or less international trade? Or a continuation of trade levels as usual?

Additional teaching materials and ideas

Natural resource management

This is a topic that usually accompanies environmental economics, so if time allows, some tips about sustainable exploitation of natural resources could be introduced. Fisheries are a good example of renewable resources, and any mineral can be used to illustrate a non-renewable resource. Forestry management is also highly appropriate, comparing the results of public management with those of private management.

The European Common Fisheries Policy (http://ec.europa.eu/fisheries/cfp/index_en.htm) provides a good description of the different instruments being used to try to avoid the disappearance of some species and to promote sustainable fishing without destroying employment.

An activity connected to this could be for students to identify an example of a national park or equivalent from their own countries, if such exists, sharing with the rest of the class how they are managed in each case: for instance, if the number of visits per year is limited or the entrance is restricted or prohibited during particular periods; if they charge an entrance fee, and in that case, how much they charge; etc. The idea is to compare different management options and, in light of the conditions of the site, suggest possible changes.

Simulations that connect economic and climate variables

En-Roads is an interactive tool that allows students to assess the results of policy actions (and their related instruments) in different economic sectors (energy, transport, buildings . . .) in an attempt to achieve the Paris Agreement goal of limiting the increase in global temperatures to 1.5 °C. Access to the tool can be gained through this link: https://en-roads.climateinteractive.org/scenario.html?v=22.9.0&p65 = 100.

These ideas are taught in climate literacy training, which is gaining momentum worldwide. This training is offered, among others, by the UN PRME working group on climate change. You can find the list of upcoming trainings here: www.unprmeclimate.org/events-1.

A real case of environmental valuation

Most of the literature uses as an example of contingent valuation the case of the Exxon Valdez oil spill in 1989 (see, for example, Harrison 2006). To find out if contingent valuation has been used again, or if a mix of methods is now being used, students could try to find out how compensation for environmental and economic damage was calculated for the Deepwater Horizon oil spill in 2010. This will help them understand the use of valuation techniques in practice instead of thinking of them as something theoretical and abstract. Using a relatively recent case will help create a connection and hopefully increase their interest in undertaking some research. The case was widely covered in the media, which will make easy to find information and to start a discussion about the long-term effects of the spill.

Blame matrix

This interesting title enables the topic of transboundary pollution to be introduced. Looking at EMEP (European Monitoring and Evaluation Program) data (http://emep.int/mscw/index_mscw.html), you will see how air pollution can move from country to country. The idea is to prevent problems like acid rain from occurring. The blame matrix transforms a vector of emissions into a vector of depositions. It can be mentioned that public policies are focused on reducing the social costs associated with acid rain and, within this framework, how cooperation should be promoted. This would involve some knowledge of game theory and the concept of the Nash equilibrium, so it would not be suitable for first-year undergraduate students. On a more basic level, games using maps to roughly calculate where emissions that originated in one country can end up may contribute to students' participation, particularly if the class/lecture/session has students of different nationalities. They can use their countries as the subject of the game. Students can calculate which country 'sends' more pollution out of its borders and which is the one being most damaged by other countries' pollution.

Further readings

Fairbrass, J. M., and N. Vasilakos (eds.) (2021), *Emerging Governance of a Green Economy. Cases of European Implementation* (Cambridge, UK: Cambridge University Press).

This book reflects on the current understanding of 'green economy' to then provide examples from European countries, covering attempts at different levels of government to implement the necessary changes to transform economies into low-carbon ones. The role of the different actors in the governance process, including private companies, and the influencing factors for decision-making explain the complexity of the transition towards a greener economy. The need to include more actors in the governance systems, to give a more prominent role to local actors, and the need to focus on issues related to social justice and a fair transition are messages that can be extracted from this reading.

Raworth, K. (2022), *Doughnut Economics: Seven Ways to Think Like a 21st-Century Economist*, 2nd edn (London, UK: Random House Business).

This book invites everyone interested in economics to challenge both the approach used to teach the discipline and the assumptions used by the models and theories that constitute the foundation of its message. Instead of focusing on reaching static balance or aiming for increases on economic growth, it makes the argument for having human well-being in equilibrium with nature as an overarching goal. One of the key features of the book is the transparent and easy language used to explain where we are and where we should be, as it questions the validity of economic systems functioning as we have learnt and lived for decades.

Schröder, P., M. Anantharaman, K. Anggraeni, and T. J. Foxon (2019), *The Circular Economy and the Global South: Sustainable Lifestyles and Green Industrial Development* (London, UK: Routledge).

This book provides examples of circular economy practices in developing countries, away from the typical case studies of big corporations in Western nations. Here the focus is on small and medium enterprises, the informal sector, and policy approaches. Interestingly, it presents a critical discussion of the narratives to circular economy, with the differences between North and South, sometimes evidencing conflicting pathways or approaches. The idea is to provide insights of how a circular economy can contribute to solve some of the big problems with development these days, including inequalities, health, urbanisation, or waste, among others.

Stavins, R. N. (ed.) (2012), *Economics of the Environment: Selected Readings*, 6th edn (New York: Norton).

This book includes a selection of papers by some of the most renowned experts in environmental economics, setting out their points of view on many of the issues surrounding natural resources, sustainability, climate change economics and policies, and corporate social responsibility, among others. Sometimes, responses to, and criticism of, previous papers are included, which could initiate an enriching discussion process to ascertain with which of the expressed positions the reader most identifies. The papers included cover a good number of years, which also facilitates the observation of changes in approach to the same issues over time.

Thomas, V., and N. Chidarkar (2019), *Economic Evaluation of Sustainable Development* (Singapore: Palgrave Macmillan).

For those who want to know a little bit more about the tools that economics uses to help evaluate the consequences of our actions in the environment, this book is a nice option. It introduces the reader to impact evaluation, an instrument widely used these days to decide if a project should go ahead or not. It looks at cost–benefit analysis, including not only economic variables but also social and environmental ones. The aim is to link the evaluation of impacts to the three pillars of sustainable development. It does so with the use of case studies to exemplify the different methodological options to measure impacts.

References

Acemoglu, D. (2021) What Climate Change Requires of Economics, *Project Syndicate*, 28 September. www.project-syndicate.org/onpoint/what-climate-change-requires-of-economics-by-daron-acemoglu-2021-09 (Accessed 21 April 2022)

Ackerman, F. (2007) *Debating Climate Economics: The Stern Review vs. Its Critics*, Report to Friends of the Earth, July. https://www.bu.edu/eci/2007/07/17/debating-climate-economics-the-stern-review-vs-its-critics/

Aldy, J.E. and R.N. Stavins (2012) The Promise and Problems of Pricing Carbon: Theory and Experience, *Journal of Environment & Development*, 21.2: 152–80.

Bayer, P. and M. Aklin (2020) The European Union Emissions Trading System Reduce CO_2 Emissions Despite Low Prices, *PNAS*, 117.16: 8804–12.

Beder, S. (1996) *The Nature of Sustainable Development*, 2nd edn (Newham, Australia: Scribe).

Bovenberg, A.L. and L.H. Goulder (2002) Chapter 23. Environmental Taxation and Regulation, in Alan J. Auerbach and M. Feldstein (eds.), *Handbook of Public Economics*, vol. 3 (Amsterdam, The Netherlands: Elsevier Science): 1471–545.

Brock, W.A. and M.S. Taylor (2005) Economic Growth and the Environment: A Review of Theory and Empirics, in P. Aghion and S. Durlauf (eds.), *Handbook of Economic Growth* (San Diego, CA: Elsevier): 1749–821.

CFI (Corporate Finance Institute) (2021) *Environmental Economics*, 10 February. https://corporatefinanceinstitute.com/resources/economics/environmental-economics/ (Accessed 16 November 2022).

Cole, M.A. and R.J.R. Elliot (2005) FDI and the Capital Intensity of "Dirty" Sectors: A Missing Piece of the Pollution Haven Puzzle, *Review of Development Economics*, 9.4: 530–48.

Economic Times (2019) Bhopal Gas Tragedy: 35 years of the Catastrophe, *The Economic Times*, 3 December. https://economictimes.indiatimes.com/news/politics-and-nation/bhopal-gas-tragedy-35-years-of-the-catastrophe/35-years-of-grief-pain/slideshow/72342988.cms (Accessed 19 September 2022).

European Commission (2013) *The EU Emissions Trading System (EU ETS). Factsheet* (European Union Publications Office). https://ec.europa.eu/clima/sites/clima/files/factsheet_ets_en.pdf, accessed 10 February 2017

European Environment Agency (2016) *Circular Economy in Europe: Developing the Knowledge Base*. EEA Report No. 2/2016. https://www.eea.europa.eu/publications/circular-economyin-europe

Fernandez, R. (2011) Corporate Governance in the EU: Opportunities of Change for a Sustainable Development, *Cuadernos Europeos de Deusto*, 45: 97–115.

Field, B.C. and M.K. Field (2013) *Environmental Economics. An Introduction*, 6th edn (New York: McGraw-Hill Education).

Global Compact (2014) *Guide to Corporate Sustainability: Shaping a Sustainable Future* (New York: United Nations Global Compact), December.

Global Reporting Initiative (2015) *G4 Sustainability Reporting Guidelines. Reporting Principles and Standard Disclosures*. https://www.globalreporting.org/resourcelibrary/GRIG4-Part1-Reporting-Principles-and-Standard-Disclosures.pdf

Grossman, G.M. and A.B. Krueger (1991) *Environmental Impacts of a North American Free Trade Agreement*, Working Paper No. 3914, National Bureau of Economic Research. www.nber.org/papers/w3914.pdf (Accessed 16 June 2014).

Hanley, N., J. Shogren and B. White (2007) *Environmental Economics in Theory and Practice*, 2nd edn (Basingstoke, UK: Palgrave Macmillan).

Hanley, N., J. Shogren and B. White (2013) *Introduction to Environmental Economics*, 2nd edn (Oxford, UK: Oxford University Press).

Harrison, G.W. (2006) *Assessing Damages for the Exxon Valdez Oil Spill*, Working Paper 06–04, University of Central Florida, Economics Department. http://citeseerx.ist.psu.edu/viewdoc/summary?doi=10.1.1.504.3840 (Accessed 1 April 2022).

HMRC (HM Revenue and Customs) (2012) *A General Guide to Landfill Tax: Notice LFT1* (London: HMRC).

Jaffe, A.B., S.R. Peterson, P.R. Portney and R.N. Stavins (1995) Environmental Regulation and the Competitiveness of U.S. Manufacturing: What Does the Evidence Tell Us? *Journal of Economic Literature*, March, 33: 132–63.

Jayaraman, T. (2019) Climate and Social Justice, *The UNESCO Courier*, July–September: 16–18.

Joseph Rowntree Foundation (2014) *Climate Change and Social Justice: An Evidence Review* (York: JRF), February.

Keiser, D.A. and J.S. Shapiro (2019) Consequences of the Clean Water Act and the Demand for Water Quality, *The Quaterly Journal of Economics*: 349–96.

Kolstad, C.D. (2009) *Environmental Economics* (Oxford, UK: Oxford University Press).

Latinopoulos, D., Z. Mallios and P. Latinopoulos (2016) Valuing the Benefits of an Urban Park: A Contingent Valuation Study in Thessaloniki, Greece, *Land Use Policy* 55: 130–41.

Laurent, E. (2020) No Environmental Economics without Social Justice, *Cogito*, 13 February 2020. www.sciencespo.fr/research/cogito/home/no-environmental-economics-without-social-justice/?lang=en (Accessed 5 April 2022).

Morrone, M. and T.B. Basta (2013) Public Opinion, Local Pollution Havens, and Environmental Justice: A Case Study of a Community Visioning Project in Appalachian Ohio, *Community Development*, 44.3: 350–63.

Niroomand, N. and G.P. Perkins (2020) Estimation of Households' and Businesses' Willingness to Pay for Improved Reliability of Electricity Supply in Nepal, *Energy for Sustainable Development*, 55: 201–9.

OECD (Organisation for Economic Co-operation and Development) (2011) Waste Generation, Recycling and Prevention, in *Greening Household Behaviour: The Role of Public Policy* (Paris, France: OECD Publishing): 81–95.

OECD/ITF (2015) *The Carbon Footprint of Global Trade: Tackling Emissions from International Freight Transport* (International Transport Forum). www.itf-oecd.org/sites/default/files/docs/cop-pdf-06.pdf

Palmer, K., W.E. Oates and P.R. Portney (1995) Tightening Environmental Standards: The Benefit – Cost or the No-Cost Paradigm, *Journal of Economic Perspectives*, Autumn, 9.4: 119–32.

Parry, I., S. Black and N. Vernon (2021) *Still Not Getting Energy Prices Right: A Global and Country Update of Fossil Fuel Subsidies* (Washington, DC: International Monetary Fund, Working Paper WP/21/236).

Pearce, D.W. and R.K. Turner (1990) *Economics of Natural Resources and the Environment* (Baltimore, MD: The Johns Hopkins University Press).

Perman, R., Y. Ma, M. Common, D. Maddison and J. McGilvray (2011) *Natural Resource and Environmental Economics*, 4th edn (Harlow, UK: Addison-Wesley).

Porter, M.E. and C. Van der Linde (1995) 'Toward a New Conception of the Environment – Competitiveness Relationship', *Journal of Economic Perspectives*, Autumn, 9.4: 97–118.

Raworth, K. (2022) *Doughnut Economics. Seven Ways to Think Like a 21st-Century Economics*, 2nd edn (London, UK: Random House Business).

Raynor, M. and D. Pankratz (2020) *A New Business Paradigm to Address Climate Change. Environmental Stewardship as a Leadership Imperative*. Deloitte Insights. A report from the Deloitte Center for Integrated Research (Deloitte Development LLC). https://www2.deloitte.com/us/en/insights/topics/strategy/corporate-climate-change-sustainability.html

ScAAN (2019) Effectiveness of Plastic Regulation Around the World, *Scientist Action and Advocacy Network*, revision 15 April. https://plasticpollutioncoalitionresources.org/wp-content/uploads/2017/03/Effectiveness_of_plastic_regulation_around_the_world_4_pages.pdf

Schröder, P., M. Anantharaman, K. Anggraeni and T.J. Foxon (2019) *The Circular Economy and the Global South: Sustainable Lifestyles and Green Industrial Development* (London, UK: Routledge).

So, R. (2014) Why We Shouldn't Subsidize the Recycling Business, *China Daily*. Hong Kong edn, 27 March. www.chinadaily.com.cn/hkedition/2014-03/27/content_17381528.htm (Accessed 30 August 2016).

Stavins, R.N. (ed.) (2012) *Economics of the Environment: Selected Readings*, 6th edn (New York: Norton).

Steffen, W., K. Richardson, J. Rockstrom, S.E. Cornell, I. Fetzer, E.M. Bennett, R. Biggs, S.R. Carpenter, W. de Vries, C.A. de Wit, C. Folke, D. Gerten, J. Heinke, G.M. Mace, L.M. Persson, V. Ramanathan, B. Reyers and S. Sorlin (2015) Planetary Boundaries: Guiding Human Development on a Changing Planet, *Science*, 347.6223: 1259855, 1–10.

Stern, N. (2006) *Stern Review: The Economics of Climate Change* (London, UK: HM Treasury).

Sullivan, R. and R. Chapman (2021) *A Guide to Investor Engagement on Plastic Packaging: Fast-Moving Consumer Goods* (Isle of Wight: UN Global Compact. Principles for Responsible Investment, in Collaboration with Ellen Macarthur Foundation).

Swiss Re (2021) World Economy Set to Lose up to 18% GDP from Climate Change if No Action Taken, Reveals Swiss Re Institute's Stress-Test Analysis. *News Release*, Zurich 22 April 2021. Swiss Re Ltd, Zurich. https://www.swissre.com/media/press-release/nr-20210422-economics-of-climate-change-risks.html

Thomas, V. and N. Chidarkar (2019) *Economic Evaluation of Sustainable Development* (Singapore: Palgrave Macmillan).

Tian, K., Y. Zhang, Y. Li, X. Ming, S. Jiang, H. Duan, C. Yang and S. Wang (2022) Regional Trade Agreement Burdens Global Carbon Emissions Mitigation, *Nature Communications*, 13: 408. https://doi.org/10.1038/s41467-022-28004-5

Tietenberg, T. and L. Lewis (2009) *Environmental and Natural Resource Economics*, 8th edn (Boston, MA: Addison-Wesley).

Turner, K. (1995) Waste Management, in H. Folmer, H.L. Gabel and H. Opschoor (eds.), *Principles of Environmental and Resource Economics: A Guide for Students and Decision-Makers* (Cheltenham, UK: Edward Elgar): 440–66.

United Nations (2015) *Resolution Adopted by the General Assembly on 25 September 2015 70/1. Transforming Our World: The 2030 Agenda for Sustainable Development*. A/RES/70/1. https://www.un.org/en/development/desa/population/migration/generalassembly/docs/globalcompact/A_RES_70_1_E.pdf.

US EPA (2010) *Guidelines for Preparing Economic Analyses* (Washington, DC: National Center for Environmental Economics. Office of Policy, US Environmental Protection Agency), 17 December (Part Updated May 2014).

World Economic Forum (2014) *Towards the Circular Economy: Accelerating the Scale-Up Across Global Supply Chains* (Isle of Wight: In Collaboration with the Ellen MacArthur Foundation and McKinsey & Company).

10

Human resources management

Developing a sustainability mindset

Daniel King and Elaine Cohen

Sustainable HRM (human resources management) is a combination of two elements: (1) *leveraging HR (human resources) tools and processes to support sustainable business objectives*, and (2) *performing HR sustainably*, that is, in a way which creates an organisational culture that is ethical, respectful, and inclusive, invests in the development of employees, and empowers them to engage at the maximum level of their capabilities (Cohen et al. 2012).

This chapter will help you to understand the role of HR teams in supporting sustainable business and the responsibility of HR teams to perform HR sustainably.

The learning outcomes of this chapter are:

- You will be able to describe how HR supports sustainable business and the connection between HRM and sustainability.

- You will be able to understand examples of the way HR practices affect society and possible ways to integrate social and environmental considerations into HR processes in order to improve the social and environmental impacts of business.

DOI: 10.4324/9781003294665-13

- You will know where to find more information and examples of good practice in the area of sustainable HRM.

- You will be able to understand some of the principles behind having a sustainability mindset.

Sustainable HR as part of sustainable business

It is increasingly clear that we are facing a global crisis around climate change with far-reaching ecological consequences that will significantly transform the business conditions for companies everywhere. Similarly, serious social issues, including racial inequities, large migrant populations, modern slavery, and as all will recognise, global public health challenges, such as the Covid-19 pandemic, are demanding urgent action from the global business community. As many of the contributors to this book have already stated, questions about how organisations are responding to these challenges are becoming more pertinent, as the consequences of organisations' impacts on the environment are now squarely in the spotlight (also see King and Lawley 2022). Consequently, there is a pressing need for deep and substantial change in how organisations operate, requiring rethinking of business models and operations, including the way they structure their workforce; design and manufacture their goods; use materials and resources, including renewable energy; manage complex supply chains; and build circular economy models, including recycling schemes, into their value chain.

One of the key features that distinguish sustainable organisations from business-as-usual organisations is that they accept **accountability for their impacts on people, society, and the environment** and demonstrate a willingness to **engage with stakeholders**, both internal and external, to gain an understanding of their expectations and assess the way business impacts their lives in a range of ways. In short, sustainable organisations require different approaches and priorities from conventional organisations, supported by new skills and capabilities.

While sustainability is often sought to be addressed from a technical perspective, with a hope that actions like the electrification of transportation or new production technologies will help to achieve net zero, the emotional, social, and cultural aspects of this transition receive less attention (Hermes and Rimanoczy 2018). Thinking in a sustainable way is a vital part of the transition that we all need in order to limit the impact of climate change and support the transition to a more sustainable planet and just society. Indeed, developing a sustainability mindset is a core aim of PRME, particularly the PRME working group on developing a sustainability mindset. 'Sustainable mindsets', a way of shifting how we are thinking (our mindset) towards sustainability, is thus an important part of organisations becoming more sustainable (Kassel et al. 2018; Hermes and Rimanoczy 2018; Rimanoczy 2021).

What has this to do with HRM? While the concept of sustainability mindsets has received most attention in terms of education, with authors arguing that management education should thus advance awareness of societal and environmental issues (Hermes and Rimanoczy 2018; Kassel et al. 2018), this chapter explores what goes on within organisations, arguing that one of the fundamental shifts that organisations need to face is for everyone in the organisation to develop a 'sustainability mindset' – and it is the role of HRM to help foster its development.

Developing a sustainability mindset

A precursor to the advancement of sustainability practice is the development of a sustainability mindset. A *sustainability mindset* is a way of thinking and being that comes from understanding the inextricable link between the natural environment and our own ability to thrive on the planet, and the interconnected nature of both on many dimensions. A sustainability mindset demands that we be reflective about our own values and adopt an approach to life (and business) that aims to produce outcomes for the greater good of all. Within this perspective of sustainable value creation, it is important that economic outcomes not be isolated from environmental and social developments. Isabel Rimanoczy argues that there are three elements to this way of thinking:

1. *The knowing* – becoming eco-literate and using systematic thinking.

2. *The being* – seeing yourself (and your actions) as part of a wider ecosystem, reflecting on your habits and values, having time for reflection, and having a larger sense of purpose.

3. *The doing* – being connected with your community, developing social sensitivity, and being innovative.

(2016: 155)

To support its development, the *PRME working group on developing a sustainability mindset* is an initiative connecting learning–teaching–research. The aim is to connect academics and practitioners interested in its development for employees and particularly students. Members of the group take existing research into developing a sustainability mindset and learn about how it can be adapted to their context. The aim is to develop a learning community of peer support to enable the members to find better ways of developing a sustainability mindset with their students (for more information, see PRME Working Group on Developing a Sustainability Mindset 2022).

Developing a sustainability mindset – the role of HR

To produce this change in mindset, sustainable HRM works by **leveraging HR tools and processes to support sustainable business**. This leveraging is the extension of the traditional 'HR business partnership role' (see Caldwell 2003). Rather than HR being the 'voice of the employees' or the 'instrument of management', or both, the more precise role of HR is to enhance organisational capability, by understanding what the business needs and what people, knowledge, skills, and culture need to be in place to deliver those needs. As companies increasingly adopt sustainable business strategies, HR's role needs to evolve, not only to be a 'business' partner, but also to become a 'sustainable business' partner.

In determining the appropriate business strategies to deliver growth and profit to the bottom line, a sustainable mindset demands consideration of both social and environmental needs, in addition to conventional economic needs. This requires active, engaged employees in transforming how the organisation is run, which is why sustainable HR is important. For instance, consider the processes of an organisation setting up a new manufacturing plant in accordance with 'green' principles. This starts with the commissioning of architects to incorporate eco-design elements that may include natural lighting, rooftop solar arrays to provide renewable energy, rainwater capture, and waste management facilities, including recycling systems, as well as modern collaborative workspaces that introduce plant life and recreational areas for more productive working. This entire design and construction process requires employees who have the skills and knowledge to lead and implement green practices. To make sustainability integral to the way the organisation is run, the mindset and outlook of the employees need to align with the organisational objectives.

This sustainability approach is vital for the organisation as a whole. Sustainability is based on fundamental elements of **good governance, ethical conduct, and compliance with the law**, while going beyond compliance with the law to generate additional opportunities to mitigate business risk, enhance business reputation, and take advantage of new business developments. In adopting a sustainability strategy, companies contribute not only to the sustainability of the planet but also to their own sustainability as businesses. This approach is changing the way businesses develop strategy; take decisions; execute processes; engage with employees, consumers, external pressure groups, and communities; and respond to the diverse expectations of all these groups in this fast-moving, transparent age of business. This requires not only a strategy for sustainable business but also a **culture** that supports strategy delivery.

Why develop a sustainability mindset – the economic case

While the ethical and moral justifications for developing a sustainability mindset are fairly self-explanatory, there are also economic justifications for being a sustainable business. From a long-term perspective, having a functioning and sustainable planet is a prerequisite for a functioning economy. Climate change is likely to bring increased droughts, floods, and temperature extremes, which will have direct impacts on all areas of the economy, including infrastructure, energy supply, agriculture, and the insurance industry, which has to pay for many of the outcomes of the changing climate. The challenge is that while transitioning to a net zero economy is essential to all of us and to generations to come, for an individual organisation, it might not be in their short-term interest. Many investors, recognising the importance of the long-term perspective, are shifting their investment portfolio to integrate low-carbon economy considerations. However, the picture is mixed, with investment fund managers BlackRock both setting up a $4.5bn climate fund at the same time as also continuing to invest in fossil fuels, which will accelerate climate change. However, the economic case is not simply about attracting investors: there is strong evidence that advancing sustainable practices in business increases profits and enhances an organisation's agility and innovative capabilities, thereby enabling it to take advantage of new business opportunities. Solar energy, for example, may require an initial investment, but over the long term, it delivers significant energy savings. Employing a diverse workforce may require initial additional recruitment efforts, but over the long term, diversity fuels innovation and competitive advantage. In fact, companies with sustainable practices can see increased employee productivity by up to 13% (Rochlin et al. 2015).

Sir Richard Branson, in his book *Screw Business as Usual*, argues that businesses should be a force for good in the world and that the conflict between doing good and being ethical is a 'false dilemma'. Whilst capitalism has 'created economic growth in the world and brought many wonderful benefits to people [it has] come at a cost that is not reflected on the balance sheet' (2011: 20–1). Being ethical and making money are therefore seen as not only possible but also desirable. For instance, research has shown that by investing in employee health and well-being, beyond the minimum requirements of law, a business will reap the benefits of improved employee motivation and productivity while contributing to a healthier and more vital society (Berry et al. 2010). By investing in community development activities, a business will make reputation gains which will serve its long-term ability to attract and retain investors and customers while strengthening the fabric of the local community from which it also draws resources (King and Lawley 2022).

Take, for instance, the recent scandal of the claims that the migrant workers who built the stadiums for the FIFA Football World Cup have endured 'persistent and widespread labour rights violations' (Pattisson 2022). As has been widely reported, many workers had unpaid wages, were not made overtime, worked in a culture of fear, and the working conditions were unsafe, with many workers who were involved in the construction having died (the exact numbers are disputed). Furthermore, some parts of the stadium are due to be dismantled after the World Cup. On moral grounds, the treatment of the workers has been criticised, as they work against the UN Sustainable Development Goals 1, no poverty; 2, zero hunger; 3, good health and well-being; 8, decent work and economic growth; 12, responsible consumption and production; and 13, climate action, due to the long-term use of the stadiums. Hosting the World Cup in Qatar has brought to attention wider human rights issues within the country, although it might also raise issues of sportswashing (where countries use sports to improve their reputation). What this scandal demonstrates is that there is increasing attention on the extent to which organisations (and countries) are acting in an ethical (and sustainable) manner.

Further, in today's 'war for talent', existing and potential **employees are searching for meaning** in their work, beyond receiving a salary at the end of each month (Ulrich and Ulrich 2010). Recent research suggests that Generation Y, people born between 1981 and 1996, who grew up in a more eco-conscious society, are more concerned with job fulfilment than financial gain, and Gen Z, those born between 1997 and 2012, are more environmentally orientated (Dabija et al. 2019), which could impact their orientation to work. Furthermore, research by Ohlrich (2015) argues that Generation Y graduates are attracted to companies not so much due to their CSR but because of the values by which the company operates. There are reports that the Covid-19 pandemic also led to many people reassessing their values and attitudes to work, with a recent survey by the insurance company Prudential finding that 48% of employees in America were rethinking their jobs due to the pandemic. This result was similar to responses to a survey in the UK by Aviva where 53% of employees wanted to change aspects of their work due to the pandemic (see King and Lawley 2022: 335). Having CSR policies therefore is not enough – it is about the wider values to attract high-quality staff.

Further research has shown that CSR 'enhances a corporation's reputation for prospective employees by increasing organizational attractiveness and firm familiarity, but also influences incumbent employees' (Gond et al. 2010: 34).

The business case for sustainability also makes claims about the potential economic benefits that can come for acting in a more sustainable manner. As the worldwide energy crisis which started in 2022 has highlighted, some sustainability measures, such as increased energy efficiency, can make very good economic as well as environmental sense. New market opportunities from more sustainable products also highlight the potential business case for more sustainable approaches.

The broader HR role in sustainability

The fundamental ability to deliver a strong sustainable business strategy lies with a company's leadership and is embodied in its **values, culture, capabilities, and communications**. This means embedding a **sustainability-enabled culture** throughout the organisation. Business leaders need to ensure that employees, the group which most influences a business's results and which is most directly influenced by the employment practices of the business, understand, engage with, and proactively advance the sustainability agenda.

HR teams are **critical partners** in making this happen. This means that HR must understand and engage with the new rules of business sustainability and align its support accordingly (Cohen 2010). For example, in a business which wishes to develop a new line of products marketed to women, a culture of **women's empowerment** within the business must be present for optimal results to be achieved. It can be argued that selling to women requires an understanding of women's needs and habits in relation to a particular product range. It is extremely challenging, if not impossible, for a business to succeed in marketing to women if women are not valued and empowered in the workplace. Helping to create **an inclusive culture** is a key role of the HR function, which, in this case, can support the achievement of specific business objectives. Not only this – there is a ripple effect in the local community when women are empowered.

Another example might be the process of achieving energy efficiencies as businesses work towards being part of a low-carbon economy. Many companies have found that the formation of '**green teams**' in the business assists in generating awareness of energy savings and recycling of waste among employees. Although they may be formed from volunteers within the business, green teams still require a framework of operation and a set of guidelines for ensuring they both deliver results and engage employees at different levels. In some cases, this might require specific training of employees, including green team leaders, or a broader communications process within the company. These are the tools that the HR function can provide, and in fact, HR is best positioned to provide such teamworking frameworks and processes. Green teams not only help a company reduce its costs and environmental impacts; they also engage employees in activities which enable them to experience additional purposeful contribution in the workplace. This has been correlated to increased retention, motivation, and engagement (IESE 2013). Not only this – there is, again, a ripple effect in the community. As employees learn the benefits of **environmental efficiencies in the workplace**, they may take this learning home and apply similar practices. This saves them money and also reduces the environmental burden of private energy consumption and waste, etc. Therefore, the role of HR in helping businesses become more sustainable can be demonstrated in different ways and requires an understanding by HR leaders and team members of **sustainable business priorities** and a sustainability mindset.

Performing HR sustainably

Equally as important as supporting business objectives is the way HR performs its traditional functions so that, even in cases where sustainable business strategy has not been specifically articulated, **HR remains accountable for its impacts on society and the environment**. The implications on society of HR decisions in almost all aspects of HR work can be far-reaching, well beyond the primary considerations of business growth and profitability. Closing a factory, for example, and laying off employees may have extensive implications for the social and economic well-being of a local community. While sustainability or HR considerations may not be enough to prevent closure, the way in which the HR leadership defines strategies to communicate, execute plans, and support employees through a life-changing event can make a critical difference to individuals and families within the community. Sustainability, in this sense, means that HR considers these implications when formulating HR policies, plans, and programmes. To implement these decisions effectively, therefore, requires a sustainability mindset.

Traditional core HR functions include recruitment and retention, training and development, compensation and benefits, organisational development and internal communications. HR has an inherent accountability to consider the **broader implications of HR decisions,** not only on employees, but also on employee families, communities, economies, and society in general (see Figure 10.1).

By recruiting a **diverse workforce** which is inclusive of different racial or ethnic groups in society, or by ensuring the recruitment of locals into key roles rather than expatriating managers for short time periods, HR plays a role in strengthening the fabric of local society. By investing in the employability of individuals in the organisation and helping them manage their own careers, HR supports a more robust economy in today's society, where 'jobs for life', once a key promise of many companies, can no longer be guaranteed. By paying a fair wage, or what is often called a '**living wage**', HR makes a difference by helping to reduce poverty in countries of operation and encouraging **investment back in the community**. By providing benefits such as health insurance and wellness programmes, HR contributes to a healthier society and reduces the burden of healthcare costs on economies and societies.

In so many ways, the decisions made by HR departments have potentially far-reaching and short- and long-term consequences for society, beyond the considerations of an individual company and its employees. While HR cannot be expected to single-handedly solve all of society's problems and inequalities, a **sustainable HR function understands the impacts it creates** and considers these broader needs when formulating policies.

Figure 10.1: Examples of the connection between HR policies and social and environmental impacts.

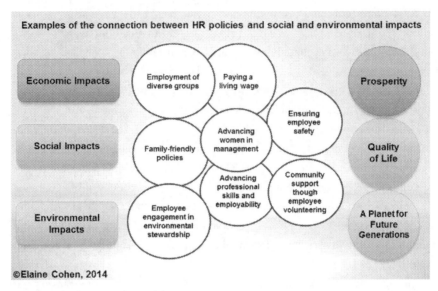

Source: Author's personal materials.

Take for example the oil and gas development company Tullow Oil plc. Tullow operates facilities in Ghana and therefore has a vested interest in helping develop a local skilled workforce that can maintain and grow its operations in the country. To this end, Tullow advances a localisation strategy, with an aim of ensuring 90% of its workforce is drawn from within the country. This strategy both supports long-term business continuity and cost-effectiveness as well as contributing to the economic and social development of their host country, Ghana. To achieve this, Tullow invests in education, training, coaching, mentoring, and career development programmes for its workforce. With its sustainability mindset, the Tullow HR team in Ghana works tirelessly to help identify opportunities for more locals as the business grows (Tullow Oil 2021).

Sustainable HR metrics

An important part of sustainable HRM is defining and tracking metrics that show how the organisation (and the HR function) is contributing to sustainable business objectives as well as operating as a responsible corporate citizen. Table 10.1

Table 10.1: Examples of HRM metrics and connection to business outcomes and value

HRM role	HRM objective	HRM metric	Business value
Values and ethics	Employees understand and behave in line with corporate values	Percentage of employees trained in values and ethics	Mitigation of risk due to unethical behaviour by employees; Improved corporate reputation and trust
		Percentage of employee responses in survey showing employee support for company values	
Recruitment	Recruitment based on diversity principles	Percentage of employees recruited by gender and by minority groups	Improved business results, innovation, and customer satisfaction
Compensation	Compensation driven by equal opportunity for men and women	Ratio of base salary men to women	Lower HR costs due to turnover, improved motivation, and trust
	Compensation linked to sustainability performance	Number of employees with sustainability targets in annual work plans	Improved execution of sustainable business strategy
Well-being	Employees fit to contribute to their maximum capability	Percentage of employees who engage in a corporate well-being programme	Reduced business health costs, lower absenteeism, improved productivity
		Percentage improvements achieved in employee well-being (health, stress, diet, etc.)	
Development	Diverse employees given opportunities to advance	Percentage of women in management positions	Improved business results, innovation, and customer satisfaction
		Percentage of minorities in management positions	
Engagement	Employees understand and act in line with sustainability strategy and principles	Percentage of employees trained in sustainability	Improved execution of sustainable business strategy
	Employees enhance corporate community relations	Percentage of employee volunteers	Employee engagement, reputation benefits, enhanced community relationships
	Employees contribute to improving environmental impacts	Percentage of employees participating in 'green' activities	Energy and material cost reductions

Source: Author's personal materials.

shows some examples of the HR contribution and the aspects of business value that can be calculated.

Opportunities for sustainable HR management

Beyond fulfilling traditional roles as mentioned earlier, HR has an opportunity to use tools provided by a sustainable business approach to **engage employees in sustainable practices**. These are practices not typically undertaken by traditional HR managers and may include supporting environmental stewardship through **green team** development or encouraging employee volunteer programmes in the community. **Raising awareness** is the first step in changing practice. **Employee volunteering programmes** offer an excellent opportunity to help develop a sustainability mindset. Volunteering programmes can help opportunities to connect with your community (the doing) and, by meeting new people, provide space to reflect on your personal values (the being) (cf. Rimanoczy 2016). The business also benefits through increased employee satisfaction, motivation, and loyalty, as well as innovative opportunities for employees to gain new experiences and enhance their skills. For example, the healthcare company GSK (GlaxoSmithKline) reports a 47% higher rate of promotion among employees who have participated in the company's PULSE volunteer programme (Korngold 2014: 122). GSK, as well as other companies, such as IBM and Intel, maintains extensive volunteer programmes which involve sending employees outside of the organisation for weeks or even months to participate in volunteer activities to support social causes, often in emerging economies. The overriding experience of these employees is one of **learning, personal growth and development, leadership**, and communication and teamworking skills, which they bring back to benefit the business. In other cases, companies maintain many different types of volunteering programmes, from a one-day annual corporate event for all employees to ongoing local activities in different operating locations. The global telecommunications networks company Ribbon Communications, for example, holds an annual HR-led Global Day of Service in which employees are offered a day of paid time off to volunteer to support social and environmental causes in their communities (Ribbon Communications 2022). In the 2021 Global Day of Service, which ran over a period of one month, 700 Ribbon employees engaged to support more than 50 non-profits in 16 countries, volunteering more than 2,500 hours of service during this month alone.

Whatever the nature or scale of volunteering activities, they universally contribute to motivation and skill development. HR must be a partner in developing such programmes in a way which meets both community needs and also strategic HR needs.

HR's role in protecting human rights

The United Nations Global Compact principles for responsible business include the following statements that that businesses should:

1. Support and respect human rights

2. Make sure they are not complicit with human rights abuses

3. Give employees freedom of association (to practice collective bargaining)

4. Eliminate forced and compulsory labour

5. Abolish child labour

6. Eliminate discrimination

(for more information, see UN Global Compact 2022)

While for many large corporations these might seem to be issues that might not concern them, on closer inspection, it can be a complex role for HR. Management of **human rights** is not something HR managers traditionally tend to consider as part of their job description. Most HR managers are conversant with labour laws or have in-house legal counsel. But human rights in a company's supply chain often go beyond the minimum requirements of law, especially if a company is operating in emerging economies, where legal frameworks are less developed or minimally enforced. This does not responsibility relate only to staff who are directly employed by the firm but also for those within the supply chain. For instance, a survey conducted by the Hult International Business School in conjunction with the Ethical Trading Initiative found that 71% of firms felt there was a likelihood of modern slavery occurring at some point in their supply chain (Lake 2016). Ensuring a supply chain free from child labour, forced labour, human rights abuses, and discrimination has now also become part of the role of HR management and goes beyond traditional relationships with suppliers and outsourcing vendors based on procurement contracts focusing on price, quality, and service. For example, many companies have established ethical sourcing policies which require suppliers to commit to maintaining human rights and employee rights in their companies. HR management has a role in assisting in the establishment, implementation, and control of ensuring human and labour rights due diligence in a company's own operations as well as advancing a similar level of control in its supply chain. For an overview of the complex range of human rights issues, including with suppliers in a global supply chain, see Unilever's Human Rights Progress Report. Given the new focus on human rights, many companies now publish accounts of their performance, relying upon HR colleagues as partners and contributors.

Diversity, equity, and inclusion

Diversity, equity, and inclusion (DEI) are complementary dimensions of a fair and just workplace. *Diversity* means engaging a workforce that is reflective of the communities in which a business operates. *Equity* means tailoring policies, processes, systems, and opportunities in ways that make it possible for all individuals to participate on an equal footing. *Inclusion* means creating a workplace culture in which differences are embraced and valued so that everyone feels they belong and are empowered to participate. Taken together, these three elements of DEI are the basis for a socially just and organisationally effective workforce.

There are many aspects of diversity. Gender diversity has long been on the organisational (and HR's) agenda, based on the realisation that women have been disadvantaged in the workplace, both in terms of their being recruited into positions of leadership and management and in terms of equal pay for equal work. Most large companies today have targets to advance gender diversity – some even go as far as to aspire to gender balance, where women will make up 50% of the workforce and 50% of the leadership. In the UK, companies are required to measure and annually report the gender pay gap – the difference in pay for women and men in same jobs. Some companies also report this at a global level.

The PRME working group on gender equality. This PRME working group was formed in 2010 by the UN Global Compact and UNIFEM, now UN Women (see www.unwomen.org). The aim of this PRME group is to 'help the private sector focus on key elements integral to promoting gender equality in the workplace, marketplace and community' (PRME working group on gender equality 2016).

Their main objectives are:

1. **Teaching:** creating an interdisciplinary network of academics, employers, and other stakeholder interested in getting gender issues on the business school curriculum and creating resources.

2. **Research:** advocating research into gender issues and creating case studies.

3. **Practice:** encouraging a wide range of PRME partners and working groups to consider gender issues and how they integrate into practice.

For further info, see: PRME Working Group on Gender Equality (2022).

Another important aspect of DEI relates to racial and ethnic minorities. In the wake of George Floyd's brutal killing by the police in May 2020, systemic racial inequities became a topic of intense focus in the media throughout the world. One aspect of this is increased awareness of the experiences of People of Colour within the workplace and how policy, practices, and cultures can end up excluding or marginalising certain groups of people. HR teams in many companies had to quickly turn their attention to their own performance on the inclusion and equitable practices for racial and ethnic minorities in the workplace and develop new strategies to meet social demands as well as explicit demands for accountability from investors.

Principle 6 of the UN Global Compact states that businesses should work on the elimination of discrimination in respect of employment and occupation. It highlights how discrimination (through conscious or unconscious bias) can arise throughout a variety of work-related activities, including recruitment, security of tenure, training, and development through to promotion, as well as through compensation and benefits policies. For example, LGBTQ policies that support same-sex partner benefits are becoming the norm. The Human Rights Campaign Corporate Equality Index publicly ranks companies on their LGBTQ-inclusive policies and practices (Human Rights Campaign 2022).

Advancing DEI has business benefits as well as ethical ones. Drawing from a diverse pool of applicants can help organisations in the 'war for talent'; it can lead to better decision-making, as a wider range of perspectives is available, and it can also mean that the organisation is more representative of its client group (King and Lawley 2022). Creating an inclusive culture can also enable everyone to achieve their potential. More diverse and inclusive teams can also lead to more original and creative thinking. Despite these tangible economic reasons, diversity, equity, and inclusion are still a challenge for many organisations. One issue is that forms of exclusion, such as microaggressions, are not always obvious. Whilst direct discrimination may be apparent, indirect forms can be harder to spot. Developing a sustainability mindset can produce a stronger awareness of such indirect forms by helping to understand forms of exclusion that might not be immediately obvious for those who have not faced similar situations (for instance, a childless man might not notice the challenges faced by women or men in bringing up children).

Employee wellness

Beyond the requirement of compliance with health and safety laws, which is often an operational, not HR, responsibility, there exists great opportunity for HR management in **advancing employee wellness in the workplace**. Wellness and well-being are concepts which are not usually mandated by law but which can help organisations care for their employees; save on healthcare costs; protect business continuity; improve employee retention, morale, and productivity; and at the same time, improve their impacts on society.

The last few years have seen an explosion in interest in well-being, with many organisations intensifying their attention on well-being during the Covid-19 pandemic as employees faced unprecedented challenges introduced by lockdowns and the increased levels of uncertainty this created (Brown et al. 2022). Furthermore, there are attitude and generational shifts with many employees: younger employees appear more comfortable speaking out about their mental health and are prepared to prioritise it. Thus, we are moving to an environment where conversations within organisations around mental health are increasingly occurring, providing opportunities to develop workplaces which encourage wellness and well-being, where HR has the potential to take the lead in shaping. HR-led mental health taskforces are now springing up in many organisations to help legitimise conversations about stress, work-related pressure, depression, and other mental health challenges and enable individuals to receive support. HR can provide tools, processes, and internal communications to help the organisation development mechanisms and approaches to think more holistically and creatively around well-being. In this way, the HR function can demonstrate a direct contribution to the business's bottom line, a perfect match of sustainability and business objectives.

Summary

The previous examples show how HR can leverage its core competencies in any company to support sustainable business objectives and perform HR sustainably. In doing so, HR must be concerned not only with the business objectives defined by management and employee needs but also with the **wider impacts of HR decisions** and performance on **communities and the environment**. The essence of this approach is for HR managers to understand the concepts, principles, and strategy of **sustainable business** and to recreate HR management processes in a way that leverages HR capabilities for the broader good, not only of the company and its employees, but also of society as a whole.

Suggested sessions

The following sessions take you through a series of activities that ask you to think about some of the types of HR issues that you might face in an organisation. In doing these activities and thinking about the social, political, and economic consequences of your actions, you are beginning the process of developing a sustainability mindset, one of the key topics for this chapter. Therefore, doing these activities, and discussing your ideas with others, is a useful way of developing yourself for your current and future roles.

Session 1: Case study – sustainable HRM reporting

Split into teams of two. Each team selects a sustainability report published within the past year by an organisation of your choice. These are freely available to download from the corporate websites of companies that report on sustainability. Each team should analyse the report and identify all the disclosures relating to employees and human resources practices. Formulate answers to the questions listed.

Report analysis questions (60 minutes)

1. What aspects of human resources practices are referenced in the report?
2. Of all the human resources elements disclosed by the company, which would be the most important for you and why, if you were:
   a. A shareholder in the company?
   b. An employee of the company?
   c. A potential recruit?
   d. A family member of an employee of the company?
   e. A local city council official in a city where a number of the company's employees are located?

3. Review commonalities and differences in the way companies report on human resources aspects of their sustainability performance. What can you infer from the content and style of their disclosures about the organisational culture of the company?

4. Review whether the disclosures related to human resources and organisational development are linked to the business performance of the company, and if so, state in what ways. What metrics connect HR performance to business results?

5. Have these disclosures increased your level of trust in this company?

6. Would you want to work for this company?

After you have answered these questions in your teams, get together as a group and review your findings. Consider the differences and similarities and the elements which have inspired greater trust in the company as a result of their sustainability disclosures.

As a group, agree on the top five characteristics of HR sustainability reporting that you feel are essential to any sustainability report on HR practices.

Session 2: Sustainable organisation culture

In a sustainable organisation, as in any organisation, the underlying culture can be both a reflection and a predictor of sustainable business results. In a sustainable organisation, values are emphasised as part of the organisation's way of operating, communications are frequent and intensive, and individuals feel instilled with a sense of purpose and are empowered to make a difference. More than concerned with their specific roles and direct business results, they are conscious of their responsibilities to society and the environment and the impacts which result from the things they do and the way they do them. These impacts are felt both internally and externally. In the sustainable organisation, values must offer a certain common ground to enable the wide engagement of employees in a shared culture which continues to respect and celebrate the diversity of individuals.

It is always difficult to assess how people understand and prioritise values and therefore what is necessary in order to motivate and frame common behaviours driven by shared values. Describing values in visual terms is often an excellent way of demonstrating alignment or otherwise, with the values which underpin a sustainable business.

In this session, participants have the opportunity to create a visual expression of the way they see sustainable organisations add the values that helped them become sustainable.

This session requires teams of four working together. The tools required are large 1 m² canvases (on easels, if possible), paints, and paintbrushes.

Each team should collaborate to create their portrait titled 'The Ideal Sustainable Company'. No more than 40 minutes should be allocated to creating the portrait.

Once all the portraits are complete, each team should present its picture to the other teams, explaining the different elements in the image and why priority has been given to certain elements. Following the presentations, a group discussion should address the following questions:

1. What were the common visual elements in the portraits?

2. What were the values that stood out as the most significant in all the portraits?

3. Did different visual elements portray the same values or different values? What does this tell us about the way values can be embedded in organisations?

4. What does this exercise tell us about the values that we see as important for sustainable organisations? Would we have created different portraits 20 years ago? Are any of these visual elements used in employer branding of companies that you are aware of?

5. Did the process of creating the canvasses engage team members in discussion about the relative importance and prioritisation of different values for sustainable organisations? Would this be a useful exercise to conduct within company teams?

Session 3: Case study – diversity and inclusion

Read the following case study. Engage in a discussion and respond as a group to the questions at the end of the case study.

Diversity and inclusion

You are the HR manager of a supermarket chain which has been expanding rapidly in your country and is poised for overseas expansion in the coming years. You know that the ability of the company to expand depends on a constant stream of recruitment of the right-quality people at all levels in the organisation. In fact, you have specific recruitment objectives which are more challenging than at any time in the past. You are very aware of the 'war for talent' and the fact that there is great competition for good people, especially university graduates. After talking with colleagues in the market, you and your HR team realise that you must proactively seek out innovative ways to attract new talent to your company. You believe that this means leveraging your reputation for sustainability more effectively during the recruitment process, as well as broadening your recruitment channels and reaching out proactively to a more diverse range of candidates from different backgrounds and minority groups.

Typically, diversity has not been a focus of your company, and no special efforts have been made to increase diversity. In fact, this is not something that you and your HR team have focused on in any way in the past. Your workforce is predominantly led by males, while most of the unskilled roles are performed by women (e.g. checkout cashiers, shelf stockers, cleaners, etc.). The workforce barely includes people with disabilities, and ethnic groups in the population are not significantly represented.

In order to compete effectively in the 'war for talent', you believe your company must significantly rethink the way it recruits and whom it recruits, in order to exploit fully the potential talent available in the market. Not only must the company now learn to recruit in a more diverse way; the organisation must also be able to take diverse candidates on board successfully and enable them to progress within the company over time. You charge yourself with delivering a plan to attract, recruit, advance, and retain diverse candidates to meet the targets defined by your CEO within three years:

- 25% of the workforce (currently 10%) should be sourced from diverse groups.
- 20% of management (currently 5%) should be women.
- 5% of management should be from diverse groups (currently zero).

It won't be easy!

Questions for discussion

1. Who is affected by this situation, and what is the impact on them? List all the relevant internal and external stakeholders and implications for them in this change in policy.

2. What tools does the HR manager have to increase diversity in recruitment processes? Which new channels can the HR manager open up? How do recruitment processes need to change?

3. What sort of organisational culture is necessary in order to attract, recruit, and retain more diverse people? What needs to be done to ensure the right culture is in place? Which key HR processes and tools are required?

4. Which tools does the HR manager have to measure the impact of this change in policy on the business results, organisational culture, employees, local communities, and the local economy? Which performance indicators should be developed to measure success?

Output required

1. State the top three actions you recommend the HR manager should advance during the next 12 months.

2. Explain why these are the most important things you should do.

3. Explain the role of the CEO and other managers in supporting this programme.

Additional teaching material and ideas

Made in Dagenham

www.imdb.com/title/tt1371155/

This movie is a dramatisation of the 1968 strike at the Ford Dagenham car plant, where female workers walked out in protest against sexual discrimination. There are several important elements in this movie which relate to the nature of power relationships in the workplace and the strength and courage it takes to drive change in support of human rights at work. While this scenario may seem rather outdated, the challenges of women in achieving equal rights are still relevant today in many workplaces, not to mention the challenges of other groups, such as the LGBT (lesbian, gay, bisexual, transgender) community. This movie can be the basis for a discussion about what needs to change in order to ensure that equal opportunity and equal rights become reality in all workplaces, and whose responsibility it is to fight for those rights.

BITC (Business in the Community) Responsible Business Tracker

www.bitc.org.uk/the-responsible-business-map/

The Business in the Community Responsible Business Tracker is a measurable tool to support organisations assess which areas they have strength in and what areas they need to work on to achieve positive societal and environmental outcomes. The BITC Tracker sees that there are five areas to being a responsible business, around purpose and values, governance and transparency, stakeholder engagement and community collaboration, value chain and digital transformation. For each area there is a desired outcome that is based on the UN Sustainable Development Goals. They see purpose-driven leaders as vital to create this healthy business. It is interesting to explore this map, the tracker.

UN Global Compact

www.unglobalcompact.org/

The UN Global Compact is a voluntary framework for responsible business based on ten principles which have been accepted by thousands of business organisations around the world. Seven of the ten principles have a clear link to HRM and HR process as they relate to upholding human rights, labour rights, and maintaining an ethical culture which opposes corruption. The UN Global Compact is rich with information, reports, and tools which can assist business in understanding the issues and developing management approaches and can be used in designing learning exercises in different areas of sustainable HRM.

UN Sustainable Development Goals

www.un.org/sustainabledevelopment/sustainable-development-goals/

The United Nations Sustainable Development Goals (SDGs) were ratified by more than 180 member nations in 2015 as a blueprint for global prosperity. The 17 goals are supported by specific targets in a range of social and environmental sustainable development areas, such as ending hunger, ending poverty, reducing social inequalities, mitigating climate change, and more. While it is designed to motivate and guide national governments in a shared sustainable development agenda, businesses around the world have galvanised support for the SDGs and are aligning their own sustainable development actions to advance the achievement of the SDGs. In all areas, HRM can be a significant partner by developing HR policies and processes to support these objectives. It is worth HR teams familiarising themselves with the SDGs, the rationale behind each, and the plans to achieve them, in order to be empowered to support their businesses effectively. The UN SDG website contains a wealth of information in each of the goal areas.

Further readings

Cohen, E. (2010), *CSR for HR: A Necessary Partnership for Advancing Responsible Business Practices* (Sheffield, UK: Greenleaf Publishing).

> The HR department can and should play an important role in CSR. This book is designed to assist practitioners in understanding how CSR is changing the HR function. It outlines the implications of the growing importance of CSR for different HR functions, examines how HR can help embed CSR, and proposes the infrastructure needed. Effectively, *CSR for HR* is a guide for HR professionals in how to adopt a CSR approach to HRM.

Cohen, E., S. Taylor, and M. Muller-Camen (2012), *HRM's Role in Corporate Social and Environmental Sustainability* (Alexandria, VA: Society for Human Resource Management).

> This report begins by examining the critical role HRM plays in sustainability and the HRM tools available to embed sustainability strategy in the organisation.

The second section introduces a road map to sustainable HRM. It outlines global business approaches to sustainability, labour standards, and specific aspects of sustainable practice, such as employee volunteering, employer branding, and green HRM. Finally, the report explores the new HR skills required for practising sustainable HRM and the applicability of sustainable HRM in different types of organisations.

King, D., and S. Lawley (2022), *Organizational Behaviour* (Oxford: Oxford University Press).

This introductory text on organisational behaviour features issues around sustainability and CSR, inclusion, and diversity (particularly around leadership) and issues on developing a more critical and sustainability mindset. It offers many real-life cases of companies that have been criticised for their actions as well as examples of organisations that are developing a growing reputation for CSR. It also includes interviews with important business leaders around the issues of sustainability (particularly in the car industry) and ethical action (in the banking sector).

Rimanoczy, I. (2021), *The Sustainability Mindset Principles: A Guide to Develop a Mindset for a Better World* (London: Routledge).

This new book introduces 12 principles for a sustainable mindset and provides guidance for educators and practitioners for how to help people develop them. While not exclusively written for HR professionals, many of these examples, checklists, tips, and tools will be directly relevant to practitioners within this field.

SHRM (Society for Human Resource Management) (2011), *Advancing Sustainability: HR's Role* (Alexandria, VA: Society for Human Resource Management).

The majority of organisations in the United States are engaged in some form of sustainable work practices, and of those that have calculated the return on investment, almost half have reported a positive outcome. This research is based on a 2010 survey of 728 HR professionals in the United States. Other noteworthy findings were that the three key drivers for these activities were contribution to society, competitive financial advantage, and environmental considerations. Moreover, one of the most important positive outcomes from sustainability initiatives was improved employee morale. In this report, you will find examples and case studies from a range of organisations and sustainable workplace practices.

Sunley, R., and J. Leigh (eds.) (2016), *Educating for Responsible Management: Putting Theory into Practice* (Sheffield: Greenleaf).

This PRME-backed book covers many of the central principles and ideas behind PRME and gives some ideas about their implications for the teaching of management education. It covers areas such as developing a responsible mindset through to the role managers can play in creating a more meritocratic workplace. It will be of interest to those that teach HR and potential future HR managers in how to help promote and develop a sustainability mindset and change management education.

References

Berry, L., A.M. Mirabito and W.B. Baun (2010) What's the Hard Return on Employee Wellness Programs? *Harvard Business Review*, December: 2012–68.

Branson, R. (2011) *Screw Business as Usual* (London: Virgin Books).

Brown, S., L. Baczor, D. Dahill, D. King and S. Couloigner (2022) *Impact of COVID-19 on Psychological Wellbeing in Occupational Contexts* (Nottingham: Nottingham Trent University).

Caldwell, R. (2003) The Changing Roles of Personnel Managers: Old Ambiguities, New Uncertainties, *Journal of Management Studies*, 40(4): 983–1004.

Cohen, E. (2010) *CSR for HR: A Necessary Partnership for Advancing Responsible Business Practices* (Sheffield: Greenleaf Publishing).

Cohen, E., S. Taylor and M. Muller-Camen (2012) *HRM's Role in Corporate Social and Environmental Sustainability* (Alexandria, VA: Society for Human Resource Management).

Dabija, D.-C., B.M. Bejan and V. Dinu (2019) How Sustainability Oriented is Generation Z in Retail? A Literature Review, *Transformations in Business & Economics*, 18(2).

Gond, J.P., A. El-Akremi, J. Igalens and V. Swaen (2010) *Corporate Social Responsibility Influence on Employees*, available at www.nottingham.ac.uk/business/ICCSR/assets/muihqm luwosf.pdf, accessed 31 March 2014.

Hermes, J. and I. Rimanoczy (2018) Deep Learning for a Sustainability Mindset, *The International Journal of Management Education*, 16(3): 460–7.

Human Rights Campaign (2022) Corporate Equality Index 2022, *Human Rights Campaign*, available at www.hrc.org/resources/corporate-equality-index, accessed 20 November 2022.

IESE (2013) Corporate Volunteering, *Expatriatus Blog*, available at http://blog.iese.edu/expatriatus/2013/11/23/corporate-volunteering-what-does-the-latest-research-say, accessed 20 November 2022.

Kassel, K., I. Rimanoczy and S. Mitchell (2018) A Sustainability Mindset Model for Management Education, in *Developing a Sustainability Mindset in Management Education* (London: Routledge): 3–37.

King, D. and S. Lawley (2022) *Organizational Behaviour* (Oxford, UK: Oxford University Press).

Korngold, A. (2014) *A Better World, Inc.: How Companies Profit by Solving Global Problems* (New York: Palgrave Macmillan).

Lake, Q. (2016) HR's Role in Combatting Modern Slavery, *HR Magazine*, available at www.hrmagazine.co.uk/article-details/hrs-role-in-combatting-modern-slavery, accessed 20 November 2022.

Ohlrich, K. (2015) Exploring the Impact of CSR on Talent Management with Generation Y, *South Asian Journal of Business and Management Cases*, 4(1): 111–21.

Pattisson, P. (2022) World Cup Stadium Workers 'Had Their Money Stolen and Lives Ruined', Says Rights Group, *The Guardian*, available at www.theguardian.com/global-development/2022/nov/10/world-cup-stadium-workers-had-their-money-stolen-and-lives-ruined-says-rights-group

PRME Working Group on Developing a Sustainability Mindset (2022) *Description*, available at www.unprme.org/working-groups/display-working-group.php?wgid=3344, accessed 15 November 2022.

PRME Working Group on Gender Equality (2022) *Description*, available at www.unprme.org/working-groups/display-working-group.php?wgid=2715, accessed 15 November 2022.

Ribbon Communication (2022) Sustainability Report 2021–2022, *Ribbon Communication*, available at https://ribboncommunications.com/sites/default/files/2022-10/Sustainability%20Report%202022%20Ribbon.pdf, accessed 20 November 2022.

Rimanoczy, I. (2016) A Holistic Learning Approach for Responsible Management Education, in *Educating for Responsible Management: Putting Theory into Practice*, edited by Sunley, R. and Leigh, J. (Sheffield: Greenleaf Publishing).

Rimanoczy, I. (2021) *The Sustainability Mindset Principles: A Guide to Develop a Mindset for a Better World* (London: Routledge).

Rochlin, S., R. Bliss, S. Jordan and C.Y. Kiser (2015) *Defining the Competitive and Financial Advantages of Corporate Responsibility and Sustainability* (Boston: IO Sustainability).

Tullow Oil (2021) *Focus on a Better Future: Tullow Oil Sustainability Report 2021* (Tullow Oil), available at www.tullowoil.com/application/files/6016/4811/4973/Tullow_Sustainability_report_interactive.pdf, accessed 20 November 2022.

Ulrich, D. and W. Ulrich (2010) *The Why of Work* (New York: McGraw Hill).

UN Global Compact (2022) *The Ten Principles of the UN Global Compact*, available at www.unglobalcompact.org/what-is-gc/mission/principles accessed 20 November 2022.

11
Sustainable marketing

Helen Goworek and Angela Green

In this chapter you will learn about ways in which businesses can conduct their marketing activities more sustainably and how we can harness our power as consumers to reduce sustainability impacts. After reading this chapter, you will be able to:

- Relate marketing theory to sustainability.

- Understand how the key aspects of marketing are linked to sustainability.

- Examine recent academic and industry developments in this field, in terms of both theory and practice.

- Understand how marketers and consumers can lower their sustainability impacts and encourage more sustainable production (SDG 12).

Introduction

This chapter aims to give an overview of contemporary developments in sustainable marketing. This topic is viewed from two perspectives: firstly, the marketing of products and services which are sustainable, and secondly, using marketing techniques which are, in themselves, sustainable. Marketing may be viewed as a

DOI: 10.4324/9781003294665-14

dynamic and popular aspect of business for students, yet its appeal may be somewhat tainted by its propensity to encourage over-consumption, which can result in the depletion of natural resources and create negative environmental impacts.

Literature on sustainable marketing is relatively limited and recent, with most of the key books on this topic having only been published since 2009 (e.g. Arnold 2009; Dahlstrom 2011; Martin and Schouten 2012; Carvill et al. 2021). However, earlier ground-breakers were writing journal articles about the topic more than a decade ago (e.g. Carrigan and Attalla 2001), thereby sowing the seeds for more recent research (Kemper and Ballantine 2019). Those researching into sustainable marketing and consumer research are often practitioners working in this field (e.g. Arnold 2009; Carvill et al. 2021; Smith 2021) or business academics, dispersed across various global regions. The chapter explains how marketers have the capacity to affect Sustainable Development Goals via many of their actions, for example, by discussing issues that enable marketing specialists to reduce their impact on climate change (SDG 13). Marketers can directly influence both consumer behaviour and production patterns to encourage lower sustainability impacts in each of these key areas (SDG 12).

Sustainability was famously defined by the United Nations Brundtland Commission (1987) as 'meeting the needs of the present without compromising the ability of future generations to meet their own needs'. This idea is easily extended to marketing, by noting that marketers must make decisions today that do not disadvantage future generations of consumers, thus promoting the notion of intergenerational justice and reflecting some of the many ethical dimensions of marketing. Marketers have been inspired by a wide range of different disciplines, and the interdisciplinary nature and systemic thinking of sustainability therefore lend themselves well to marketing's eclectic mix of influences, drawing as it does from the fields of psychology, sociology, accountancy, finance, political science, design and geography, etc. Marketing has a key role to play in a business's approach towards sustainability, since it is the main interface between the organisation and consumers (Martin and Schouten 2012). Lunde (2018) proposes an integrated model of sustainable marketing (referred to as GREEN) that includes macro-marketing issues as well as the more common strategic and tactical marketing issues. However, it should be acknowledged that a tension exists between marketing's goal of encouraging consumption and sustainability specialists' aim to reduce consumption of resources, as explored by Bolton (2021). Nevertheless, sustainability has clearly become a significant issue for consumers. The Ethical Consumer Markets Report has provided updates on ethical spending in the UK for over 20 years, and its latest report demonstrates that expenditure grew significantly from £11.2 billion in 1999 to £122 billion in 2020 (Co-operative Bank 2021). Sustainable consumer behaviour has therefore become a key area of interest within the marketing literature, making it the focus of various studies (e.g. Wrigley 2008). Marketers can gain an understanding of how to influence the implementation of sustainable production patterns, consequently facilitating sustainable consumption, to meet SDG 12.

Marketing focuses on the creation of value, which can be viewed more broadly than solely from a financial perspective, since sustainability also has a high level of value in connection to the continued prosperity of society. Indeed, **sustainable marketing** is defined by Martin and Schouten (2012: 10) as 'the process of creating, communicating and delivering value to customers in such a way that both natural and human capital are preserved or enhanced throughout'. A subsection of sustainable marketing is **green marketing**, since it concentrates on environmental sustainability, described by Dahlstrom (2011: 5) as 'the study of all efforts to consume, produce, distribute, promote, package and reclaim products in a manner that is sensitive or responsive to ecological concerns'. The term 'green marketing' could be criticised, however, for being limited to environmental issues, without comprising important social sustainability issues, as well as potentially giving consumers and investors the impression that it is linked to 'greenwashing'. Dahlstrom (2011) exhorts governments, non-governmental organisations, consumers, retailers, manufacturers, and service firms to engage in green marketing due to a variety of factors:

- Environmental benefits
- Support for developing economies
- Consumer benefits
- Strategic benefits for organisations
- Product benefits
- Production process benefits
- Supply chain benefits

More recently, Papadas et al. (2017) have described green marketing as having three key dimensions, consisting of strategic, tactical, and internal orientations.

This chapter's session content will draw both from students' business knowledge and their experiences as consumers. The key points are based on the standard marketing mix framework: product, price, promotion (i.e. marketing communications), and place (i.e. distribution channels). Though additional marketing paradigms such as relationship marketing have emerged (see following text), the marketing mix is deemed as being suitable for framing such a complex subject, since business students are very likely to have prior knowledge of it. Sustainability can be built into products (or services) at the development stage, and it also has relevance to the rest of the marketing mix. Overall, this chapter will review ways in which marketers can address sustainability issues in both their everyday practice and longer-term strategy. In doing so, it focuses largely on PRME principle 1 and principle 3, by developing students' capabilities to generate sustainable value for businesses, facilitated by the provision of relevant educational materials.

Sustainable marketing strategy and planning

Creating a marketing strategy is generally the responsibility of marketing managers or directors, derived from the corporate strategy that is usually devised by an organisation's senior management team. For marketing strategy to be effective, it needs to be aligned closely with the overall corporate strategy and the strategies of other divisions within the organisation, such as finance, procurement, human resources management, design, and logistics. The inclusion of a sustainable approach within the corporate strategy can facilitate the development of a marketing strategy that recognises the significance of lessening the company's sustainability impacts and thereby assist in enhancing the organisation's overall sustainability performance. It has become standard practice for retailers, as well as many companies in other sectors, to incorporate CSR (corporate social responsibility) policies into their corporate strategies, thus making societal marketing (a close relation to social marketing) more widespread, as long as those policies are implemented in practice. Since the **marketing planning** process includes an audit of the environment in which the organisation operates, incorporating both external and internal factors, sustainability is a key factor to be taken into account. Marketers have traditionally worked within (and often encouraged the existence of) a linear economy, that is, a system that largely draws upon raw materials to manufacture products, which are disposed of after usage, even if those products are still usable. However, the concept of the circular economy is becoming increasingly significant in relation to sustainable consumption, in that consumers can reuse, recycle, repurpose, and re-sell products to extend goods' useful lives (see Claudy and Peterson 2022).

Figure 11.1: Stratasys 3D printer (left) and *Crania Anatomica Filigre,* 3D-printed artwork by Joshua Harker (right).

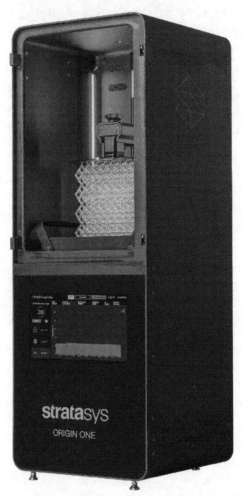

Source: Courtesy of Stratasys (left) and Joshua Harker (right) (www.joshharker.com).

Of the PESTEL factors (political, economic, societal, technological, environmental, and legal) that are investigated by marketers when assessing the macro-environment, ecological issues are the most obvious factors to examine in relation to sustainability, in line with SDG 15 (which aims to protect and restore the use of ecosystems). However, a broader approach can be taken by recognising that each of the PESTEL macro-environmental areas can also be considered in terms of sustainability. For example, technological advances can be used to make products and processes more environmentally sustainable. Innovative digital technology such as design software or 3D printing have become more widely accessible (see Figure 11.1) and can lessen the wastage and use of materials for prototypes, with the extra advantage of speeding up the process. Nevertheless, these technologies are likely to reduce, rather than eliminate, sustainability impacts, since fossil fuels are needed to operate them, for example, the energy, plastic, and embodied carbon involved in 3D printing. 3D printing has applications for art, prototyping, and production (see artwork by Joshua Harker in Figure 11.1) and has been used in house construction in Amsterdam, employing a bioplastic made from 75% plant oil blended with microfibre (Nield 2014), and in Germany, where the first building to meet the approval of national building regulations was constructed in 2020 (PERI 2020).

Furthermore, marketing strategies usually begin with STP (**segmentation, targeting, and positioning**). Segmentation divides consumers into groups with similar needs and characteristics. Organisations can then target these selected market segments by devising an appropriate marketing mix which aims to place the company, brand, or product in a particular position in the consumer's mind. Encouraging consumers to perceive sustainability as an integral component of a brand's market position is becoming a key feature of many organisations' STP strategies. When marketing plans are devised to put strategies into practice, they can have a substantial impact on customers, the environment, and society in general, as discussed in the following.

Sustainable consumer behaviour

Consumer behaviour (CB) is the study of who buys and what, how, when, where, and why they buy (Jobber and Ellis-Chadwick 2019) and, increasingly, how they dispose of, repurpose, and select new or used products. The consumption of products and services clearly has significant sustainability impacts, with effects stretching well beyond the realms of marketing and business. Traditional CB models are predicated on the notion that marketers should seek to increase sales of products and services, and consequently, a need exists for contemporary models that incorporate sustainability issues. One of the most widely used CB theories is the CDP (**consumer decision process**). Developed by Engel et al. (1968), this theory assumes that consumers follow a series of logical, rational steps when making consumption decisions.

Figure 11.2: The CDP (consumer decision process) model.

1. Need recognition

2. Information search

3. Pre-purchase evaluation of alternatives

4. Purchase

5. Consumption

6. Post-consumption evaluation

7. Divestment

Source: Adapted from Blackwell et al. (2001).

Consumer decision-making

The CDP model originally included five phases: problem recognition, information search, evaluation of alternatives, purchase, and post-purchase use. Tellingly, this version was inspired by earlier models of buyer behaviour in industrial markets (Robinson et al. 1967; Webster and Wind 1972) which did not acknowledge the disposal of products after the purchase decision. A more recent adaptation with further steps developed by Blackwell et al. (2001) includes consumption, post-consumption evaluation, and divestment (i.e. disposal) stages (see Figure 11.2). This updated model encourages marketers to reflect on the longer-term impacts of their products on the environment and also has the potential to address sustainability issues more fully, for example, by including more sustainable options in the 'evaluation of alternatives' phase, and is therefore compatible with consumption within a circular economy. Using this model, marketers can look beyond the current marketplace to consider how the resources used in products and services today can avoid disadvantaging future generations of consumers.

There appears to be a prevailing view in many societies that a high level of consumption equals success, leading to conspicuous consumption, where purchases are displayed ostentatiously and shopping is perceived as a leisure activity. These attitudes towards purchasing are frequently stimulated by marketing activity to persuade shoppers to spend more, an unsustainable situation that leads to unnecessary usage of raw materials, particularly fossil fuels used in the manufacture and delivery of products.

Market segmentation in terms of sustainability

Market segmentation is traditionally based on consumers' demographic, psychographic, geographic, or behavioural characteristics. Demographics are factual details about consumers, such as age, whereas psychographics are aspects of lifestyle and behavioural segmentation that group consumers by their frequency of use of a product or service, for example, loyal or occasional customers. In various countries, market segmentation categories based primarily on the sustainability of consumers' behaviour have been developed. An example of this is the Framework for Pro-environmental Behaviours developed for the UK government (Defra 2008) categorising consumers into seven different groups from the sustainability-orientated 'positive greens' through to the opposite extreme:

1. Positive greens

2. Waste watchers

3. Concerned consumers

4. Sideline supporters

5. Cautious participants

6. Stalled starters

7. Honestly disengaged

Figure 11.3 describes the characteristics of each of these categories and positions them in terms of their willingness and ability to act in a sustainable manner. This type of model assists marketers in identifying, understanding, and consequently responding to customer requirements, thus enabling sustainable CB by the provision of products and services, allowing more sustainable purchase decisions to be made. It is anticipated that the proportion of the population in each category will change over time and be dependent upon the location of the market. Through the use of STP, marketers can understand that different groups of consumers have different value 'equations'. When framed around value, the marketing mix then becomes the means through which marketers match the different value equations for different groups of consumers. The various consumer segments in the framework in Figure 11.3 each have different value equations, thereby requiring different marketing mixes.

Studies have been conducted to investigate consumers' lack of willingness to purchase products with low sustainability impacts. For example, according to Eckhardt et al. (2010: 426), 'many consumers profess to want to avoid unethical offerings in the marketplace yet few act on this inclination'. Although people

Figure 11.3: A framework for pro-environmental behaviours.

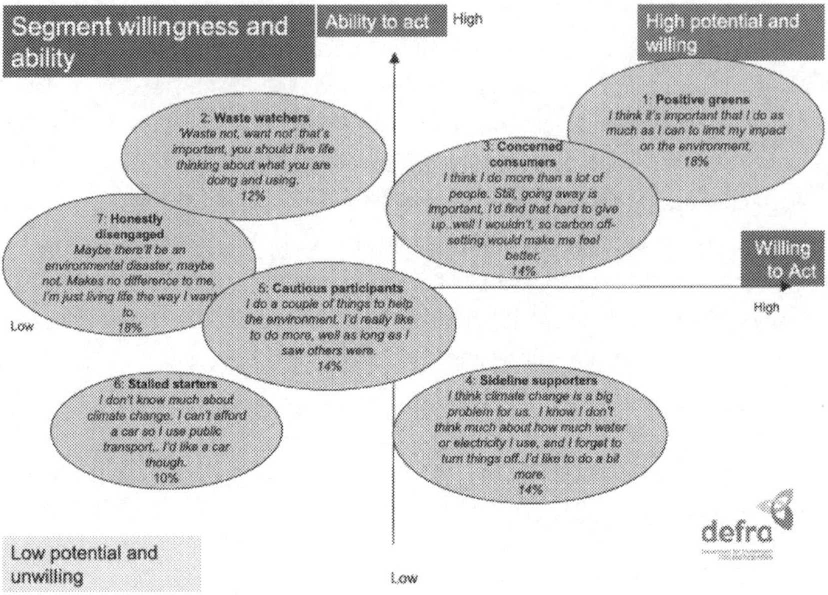

Source: Defra (2008).

do not appear to wish to be viewed as behaving unethically, there is a disconnect between their behaviour and their professed opinions, widely known as the 'attitude–behaviour gap'. Some people in Eckhardt et al.'s (2010: 434) research did change their behaviour, but they were exceptions, and all respondents offered justifications for unethical behaviour. The authors therefore concluded:

> The nature of the rationales suggests that simply making information available to consumers about the ethical nature of their purchases, or even using moral appeals to try and invoke behavior change, will not likely engender anti-consumption of unethical or irresponsible brands. . . . Strong emotional appeals rather than rational or moral appeals may have a better chance of making the luxury of consumer ethics more appealing and the case for action more compelling.

However, in the UK, a more recent study exploring factors that might help consumers adopt more sustainable shopping behaviours reported that 25% of consumers wanted to see advertising that positioned sustainability as the norm and as desirable (Deloitte 2021).

Another study in this area compared **sustainable consumption** patterns in different markets. McDonald et al. (2009: 141) found that sustainability criteria are used inconsistently across product sectors:

> For example, the same consumer may prioritise environmental criteria in his/her purchase of FMCGs [fast-moving consumer goods], consider them when buying white goods or flights, but ultimately sacrifice them in favour of availability or convenience, and not take them into account at all during the purchase of small electrical products. Equally, consumers focus on different green or ethical criteria in different product sectors.

CB is already a complex area that marketers are seeking to understand with the assistance of various methods, including **consumer neuroscience** (Serrano and de Balanzo 2011), and issues of sustainability and ethics add a further dimension of complexity to these issues that researchers have begun to explore (e.g. Smith 2021).

Sustainable products and brands

There is a lack of consensus about what constitutes sustainable products and brands. The terms 'green' and 'eco' have been widely applied to products, but since they have no precise definition, it is not clear to consumers whether they are made entirely of renewable resources or simply have less impact on the environment than competing merchandise. Martin and Schouten (2012: 140) define a **sustainable brand** as being 'economically enduring and its associations in the minds of customers and other stakeholders rightfully include social justice and ecological sustainability', thereby aligning such brands with Elkington's (2004) 'triple bottom line' (environmental, social, and financial sustainability).

Certain brands are inherently sustainable, having been built on sustainable values, for example, the Body Shop and Howies. Other brands and retailers take a more limited approach to sustainability by offering a small selection of 'environmentally friendly' or Fair Trade products, such as Adidas's FutureCraft shoe, which is 100% recyclable (Adidas 2019). Most major car brands have incorporated improved fuel efficiency and more sustainable design into their product ranges in recent years, including hydrogen fuel cell cars from Hyundai and Toyota. The automotive industry clearly has a great deal of scope for improvement in terms of its impact on the environment, and it is now becoming standard practice for concept cars to include more sustainable features as we head towards legislation that will substantially change this market, for example, banning the sale of diesel and petrol cars in the UK from 2030. Many major brands and retailers in other product sectors, such as Nike and Marks & Spencer, also seek to incorporate sustainable values within their brand images. This trend is likely to have been prompted by criticism from pressure groups and consumers against major brands, which escalated during the 1990s. Various studies suggest that a socially responsible approach to business could be related to strong business performance. For example, Martin and Schouten (2012: 139) state that 'a study by Interbrand finds a correlation between CSR and brand value', and Waddock and Graves found a positive link between CSR and financial performance as long ago as 1997. More recently, a study by Papadas et al. (2019) also revealed that internal green marketing has the potential to enhance an organisation's competitive advantage.

Sustainable products can be environmentally or socially sustainable, and some brands combine both aspects, for example, People Tree garments are manufactured only by Fair Trade companies, as well as being made from materials such as organic cotton. Handmade cosmetics retailer Lush sells 'charity pots' of hand-and-body moisturiser in its stores, donating the selling price (minus sales tax) to charity (see Figure 11.4). The lotion contains organic ingredients and is socially sustainable through offering grants from its proceeds to groups in the UK and overseas that aim for long-term positive change to human rights, the environment, and animal protection, some of the groups being featured on the recycled/recyclable pots. Sustainable products have been criticised for being unfashionable in previous decades, but many now combine strong design with sustainable materials, offering functional and aesthetic properties alongside sustainability.

Environmentally sustainable products can take various forms, being made of materials which are recycled, recyclable, reused, repurposed, or a combination of more than one of these aspects, many of which are compatible with a circular economy. For example, Freitag makes durable messenger-style bags from recycled truck tarpaulins, and former fashion label 'From Somewhere' designed clothing from pre-consumer waste fabric from luxury brands, thus saving it from disposal. More recently, North Face has produced clothing made from plastic bottles collected from the foothills of the Himalayas and Alps.

Durability is perhaps a less-conventional way of viewing sustainable products, by manufacturing them for longevity rather than disposability (Cooper 2010). Products and services can therefore have sustainability built into them via various processes

Figure 11.4: Charity pots from Lush incorporate both environmental and social sustainability.

Source: Courtesy of Lush.

and choices of materials, with marketers and designers being central to sustainable decision-making. Product development can adopt a 'cradle to cradle' approach, which advocates extending the life cycle of products or materials through their reuse, in preference to the prevalent 'cradle to grave' method of disposing of items before the end of their usable life (Braungart and McDonough 2009). Furthermore, retailers and brands can implement a policy to 'choice-edit' products to include an offer to customers that only consists of environmentally and socially sustainable products.

The concept of extended producer responsibility (EPR) is a policy approach in which organisations retain responsibility for products after their sale and usage by consumers (OECD 2022). EPR is intended to incentivise the reduction of waste by companies, aligning with the motivation to engage in more sustainable new product development and the macro-environmental trend towards sustainable consumption behaviour, aiming towards increasing integration of products within the circular economy.

Sustainable integrated marketing communications

This section discusses how sustainable products can be promoted to customers. Integrated marketing communications (IMC), largely synonymous with the 'promotion' element of the 4Ps, consists of five core tools: advertising, public relations (PR), direct marketing, personal selling, and sales promotion (Baines et al. 2022). Sustainable IMC can be viewed from two main perspectives: the promotion of sustainable products and services and promoting products and services using sustainable methods. A key IMC issue is that overstating the sustainable values of products has led to accusations of **greenwashing** against the brands that sell them. Companies may also be accused of 'greenwishing' if they are overly optimistic in stating the proximity to achieving their sustainability goals. Many companies have therefore become somewhat reticent about making claims that reveal the sustainable nature of products. Consequently, consumers can find it even more difficult to discover which products they could purchase to enable them to lessen their sustainability impacts, yet they would be willing to receive more information to allow them to do so (Fisher et al. 2008; Deloitte 2021).

Advertising is likely to be the most high-profile aspect of promotion to consumers and may often be seen as synonymous with marketing. It is undoubtedly a major element of the marketing communications mix, involving *promotion where space or time in a media channel is paid for by the advertiser*, for example, in a TV advert or in a banner advert or promoted content on social media. Advertising is therefore an area of promotion where brands have a high level of control in that they make their own decisions on the messages, visual imagery/audio content, location, and media vehicle/s in which they advertise, leading to it being a relatively expensive choice in comparison to other methods of promotion. However, with significant changes in the proportions of different media channels being viewed by consumers, advertising has become less important overall than in previous years, compared to other promotional techniques. It is therefore essential for marketers to be aware of these changes in order to implement effective and sustainable marketing communications campaigns. Market penetration of digital technologies is growing rapidly, and globally, most people had online access by 2017 (Ryan 2017). Digital technologies like the internet, email, and social media are providing ways for marketers to connect and build relationships in a more sustainable format than traditional print and broadcast media. There has been a tendency in recent years to move away from relying on the 'hard sell' of broadcast and print advertisements towards digital advertising and 'soft sell' forms of promotion, such as online PR (**public relations**) and **word-of-mouth** (Meerman-Scott 2020). *PR differs from advertising in that the space in which the brand or product discussed is not paid for.* For example, an article written about a brand by a journalist in a newspaper or a positive post about a sustainable product on social media (where no payment has been made to the social media platform itself for the post). Social media and mobile apps have been particularly useful to organisations looking to build deeper levels of attachment with their customers (Hollebeek et al. 2014; Kim and Baek 2018). Consumers can use digital technologies to share, interact, connect, and exchange information with brands and other customers. Often, the main purpose of these interactions is not to close a sale but to create added value to the consumer in some other way (Gill et al. 2017). Using these methods, businesses can showcase their position on sustainability, highlight the measures they are taking to improve sustainable practice, and generally demonstrate how they add value to the consumer and the environment. The clothing brand Patagonia (eu.patagonia.com) uses its digital tools to promote its stance on anti-consumerism, which is interesting for a clothing retailer, whom you might expect to want to sell more. Instead, it provides information on how consumers can repair, reuse, or recycle their clothing. These digital methods, usually facilitated by the internet, could be considered to be more sustainable than using printed promotional material, although this may not always be the case, since computers generate carbon emissions in their manufacture and transportation (i.e. embodied carbon: see Chapter 5), and they may use fossil fuels as an energy source, whereas print media can be both renewable and recyclable.

Social media has provided consumers with new ways to explore, assess, and purchase goods and services. It has supplied the means for consumers to communicate directly with brands but has also enabled the formation of brand communities where consumers can contact one another. In its broadest sense, it incorporates interactive internet-based technologies, like **blogs** and **micro-blogs** (e.g. Twitter, Tumblr, and Reddit), **social networking sites** (e.g. Facebook and Instagram), **collaborative platforms** (e.g. Wikipedia and Google Drive), **content community sites** (e.g. YouTube and Flickr), and sites dedicated to feedback (e.g. Tripadvisor and Trustpilot) (Mangold and Faulds 2009; Alves et al. 2016).

Influencer marketing is a strategy that leverages the reach and credibility of social media influencers, including Instagrammers, YouTubers, bloggers, etc., to augment marketing efforts and communicate with wider audiences. Influencers have the power to affect the buying behaviour of others, and if chosen correctly by brands, they can create considerable impact. Marketers can use digital tools, such as www.buzzsumo.com, to identify key influencers in a chosen field. In return for free products or financial benefits, influencers are compensated for posting comments about brands on their own channels. Brands wanting to communicate their sustainability messages to others might work with key influencers who have a large following in this area. Technically, using influencers for promotion is a PR technique, rather than advertising, since the media space itself (i.e. the social media platform) is not usually paid for by the organisations who are promoting their products. However, this can potentially be at least as expensive as advertising, since the influencer is usually paid by the relevant brand for sharing social media posts with followers. Marketers have an opportunity to distribute their communications budgets amongst various influencers (or 'micro-influencers' who have smaller numbers of followers, specifically focused on a relevant area) to connect more effectively with highly targeted consumer groups than traditional media may allow.

Hashtags were originally introduced to help users structure and organise content on social platforms, but they have since become an integral part of contemporary communications (Rauschnabel et al. 2019). The hashtag is the hash symbol (#) followed by a specific word or phrase (with no gaps or punctuation) that is used to identify a topic, often found in messages posted on social media. They can be used to increase engagement by linking people to larger conversations on particular topics. Identical hashtag phrases can be used by marketers across different social media platforms, making it easy for consumers to remember and search. Within the area of sustainability, some of the common hashtags used include: #Sustainability, #Environment, #ClimateChange, #greenbusiness, #ecofriendly, and #recycling (London School of Public Relations 2020).

Unlike traditional forms of one-way marketing communication, digital engagement initiatives tend to be interactive and elicit participative experiences (Gill et al. 2017), often encouraging consumers to create **user-generated content (UGC)** and upload it to their social platforms. UGC may be viewed as more credible and therefore more influential, as it is not created by the brand or organisation (Roma and Aloini 2019; Geurin and Burch 2017) and often includes uploading photographs or reviews about products and services, which are then used by the brand in their promotion. However, one of the challenges with this method is the lack of control a business might have over content that is uploaded (Geurin and Burch 2017). **Word-of-mouth communication** is considered to be one of the most

impactful forms of promotion, since unpaid comments from consumers can create a more robust image of authenticity and reliability. Electronic word-of-mouth
(eWoM) messages can now be distributed more rapidly than in previous generations by using social media, which can be advantageous for companies but can also
accelerate the circulation of criticism of a brand, for example, regarding unsustainable features of products or greenwashing claims.

Virtual reality (VR) is a technology that provides marketers with the opportunity to create digital experiences in place of physical ones. Consumers can be fully
immersed in a virtual computer-generated environment that is usually accessed
through a VR headset, thus potentially saving the usage of resources required in
the creation of real-life surroundings used for marketing purposes.

Augmented reality (AR) is another emerging marketing trend that uses technology to overlay (i.e. augment) sound, graphics, or text over the real world.
Unlike VR, it doesn't take consumers to a digital world as such but adds elements
to supplement their existing real world. In contrast to VR, AR doesn't require a
headset and can usually be seen by using a mobile device. For example, the banana
brand Chiquita used blue stickers on its bananas to take shoppers and retailers on
a journey to learn about the brand's commitment to sustainability. It is clear that
VR and AR technologies can provide scope for future marketing activity. The
additional benefit afforded by these tools is that they can be considered sustainable
methods. For example, consumers can use VR to visit places in different countries
or locations, thus reducing the need to travel.

Direct marketing involves promotional messages being communicated directly
to individual consumers, traditionally sent via post, typically to an organisation's
existing or potential customers. Direct marketing can now be distributed more sustainably and economically by email, thus saving on paper, printing, postage, and
distribution associated with mailshots (Goworek and McGoldrick 2015). Direct
marketing is often used as a key component of **relationship marketing (RM)**,
which is viewed as an alternative method of engaging with consumers rather than
focusing on the marketing mix. Derived from business-to-business (B2B) marketing, as well as from traditional relationships between tradespeople and customers,
RM is defined by Blythe (2013: 368) as 'the practice of concentrating on the lifetime value of customers rather than their value in the single transaction'. Building
up this longer-term relationship often involves personalised communication being
sent to consumers via direct marketing messages, which can help convey organisations' sustainability values.

Sustainable pricing

As consumers seek to purchase increasing numbers of products, under the pressure of marketing stimuli and peer groups, retailers and brands may reduce prices to fulfil their customers' desire to buy more. This can lead to the production of excessive amounts of products that not only use up valuable raw materials but can also lead to more pollution from manufacturing as well as increased landfill waste. Reduced prices are also central in problems concerning social sustainability, with competitive prices driving manufacturers to pay low wages and offer poor working conditions. Problems with low prices are not restricted to the cheaper, so-called 'value' end of the mass market, as illustrated by the tragic Rana Plaza factory collapse in Bangladesh in 2013, which resulted in more than 1,000 deaths and many injured victims. Products were manufactured in this building not only for low-priced retailer Primark but also middle mass-market companies Inditex and Mango, among others. Therefore, paying a mid-level retail price for a product is no guarantee that it has been made by operatives with good employment conditions, and the purchase price does not indicate the cost price that has been paid by the retailer to the supplier. Although minimum wages were increased in Bangladesh after the disaster, this does not ensure that all their factories will give pay rises (Thomasson 2014), and it does not address safety issues or in any way compensate for the devastation and loss of life which has occurred. Consequently, at New York Fashion Week in February 2014, activists projected photos of victims of the Rana Plaza disaster onto the Lincoln Center to publicise the real price of non–socially sustainable fashion (Malik Chua 2014).

Marketing managers, buyers, designers, technologists, and merchandisers working for manufacturers, brands, and retailers can all take on responsibility for questioning and investigating whether operatives in (and beyond) the clothing sector have decent wages and working conditions that allow SDG 8 to be met by promoting sustainable economic growth and decent employment. Organisations and their employees can share and learn good practice by becoming members of relevant industry bodies and non-government organisations (NGOs) that promote sustainability issues, such as the Ethical Fashion Forum (www.ethicalfashionforum.com) and the Ethical Trading Initiative (www.ethicaltrade.org). Membership of these organisations can enable businesses to acquire the knowledge to meet principles 3 to 6 of the UN Global Compact (www.unglobalcompact.org/what-is-gc/mission/principles) more effectively.

An obvious issue with the pricing of sustainable products and services is that they are frequently perceived as being more expensive than standard items. This can be the case when, for example, products or their components are organic, leading to lower yields for land in comparison to produce grown using pesticides, as well as payment for the process of organic certification. Similarly, premiums paid to farmers for **Fair Trade** goods or socially responsible donations to the community where products are manufactured inevitably add extra costs. However, a sustainable approach to business also has the potential to reduce costs, for example, by eliminating waste or using recycled products or more energy-efficient transportation. High costs may also be associated with sustainable products because many have been introduced at the higher end of the market and products can consequently become more cost-effective when they reach the mass market, due to achieving economies of scale. Through advance planning, it is possible for the costs associated with sustainability to be 'designed out' of products, for example, incorporating solar panels into buildings during construction is more economical than adding the panels at a later stage. Manufacturers are able to calculate more realistic product costs by considering their full impact on the environment, using **life cycle assessment**, defined by Dahlstrom (2011: 137) as 'accounting for production and processing as well as resource energy, usage, emissions and waste'. Through the process of segmentation and targeting, sustainable marketing seeks to meet the needs of consumer segments that are willing to pay higher prices precisely because this consumer segment finds value in the sustainable goods which they purchase, for example, Fair Trade coffee or electric bicycles.

Sustainable distribution channels

Distribution channels for products and services have several facets relating to environmental and social sustainability issues: the use of materials in the selection of products they offer, the materials used to construct the retail environment, and the social sustainability of employees in manufacturing, transportation, warehousing, and retailing. Although all types of organisation can address sustainability, retailers are uniquely positioned in the distribution chain at the nexus between suppliers and consumers, interacting directly with both of these stakeholder groups and thus being able to exert a strong influence upon their sustainability impacts. **Etailing** (online retailing) has become a key part of the retail market, and this is growing further through the widespread use of mobile devices (m-tailing), which was accelerated by the safety of shopping from home during the Covid-19 pandemic. Since it acts as a filter between suppliers and consumers, as well as being a significant source of private sector employment, retailing is an industry which can have the greatest potential impact upon society and its ability to behave sustainably, possibly even more so than any other societal group.

The following list proposes techniques that can be used by retailers to exert a positive influence on sustainable practice:

- Encouraging suppliers to behave more sustainably in the ways that they source, manufacture, and deliver products (see Chapter 10).

- Choice-editing by sourcing and selling products that offer only environmentally and socially sustainable choices to consumers (see earlier text).

- Minimising energy consumption in distribution and premises.

- Implementing sustainable store design (or sustainable online retailing).

- Minimising disposal of waste, particularly to landfill.

- Recycling or using recycled/repurposed materials in products and premises.

- Educating and enabling consumers to behave more sustainably.

Retailers can educate customers by offering sustainability guidelines online or in-store for their customers to act upon, to alter ingrained habits. Each of the tactics listed has financial implications for retailers, but they are not all negative, as many could be implemented at relatively low cost or help reduce costs. Implementing these techniques could decrease the possibility of legislation or regulations regarding sustainability being imposed on retailers in the future (Goworek et al. 2012). However, many companies may welcome the introduction of legislation to ensure a more 'level playing field' among competitors.

Conclusion

The consequences of living unsustainably have been represented by the film business in the form of disaster movies (Blincoe 2009), thus potentially making consumers feel helpless to act. Rather than presenting the world as hurtling inevitably towards adversity, more positive motivation can be given to consumers with examples of scenarios in which sustainable behaviour could potentially avert such a crisis. In higher education, business and marketing academics can create and disseminate such scenarios via curricula, assignments, and employment opportunities which can enable them to address the PRME principles. Marketing educators have numerous opportunities to encourage others to behave more sustainably within their institutions and as consumers, such as:

- Seeking out literature on sustainable marketing to incorporate into module reading lists, post on intranet pages, order for the library, and share with colleagues in their own departments and at other universities.

- Passing on information to encourage sustainable CB in students who are in other departments.

- Facilitating opportunities for staff to meet to discuss sustainable marketing issues.

- Encouraging the formation of student groups interested in sustainability and marketing, for example, by booking rooms or offering online events.

- Disseminating information to friends and relatives about behaving more sustainably as consumers.

- Generally encouraging the purchase of products which have low sustainability impacts.

Organisations often take action in response to sales figures, complaints, and negative publicity, and therefore, consumers also have the potential power to encourage businesses to behave more sustainably through the following actions:

- Buying products which have low sustainability impacts, to encourage companies to offer more of them in future.

- Buying fewer products overall but selecting goods which are more durable.

- Asking questions of businesses about sustainability, for example, whether they sell Fair Trade merchandise or avoid using palm oil.

- Contacting companies to complain when they offer limited or no ranges of sustainable products.

- Posting reviews about products or services in relation to their sustainability on companies' websites or third-party review websites.

- Contacting the media about experiences with businesses in relation to sustainability.

In conclusion, the **extended marketing mix**, or 'seven Ps', can be applied to services marketing, with the addition of people, physical environment, and process. It could be argued that, alternatively, the three Ps of the triple bottom line, 'people, planet, and profit', could be added to the traditional '4Ps' marketing mix to make a new seven Ps framework for the sustainable marketing of products and services.

Suggested sessions

Session 1: Sustainable products

In this session you will investigate your own behaviour in relation to sustainability and the products you buy. The activities in sessions 1 and 2 address SDG 12, which aims to 'ensure sustainable consumption and production patterns'.

Activity 1 (15 minutes)

Working in pairs or small groups, list specific examples of your own sustainable practice relating to the products you buy, for example, buying durable goods, choosing products made from renewable, recycled, or repurposed materials, and recycling products afterwards. You can also include sustainable practices you've heard of other people using, or you could create new ideas.

Activity 2 (10 minutes)

Now, describe and discuss some of the things you do where the sustainability impacts could be improved, for example, where you send used materials to landfill or purchase products from unsustainable sources.

Activity 3 (30 minutes)

Consider what influenced (or could influence) you to adopt the practices in activity 1. What are the barriers to you behaving more sustainably when shopping, consuming, or disposing of products, in relation to the outcomes of activity 2? Make suggestions of ways in which these barriers could potentially be removed. For example, this could involve policy changes by retailers, your university/college, companies, the government, and you or your peer group. As a result of this discussion, specify three key suggestions for removing barriers to consumers behaving more sustainably, to discuss with the rest of the session group.

Session 2: Sustainable consumer behaviour exercise

In this session you will investigate your behaviour as a consumer in relation to sustainable consumption.

Activity: sustainable CB focus group (55 minutes)

Split the session group into teams of around eight to ten students. One person in each team should be appointed as a moderator, and another should take on the role of note-taker, leaving six to eight people to take part in a focus group. The briefing for the activity should take up to five minutes. The moderator needs to manage the discussion without offering their own views, to avoid influencing the group's perceptions, whilst keeping the discussion on track. Group members should be allowed to offer their opinions, and all of them should be drawn into the conversation at some point by the moderator (except for the note-taker).

The moderator should introduce the topic of sustainable CB and read the questions that follow to the group, allowing each question to be explored by the participants before moving on to the next one. Prompts can be used to extend the conversation. Each group should discuss the issues in these questions for around 30 minutes. The note-taker should make notes on the key points of the discussion, to summarise participants' views. It is not essential for each group to complete all the questions, as long as there has been interaction and debate about sustainability issues between group members. The lecturer can observe part of each group's discussion and may wish to support the moderator in ensuring that all participants become involved.

After the group discussions, the next ten minutes should be taken up with feedback by the note-taker and moderator of each group, summarising the views of the participants to the whole session group and noting where the groups had responses in common with each other. This could include the written notes being shown on a visualiser. In the final ten minutes, the whole session group should be drawn together by the lecturer and asked to discuss potential implications of the findings from this session for manufacturers and retailers.

Discussion group questions

These questions have been adapted from those used within a study funded by Defra (Fisher et al. 2008) to establish the public's understanding of sustainable clothing consumption. The full report and appendices are available to download online at: Science Search (defra.gov.uk) (see Appendices, p. 35, in the report).

Introduction by moderator

This discussion session is about the sustainability impacts of clothing. We will discuss how you obtain your clothes, how you look after them, and what you do when you no longer need them. We want to encourage you to be open and honest with your contributions and feel free to disagree, but please respect the fact that other people are entitled to hold different views from you, by only speaking one at a time. Also, we will aim to enable everyone to contribute equally to the discussions. What you say is to be considered confidential within this session group.

Key questions

1. **Obtaining clothes.** First of all, we're going to talk about buying clothes. What kind of information informs your clothing purchasing decisions (e.g. adverts, magazine articles, brochures, seeing new clothes on friends)?

2. Do you feel that you usually buy clothes having recognised a need for some or for the pleasure of shopping?

3. Do you always buy your own clothes, or do your family or partner ever buy them for you?

4. What kind of clothes would you think of as 'sustainable' and why? Does anything influence your decisions about which clothes are sustainable? (Use these prompts if needed: brand, fabric [e.g. organic], durability, and manufacturing conditions.)

5. Do any of you buy sustainable clothing? If so, can you give some examples (e.g. sustainable brands and fabrics)?

6. **Clothing use and maintenance.** Next, we want to consider issues to do with washing, drying, and caring for your clothes. What are the usual elements in your laundry routine? (Prompt if necessary by asking whether they sort, wash, dry, and iron or dry-clean.)

7. Do you separate different types of items (e.g. colours and fabrics)? If not, why?

8. Do you always use a washing machine or sometimes hand-wash?

9. Which machine wash temperature do you use and why?

10. How do you dry your clothes? (Prompts: tumble drying, line drying, using an indoor clothes airer.)

11. If you normally use a tumble dryer, what are your reasons for doing this? Do you consider the money or energy involved in using it?

12. Do you or anyone else in your household ever repair clothes? If not, what puts you off doing this? (Prompts: lack of skill, equipment, or time or it's cheaper/easier to replace them.)

13. **Disposing of clothes.** What influences how long you keep clothing? (Prompts: it's gone out of fashion, worn out, or a poor fit.)

14. What sort of clothes do you put in the rubbish bin? What do you do with other types? (Use prompts if needed, for example, give to a charity shop or jumble sale, put it in a clothing recycling bin/bank, give it away to friends or family, take it to a clothes exchange party, sell it via a car boot sale, eBay, Amazon, etc.)

See also 'Which (2022) Washing Machine Temperature Guide', 28 September 2022, available online at: https://www.which.co.uk/reviews/washing-machines/article/washing-machine-temperature-guide-aLiyf2p96y4d

Session 3: Sustainable retailing exercise

This session will focus on the ways in which retailers can behave more sustainably, addressing sustainable industrialisation (SDG 9) and the impacts of climate change (SDG 13). This also relates to PRME principle 2, to incorporate global social responsibility values within curricula.

Working in small teams of two to four students, select a bricks-and-mortar retailer that you believe has the potential to improve its sustainability impacts. This could be one which is already improving its sustainability impacts or one which does not seem to have done this at all. This retailer could be selected at the previous session so that students have the opportunity to visit one of the company's branches beforehand and to look for ideas of good practice in terms of sustainability in other organisations, as well as assessing the company's website.

Teams may all choose the same retailer or different ones. This source could be used as background reading: 'Timberland opens new purpose-led flagship', News, Dalziel & Pow (dalziel-pow.com).

Activity 1 (10 minutes)

Each team should establish areas in which the retailer has room for improvement in terms of behaving sustainably. This could fall into two main areas:

- Store environment (e.g. energy use in lighting and heating, as well as the sustainability of materials used in the store's fixtures)

- Products and services (e.g. the availability of environmentally sustainable or Fair Trade products)

Activity 2 (45 minutes)

For up to 30 minutes, you should discuss ways in which the retailer can improve its sustainability impacts in these respects. See the section on 'sustainable distribution channels' for inspiration. You can use good practice from other organisations for ideas, and the financial viability of your suggestions should be taken into account. Suggestions from each team should be presented informally to the rest of the session group for ten minutes, through verbal discussion or through a list of ideas on a flip chart. For the last five minutes, as a result of the discussion, the session group should sum up key ways in which retailers in general can improve their sustainability impacts.

Additional teaching material and ideas

1. Apply the CDP model (Figure 11.2) to shopping for vegetables that are either organic or imperfect (usually referred to in UK supermarkets as 'wonky veg'). Consider each one of the model's stages and decide whether it is relevant to this type of purchase. Suggest ways in which the model could be adapted to take sustainability into account, for example, by removing or renaming any of the seven stages or adding in new stages.

2. Sustainable Brands conferences take place in San Diego and in other parts of the world. Delegates can attend in person, but it is also possible to register to watch a live stream of these events, with selected footage available on the organisation's website at: https://sustainablebrands.com/events. Watch an extract from a recent Sustainable Brands conference and discuss the possible effects on brands of these issues.

3. Watch this video about Nike recycling trainers, then investigate the criticism that has been levelled at the company by ethical campaigners in the past, using an internet search. Assess the effectiveness of Nike's subsequent initiatives to enhance their sustainability credentials: https://www.nike.com/help/a/recycle-shoes.

4. The Copenhagen Fashion Summit (Global Fashion Agenda), organised in conjunction with the Danish Fashion Institute, focuses on the need for more sustainable approaches within the fashion industry, from manufacturers to retailers and the media. Presentations and interviews have been given by key figures from sustainable fashion organisations and high-profile brands, and an international team of students collaborated on the Youth Fashion Summit project, calling for the fashion industry to take urgent action to address the UN's 17 Sustainable Development Goals. You can listen to speeches from the summit and access further content here: www.youtube.com/c/globalfashionagenda.

5. Pressure groups, such as Labour Behind the Label, have criticised retailers for a lack of transparency about where their products are sourced and the employment conditions in which their operatives work. Discuss potential reasons that retail businesses don't usually reveal this information to consumers, and consider the effects that being more transparent about their sources could have on their products, pricing, and promotion (https://labourbehindthelabel.org).

Further readings

Belz, F. M., and K. Peattie (2012), *Sustainability Marketing: A Global Perspective*, 2nd edn (Chichester, UK: Wiley and Sons).

>This seminal text offers an in-depth exploration of sustainability marketing and the ways in which it can address socio-ecological problems. It begins by discussing key marketing issues and a framework for sustainability marketing, then covering values, marketing strategies, CB, the marketing mix, and the future of sustainability marketing.

Blowfield, M. (2013), *Business and Sustainability* (Oxford, UK: Oxford University Press).

>This textbook covers a broad range of sustainability issues relating to business and management, the most relevant chapter for marketers focusing on innovation, planning, and design. Snapshots and extended case studies are included to demonstrate how sustainability strategies can be developed and implemented in practice.

Carvill, M., G. Butler, and G. Evans (2021), *Sustainable Marketing: How to Drive Profits with Purpose* (London: Bloomsbury).

>This book is written by practitioners to offer contemporary industry insights into sustainable marketing practice, supported by case studies on B Corps. Each chapter offers viable action points for companies to improve their sustainability impacts.

Martin, D., and J. Schouten (2012), *Sustainable Marketing* (Upper Saddle River, NJ: Prentice Hall).

>This definitive textbook comprises all the aspects you would expect to find in a standard marketing textbook, viewed from a sustainability perspective, forming a comprehensive guide to the topic with innovative cases and a broad range of academic references.

Sharma, R. R., T. Kaur, and A. S. Syan (2021), *Sustainability Marketing: New Directions and Practices* (Bingley: Emerald Group Publishing).

>This book investigates growing consumer markets for sustainable products and the strategies required to meet such consumers' needs, focusing on the benefits of sustainability in relation to competitive advantage and the triple bottom line.

Recommended industry sources

Advertising Standards Authority Home – https://www.asa.org.uk/

Advertising Standards Council of India – https://asci.social/

Data and Marketing Association DMA – https://dma.org.uk/

Green Business Bureau greenbusinessbureau.com What Is Sustainable Marketing and Why Is It Important in 2022 – https://greenbusinessbureau.com/business-function/marketing-sales/what-is-sustainable-marketing-and-why-is-it-important-in-2021/

The Market Research Society – https://www.mrs.org.uk/

Mintel (Market Intelligence) – https://www.mintel.com/

References

Adidas (2019) Adidas Unlocks a Circular Future for Sports with Futurecraft.loop: A Performance Running Shoe Made to Be Remade. *adidas.com News*, 17th April.

Alves, H., C. Fernandes, and M. Rapso (2016) Social Media Marketing: A Literature Review and Implications. *Psychology of Marketing*, 33(12), 1029–38.

Arnold, C. (2009) *Ethical Marketing and the New Consumer* (Chichester, UK: Wiley).

Baines, P., P. Antonetti, and F. Rosengren (2022) *Marketing*, 6th edn (Oxford: Oxford University Press).

Blackwell, R.D., P.W. Miniard, and J.F. Engel (2001) *Consumer Behavior*, 9th edn (Mason, OH: Thomson South Western Publishing).

Blincoe, K. (2009) Re-Educating the Person. In A. Stibbe (ed.), *The Handbook of Sustainability Literacy: Skills for a Changing World* (Totnes, UK: Green Books). 204–8.

Blythe, J. (2013) *Consumer Behaviour*, 2nd edn (London: Sage).

Bolton, R.N. (2021) The Convergence of Sustainability and Marketing: Transforming Marketing to Respond to a New World. *Australasian Marketing Journal*. Advance online publication. https://doi.org/10.1177/ 18393349211005200

Braungart, M., and W. McDonough (2009) *Cradle to Cradle: Re-Making the Way We Make Things* (London: Vintage).

Carrigan, M., and A. Attalla (2001) The Myth of the Ethical Consumer: Do Ethics Matter in Purchase Behaviour? *Journal of Consumer Marketing*, 18(7), 560–78.

Carvill, M., G. Butler, and G. Evans (2021) *Sustainable Marketing: How to Drive Profits with Purpose* (London: Bloomsbury).

Claudy, M., and M. Peterson (2022). Sustainability: Understanding Consumer Behavior in a Circular Economy. In L.R. Kahle, T.M. Lowrey, and J. Huber (eds.), *APA Handbook of Consumer Psychology*, 1st edn (Washington, DC: American Psychological Association). Chap. 15, 373–92.

Cooper, T. (2010) *Longer Lasting Products: Alternatives to the Throwaway Society* (Farnham, UK: Gower).

Co-operative Bank (2021) *Ethical Consumerism Report*. Ethical Consumerism Report 2021. https://www.co-operative.coop/ethical-consumerism-report-2021, accessed 26th April 2022.

Dahlstrom, R. (2011) *Green Marketing Management* (Andover, UK: South-Western Cengage).

Defra (2008) *A Framework for Pro-Environmental Behaviours*. http://archive.defra.gov.uk/evidence/social/behaviour/documents/behaviours-jan08-report.pdf, accessed 23rd January 2014.

Deloitte (2021) *Changes and Key Findings in Sustainability and Consumer Behaviour in 2021*. https://www2.deloitte.com/uk/en/pages/consumer-business/articles/sustainable-consumer.html

Eckhardt, G.M., R. Belk, and T.M. Devinney (2010) Why Don't Consumers Consume Ethically? *Journal of Consumer Behaviour*, 9, 426–36.

Elkington, J. (2004) Enter the Triple Bottom Line. In A. Henriques, and J. Richardson (eds.), *The Triple Bottom Line: Does It All Add Up?: Assessing the Sustainability of Business and CSR* (London: Earthscan). 1–16.

Engel, J.F., D.T. Kollat, and R. Blackwell (1968) *Consumer Behavior* (New York: Rinehart & Winston).

Fisher, T., T. Cooper, S. Woodward, A. Hiller, and H. Goworek (2008) *Public Understanding of Sustainable Clothing.* http://randd.defra.gov.uk/Default.aspx?Menu=Menu&Module=More&Location=None&Completed=1&ProjectID=15626, accessed 30th November 2013.

Geurin, A.N., and Burch, L.M. (2017) User-Generated Branding via Social Media: An Examination of Six Running Brands. *Sport Management Review*, 20, 273–84.

Gill, M., S. Sridhar, and R. Grewal (2017) Return on Engagement Initiatives: A Study of a Business-To-Business Mobile App. *Journal of Marketing*, 81(4), 45–66. https://doi.org/10.1509/jm.16.0149.

Goworek, H., T. Cooper, T. Fisher, S. Woodward, and A. Hiller (2012) The Sustainable Clothing Market: An Evaluation of Potential Strategies for UK Retailers. *International Journal of Retail & Distribution Management*, 40(12), 935–55.

Goworek, H., and P.J. McGoldrick (2015) *Retail Marketing Management: Principles and Practice* (Harlow, UK: Pearson).

Hollebeek, L.D., M.S. Glynn, and R.J. Brodie (2014) Consumer Brand Engagement in Social Media: Conceptualization, Scale Development and Validation. *Journal of Interactive Marketing*, 28(2), 149–65.

Jobber, D., and F. Ellis-Chadwick (2019) *Principles and Practice of Marketing*, 9th edn (Harlow, UK: McGraw Hill).

Kemper, J.A., and P.W. Ballantine (2019). What Do We Mean by Sustainability Marketing? *Journal of Marketing Management*, 35(3–4), 277–309.

Kim, S., and T.H. Baek (2018) Examining the Antecedents and Consequences of Mobile App Engagement. *Telematics and Informatics*, 35(1), 148–58. https://doi.org/10.1016/j.tele.2017.10.008.

London School of Public Relations (2020) *Maximise Your Social Media Reach with LSPR's Recommended CSR and Sustainability Hashtags* [blog]. www.lspr-education.com/blog/maximise-your-social-media-reach-with-lsprs-recommended-csr-and-sustainability-hashtags, accessed 9th April 2022.

Lunde, M.B. (2018). Sustainability in Marketing: A Systematic Review Unifying 20 Years of Theoretical and Substantive Contributions (1997–2016). *AMS Review*, 8(3), 85–110.

Malik Chua, J. (2014) Activists Project Photos of Rana Plaza Victims at New York Fashion Week. *Ecouterre*, 7 February. www.ecouterre.com/activists-project-photos-of-rana-plaza-victims-at-new-york-fashion-week/, accessed 10th February 2014.

Mangold, W.G., and D.J. Faulds (2009) Social Media: The New Hybrid Element of the Promotion Mix. *Business Horizons*, 52, 357–65.

Martin, D., and J. Schouten (2012) *Sustainable Marketing* (Upper Saddle River, NJ: Prentice Hall).

McDonald, S., C. Oates, M. Thyne, P. Alevizou, and L.A. McMorland (2009) Comparing Sustainable Consumption Patterns Across Product Sectors. *International Journal of Consumer Studies*, 33, 137–45.

Meerman-Scott, D. (2020) *The New Rules of Marketing and PR*, 7th edn (Hoboken, NJ: Wiley and Sons).

Nield, D. (2014) A Full-Size 3D House is Under Construction in Amsterdam. *Digital Trends*, 30 March. www.digitaltrends.com/cool-tech/full-size-3d-printed-house-construction-amsterdam/#!B0tJq, accessed 31st March 2014.

OECD (2022) *Extended Producer Responsibility* (Paris: Organisation for Economic Co-operation and Development).

Papadas, K.K., G.J. Avlonitis, and M. Carrigan (2017) Green Marketing Orientation: Conceptualization, Scale Development and Validation. *Journal of Business Research*, 80, 236–46.

Papadas, K.K., G.J. Avlonitis, M. Carrigan, and L. Piha (2019) The Interplay of Strategic and Internal Green Marketing Orientation on Competitive Advantage. *Journal of Business Research*, 104, 632–43.

PERI (2020) *3D Construction Printing*. www.peri.com, accessed 23rd April 2022.

Rauschnabel, P.A., P. Sheldon, and E. Herzfeldt (2019) What Motivates Users to Hashtag on Social Media? *Psychology of Marketing Journal*, 36(5), 473–88. https://doi.org/10.1002/mar.21191

Robinson, P.J., C.W. Faris, and Y. Wind (1967) *Industrial Procurement* (New York: Allyn and Bacon).

Roma, P., and D. Aloini (2019) How Does Brand-Related User-Generated Content Differ Across Social Media? Evidence Reloaded. *Journal of Business Research*, 96, 322–39.

Ryan, D. (2017) *Understanding Digital Marketing, Marketing Strategies for Engaging the Digital Generation*, 4th edn (London: KoganPage).

Serrano, N., and C. de Balanzo (2011) Neuroscience and Communication Strategy: Redefining the Role of the Unconscious. In *Tripodos* (Universitat Ramon Llull). www.raco.cat/index.php/Tripodos/article/view/247474, accessed 20th March 2014.

Smith, M.E. (2021) *Inspiring Green Consumer Choices: Leverage Neuroscience to Reshape Marketplace Behavior* (London: Kogan Page).

Thomasson, E. (2014) Inspections Highlight Safety Risks at Bangladesh Factories. *Reuters*, 10 March. www.reuters.com/article/2014/03/10/us-bangladesh-inspections-idUSBREA2914920140310?feedType=RSS, accessed 24th March 2014.

United Nations Brundtland Commission (1987) *Academic Impact: Sustainability* (United Nations). https://www.un.org/en/academicimpact.

Waddock, S.A., and S.B. Graves (1997) The Corporate Social Performance – Financial Performance Link. *Strategic Management Journal*, 18(4), 303–19.

Webster, F.E., and Y. Wind (1972) *Organizational Buying Behavior* (New York: Prentice Hall).

Wrigley, P. (2008) Ethics Must Stay High on the Agenda. *Drapers*, 27 November. www.drapersonline.com/news/ethics-must-stay-high-on-the-agenda/1936268.article#.U5HEvhsU_IU, accessed 27th November 2013.

12
Crowdsourcing for sustainable solutions[1]

Lorinda R. Rowledge

This chapter examines some of the powerful ways in which open innovation and crowdsourcing are applied to solving environmental, social, and economic sustainability challenges, then outlines critical success factors. You will learn how businesses, governments, non-governmental organisations (NGOs), and academic institutions are tapping into the collective intelligence of the 'crowd' to develop innovative technological and social solutions for ecological and social justice problems. The content and exercises in this chapter will prepare you to:

- Describe what crowdsourcing is and the different ways it is applied.

- Describe the rationale for open innovation and crowdsourcing as an important approach to innovation in general and for sustainability and social innovation challenges in particular.

- Describe and analyse examples of crowdsourcing applied to finding innovative solutions that advance sustainable and socially just businesses, economies, and lifestyles.

DOI: 10.4324/9781003294665-15

- Share insights and learning from personal experience participating in a crowdsourcing challenge.

- Discuss the implications of open innovation and crowdsourcing for leadership.

- Outline ways crowdsourcing can be used to mitigate and adapt to the impacts of climate change.

- Argue that open innovation and crowdsourcing are not only helpful but also essential in society's efforts to address the impacts and issues of climate justice.

This chapter is particularly focused on the first three principles of the Principles for Responsible Management Education (PRME 2017):

1. **Purpose:** We will develop the capabilities of students to be future generators of sustainable value for business and society at large and to work for an inclusive and sustainable global economy.

2. **Values:** We will incorporate into our academic activities and curricula the values of global social responsibility as portrayed in international initiatives, such as the United Nations Global Compact.

3. **Method:** We will create educational frameworks, materials, processes, and environments that enable effective learning experiences for responsible leadership.

Introduction

There is growing conviction among business leaders, investors, consumers, employees, and other stakeholders that we need urgent, transformational change if we are to avert ecological catastrophe, build a more socially just world, and importantly, ensure business success in the 21st century. Fortunately, a movement towards open innovation, propelled by emerging crowdsourcing technology platforms, is engaging our collective intelligence and commitment in developing the needed breakthrough innovations. This chapter outlines the strategic context and need from a business perspective, defines open innovation and crowdsourcing, and then summarises inspirational examples of crowdsourcing applied to advancing business sustainability and social innovation. Finally, I discuss the implications of open innovation for organisational leadership.

The strategic context

Business leaders can no longer ignore shifting investor, customer, and employee expectations or the existing and potential consequences of climate change and threats to business-critical natural resources. They face increasingly rigorous corporate customer requirements and consumer demands to reduce environmental impacts, offer more sustainable products, and demonstrate corporate social responsibility. Many are struggling to avoid brand value hits from sustainability-related issues, such as leaks, pollution, allegations of safety failures, child labour, or poor working conditions in their supply chains. Investors, concerned about exposure to such risks within their financial portfolios, are applying pressure on companies for more transparency and disclosure of sustainability-related impacts, risks, and strategies for reduction, mitigation, improvement, and adaptation. Further, business leaders are increasingly aware that employees are invested in meaningful work and making a contribution to the world. Progressives among them have seen cost savings from energy, water, materials, and waste reduction and have achieved competitive advantage with more sustainable technologies and products. The true leaders see the business opportunities in sustainability challenges, strive to create shared value not only for investors but also for other key stakeholders, and see the role of business as helping to solve the world's problems.

If businesses are to remain competitive, reduce risk, meet customer and market expectations, attract and retain top talent, and bring inspiring, innovative products and solutions to the marketplace, we need to reinvent our industrial system to be more environmentally, socially, and economically sustainable. Transformational change is also needed if we are going to stop human-driven climate change, loss of biodiversity, poverty, injustice, violence against women, and other global problems. What is required is nothing less than redesigning our business models, product designs, production processes, human resource practices, and lifestyles such that they stop harming and instead start restoring ecosystems and helping people and communities flourish. While the problems may initially seem insurmountable, our ever-deepening wisdom about the principles and strategies for sustainability, combined with caring and committed people all over the globe with unbounded creativity, provides ground for optimism. There are improvements, for example, in:

- Impact assessment, disclosure, and reporting (as of 2015, over 5,000 companies are reporting their carbon-related impacts and risks to CDP (www.cdp. net), and in 2013, 93% of the global 250 largest companies reported on their sustainability impact, performance, and plans).

- Integration of sustainability into core business strategy in companies such as Unilever, GE, Patagonia, Interface, and Marks & Spencer.

- Reductions in both intensity of and total energy use, carbon footprint, and water use.

- Application of design for environment to new product design, such as the hybrid gas-electric Toyota Prius or the Method naturally derived plant-based cleaning products.

- Understanding of the opportunity within closed-loop value chains and the circular economy: for example, the Ellen MacArthur Foundation (www. ellenmacarthurfoundation.org) is building partnerships to accelerate the transition to a circular economy, and Jaguar Land Rover, Novelis, and other partners are collaborating on a closed-loop value chain for REALCAR (Jaguar Land Rover and Novelis 2016).

- Decades of attention to human rights and safety abuses in global supply chains have led to extensive systems for improvement and auditing.

- Efforts to create sustainable cities around the globe.

- Mechanisms to track and respond to impacts of severe climate events (likely exacerbated by change).

These and other examples like them have traditionally been developed by a dedicated group of experts within the organisation. This chapter is about the amplified opportunity and impact potential if we dramatically expand the creative resources engaged in discovering, developing, and accelerating design and implementation of these solutions through open innovation and crowdsourcing.

Definitions of open innovation and crowdsourcing

Innovation is generally defined as a new idea, device, or method and as the act or process of introducing new ideas, devices, or methods (Merriam-Webster 2017). In a business context, the meaning of innovation is often broadened to include how an idea or invention is utilised in a new product or solution to create a desired impact. For example, Michael Katz defines *innovation* as:

> The successful generation, development and implementation of new and novel ideas, which introduce new products, processes and/or strategies to a company or enhance current products, processes and/or strategies leading to commercial success and possible market leadership and creating value for stakeholders, driving economic growth and improving standards of living.
>
> (Katz 2007)

Academics, consulting firms, and business magazines distinguish between different forms or application areas of innovation (such as product/service, technology, production process), types or levels of innovation (such as incremental, breakthrough, transformational), and steps in the innovation process (such as idea generation and mobilisation, advocacy and screening, experimentation and testing, commercialisation, diffusion and implementation) (Mariello 2007). While there is considerable benefit to be gained from examining many such frameworks of analysis, the focus here is twofold: the overall approach to innovation and how leading corporations are innovating the innovation process itself.

Corporations have traditionally looked to their research and development (R&D) departments for new technologies and product development and to manufacturing engineers and process improvement experts for operational improvement. Governments have relied on subject matter experts, elected officials, and experienced public servants to develop policy. Since the early 2000s, open innovation has emerged as a popular alternative approach that combines internal resources with those outside the organisation.

Henry Chesbrough, professor at UC Berkeley's Haas School of Business, introduced the concept of open innovation in his 2003 book, *Open Innovation: The New Imperative for Creating and Profiting from Technology*, and later defined *open innovation* as a more participatory, more decentralized approach to innovation, based on the observed fact that useful knowledge today is widely distributed, and no company, no matter how capable or how big, could innovate effectively on its own. . . . Open innovation is the use of purposive inflows and outflows of knowledge to accelerate internal innovation, and expand the markets for external use of innovation, respectively.

(Chesbrough 2011)

Essentially, what this means is that organisational boundaries are more permeable. Organisations are inviting external experts, inventors, entrepreneurs, customers, and others to help find innovative solutions. These selected 'crowds' are participating in analysing challenges and generating, screening, testing, and diffusing innovative solutions.

Crowdsourcing, an element of open innovation, is defined as 'the practice of obtaining information or input into a task or project by enlisting the services of a large number of people, either paid or unpaid, typically via the Internet' (Oxford Dictionaries 2017). The term reflects the notion of outsourcing creative or analytical work to the 'crowd'. It is based on the principle that good ideas can come from anywhere and that innovation should no longer be restricted to R&D departments or innovation labs. A popular non-profit dedicated to sharing information about crowdsourcing and crowdfunding defines *crowdsourcing* as 'the process of connecting with large groups of people via the internet who are tapped for their knowledge, expertise, time or resources' (Esposti *et al.* 2013: 17). There are many examples of companies and organisations leveraging open innovation and crowdsourcing to find innovative solutions for sustainability and social justice challenges, such as Unilever's Foundry ideas for meeting its Sustainable Living Plan goals (Unilever 2017), GE's Ecomagination and Healthymagination, the Ocean Health XPRIZE contest, and Nike's Launch campaign for more sustainable fabric. Similarly, governments around the world are crowdsourcing citizen input into policies and city strategic plans.

United Nations (UN) Sustainable Development Goal (SDG) 17, 'partnership for the goals', states that there is a need to 'strengthen the means of implementation and revitalise the global partnership for sustainable development' (United Nations 2016). As such, this can help drive forward existing crowdsourcing projects as well as encourage new initiatives. This is explained further in target 17.16, which calls for action to 'enhance the global partnership for sustainable development, complemented by multi-stakeholder partnerships that mobilise and share knowledge, expertise, technology and financial resources, to support the achievement of the sustainable development goals in all countries, in particular developing countries' (United Nations 2016).

The next section describes different types of crowdsourcing and why it is such a powerful approach, then outlines examples of crowdsourcing applied to sustainability in particular.

Types of crowdsourcing

While authors, thought leaders, and practitioners vary somewhat in their descriptions of different types of crowdsourcing, the basics are widely shared. There are essentially six types of crowdsourcing:

1. **Crowd labour.** Access external labour to complete a job or task, for example, building Wikipedia, translating works into many languages, or accessing content writers via sites such as crowdcontent.com.

2. **Crowdfunding.** Raise capital from the general public through many participants pooling financial resources, popularised through sites such as Kickstarter.com or Indigogo.com.

3. **Crowd creativity.** Recruit artistic, creative, or design input to develop branding, communications, design, or creative solutions, such as a corporate logo or advertising video.

4. **Crowd innovation.** Generate ideas or develop solutions to a problem or part of a problem, for example, the Ansari XPRIZE offered $10 million to the team best able to build a reusable manned vehicle capable of carrying three people 100 km above the surface of the Earth and back twice in the span of two weeks, effectively launching the commercial private space industry.

5. **Crowd wisdom.** Share and assemble information and/or access distributed knowledge. This includes **citizen science**, soliciting public input on scientific processes – data collection, analysis and interpretation, technology and app development, problem-solving, and finding scientific discoveries;

crowd mapping, obtaining geographic information to produce meaningful collaborative maps, such as Ushahidi (www.ushahidi.com); and **customer crowdsourcing**, gathering customer needs, preferences, opinions, input, feedback, and testing, such as My Starbucks Idea (http://mystarbucksidea. force. com).

6. **Crowd governance.** Solicit public input into policy-making, prioritising, and decision-making, and crowd voting – obtain communities' ratings of various options by providing judgements about relative values or analyses against established criteria (Bott *et al.* 2011; DigitalGov 2017). This can involve civic engagement and community building, supporting participatory governance, participation in the political process and policymaking, input into community issues, and/or social activism.

Why crowdsourcing is a powerful approach

A recent report, *The State of Crowdsourcing 2016* (Roth *et al.* 2016), found that those Interbrand 'Best Global Brands' already using crowdsourcing in a significant way between 2004 and 2014 increased their usage by over 30% from 2014 to 2015, that the fast-moving consumer goods (FMCG) sector is leading the application of creative crowdsourcing (followed by consumer electronics), and that the fastest-growing application is ideation (crowdsourcing for ideas). The report found the 20 leading major brand consumer products companies using crowdsourcing, in order of most use, are: Coca-Cola, Danone, Nestlé, Pepsi, Samsung, Hewlett-Packard, Ford, Nokia, Toyota, General Electric, Microsoft, Google, J&J, Budweiser, Chevrolet, Shell, Intel, Phillips, Santander, and Nescafé (Roth *et al.* 2016). Let's look at what is driving this increased interest in crowdsourcing.

For businesses, open innovation and crowdsourcing can provide a number of advantages over traditional approaches, all of which impact the bottom line:

- Improved discovery and development of new technologies, approaches, and creative solutions, enhanced by greater diversity of problem-solvers and a wider pool of intellect addressing the issue.

- Accelerated time-to-market and opportunities for first-to-market advantages, which also mean competitive advantage and a more agile organisation able to adapt to changing customer needs and business environments.

- Higher hit rate of new product development (and new solution development) from greater breadth of ideas considered, more knowledge and know-how brought to bear, and a high level of experimentation, testing, and consumer/user feedback throughout the design process (this also reduces the risk of innovation and enables faster abandonment of, and greater learning from, failed ideas).

- Cost reduction from faster time-to-discovery, participating teams willing to donate or invest time (often incentivised by the chance they might win prizes), or external sources willing to work for no or reduced fees.

- Participation and engagement increasing the likelihood of behaviour change, which is important, given that 'innovation' refers to the *entire* innovation process from ideation and invention through design, engineering, production, go-to-market strategy, sales, and distribution, to market adoption.

- Open innovation stimulating more transformative solutions and business models because it engages the broader business/organisational ecosystem in better understanding:

- The system dynamics related to the challenge, problem, or opportunity

- The strategic, operational, and contextual aspects of every stage of the life cycle

  - The full range of potential alternatives

  - 'Ground-truth' information and data

  - Collective insights drawn from prototyping and experimentation

While no company is truly sustainable and all these companies still have significant negative environmental and social impacts, many of them are genuinely working to find sustainability-focused improvements and innovations.

There are parallel advantages for non-profits, foundations, and mission-driven businesses, such as gaining new, more innovative approaches, a deeper understanding of the context in which their planned services are being delivered/received, and insights about the most effective design and approach.

Innovation and sustainability

It is a 'no-brainer' to apply these advantages of open innovation and crowdsourcing to almost every sustainability challenge facing companies, organisations, governments, and civil society. Crowdsourcing has already been demonstrated to be effective at involving scientists, social workers, inventors, technology developers, and citizens around the globe in finding innovative solutions to environmental, sustainability, and social justice–related challenges. In addition to outlining many of these general examples of crowdsourcing solutions to social and environmental sustainability, the chapter also focuses on open innovation applied to mitigating and adapting to climate change and understanding and confronting climate justice.

As mentioned previously in this chapter, crowdsourcing initiatives are, in their very nature, intrinsically linked to SDG 17, 'partnership for the goals'. In fact, target 17.17 asks that we 'encourage and promote effective public, public – private and civil society partnerships, building on the experience and resourcing strategies of partnerships'. Table 12.1 illustrates how crowdsourcing can help work towards the achievement of not just one but all those goals.

Table 12.1: Examples of crowdsourcing applied to sustainability

CROWD LABOR	
Company/Organisation Website/link	**Crowdsourcing Initiative**
ORANGE http://www.100open.com/orange-launches-do-some-good/ See youtube video https://www.youtube.com/watch?v=3R-MiWTUqYE	**"DO SOME GOOD"** Orange's crowdsourcing 'micro volunteering' app encourages UK citizens to volunteer for 5 minute, bite-sized actions on their mobile device (Orange UK 2011). Within a year from launch, the campaign had activated 25,000 volunteers and over 30 charity partners. This built on the company's 'Making Minutes Matter' campaign (Ward-Smith 2010). Orange is quoted as having calculated that if one million people gave five minutes each to a voluntary activity that would amount to 9.5 years of time. http://ivo.org/post/making-minutes-matter-orange-mobile-micro-volunteering-548768a49108686207659dc3 Goal 17: Partnership for the Goals

CROWD LABOR	
TED http://www.ted.com/about/programs-initiatives/ted-open-translation-project	**OPEN TRANSLATION PROJECT** – TED Outsourcing the work of creating subtitles in different languages through their ' Open Translation Project' (OTP). By May, 2016, 21,204 volunteer translators around the globe had completed 92,419 translations of TED presentations in 111 languages. Goal 10: Reduced Inequalities
ZOONIVERSE https://www.zooniverse.org/	**ZOONIVERSE** states it is the world's largest and most popular platform for people-powered research. Volunteers of 'citizen scientists' assist professional researchers, accelerating research and new discoveries by supporting information analysis and pattern recognition. Examples related to sustainability include categorizing bat calls, photographing orchids to determine impacts of climate change, observing plankton, and watching penguins. Goal 13: Climate Action, Goal 14: Life Below Water, Goal 15: Life on Land

CROWD CREATIVITY	
Company/Organisation Website/link	Crowdsourcing Initiative
COCA COLA FRANCE	**DURABLE DESIGN CONTEST** invites students to design objects with recycled beverage packaging. Goal 12: Responsible Consumption and Production
DELL	**GO GREEN CHALLENGE** in India 'invited citizens to make online submission of photographs, videos and other innovative depictions of key issues, concerns or thoughts on green technology' (CXOtoday 2010). Goal 9: Industry, Innovation and Infrastructure
LEGO **https://ideas.lego.com/**	**LEGO IDEAS** Fans and users of Lego are invited to create Lego sets. Winning ideas are developed. Some have focused on reducing sexism and promoting women in science, as well as creating sets with solar energy themes. See also Lego CUUSOO. Goal 5: Gender Equality, Goal 7: Affordable and Clean Energy

(Continued...)

CROWD LABOR	
CITI	**CITI'S 'KIVA MICROFINANCE' CONTEST** was a contest launched on Tongal, asking people to submit ideas for 30–90 second videos that would engage students and educators to participate in Kiva U, a virtual community that harnesses the energy, passion, and creativity of students and educators to address the world's critical problems through microfinance. The 30–90 second videos should educate viewers on what Kiva U is and answer the question, "How can youth change the world through microfinance?" Goal 4: Quality Education, Goal 8: Decent Work and Economic Growth

CROWD INNOVATION – Competitions, Grand Challenges, IdeaMarkets, Innovation Foundaries, Hackathons, and Jams

Company/Organisation Website/link	Crowdsourcing Initiative
GE	**ECOMAGINATION** represented a significant commitment by GE to the investment, development, and marketing of green technology. Ten years after the launch, by the end of 2014, GE had invested $15 billion in Ecomagination Research & Development (R&D), which generated $200 Billion in revenue, greenhouse gas reductions, water use reduction, and cost savings. Importantly, GE's approach was to apply open innovation to achieve their technology and revenue goals. GE held, and continues to sponsor, open challenges to innovators around the world focused on a wide range of clean technology and environmental challenges. http://www.ge.com/about-us/ecomagination/strategy Goal 9: Industry, Innovation and Infrastructure **OIL SANDS GHG EMISSION ECOMAGINATION CHALLENGE** is a $1 Million Cdn Open Ecomagination Challenge (GE 2017) to reduce GHG Emissions in the Canadian Oil Sands (NineSigma 2015). https://ninesights.ninesigma.com/web/ecomaginationinnovation/home Goal 7: Affordable and Clean Energy

CROWD LABOR	
	HEALTHYMAGINATION was launched by GE, applying the same open innovation/ crowdsourcing approach to global health issues. Their goal was launching at least 100 innovations that lowered cost, increased access, and improved quality of healthcare (GE 2009). http://www.ge.com/pdf/investors/ events/05072009/ge_healthymagination_pr.pdf Goal 3: Good Health and Well-Being
GE and UNDER ARMOUR http://www.ninesights.com/community/ grand-challenges#sthash.EbIJIXA3.dpuf	**HEAD HEALTH CHALLENGE II**, a collaboration by the NFL, Under Armour, and GE, focuses on identifying breakthrough technologies and approaches that will result in preventing, monitoring and identifying trauma, engineered safety solutions, and training protocols in order to make sports safer for athletes (Malouf 2015). Military and civilian markets may also benefit from innovations. Up to $10 million will be awarded for solutions that produce advancements in preventing, measuring and detecting brain injury, innovative brain protective materials and devices, and training methods that result in behaviour modifications. Goal 3: Good Health and Well-Being
TOYOTA	**IDEAS FOR GOOD CHALLENGE** involves Toyota asking the public to imagine new ideas for using Toyota's technology to help benefit humanity (Nichols 2012). Members of the public will submit an idea based on one of five Toyota technologies: T.H.U.M.S. (Total Human Model for Safety), Solar Powered Ventilation System, Hybrid Synergy Drive, Advanced Parking Guidance System, and Touch Tracer Display. https://www.behance. net/gallery/Toyota-Ideas-For-Good/5967749 Winning ideas included redesigned bike helmets, an automated firefighting ladder, and a power plant gym (Toyota 2011). http://corporatenews. pressroom.toyota.com/releases/ winners+ideas+for+good+may+2011.htm Goal 9: Industry, Innovation and Infrastructure

(Continued...)

CROWD LABOR	
X-PRIZE http://oceanhealth.xprize.org/	**TURNING THE TIDE ON OCEAN HEALTH** Wendy Schmidt and X-Prize teamed up to launch a $2 million global competition focused on creating pH sensor technology that affordably, accurately, and efficiently measures ocean chemistry (XPRIZE 2017). Goal 14: Life Below Water
 http://www.nyasatimes.com/2013/11/14/malawi-scoops-healthcare-innovation-award-for-developing-countries/	GlaxoSmithKline partnered with Save the Children in launching a $1 million grassroots **Healthcare Innovation Award** with the ambitious goal of saving the lives of millions of children in developing countries (GSK 2015). The challenge, open only to organisations from developing nations, solicited approaches with proven results at reducing under-5 child deaths that are sustainable and have the potential to be replicated and scaled. Malawi won the highest funding of $400,000 for a simple device for helping newborn babies breathe that can be produced at a fraction of the cost of similar versions in use in developed nations. Goal 1: No Poverty, Goal 3: Good Health and Well-Being
SONY http://www.theguardian.com/sustainable-business/sony-untapped-audience-crowdsourcing-project	ONE PLANET INITIATIVE: Together with the award-winning design firm Ideo and the World Wildlife Fund, **Sony's Open Planet Initiative** contest (Beavis 2011) solicited ideas for how the company's products could be repurposed to tackle environmental problems. The competition focused on ideas to address carbon-intensive challenges such as food production, housing, and transport to identify one winning idea that would be developed into a working prototype. Goal 13: Climate Action, Goal 14: Life Below Water, Goal 15: Life on Land

CROWD LABOR

Unilever

http://www.unilever.com/innovation/
collaborating-with-unilever/challenging-and-
wants/

UNILEVER FOUNDRY: Unilever invited ideas for new designs and technologies that help improve products and production to meet its **Sustainable Living Plan** goals (Sustainable Brands 2016). In 2010 Unilever, the giant personal care and food products company with more than 1,000 brands used by more than two billion people on a given day, announced its **Sustainable Living Plan**, setting ambitious goals for making its products and production systems more environmentally and socially sustainable. Recognizing the company would need help if it is to meet its targets; Unilever used crowdsourcing to invite partners to suggest new designs and technologies that help improve products and production in 12 areas of 'wants': 1. Cleaning up fat, 2. Safe drinking water, 3. Fighting viruses, 4. Better packaging, 5. Sustainable washing, 6. Less salt, 7. Toothpaste that amazes your mouth, 8. Preserving food naturally, 9. Storing renewable energy, 10. Sustainable shower sensation, 11. Change consumer behavior, and 12. Long-lasting green colour for herbs and vegetables (Godelnik 2012). Unilever Foundary has a powerful 'Pitch-Pilot-Partner' approach aimed at getting new ideas to market rapidly.
Goal 12: Responsible Consumption and Production.

IDEO
https://www.ideo.org/amplify
https://openideo.com/

OPEN IDEO AMPLIFY PROGRAM, sponsored by the UK Department for International Development is a five-year, 10 Challenge program focused on improving the lives of the billion people living in extreme poverty around the world. In May 2016, the Agricultural Innovation Challenge was requesting ideas from people who had worked in the sector for at least one year. The challenge question is *How might we improve the livelihoods of small-scale farmers by reducing food waste and spoilage?* All challenges follow the structure of IDEO's powerful human-centered design process (Open IDEO 2016).
https://challenges.openideo.com/challenge/
agricultural-innovation/beneficiary-feedback
Goal 1: No Poverty. Goal 2: Zero Hunger

(Continued...)

CROWD LABOR	
CROWD WISDOM – Citizen Science and Map-Making	
Company/Organisation Website/link	**Crowdsourcing Initiative**
USHAHIDI https://www.ushahidi.com/	CRISIS MAPPING originally developed in 2008 to map reports of post-election violence in Kenya (Ushahidi 2017). 'Partner with leading foundations and organizations to increase access to information, empower citizens, and protect marginalised communities'. Example: 'Making all voices count' working for open, effective and participatory government. Goal 16: Peace and Justice Strong Institutions
CITI	**CITI'S 'KIVA MICROFINANCE' CONTEST** was a contest launched on Tongal, asking people to submit ideas for 30–90 second videos that would engage students and educators to participate in Kiva U, a virtual community that harnesses the energy, passion, and creativity of students and educators to address the world's critical problems through microfinance. The 30–90 second videos should educate viewers on what Kiva U is and answer the question, "How can youth change the world through microfinance?" Further, Citi and Kiva partnered to engage students and educators in improving financial inclusion globally (Citigroup 2013). http://finance.yahoo.com/news/citi-kiva-launch-kiva-u-123000220.html Goal 4: Quality Education, Goal 8: Decent Work and Economic Growth
RED CROSS	Red Cross, Doctors without Borders, UN are collaborating on Humanitarian 'OpenStreetMap' (OSM) Team (Humanitarian OpenStreetMap Team (HOT) 2017), crowdsourcing detailed maps of Sierra Leone, Guinea, and Liberia, the three West African countries hardest hit by EBOLA. Given the lack of incentive for financial return, Google Maps in these West African countries were extremely incomplete, greatly hampering organisations working to provide medical personnel and equipment. https://www.openstreetmap.org/#map=5/51.500/-0.100 Goal 3: Good Health and Well-Being, Goal 10: Reduced Inequalities

CROWD LABOR	
CROWD GOVERNANCE	
GOVERNMENT Website/link	**Crowdsourcing Initiative**
	The UN crowdsourced citizen input into the Sustainable Development goals. This has been characterised as an initiative to rectify the democratic deficit in governance.[1] The author summarises the potential of crowdsourcing in governance as 'civil society can enhance the prospects for increased legitimacy among international environmental institutions by "(1) collecting, disseminating, and analyzing information; (2) providing input to agenda-setting and policy development processes; (3) performing operational functions; (4) assessing environmental conditions and monitoring compliance with environmental agreements; and (5) advocating environmental justice"' (citing Gemmill and Bamidele-Izu 2002). For an inspiring presentation about this see ONE.org Co-Founder Jamie Drummond's TED talk. Drummond (2012)[2]
Challenge.gov	The US government now has hundreds of open challenges, soliciting citizen input ideas on such challenges as improving air quality, managing stormwater on campus, and keeping our earth green and clean. Goal 6: Clean Water and Sanitation, Goal 11: Sustainable Cities and Communities
CROWDFUNDING	
Company/Organisation Website/link	**Crowdsourcing Initiative**
GoldieBLOX https://www.kickstarter.com/projects/16029337/goldieblox-the-engineering-toy-for-girls	GOLDIEBLOX launched Kickstarter campaign to raise capital for development of this engineering toy for girls (GoldiBlox 2017; Sterling 2012). Goal 5: Gender Equality

[1] Joshua Chad Gellers, Crowdsourcing Sustainable Development Goals from Global Civil Society: A Content Analysis
[2] http://www.ted.com/talks/jamie_drummond_how_to_set_goals_for_the_world?language=en

Crowdsourcing the 2030 Sustainable Development Goals: a case study

In 2012, the UN secretary-general put out a general call inviting participation in defining a new set of targets subsequent to the Millennium Development Goals (MDGs), which were due to conclude in 2015. These new targets would be the Sustainable Development Goals (SDGs), officially known as *Transforming Our World: The 2030 Agenda for Sustainable Development*.

In support of this, ONE (www.one.org), an international campaigning and advocacy organisation with 7 million members, led a major initiative to enable widespread grassroots input and engagement in building a collective vision of 'The World We Want' (www.worldwewant2015.org). In January 2013, ONE publicised and delivered to the UN High Level Panel the report *Open for Development* (ONE 2013a), advocating on behalf of ONE and several other agencies the position that '[o]penness – especially transparency, accountability and public participation – must be at the heart of the post-2015 development framework' (ONE 2013b: 2). At the heart of this was ONE's belief that 'the path to ending extreme poverty must be one that factors in the voices of those actually living in extreme poverty' (ONE 2013a). The authors commended the 'unparalleled rates of progress' on most of the MDGs but noted that, because of the top-down design of the MDGs, several important needs and priorities of ordinary citizens, especially the target beneficiaries, were not included.

By April 2013, ONE Africa Director Dr Sipho Moyo reported that almost 120,000 people had signed the 'Open for Development' petition (Moyo 2013), while 144,000 had given their ideas to the 'You Choose' campaign about what development should look like in their countries (Nkombo 2013). This input was delivered directly to world leaders, who were also told that 'ONE's You Choose survey is being adapted to contribute to the UN's My World process of soliciting citizens' views on the future of development' (Moyo 2013).

In addition to the African 'You Choose' campaign, the UN launched the 'MY World 2015' survey, where 'over ten million people shared their hopes and dreams with the UN to help shape the Sustainable Development Goals (SDGs)' (UN SDG Action Campaign 2016). It is important to note that the website survey was supplemented by on-site surveying in developing countries using paper ballots, and this offline outreach yielded nearly six times as many participants as online methods (Gellers 2015: 23). The myriad of consultative processes is described in a UN report titled *The Global Conversation Begins* (UN Development Group 2013).

Mitchell Toomey, Director of the UN SDG Action Campaign, commented:

> In September of last year (2015) the world witnessed an his-
> toric moment – leaders from every member state of the United
> Nations unanimously ratified a bold and comprehensive 2030
> Agenda and the Sustainable Development Goals (SDGs). This
> agreement emerged not only from the negotiating chambers at
> the UN but also from a radical and far reaching global conversa-
> tion that eventually included more than ten million people and
> thousands of civil society organisations (CSOs), largely through
> the MY World 2015 survey. The mix of new and old techniques
> opened the negotiation process to a vivid display of the variety
> of experiences, knowledge and organisational forms which popu-
> late the civic space and left member states buoyed by the energy
> and enthusiasm of people worldwide, ultimately resulting in a far
> reaching, complex and ambitious agenda for action.
>
> (Toomey 2016)

There is little question that this effort to broaden participation in environmental and social governance through crowdsourcing the SDGs was wildly successful.
It is also worth examining more rigorously, as Josh Gellers at the University of
North Florida has done. His conclusion is that although this case of engaging civil
society was unprecedented in scope and crowdsourcing is 'a promising new form
of global civic engagement, certain challenges must be addressed in order to maximise its participatory capacity' (Gellers 2015: 22).

Gellers's analysis of the e-discussions and report revealed 'there exists a per-
ceptible demographic imbalance among contributors to the MY World survey
and considerable dissonance between the characteristics of participants in the
e-discussions and those whose voices were included in the resulting summary report'
(p. 1). The civil society participants were primarily English-speaking from more
developed nations. Gellers makes the following recommendations (pp. 23–4):

- Encourage participation through both digital and physical outreach activities to strengthen fairness and improve participation from lower ranks of the
  HDI (Human Development Index)

- Allow for multiple submission pathways in the same participatory platform
  (e-discussion, text, paper, tweets, etc.)

- Emphasise the contributions of the world's most vulnerable, marginalised groups by recruiting participants, enabling contributions, publishing communications and reports in multiple languages, and actively engaging individuals from the least developed areas and those most likely to be impacted by decisions

Crowdsourcing 2030 Agenda and the SDGs is a powerful example of a more inclusive, engaging, and democratic political process.

Climate change is one of the most urgent and critical crises facing humanity. The nearly 3,000-page report released by the IPCC (Intergovernmental Panel on Climate Change) in April 2022 warned that:

> Without immediate and deep emissions reductions across all sectors, limiting global warming to 1.5 °C (2.7 °F) is beyond reach. In the scenarios assessed, limiting warming to around 1.5 °C requires global greenhouse gas emissions to peak before 2025 at the latest, and be reduced by 43% by 2030; at the same time, methane would also need to be reduced by about a third.

Recent United Nations IPCC reports provide compelling scientific evidence that we are already experiencing what will only be increasing catastrophic impacts of climate change, our mitigation efforts are not on track for adequately limiting greenhouse gas emissions, and our window for achieving the required transformational change is rapidly vanishing (United Nations Climate Reports, 2023).

Exploring how open innovation and crowdsourcing can be used to assess, mitigate, and respond and adapt to climate change impacts is a book (or more) in itself. In what follows we provide several illustrative examples.

Examples of open innovation and crowdsourcing to mitigate, respond, and adapt to climate change

Climate CoLab and Wazoku (InnoCentive) Contests

MIT's Climate CoLab was created in 2009 to 'harness the collective intelligence of thousands of people from all around the world to address complex societal problems, starting with global climate change' (www.climatecolab.org/page/about).

Climate CoLab operated as an open platform for community members to join, submit climate-related contests, propose solutions, and participate by supporting, sharing, and voting on proposals.

In August 2022, MIT's Climate CoLab, which crowdsourced ideas for addressing climate change, spun out and migrated to Wazoku's InnoCentive, bringing together a community of more than 500,000 to address global sustainability issues. Wazoku's innovation platform is Idea Spotlight (www.prnewswire.com/news-releases/mit-center-for-collective-intelligences-climate-colab-spins-out-and-migrates-to-wazokus-global-challenge-community-innocentive-301602340.html).

In February of 2020, the open innovation breakthrough platform InnoCentive was acquired by Wazoku to create the world's most comprehensive and powerful innovation platform and community (www.wazoku.com/showcases/climate-colab/).

Climate CoLab's past and current contests include topics such as energy efficiency, transitioning to a circular economy, climate resilience, community adaptation to climate impacts, mobilising climate action and behaviour change, and sustainable transportation, agriculture, and construction to name but a few.

Citizen science

Citizen science is a powerful way of engaging people in working together to gather data on environmental and social climate impacts. All over the planet, citizens, community members, students, lay scientists, constituents, residents – basically people outside of professional funded scientific research organisations – are providing critical data. The focus ranges from birdwatching to hurricanes, from the microscopic to the stars. Teams of citizen scientists, some of which include professionals, are undertaking projects to reduce the threat of climate change. These projects are generally more engaging, inclusive, participative, and sensitive to on-the-ground variation and cultural context than top-down initiatives. In many cases, they result in more creative and effective solutions.

ISeeChange: community science at work

The crowdsourcing platform ISeeChange was founded to connect people to the importance of climate change to their daily lives. It is just one of many examples of using crowdsourcing for gaining information of citizens and community members as key stakeholders. Local community members share data, stories, and photos on weather impacts, such as flooding, droughts, heat-related illness, and wildfires. The ISeeChange website provides a number of project examples, including the NOLA Heat Map in the city of New Orleans. The project is a 'collaboration between Johns Hopkins Bloomberg School of Public Health, ISeeChange, RAND . . ., the Louisiana Department of Health and the NOLA Health Department. This work is guided by a Community Advisory Panel which is led by community partners and supported by a grant from the National Institute of Environmental Health Sciences' (www.iseechange.org/).

Examples of open innovation and crowdsourcing to mitigate, respond, and adapt to climate change

Crowdsourcing projects to achieve the UN Sustainable Development Goals

In 2022, Crowd4SDG ran Open17 Challenge on Climate Justice, inviting ideas, prototypes, or projects that use crowdsourcing (in this case, citizen science) to tackle a specific climate justice issue. Some applicants received a small prize, then 50 were chosen for team coaching to develop their project and compelling pitch. Promising projects were provided an intensive online workshop organised by CERN IdeaSquare and Crowd4SDG partners aimed at producing a working prototype of the citizen science project. Winning teams, selected based on **novelty** of the specific challenge, **relevance** to climate justice, **feasibility** 'with a few like-minded people', and **crowdsourcing** used to inspire large numbers of people to engage or take collective action, received expenses to participate in the conference in Geneva in March 2023 (https://home.cern/news/news/knowledge-sharing/call-crowdsourcing-projects-pursuing-un-sustainable-development-goals).

Harlem Heat Project

The Harlem Heat Project engages residents to collect temperature and humidity data and use narrative journalism to 'tell the story of urban heat islands in New York City. The data was used to tell the story of disproportionate risks to extreme heat for lower-income and communities of color as a result of increasing temperatures from climate change' (www.adaptationclearinghouse.org/resources/harlem-heat-project-new-york-city.html).

This project raised awareness about the dangers of heat as a 'silent killer'. In community workshops, participants shared stories about difficulties paying electricity bills, inadequate air conditioners, and problems accessing cooling centres.

It is inconceivable that we can adequately address the impacts and issues of climate change and climate justice without deep engagement and leadership by those peoples most impacted. Open innovation and crowdsourcing are thus particularly essential for addressing the gap in integrating climate justice into mainstream climate change mitigation and adaptation initiatives.

Implementation success factors

The successful implementation of crowdsourcing for sustainability-related challenges has a number of specific requirements and recommendations (above and beyond all the typically expected implementation guidelines):

- Deep authenticity and commitment to the stated sustainability-related objectives: the goal must be to drive social, environmental, and economic innovation, achieve results, and truly make an impact (be alert to the danger that challenges and campaigns might be primarily public relations stunts to enable the company to mask unsustainable practices).

- Integration with a broader sustainability/corporate social responsibility commitment and plan that is seen as an integral part of the core business strategy.

- Openness to genuine partnership and collaboration with a wide range of stakeholders and interest groups.

- Systems analysis and contextual knowledge-sharing as an element of the overall process.

- Transparency about the corporate interests and benefits, decision-making processes, assessment processes, and findings: sustainability advocates, and increasingly, consumers in general, are ever more sophisticated, and failure to deliver on expectations can quickly devolve into a social media disaster.

- Focus on community building, both online and in person.

- A focus on accessing and encouraging the voices of marginalised peoples.

- Leading actively throughout the process.

- Following up on promises and driving to implementation.

- Assessing not just ideas and comments but also the results and impact catalysed by the crowdsourcing initiative.

- Learning and embracing cross-cultural competency.

- Balancing the power and sharing or giving over leadership through every stage.

Suggested sessions

Session 1: What is open innovation?

In this session you will focus on reinforcing your understanding of the definition of *open innovation* and how open innovation differs from more traditional approaches. This session requires access to the internet and/or library, although if absolutely needed, the chapter will suffice.

Activity 1 (20 minutes)

Note to faculty: This activity can also be done as a homework assignment. If so, move directly to activity 2 and allow 30–40 minutes for that and 20–30 minutes for sharing and discussing with the entire class.

1. Research the topics of 'open innovation' and 'closed innovation'.

2. Quickly develop:

   a. A description of each
   b. A statement about how they are different
   c. A statement about why open innovation might be advantageous from a business perspective

Activity 2 (20 minutes)

Select a partner from the class. Take turns starting each topic and modifying your statements to come up with the best 'shared' statements. Be prepared to share your statements with the rest of the class.

1. What is *open innovation*?

Definition of open innovation:

....

....

....

....

2. What is *closed innovation*?

Definition of closed innovation:

....

....

....

....

3. How are open and closed innovation different?

Explanation of how they are different:

....

....

....

....

4. Why might a business use open innovation?

Statement of why open innovation might be advantageous from a business perspective:

....

....

....

....

5. Bonus: Why might a government use open innovation?

Statement of why open innovation might be advantageous for governance:

....

....

....

....

Resources

Chesbrough, H. (2003), *Open Innovation: The New Imperative for Creating and Profiting from Technology* (Boston, MA: Harvard Business School Press).

Chesbrough, H. (2011), 'Everything You Need to Know About Open Innovation', *Forbes*, www.forbes.com/sites/henrychesbrough/2011/03/21/everything-you-need-to-know-about-open-innovation/#4a4e897b20b4, accessed 29 January 2017.

GE (2017), 'GE Open Innovation', www.ge.com/about-us/openinnovation, accessed 12 February 2017.

Ideascale (2017), 'Open Innovation', https://ideascale.com/service/open-innovation/, accessed 12 February 2017.

NineSigma (2013), 'What Is Open Innovation?', www.ninesigma.com/open-innovation-resources/what-is-oi, accessed 12 February 2017.

Session 2: LAUNCH case example

In this session you will do a deep dive into LAUNCH, a 'collective genius for a better world' platform sponsored by Nike, NASA, the US Department of State, and the US Agency for International Development.

Activity 1: Examine the LAUNCH challenges through five short videos (30 minutes)

As you watch the following videos, pay attention to and jot down:

- Your emotional reactions

- What you see as strengths of the LAUNCH approach

Suggestion: Fold a piece of paper in half with an area for each of these two topics.

1. Show video *What Is LAUNCH?* (48 seconds duration) https://vimeo.com/37685294.

2. Show video *Nike: NASA LAUNCH* (2:36 minutes duration) https://vimeo.com/55494526.

3. Show video *LAUNCH: Water* (1:10 minutes duration) https://vimeo.com/10208446.

4. Show video *LAUNCH 2020* (3:34 minutes duration) https://vimeo.com/64939206.

5. Show video *What Is the LAUNCH Forum?* (11 minutes duration) https://
    vimeo.com/52700355.

Activity 2: Discuss the emotional appeal of the LAUNCH approach to innovation by creating a 'LAUNCH emotional impact wall' (5 minutes)

As a class, select two volunteers to quickly write down other students' words that describe their emotional reactions to the videos on a whiteboard, blackboard, or chart paper.

Activity 3: Identify and discuss the strengths of the LAUNCH approach to innovation (10 minutes)

As a class, identify what you see as the strengths of the approach taken by LAUNCH that might inform other innovation campaigns for sustainability. Discuss your insights about the design of a successful crowdsourcing initiative, especially one related to sustainability.

Activity 4: Review the LAUNCH process to innovation (10 minutes)

Review the LAUNCH process by referring to Figure 12.1.
   Additional resources related to LAUNCH innovation challenges:

1. Examine the LAUNCH website home page: www.LAUNCH.org.

2. Read about the background of LAUNCH: www.launch.org/about.

3. See the LAUNCH case covered in more detail in Rowledge (2020).

4. Examine current and past LAUNCH challenges: www.launch.org/
    challenges.

Session 3: Implications of crowdsourcing for organisational leadership

In this session you will examine the role of leaders in innovative organisations and the implications that open innovation and crowdsourcing have for leadership. You will identify new or additional competences and attitudes needed by leaders.

Figure 12.1: LAUNCH methodology and value.

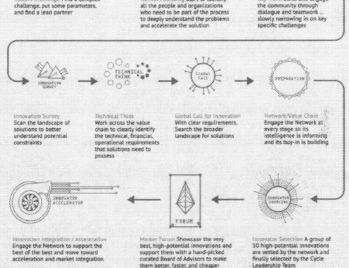

Source: LAUNCH (2017).

Activity 1: Discussion of characteristics of exceptional leaders (10 minutes)

1. Think about the question: 'What are the first characteristics that come to mind when you think about an exceptional leader?'

2. Capture the answers of the entire class to this question on a whiteboard, blackboard, or screen that everyone in the class can read. Treat this as a brainstorming exercise – no right or wrong answers.

Activity 2: Small group exploration of key qualities and roles for leaders of open innovation (30 minutes)

In small groups, discuss three questions using the following instructions:

1. Now that you know more about crowdsourcing and its potential to accelerate innovation, engagement, and progress in solving some of the most difficult

challenges faced by business and the world, what different or additional qualities does a leader need to have?

2. What is the role of leadership in open innovation?

3. How might we build these qualities?

Activity 3: Small group exploration of key qualities and roles for leaders of open innovation (15 minutes)

1. In each small group, share the key points from their discussion. Discuss insights and implications.

2. *Extension activity or assignment.* Individually, form a personal goal and then a development plan for developing one or more of these leadership competences related to leading a culture and practice of open innovation. Then find a coaching buddy and agree to support each other in achieving this goal.

Session 4: Open innovation and sustainability team assignment and presentation

In this session you will present your research and insights regarding open innovation and sustainability using a team assignment with A and B versions.

Find a partner with whom to do this team assignment. If needed, one team could have three members. Plan to spend 15 minutes, making sure everyone in class understands the assignment. You will then spend about 10 hours researching and preparing a presentation, followed by 55 minutes total in a class setting for team presentations and discussion.

This assignment is intended to increase your knowledge of crowdsourcing (in general and applied to sustainability) through more in-depth analysis, experience, and preparation and delivery of presentations to fellow students. The assignment inspires you to do a deeper dive into a selected crowdsourcing challenge or gives you direct experience as a participant in a crowdsourcing initiative of your choice.

Learning objectives

On completing this assignment, you will be able to:

- Conduct internet research on and identify examples of open innovation and crowdsourcing applied to sustainability and social justice–related issues.

- Demonstrate your expanded knowledge by presenting an example of crowdsourcing applied to sustainable business and social innovation.

Note: This activity is best done as a team homework assignment presented and reviewed in class. Working in pairs (rather than a larger team) will reduce the coordination requirement and optimise the time each student is directly engaged with the assignment. The level of performance expectations can increase with the level of the class, especially with respect to expectations about critical thinking, strategic analysis, and ability to offer creative and innovative solutions. This can also be scaled to be a major multi-week assignment, with either more extensive engagement in a crowdsourcing challenge or writing a case study.

Resource

Rowledge, L. R. (2020), *CrowdRising: Building a Sustainable World Through Mass Collaboration* (Abingdon, Oxon and New York, NY: Routledge, 2020).

Activity 1: Read over the assignment and select a partner (15 minutes)

Assignment directions:

1. As a two-person team:
   a. Conduct research to find and review examples of crowdsourcing applied to sustainable business and social innovation. There is a list of potential challenges in Table 12.2 but feel free to select a different challenge in which you may be interested.
   b. Select one challenge to (a) review and/or (b) participate in and make a contribution towards.

2. Incorporating the guidelines that follows, either:
   a. Prepare a five-minute presentation (or poster board presentation) summarising the crowdsourcing challenge, process, and where available, winning ideas.

    b. Make a contribution to a sustainability crowdsourcing challenge and prepare a five-minute presentation.

3.   The number of members in each group will be determined by the class size and the presentation time and format. For example, if there are 20 students in pairs presenting for 5 minutes each, then it will take 50 minutes. Alternatively, if there are 40 or more students, you could change the assignment to a poster session and do half the class as presenters, the other half as audience, then switch.

4.   In both cases A and B, the presentation should include:

- Name, description, goals, and presenting question of the open innovation/ crowdsourcing initiative
- Sponsoring organisation(s)
- Intended participants, audience
- Clear statement of how this initiative is related to innovation to address sustainability, social justice, or global problems, challenges, or opportunities
- Description of the structure and process of the challenge and what type of crowdsourcing it involves

Table 12.2: Crowdsourcing examples

A: Review, summarise, report	B: Review, participate, report
The Counted	**Zooniverse** (see Table 12.1)
A project by *The Guardian* to count people killed by police and other law enforcement agencies in the USA and tell their stories (www.theguardian.com/us-news/ng-interactive/2015/jun/01/the-counted-police-killings-us-database).	The Zooniverse lets everyone take part in real, cutting-edge research in many fields across the sciences, humanities, and more. **Contribute to new research.** There's no previous experience required; just pick a project and get started right away (www.zooniverse.org/projects ng-interactive/2015/jun/01/ about-the-counted).
LAUNCH (see session 2) Select any one of the major annual topics to review.	**OpenIDEO** (see Table 12.1) Select any one of the major annual topics to review.
XPRIZE (see Table 12.1) Select any one of the major annual topics to review.	**Unilever Foundry** (see Table 12.1) Select any one of the major annual topics to review.
Dell Go Green Challenge (see Table 12.1) Select any one of the major annual topics to review.	**My Starbucks Idea** Review and then contribute an environmental or social sustainability idea (http://mystarbucksidea.force.com).

- Examples of noteworthy or winning solutions proposed by the crowd
- Key learning or takeaway(s)

Again, you are encouraged to find other challenges to review and/or participate in.

Activity 2: Crowdsourcing sustainability examples presentations (55 minutes)

Each pair of students should present their example in five minutes, either sequentially for the entire class or in a poster session with half the class presenting while half is audience, then switching.

Additional teaching material and ideas

40 Examples of Open Innovation and Crowdsourcing http://innovation excellence.com/blog/2012/08/13/40-examples-of-open-innovation-crowdsourcing/

As either in-class or homework assignment, go to this website and follow up on ONE of the crowdsourcing examples, looking for sustainability-related applications. At the end of 30 minutes' research, create a summary list of examples and the links to more information (potentially using Google Docs so you can share it with the class).

Let's Crowdsource the World's Goals (Drummond 2012) www.ted.com/talks/jamie_drummond_how_to_set_goals_for_the_world?language=en

Watch this video, then work in groups of two to three to identify other potential examples where crowdsourcing might be used to obtain input from the people impacted by policy, programmes, or decisions. Each group should then share their ideas, creating a master list at the front of the class (two students could serve as recorders).

Federal Crowdsourcing and Citizen Science Catalog of projects https://ccsin-ventory.wilsoncenter.org

Look for projects near the area where you live or like to visit. Can you think of a 'citizen science' crowdsourcing project you think would be a valuable contribution?

Sustainable Brands article on BwareIT

www.sustainablebrands.com/news_and_views/startups/sustainable_brands/unilever_foundry_indiegogo_partner_crowdfund_sustainabili

Additional Resource:

www.unileverusa.com/news/press-releases/2016/unilever-foundry-and-indiego go-launch-crowdfunding-partnership.html

Read this article, and discuss how Unilever has partnered with the crowdfunding platform Indiegogo to launch and scale sustainability ideas and solutions identified through the Unilever Foundry.

Examine examples of open innovation and sustainability

1. Review different types and examples of crowdsourcing, then develop a master list of examples applied to sustainability challenges.

2. Deepen your understanding of crowdsourcing: watch the video called *Crowdsourcing and Crowdfunding Explained* (3:48 minutes duration) on www.youtube.com/watch?v=-38uPkyH9vI.

Group work

1. Identify sustainability-related crowdsourcing initiatives (30 minutes). Provide the following instructions and allow time for students to gather in groups:

    In groups of about four people, identify one or more exciting examples of *sustainability-related* crowdsourcing initiatives. Bonus points for new examples not identified in this chapter. To the extent possible, use the internet for your research. Prepare a 2-minute presentation on the example(s) you are most excited about to give to your classmates 25 minutes from now.

2. Group presentations of exciting sustainability-related crowdsourcing initiatives (15 minutes)

    Each group should present the example of crowdsourcing applied to sustainability that the group is most excited about. As each group presents examples, record them under the type of crowdsourcing that most closely defines each initiative described according to the six types outlined in this chapter.

Further readings

Chesbrough, H. (2003), *Open Innovation: The New Imperative for Creating and Profiting from Technology* (Boston, MA: Harvard Business School Press).

> In this book, Henry Chesbrough suggests starting with building an appreciation for the merits of the traditional industrial R&D paradigm before launching into its issues and problems. He presents four course modules and summarises innovation case studies appropriate for a wide range of somewhat-sophisticated management topics. Module 3 addresses the innovation processes that companies use to source ideas and technologies from the external environment given knowledge is now widely distributed. Chesbrough also introduces the concept that 'technology has no economic value absent a business model'.

Plastrik, P., M. Taylor, and J. Cleveland (2014), *Connecting to Change the World: Harnessing the Power of Networks for Social Impact* (Washington, DC: Island Press).

> This book is a guide to building and managing networks for social impact. Aimed primarily at leaders of non-profits, it describes important considerations for building and designing effective social-impact networks. Critical within this are purpose; membership; value propositions; coordination, facilitation, and communication; resources; governance; assessment; and operating principles.

Rowledge, L. R. (2020), *CrowdRising: Building a Sustainable World Through Mass Collaboration* (Abingdon, Oxon and New York, NY: Routledge).

> *CrowdRising* introduces the convergence of society's and business's need for transformational change towards sustainability and social justice with the emerging technological capability and leadership insights necessary to achieve business sustainability and solve global challenges. Open innovation and crowdsourcing, applied to tapping our collective knowledge, wisdom, and power, are endorsed as the window of hope. The book provides in-depth case studies and a myriad of examples of crowdsourcing used for:
> - Catalysing innovative solutions to scientific, technological, and societal challenges (Chapter 3)
> - Soliciting customer vision, insights, and action (Chapter 4)
> - Engaging employees in improvement, innovation, and activism (Chapter 5)
> - Gathering citizen input and democratising governance (Chapter 6)
> - Activating student initiative for good (Chapter 7)
> - Co-creating strategy for environmental, social, and economic sustainability (Chapter 8)

CrowdRising provides guidance for designing and implementing open innovation and crowdsourcing campaigns and highlights selected crowdsourcing platforms. The book closes with the importance and potential of open innovation for co-creating a positive future.

References

Beavis, S. (2011) *Sony: Engaging Untapped Audience Through Crowdsourcing*, www.theguardian.com/sustainable-business/sony-untapped-audience-crowd sourcing-project, accessed 29 January 2017.

Bott, M., B.-S. Gigler and G. Young (2011) *The Role of Crowdsourcing for Better Governance in Fragile State Contexts*, www.scribd.com/document/75642401/The-Role-of-Crowdsourcing-for-Better-Governance-in-Fragile-State-Contexts, accessed 12 February 2017.

Chesbrough, H. (2003) *Open Innovation: The New Imperative for Creating and Profiting from Technology* (Boston, MA: Harvard Business School Press).

Chesbrough, H. (2011) 'Everything You Need to Know About Open Innovation', *Forbes*, www.forbes.com/sites/henrychesbrough/2011/03/21/everything-you-need-to-know-about-open-innovation/#4a4e897b20b4, accessed 29 January 2017.

Citigroup (2013) *Citi and Kiva Launch Kiva U to Engage Students and Educators in Global Effort to Expand Financial Inclusion* [Press Release], www.citigroup. com/citi/news/2013/130827a.htm, accessed 12 February 2017.

CXOtoday (2010) 'Dell Encourages Green Behavior in Consumers', *CXOtoday*, www.cxoto day.com/story/dell-encourages-green-behavior-in-consumers/, accessed 12 February 2017.

DigitalGov (2017) *Federal Crowdsourcing and Citizen Science*, www.digitalgov.gov/communities/ federal-crowdsourcing-and-citizen-science/, accessed 29 January 2017.

Drummond, J. (2012) *Let's Crowdsource the World's Goals* [Video], www.ted.com/talks/jamie_ drummond_how_to_set_goals_for_the_world?language=en, accessed 30 January 2017.

Esposti, C., D. Albert and D. Evans (2013) *Enterprise Crowdsourcing: Changing the Way Work Gets Done*, https://sustainabledevelopment.un.org/content/documents/211617%20 Goals%2017%20Partnerships.pdf, accessed 12 February 2017.

GE (2009) *GE Launches "Healthymagination"; Will Commit $6 Billion to Enable Better Health Focusing on Cost, Access and Quality* [Press Release], www.ge.com/pdf/investors/ events/05072009/ge_healthymagination_pr.pdf, accessed 29 January 2017.

GE (2017) *Ecomagination Strategy*, www.ge.com/about-us/ecomagination/strategy, accessed 29 January 2017.

Gellers, J.C. (2015) *Crowdsourcing Sustainable Development Goals from Global Civil Society: A Content Analysis*, https://ssrn.com/abstract=2562122, accessed 30 January 2017.

Gemmill, B. and A. Bamidele-Izu (2002) 'The Role of NGOs and Civil Society in Global Environmental Governance', in D.C. Esty and M.H. Ivanova (eds.), *Global Environmental Governance: Options and Opportunities* (New Haven, CT: Yale Center for Environmental Law and Policy): 1–24.

Godelnik, R. (2012) 'Can Crowdsourcing Really Work for Unilever?', *TriplePundit*, www. triplepundit.com/2012/04/crowdsourcing-really-work-unilever/, accessed 12 February 2017.

GoldiBlox (2017) *About*, www.goldieblox.com/pages/about, accessed 12 February 2017.

GSK (2015) *Healthcare Innovation Award 2015*, www.gsk.com/en-gb/responsibility/ apply-for-healthcare-innovation-award/, accessed 12 February 2017.

HOT (Humanitarian OpenStreetMap Team) (2017) *About*, https://hotosm.org/ about, accessed 12 February 2017.

IPCC (2022) *Climate Change 2022: Mitigation of Climate Change. Contribution of Working Group III to the Sixth Assessment Report of the Intergovernmental Panel on Climate Change*, P.R. Shukla, J. Skea, R. Slade, A. Al Khourdajie, R. van Diemen, D. McCollum, M. Pathak, S. Some, P. Vyas, R. Fradera, M. Belkacemi, A. Hasija, G. Lisboa, S. Luz, J. Malley (eds.), (Cambridge, UK: Cambridge University Press) doi: 10.1017/9781009157926, https://www. ipcc.ch/report/ar6/wg3/

Jaguar Land Rover and Novelis (2016) *Collaboration for a Closed-Loop Value Chain: Transferable Learning Points from the REALCAR Project*, www.cisl.cam.ac.uk/publications/ publication-pdfs/cisl-closed-loop-case-study-web.pdf, UK: accessed 29 January 2017.

Katz, B. (2007) *The Integration of Project Management Processes with a Methodology to Manage a Radical Innovation Project* (MscEng thesis, Department of Industrial Engineering, University of Stellenbosch) cited in S.J. Marais and C.S.L. Schutte (n.d.) *The Development of Open Innovation Models to Assist the Innovation Process*, www.academia.edu/219234/

The_Development_Of_Open_Innovation_Models_To_Assist_The_Innovation_Process, accessed 29 January 2017.

LAUNCH (2017) *Our Process*, www.launch.org/process, accessed 31 January 2017.

Malouf, A. (2015) *The Head Health II Final Winners Announced*, https://ninesights.ninesigma. com/web/head-health/supportforum/-/message_boards/message/14135951, accessed 12 February 2017.

Mariello, A. (2007) 'The Five Stages of Successful Innovation', *MIT Sloan Management Review*, http://sloanreview.mit.edu/article/the-five-stages-of-successful-innovation/, accessed 29 January 2017.

Merriam-Webster (2017) *Innovation*, www.merriam-webster.com/dictionary/innovation, accessed 29 January 2017.

Moyo, S. (2013) *How We Delivered African Voices Directly to World Leaders*, www.one.org/ international/blog/how-we-delivered-african-voices-directly-to-world-leaders/, accessed 31 January 2017.

Nichols, J. (2012) *Toyota Ideas for Good*, www.behance.net/gallery/5967749/Toyota-Ideas-For-Good, accessed 29 January 2017.

NineSigma (2015) *GE GHG Ecomagination Innovation Challenge: Energy Efficiency Solutions for Canada's Oil Sands*, https://ninesights.ninesigma.com/web/ecomaginationinnovation/ home, accessed 29 January 2017.

Nkombo, N. (2013) *Make Yourself Heard with ONE's New "You Choose" Campaign Says D'banj*, www.one.org/international/blog/make-yourself-heard-with-ones-new-you-choose-campaign-says-dbanj/, accessed 31 January 2017.

ONE (2013a) *Open for Development*, https://www.imf.org/external/np/exr/consult/2013/ transpol/pdf/onehelp.pdf, accessed 23 March 2023.

ONE (2013b) *Open for Development: Achieving Greater Post-2015 Results Through an Open Design Process, Monitoring System and Data Portals*, https://s3.amazonaws.com/one.org/ images/ONE_HLP_Report_-_FINAL.pdf, accessed 31 January 2017.

Open IDEO (2016) *Beneficiary Feedback*, https://challenges.openideo.com/challenge/ agricultural-innovation/beneficiary-feedback, accessed 30 January 2017.

Orange UK (2011) *Do Some Good: Interviews* [Video], www.youtube.com/ watch?v=3R-MiW TUqYE, accessed 29 January 2017.

Oxford Dictionaries (2017) *Crowdsourcing*, www.oxforddictionaries.com/us/definition/ american_english/crowdsourcing, accessed 29 January 2017.

PRME (Principles for Responsible Management Education) (2017) *Six Principles*, www.unprme. org/about-prme/the-six-principles.php, accessed 29 January 2017.

Roth, Y., F. Pétavy and M. Braz de Matos (2016) *The State of Crowdsourcing in 2016*, https:// en.eyeka.com/resources/reports?download=cs_report_2016.pdf #CSreport2016, accessed 12 February 2017.

Rowledge, L.R. (2020) *CrowdRising: Building a Sustainable World Through Mass Collaboration* (Abingdon, Oxon and New York, NY: Routledge).

Sterling, D. (2012) *GoldieBlox: The Engineering Toy for Girls*, www.kickstarter.com/projects/ 16029337/goldieblox-the-engineering-toy-for-girls, accessed 30 January 2017.

Sustainable Brands (2016) 'Unilever Foundry, Indiegogo Partner to Crowdfund Sustainability Solutions', *Sustainable Brands*, www.sustainablebrands.com/news_and_views/startups/ sustainable_brands/unilever_foundry_indiegogo_partner_crowdfund_sustainabili, accessed 30 January 2017.

Toomey, M. (2016) *A People-Powered Agenda*, https://sdgactioncampaign.org/2016/05/27/a-people-powered-agenda/, accessed 31 January 2017.

Toyota (2011) *Five Winners Selected in Toyota "Ideas for Good" Challenge* [Press Release], http:// corporatenews.pressroom.toyota.com/releases/winners+ideas+for+good+may+2011.htm, accessed 29 January 2017.

UN Development Group (2013) *The Global Conversation Begins: Emerging Views for a New Development Agenda*, www.undp.org/content/dam/undp/library/MDG/english/global-conversation-begins-web.pdf, accessed 31 January 2017.

UN SDG Action Campaign (2016) *SDGs: A People-powered Agenda – Leave No One Behind*, https://sdgactioncampaign.org/2016/07/18/sdgsexhibition/, accessed 31 January 2017.

Unilever (2017) *Open Innovation*, www.unilever.com/about/innovation/open-innovation/, accessed 12 February 2017.

United Nations (2016) *Sustainable Development Goal 17*, https://sustainabledevelopment. un.org/sdg17, accessed 12 February 2017.

United Nations Climate Reports (2023) https://www.un.org/en/climatechange/reports? gclid=Cj0KCQiA1NebBhDDARIsAANiDD2JVyK_5YfTGYat-00Bvwwom96Bvx 5RlcG80RO-olc17TvQqwucWD4aAnoxEALw_wcB, accessed 23 March 2023.

Ushahidi (2017) *About Ushahidi*, www.ushahidi.com/about, accessed 12 February 2017.

Ward-Smith, J. (2010) *"Making Minutes Matter": Orange Mobile Micro Volunteering*, http:// ivo.org/post/making-minutes-matter-orange-mobile-micro-volunteering-548768a 49108686207659dc3, accessed 29 January 2017.

XPRIZE (2017) *Wendy Schmidt Ocean Health XPRIZE*, http://oceanhealth.xprize.org, accessed 29 January 2017.

Note

1   This chapter summarises analyses and cases covered in more detail in Rowledge (2020).

13

Sustainable operations management

Roy Stratton, Maggie Zeng, Aquila Yeong, and Talal Alsharief

Operations management is concerned with creating the value delivered by the organisation and therefore is more directly responsible for how the resources (human, material, and energy) are effectively used in this process.

Five performance objectives (cost, quality, speed, dependability, and flexibility) (Slack et al., 2019) have traditionally been attributed to the operations function, but the cost objective commonly dominates decision-making, which can encourage wasteful short-term and local cost-focused decisions at the expense of the other performance objectives. Over the decades, industry practice has emerged that has proved effective at reducing this waste by adopting more systems-based approaches centred on reducing variability through quality management/Six Sigma and improving flow through lean thinking (Womack and Jones, 1996; Bicheno and Holweg, 2020). These developments are very well aligned with a wider systems perspective, improving alignment and eliminating waste across the supply chain, which is consistent with the sustainability objective commonly referred to as 'lean and green' (Piercy and Rich, 2014).

DOI: 10.4324/9781003294665-16

However, the sustainability agenda goes beyond this, adding a wider systems perspective that embraces the product and process design, covering the entire product cycle. This is reflected in Figure 13.1, which corresponds with the UN Sustainable Development Goals (Giannetti et al., 2020).

This simple illustration helps explain the need to move from a linear to a circular model where, as in nature, there is an embedded waste recycling process.

This wider perspective is not clearly embraced in the five performance objectives referred to earlier, and a sixth operations management objective is needed that Jimenez and Lorente (2001) termed 'environmental performance'.

With this wider perspective, this chapter will look into how these six objectives can be effectively managed, extending the 'lean and green' manufacturing practice to embrace the circular economy incorporating life cycle assessment and sustainable product design (Lacey et al., 2020).

On completion of this chapter, students should be able to:

- Understand the difference between traditional operations management and sustainable operations management.

Figure 13.1: Goods and services life cycle.

- Discuss the contribution that sustainable operations management can make to overall performance.

- Classify sustainable operations management practices in different organisations and identify different options in how to achieve Sustainable Development Goal 12, 'ensure sustainable consumption and production patterns'.

Introduction

The sustainability agenda demands a shift in operations management thinking that goes beyond the systems approaches often characterised by lean thinking. This involves taking a long-term view that encompasses the entire product cycle, so moving from a linear economy (take, make, waste) to a circular economy. The circular economy is where products and materials are kept within productive use for as long as possible and, at the end of use, effectively recycled or looped back. This is contrary to local short-term rather than systems thinking that naturally dominates operations and supply chain management. This shift in thinking needs to be supported by government regulation, but addressing this challenge also brings opportunity to develop creative solutions. The concept of circularity effectively captures this new paradigm and is gaining practical favour, and in 2020, France established a comprehensive anti-waste law to shift the country's production, distribution, and consumption systems from a linear to a circular economic model, urging enterprises of all sizes, towns, and consumers to eliminate waste and adopt more circular behaviours (Ellen MacArthur Foundation, 2022a; Atasu et al., 2018; Blunck, 2016).

The chapter is structured as follows: Firstly, key circular economy business models are outlined before considering three operational aspects that are key to transitioning to the circular economy. These aspects are then viewed through the lens of operations theory before considering specific action more closely allied to the operations function.

Business models to support circular systems

Lacey et al. (2020) proposes the following six business models as a means of considering opportunities to engage circularity.

Circular inputs

A first step is to consider using resources in the process that are naturally circular, such as renewable energy and biological materials that naturally decompose (Marshall et al., 2022).

Sharing platforms

Poor utilisation of resources can be addressed by the use of sharing platforms. The sharing platforms have given many consumers access to more and frequently less-expensive alternatives of goods and services across numerous industries. This ability to share has been enhanced through smart technology in our pockets. Why not share your car or the ability to park on your drive at home? Airbnb utilised the internet to enable a means of better utilising spare capacity in the form of accommodation; originally starting with an airbed, this has grown to embrace any accommodation worldwide. Since its launch in 2009, Airbnb has grown rapidly as one of the most popular platforms for the sharing economy. In 2018, Airbnb had a market value of close to $31 billion, a profit of $2.6 billion, and revenues of $93 million. This ability to utilise capacity through sharing peer to peer has clear benefits but is also being used in business resource sharing (Ferreira et al., 2022).

Product as a service

If we take the concept of sharing further, why should the end user own the product? Can a delivery system be devised where the physical product ownership does not change? How could the delivery system be designed so the end user pays for the benefits of use rather than ownership? This is commonly referred to as servitisation of a product, and more attention is given to this later. Sometimes referred to as 'pay per click', we see this in high-capital-cost items and notable Xerox photocopiers, where you pay per copy, and gas turbine–powered commercial aircraft where the charge is based on time in flight. There are many circular benefits, but the model requires an ongoing relationship with the customer, whose usage now has a direct input to the suppliers' delivery system. Such transitions have radical implications as they positively impact overall performance. For example, Rolls-Royce traditionally made money through the sale of spares, often selling the initial aircraft engines at a loss. This created a perverse contradiction where a less-reliable engine was potentially more profitable. They introduced the power-by-the-hour service model, partly because their engines were so reliable, and with this new business model, the contradiction was eliminated, so encouraging longer service life. By charging airlines based on usage, it was Rolls-Royce's responsibility to monitor continuously and service the engines as required (Aubertin, 2019).

As illustrated, moving to a service-based model has major implications on how the new business operates, opening up significant sustainability benefits (retained ownership and control, repair and overhaul performance aligned with customer benefits, etc.).

Product use extensions

The products we buy, such as white goods in the kitchen, are often very expensive to repair, and when something goes wrong, it is tempting to replace and recycle (remember, recycling is the poorest means of closing the loop). IKEA kitchen goods come with a five-year repair warranty. This requires a repair service to be on call to repair machines promptly in your home. With this commitment in place, as with servitisation, there is an implicit incentive to minimise this cost by improving the reliability. This also provides the OEM with valuable data on reliability and where improvement is needed. This can be taken further by designing the machine to enable self-maintenance increasingly aided by YouTube videos. Dyson is notable for designing their vacuum cleaner products to enable user maintenance, supported by free support over the phone with replacement parts through the post whilst under guarantee.

Resource recovery

The final cycle concerns recovery of the resources in the product. It is important to carefully consider how a product's design supports this process, including reverse logistics. This involves getting the product to a location capable of doing this effectively, which is greatly assisted if the OEM retains ownership, as in the servitisation model. For example, the partnership between Hewlett Packard (HP) and Sinctronics has established a robust reverse logistics scheme enabling recovery and the creation of value out of HP's end-of-use electronic equipment. This has resulted in numerous benefits, including a 50% reduction in collection time for end-of-life products, a 30% reduction in client expenditures, and 97% of materials collected by Sinctronics being recovered to be immediately reintroduced into the supply chain (Ellen MacArthur Foundation, 2022b).

Key aspects of operational improvement

Having considered the classic circular business models, let us consider the transition required at a more theoretical level by identifying key aspects we will then use within a wider theoretical model closely allied to the operations perspective.

> **Trade-offs.** Customers have different priorities and are willing to pay more; therefore, it is important to align delivery systems to meet the needs of different customer priorities (e.g. fair trade, organic goods, and electric/hybrid cars).

Strategy is about making trade-off choices that are consistent with the institutional environment in which they operate. This includes legal (laws, regulations, policy initiatives, political climate, etc.), market forces (customer demand and preferences, competition, unions), evaluation criteria (profits, certification, KPIs, standards, etc), and societal values and norms (acceptable behaviour, best practice, etc).

Business and operations strategy work to acknowledge these factors, and clearly these are changing, but not fast enough. For example, what level of incentive is needed to encourage the adoption of electric cars or public transport? Will changing societal attitudes towards fast fashion and the associated waste need to be complimented by regulation?

> **Technology.** Developing and using new technology that improves multiple performance objectives in the long term. This is particularly evident in our use of physical technology, for example, solar panels, battery technology, and LED light bulbs, but most importantly, digital technology and biological technology is rapidly developing (Lacey et al., 2020).

For example, Johnson & Johnson successfully automated 60 global operations via intelligent automation, freeing up employees' time to work on high-priority projects rather than routine busy work and producing insights that employees can use to make better decisions and increase compliance, quality, and speed (Mixson, 2021). However, technology comes in many forms, computing technology and particularly smartphones providing a technological capability that needs to be effectively exploited through software applications that enable changes in practice, policy, and behaviour. This may simply be renting out your car or parking space through an app or adopting a paradigm shifting circular business model.

> **System design.** Designing products and delivery systems that embrace a wider systems perspective reflected in the circular economy business models. Inertia in adopting such models is rarely limited by technology but by the need for creative redesign

that encompasses the overall life cycle to improve reliability, reparability, reuse, and upgrade.

Changes to the delivery system design can simply challenge custom and practice, such as specifying best-before dates or selecting fruits and vegetables that conform to acceptable shape norms. On the other hand, it also includes the coordination of the product and the logistics process design. So designing parts for ease of upgrade rather than disposal. The bottom line benefits could include customer loyalty or even customer lock-in with a service relationship over a longer product lifetime and lower disposal costs, particularly in countries that mandate product takeback.

These three aspects to improving sustainable performance have been usefully embraced through operations management theory that can usefully aid our thinking about how they interplay as we seek sustainability.

Theory of performance frontiers

The theory of performance frontiers (TPF) (Schmenner and Swink, 1998) originally emerged as a means of explaining the shift in thinking associated with the lean flow–based management approach referred to earlier. This encompasses systems thinking that can be readily extended to embrace the wider global perspective encompassing sustainability and the circular economy.

The theory represents the interplay between the three aspects represented using two different trade-off frontiers. The limiting trade-off is represented by the technology frontier, where new technology enables these trade-off limitations to effectively move to the right, so improving environmental performance at lower cost. However, this figure, as the original, uses the operating frontier to acknowledge how current practice operates far short of the technology limits. Lean and the TPS demonstrated the opportunity to significantly improve performance through more effectively capitalising on the existing technology (assets in original model); hence, the operating frontier was moved to the right through the adoption of new policies, measurements, and behaviours that effectively comprised a paradigm shift in thinking.

Let us reflect on how these three aspects relate to environmental sustainability.

Firstly, the model utilises the concept of **trade-offs** between the performance objectives. This is represented by the frontiers that illustrate how improved quality, speed, environment, etc. can be achieved at the expense of higher cost. This is easily illustrated by the cost of clothing that is eco-friendly, the cost of a product that has high reliability and a long life (e.g. Miele white goods), or the building of a house to a high performance, for example, quality or energy rating (e.g. additional levels of insulation). This concept of performance trade-offs underpins operations strategy and, with it, the need to align performance objectives with the market priorities. It is therefore important to acknowledge trade-off choices as well as the need for strategic focus in acknowledging wider and longer-term systems perspectives.

The second and third aspects (**technology and system design**) are reflected in the two trade-off frontiers (technology and operating, respectively).

The potential of new technology enables the trade-off curve to be repositioned, effectively moving the frontier to the right. So representing improvement on all fronts simultaneously due to enhanced technology. However, this frontier only represents the potential performance offered by the technology, with the actual performance (operating frontier) being further to the left.

The operating frontier represents the actual performance achieved and illustrates the need to align policies, measures, behaviours, and effective management if the full potential of the available technology is to be exploited.

If you consider Figure 13.2, 'A0' is performance that is rather ad hoc and had never represented good practice. 'A1' represents a position on an operating frontier reflecting performance akin to traditional values, policies, measures, and behaviours. These are typically centred on local performance embedded in the traditional linear model. Figure 13.2 therefore illustrates how operations can move from position A1 to A2 by adopting different values, measures, policies, and behaviours, so embracing means of extending product life, utilising sustainable resources, etc.

The model effectively illustrates the relationship between these three aspects of operational improvement:

- Performance trade-offs need to be acknowledged as strategic incentives help to focus attention.

- Technology provides the means of improving performance on all fronts, thereby breaking traditional trade-offs, as reflected in the asset frontier.

Figure 13.2: An interpretation of the theory of performance frontiers.

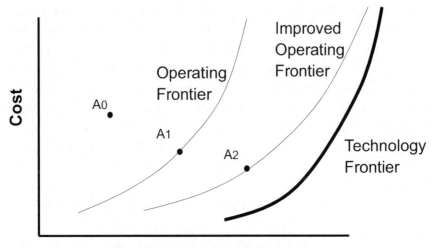

Source: Schmenner and Swink (1998, modified).

- A paradigm shift in how the delivery system is designed is commonly required to move the operating frontier, and it is rare for the technology frontier to be the limiter as it takes time for system redesign to capitalise on the potential of such technology, as reflected in the circular economy business models outlined earlier.

Lean and green manufacturing

Following *The Machine that Changed the World* (Womack et al., 1990), Womack and Jones (1996) introduced the Western world to *lean thinking* by addressing the revolution in manufacturing production systems presented by the Toyota production system. Compared to traditional 'mass production' manufacturing systems epitomised by batch-and-queue methods, lean systems focus on just-in-time, waste elimination, value stream, and continuous improvement. Empirical evidence shows that companies that adopt the lean manufacturing philosophy centred on flow are also benefiting the environment by becoming more resource- and energy-efficient through pollution prevention, waste reduction, and recycling opportunities (Bergmiller and McCright, 2009).

Because lean focuses on reducing non-value-added activities and producing only the amount of a product that is needed, systematic improvements combine well with sustainable operations. Lean results in an operational and cultural environment highly conducive to the minimisation of waste and pollution, thus providing an excellent platform for environmental management tools, such as LCAs and design for environment (Arturo Garza-Reyes, 2015).

Lean practices are aimed at providing the right materials at the right time to support manufacturing needs by focusing on reducing excess inventories of raw or work-in-process materials that are not immediately consumed by the production cycle. Significant reductions in waste material delivered to landfill have come about through cell-based manufacturing processes that signal a pull for materials based on demand of a product. This has also led to a reduction in raw materials consumed. By using this process-focused approach, managers have the luxury of adopting a more holistic view regarding change. Both lean and green focus on minimising waste and time, resulting in an improvement in quality of the product. The former considers waste as no value to the customer, and the latter considers it as the extraction and subsequent disposal of resources at a rate and in a form which is environmentally sustainable. The belief is that all companies can make minor operational changes that will exponentially reduce costs and improve sustainability.

Lean and green practices share common goals and values, so this collaboration could also stretch to non-manufacturing companies. What company would not welcome a reduction in waste (be it time, energy, or resources) that leads to rising profits, as well as developing the maturity to embed environmental responsibility within its processes? The implementation of lean and green practices would lead to companies being more competitive and environmentally friendly. In this way, companies can also contribute to Sustainable Development Goal (SDG) 12, 'ensure sustainable consumption and production patterns', but also other SDGs, such as SDG 13, 'climate action'.

The following approaches explain in more detail how this transition can be achieved.

Life cycle assessment

Life cycle assessment is a process of evaluating the total cost and environmental burdens associated with a product, process, or activity. This is achieved by identifying and quantifying energy and materials used and wastes released to the environment, with a view to identify and evaluate opportunities to affect improvements. The assessment includes the entire life cycle of the process, product, activity, or service system, encompassing extracting and processing raw materials, manufacturing, transportation and distribution, use, reuse, maintenance, recycling, and final disposal (SETAC, 1993).

Life cycle assessment (LCA), often referred to as 'cradle-to-grave' assessment, was developed as an analytical tool, is practised globally, and has been standardised by ISOs 14040 and 14044. By following the course of all inputs (e.g. processing of raw materials, use of energy, water, and fuel) and outputs (e.g. consumer products, waste to landfill, CO_2 emissions, heat and energy loss), this system will enable companies to assess and identify the environmental impacts of a product or activity over its entire life cycle.

A fully comprehensive LCA should include every material component and process to assess both their direct and indirect impacts. This data is then placed in a hierarchy based on its impact category, that is, global warming, acidification, carcinogens, etc. By implementing LCAs, firms are able to systematically organise complex data from comprehensive environmental, economic, and social categories as well as identifying the trade-offs between the three sustainability pillars, life cycle stages, impacts, products, and generations throughout the product's entire life cycle (Ciambrone, 2019). For example, Table 13.1 provides a life cycle assessment for a pair of jeans, focusing on the effects of resource extraction, manufacturing, packing, logistics, and the end of life of the jeans, where they are either reused or end up in a landfill.

Levi's is a pioneer in the clothing industry having conducted an LCA in 2007, and sustainability has been embedded in the company's policy and operations practice (Thorpe, 2011). For example, Levi's identified that a pair of jeans consumed 919 gallons of water during its lifetime, and 49% of water usage was during the early stages, when the denim was still in its cotton, plant form. In other words, just under half the amount of water it will be exposed to occurs during its raw material stage, and this led Levi's to educate its farmers in China,

Table 13.1: Life cycle assessment for a pair of jeans

Cotton	Water, pesticides, herbicides, fertiliser, energy use
Spinning	Energy consumption, dust, waste material
Dying/weaving	Chemical use, dyes, wastewater, energy
Other materials	Zips, button, label, rivets
Garment production	Material waste, ethical labour condition, energy use
Packaging	Plastic packaging
Transport	Different transportation modes, energy consumption, gas emission
Use, care, and maintenance	Water, wash chemical, energy consumption
End-of-life	Landfill, reuse, unravelling into fibres

Source: Adopted from Thorpe (2011).

India, Brazil, and other places on how to grow cotton with less water and how to process the stonewashing of jeans without using any water at all. Levi's later joined the Better Cotton Initiative, a non-profit organisation, in 2009, with the aim of reducing the negative environmental impact of clothing manufacturers. A 'green wash initiative' was also launched in order to encourage consumers to wash their jeans less and to wash in cold water to further reduce water consumption (see Figure 13.3).

Tropicana undertook an LCA and found that rather than its carbon footprint being mainly due to the transportation of heavy juice containers, evidence showed that it was actually the agricultural inputs needed to grow its oranges (Martin, 2009). This has now changed the company's attitude towards how to reduce its carbon footprint: rather than focusing on the fuel efficiency of its distribution vehicles, it now concentrates on sustainable agricultural practices, that is, reduced fertiliser use. The information provided by LCAs can be a valuable insight into alternative ways of cutting costs and waste, raising profits, gaining a competitive advantage, and improving operations practices, while at the same time reducing environmental impact. In addition, by identifying the source and relative magnitude of environmental impacts, this data can shape the innovation agenda. It highlights fertile areas that are ready for improvement and can help drive the outcomes of competing new ideas.

Figure 13.3: Life cycle of Levi's 501 jeans.

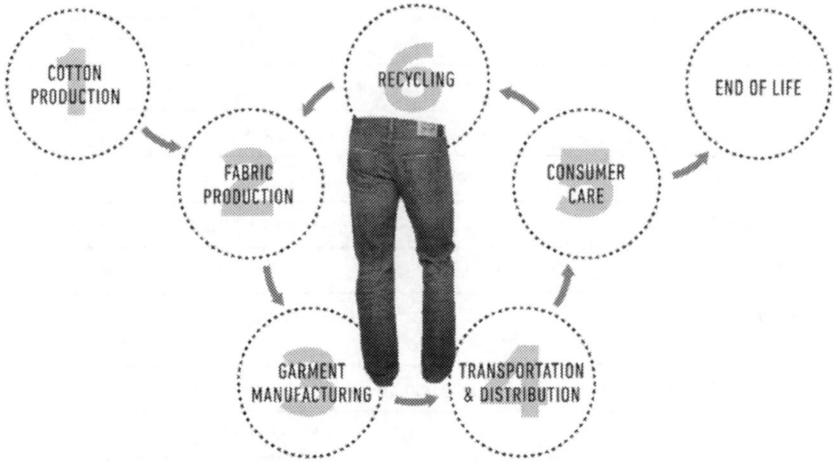

Source: Adopted from Levi Strauss & Co.

Sustainable product design

Sustainable product design is an approach whereby the design stage of a product is intended to be more sustainable (Armad et al., 2018). By doing this, there is equilibrium between the demands of the environment, social responsibility, and economic needs while still demonstrating the traditional product requirements, for example, quality, market, technical, cost issues, etc. We have to accept the reality of the business environment: it has always been about profit, and companies need profit for their continued existence, so the move towards a more sustainable approach will not occur overnight. However, with a gradual integration of environmental requirements into the product development process at every stage, this will eventually bring about a new ethos within businesses and companies will no longer see sustainability as a harbinger of extra restraints or extra costs, but maybe they will see it as a way of entering a new market and a way of opening up new and alternative revenue streams (Unruh and Ettenson, 2010b).

Traditionally, taking into account environmental demands was viewed as a necessary evil, bringing with it extra restraints and costs, and as a result, environmental assessments were usually conducted during the latter stages of the development process. This means that they were not integrated into existing development activities, which would naturally increase costs, thus completing the self-fulfilling prophecy. Companies that legislate for sustainable product design are able to reduce their environmental impact at the design phase and experience fewer disruptions in disposals later on. This enables the company to clear up the possible causes of environmental impact rather than merely masking the symptoms (Laurenti et al., 2015). There are several different strategies that can be employed to design products more sustainably:

- **Economic use of materials.** This involves using less material or the reuse or recycling of nature resources as a material input for a product. H&M launched 'The Conscious Collection' in 2001, in which all the items, including blouses, T-shirts, dresses, and trousers, were made from organic linen, polyester recycled from PET bottles, textile waste, and Tencel (Dishman, 2013). This was also demonstrated by Nike, who redesigned some of its footwear to have mechanically locking soles, meaning no glues or solvents were used in the production system (Nike, 2013).

- **Design for ease of repair/disposal.** This approach focuses on design for dismantling, reuse, and recycling (Unruh and Ettenson, 2010b). For example, Nike introduced insertable booties and removable logos, which, together with the mechanically locking soles, make its shoes easy to dismantle and further simplify the recycle process (Nike, 2013). IKEA specialises in developing repairable and adaptable designs (Laurin and Fantazy, 2017; Bodreau, 2021). This is a technique to enable firms to understand the process, from the beginning of production to the end of consumption, and the resulting environmental impact (Unruh and Ettenson, 2010b). Companies therefore need to consider all design processes, from the concept to manufacturing, packaging options and transportation, and finally, use and disposal of products. Xerox adopted a programme of asset recycle management that takes back leased copiers to recondition and reassemble them into 'new' machines through a remanufacturing process (Rothenberg, 2007).

- **Innovative environmental product design.** This is a sustainability-driven design that balances both customers' expectations as well as the needs of the environment (Unruh and Ettenson, 2010b). Such sustainability-driven innovative product designs help firms redefine their market scope and drive more economic returns (Unruh and Ettenson, 2010b). Waste organic materials that end up in landfill are now being explored for reuse. For example, orange peel contains cellulose that can be extracted to make fabrics like rayon, milk contains proteins that can be extracted to make the fabric Lanatil, grape skins are used to create a leather-like fabric, and paper is made from pasta by-products (Ellen MacArthur Foundation, 2022c). Many other innovative designs, such as biomimicry, nanotechnology, and 3D printing, develop fast as new ways to tackle resource scarcity. For example, one of the plastic filaments used in 3D printing is polylactic acid, which is made from renewable resources, such as cornstarch or sugar cane. Many organisations are eyeing up 3D printers as a means of revolutionising their manufacturing processes and addressing the triple bottom line of people, planet, and profit (Maxey, 2014).

Yet implementing a sustainable product strategy can be challenging due to misconceptions about cost versus benefits. Product design is the natural and best place to implement sustainable design, as it causes the least amount of disruption to businesses. Many firms engage in widespread sustainable product design to optimise natural resource efficiencies, reduce cost, simplify the operational process, and stimulate innovation. Proactively embracing a sustainability strategy will allow organisations to gain a competitive edge over their rivals.

Servitisation

The term *servitisation* has recently been adopted to describe where an OEM moves from selling a product with no customer inputs to one where the physical product (e.g. aircraft engine) is part of the offering, which often means ownership of the physical product is not transferred (Rothenberg, 2007). As already discussed, this can require a radical rethink to maximise the benefits of such a change, which may include incorporating other models, such as product life extension and sharing. However, the concept of servitisation is not new, as expensive products requiring expert maintenance have traditionally fitted. This includes photocopier contracts where the customer pays per copy or, more generically, per click. TVs in the early years up until the 1970s were commonly rented, due in part to the poor reliability. However, the term emerged later (Vandermerwe and Rada, 1988), where companies developed competitive edge by offering customer-focused 'bundles', which consist of 'goods, services, support, self-service, and knowledge'. This can be seen as 'transformational processes whereby a company shifts from a product-centric to a service-centric business model and logic' (Kowalkowski et al., 2017). This allows a company to offer more complex value propositions (Smith et al., 2014; Szasz and Seer, 2018).

Some of the classic servitisation examples are 'pay-per-flying-hour' by Rolls-Royce, 'pay-per-user' by Xerox, and 'availability-based' and 'performance-based' service contract by Alstom (Emerald, 2020).

Servitisation has been explored by researchers from various disciplines, such as manufacturing, marketing, and engineering (Baines et al., 2016). Based on the motivation and outputs, Pawar et al. (2009) summarised servitisation into three main streams: (1) the 'product–service system', which emphasises the reduction in negative environmental impact of consumption through the combination of products and services (White et al., 1999); (2) the 'integrated solutions', where financial gain is improved by integrating both products and services into a solution, through a company's skills and knowledge; and (3) the 'experiential services', where the products and services are a means to co-create value with customers.

In the classic case of Xerox, the OEM retains ownership of the photocopier and the customer simply hosts the machine, paying a monthly fixed fee and a per-copy charge. Xerox are responsible for maintaining the machine and supplying the toner, etc., which can be managed remotely these days with the internet of things (IOT). An upgrade or termination of the contract results in the copier being returned, where it may be incorporated in another service contract or otherwise reused before recycling. In this way, servitisation enables the operating frontier to be moved further to the right concerning sustainability. Thus, servitisation is also viewed as a business model which aligns with circular economy (Probst et al., 2016).

Conclusion

The adoption of a systems approaches, such as TQM (Total Quality Management), lean, and Theory of Constraints (TOC), has enabled the operating frontier to move closer to the asset frontier (Figure 13.2), hence improving overall performance. This includes the workforce, who are encouraged to creatively engage with developing and implementing improvements. Adopting sustainability perspective extends this systems view to consider wider business models, encouraging service provision that extends and more effectively utilises physical products commonly with OEM ownership of the life cycle, enabling more effective recycling. Although technology can be used to immediately improve discrete elements of the overall performance, including sustainability, it is important to exploit the synergies associated with integrated systems thinking that continually improves the performance through moving the operating frontier using existing technologies but new thinking.

Many organisations have been striving to improve efficiency and productivity through sustainable operations management, such as life cycle assessment, sustainable product design, and lean and green manufacturing practice. It is evident that adding environmental criteria as part of the operation's performance objectives helps firms to reduce waste, improve efficiency, drive innovation, shorten product lead time, and establish both tangible and intangible value. Companies that fail to capture this opportunity will face increased regulatory and social pressure, while those that embrace it and master it will enjoy competitive advantages and gain more market share. There are many examples relating to the sound management of chemicals and wastes in production under SDG 12 of the Sustainable Development Knowledge Platform (https://sustainabledevelopment.un.org/sdg12).

Suggested sessions

Session 1: Realignment and shifting frontiers in response to the Sustainable Development Goals

The aim of this session is for students to understand the difference between realignment and the movement of the performance frontiers (asset and operating) as described earlier.

Activity 1 (20 minutes)

Discuss which statements from the following list represent trade-off positioning, the movement of the operating, and the asset frontier.

- Promoting products based on sustainable performance
- Adopting new technology, such as solar panels
- Minimising packaging through redesign
- Equipping employees to problem-solve
- Avoiding wastage through developing a regular replenishment system
- Reducing energy usage through the use of lower-wattage LED lighting
- Reducing supply chain wastage through enhanced supply chain communication
- Changing marketing promotions to avoid wasteful fluctuating demand patterns
- Reducing the inventory through more frequent deliveries from local suppliers
- Enabling working from home
- Marketing on the basis of reliability

- Marketing on the basis of water usage

- Enabling employee engagement

- Redesigning a product/process to eliminate waste

- Continuous improvement

- Introducing a system that encourages a clean and tidy environment

- New investment in waste treatment

- Designing products for long life and user repair

Activity 2 (10 minutes)

Choose three statements from the previous list that illustrate each of the approaches, and use graphs similar to Figure 13.2 to illustrate how the performance improved.

Activity 3 (10 minutes)

Read the targets identified for SDG 12 in this overview: https://sustainabledevelopment.un.org/sdg12.

Which targets are linked to the example you have drawn in activity 2?

Activity 4 (20 minutes)

Look at the other SDGs in the Sustainable Development Knowledge Platform https://sustainabledevelopment.un.org/sdgs.

Are any of them also addressed in the examples you have chosen? How would you improve it further to address more SDGs? Draw a final graph to show your improvements.

Session 2: Life cycle assessment

This session provides a set of activities using LCA techniques to encourage students to take a more proactive attitude towards sustainable operations and to creatively consider how environmental performance can be achieved with no trade-offs.

Activity 1 (10 minutes)

1. During a student's typical day, can you identify opportunities to carry out sustainable practices, that is, ethical food consumption, turning off the lights, food recycling, using a bike rather than driving?

2. Compare the differences in your accounts and discuss them with your peers.

Activity 2 (40 minutes)

1. Form different groups, and apply and analyse the LCA for two products: a carton of orange juice from a supermarket and a cup of coffee sold in a coffee shop.

2. Draw the LCA maps for the orange juice and a cup of coffee on the whiteboard, and compare and contrast the differences.

3. Discuss how organisations can benefit from conducting an LCA for these two products.

Session 3: Sustainable operations management

The session will give an overview of how sustainability is practised and executed through operations management within different organisations. This session includes online evaluation of company websites and should therefore be carried out in a computer laboratory or with the help of laptops/tablets.

Activity 1 (30 minutes)

Form groups and choose two different companies from the following list (each company can only be selected by one group).

- IKEA
- Dell
- Walmart
- Levi's

- Brita

- GE

- BP

- Marks & Spencer

- Amazon

While conducting online research of their chosen companies, you need to analyse how the companies are working towards the goal of sustainability through their respective operations, and answer the following questions:

1. What are the sustainable operations management practices you find in each company's business model?

2. How do these sustainable operations management practices differ from traditional ones? (Or what are the key differences between sustainable and traditional operations management practices in your chosen organisation?)

3. Does sustainable operations management constrain or drive your selected organisations' profitability?

4. What are the benefits that could be derived from running sustainable operations management for your selected organisations?

5. What SDGs have been incorporated into their sustainability strategies?

Activity 2 (20 minutes)

Each group then summarises (maybe on a poster) their findings, or each group could produce a mini presentation based on their findings. Alternatively, their posters could be displayed, and students are free to look at the other groups' work.

Session 4: Explore sustainability/circular opportunities within the campus

As mentioned earlier in this chapter, various business models can be used to support circular systems. Students are encouraged to conduct a mini investigation to identify any potential ideas/initiatives towards sustainability in their daily activities at the university and on campus. Keep in mind the following circular models that may be useful in supporting your idea:

- Circular inputs
- Platform sharing
- Product as a service
- Product use extensions
- Resource recovery

Use the following table to help you organise your ideas/initiatives, and fill in the required fields.

What ideas/initiatives do you perceive are opportunities for a circular economy?	
Why do you think these are important initiatives?	
What circular models can be most useful to support your ideas?	
What are the operations implications associated with introducing such changes?	
Determine how this initiative will help attain Sustainable Development Goal 12: 'ensure sustainable consumption and production patterns'.	

Workshop: case study comparison and analysis

The Ellen MacArthur Foundation was established in 2009 with the goal of expediting the transition to a circular economy. Its network provides a diverse range of global circular economy examples and case studies demonstrating new business models, policies, and strategies for building and scaling a circular economy. Students are encouraged to visit https://ellenmacarthurfoundation.org/topics/circular-economy-introduction/examples and explore how different circular business models are used to reduce and reuse waste while significantly enhancing resource utilisation. Students must then select two case study examples in the same industry and respond to the following questions:

1. What evidence of supporting circular systems do you find in each model?

2. Analyse and compare each company's business model to design a more sustainable product or service.

3. How do these business models reflect a shift in operations management thinking?

Additional teaching material and ideas

Product design game
Activity 1: Students are required to undertake a mini investigation involving products in their everyday life to explore and identify the most and least sustainable product design, and then to discuss their reasoning.

Activity 2: Students are then encouraged to identify the best way for the least sustainable product design to be improved.

Exploring case evidence
An article from the MIT *Sloan Management Review*, 'The Mini-Cases: 5 Companies, 5 Strategies, 5 Transformations' (Fromartz, 2009), provides students with a range of case studies to rethink how companies could utilise OM to achieve their goal of becoming a sustainable organisation. Students can be divided into five

groups, with each group allocated one case. Students can then discuss within their groups, and then with the whole class, to compare and contrast the differences and similarities among the five cases.

Video evidence

There are a variety of clips available, for example:

- www.youtube.com/watch?v=fGhoInz-VUs

  (a good overview of life cycle assessment)

- https://youtu.be/2s8wqa_lvoQ

  (McDonald's sustainable sourcing achievements)

- www.youtube.com/watch?v=U9OT9O5-7ZQ

  Electric car battery life cycle (Reuse, Repurposing, Recycling, Reduction)

Activity 1: This virtual aid will help students gain more understanding of what constitutes sustainable product design.

Activity 2: Students are divided into teams. Their brief is to choose a target company and select one of their products and make a pitch to that company on ways of improving sustainable product design.

Activity 3: Winners will be selected by a *Dragons' Den*–style presentation, with teachers playing the role of board members who will make a decision based on the quality and originality of the students' pitch.

Accepting the challenge

Students are to play the role of a professional consultant for a local company and advise it on ways of solving the sustainability operations challenge. In 2013, Maggie Zeng held a **sustainability essay competition** and involved Cheltenham Racecourse as the project sponsor. The managing director of the racecourse was invited as a guest speaker and gave a presentation to the students on the current status of the racecourse and its main operations sustainability challenges. Many of the students had previous employment experience of working for the racecourse so had already developed a good level of understanding of its business operations. The students were required to adopt the role of consultant and provide solutions to the challenges mentioned, with a £500 prize awarded to the student who offered the best solution.

The campus lab

Students are required to take a tour of their university and note down their observations.

- What are the evidences of green practices within the campus? How would you classify these?

- For example:

  - Solar panels on roof?

  - Hire a bike for the year at a subsidised price?

  - Ensuring excess food is minimised and disposed of sustainably?

Students will then need to categorise their observations of green and lean practices into two categories and put them on Post-it notes on the board, where two overlapping circles are drawn.

Students will then compare the similarities between lean and green within a university context by answering the following questions:

- What is the evidence that this university is a sustainable one?

- Are there any overlapping characteristics between lean and green universities?

- What are the benefits of being a lean and green university?

Further readings

Atasu, A., V. Agrawal, M. Rinaldi, R. Herb, and S. Ulku (2018), 'Rethinking sustainability in light of the EU's new circular economy policy', *Harvard Business Review*, July.

> Many companies lack access to used products, they aren't able to refurbish or recycle used products in a cost-effective way, their products are not designed with circularity in mind, and their customers discount the value of refurbished or remanufactured products. But these obstacles can be overcome. Companies can take three actions to build strong CEs: creating modular products, developing a refurbishing infrastructure, and leasing. Companies that aren't succeeding in building CEs often adopt some of these approaches, but never all three in coordination. It is the combination of all three approaches that improves access to products, reduces costs, and increases value to the consumer. Together, they create the scale needed to make CEs profitable.

Blunck, E. (2016), 'Germany BMW's sustainability strategy of evolution and revolution towards a circular economy', in V. Anbumozhi and J. Kim (eds.), *Towards a circular economy: Corporate management and policy pathways*. ERIA Research Project Report 2014–44, Jakarta: ERIA, pp. 75–92. Available at: www.eria.org/RPR_FY2014_No.44_Chapter_6.pdf, accessed 16 November 2022.

   Insight into a major car company's approach to sustainability and the opportunities in innovation whilst government policy is driving the timescales.

Lacy, P., J. Long, and W. Spindler (2020), *The circular economy handbook: Realising the circular advantage*, London: Palgrave Macmillan.

   A useful handbook written by Accenture consulting employees that very practically presents the need and opportunity to embrace business models aligned with the need for circular rather than linear thinking.

Ellen Macarthur Foundation.

   A charity launched in 2010 committed to creating a circular economy and providing an informative website with many case illustrations and educations sources relating to applying the circular business models with an operations perspective (https://ellen-macarthurfoundation.org/topics/circular-economy-introduction/overview).

Marshall, D., A. O'Dochartaigh, A. Prothero, O. Reynolds, and E. Sacchi (2022), 'Why businesses need to embrace the bioeconomy', *MIT Sloan Management Review*, November.

   Companies seeking more sustainable product strategies should explore using biological (nonfossil) resources, waste streams, and manufacturing by-products. New materials technologies and processes are replacing fossil-based ingredients with bio-based alternatives from the agriculture, forestry, and marine industries.

Piercy, N., and N. Rich (2014), 'The relationship between lean operations and sustainable operations', *International Journal of Operations and Production Management* 35.2: 282–315.

   This research paper provides a comprehensive review of the literature relating lean and sustainability before using case studies to clarify the underlying strategic relationship between lean and sustainable operations.

Rothenberg, S. (2007), 'Sustainability through servicizing', *MIT Sloan Management Review* 48.2: 83–91, Winter.

   This article uses different examples of how companies have taken advantage of a business model that allows for growth by educating society to switch from high to low consumption of its products. Examples show that by adopting a low product consumption business model, companies can make their business more profitable by focusing on services that extend the efficiency and value of their product.

Unruh, G., and R. Ettenson (2010a), 'Growing green: Three smart paths to developing sustainable products', *Harvard Business Review*: 94–100, June.

   This article offers a holistic and practical framework for integrating sustainability product design strategies into an organisation's business portfolio. It provides a good range of case studies to illustrate the three steps of green growth (accentuate, acquire, and architect) as part of a company's business activities and offering to assist managers in crafting a sustainable business strategy.

References

Armad, S., K.Y. Wong, M.L. Tseng, and W.P. Wong (2018) 'Sustainable product design and development: A review of tools, applications and research prospects', *Resources, Conservation and Recycling* 132: 49–61, May.

Arturo Garza-Reyes, J. (2015) 'Lean and green – a systematic review of the state of the art literature', *Journal of Cleaner Production* 102: 18–29.

Atasu, A., V. Agrawal, M. Rinaldi, R. Herb, and S. Ulku (2018) 'Rethinking sustainability in light of the EU's new circular economy policy', *Harvard Business Review*, July.

Aubertin, C. (2019) 'From product to product-as-a-service, medium', *The Startup*. Available at: https://medium.com/swlh/from-product-to-product-as-a-service-37baed471cd6, accessed 25 September 2022.

Baines, T. et al. (2016) 'Servitization: Revisiting the state-of-the-art and research priorities', *International Journal of Operations & Production Management* 37.2: 256–78.

Bergmiller, G.G., and P.R. McCright (2009) *Are lean and green operations synergistic?* Paper Presented at the 2009 Industrial Engineering Research Conference, Miami, FL, May.

Bicheno, J., and M. Holweg (2020) *The lean toolbox*, Buckingham: PICSIE Books.

Blunck, E. (2016) 'Germany BMW's sustainability strategy of evolution and revolution towards a circular economy', in V. Anbumozhi, and J. Kim (eds.), *Towards a circular economy: Corporate management and policy pathways*. ERIA Research Project Report 2014–44, Jakarta: ERIA, pp. 75–92. Available at: www.eria.org/RPR_FY2014_No.44_Chapter_6.pdf, accessed 16 November 2022.

Bodreau, A. (2021) *Large companies are leveraging circular design to transform their businesses: This is how IKEA and DS Smith are doing it.* Available at: https://ellenmacarthurfoundation.org/articles/how-circular-design-guidelines-unlock-organisations-potential-for-change, accessed 22 November 2022.

Ciambrone, D.F. (2019) *Environmental life cycle analysis*, Boca Raton: CRC Press.

Dishman, L. (2013) *Inside H&M's quest for sustainability in fast fashion.* Available at: www.forbes.com/sites/lydiadishman/2013/04/09/inside-hms-quest-for-sustainability-in-fast-fashion/, accessed 11 December 2013.

Ellen MacArthur Foundation (2022a) *France's anti-waste and circular economy law, how to build a circular economy.* Available at: https://ellenmacarthurfoundation.org/frances-anti-waste-and-circular-economy-law, accessed 25 October 2022.

Ellen MacArthur Foundation (2022b) *Creating a reverse logistics ecosystem.* Available at: https://ellenmacarthurfoundation.org/circular-examples/creating-a-reverse-logistics-ecosystem, accessed 5 October 2022.

Ellen MacArthur Foundation (2022c) *High value products from organic waste.* Available at: ellenmacarthurfoundation.org, accessed 14 November 2022.

Emerald (2020) *What is servitization of manufacturing? A quick introduction.* Available at: www.emeraldgrouppublishing.com/opinion-and-blog/what-servitization-manufacturing-a-quick-introduction, accessed 22 October 2022.

Ferreira, W.S., G.M. Vale, and V.S. Corrêa (2022) 'Diffusion of innovation in technological platforms: The Uber case', *BAR – Brazilian Administration Review* 19.3. Available at: https://doi.org/10.1590/1807-7692bar2022210101.

Fromartz, S. (2009) 'The mini-cases: 5 companies, 5 strategies, 5 transformations', *MIT Sloan Management Review* 51.1: 41–5, October.

Giannetti, B.F., F. Agostinho, J.J. Cabello Eras, Z. Yang, and C.M.V.B. Almeida (2020) 'Cleaner production for achieving the sustainable development goals', *Journal of Cleaner Production* 271: 122127.

Jimenez, J., and J. Lorente (2001) 'Environmental performance as an operations objective', *International Journal of Operations and Production Management* 21.12: 1553–72.

Kowalkowski, C. et al. (2017) 'Servitization and deservitization: Overview, concepts, and definition', *Industrial Marketing Management* 60: 4–10.

Lacey, P., J. Long, and W. Spindler (2020) *The circular economy handbook*, London: Palgrave Macmillan.

Laurenti, R., R. Sinha, J. Singh, and B. Frostell (2015) 'Towards addressing unintended environmental consequences: A planning framework', *Sustaiable Development* 24.1: 1–17.

Laurin, F., and K. Fantazy (2017) 'Sustainable supply chain management: A case study at IKEA', *Transnational Corporations Review*. https://doi.org/10.1080/19186444.2017.1401208.

Levi Strauss & Co. Available at: www.levistrauss.com/wp-content/uploads/2015/03/Full-LCA-Results-Deck-FINAL.pdf, accessed 21 November 2022.

Marshall, D., A. O'Dochartaigh, A. Prothero, O. Reynolds, and E. Sacchi (2022) 'Why businesses need to embrace the bioeconomy', *MIT Sloan Management Review*, November.

Martin, A. (2009) 'How green is my orange', *The New York Times*. Available at: www.nytimes.com/2009/01/22/business/22pepsi.html, accessed 22 November 2022.

Maxey, K. (2014) *3D printer filament recycling is super green*. Available at: www.engineering.com/3DPrinting/3DPrintingArticles/ArticleID/7273/3D-Printer-Filament-Recycling-is-Super-Green.aspx, accessed 11 March 2014.

Mixson, E. (2021) *Johnson & Johnson: A crash course in tech-enabled business resiliency, intelligent automation network*. Available at: www.intelligentautomation.network/resiliency/articles/johnson-johnson-a-crash-course-in-tech-enabled-business-resiliency, accessed 5 May 2021.

Nike (2013) 'Through the years: Nike's history of sustainable innovation', *The Guardian*. Available at: www.theguardian.com/sustainable-business/nike-history-sustainable-innovation, accessed 11 December 2013.

Pawar, K.S., A. Beltagui, and J.C.K.H. Riedel (2009) 'The PSO triangle: Designing product, service and organisation to create value', *International Journal of Operations & Production Management* 29.5: 468–93.

Piercy, N., and N. Rich (2014) 'The relationship between lean operations and sustainable operations', *International Journal of Operations and Production Management* 35.2: 282–315.

Probst, L. et al. (2016) 'Servitization – pay-per-use', *The European Union*. Available at: https://ec.europa.eu/docsroom/documents/16595/attachments/1/translations/en/renditions/native, accessed 15 October 2022.

Rothenberg, S. (2007) 'Sustainability through servicizing', *MIT Sloan Management Review* 48.2: 83–91, Winter.

Schmenner, R.W., and M.L. Swink (1998) 'On theory in operations management', *Journal of Operations Management* 17: 97–113.

SETAC (Society of Environmental Toxicology and Chemistry) (1993) *Guidelines for life-cycle assessment: A code of practice*, SETAC workshop in Sesimbra, Portugal, 31 March–3 April.

Slack, N., and A. Brandon-Jones (2019) *Operations management*, 9th ed., Harlow: Pearson.

Smith, L., R. Maull, and I.C.L. Ng (2014) 'Servitization and operations management: A service dominant-logic approach', *International Journal of Operations & Production Management* 34.2: 242–69.

Szasz, L., and L. Seer (2018) 'Towards an operations strategy model of servitization: The role of sustainability pressure', *Operations Management Research* 11: 51–66.

Thorpe, L. (2011) 'Levi Strauss & Co: The Levi style with a lot less water', *The Guardian*. Available at: www.theguardian.com/sustainable-business/levi-rethinking-traditional-process-water, accessed 22 November 2022.

Unruh, G., and R. Ettenson (2010b) 'Winning in the green frenzy', *Harvard Business Review*: 110–16, November.

Vandermerwe, S., and J. Rada (1988) 'Servitization of business: Adding value by adding services', *European Management Journal* 6.4: 314–24.

White, A.L., M. Stoughton, and L. Feng (1999) *Servicizing: The quiet transition to extended product responsibility*, Boston, MA: Report for US Environmental Protection Agency, Tellus Institute.

Womack, J.P., and D.T. Jones (1996) *Lean thinking: Banish waste and create wealth in your corporation*, New York: Simon & Schuster.

Womack, J.P., D.T. Jones, and D. Roos (1990) *The machine that changed the world: The story of lean production*, New York: Harper Collins Publishers.

14
Sustainable supply chain management

Lynn Oxborrow

Supply chain management and the principles of PRME

Because of its influence on all aspects of materials, production, transport, and contracted services – from extraction, agriculture, or service conception to consumption and reuse or disposal – improving supply chain management is integral to achieving the PRME principles. This is increasingly important because of the international complexity of many supply chains, the nature of inter-organisational relationships that make up supply chains, and the increasing need for sustainability reporting to extend to scope 3 – largely represented by the supply chain.

Across this international and multi-organisational complex, sustainable supply chain management relates to all four issues covered by the UN Global Compact: the treatment of labour together with upholding human rights, managing environmental challenges and impact on climate change, and reducing corruption. Information and resources can be found at *Supply Chain Sustainability: A Practical Guide for Continuous Improvement*, 2nd ed., UNGC, 2015.

The potential for sustainable supply chain management to contribute to Sustainable Development Goals (SDGs) is also comprehensive, because of the scope and complexity of global supply chains. However,

DOI: 10.4324/9781003294665-17

there is a clear link between SDGs, such as goal 8, *decent work and economic growth,* and goal 12, *responsible consumption and production.* Furthermore, effective supply chains rely on *partnership*, so goal 17 is also an aspiration.

What is supply chain management?

Supply chain management has come to public prominence during the Covid-19 pandemic (2020–2022), and since, because the global crisis has exposed both the risk and the potential that supply chain management brings. During the pandemic, factory closures in countries such as China, reduced shipping and transportation, changes to working patterns and the delivery models of industries, such as retail and hospitality, all contributed to disruption that has illustrated the vulnerability of the global supply chain system. This led to shortages of materials and components as diverse as:

- Computer chips and petfood packaging

- Rationing of products such as toilet roll and hand sanitiser

- Growth in demand for standard goods or services in new formats, such as flour in domestic rather than industrial quantities and logistics for online shopping

- Waste in sectors such as agriculture and horticulture due to labour shortages

In contrast, the rapid implementation of the vaccine supply chain, which encompassed ramping up the supply of high-performance glass phials (The New Yorker, 2020) and implementing cold-chain systems to preserve deep frozen vaccines (Insider, 2020), represented the ability of innovative and effective supply chains to be agents of change (McKinsey & Company, 2021).

In general terms, **supply chain management** can be defined as 'the management of upstream and downstream relationships with suppliers and customers to deliver superior customer value at less cost to the supply chain as a whole' (Christopher, 2011). In this context, **upstream** to **downstream** represents the predominant flow of materials from their upstream source in agriculture, material extraction, or knowledge to finished goods or services at the point of consumption. Information flows in both directions, and there should, of course, be a fair financial exchange from downstream to upstream in return for the goods and services provided. The discipline of supply chain management therefore incorporates numerous business functions ranging from product design, production, and facilities management, as discussed in Chapter 13, to procurement and logistics, discussed in Chapter 8, with close links also to marketing, human resources, finance, and distribution.

Trends in supply chain management have seen a rapid growth in **outsourcing** since the 1980s and 1990s, when markets in developed economies began to mature and become increasingly price-sensitive, international trade liberalisation was facilitated by the **World Trade Organization,** and transport and communications became more globally accessible. This enabled lead organisations to commission third-party suppliers to carry out specific activities; **offshoring,** where such activities are undertaken in a different country from the sourcing organisation; and **global sourcing,** where the supply chain spans different countries (Slack et al., 2013). Together with the growth in consumerism across the globe, these developments have resulted in growing levels of supply chain activity, made more complex by its global nature, and consequently with greater opportunity to impact upon social, environmental, and economic sustainability issues, both positively and negatively. The opportunity is clear for supply chains to impact upon **SDG 12, 'responsible consumption and production',** by ensuring sustainable consumption and production patterns through resource efficiency, waste reduction, effective logistics, and inter-organisational relationships, as well as taking responsibility for waste and post-consumer supply chains through the **circular economy** (World Economic Forum, 2014).

The concept of **sustainable supply chain management** relates to how lead companies and their suppliers manage and improve working conditions, labour standards, and prevent the violation of human rights at any point across the supply chain, including at suppliers' production and delivery facilities. Referred to as social sustainability, this includes addressing SDG goal 8, **decent work and economic growth,** by imposing **international labour standards,** such as securing workers the local minimum wage, reasonable working hours and overtime payments, the right to collective bargaining, freedom of association, and health and safety at supplier facilities. This chapter therefore deals with two broad aspects – **social** and **environmental** sustainability within the supply chain – and adopts the following definition of sustainable supply chain management:

> Management of raw materials and services from suppliers to manufacturer/ service provider to customer and back with improvements of the social and environmental impacts explicitly considered.
>
> (SBC, 2003: 6)

This reflects the importance of designing sustainable practices and standards into the supply chain rather than seeing these as optional added extras and an implicit requirement for effective performance improvement.

For those organisations that lead or are involved in complex supply chains, the incentive to implement sustainable supply chain management depends on a set of risk factors, notably their exposure to consumer criticism for poor practice. This is exacerbated in high-risk products, such as precious metals; high-risk sectors, such as clothing; and whose suppliers are located in high-risk countries, including the Democratic Republic of Congo (DRC). Managing those variables can substantially reduce organisational vulnerability to sustainability violations throughout the supply chain (UNGC, 2009; Lund-Thomsen and Lindgreen, 2014) but may come with other risks, such as increased costs or slowing down supply.

Environmentally sustainable supply chain management

Environmental or **green supply chain management** (GSCM) is defined as 'integrating environmental thinking into supply-chain management' (Srivastava, 2007: 54–5). In practice, this means:

- Saving energy and reducing carbon emissions in production, service delivery, and logistics while achieving economies of scale.

- Efficient equipment and adopting waste reduction strategies referred to as **lean and green,** discussed in Chapter 13.

- Reducing embedded energy in products, their use and after-use, for example, by sourcing alternative materials and packaging, using alternative energy sources, retaining the value of materials through reuse, recycling or sensitive disposal; utilising local production or making environmentally sustainable transport choices.

Some generic supply chain concepts, such as network design, logistics management, waste minimisation, and order fulfilment strategies, can, therefore, help achieve sustainable supply chain management (Liu et al., 2012; Sharma et al., 2010). Meanwhile, SSCM is fundamental to the physical implementation of the circular economy (World Economic Forum, 2014).

There is a lack of consensus regarding the key **drivers** to instituting a sustainable supply chain, whether legislative, commercial, or environmental. At the same time, there are also counter-arguments against the benefits, such as the potential link between green products and services and market failure because end users perceive products to be more expensive, functionally or aesthetically inferior, or too slow to market to be competitive.

Achieving net zero: pillar 1

To achieve the 1.5 °C ambition to reduce climate change, halve emissions by 2030, and stand any chance of reaching net zero by 2050, supply chain obstacles need to be overcome. The **Exponential Roadmap Initiative** has produced a supply chain engagement guide to help organisations lead their supply chain partners towards net zero. The roadmap is set out in four 'pillars', each representing a deeper commitment and intensity of actions towards greenhouse gas (GHG) emissions.

Pillar 1 encourages prime supply chain stakeholders to lead by example and start by internally addressing aspects of their buildings, transport fleet, operations, systems and processes, materials use, as well as installing clean energy wherever possible. Key aspects include setting targets, installing measures, and sharing results to influence suppliers (Falk et al., 2022).

Supply chain design

Network design determines **location choices** for key supply chain activities. Creation of global supply chains involves **offshore sourcing**, usually to low-labour-cost economies, impacts upon transport emissions, and some loss of control over the actions of suppliers. **Back-shoring,** or returning to local supply sources, is controversial, as any reduction in GHG emissions is offset against higher financial costs and the potential social costs of removing job-creating activities from developing economies. In some sectors, such as footwear manufacture, local infrastructure has declined irreversibly, so a compromise is to reduce supply chain lead times and environmental impacts by **near-shoring** or relocating key activities to countries closer to the point of consumption (Mangan and Lalwani, 2016).

A different approach is just-in-time delivery, where component deliveries are required in small quantities, every few hours, to meet specific demand patterns and avoid costly inventory, so key suppliers are clustered around the final assembly plant. While the motivation is to provide operational efficiency, this practice can also reduce the long-distance transportation impact on the environment while managing sustainable logistics for local, frequent just-in-time deliveries (Brindley and Oxborrow, 2014; Slack et al., 2013). In the food industry, information sharing with local suppliers reduces unsustainable surplus production, food waste, and unnecessary food miles in **build-to-order** systems.

Achieving net zero: pillar 2

To achieve the 1.5 °C ambition to reduce climate change, suppliers must halve emissions by 2030 and target achieving net zero by 2040. Integrated strategies between buyer and supplier organisations are needed, with a clear plan to reduce scope 3 emissions, with metrics and collaboration, to put plans into place. At pillar 2, priorities include components and materials, machinery, logistics, facilities, IT, and consultancy services.

Key activities at **pillar 2** include identifying priorities by mapping the value chain, agreeing measures and project milestones, allocating resources and implementing plans step by step, regular reviewing and sharing of results to inform stakeholders and future plans (Falk et al., 2022; SBC, 2014).

WWF supplier assessment on climate impact

The World Wildlife Fund, through its *For Your World* campaign and the *Exponential Roadmap Initiative,* has developed a toolkit to improve the sustainability performance of suppliers (WWF, n.d.).

The questionnaire asks about suppliers' goals, measurements for scope 1 and scope 2 emissions, and strategies to reduce these. Suppliers are also asked whether their emissions are externally verified and what proportion is attributable to the customer concerned.

Logistics and distribution

Distance and network design, in turn, impact upon **logistics** – the planning, control, and implementation of moving goods and exchanging information throughout the supply chain, or getting the right product to the right place at the right time, as discussed in Chapter 8. Transporting goods less often, in larger volume, is considered to be more cost-effective and less environmentally damaging. However, this may not be consistent with supply chain models, such as just-in-time and the rapid fulfilment of online orders.

The trend for **consolidation** is increasingly evident in global shipping, with a growing number of super-ships that can carry more freight, use more sustainable power sources, and reduce the cost per item shipped (Mangan and Lalwani, 2016).

However, these huge ships can only operate in the world's largest ports, and so consolidation also involves developing **hub-and-spoke** models of storage, transport, and distribution along the supply chain, to offload and redistribute goods into local distribution systems. While some parts of these local supply chains may be by rail, the majority uses road haulage. Some items, whether due to the need for speed, such as in fast fashion, or because of unplanned supply delays, are transported by airfreight, at considerable environmental cost (ibid.).

The incident of the *Ever Given*

The vulnerability of the bulk shipping supply chain was illustrated by the crash of the 400-meter long *Ever Given* super container ship into the banks of the Suez Canal in March 2021. As well as the delayed delivery of the goods on board, the trapped *Ever Given* also prevented nearly 400 other ships from travelling from the Far East to Europe, causing a delay of weeks in some cases and a backlog to receive and redistribute billion dollars of vital goods, including food, fuel, and medicines, at Europe's major ports.

While the enquiry is still underway, one contributary cause of the shipping disaster is known to be high winds at the time of the accident. Super ships have proven to be extremely vulnerable to such extreme weather events, attributable to climate change, and this is not the only instance of ships veering off course. Over 2,500 shipping incidents are reported annually (BBC, 2022).

In integrated supply chains, specialist 3PL (**third-party logistics**) providers introduce the latest technology for warehouse and distribution management, as well as helping identify opportunities for the sharing of resources between compatible stakeholders. A 3PL provider might enable a Christmas gift company and a garden centre chain with different seasonal peaks to share their warehouse facilities, or suppliers to an automotive plant to share transport for just-in-time delivery. Another example would be filling the base of a truck with heavy bottles and cans of beverage to supply the catering trade and then using space above to 'top-stow' light items, such as crisps (Mangan and Lalwani, 2016).

Choice of **mode of transport** (road, rail, air or sea freight, etc.), fuel-efficient vehicle designs, reducing vehicle emissions, and switching to alternative fuels can all help reduce the environmental impact of logistics, for example, McDonald's use of recycled cooking oil to power their biodiesel fleet.

Circular economy supply chains

Circular supply chain initiatives

An increasing array of organisations are reclaiming, recycling, and reusing materials within their supply chains.

- Nike has developed a programme started in 1992 to repurpose unused materials, manufacturing waste, and used trainers into *Nike Grind* (Nike, 2021) – a substrate that can then be made into a range of surfaces, from skateboard grip tape to 4G sports pitches, construction materials, to protective phone cases.
- McDonald's delivery fleet is 28% powered by biofuel, of which 37% was generated from used cooking oil in 2019 (Verdict Food Service, 2019). The retailer is now collaborating with Miele to recapture grease from its washing machines to increase the supply of biofuel while reducing the impact on sewers.

The **circular economy** (Ellen MacArthur Foundation, 2020) is a growing phenomenon in sustainable supply, as legislation, cost pressure, and shortage of materials make it more viable for all kinds of recycled items to be recaptured to retain value in the supply chain – sometimes as completely different products. The circular supply chain can be defined as collecting and moving goods from their normal end-of-life for the purpose of capturing value from waste, reuse or refurbishment, or managing their disposal (see Mehrmann, 2008). The circular process can encompass the collection of packaging materials for reuse, materials for integration into new products, or obsolete or surplus products to be disassembled into constituent parts and repurposed. It can also include reclaiming fuel, water, or waste to be recycled or used in energy generation. Recycled goods, particularly valuable metals, are increasingly exported to global manufacturing locations for sorting, reprocessing, and reintegration into new products; others, such as clothing, find a second-hand market in developing economies. However, the supply chain for these processes has to be designed, just like any other, and exposes a further trade-off between environmental and social benefits. For example, the export of second-hand clothing potentially competes with job-creating local production and has been banned in some African countries, such as South Africa and Nigeria.

Achieving net zero: pillar 3

To achieve the 1.5 °C ambition to reduce climate change, emissions embedded in the products or services produced in the supply chain must halve by 2030, with a target of achieving net zero by 2040. To achieve this means developing products and services that enable customers and users to reduce their carbon emissions through use and disposal, while lead companies pivot their business model in favour of shared ownership, services, and circular supply chains.

At **pillar 3**, a key priority is to include customers in designing game-changing products and services, communicating vision and purpose and inventive business models, and setting goals, measurement of progress, and investment in innovative solutions (Falk et al., 2022).

Social sustainability in the supply chain

Social aspects of sustainable supply chain management govern the way that **working conditions** of those labouring in primary industries, supplier facilities, logistics, and distribution can be improved. Some high-profile global brands have been the subject of media exposés highlighting issues of child labour, forced labour, poverty wages, excessive overtime, and general exploitation of workers in their supply chains (Greenberg and Knight, 2004). These companies, such as Nike, Levi, the Gap, and Apple, apply their branding, marketing, and distribution to consumer goods sold globally but sourced from complex networks of suppliers in developing countries (Bair and Palpacuer, 2012). Meanwhile, the march of globalisation and sourcing has fuelled fears that well-paid, well-regulated jobs in a range of skilled roles could be outsourced from secure countries in the West to countries in Latin America, Asia, and Africa whose governments might not care about the well-being, health, and safety of their workforce (Khara and Lund-Thomsen, 2012).

These developments sparked concerted campaigns by trade unions, student organisations, media outlets, and NGOs (non-governmental organisations) against the exploitation of workers in developing countries in order to produce cheap goods for Western consumers (Bair and Palpacuer, 2012). To respond to these allegations – and protect their **brand value** – many high-profile Western brands started developing so-called **corporate codes of conduct**, ethical guidelines which specify the social and environmental conditions under which goods and services are to be produced at supplier facilities in developing countries, as discussed next.

Codes of conduct vs collaboration

Sustainable supply chain initiatives can be implemented in two broad ways. Typically, the **codes of conduct** of powerful brands and retailers set out conditions of supply and are usually imposed on suppliers by powerful buying organisations or brands. They state that suppliers must employ workers on a regular contract, that workers must be paid the minimum wage and for any overtime work, that no child labour is employed, and a host of other similar criteria. These criteria were often based on international labour standards as specified in the conventions of the ILO (**International Labour Organization**), an agency of the United Nations entrusted with protecting the rights of workers worldwide (Lund-Thomsen, 2008), and have helped factory-based workers maintain fair pay and conditions, with fewer occupational health and safety accidents within supplier factories.

However, codes of conduct have been less influential on workers' freedom to join trade unions or collectively bargain with their employers about their working conditions (ibid.), where implementation and monitoring are ineffective (UN Global Compact and BSR, 2014), and where workers are employed further upstream in the supply chain and excluded from codes of conduct designed to regulate **first-tier suppliers** (ETI, 2006). Women and underage workers are more likely to be limited to semi-formal factories or homework, out of sight of the brands, their codes of conduct, and monitoring systems (ibid). Furthermore, asymmetrical power within buyer–supplier relationships is a characteristic of many supply chains (Talay et al., 2018) through which the lead partners impose their standards and expectations, both commercial and ethical, while weaker partners, often suppliers, have little influence on practice or improvements. This can lead to conflicts of interest, especially where expectations of low prices, fast delivery, and response to changes undermine sustainable objectives.

Alternatively, introducing new and innovative sustainability solutions into the supply chain is seen to depend on more collaborative relationships, sharing of information, and working towards common goals (Vachon and Klassen, 2006), and suppliers are more likely to adopt good practice if they have good relationships with the customers who request those improvements and have bought into management system standards or lean thinking (Short and Toffel, 2021). Implementing a successful, sustainable supply chain therefore requires marketing and purchasing functions working together (Sharma et al., 2010), senior management buy-in, a supportive organisational culture, and inter-functional cooperation (Krause et al., 2009), with a wider set of performance objectives beyond economic measures (Seuring and Muller, 2008). Achieving a sustainable supply chain has therefore become a multi-disciplinary task, encompassing relationships, networks, channels, and partnerships (Srivastava, 2007) throughout the sourcing and processing stages, delivery of goods and services to the final consumer, and any circular supply chain activity.

Modern slavery

Modern slavery is defined as 'the **exploitation of a person** who is deprived of individual liberty anywhere along the supply chain, from **raw materials extraction to the final customer**, for the purpose of service provision or production' (Gold et al., 2015: 5). In the supply chain, modern slavery epitomises poor practice in social supply chain management and includes child trafficking and child labour, debt bondage (where individuals are forced to work to pay off debt often incurred to buy passage to safer countries), and forced labour.

While a number of the richest economies introduced legislation to reduce modern slavery during the 2010s, by 2021 an estimated 10 million more people were trapped in modern slavery compared to 2016 global estimates (ILO, 2022) – a rise to 49.6 million people. This includes 3.3 million children in forced labour, even though target 8.7 of the **Sustainable Development Goals** has committed to ending child labour by 2025.

Tackling forced labour should include measures to improve workers' freedom of association while also reducing the factors that make some people, often women, children, and migrants, vulnerable to exploitation, as well as enhancing enforcement to ensure compliance and rehabilitation for victims. Within business operations and supply chains, the ILO recommends identifying small and informal enterprises, often sub-contracted upstream in supply chains. Improvements should be focused on 'hotspots', where the risk, severity, and scale of forced labour and human rights exploitation are highest, especially in high-risk sectors and locations (ibid.).

Modern slavery in the supply chain

Almost 50 million people are thought to be victims of modern slavery, of which 27.6 million are in forced labour, and 3.3 million are children. Forced labour has increased since Covid-19 due to indebtedness and falling working conditions combined with a predisposition to extreme poverty. Other crisis situations, including climate crises, are known to increase the risk of forced labour (ILO, 2022).

Of the total adults in forced labour, five sectors account for the majority of cases, including services, manufacturing, construction, agriculture, and domestic work. Other sectors, such as mining and quarrying and fishing, are among those that contribute to hundreds of thousands of further workers affected by forced labour. Workers in manufacturing and construction are most likely to be over-represented compared to population averages in many economies.

In the UK, under the **Modern Slavery Act 2015** (Advice Gov, 2021), large organisations must produce an annual statement of the steps they have taken, including due diligence and staff training, to ensure that slavery and human trafficking are not taking place, internally or in their supply chains, including scope 3.

Some organisations are identifying surprisingly high-risk supply chains, such as the production of computers and mobile phones, which sometimes involve mineral extraction or assembly in regions identified by the Global Slavery Index as associated with conflict or labour exploitation (Walk Free Foundation, 2018).

One reason for a lack of improvement is that Western multinational companies tended to use **purchasing practices** and corporate codes of conduct that contradicted one another (Barrientos and Smith, 2007). For example, a Western retailer's procurement staff might ask a supplier to reduce its prices or face the risk of losing an order. At the same time, the retailer's sustainability department might ask the same supplier to increase worker's wages or at least ensure that workers are paid fairly (ETI, 2006). Moreover, peaks and troughs in seasonal demand in the West create employment insecurity in developing country export industries, where first-tier suppliers vary capacity requirements according to orders received from their buyers. Alternatively, suppliers might subcontract work to smaller suppliers to avoid any legal requirement that workers should be offered more permanent contracts within their factories (Khara and Lund-Thomsen, 2012). Finally, international brands increasingly place orders at the last minute, thus compelling their offshore suppliers to force employees into doing excessive overtime work. The resulting outcomes illustrate how suppliers have to devise innovative, often counterproductive, strategies in order to survive. For example, during social audits, suppliers might coach workers to ensure they gave favourable answers or avoided details about their treatment, working conditions or pay, in some cases in fear of losing their jobs (HRW Human Rights Watch, 2022).

Examples such as these highlight the difficulties and complexities inherent in sustainable supply chain management and the challenges that must be addressed. Often, there are trade-offs between commercial and social considerations which are not easily reconciled. At the same time, even well-intended corporate codes of conduct might do more harm than good to workers in instances where they are implemented without due consideration for **local social and environmental circumstances** (Lund-Thomsen, 2008). For instance, Western retailers may impose regulations relating to child labour, resulting in child labourers being fired and therefore unable to supplement family income. This could force children into even worse types of occupation, such as prostitution or bonded labour.

Such examples illustrate that implementing **'global' ethical guidelines** of companies in **'local contexts'** often requires considerable knowledge of the context in which the supplier is operating, the ability to handle dilemmas, and the ability to devise concrete, practical solutions to real-life challenges faced upstream in the global supply chain in developing countries (Lund-Thomsen and Lindgreen, 2014).

Examples of poor labour conditions within supply chains

Treatment of immigrant labour in the Middle East under the **Kafala System** (HTS, 2022a) has come to public attention through the poor working conditions and lack of freedom of construction workers in football's 2022 World Cup supply chains. While still under investigation, reports suggest that workers are unable to leave employment or the country, take adequate breaks, and in some cases, are forced to work throughout the day in extreme heat and with little water, even though there is legislation against this.

During the Covid-19 pandemic, clothing retailers and brands and many first-tier factories were forced to close. However, the nature of the global supply chain meant that large quantities of goods were at various stages of materials supply, manufacturing, or shipping. Many retailers cancelled their orders, and some ceased trading altogether, often with little notice or payment to suppliers. The implications for factory workers, already often working in very challenging conditions and for low pay, encouraged the Ethical Trading Initiative (ETI) to produce guidance for brands and sourcing companies (ETI, 2020).

Meanwhile, clothing manufacturers in the UK city of Leicester highlighted the poor working conditions that exist everywhere. Factories failing to adhere to health and safety legislation, social distancing, and suspension of non-essential work were attributed with helping to facilitate the spread of Covid-19 in the city. The suppliers blame their retail customers for continuing to demand fast-response items to support growing online demand (Financial Times, 2020).

Social sustainability meets climate change

Some links between modern slavery and climate change are beginning to emerge, with interesting supply chain consequences. These examples relate to the chapter content:

Unethical cobalt mining

Cobalt is an essential material used in many green technologies, such as electric vehicle batteries. According to HTS, 70% of cobalt mined globally is sourced from the Democratic Republic of the Congo, DRC, which in return is a major source of international investment and economic growth, providing income for hundreds of thousands of the population. However, the mining industry in the DRC is synonymous with human rights violations, exploitation of workers, and child labour, while cobalt mining specifically is linked with poor working conditions and damaging public health (HTS, 2022b).

Deep-sea fishing

Intensely farmed fishing practices are driven by growing global demand for cheap seafood products in the supply chain and associated with a harmful reduction in marine biodiversity. This has, in turn, led to an increase in labour exploitation in the ocean-fishing fleets of countries such as Thailand, where reduced catches have seen economic viability, and therefore, wages and working conditions fall dramatically, leading to an increase in modern slavery (Rights Lab, 2018). This situation is exacerbated in that many of those exploited by debt bondage in the Thai fisheries are migrants displaced from agricultural regions in poorer countries such as Cambodia because climate change has perpetually caused their crops to fail. The Walk Free Foundation's Global Slavery Index (2018) highlights that modern slavery is particularly virulent in deep-sea fisheries, as those exploited can be switched from ship to ship while at sea, evading the risk of escape or exposure of the abuse.

Burner boys in the circular economy

Transition to the circular economy is another area where environmental and social good practice could and need to diverge in the quest for climate change. Circular economy principles are growing rapidly in supply chains and, indeed, often require the development of new global supply chain systems and reverse logistics. This growth offers considerable scope for job creation, since 'as a stepping stone, remanufacturing and repair of goods is more labour-intensive than resource extraction' (ILO, 2022: 20). The e-waste supply chain highlights the condition of 'burner boys', marginally self-employed workers who extract tiny copper particles by burning the plastic from redundant electric cables. They work for low pay within the informal economy, in hazardous conditions that generate harmful emissions and by-products, pollute water supply, and damage their own health (Wired, 2020).

Supply chain traceability and transparency

In the context of supply chain sustainability, **traceability** is defined as '[t]he ability to identify and trace the history, distribution, location and application of products, parts and materials, to ensure the reliability of sustainability claims, in the areas of human rights, labour (including health and safety), the environment and anti-corruption' (UNGC, 2014: 6).

Various approaches to traceability are in use, depending on product and supply chain context, but in common they all use data systems to enable businesses to maintain knowledge of each step of the supply chain in order to underpin claims of sustainability, quality, and authenticity. The benefits include efficiency savings through risk reduction, process improvements, and securing supply; appeasing stakeholder pressure to achieve sustainability goals; demonstrating adherence to regulations and standards; and helping preserve natural resources. Well-known examples include:

- Fairtrade Labelling Organizations (such as for coffee, tea, cocoa)
- Forest Stewardship Council (FSC for timber)
- Organic food labels (such as cotton, fruit, and vegetables)
- Marine Stewardship Council (MSC for fish and seafood)

Implementation of traceability schemes involves high levels of collaboration and engagement with senior managers to establish the business case, stakeholder organisations to access existing systems and knowledge, and internal teams and suppliers to identify issues, collect data, and implement improvements.

Whether or not organisations subscribe to formal traceability standards, consumers, customers, and stakeholders increasingly expect to know more about the origins of products and services to address concerns about quality, safety, ethics, and the environment. **Transparency** in the supply chain involves making details about the provenance of products and materials available to customers and stakeholders and is enabled by tracking technologies, such as RFID (radio frequency identification devices) and the internet of things, with a growing array of sophisticated tracking tools creating new supply chains in access to data, data management, and security and new payment methods, including blockchain. Analysts predict that revealing product origins will become an important part of building trust and reputation and can help protect businesses against substitution and counterfeiting (New, 2010). Some examples are illustrated in what follows.

Transparency and traceability in the IT supply chain

Hewlett-Packard (HP) has published a list detailing where its final-assembly suppliers are located, the number of workers, products made, and links to the suppliers' own sustainability policies. HP also lists a range of component suppliers and smelters on their website. An increasing number of leading companies are making some of their supply chain details **transparent** in this way (HP supplier list, 2021).

In the United States, the Dodd-Frank Act (2010) obliges companies to ensure they avoid sourcing tin, tungsten, tantalum, and gold (T3G) extracted from conflict zones around the Democratic Republic of Congo (DRC), where child labour and other forms of modern slavery are common and financial proceeds support the militia. HP publish progress in converting their supply chain to be free of T3G from high-risk zones, currently down to just 2%, with a range of initiatives, including recycling, to maintain improvements. Intel has traced 100% of the smelters in its supply chain and is one of the first companies to achieve this level of **traceability**. Intel has audited many suppliers to improve conditions, supported a multi-stakeholder initiative, and since 2014, begun to design and manufacture microprocessors that are free of DRC conflict minerals (BWAA, 2016).

Tackling corruption in the supply chain

Another area of increasing concern in sustainable supply chain management, **corruption**, can take a number of forms. These include financial incentives or gifts to buyers to influence supplier selection decisions; selecting suppliers because of personal relationships; incentivising buyers, officials, or verifiers to overlook poor quality or substitutes; or falsely accepting non-compliance when checking health and safety, environmental or ethical standards, or providing customs clearance. Addressing corruption enables businesses to improve quality, avoid compensation and litigation costs, develop a sustainable business environment, and enhance reputation (UNGC, 2010). However, the complexities of the global supply chain, spanning diverse cultural norms and different legal frameworks, exacerbate the challenge. Some experts advocate greater simplicity, transparency, and shortening of the supply chain, as well as adoption of codes of conduct and re-education for suppliers and employees.

The future of supply chain sustainability

The chapter has introduced aspects of sustainable supply chain management, particularly linking to social and environmental concerns. It went on to discuss some of the practicalities and trade-offs experienced by supply chain managers in adopting the principles of the Global Compact and supporting the SDGs.

408 Sustainable Management

Critical aspects of change in the future include:

- Addressing trade-offs, for example, between cost and sustainability, or social and environmental sustainability

- Strengthening supply chain relationships so that buyers and suppliers can work together to implement learning and improvements

- Improving traceability and transparency, with better monitoring and enforcement in known hotspots

- Adoption of new technologies and data systems to enable improvements in environmental performance, new developments to support circularity, and monitoring of social improvements

- Collaboration, knowledge sharing, and working for a common good to reduce the impact of supply chains on environmental sustainability and the supply chain risks imposed by climate change and poor social sustainability

Achieving net zero: pillar 4

To achieve the 1.5 °C ambition to reduce climate change, industry leaders need to contribute towards scaling the ambition and potential to make a real difference.

At **pillar 4**, a key priority is for stakeholders to share their knowledge and experience, invest in technology and expertise, and become advocates and lobbyists to accelerate demand, beyond the normal reach of their organisations (Falk et al., 2022).

Case study: Nestlé

Nestlé is a corporate **pillar 4** advocate. The corporation's sustainability portal shares a range of projects and their outcomes, explaining how internal processes, supply chain partners, customers, and stakeholders are able to contribute to achieving net zero, as well as social sustainability and Corporate Shared Value (CSV).

Pillar 1: Nestlé brands have reduced GHG emissions by 4 million tonnes and sourced 63% of electricity from renewable sources.

Pillar 2: 97% of Nestlé ingredients are assessed as deforestation-free, and there are plans to introduce reforestation initiatives in its supply chains.

Pillar 3: Introducing plant-based products and brands is expected to help achieve net zero by 2050. Plant-rich foods are better for health and the environment, and Nestlé aims to eliminate deforestation from its supply chains by 2022, while the ambition to make every cup of Nespresso carbon-neutral will help both consumers and corporate customers change their sustainable behaviours.

Pillar 4: Nestlé will expand its advocacy with government, NGOs, farmers, suppliers, and communities to ensure all sectors move more quickly toward this target.

Suggested sessions

Session 1: Supplier selection for sustainable supply chains

Objective: To develop a simple framework for selecting suppliers able to meet social and environmental requirements

Activity 1

Search online for brands and retailers, such as Hewlett-Packard (HP, 2021), that publish lists of suppliers. What can you find out about the capabilities of these suppliers, their location, and their approach to sustainability?

Activity 2

Develop a framework or scorecard that can be used to objectively assess whether a potential or existing supplier is able to meet the needs of a sustainable supply chain.

1. Study the supplier selection framework in the following and watch the video: AT&T video: Sustainable Supply Chain Management – A Big Deal for Big Business (www.mnn.com/green-tech/gadgets-electronics/sponsorvideo/sustainable-supply-chain-management-a-big-deal-for-big).

2. With a specific case company in mind (such as IKEA, Nike, Hewlett-Packard, M&S), make a list of the sustainability factors that buyers might add to the framework so that it can be used to shortlist suppliers for the sustainable supply chain of a chosen product. These might include a traceability standard, approaches to workers' rights or modern slavery, approaches to manage upstream suppliers.

3. For your chosen company, rank all the main selection criteria from most important to least, and assign each category a weighting to ensure that

important criteria are most influential in your decision. Weightings should total 100% when all categories are added together. What weighting will you give to sustainability factors?

4. You can now apply scores for potential suppliers against your grid based on their **performance, capabilities, or tendering information. To obtain a weighted ranking,** multiply each score by the weighting percentage. Which supplier should you choose?

5. Now try changing the weightings based on different priorities. How does this affect your decision?

Supplier selection draft framework

A Selection criteria	B Category weighting	C Supplier score 1 low, 5 high	D Weighted score (B × C)
Management capability			
Management capability			
Worker relationships			
Financial security			
Return on investment			
Indebtedness			
Cost structure			
Costs relative to industry norm			
Cost transparency			
Cost reduction			
Quality assurance systems			
Quality system certification			
Continuous improvement			
Delivery performance			
Delivery accuracy and on-time			
Flexibility/ JIT			

(continued...)

A Selection criteria	B Category weighting	C Supplier score 1 low, 5 high	D Weighted score (B × C)
Product/process innovation			
Product–service mix			
Technological innovations			
Product development/R&D			
IT and communications			
EDI/EPOS/RFID capability			
Computer-aided design/3D			
Sustainability			
x			
y			
z			
Total	**100%**		

Session 2: Ten questions to ask companies about their sustainable supply chain

In this session, you are asked to make an initial, desk-based assessment of whether an importing company in a developed country is using sustainable supply chain management practices. The toolkit includes ten questions that allow you, as a learner, to find out whether a given importing company, for example, a retailer or a supermarket, is in compliance with ethical procurement policy. Select a company and try to find out whether they live up to Oxfam Australia's ethical procurement policy and/or the WWF's GHG emissions management. The questions are summarised here and can be downloaded in more detail from:

Oxfam n.d.: 10 Questions_for_Companies_about_Labour_Practices: https://oxfam.app.box.com/s/ocbkeyl04rm5u374r6mmcyf8vt68a3db

WWF, n.d.: Emission Possible Toolkit – Example Questionnaire.pdf (wwf.org.uk)

1. Does the company have a supplier code of conduct to guide suppliers through the implementation of human rights for their workers? Is it publicly available?

2. Does the company publish a list of its suppliers and their locations? Supply chain transparency enables stakeholders and external observers to monitor developments, but does the company agree?

3. Are core ILO conventions ratified in the countries where the company's suppliers are based? This should give workers the right to freedom of association.

4. Does the company have a good system to audit factory conditions and workers' wages? This may involve local unions rather than private suppliers, with workers interviewed away from their place of work so that they can speak without risk or pressure.

5. Do workers have permanent contracts and job security, right to join a union, awareness of their rights, and ability to raise a grievance?

6. Does the company have transparent GHG emissions monitoring and targets to reduce these emissions?

7. What methodology and reporting tools have been used to calculate emissions and any improvements?

8. What are the companies' scope 1 and scope 2 emissions in CO_2e for the baseline and current years? How have these changed?

9. Has the company started to report on scope 3 emissions? And if so, what does the data show?

10. Is the implementation of the code of conduct and/or the GHG emissions data being audited by a third party? Is the audit process transparent and are reports available?

Session 3: Complex challenges for materials in the circular economy

Listen to the Circular Economy Podcast from Catherine Weetman:

No. 78 with Colin Church – complex challenges for materials

This podcast features guest expert **Colin Church, Chief Executive of the UK Institute of Materials, Minerals, and Mining (IOM3)**. The podcast touches on a range of topics, from the economic, social, and political aspects of circular economy to supply chain issues, especially relating to upstream materials and recycling; the role of technologies, including blockchain and life cycle assessment tools; consumers, consumption, and use of products and packaging; and the role of sand as a critical material!

The podcast is around 45 minutes long, so stop every 10 minutes (up to 38 minutes) or so to discuss each of the following in turn:

1. How can the conflicting sustainable and social aspects of the circular economy be balanced? How can materials and the benefits/costs of circularity be shared more fairly?
2. What are the supply chain challenges of creating a circular economy supply chain, and how can these be overcome?
3. What is the role of knowledge, technology, and monitoring systems in creating a circular economy? What obstacles need to be solved, and how can these tools be used more effectively?
4. How can the circular economy and end-of-life management be financed, resourced, and scaled?

Access the full range of Catherine Weetman podcasts here: Circular Economy Podcast on Apple Podcasts.

Additional teaching material and ideas

'Where from?' icebreaker

This is a way to encourage students to get to know each other and learn more about sustainable supply chains. In pairs or threes, examine labels in the clothes you are wearing, the snacks in your cafeteria, or the contents of your bag. Map where each of your items has come from, and then identify any aspects of sustainability that might relate to the items and their supply chains, such as transport, packaging, materials, production processes, waste or recycling, skills, working conditions, etc. The groups can compare notes by presenting their most interesting and surprising 'finds'.

Topics for debate

The trade-off choices between commercial and sustainable pressures in the supply chain provide fertile territory for class debate. Topics to explore could include:

1. Slow fashion vs fast fashion: How can the social and environmental impacts of our high levels of consumerism be addressed in today's global society?

2. Is it possible to have environmentally and socially sustainable cocoa/fashion/ e-waste recycling processes/electric car batteries?

3. Local or global: evaluate the social and environmental impact of importing fresh food to Europe from Kenya.

4. Does creating circularity in the supply chain really reduce GHG emissions?

5. Do codes of conduct prevent modern slavery and forced labour in labour-intensive industries?

Multimedia resources

If you prefer to watch video material, the following provide a short introduction to environmental and ethical sustainability in the supply chain, respectively:

What is a circular economy? | Ellen MacArthur Foundation. The Ellen MacArthur Foundation portal includes a range of different articles, reports, videos, and podcasts.

Circular Economy Podcast on Apple Podcasts. Catherine Weetman's series of discussions with experts and professionals in all things to do with the circular economy, over 90 circular economy podcasts.

Freedom United (2017), Slavery in Supply Chains. A closer look at the cotton industry illustrates the breadth of modern slavery issues found in the supply chain for cotton products and relates these to supply chain operations: Slavery In Supply Chains – A closer look at the Cotton Industry – 2017 – YouTube.

The Global Slavery Index (2016) provides a comprehensive range of resources, interactive maps, and research findings related to the incidence of modern slavery across the globe: www.globalslaveryindex.org/index/.

Further readings

BSR/UN Global Compact, 2015, *Supply Chain Sustainability: A Practical Guide for Continuous Improvement*, 2nd Ed. New York: UN Global Compact.

> The UN report provides a practical way to understand some of the major issues affecting the supply chain and access relevant tools and techniques for making improvements. The report details various standards and improvement projects, illustrated with case examples. The first edition is available in several languages.

Golman, M., and C. Ernst, 2022, *Future of Work, Emerging Sectors and the Potential for Transition to Formality*. Geneva: ILO.

> This position paper sets out many of the issues facing employment in the future, focusing on the transition from informal to formal employment for up to 2 billion workers. Along the way, it explains the potential effects of political and social challenges, as well as changes, such as technology, digitisation, and climate change. Section 2 specifically discusses new sectors presenting both formal and informal work opportunities, including renewable energy, circularity, waste and recycling, and sustainable tourism.

ILO/Walk Free/IoM, 2022a, *Global Estimates of Modern Slavery: Forced Labour and Forced Marriage: Executive Summary*. Available [online] at: Global Estimates of Modern Slavery: Forced Labour and Forced Marriage   **Executive Summary:** wcms_854795.pdf (ilo.org)

ILO/Walk Free/IoM, 2022b, *Global Estimates of Modern Slavery: Forced Labour and Forced Marriage*. Geneva: ILO. Available [online] at: wcms_854733.pdf (ilo.org)

> This report explores the fate of the 50 million people trapped in modern slavery in 2021. Of these, 28 million people were in forced labour – up by 10 million compared to 2016 global estimates. The report discusses the reasons and provides detailed case studies that illustrate why this is such a complex problem. A range of recommendations is proposed.

Molthan-Hill, P., et al., 2022, *The Handbook of Carbon Management: A Step-by-Step Guide to High-Impact Climate Solutions for Every Manager in Every Function. Chapter 8: Procurement and Supply: Pushing the Boundaries to Remove Carbon.* Available [online] at: www.routledge.com/The-Handbook-of-Carbon-Management-A-Step-by-Step-Guide-to-High-Impact-Climate/Molthan-Hill-Winfield-Howarth-Mazhar/p/book/9781032227603

> Procurement and supply account for 70% of business revenue and most of their GHG emissions. Much of these are in 'scope 3', or the supply chain, and often considered outside of the organisation's control, but initiatives, standards, and collaboration can make a difference, with subsequent reductions providing mutual benefit. This practical chapter will help you design an emissions-reduction strategy for the supply chain.

Weetman, C., 2022, *A Circular Economy Handbook for Business and Supply Chains: Repair, Remake Redesign, Rethink.* London: Kogan Page.

> This book is described as essential to anyone considering developing a circular supply chain. It discusses the drivers, tools, and techniques for creating a circular supply chain, illustrated with details and examples, but Weetman also questions some of the trade-offs and limitations and challenges that need to be overcome – for example, what impact on GHG emissions the circular economy really makes?

The book is accompanied by a series of over 90 circular economy podcasts. Circular Economy Podcast on Apple Podcasts.

References

Advice Gov, 2021, *Modern Slavery Act and Procurement Explained*, Advice Gov. Available [online] at: https://advice-gov.co.uk/insights/modern-slavery-act/

AT&T Video. *Sustainable Supply Chain Management – A Big Deal for Big Business.* Available [online] at: www.mnn.com/green-tech/gadgets-electronics/sponsorvideo/sustainable-supply-chain-management-a-big-deal-for-big.

Bair, J., and F. Palpacuer, 2012, 'From Varieties of Capitalism to Varieties of Activism: The Anti Sweatshop Movement in a Comparative Perspective', *Social Problems* 59.4 (November): 522–43.

Barrientos, S., and S. Smith, 2007, 'Do Workers Benefit from Ethical Trade? Assessing Codes of Labour Practice in Global Production Systems', *Third World Quarterly* 28.4: 713–29.

BBC, 2022, 'Why Ships Crash', *BBC Two*, 18 January. Available [online] at: www.bbc.co.uk/programmes/m0013p1f

Brindley, C., and L. Oxborrow, 2014, 'Aligning the Sustainable Supply Chain to Green Marketing Needs: A Case Study', *Industrial Marketing Management* 43: 45–55.

BWAA (Baptist World Aid Australia), 2016, *Electronic Industry Trends-The Truth Behind the Barcode*. Available [online] at: www.ituc-csi.org/IMG/pdf/electronics-industry-trends-report-australia.pdf

Christopher, M., 2011, *Global Logistics and Supply Chain Management*. London: FT Prentice Hall.

Ellen MacArthur Foundation, 2020, *What Is a Circular Economy?* Available [online] at: https://ellenmacarthurfoundation.org/topics/circular-economy-introduction/overview

ETI (Ethical Trading Initiative), 2006, *ETI Code of Labor Practice: Do Workers Really Benefit?* Brighton, UK: University of Sussex, Institute of Development Studies.

ETI (Ethical Trading Initiative), 2020, *ETI Publishes Guidance to Apparel and Textile Members on Payment of Orders to Workers*. Ethical Trading Initiative. Available [online] at: www.ethicaltrade.org/blog/eti-publishes-guidance-to-apparel-and-textile-members-payment-orders-to-workers, accessed 6 April 2020.

Falk, J. et al., 2022, *Business Playbook*. Exponential Roadmap Initiative. Available [online] at: https://exponentialroadmap.org/wp-content/uploads/2022/10/1.5C-business-playbook-v2.1_digital_Ny-ISBN-1.pdf

Financial Times, 2020, *Leicester's Dark Factories Show Up a Diseased System*. Available [online] at: www.ft.com/content/0b26ee5d-4f4f-4d57-a700-ef49038de18c

Freedom United, 2017, Slavery in Supply Chains. A closer look at the cotton industry, YouTube.

Global Slavery Index, 2016, *Modern Slavery: A Hidden Everyday Problem*. Available [online] at: www.globalslaveryindex.org/index/

Global Slavery Index, 2018, *04 Spotlight on Sectors*. Available [online] at: https://downloads.globalslaveryindex.org/ephemeral/4_Spotlight-on-Sectors-1669254322.pdf

Gold, S., A. Trautrims, and Z. Trodd, 2015, 'Modern Slavery Challenges to Supply Chain Management', *Supply Chain Management: An International Journal* 20.5: 485–94.

Greenberg, J., and G. Knight, 2004, 'Framing Sweatshops: Nike, Global Production, and the American News Media', *Communication and Critical Cultural Studies* 1.2 (June): 151–75.

HP, 2021, *HP Supplier List*. Available [online] at https://h20195.www2.hp.com/V2/GetPDF.aspx/c03728062.pdf

HRW Human Rights Watch, 2022, *Social Audits No Cure for Retail Supply Chain Labor Abuse*, November 15. Available [online] at: Social Audits No Cure for Retail Supply Chain Labor Abuse | Human Rights Watch (hrw.org)

HTS Human Trafficking Search, 2022a, *The Kafala System: An Issue of Modern Slavery*. Available [online] at https://humantraffickingsearch.org/the-kafala-system-an-issue-of-modern-slavery/

HTS Human Trafficking Search, 2022b, *A Green Transition but at What Cost? Cobalt Mining in the DRC*. Available [online] at: https://humantraffickingsearch.org/resource/a-green-transition-but-at-what-cost-cobalt-mining-in-the-democratic-republic-of-congo/

ILO, 2022, *Future of Work, Emerging Sectors and the Potential for Transition to Formality*. Available [online] at: www.ilo.org/wcmsp5/groups/public/-ed_emp/documents/publication/wcms_855420.pdf

Insider, 2020, *Pfizer's Vaccine Relies on a 'Cold Chain' That Keeps the Shots Colder Than a Freezer*. Available [online] at: www.businessinsider.com/vaccine-cold-chain-why-coronavirus-shot-needs-to-be-cold-2020-11?r=US&IR=T, accessed 13 November.

Khara, N., and P. Lund-Thomsen, 2012, 'Value Chain Restructuring, Work Organization and Labour Outcomes in Football Manufacturing in India', *Competition and Change* 16.4 (October): 261–80.

Krause, D., S. Vachon, and R. Klassen, 2009, Introduction and Reflection on the Role of Purchasing Management, *Journal of Supply Chain Management* 45.4: 18–25.

Liu, S., D. Kastriratne, and J. Moizer, 2012, 'A Hub and Spoke Model for Multi-Dimensional Integration of Green Marketing and Sustainable Supply Chain Management', *Industrial Marketing Management* 41: 581–8.

Lund-Thomsen, P., 2008, 'The Global Sourcing and Codes of Conduct Debate: Five Myths and Five Recommendations', *Development and Change* 39.6: 1005–18.

Lund-Thomsen, P., and A. Lindgreen, 2014, 'Corporate Social Responsibility in Global Value Chains: Where are We Now and Where are We Going?', *Journal of Business Ethics*, 123.1, 11–22.

Mangan, J., and C. Lalwani, 2016, *Global Logistics and Supply Chain Management*, 3rd Ed. London: Wiley.

McKinsey & Company, 2021, *The Risks and Challenges of the Global Covid-19-Vaccine Roll-Out*. Available [online] at: www.mckinsey.com/business-functions/risk/our-insights/the-risks-and-challenges-of-the-global-covid-19-vaccine-rollout, accessed 26 January.

Mehrmann, J., 2008, *Reverse Logistics in Supply Chain Management*. Available [online] at: www.improvementandinnovation.com/features/article/reverse-logistics-supply-chain-management/

New, S., 2010, 'The Transparent Supply Chain', *Harvard Business Review*, October. Available [online] at: https://hbr.org/2010/10/the-transparent-supply-chain, accessed 1 September 2016.

The New Yorker, 2020, *The Race to Make Vials for Coronavirus Vaccines*. Available [online] at: www.newyorker.com/magazine/2020/12/07/the-race-to-make-vials-for-coronavirus-vaccines, accessed 7 December 2020.

Nike, 2021, *Made with Nike Grind*. Available [online] at: www.nikegrind.com/made-with-nike-grind/

Oxfam, n.d., *10 Questions_for_Companies_About_Labour_Practices*. Available [online] at: https://oxfam.app.box.com/s/ocbkeyl04rm5u374r6mmcyf8vt68a3db

Rights Lab, 2018, *Modern Slavery, Environmental Destruction and Climate Change: Fisheries, Field, Forests and Factories*. University of Nottingham, Royal Holloway University of London, and the Independent Anti-Slavery Commissioner. Available [online] at: www.antislaverycommissioner.co.uk/media/1241/fisheries-field-forests-factories.pdf

SBC (Sustainable Business Council), 2003, *Business Guide to a Sustainable Supply Chain: A Practical Guide*. Available [online] at: www.sbcvaluechain.org.nz/__data/assets/pdf_file/0005/54914/Sustainable-Supply-Chain-Guide.pdf

SBC (Sustainable Business Council), 2014, *Value Chain Guide*. Available [online] at: www.sbcvaluechain.org.nz/

Seuring, S., and M. Muller, 2008, 'Core Issues in Sustainable Supply Chain Management: A Delphi Study', *Business Strategy and the Environment* 17: 455–66.

Sharma, A., G.R. Iyer, A. Mehrotra, and R. Krishnan, 2010, 'Sustainability and Business-to-Business Marketing: A Framework and Implications', *Industrial Marketing Management* 39: 330–41.

Short, J.L., and M.W. Toffel, 2021, 'Manage the Suppliers That Could Harm Your Brand: Know when to avoid, engage, or drop them', *Harvard Business Review*, March–April 2021. Available [online] at: Manage the Suppliers That Could Harm Your Brand (hbr.org)

Slack, N., A. Brandon-Jones, and R. Johnston, 2013, *Operations Management*. Harlow, UK: Pearson.

Srivastava, S.K., 2007, 'Green Supply Chain Management: A State of the Art Literature Review', *International Journal of Management Reviews* 9.10: 53–80.

Talay, C., L. Oxborrow, and C. Brindley, 2018, An Exploration of Power Asymmetry in the Apparel Industry in the UK and Turkey. *Industrial Marketing Management* 74: 162–74. ISSN 0019-8501.

UNGC, 2009, *The Business and Its Supply Chain – A Management Alternative: Guide for the Responsible Management of the Supply Chain*. Spain: United Nations Global Compact Network. Available [online] at: www.unglobalcompact.org/library/100

UNGC, 2010, *Fighting Corruption in the Supply Chain: A Guide for Customers and Suppliers*. United Nations Global Compact. Available [online] at: www.unglobalcompact.bg/wp-content/uploads/2014/05/131.pdf

UNGC, 2014, *A Guide to Traceability: A Practical Approach to Advance Sustainability in Global Supply Chains (English)*. UN Global Compact and BSR. Available [online] at: https://d306pr3pise04h.cloudfront.net/docs/issues_doc%2Fsupply_chain%2FTraceability%2FGuide_to_Traceability.pdf.2014:62014

UNGC, 2015, *Supply Chain Sustainability – A Practical Guide for Continuous Improvement*, 2nd Ed. United Nations Global Compact and BSR. Available [online] at: www.unglobalcompact.org/docs/issues_doc/supply_chain/SupplyChainRep_spread.pdf

Vachon, S., and R. Klassen, 2006, 'Extending Green Practices Across the Supply Chain', *International Journal for Operations and Production Management* 26.7: 795–821.

Verdict Food Service, 2019, *McDonald's UK to Turn Waste into Biofuel and Reduce Fatbergs*. Available [online] at: www.verdictfoodservice.com/news/mcdonalds-turn-waste-biofuel/

Walk Free Foundation, 2018, *Highlights*. Global Slavery Index. Available [online] at: www.globalslaveryindex.org/2018/findings/highlights/

World Economic Forum, 2014, *Towards the Circular Economy: Accelerating the Scale-Up Across Global Supply Chains*. Available [online] at: https://www3.weforum.org/docs/WEF_ENV_TowardsCircularEconomy_Report_2014.pdf

Wired, 2020, 'Your Old Electronics Are Poisoning People at This Toxic Dump in Ghana', *Wired UK*. Available [online] at: www.wired.co.uk/article/ghana-ewaste-dump-electronics

WWF, n.d., *Emission Possible Toolkit – Example Questionnaire*. Available [online] at: www.wwf.org.uk/sites/default/files/2021-04/Emission%20Possible%20Toolkit%20-%20Example%20Questionnaire.pdf

ADDING CORE TOPICS
TO THE CURRICULUM

15

Climate change and greenhouse gas management

Richard Holmes, Al Dharmasasmita, Helen Puntha, and Ellie Kennedy

This chapter introduces the global challenge of climate change as it relates to business activity, with specific focus on how business approaches 'carbon management'/ greenhouse gas (GHG) management. It considers how businesses impact and are affected by climate change. It also discusses the key steps business organisations can take to identify and measure their GHG emissions, enabling them to be more efficient in their processes, which, in turn, can lower their production and/or running costs.

The opening section of this chapter is written as a general introduction, with enough detail to give you a working understanding of what is required to complete the activities. More detail is provided in the subsequent sections, followed by material for teaching units, learning activities, and further recommended reading.

In this chapter you will learn:

• How climate change is connected to business and vice versa.

DOI: 10.4324/9781003294665-19

- Why 'carbon management' can help businesses minimise their impact on the climate as well as reduce energy and other running costs.

- How organisations can measure their impact on the climate.

- What actions organisations and individuals can take to reduce their climate impact and save money.

So let's get started.

What is climate change, and how does it relate to businesses?

Businesses contribute to climate change by emitting gasses into the atmosphere which contribute to global heating or the greenhouse effect. These are known as greenhouse gasses (GHG). It has been recognised for many decades that these gasses have an insulating effect in the atmosphere, which prevents heat radiating from Earth into space. Having more than the natural level of these gasses in the atmosphere adds to the insulating effect, trapping additional energy and raising temperatures across the globe. Currently, the world is about 1.1°C above pre-industrial temperatures. An international body of scientists and other experts (IPCC: Intergovernmental Panel on Climate Change) has concluded that it would be dangerous to exceed 1.5°C. This figure was brought into public awareness through the 2015 Paris Agreement.

Well, 1.5°C doesn't sound like a lot, does it? Such a small number can make the issue seem overblown or exaggerated. In fact, it is the additional energy trapped inside the atmosphere causing the rise in temperature which is the real problem. That extra energy affects how much heat and water vapour the atmosphere contains, how they move around the planet and change weather patterns through, for example, hurricanes, flooding, and drought.

Instead of describing the problem in terms of temperature rise, perhaps we should explain that the energy being trapped inside the atmosphere today because of human activity is the equivalent of five atomic bombs per second (Nuccitelli 2020). Perhaps it isn't surprising that this will have a significant impact on temperature and weather.

In order to limit global warming to 1.5 °C, the IPCC stresses that the world needs to halve CO_2 emissions by around 2030 and reach net zero CO_2 emissions by mid-century. Often, commentators concentrate on achieving net zero in 2050, not realising that the reductions need to be planned immediately – with the first aim to **halve the emissions by 2030!** This is quite an ambitious task, but one that is possible with everyone contributing.

While businesses contribute to the causes of climate change, they are also impacted by it. Many businesses are affected directly by changes to weather. For example, tourism depends on a predictable climate to attract visitors, while agriculture relies on certain conditions for efficient growth and harvesting of crops. Other organisations are affected indirectly, via their supply chains. The hospitality industry is dependent on agriculture for food and drink ingredients, while the construction industry depends on a reliable supply of timber.

Often, the climate is seen as a distant idea, difficult to define, and which doesn't seem to connect with our daily lives. When we do become more aware of the impact of our actions, the solution which is often presented to us can be over-whelming – that we should make better choices as consumers in everything we buy. Given that we will each purchase many thousand items in our lifetime, the task at hand in each of us identifying the impact of every one of these actions is rather ambitious, if not impossible.

Wouldn't it be easier if the businesses providing the products and services ensured that they had minimal impact to begin with?

That's where greenhouse gas management, sometimes known as carbon management, comes in.

Carbon management is the process by which organisations identify the impacts they have on the climate and take action to reduce them to a minimum. This is sometimes known as developing a **carbon management action plan (CMAP)**.

To do this, a business would have to do the following:

1. Measure their impact by identifying and quantifying greenhouse gas emissions (GHG).

2. Set targets to reduce these emissions. For example, 50% by 2030 or net zero by 2050.

3. Identify actions that can be taken to reduce emissions.

4. Implement these actions.

5. Continue to monitor their impact to prevent it rising again.

Table 15.1: The six major human-made GHGs and the common sources of their emissions

Carbon dioxide (CO_2) One of the main contributors to climate change, especially through deforestation, the burning of fossil fuels (e.g. oil, gas, and coal), and other changes in land use.		
Methane (CH_4) Produced naturally when vegetation is rotted in the absence of oxygen or when burnt. The majority is released through cattle farming, production of oil and gas, and landfills.		**Nitrous oxide (N_2O)** Released by chemical fertilisers and the burning of fossil fuels.
Hydrofluorocarbons (HFCs) Chemical by-products and also used in some refrigeration equipment.	**Perfluorocarbons (PFCs)** Manufactured and chemical compounds used in various medical and other applications.	**Sulphur hexafluoride (SF_6)** Manufactured compound used in specialised applications, for example, insulation for high-voltage electrical equipment.

Source: Adapted from Lingl et al. (2010).

Carbon management

Businesses, like individuals, contribute to climate change through the production of greenhouse gasses, often referred to as 'carbon emissions'. The terms 'carbon' and 'greenhouse gas' are often used interchangeably, and for the remainder of this chapter, we will refer to 'carbon' as a synonym for GHGs.

Organisations emit carbon either directly by, for example, burning fossil fuels for heating (gas) or for transport (petrol) or indirectly through purchase of electricity. They can also contribute indirectly to further emissions via third parties, such as consumers or suppliers (Lingl et al. 2010). Figure 15.1 depicts the sources of carbon emissions globally.

To reduce carbon emissions, organisations should reduce their 'carbon footprint'. A *carbon footprint* is the total amount of emissions produced by an individual, an organisation, a country, etc., as measured in CO2e, or 'carbon dioxide equivalent' (sometimes called 'tCO2e', that is, tonnes of CO2 equivalent). The universal unit for measuring carbon is tCO2e.

A carbon footprint is calculated by converting the amounts of the various GHGs into equivalent amounts of CO_2 based on the extent to which they have a higher global warming potential. Once aware of their carbon footprint, organisations may

Figure 15.1: Global carbon emissions by 2018 based on sectors.

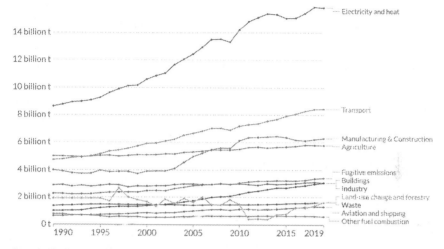

Greenhouse gas emissions by sector, World

Emissions are measured in carbon dioxide equivalents (CO2eq). This means non-CO2 gases are weighted by the amount of warming they cause over a 100-year timescale.

Source: Our World in Data based on Climate Analysis Indicators Tool (CAIT).
OurWorldInData.org/co2-and-other-greenhouse-gas-emissions • CC BY

Source: https://ourworldindata.org/.

set targets to reduce their emissions, such as achieving 'net zero' or 'zero carbon' by a chosen date.

- Net zero carbon. All carbon emissions are reduced in line with the Paris Agreement 1.5 °C trajectory, with residual emissions offset through carbon removals or avoided emissions.

- Zero carbon. Eliminating all carbon emissions without the use of offsets.

Mini Activity

Based on the information in the previous paragraph, which route do you think is best for organisations to take to address their carbon emissions? Discuss.

Identifying emissions

In order to reduce their impact on the climate, businesses need to identify the sources of their carbon emissions. For example, the amount of electricity used in a factory, fuel used in business travel, or emissions from production, consumption, and disposal of food.

While most organisations emit carbon from similar areas, the extent to which carbon management will benefit a business is very much specific to them. It is important to understand an organisation's business model while applying carbon management. You should understand how the business is structured and managed as well as which processes will contribute to carbon emissions. Small microbusinesses (e.g. less than ten people) will be managed very differently from large corporations.

There are many benefits to organisations in managing carbon.

Key advantages include:

- Costs savings

- Compliance with regulations

- Brand enhancement

Disadvantages would include rising costs, fines for not complying with regulations, and losing market share to greener competitors.

Initiating a carbon management action plan (CMAP) need not require much in the way of resources. However, commitment from management is fundamental. Someone, preferably a team, must be assigned responsibility for the overall CMAP. For larger bodies, this might be a bigger team of people. For smaller microbusinesses (e.g. less than ten people), it may simply be the responsibility of the owner.

Whilst many carbon management measures cost very little, making meaning-ful reductions will require financial investment. Many investments can provide a better return than banks or shares, as illustrated by the following case study on 'Facelift Access Hire'.

Case study 1: Facelift Access Hire (Earley 2013)

Facelift Access Hire has reduced its carbon footprint by 403 tonnes a year through simple yet effective changes.

After researching how energy and resources were being used, Facelift introduced measures to generate energy savings.

The company upgraded its 26-tonne trucks to more fuel-efficient vehicles, providing diesel fuel savings of 4,550 litres per month. They also saved a further 960 litres of diesel each month by using lighter Transit vans. The managing director changed his car from a Porsche Cayenne to a Vauxhall electric vehicle.

Facelift installed a wood boiler, saving 22,000 litres of diesel oil per year. It also added movement sensors and LED lighting to its depots, saving £5000.

Facelift installed waterless urinals, saving 200,000 litres of water per year. They recycle electronic equipment and printer cartridges and have switched to a paper-free policy, saving 16,000 kilograms of paper per year (Earley 2013).

Measuring carbon emissions

In order to manage something effectively, it must be measured.

It is essential for an organisation to measure and assess its current situation through an 'emission inventory'. This needs to be undertaken by every business in order to know where it is starting from and what to measure progress against.

The emission inventory process involves quantifying an organisation's major emissions, such as energy used by office buildings and factory plants and emissions from the vehicles and air travel. Data will be gathered from various sources, including utility bills and interviewing colleagues about travel methods. The emissions are then quantified, in tonnes CO_2e.

The emissions should be assessed over a 12-month period. As well as documenting the total annual emissions, it is useful for an organisation to have a percentage breakdown of emissions and to know the sources of those emissions. It can then prioritise actions by targeting areas of greatest emissions first. Figure 15.2 illustrates what the resulting emissions breakdown might look like for two different businesses. Perhaps the 'large retailer' would concentrate initially on reducing emissions from heating or lighting, while the 'small office-based company' might focus on business travel?

Figure 15.2: Example of inventory results of companies per year.

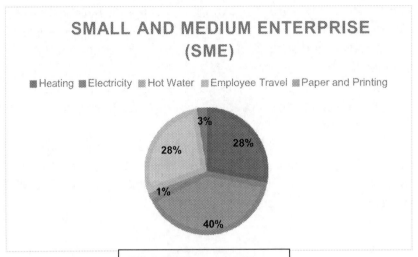

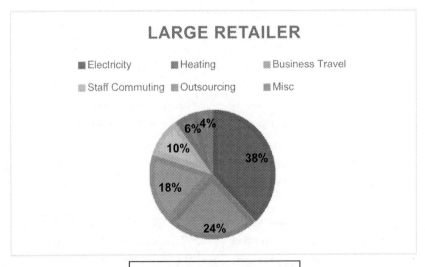

How to measure emissions: the Greenhouse Gas Protocol

For a business to assess and quantify emission sources, it needs to follow an agreed method. This is because it is not always possible to measure everything and to allow comparisons to be made between companies and over time. The Greenhouse Gas Protocol (GHGP) is the internationally agreed method for counting and reporting GHG emissions (UNFCCC 2014).

Companies can follow four basic steps for their CMAP (Ranganathan et al. 2004):

1. Establish an emission boundary.

2. Collect activity data.

3. Calculate emissions.

4. Quality control.

Establishing an emissions boundary

This is the first step. Due to the complex nature of businesses, it is not always possible to calculate all the emissions associated with their activity. It may be difficult or impossible to quantify the emissions from a complex supply chain or organisational structure. Therefore, two boundaries need to be decided upon: organisational boundary and operational boundary.

Organisational boundary

Which part of the organisation is to be assessed? All the organisation or just a subsidiary? Every site or just a single site?

Operational boundary

Which sources of emissions are to be counted towards the overall carbon annual total? For example, amount of (office) paper used, company cars, raw materials, energy used, food consumed on premises, employee business travel, employee commute, etc. From there, the organisation can decide which emission sources they would like to address.

In an ideal world, all emissions associated with an organisation's operations would be assessed. However, it might be impractical to do this. Emissions are

Figure 15.3: The three scopes of emissions according to the Greenhouse Gas Protocol.

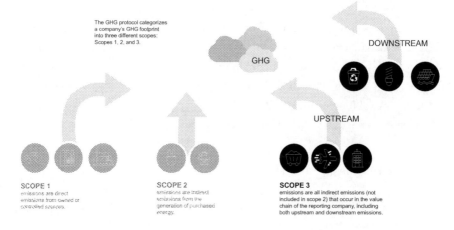

The GHG protocol categorizes
a company's GHG footprint
into three different scopes:
Scopes 1, 2, and 3.

GHG

DOWNSTREAM

UPSTREAM

SCOPE 1
emissions are direct
emissions from owned or
controlled sources.

SCOPE 2
emissions are indirect
emissions from the
generation of purchased
energy.

SCOPE 3
emissions are all indirect emissions (not
included in scope 2) that occur in the value
chain of the reporting company, including
both upstream and downstream emissions.

Source: www.bsr.org/images/inline/2020-04-02-scope3-report-infographic.jpg (2022).

placed in one of three categories, which have been defined as the three scopes of emissions (see Figure 15.3).

1. Processes the organisation has direct control over, for example, fuel that the organisation uses to run manufacturing equipment, to heat buildings, or to run a vehicle are known as 'scope 1'.

2. 'Indirect GHG emissions' over which the organisation has indirect control, such as purchased electricity, are known as 'scope 2'.

3. Emissions generated by third parties, such as consumers or suppliers, are known as 'scope 3'. While the business cannot control these directly, it can influence them by changing suppliers or working with existing suppliers to encourage them to reduce their emissions.

Companies need to look at all three scopes to manage their GHG emissions effectively. For the majority of organisations, scope 3 will prove to be difficult, with scopes 1 and 2 sometimes being the only sources assessed.

Further illustrations of the three scopes can be found in Table 15.2 and 15.3.

Once we have decided which sources of emissions to assess, the next step is to collect data on the activities that generate emissions (Lingl et al. 2010: 16). The data can be found on various sources, such as utility bills or transport mileage claims. These data might be expressed as kilometres/miles driven, kilowatts, or

Table 15.2: Different types of scopes

Scope 1	Emissions directly controlled by the company; it is all about *fuel combustion*, for example, purchased heat (gas).
Scope 2	Emissions partly controlled by the company, for example, purchased electricity.
Scope 3	Everything else outside scopes 1 and 2 and is **within the value chain** of the company, for example, purchased goods for the office kitchen, outsourced printing, and delivery.

litres/gallons of fuel consumed. It is important to note the unit used for each type of data collected for carbon conversion later.

This activity is the most time-consuming section in the development of a GHG inventory.

As the success of an organisation's CMAP is highly dependent on this process, the data needs to be collected carefully and the calculation needs to be accurate. For areas where exact data is missing, we need to make realistic estimates. Table 15.4 shows some of the common sources of GHG emissions, where this information can usually be found, and the common units used.

When all appropriate data (activity data) has been collected, we then calculate all the emissions. The universal formula is:

(activity data) × (carbon conversion factor) = carbon emissions

By using emission factors, the data can be converted into carbon emissions values, expressed in kilograms or tonnes of CO_2e. For example, using the emission factor for flights, it is possible to calculate that for one passenger to travel 17,040 kilometres by plane from Birmingham, UK, to Sydney, Australia (distance calculated using www.distance.to/), their carbon emission is:

17,040 km × 0.140625 kg CO_2/km* = 2,396.25 kg CO_2e

As 1,000 kg = 1 tonne

So 2,396.25 kg CO_2e/1,000 = 2.4 tonnes CO_2e (always leave the final unit as *tCO_2e*, which is the unit used globally when recording carbon management data)

That is for a one-way flight per person. For a return flight, double it.

*Where did the 0.140625 kg CO_2/km come from? I hope you have asked that! Read on to find out.

Can you guess what the 'e' in *tCO_2e* stands for?
Why do you think this is so? (Hint: think back to what causes *GHG* emissions.)

Table 15.3: Further examples of emissions scopes

Scope 1 Direct GHG emissions (company-owned or controlled sources)	Scope 2 Indirect GHG emissions (purchased electricity, heat, or steam)	Scope 3 Indirect GHG emissions (other sources)
Generation of own heat, steam, and electricity	Purchased electricity (from a utility company)	Transportation of goods and materials in vehicles **owned or controlled by third parties** (e.g. shipping services)
Transportation of materials, goods, products, waste, and employees in **company-owned or controlled** vehicles, planes, ships, etc.	Purchased steam	Extraction and production of materials and products (e.g. paper/gypsum) purchased by the business
Emissions from chemicals, such as HFCs, used in refrigeration and air-conditioning equipment		Outsourced activities, such as delivery, design, printing, etc.
Manufacturing and chemical processing (using machines that can be controlled by the company)		End use and disposal of company products
Combustion of fuel in furnaces, boilers, or generators		Transportation of people in vehicles owned or controlled by third parties (e.g. business travel and employee commuting on public buses/trains)
Fugitive emissions either intentionally or unintentionally released (e.g. leaks from equipment joints that can be repaired by the company)		Consumption of purchased electricity, heat, or steam in a leased operation not owned or controlled by the company (e.g. company in a leased building where utilities are included in the rent)
Purchased heat whereby the boiler is on site		Purchased goods for office use (e.g. electrical devices, kettle and microwave for the office kitchen, and printer)

Source: Adapted from Lingl et al. (2010: 12).

Carbon conversion factors can usually be found on government websites. In the UK, they are available on the UK government's site: www.gov.uk/government/collections/government-conversion-factors-for-company-reporting (UK Government 2022).

Table 15.4: Common sources of emissions: where information can be found, and the units represented

Source of emission	Where emission data can be found	Data units
Purchased electricity	Utility bills, online accounts of companies	kWh, MWh
Purchased heat (with boiler on site)	Utility bills, online accounts of companies	GJ, MWh, therms, BTUs, lbs of steam
On-site heat generation	Utility bills, storage tank logs, online accounts of companies, fuel purchase records, and invoices	Litres, GJ, gallons, m³, kg, BTUs, cubic ft, lbs
Company-owned vehicles	Fuel purchase records, fuel tank logs	Fuel type and amount (litres/gallons), or km/miles travelled and the vehicle make/model/year
Business travel (air)	Online calculators are available and can be used to find distances that flights have covered	Km/miles flown, or fuel used (in case of charter flights)
Business travel (vehicles)	Expense claims, accounting receipts	Fuel type and amount (litres/gallons), or km/miles travelled and the vehicle make/model/year
Employee commuting	Employers travel to work surveys	Km/miles travelled and mode of transportation, of fuel type and amount depending on the type of vehicles used
Freight transport	Delivery invoices, shipping invoices	Kg/lbs/tonnes and km/miles transported, mode of transport (lorries, trucks, air, ship, rail)
Leased premises	Where tenants do not receive utility bills, calculations can be done based on the size of the premises	m² or sq. ft and the number of days the property has been leased
Fugitive emissions (refrigeration equipment, air-conditioning, pipelines, etc.)	Government and industry publications, equipment specifications/manuals	Varies
Material inputs	Receipts of purchase, suppliers, life cycle analysis	Varies
Outsourced services	Information from suppliers or an organisation can collaborate with them to measure data	Varies

Source: Adapted from Lingl et al. (2010: 17).

There are different conversion factors for every year. What does this mean? Yes, the conversion factor (for any business process) changes annually. Why do you think this is so? Discuss this in class.

For a precise calculation, it is necessary to use the correct conversion factor for the correct year and the original units (e.g. km) on the spreadsheet.

In the case of the previous example of flying from Birmingham to Sydney, there are a few factors to be aware of:

1. The conversion factor for 2022 has been used, presuming the travel was in 2022.

2. The correct conversion factor for kilometres (km) was used, not miles (m).

3. Passenger travel in economy class was assumed. Premium, business, or first class would have used different conversion factors. Why is this so, do you reckon?

Quality control of the emissions inventory

The organisation needs to make sure that all data collected is reliable and recorded in a methodical way.

Setting targets

For companies to be successful in reducing their carbon emissions, they will need to set targets.

Targets help quantify what it is trying to achieve and how to achieve it. Goals give organisations something to aim for to help measure success. Without targets, organisations can lose focus and not make any progress. Four questions to ask when setting goals:

1. How much will we reduce our carbon emissions? This needs to be clear.

2. By when will we do it? A target date means everyone knows the deadline.

3. What year is the baseline?

4. How does the goal align with the overall strategy?

For example, a catering company aiming to reduce its emissions by 30% by 2025 compared with 2022, or a bus company aiming to make its operations carbon-neutral in ten years.

Reducing GHG emissions and going net zero

Having identified and quantified emissions sources across a whole organisation, management may decide to set a target to reduce emissions, such as one set in line with the Glasgow Climate Pact. They may wish to become completely net zero or carbon negative by, for example, generating excess energy from renewable sources.

Carbon reductions can be made by adjusting processes, activities, and facilities. Similar to when individuals reduce their energy consumption in the home.

Case study 2: Sainsbury's

J Sainsbury plc uses specialist IT systems in its Hythe branch to reduce energy use in heating, ventilation, and lighting.

The store uses night blinds on chiller cabinets and lower lighting levels at different times of day. Within six months, there was a 12% energy reduction.

The site has a biofuel generator plus photovoltaic cells. It generates heat and hot water from a biomass boiler.

The store's target of a 60% reduction in energy use has been exceeded.

By 2030, they aim to use renewable heat in the majority of super-markets and convert to natural refrigerants. They work with suppliers to reduce value chain emissions by 30% by 2030 (Fox 2012).

Identifying carbon reductions

Which carbon reduction measures are appropriate for a particular organisation will depend on where its emissions arise from, the efficiency of those processes, and the possibilities for improving or finding alternatives.

Specific measures are identified by carrying out a carbon audit of the organisation. This could mean surveying a building to identify any areas for improvement in insulation, heating, lighting, or equipment used. It could also mean assessing an organisation's management structure or where food or energy wastage might be identified in food production.

Opportunities fall into two main categories, human behaviour and technical.

Human behaviour can range from how the organisation is managed through to how the actions of individual members of staff can impact carbon emissions, such as cooking habits within a catering facility or driving technique in a haulage company.

Further examples of possible areas for behavioural improvement might include the following.

Management

- Development of a carbon management policy.

- Assigning responsibility for carbon management to relevant staff.

- Providing funding for improvements.

- Providing staff training.

- Monitoring of carbon emissions.

- Changing procedures, such as production line processes, or enabling home working.

Individuals

- Setting thermostat temperature to lower settings for heating or higher for air-conditioning.

- Wearing suitable clothing for the time of year and temperature.

- Changing eating habits and waste produced when preparing food.

- Switching lighting and appliances off when not in use.

Technical improvements can include physical improvements to buildings, such as insulation, lighting, heating, or renewable energy generation, such as solar panels.

Further examples of possible areas for technical improvement might include:

- Replacement of gas boilers with heat pumps.

- Upgrading transport fleet to electric alternatives.

- Replacement of a production line in a factory.

Improvement actions can be further divided by their cost:

- No or low cost
- Medium Cost
- Capital Investment

Or the length of time they take for the savings to cover the investment (payback period):

- Short term
- Medium term
- Long term

Communicating the carbon management programme

Communication is fundamental. Members of the staff need to be kept aware of the programme. Effective communication ensures that greenwashing can be avoided and the reputation of the organisation is not put at risk. Any idea what 'green-washing' is? If not, it will be explained in the next few pages.

The following factors of communication, adapted from Lingl et al. (2010), can help companies in their CMAP:

Principles of good communication:

1. 'Inside out'. Organisations need to communicate internally first. This ensures that all staff members are kept in the loop.

2. Authenticity. That is, 'do what you say you are doing/going to do'. Failure to do so will erode trust and can be seen as greenwashing.

3. Be specific. Provide detailed and precise information about carbon emissions.

4. Gain the right knowledge and proficiency required.

5. Obtain assurance from independent and accredited third parties. Accreditations also reassure other stakeholders that the company is not merely greenwashing.

6. Seeing is believing. The more an organisation can 'show' what it is doing—for example, solar panels on an organisation's building or a fleet of hybrid vehicles.

The term 'greenwashing' is used when companies make false claims about their emissions management or downplay their negative effects on the environment.

When you see a picture of a field or a forest on a product's packaging, what comes to your mind? Do you think of environmental responsibility? Or are you immediately suspicious?

Have a look at these examples of greenwashing and the consequences for business organisations:

https://truthinadvertising.org/articles/six-companies-accused-greenwashing/

https://thesustainableagency.com/blog/greenwashing-examples/

Conclusion

Climate change is already having catastrophic effects. Greenhouse gasses are major contributors to climate change. By managing these emissions, businesses can contribute to the long-term sustainability of their operations and the planet. All business organisations can address climate change by creating a coherent carbon management action plan (CMAP). This is especially important if they want to have a competitive advantage. Tools and frameworks can help with this, some of which have been introduced in this chapter. Taking positive steps now can help organisations reduce costs, gain recognition, and protect the Earth for future generations.

Offsetting

Offsetting can be defined as an act that 'negates, or offsets, the same amount of carbon emissions released into the atmosphere'.

Individuals can take part in carbon offsetting (Weforum 2019). For example, when booking a flight, you pay an additional fee which will be invested in clean energy projects or tree-planting. One flight company is discontinuing this option (see case study by Taylor 2009). Why do you think this is the case?

Table 15.5: Opportunities and risks in implementing carbon management

Risks	Issues for business (drivers)	Opportunities
Continued expenditure related to high fuel and energy costs	**Fuel and energy costs**	Cost savings Improved operational efficiencies
Being the target of a public campaign	**Reputation**	Brand enhancement
Increased challenges in recruiting and training new employees Higher employee costs related to lower productivity and efficiency	**Employees**	Attracting new employees who are looking for companies with strong sustainability programmes Motivating employees Enhancing employee wellness
Carbon taxes and other measures Requirements to meet energy efficiency standards Limits on emissions due to international standard	**Regulations**	Benefiting from government incentive programmes Early movers may be able to influence Flexibility to choose a course of action
Losing customers/consumers who switch to competitors that are more carbon-focused	**Products, services, and technologies**	Taking advantage of the growing demand for climate-friendly products and services
Exposure to high shipping costs due to higher fuel costs Costs of carbon-intensive production for suppliers being passed along to the company	**Supply chain**	Managing transportation in the supply chain reducing fuel consumption and carbon Choosing suppliers with low-carbon products and services
Shareholders demanding measures for addressing climate change Shareholders' concern about climate change and risk exposure Funders' request for carbon action plans to see the steps taken to address carbon emissions	**Investors/funders**	Meeting corporate social responsibility goals Attracting new investors who want to invest in progressive, well-managed, and innovative companies Getting more grants and/or funds from funders
Losing out to competitors who make carbon management a priority	**Awards**	Winning awards related to carbon management

Note: An assessment against the areas shown can help to explain how the risks apply specifically to the organisation concerned, and how these risks can then be turned into opportunities.

Source: Adapted from Lingl et al. (2010: 3).

Suggested sessions

Session 1: Your own carbon footprint

In this session, you will learn to apply the principles of carbon management to your own life and save costs.

This session will address the following Sustainable Development Goals (SDGs):

- Goal 3, good health and well-being

- Goal 12, responsible consumption and production (ensure sustainable consumption and production patterns)

- Goal 13, climate action (take urgent action to combat climate change and its impacts)

Activity 1: Your home's carbon footprint – food waste (30 minutes)

Thirty percent of the food produced for human consumption is wasted globally (https://wrap.org.uk/taking-action/food-drink). Some countries are even higher (e.g. in America, it could be nearer to 40% according to www.epa.gov/sustainable-management-food/united-states-2030-food-loss-and-waste-reduction-goal). Sometimes ingredients are shunned because they are imperfect; other waste occurs because people buy too much.

What percentage is wasted in your household? What happens to your leftovers? Do they end up in a landfill, producing methane (a greenhouse gas)? In the UK, approximately 40% of wasted food ends up in a landfill (www.vision2020.info/ban-food-waste/).

In this activity, we ask you to do an audit **before** the session (elements 1 and 2 in what follows), then the time in the session can be used to draw up an action plan to reduce your own food waste (activities 3–7).

Before the session:

1. Work out how much food you waste in a typical week – keep a log for a fortnight if possible. Remember to include *anything* that you throw away:
   a. From the fridge

  b. Vegetable peelings

  c. Jars going mouldy in the cupboard

  d. Plate waste

  e. Surplus cooked food

2. Once you have your baseline of the waste generated, aim to reduce it (maybe weigh it over a few weeks or aim to save a certain amount of money).

During the session:

3. Draw up a menu plan and a shopping list.

4. Plan to incorporate leftovers into subsequent meals or consider giving away spare food to others – using the Olio app or similar: https://olioex.com/.

5. Make sure you have suitable containers to store your leftover ingredients.

6. If you live with others, plan to share the cooking and pool ingredients – you should also find you are saving energy.

7. If you are going away, plan to offer spare ingredients to others in the household, or even neighbours.

Continue to monitor your food waste; hopefully, it will have reduced! Once you have looked at your own habits, you could try to involve other members of your household.

Useful resources:

www.bbcgoodfood.com/howto/guide/how-reduce-food-waste

https://fareshare.org.uk/tips-for-reducing-food-waste/

Activity 2: Your carbon footprint – electricity (30 minutes)

Energy prices are rising, and many countries are trying to find ways to decrease their dependence on fossil fuels. In Europe, some countries have set targets to reduce their consumption of gas (Jack and Zimmerman 2022, www.politico.eu/article/eu-countries-save-energy-winter/).

For this exercise, we will explore what households could do to reduce their own usage of electricity. Please use where you live for your calculations. The audit of your current electricity usage will need to be done before the session (elements

1 and 2). Elements 3–4 can be drawn together into an action plan in the session itself. Element 5 is an activity after the session to stay on target.

Before the session:

1. Start by working out your current usage of electricity. If you have a smart meter for your electricity, use that. If not, use your last couple of utility bills. This is your baseline.

2. Try to work out whether any specific activities use the most energy. If you live with others, make sure they are aware of the overall current usage.

During the session:

3. Draw up a plan of action. Aim to reduce your usage by a certain percentage or a specific number of kWh. This should also save you money!

4. For example, you could:
    a. Use your appliances more efficiently – cook together to avoid putting the oven on at different times.
    b. Use different appliances – the microwave or a slow cooker.
    c. Take advantage of a lower tariff – some energy suppliers charge less at night.
    d. Turn down the heating by 1° (and switch it off when everyone is out).
    e. Take quick showers, not long baths.
    f. Switch off all lights when leaving a room, and turn off appliances completely.

5. Check usage every two weeks (for example) to ensure you are on target.

> **Useful resources:**
>
> www.moneysupermarket.com/gas-and-electricity/energy-saving-tips/
>
> www.politico.eu/article/eu-countries-save-energy-winter/

Session 2: Perspectives on carbon management

In this session, you will discuss how business activities are connected to climate change. You will learn about carbon reporting as well as carbon management as a whole.

This session will address the following Sustainable Development Goals (SDGs):

- Goal 11, sustainable cities and communities (make cities and human settlements inclusive, safe, resilient, and sustainable).

- Goal 12, responsible consumption and production (ensure sustainable consumption and production patterns).

- Goal 13, climate action (take urgent action to combat climate change and its impacts).

Activity 1: Effects of human activity on climate change (5 minutes)

There are six GHGs whose abundance in the atmosphere has increased (IPCC 2022), listed in the following table. Draw a line to match each gas with the business activity that typically causes it. One pair is highlighted as an example.

Bonus question: Do you know which GHG is over 20 times more potent than CO_2? (Clue: it has something to do with cows.)

Activity 2: Effects of climate change on business (10 minutes)

Table 15.6: GHGs whose abundance in the atmosphere has increased

Greenhouse gas	Typical activity
Hydrofluorocarbons (HFCs)	Released by cattle farming, landfills, rice farming and the production of oil and gas
Carbon dioxide (CO_2)	Chemical by-products also used in some types of refrigeration equipment
Sulphur hexafluoride (SF_6)	Manufactured compound used in some specialised applications, like insulation for high-voltage electrical equipment
Nitrous oxide (N_2O)	Manufactured chemical compounds used for a variety of medical and other applications
Methane (CH_4)	**Emitted through burning of fossil fuels, like coal, oil, and gas, and also as a result of deforestation and other land-use changes**
Perfluorocarbons (PFCs)	Released by chemical fertilisers and burning fossil fuels

1. Climate change affects global supply chains. Can you think of ways in which the following extreme weather events could cause shortages in the UK: (a) typhoons in China and (b) drought in Germany?

2. Look at Figure 15.4 in this chapter, which gives some examples of impacts of climate change. Work with a classmate to brainstorm the consequences of climate change on business organisations, such as:

- An international clothing retailer
- A local greengrocer
- An airline
- A manufacturer of a product of your choice
- A bank

Activity 3: Perspectives on carbon reporting (25 minutes)

Businesses may be affected directly by climate change and indirectly via government regulations, such as emissions caps and environmental taxes. Government policies often focus on measuring and reducing carbon emissions. Since 1 April 2019, all quoted companies in the UK must report on their carbon emissions under the **Streamlined Energy and Carbon Reporting (SECR)** policy as part of mandatory carbon reporting.

1. Your tutor will assign you one of the following roles:
   - A 'Friends of the Earth' representative
   - A representative of Defra (the UK Department for Environment, Food, and Rural Affairs)
   - A representative of the CDP (Carbon Disclosure Project)
   - The CEO of a quoted company
   - The CSR (corporate social responsibility) manager of a quoted company
   - The manager of an independent second-hand appliance shop

Read the information that follows on mandatory carbon reporting and spend ten minutes considering the perspective of your assigned role regarding mandatory carbon reporting. Imagine you are that person and what you think about the following:
   - How do you view the relationship between carbon reporting and climate change?

- What do you think about the fact that carbon reporting is mandatory for quoted companies?
- What will you gain/lose professionally from mandatory carbon reporting?
- What, if any, are the conflicts of interest/competing pressures for you in terms of your stance on carbon reporting? (Consider any conflicts of interest within your professional practice and any conflicts between your personal/ professional stance.)

2. Compare your notes and ideas with others who have been assigned **the same role as you**. Based on the discussion, amend your notes as necessary.

3. Form mixed groups in which **all the different roles are represented**. Share your perspectives in turn within your group – speak as if you are that individual.

You can find out more about mandatory carbon reporting on the following websites:

UK Government Environmental Reporting Guidelines www.gov.uk/government/ publications/environmental-reporting-guidelines-including-mandatory-green house-gas-emissions-reporting-guidance [Accessed 6 November 2022].

SECR Explained www.carbontrust.com/news-and-events/insights/secr-explained-streamlined-energy-carbon-reporting-framework-for-uk [Accessed 6 November 2022].

Activity 4: Discussion on perspectives (10 minutes)

Discuss as a class why different groups/individuals have varying perspectives on carbon management.

Session 3: First steps to managing carbon emissions

In session 2, you explored how business activities can contribute to and be affected by climate change, and you considered different perspectives on carbon management. In session 3, you will consider three scopes of emissions to explore how companies can map their emissions in detail.

This session will address the following Sustainable Development Goals (SDGs):

- Goal 9, industry, innovation, and infrastructure (build resilient infrastructure, promote inclusive and sustainable industrialization, and foster innovation).

- Goal 11, sustainable cities and communities (make cities and human settlements inclusive, safe, resilient, and sustainable).

- Goal 12, responsible consumption and production (ensure sustainable consumption and production patterns).

Activity 1: Brief discussion (5–10 minutes)

To refresh ideas from session 2 and consider some next steps, brainstorm in small groups or as a class:

- Why do business organisations try to reduce their carbon emissions?

- What might an organisation do to reduce its emissions?

- What are the potential risks and benefits of these actions for the organisation?

Introducing the three scopes for measuring emissions

An organisation attempting to reduce its GHG emissions will need a complete picture of the emissions produced. However, it can be difficult to quantify an organisation's emissions, particularly with multipart supply chains or complex organisational structures. Furthermore, some emissions associated with an organisation may be outside its control, and so it can be helpful to categorise emissions according to the amount of control the organisation has over them. For more detail, read the part of this chapter on establishing an emissions boundary.

Activity 2: Activities within each scope (3–5 minutes)

With a partner, suggest one or two additional business activities which may fall into each of the three scopes.

Identifying the three scopes for measuring emissions

The University of British Columbia (UBC 2012) is trying to minimise its emissions. What follows is a partial inventory of emissions for UBC's Vancouver campus: the right-hand column categorises the relevant activities according to the scopes of control.

Table 15.7: Partial inventory of emissions for UBC's Vancouver campus

Component	Usage data	Emissions (tCO$_2$e)	Scope (1, 2, or 3)
Paper	98,906 PKG	572	3
Ancillary buildings: electricity[a]	50,344,856 kWh	1,251	2
Staff air travel (including research and conference travel)		19,772	3
Natural gas direct use (core buildings)	84,004 GJ	4,214	1
Core buildings: electricity	156,491,863 kWh	3,887	2
Commuting		30,757	3
Natural gas direct use (ancillary buildings)[a]	94,859 GJ	4,758	1
Biomass facility (core and ancillary buildings)[a]	75,502 GJ	261	1
Building life cycle		11,705	3
Solid waste		TBD	3
Total campus emissions offset[b]			

[a] Ancillary buildings include student housing, conference rooms, and athletics facilities.
[b] This table shows some of the campus emissions that were offset in 2012. For a full list, see UBC 2012.

Activity 3: categorising activities according to the three scopes (15–20 minutes)

Read through the following Yum Scrum restaurant case study, and with a partner, identify which of its activities could be categorised under each of the three scopes.

Scope 1 (full control)	Scope 2 (indirect/less control)	Scope 3 (minimal control)

Case study: Yum Scrum restaurant (Compiled by Dharmasasmita 2014)

Yum Scrum is a restaurant in the UK that offers an 'all-you-can-eat' buffet. It is open seven days a week, from midday to 1:00 a.m., including public holidays. For lunch, served from 12:00 p.m. to 5:00 p.m., the restaurant charges £10.99, while dinner, from 5:00 p.m. to 1:00 a.m., costs £17.99, excluding drinks. The company owns the restaurant building. The chef produces food of good quality, and the restaurant is popular. Food is prepared in a kitchen and transported to the respective hot and cold buffet units, where diners serve themselves. Customers can also buy food to take away.

During its opening hours, the restaurant keeps the lights on, including those in the lavatories. The same applies to the heating in the washrooms and dining area during the winter season. Consequently, the heat from the dining area sometimes affects food quality. At off-peak times, the food on the cold buffet unit needs to be changed more frequently to avoid complaints (and possible lawsuits) from customers, resulting in increased production costs and food waste. The management and some members of staff have noticed that the buffet units which keep the food warm have to remain switched on throughout the restaurant opening hours. Some staff take the initiative to turn the heat down or off during off-peak times, but not everyone does. The cost of keeping the buffet warm all day affects the restaurant's profit. In the beverage section, some members of staff make the extra effort to ensure that the refrigeration units are closed. There have been times, however, when the refrigeration units are left ajar, especially during busy periods.

Where its supply chain is concerned, Yum Scrum gets its ingredients from the cheapest sources. Hence, its suppliers can be from anywhere in the UK and beyond. Since negotiations sometimes need to take place face-to-face, management often travel to these areas to get the best deals. Topics such as sustainable fishing and farming are increasingly highlighted in the media, and the public is becoming aware of these issues.

Yum Scrum has hired a cleaning company to clean after the restaurant has closed. However, in order to cut costs, the cleaning company only cleans the dining and buffet area twice a week. So far, there have been no complaints from customers about hygiene. They are also considering how they can increase their profit margins. New legislation on emissions has meant that Yum Scrum restaurant will need to look into its practice and processes to avoid paying a fine.

The staff and management are aware of rising energy costs, and management discuss it verbally with staff on a regular basis. All staff are aware of what to do to save energy, but no one is in charge. Energy consumption is checked against gas and electricity bills on a quarterly basis to ensure the company is not being overcharged. Although monies are available for investment, only essential upgrades and maintenance are actually implemented, such as replacement of light fittings when they fail.

Compare your answers with another pair's. Where you have different answers, discuss and try to justify your point of view. Adjust your answers if the other pair's reasoning is more convincing.

Activity 4: Applying your analysis (15–20 minutes)

Based on your analysis of the Yum Scrum case study so far, work in small groups to discuss the following questions:

1. Which of Yum Scrum's activities would be easiest to change in order to reduce emissions, and which would be most difficult?

2. Change in which areas(s) would have the greatest effect on total emissions?

3. What particular strategies would you use to bring about change in your chosen area(s)?

4. Change in which area(s) would have the greatest effect on other areas of business, for example, staff morale, public image, customer satisfaction?

5. What disadvantages might be created in other areas of scope by reducing the emissions in certain areas?

Use your notes from the discussion to make some recommendations and present them to the class.

Additional teaching material and ideas

Work-based learning: students solving sustainability challenges through strategic business partnerships

Molthan-Hill, P., Robinson, Z. P., Hope, A., Dharmasasmita, A., and Mcmanus, E. (2020), 'Reducing Carbon Emissions in Business Through Responsible Management Education: Influence at the Micro-, Meso- and Macro-Levels', *International Journal of Management Education* 18.1: 100328. ISSN 1472–8117.

Molthan-Hill, P., and Robinson, Z. (2021), 'Assessing Competencies for Future-Fit Graduates and Responsible Leaders', in *Assessment and Feedback in a Post-Pandemic Era: A Time for Learning and Inclusion* [P. Baughan (ed.)] (York: Advance HE), pp. 196–213. ISBN 9781916359352.

The importance of partnerships between business schools, local companies, and other organisations has grown in recent years and is the basis of principle 5 of PRME. These articles summarise a replicable model that other business schools and universities could integrate into their curriculum. The focus of the described greenhouse gas management project is on Sustainable Development Goal 13 (climate action), but the partnership model could also be used to address other Sustainable Development Goals. Students directly apply the concepts they encounter in a real-life business. The deployment of such work-based learning in the core curriculum at Nottingham Business School is described, showing how this aids the development of employability skills of the students. Furthermore, the partnership, which won the Guardian University Award in Business Partnership 2015, is described, and recommendations are included on how to set up something similar.

Sustainable Development Goals

Sustainable Development Goal (SDG) 13 calls for countries to:

> Take urgent action to combat climate change and its impacts.

This includes adhering to the UNFCCC through the Glasgow Climate Pact, which calls for carbon net zero by 2050 (UNFCC 2021). Linked to this is Goal 7, which is to:

> Ensure access to affordable, reliable, sustainable, and modern energy for all.

Goal 7 has specific targets relating to improving energy efficiency and promoting clean energy research and technology.

Read goals 7 and 13 again and have a look at the Glasgow Climate Pact (https://ukcop26.org/the-glasgow-climate-pact/), then undertake the discussion that follows.

Discussion:

1. Why is combatting climate change important for the following?
   a. Successful business and trading
   b. Sustainable development (and vice versa)

2. How might goal 7 relate to goal 13 – that is, how does ensuring access to affordable, reliable, sustainable, and modern energy for all relate to taking urgent action to combat climate change and its impacts?

3. What are the opportunities for business organisations with regard to supporting SDG goal 7 and its targets?

Risks, adaptation issues, and prospects

- Read through the projected impacts and risks for the various continents and regions as identified in IPCC 2022: 8–19.

- Choose an area of business you are interested in, and consider the relationships between your business and climate change in terms of risks, adaptation issues, and prospects.

- Discuss your thoughts with another student, preferably a student whose work or supply chain is based in another region or continent.

In addition to the IPCC document, you may wish to refer to the risks and opportunities listed in Table 15.5 earlier in the chapter.

Climate change and the case of the strawberry yogurt

The IPCC has stated that '[c]limate change will increasingly put pressure on food production and access, undermining food security and nutrition (high confidence)' (IPCC 2022: 14). Imagine you are a producer of strawberry yogurt. Consider the relationships between your business and climate change at each stage of the food life cycle, namely, production, processing, distribution, retailing, consumption, and waste. Consider:

- The likely sources of your three main ingredients: strawberries, sugar, and milk.
- The relationships between the different stages of the food life cycle.
- How your business is affecting climate change and how climate change is affecting your business.

Dimensions of action on climate change

Jonathan Rowson (2014) identifies seven dimensions for action on climate change: science, law, money, technology, democracy, culture, behaviour. Discuss in small groups how each dimension is relevant to how businesses can help combat climate change. Then, rank the dimensions according to which you think is most import-ant. Compare your answers with those of another group, and discuss your rationales.

Strong statements

Consider each of the following statements in turn and decide how strongly you agree/disagree with each one:

- Business is responsible for the world's environmental problems.
- Trying to regulate climate change is like rearranging deckchairs on the *Titanic*.
- Carbon offsetting is an effective way of halting climate change.
- Carbon management is anti-capitalist.
- We can eat money.
- Mandatory carbon reporting is harmful to business.

Draw an imaginary line on the floor where one end of the line represents 'strongly agree' and the other end 'strongly disagree'. Stand at the point on the line where your agreement lies. Compare your position with those on each side of you, and try to convince them of your point of view. Move to a different point on the line if you change your mind based on discussion. If you don't have space in the classroom to make a line, do a show of hands or use online voting or a clicker system. At the end of the activity, reflect on which opinions you kept and which you changed, and why.

Emissions report

Choose an area of business where you have worked or would like to work, and list the main activities of that business. Skim the US Environmental Protection Agency's information on greenhouse emissions (www.epa.gov/ghgemissions/over view-greenhouse-gases), and list the likely main greenhouse gas emissions of that business area, based on your list of activities. Create a single PowerPoint slide to summarise your ideas.

Carbon neutrality

Nottingham Trent University in the UK has set itself the goal of being carbon net zero across all three scopes by 2040 (www.ntu.ac.uk/about-us/strategy/sustainability). Discuss in small groups the advantages and disadvantages of this, and report back to the group. You may wish to refer back to the risks and opportunities listed in Table 15.5 and also the projected impacts and risks identified by the IPCC (2022).

Carbon literacy

For a more thorough general understanding of climate change, a new carbon literacy course has been released on Future Learn (www.futurelearn.com/courses/climate-literacy-and-action-for-all).

Further readings

Berners-Lee, M. (2020), *How Bad Are Bananas: The Carbon Footprint of Everything* (London: Profile Books).
Provides information about the carbon footprints of a huge variety of products and activities while challenging beliefs and ideas about sustainability and sustainable living.
Carbon Trust (2022), *A Guide to Carbon Footprinting for Businesses*. www.carbontrust.com/resources/a-guide-carbon-footprinting-for-businesses [Accessed 23 November 2022].
This publication describes how businesses can calculate a carbon footprint at an organisational or product level.
Greenhouse Gas Protocol (2016), *The Greenhouse Gas Protocol: A Corporate Accounting and Reporting Standard*, rev. ed. www.ghgprotocol.org/standards/corporate-standard [Accessed 6 November 2022].
An accounting tool to manage GHG emissions. A partnership between the World Resources Institute and the World Business Council for Sustainable Development.

Jaber, D. (2021), *Climate Positive Business: How You and Your Company Hit Bold Climate Goals and Go Net Zero*, 1st ed. (London: Routledge). https://doi.org/10.4324/9781003191544

> This book provides you with the tips, tools, and techniques to tackle your company's carbon footprint. The book will equip you to think critically about GHG reduction, carbon offsets, and carbon removal.

Lingl, P., D. Carlson, and the David Suzuki Foundation (2010), *Doing Business in a New Climate: A Guide to Measuring, Reducing, and Offsetting Greenhouse Gas Emissions* (London: Earthscan).

> This book offers advice on how business organisations can reduce their impact on climate change and save money at the same time. It includes case studies of over 50 leading businesses and provides additional resources for businesses and other organisations looking to reduce their GHG emissions.

Molthan-Hill, P., F. Winfield, R. Howarth, and M. Mazhar (2023), *The Handbook of Carbon Management: A Step-by-Step Guide to High-Impact Climate Solutions for Every Manager in Every Function* (Abingdon: Routledge).

> Every manager and every employee in every function. This book was written by experts in the field of sustainability in business to show you how to embed climate solutions and reduce greenhouse gas emissions.
>
> Everyone needs to know the best climate solutions for their organisation. This book provides you with implementation plans and inspiring case studies, with practical and helpful tools that will help you scale up climate solutions. If you are an owner of a company or an executive in any organisation, you will benefit from this step-by-step guide on how to set up your own greenhouse gas management plan and how to reduce the greenhouse gas emissions of your whole organisation. We explain key terms, such as *net zero, carbon-neutral, carbon emissions equivalents*, and the *three scopes*. We look at the bigger picture in this book and also how you could effect change.

This is the first book to offer an easy-to-implement approach to decarbonise organisations and transform societies and is appropriate for managers at any level. This book can also be used in business schools to inspire future managers and business leaders. Last, but not the least, everyone can find ideas here that they can implement in their personal lives.

References

EAUC (2016) *University on Its Way to Carbon Neutral Status*. www.eauc.org.uk/university_on_its_way_to_carbon_neutral_status [Accessed 6 November 2022].

Fox, N. (2012) 'Sainsbury's: Working Smarter, not Harder', *The Guardian*. www.theguardian.com/sustainable-business/best-practice-exchange/sainsburys-working-smarter-not-harder [Accessed 6 November 2022].

IPCC (Intergovernmental Panel on Climate Change) (2022) 'Climate Change 2022: Impacts, Adaptation, and Vulnerability', in *Contribution of Working Group II to the Sixth Assessment Report of the Intergovernmental Panel on Climate Change* [H.-O. Pörtner, D.C. Roberts, M. Tignor, E.S. Poloczanska, K. Mintenbeck, A. Alegría, M. Craig, S. Langsdorf, S. Löschke, V. Möller, A. Okem and B. Rama (eds.)] (Cambridge, UK and New York, NY: Cambridge University Press), p. 3056. https://doi.org/10.1017/9781009325844. www.ipcc.ch/report/ar6/wg2/ [Accessed 6 November 2022].

Jack, V. and A. Zimmermann (2022) 'Here's What EU Countries Are Doing to Save Energy Ahead of Winter', *Politico*, 4 August. www.politico.eu/article/eu-countries-save-energy-winter

Lingl, P., D. Carlson and the David Suzuki Foundation (2010) *Doing Business in a New Climate: A Guide to Measuring, Reducing, and Offsetting Greenhouse Gas Emissions* (London: Earthscan).

Nuccitelli, D. (2020) 'Earth Is Heating at a Rate Equivalent to Five Atomic Bombs Per Second. Or Two Hurricane Sandys', *Bulletin of the Atomic Scientists*, 3 February.

Ranganathan, N.R. et al. (2004) *Greenhouse Gas Protocol: A Corporate Accounting and Reporting Standard*, rev. ed. WBCSD/WRI, 2004. SBN 1-56973-568-9. https://ghgprotocol.org/corporate-standard

Rowson, J. (2014) 'The Seven Dimensions for Action on Climate Change', *The Guardian*, 14 February. www.theguardian.com/sustainable-business/behavioural-insights/2014/feb/14/seven-dimensions-action-climate-change [Accessed 7 November 2022].

Taylor, J. (2009) *Ethical Travel Company Drops Carbon Offsetting*. www.independent.co.uk/environment/green-living/ethical-travel-company-drops-carbon-offsetting-1816554.html [Accessed 3 November 2022].

UBC (2012) *The University of British Columbia: GHG Inventory*. http://sustain.ubc.ca/campus-initiatives/climate-energy/ghg-inventory [Accessed 3 November 2022].

UK Government (2022) *UK Government Conversion Factors for Company Reporting of Greenhouse Gas Emissions*, www.gov.uk/government/collections/government-conversion-factors-for-company-reporting [Accessed 6 November 2022].

UNFCCC (2014) *Greenhouse Gas Inventory Data*. http://unfccc.int/ghg_data/items/3800.php [Accessed 6 November 2022].

UNFCCC (2021) *Glasgow Climate Pact*. https://ukcop26.org/the-glasgow-climate-pact/ [Accessed 6 November 2022].

Weforum (2019) *What Is Carbon Offsetting?* www.weforum.org/agenda/2019/06/what-is-carbon-offsetting/ [Accessed 30 September 2022].

16

Stakeholder engagement and corporate peacemaking

Natalie Ralph and Ellie Kennedy

Stakeholder engagement is essential for sustainable business. In all markets, most companies benefit from peace and stability, while violent conflict is detrimental to sustainability. This chapter proposes how stakeholder engagement can support peacemaking in conflict-prone markets through CPM (corporate peacemaking), particularly relevant in the context of global crises, such as climate change fuelling societal stress. CPM helps bring disputing parties together for peace talks to halt/prevent violent conflict. CPM can demonstrate corporate responsibility, build peace and good relations with and *between* stakeholders, and protect the company and its reputation. This chapter outlines concepts in stakeholder theory/engagement and then illustrates how companies can conduct CPM by applying a framework of 14 interventions. A CPM case study in Colombia is presented, then session plans (with more case studies and scenarios), additional activities, and further readings. Students learn to discuss concepts in stakeholder theory and CPM, understand various approaches to peace, identify stakeholders/conflict actors to engage, and apply the CPM framework to

DOI: 10.4324/9781003294665-20

case studies and scenarios. This chapter particularly contributes to Sustainable Development Goal (SDG) 16 while indicating links to climate change (SDG 13).

Introduction

Stakeholder engagement is essential for responsible business in today's highly networked world. In conflict-prone markets, this chapter proposes, stakeholder engagement encompasses an added, critical role for managers: supporting peace. Most companies benefit from peace, while violent conflict erodes the sustainability of most economic activity, both directly and through destabilising the natural environment and social cohesion. Climate change, pandemics, energy (in)security (a prominent issue highlighted by the Russia–Ukraine war), and other global crises demand constructive business responses. Climate change is a potential threat-multiplier, escalating instability where socio-political inequality and poor governance and economic development exist. It may augment competition over land, food, water, and fuel (IEP 2022a). Climate and environmental sustainability initiatives, however, can enhance peacebuilding simultaneously through collaborative 'environmental peacebuilding' (Ide 2022). Covid-19 has demonstrated that societal stress can culminate in social dislocation and could catalyse violence in any country, including those deemed peaceful. Business leader and IT entrepreneur Steve Killelea states:

> Without peace, it will not be possible to achieve the levels of trust, cooperation or inclusiveness necessary to solve . . . [global] challenges, let alone empower the international institutions and organisations necessary to address them. Therefore, peace is the prerequisite for the survival of humanity as we know it in the 21st century.
>
> (Killelea 2022)

Killelea, an example of a business leader supporting peace, established the Institute for Economics and Peace (IEP) in 2007. The Institute addresses the economic cost of violence and offers a 'Pillars of Peace' framework for business and other institutions to support positive peace – the societal attitudes, structures, and institutions reinforcing peaceful society (IEP 2022b). This contrasts with negative peace – defined as the absence of war and violent conflict but where structural violence (see next) remains, such as gender inequality or racism.

In 2013, the United Nations (UN) Global Compact, the agency which engages business in the UN's international work, established the 'Business for Peace' (B4P) platform. Businesses from around the world and 18 of the Global Compact's local networks joined the platform from such countries as Iraq, Sudan, and Turkey, seeking to support peace in conflict-prone markets (see Colombia case later; Business for Peace 2022).

Later in 2018, the Global Compact launched an 'action platform' to help companies contribute to Sustainable Development Goal 16 (SDG 16), aimed at building peace, justice, and strong institutions. The platform illustrates how companies can support SDG 16's targets and report on their activity (PeaceNexus 2020). For example, target 16.1 states, 'Significantly reduce all forms of violence and related death rates everywhere.' Examples of business activities outlined include ensuring corporate culture and policies underpin risk management and conflict-sensitive business practices, enabling spaces for cooperation between cultural and religious groups, and creating job opportunities for youth vulnerable to recruitment in violence (UN Global Compact 2022). In 2022, the Global Compact prioritised forming two task forces to increase business engagement and national-level policy dialogues on SDG 16 business action.

Sustainable Development Goal 16

Global sustainability is focused around the 17 Sustainable Development Goals (SDGs) launched in 2015 as a continuation of the Millennium Development Goals (2000–2015). Momentously, SDG 16 calls governments, *business*, and civil society to:

Promote peaceful and inclusive societies for sustainable development, provide access to justice for all, and build effective, accountable, and inclusive institutions at all levels.

Guidance for business on SDG 16 includes outlining steps firms can take to identify *specific* actions that address conflict drivers and build peace, while measuring, evaluating, and communicating these actions. Business approaches can involve promoting economic development, social cohesion, and dialogue; supporting peace processes; and building skills and partnerships (Business for Peace and CDA 2015).

In 2007, Sir Richard Branson, Head of the Virgin Group of companies, musician Peter Gabriel, and former South African President Nelson Mandela created the Elders (2022). The Elders brings together diplomatic leaders, such as the former president of Liberia Ellen Johnson Sirleaf, to help catalyse peace processes in conflict-affected countries. This demonstrates a business leader advocating infrastructure for peacemaking (although Branson more recently received criticism for his resource-intensive spaceflights programme).

These examples demonstrate stakeholder engagement supporting peace, including on occasion, peacemaking. This latter may be termed CPM (corporate peacemaking). Intra-state conflict arises within or between communities, or between armed groups and/or the government. CPM is proposed as a strategy for helping to build peace and good relations with and *between* stakeholders, demonstrating responsibility, and protecting the company and its reputation. CPM (either directly or indirectly) aims to bring disputing parties in intra-state conflict together in peace talks to prevent or halt violent conflict.

It is important to distinguish CPM from CPB (corporate peacebuilding) and structural peacebuilding. *CPB* is the umbrella term for both structural peacebuilding and peacemaking. Structural peacebuilding addresses the underlying structural issues which cause grievance and conflict. These arise when society's socially constructed institutions, such as government, police, and universities, provide some people with material resources, representation, and a voice in matters affecting their well-being and status while depriving others (Christie and Wessells 2008: 1957).

Structural peacebuilding by companies includes support for equitable economic and business development (e.g. jobs for youth and ex-combatants), democracy and good governance (e.g. capacity-building for transparent local government), promoting decolonisation and human rights (such as those of indigenous groups or employees), disarmament and demobilisation programs, and environmental sustainability.

In contrast, direct physical violence requires *peacemaking* between conflict parties. Peacemaking concentrates on the political/diplomatic, relational, and reconciliation aspects of peace work. It builds peaceful relations between conflict parties and communities, progresses peace processes, and helps parties reach a peace agreement. Peacemaking is more critical at certain times, such as an immediate response for preventing fighting between belligerents. This chapter primarily discusses CPM for promoting peace.

The PRME Business for Peace working group

The 'PRME Business for Peace working group' builds understanding of specific business contributions to peace (taking a broad, multidimensional approach to peace, such as poverty reduction). Members aim to create applied research and tools, including case studies and curriculum for management education. Members access webinars, resources, and networking (PRME 2022a, 2022c). Similarly, the 'PRME working group on business and human rights' provides resources (PRME 2022b).

Research on business and peace is a maturing field, with two decades of focused study. However, as Miklian (2017) states, there remains a need for clearer definitions of ethical, proactive business action in conflict contexts and how to address unintended negative consequences of business activity.

This chapter provides concepts in stakeholder theory and engagement as applied particularly in conflict-prone areas. You will encounter examples of stakeholder engagement for corporate peacemaking, activities, and prompts to help you consider how you might apply such strategies to promote peace, including when facing challenges arising from climate change. This chapter does not give hard and fast rules or answers: you must draw your own conclusions, carefully considering whether and how you, as a corporate manager, might apply CPM in different conflict situations.

Stakeholder engagement

In R. Edward Freeman's (2010: 52–3) book *Strategic Management: A Stakeholder Approach*, originally published in 1984, this pre-eminent advocate of stakeholder theory defines *stakeholders* as groups or individuals who affect, or are affected by, the attainment of an organisation's goals. Stakeholders can include the full range of individuals/groups that companies may engage with, including shareholders, employees, customers, social justice and environmental non-governmental organisations (NGOs), suppliers, communities, the natural environment, governments, and armed groups or terrorist groups when they substantially affect operations.

In the traditional managerial (or shareholder) model of the firm, owners (shareholders) are the primary group, and management is responsible for prioritising maximised value for the owners. This is exemplified by Milton Friedman's (1962) famous declaration that the business of business is 'mak[ing] as much money for their shareholders as possible'. Contrary to this, the stakeholder model proposes that all those affected by the firm's pursuit of its goals must have their legitimate interest in the company acknowledged, and the firm must maximise value for these 'stakeholders'. Stakeholder theory can be viewed as a normative theory advocating, to varying degrees, firms are *morally obligated* (Crane *et al.* 2013: 133–9) to consider stakeholder interests – with growing urgency in an era of climate emergency, intergenerational responsibility, and the SDGs (Idowu 2021; Maak *et al.* 2022). Stakeholder theory has gained traction since the 1980s among those who question the sustainability of prioritising shareholders' wealth over other interests related to business. A limited application of the theory involves considering other interests, but not necessarily engaging these interests to influence company decision-making.

On the other hand, stakeholder theory can be applied as an analytical and proactive tool to identify and engage stakeholders (Crane *et al.* 2013). A company should identify its stakeholders and, wherever possible, engage them to identify their interests and influence, have processes in place to engage stakeholder concerns, and aim to benefit both the company and stakeholders. Companies benefit from preserving their license to operate, gaining knowledge on issues from external actors and improving long-term, innovative decision-making. Stakeholders benefit from companies *cooperatively* engaging with their needs and interests and, ideally, taking these into account (Maak *et al.* 2022; Idowu 2021).

Standards like ISO 26000 and AA 1000 help companies develop strategies for stakeholder engagement and sustainability. Firms report publicly through processes provided, for example, by the Global Reporting Initiative. Companies potentially use digital tools to predict and measure engagement performance and engage stakeholders via social media, sustainability or corporate social responsibility (CSR) annual reports, partnerships, and community meetings.

Ignoring stakeholders' interests can damage a firm's reputation, share price and sales, while risking costly legal battles. Examples include the landmark Dutch court ruling forcing Royal Dutch Shell to reduce its emissions by 2030 (Harrabin

2021), and reputation-damaging campaigns by NGOs such as Global Witness's work to draw attention to 'conflict diamonds/minerals' (www.globalwitness.org).

It can, however, be difficult to assess which stakeholders to prioritise and to balance competing stakeholders' claims. Mitchell *et al.*'s (1997) seminal model assesses stakeholder 'salience' based on a stakeholder's power, legitimacy, and urgency. *Power* is the ability to influence the company, *legitimacy* derives from having a legal claim or moral argument against the company, and *urgency* concerns how time-sensitive or critical a claim is. This model assists managers to prioritise stakeholders' claims, taking into account the changing environment.

Stakeholder engagement in conflict-prone markets

In conflict-prone markets, corporate actors can benefit from engaging stakeholders to promote peace and ensure companies do not cause or exacerbate conflict (Ganson 2022). Many companies have been accused of ignoring, manipulating, or being complicit in the abuse of stakeholders, such as local communities and political groups. Companies have either deliberately or unwittingly increased tensions over revenues, jobs, or the destruction of local environments and livelihoods, allowed security personnel to respond violently to protesters, or provided revenue to undemocratic host governments who have used the money to buy weaponry to suppress civilians (OHCHR 2022).

However, civil society is increasingly powerful in demanding that companies address their negative impacts on communities by adopting conflict-sensitive business practices and respect for human rights (Hlatky *et al.* 2021; OHCHR 2022). Conflict-sensitive practices consider the conflict context, its actors and dynamics, and the interaction between any business intervention and its context. This helps avoid negative impacts and maximise positive effects (CDA 2022). Amid violent conflict, human rights cannot be enjoyed. Supporting peace processes to reduce violence may be the most immediate way to halt human rights abuses.

Most companies benefit from peace, transparent and accountable government, a strong civil society, and an independent judiciary system to maintain rule of law. They gain from infrastructure supporting healthcare, education, and transport. In contrast, conflict impedes business operations by such practices as employee kidnapping, destruction of company installations, reduced production, or closure of operations. Consequences can include raised international insurance premiums, diminished profits, and low employee morale.

Noting this, it is likely that promoting peace can benefit both large and small companies. Rather than addressing domestic businesses, this chapter primarily focuses on CPM by TNCs (transnational corporations), business organisations (with TNCs as members), or business leaders representing TNCs. When considering TNCs, characteristics such as company ownership structure, sector, and size will influence how a company supports peacemaking.

The following presents a framework for peacemaking by corporate actors, outlining 14 interventions they might potentially apply in intra-state conflict.

The 14-intervention corporate peacemaking framework

The 14-intervention CPM framework is the culmination of research on case studies of CPM and a cross-fertilisation of concepts from business and peace theory, peace and conflict studies, conflict resolution, diplomacy, and peace psychology (Ralph 2015).

The framework is an exploration of potential interventions only. Some interventions have been implemented by corporate actors, while others are hypothetical. Some interventions may only be effective in certain situations. Other interventions might only receive support from TNCs while actually being led by more traditional peace actors, such as professional mediators, the UN, or conflict-resolution organisations. The framework is illustrated in Figure 16.1 in the form of a jigsaw puzzle, showing that this conceptual framework remains unfinished, possibly awaiting other interventions and pieces of the puzzle.

From collective action to shuttle diplomacy (interventions 1–7)

Through **intervention 1**, collective action between TNCs and/or with domestic businesses and civil society organisations, CPM gains credibility and influence. For example, the Northern Ireland branch of the CBI (Confederation of British Industry), a non-party-political organisation promoting business interests, supported the (successful) peace processes in the 1990s to end the violence in Northern Ireland.

Figure 16.1: The 14-intervention corporate peacemaking framework.

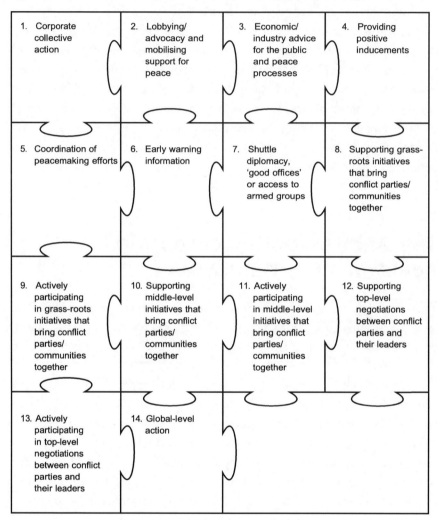

To gain influence, the CBI partnered with other trade and industry organisations, such as the Institute of Directors and the Hotel Federation (Banfield *et al.* 2006).

Applying **intervention 2**, corporate actors focus on lobbying and advocacy with the conflict parties, public, or other businesses to mobilise them to work towards peace. The Northern Ireland CBI's advocacy, for example, included writing *Peace: A Challenging New Era*, referred to as 'the peace dividend paper', which outlined an economic rationale for peace. Politicians and the media adopted the concept of a 'peace dividend', which then infused new momentum into the peace processes (Tripathi and Gündüz 2008; Nelson 2000).

Intervention 3 includes providing economic or industry advice that supports peace, either in the public realm (per the CBI example earlier) or in peace negotiations, such as providing information for negotiations on the revenues gained from particular natural resources under dispute in a conflict (Shankleman 2007).

By applying **intervention 4**, corporate actors provide 'positive inducements' to enable or encourage the conflict parties to come to the negotiating table. This may include funding, transportation, equipment, accommodation, increased investment, aid, or economic development projects. This intervention is controversial; transparency and compliance with laws such as the UK Bribery Act 2010 will be crucial (Haufler 2001).

Intervention 5 includes corporate support or leadership for the (often lacking) coordination of activities by multiple peace actors in a country. The Colombian business organisation FIP (Ideas for Peace Foundation), for example, produced databases on Colombian peace negotiations to record and understand the roles of various peace actors, potentially facilitating coordination (Sweetman 2009; see Ralph and Kennedy 2014 for additional reference – the original URL/reference is no longer available).

Applying **intervention 6**, companies provide information for the early warning of conflict. An organisation could be funded or established to collate data from businesses located in conflict-prone areas to inform wider early warning systems (Sweetman 2009; Nelson 2000).

With **intervention 7**, corporate actors conduct shuttle diplomacy, provide 'good offices', and/or provide access to armed groups to build trust between parties (Tripathi and Gündüz 2008; Nelson 2000). In Aceh, Indonesia, Juha Christensen, who headed up a Swedish pharmaceutical/healthcare technology company with interests in Indonesia, used his contacts with key people to undertake shuttle diplomacy, relaying information between the Free Aceh movement and the Indonesian government. This partly assisted a peace agreement in 2005 that ended the civil war (Braithwaite *et al.* 2010; Iff *et al.* 2010).

Grassroots to global interventions (interventions 8–14)

TNCs have international reach, and their influence ranges from the global level to the national and local levels in a country. When discussing CPM activities that can be conducted at different levels of a society, the adaption of John Paul

Lederach's (1997; see also Killick 2000) conceptual societal structure for building peace is beneficial.

Lederach describes society as a pyramid, which includes the national, top-level peace process and its (relatively few) political leaders, mostly applying direct negotiations between leaders of warring parties. These negotiations aim for a ceasefire and peace agreement. The pyramid's base represents grassroots communities and leaders and their often-numerous yet less-visible peace initiatives. In the middle level are actors, such as business leaders, academics, and religious, ethnic, and humanitarian leaders. Middle-level actors are well-placed to link grassroots with top-level processes and often have relationships with counterparts across the conflict divide (Lederach 1997). To represent all possible CPM activities, the apex here reflects global-level action.

Within a country, a TNC's executives may be middle-level leaders, but they can act at the top and middle levels of a society and *support* grassroots activity. At the local level, company workers/managers might engage in grassroots activity in their local communities (see Figure 16.2).

Usually implemented by community leaders, grassroots approaches (**interventions 8 and 9**) use networks such as church associations. They build pressure from 'the people' to encourage peace processes. For example, a travelling 'Circus of Peace' in Mozambique used drama to explore the challenges of war, possible reconciliation, and conflict resolution skills (Lederach 1997: 52–5). Company workers could initiate or support such activities with the additional support (including funding) of the company or a collective of companies.

Conflict resolution activities at the middle level of society (**interventions 10 and 11**), such as behind-the-scenes conflict resolution workshops, can build relationships across society and prepare the ground for agreements between top-level leaders. In conflict resolution workshops, middle-level leaders are invited because of their knowledge of the conflict and proximity and influence with top-level decision-makers. Workshops do not replace formal, top-level negotiations but broaden participation in the peace process and encourage participants to analyse problems and seek creative solutions (Ralph and Conley-Tyler 2006; Lederach 1997). In the 1990s, to support peace negotiations in South Africa to end apartheid, the Consultative Business Movement, with international and domestic companies as members, organised forums on peace, development, and the economy. These brought together societal leaders from across the conflict divide, often deeply suspicious of one another, and helped them develop solutions and build trust (Hutchings 2017; Ganson 2017; Fourie and Eloff 2006;

Figure 16.2: Conceptual structure for corporate peacemaking.

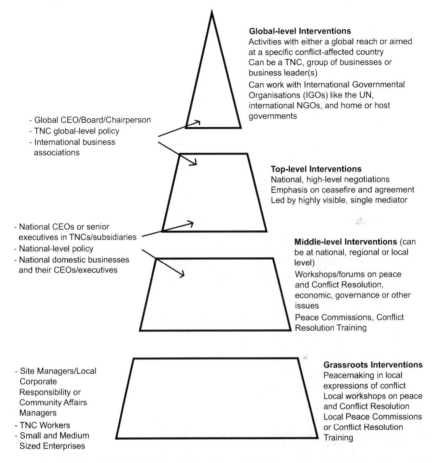

Source: Adapted from Killick's (2000) use of Lederach's (1997) conceptual pyramid of the societal structure for peacebuilding to demonstrate roles for business leaders.

see Ralph and Kennedy 2014 for references – the original URL/reference is no longer available).

In national-level negotiations between conflict parties' top-level leaders (**interventions 12 and 13**), corporate actors either support or actively participate by providing advice and mediation (see the Colombian and South African case studies that follow). Further research into these potential interventions is needed to identify best practices and ways to curb corporate interests negatively influencing peace negotiations (Ralph 2015). Corporate actors could underline that they want a business-friendly environment but, beyond this, are neutral and genuinely support democratic, inclusive peace processes (Fourie and Eloff 2006; see Ralph and Kennedy 2014 for references – the original URL/reference is no longer available). This unfortunately is not always the case; they are *not* always neutral. Further, to counter self-interest and increase credibility, corporate actors can work as a collective with domestic businesses and simply support the preparation of these negotiations (intervention 12). This could include assisting logistics, administration, funding, or capacity-building in peace-process design and mediation for the conflict parties (FIP 2022; Ganson 2017; Nelson 2000).

When taking action at the global level (**intervention 14**), corporate actors may promote peace generally, or within a particular country. Support could be given to international business associations, the UN, governments, NGOs, and others to promote peace.

This chapter does not recommend that any company undertake these activities without very careful consideration of their impacts on a conflict, a country, its communities, and the company/employees themselves. Any activity by a corporate actor should be well considered, alongside experienced peace actors, and relevant partners, and within international/national legal and ethical standards.

This 14-intervention CPM framework is useful for examining existing corporate responses to intra-state conflict as well as considering potential future interventions by corporate actors. The following empirical case study applies the framework to examine CPM interventions in a particular period of a long-standing conflict in Colombia.

Case study: Colombia

Colombia suffered widespread violence for half a century prior to a peace agreement in 2016 between the Colombian government and FARC (Revolutionary Armed Forces of Colombia). Initially, this agreement reduced violence. By 2022, some former and newly established armed groups and other actors were inflicting violence against Colombians, yet many Colombians continue peace efforts (Human Rights Watch 2022).

This case study addresses the period during President Pastrana's administration between 1998 and 2002 (and relevant activity leading up to the 2016 peace agreement), when there began unprecedented participation in peace processes by international and Colombian business, including through the peace-focused business organisation FIP (Ideas for Peace Foundation) (FIP 2022; personal conversation with A. Guáqueta, former Academic Director, FIP, 19 July 2008; Rettberg 2007, n.d.). The main conflict parties were the Colombian government, paramilitary groups, and the dominant Marxist guerrillas FARC and ELN (National Liberation Army). Colombian citizens, both rich and poor, were victims of this violence.

Illustration of CPM interventions

Interventions 1 and 2: Corporate collective action; peace advocacy

President Pastrana established a negotiating team to develop contacts with FARC. Four high-ranking Colombian business executives, in turn, held positions on the team. TNCs were linked to this business involvement via FIP, which was established in 1999 to provide advice on organising negotiations to the government team. TNCs comprised a number of FIP's founders, executive committee, and membership. Founders included, for example, the US oil company Occidental Petroleum Corporation and the mining company Cerrejón, while representatives on the executive committee included the brewer SABMiller. FIP's founders aimed to encourage broader business backing for peace negotiations, a commitment that continued to be a priority over the years (conversation with Guáqueta; Rettberg n.d.; Guáqueta 2006).

FIP also partnered with the UN Global Compact and UK-based IBLF (International Business Leaders Forum, now the IBLF Global, www.iblfglobal. org/) to organise events that brought TNCs invested in Colombia together with civil society and government. The events supported peace by finding ways to address social and economic issues within a conflict context (Ralph 2015; UN Global Compact 2013; see Ralph and Kennedy 2014 for additional reference – the original URL/reference is no longer available).

Intervention 5: Coordination of peacemaking efforts

As stated previously, FIP recorded the roles of the many peace actors involved over the years, potentially facilitating coordination (see Ralph

2015; Ralph and Kennedy 2014 – the original URL/reference is no longer available).

Intervention 12: Supporting top-level negotiations

FIP and its researchers provided technical and process advice to Pastrana's negotiating team for negotiations with FARC (conversation with Guáqueta). Through their leadership and membership in FIP, TNCs and domestic firms were able to support this intervention.

Nonetheless, by 2002, the peace talks had broken down for a number of reasons. For example, despite participating in the negotiations, FARC issued 'Law 002', demanding a 'peace tax' from wealthy Colombians who otherwise risked being kidnapped by FARC. This led to broad criticism of the peace process. Furthermore, disunity across the business sector as a whole, resulting from the connection of some firms to paramilitary groups and the illegal drugs trade, and from the weak representation of business in business associations, meant that no broad and unified business peace movement developed. In general, business was ambivalent towards a peaceful solution to the conflict and organising itself to influence the peace talks (Rettberg 2007; Guáqueta 2006; Arnson and Whitfield 2005). A new government in 2002 led by President Uribe replaced the peace talks with a decade-long, hard-line military strategy. FIP continued its peace efforts, including supporting **structural peacebuilding**, focusing on economic development, strengthening institutions, and assisting internally displaced persons and ex-combatants (FIP 2016).

Negotiations began again in 2012 between the Colombian government (under President Santos) and FARC (and 'talks about talks' with the ELN) (BBC 2016). In 2013, the Global Compact's local network in Colombia hosted the first country-level event of the 'Business for Peace' platform (**interventions 1 and 2**). A panel, which included the president of FIP, highlighted 'the importance of public – private partnerships to generate solutions that foster peace'. Riding on the momentum of the Colombian peace talks (that culminated in the 2016 peace agreement), the event held multi-stakeholder dialogues to identify business strategies to support Colombia's peace process, stability, and socioeconomic development (UN Global Compact 2013).

Suggested sessions

Session 1: CPM and stakeholder engagement

In this session, you will learn to explain and use keywords associated with the topics of stakeholder engagement and CPM, discuss issues associated with these topics from different value perspectives, and differentiate between structural peacebuilding (such as economic interventions) and peacemaking (political/diplomatic interventions) in areas of conflict.

Activity 1 (5–10 minutes)

Thinking about stakeholder engagement in general (i.e. not necessarily in a conflict environment), tell a partner:

1. What are stakeholders (give some examples)?

2. What is stakeholder engagement?

3. Why is this important for business?

Activity 2a (5–10 minutes)

Figure 16.3 shows some possible stakeholders in a region of conflict (i.e. armed struggle). Discuss in small groups what effects armed conflict might have on each of the stakeholders (two boxes are left blank for you to add your own suggestions for other stakeholders).

Discussion point example: 'Armed conflict could create a lot of problems for **local government** because they are responsible for infrastructure, such as telecommunications and roads, and these can be destroyed and disrupted by violent conflict.'

Activity 2b (5–10 minutes)

In the previous activity, you considered the effects of conflict on stakeholders. However, stakeholders can influence situations as well as be affected by them.

Figure 16.3: Possible stakeholders in a region of conflict.

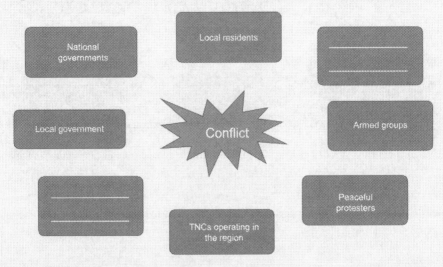

They are called stakeholders because their actions can also be driven by the *stake* that each *holds* in the situation. Thinking about the stakeholders you have been discussing, which ones might have a stake in exacerbating conflict, and which might have a stake in promoting peace? Why?

Discussion point example: 'Local businesses are likely to want peace, as violence can make it difficult or dangerous for them to operate normally. However, some might have a stake in prolonging a conflict, such as businesses that provide food or entertainment to soldiers.'

Activity 3 (5–15 minutes: see teacher notes for shorter and longer approaches)

TNC involvement in conflict can take different forms and have different effects. Read the three case studies that follow, all of which show examples of stakeholder engagement in conflict-prone areas. Identify which intervention(s) promote(s) peace and which exacerbate(s) conflict.

Case A: Kube Energy

The Norwegian company Kube Energy leases off-grid solar energy systems to peace and humanitarian operations, communities, governments, and businesses in conflict-prone countries with low electrification, such as South Sudan and Kenya.

Shifting from expensive diesel generators to solar, organisations reduce energy costs and carbon emissions while paying monthly energy fees without having to own or maintain systems. Kube Energy covers upfront costs and operates the system, offering technical/financing options, such as power purchase agreements. Peace and humanitarian operations (e.g. refugee camps) require electricity generation to power food storage, water pumps, clinics, schools, and lighting (Kube Energy 2022).

Case B: Lonrho in Mozambique

Mozambique suffered a civil war from 1975 until 1992. In the 1980s, following spiralling security costs, 'Tiny' Rowland, CEO of the mining TNC Lonrho (became Lonmin, then acquired in 2019 by Sibanye-Stillwater), conducted shuttle diplomacy between the leaders of key groups in the conflict. Lonrho supplied one group with a jet to transport representatives to negotiations, and millions of dollars to enable the group to transform into a political party and encourage it to remain in talks. During difficult negotiations, Rowland organised meetings, gave advice, and encouraged the groups' leaders until they reached an agreement (Banfield *et al.* 2006; Wenger and Möckli 2003; Vines 1998). However, Lonrho's activities were highly controversial. Further, in 2012 in South Africa, Lonmin was accused of being responsible for the 'Marikana miners' strike', where over 100 striking Lonmin employees were shot by police, with Lonmin remaining in severe controversy (London Mining Network 2019).

Case C: Democratic Republic of Congo Mining

The Democratic Republic of Congo (DRC) supplies much of the world's copper and cobalt. In the Katanga region, Congolese miners often work with poor safety provisions and child labour. With inadequate legal protection, local communities are forcibly removed. Artisanal miners are removed from mining areas, at times with violence (van Dorp and Bwenda 2021).

The previous Kube Energy case is an example of *structural peacebuilding*. Lonrho is an example of *peacemaking* but demonstrates the importance of taking a broader, long-term view when analysing companies' impacts. They may work for peace in one area/region while having a negative impact in another time and place. Structural peacebuilding and peacemaking take place in regions of conflict. Although these concepts are connected, they are not the same thing. To understand the difference, consider the following definitions:

- **Structural peacebuilding** involves helping to provide what a society needs to function fairly and effectively. This can include government capacity-building, equitable economic development, promoting human rights, and environmental regeneration. Corporations can get involved by, for example, providing jobs for women, youth, and ex-combatants, helping local development and environmental initiatives, and teaching their security forces about human rights.

- In contrast, **peacemaking** concentrates on the political/diplomatic, relational, and reconciliation aspects of peace work. It builds peaceful relations between conflict parties and communities, progresses peace processes, and helps parties reach a peace agreement.

Activity 4 (10 minutes)

Following are some activities that can promote peace. Work in groups to allocate each activity to the relevant category in the table that follows (an example of each has been filled in for you).

- Economic advice for negotiations
- Conflict resolution workshops
- Providing funds for hospitals or schools
- Protecting the local environment
- Lobbying for peace
- Supporting mediation between disputants
- Offering fair employment terms
- Early warning information on rising conflict
- Creating jobs for marginalised groups

Structural peacebuilding	Peacemaking
Helping local government be more transparent and accountable to its constituents	Supporting grassroots initiatives that bring disputing communities together for talks

Activity 5 (15–30 minutes)

Discussion:

1. Based on what you have learned so far, to what extent do you think companies are likely to get involved in (a) structural peacebuilding and (b) peacemaking? Why do you think they get involved (or not) with these interventions? In what ways might their involvement depend on the particular conflict?

2. Of the stakeholders in activity 2, which would be easier/more difficult to engage with? What might be the benefits and dangers of engaging with each group? What else might companies take into account if considering engaging with armed groups?

3. Of the types of engagement discussed today, which are probably more difficult? How beneficial will each type of intervention be over the long term for both the company and the region's people?

Session 2: Applying the 14-intervention CPM framework

In this session, you will identify and discuss interventions from the 14-intervention CPM framework by means of examples. You will learn about corporate involvement in peacemaking in South Africa and reflect on and critically discuss key aspects of corporate involvement in peacemaking.

It is recommended you read the detailed explanation of the 14-intervention CPM framework in this chapter in preparation for this session.

Activity 1 (5 minutes)

Complete column 3 of the following table (see next page) with ideas learned from the previous session and/or your own thoughts.

Activity 2 (5 minutes)

Before you read a case study on South Africa, what do you already know about the conflict and peace process in that country?

When operating in conflict-prone areas, companies can:	Do nothing	What are the risks and the benefits?
	Check their supply chains	Give an example; what are the types of risk involved in supply chains linked to conflict-prone areas? How can risk be reduced?
	Get involved in structural peacebuilding	Give a real or hypothetical example.
	Help with peacemaking	Give an example; what are the risks and benefits?

Discuss in small groups:

1. From 1948 to 1994, the South African political system was known as **apartheid**. What does this mean, and why did many people object to it?

2. Have you heard of the following: Archbishop Desmond Tutu, Nelson Mandela, P. W. Botha, F. W. de Klerk, and the ANC (African National Congress)? What do you know about them?

3. Some governments, businesses, and individuals used **divestment** and **sanctions** to protest the South African political system. What do these involve, and how do you think they affected South African businesses and international corporations with interests in South Africa?

4. What was the final outcome of this situation?

Activity 3 (5 minutes)

Read the following case study, which provides background information on the South Africa situation:

1. What information can you add to your previous discussion about South Africa's recent history?

2. What was the CBM (Consultative Business Movement), and why was it formed?

Case study: Consultative Business Movement, South Africa

Three decades before the Black Lives Matter movement created a global impact, the majority-Black population in South Africa had few rights, and Afrikaner (White settler) minority rule was maintained. Apartheid, or racial segregation, in South Africa was enforced by the ruling party, the NP (National Party), between 1948 and 1994. Apartheid led to resistance, violence, and the killing of many Black protesters. International protests and trade sanctions were established against South Africa, reducing investment and growth and forcing many TNCs to divest. In 1990, the NP president de Klerk agreed to negotiations. These led to democratic elections in 1994, the end of apartheid, and the election of the ANC (African National Congress), with Nelson Mandela as leader.

In 1988, a group of businesspeople faced great danger when bringing together representatives of some domestic and international businesses in South Africa to form the CBM (Consultative Business Movement). The CBM was a non-party-political movement led mostly by representatives of domestic businesses. Its objectives were peace, democracy, economic growth, and the end of international sanctions. Many of the businesses realised they needed to participate in the peace processes to encourage negotiations and to meet all political parties to ensure an inclusive peace process and the outcome of a business-friendly economy (Hutchings 2017; Ganson 2017; Ralph 2015; Fourie and Eloff 2006). As CBM members, TNCs supported peacemaking through their membership, roles on the CBM 'board', or actively participating in the CBM's peacemaking interventions. TNCs included Anderson Consulting, Arthur Andersen and Associates, Anglo American, Cadbury, Ernst & Young, Kellogg's, Siemens, Toyota, BP, Caltex Oil, Shell, and Unilever (personal conversation with T. Eloff, former Executive Director, CBM, 28 August 2008; personal conversation with G. Hutchings, Director (Memberships), National Business Initiative, formerly CBM, 3 July 2008; Ralph 2015; see Ralph and Kennedy 2014 for additional references – the original URL/reference is no longer available).

Activity 4 (5 minutes)

Strategies used to engage stakeholders in conflict situations with the aim of bringing about peace can be called **interventions**. Before you complete the next activity, shut your book and, with a partner, try to guess some of the interventions which the CBM might have used, and not used, in this situation.

Activity 5 (15 minutes)

Table 16.1 (see below) is a list of the actual interventions used by the CBM in South Africa. Using the 14-intervention CPM framework described earlier in this chapter, identify which of the framework's interventions is illustrated in each point, and write in the relevant name and number. An example is done for you.

Activity 6 (5 minutes)

Return to your speculations on possible CBM interventions in activity 4. How accurate were your guesses as to the strategies used?

Activity 7 (15 minutes or longer)

To consolidate and reflect on what you have learned so far, jot down some thoughts on the following questions, and then debate them in small groups or in a whole-class setting:

1. Based on what you have learned so far, do you think companies should get involved in conflict mediation? Why/why not?

2. What key skills and knowledge might companies have that could help bring about a successful outcome (e.g. conflict resolution, facilitation, local knowledge, etc.)?

3. In what situations should company representatives simply enable others to mediate, and in what situations might they take a direct part in mediations?

4. How might companies approach mediation at the grassroots level differently from mediation at the top levels?

5. Besides mediation, what else can company representatives do to support peace negotiations?

Table 16.1: CBM interventions in the South Africa peace process

The CBM . . .	Name(s) and number(s) of intervention(s) from the CPM framework illustrated here
Worked with the South African Council of Churches and Chamber of Business, unions, political parties, women's groups, and NGOs to build pressure for talks	Intervention 1: Corporate collective action
Took a non-partisan, inclusive approach, holding hundreds of meetings to meet separately the various groups that could help create peace	
Maintained communication flows between the conflict's political parties, particularly when the negotiations stalled, to ensure the negotiations could continue	
Organised regional and national forums addressing economic and development issues, providing advice throughout, and building consensus on solutions that could be fed into the national (top-level) negotiations	
Supported the establishment of local dispute resolution committees, run by community leaders to mediate in local incidences of the violence	
Helped create regional dispute resolution committees, which mediated conflicts at the regional level, preventing violence from spreading and derailing top-level, constitutional negotiations	
Donated financial resources	
At least one TNC representative took a leadership role in a regional dispute resolution committee	
Provided process and administrative support for the national negotiations between the top political leaders of the conflict parties	
Actively participated in national negotiations: for example, John Hall, a CBM member and domestic businessperson, was a co-chair in initial peace talks alongside Archbishop Desmond Tutu	
Observed the national negotiation process, identifying any stumbling blocks that could stall the process, and encouraged the parties to reach an agreement	

Source: Fourie and Eloff 2006; Collin Marks 2001; see Ralph and Kennedy 2014 for additional references (the original URL/reference is no longer available). See also Hutchings 2017; Ganson 2017; Ralph 2015.

Session 3: Role-play – companies and stakeholders in Colombia

In this session, you will critically apply relevant interventions from the 14-intervention CPM framework to a conflict scenario. You will role-play a meeting between international companies and create a proposal for corporate support of peacemaking.

Before you commence this session, you may find it useful to read and make notes on the Colombia case study earlier in this chapter.

Activity 1: Refresher quiz (5–10 minutes)

Quiz a classmate on what you have learned about corporate peacemaking (CPM) so far. You can use the following questions as a guide or make up your own:

1. What are the main differences between structural peacebuilding and peacemaking?

2. Name at least one company that has been involved in CPM and the region in which it has done this.

3. How many interventions from the 14-intervention CPM framework can you remember without looking at your book/notes?

4. What are the main reasons companies might get involved in CPM?

5. What are the main risks or dangers when companies get involved in CPM?

Activity 2 (15 minutes – ideally done before the session as a prep task)

Research on Colombia. Later, you will role-play a discussion between companies operating in Colombia about possible CPM interventions. To prepare for this, first read the case study on Colombia earlier in this chapter. Make notes on:

1. The background to the conflict (first and second paragraphs of the case study)

2. Key details of the interventions which have been applied (remaining paragraphs)

Alternatively, if you have pre-read the case study before the session, take a few minutes now to refresh your memory by reading your notes and comparing them with a classmate's. Can your partner help add or clarify any points in your notes?

Activity 3: Role-play (spend about half the remaining session time on the prep activities [3a-c] and half on the role-play [3d-e])

A group of TNCs operating in Colombia has decided to work together to help promote peace in the country. Senior representatives from each TNC involved will meet and present their ideas to each other. Complete the following steps to prepare for, and carry out, the presentation, and engage in a follow-up discussion.

Activity 3a: Work in groups. First, choose one of the companies that follow. Your group will represent this company in the 'meeting' later on. Read the paragraph provided to learn about your company's activities in Colombia. (Alternatively, you may choose to act as another international company, representing a different sector, but the company must be one that exists in real life and operates or could potentially operate in Colombia.)

Nestlé

Nestlé is a Swiss food and beverage TNC providing products like coffee, baby foods, and cereals. In Colombia, Nestlé purchases milk and coffee from rural communities (Reuters 2017; *regional challenges to Nestlé*, see FairWorld Project 2019). Nestlé Colombia claims to help reduce violence and crime where it operates and supports related projects. 'The Peace Observatory' gathers local information on violence in the 'El Valle' subregion to prepare prevention programmes. 'Equity peacemakers' enhance capabilities in conflict resolution in the community. A leadership school provides young people with skills in leadership and citizen participation (UN Global Compact 2020).

Microsoft

Headquartered in the United States and based in the capital, Bogotá, in Colombia, Microsoft develops computer products and services (e.g. Windows, Office, and Xbox). Internationally, its stated CSR foci are inclusive economic opportunity, fundamental rights of people, addressing climate change, and increasing trust in technology (e.g. protecting privacy). Examples include helping to ensure young refugees receive education, supporting rural projects in Colombia to increase women's internet use and economic opportunities, supporting social entrepreneurs, and using its 'Planetary Computer' to provide local information on land use and forest size to assist climate change mitigation (Microsoft 2020).

Coca-Cola

Headquartered in the United States, Coca-Cola is a beverage company providing non-alcoholic drinks (e.g. water and fizzy drinks). The company's sustainability foci include water security, sustainable packaging, diversity and equity, human rights, and sustainable sourcing of agricultural ingredients. Examples include supporting circular economy approaches for packaging, economic empowerment of women entrepreneurs, and (following accusations of complicity in attacks on workers in partner bottler firms, with firms paying a paramilitary group) promoting human rights and ensuring safe, responsible workplaces across its supply chain (teleSUR 2016; Coca Cola 2021).

Activity 3b: Identifying key stakeholders. The following table lists some key stakeholders in the Colombia situation. Discuss and prioritise which of these stakeholders your company will engage with in your peacemaking endeavours.

1. What are their interests and influence in the conflict?

2. How might your company affect them and vice versa?

3. How might you prioritise their claims on your company's attention?

4. Which stakeholders should you preferably not engage, or definitely *not* ignore, and why?

Possible stakeholders mentioned in the case study	Other stakeholders to consider
FIP, UN Global Compact and its Colombian local network, IBLF (or similar organisation to IBLF working in Colombia)	Local communities; local government; police; religious, human rights, environmental, and labour groups; Colombian or international peace-focused NGOs; media; academia; Colombian government and other political parties; Colombian armed groups/criminal organisations; Colombian national and small businesses; other state governments and their embassies in Colombia

Activity 3c: Your group represents senior management at the Colombian headquarters of your chosen company. You have decided to work with other companies operating in Colombia to contribute to violence reduction and building peace. You are preparing a presentation for a meeting with these companies. Write a proposal in bullet points, and prepare to present your proposal to representatives of these other TNCs. Include the following information:

1.   Who are the key stakeholders where your company is concerned?

2.   What interventions from the 14-intervention CPM framework will you use with each stakeholder (including ones which could bring your stakeholders together for peacemaking)?

3.   How will you employ your chosen interventions?

4.   Who in your company will carry out this work?

5.   What expertise already exists in your company to carry out this work, and what additional skills/training will be needed? Will you partner with other organisations more experienced in peacebuilding? Which organisation(s)?

Activity 3d: Meet the representatives of the other companies and present your solutions to each other.

Activity 3e: Based on yours, and the other groups', proposals, discuss all together whether it is possible for your companies to cooperate in collective action to foster peace in Colombia.

Additional teaching material and ideas

Film *2040*

This film explores what the future could be like by 2040 if we implemented the best solutions available now to live harmoniously with the planet.

Watch the film *2040* (Madman Entertainment 2019: https://play.google.com/store/movies/details?id=DTO96hTODGc.P) and note down the solutions advocated. In groups, share your initial thoughts on the solutions and how they relate to business.

Look at 'Activate Your Plan' (https://whatsyour2040.com/#activate-plan) and watch the 'Corporate Program' video. Playing the role of a representative of a company of your choice, discuss in pairs how you could activate a plan for 2040 for your chosen business. Does your plan support peaceful relations and/or a sense of community in your area/country?

Research report on the Russia–Ukraine war

Research the Russia–Ukraine conflict, either in groups or individually. You must identify the major conflict parties, their goals, needs, and interests, and any other stakeholders in the conflict that could affect a peace process. Note that this conflict is an international conflict across Russia–Ukraine borders and is affecting many other countries, particularly regarding energy and food security. This is different from an internal conflict – an intra-state conflict – that is foremost fought between conflict parties within a country. Choose a company that is/has been invested in the Ukraine (or develop a hypothetical company). Then, identify your company's main stakeholders within the Ukraine, Russia, and internationally, and describe how your company might apply structural peacebuilding or interventions from the CPM framework to assist peace and/or Ukrainian refugees outside of Ukraine, showing which stakeholders might be involved and how. You can either present the results of your research in a later session or write a report.

Sustainable Development Goal 16

Sustainable Development Goal (SDG) 16 calls governments, business, and civil society to '[p]romote peaceful and inclusive societies' (see earlier vignette). Without peaceful, inclusive societies, climate change mitigation and sustainability have no 'enabling environment' (UN Global Compact 2020: 1).

Goal 16's targets aim to encourage accountable institutions, rule of law, equal access to justice, and reduced corruption to prevent violence, terrorism, and crime, for example.

Discussion:

1. Why are peaceful and inclusive societies important for the following?
    a. Successful business and trading
    b. Addressing climate change and sustainable development

2. Why are accountable institutions, rule of law, justice, and reduced corruption important for peaceful societies?

3. How might a company support SDG Goal 16 and its targets? (Find ideas from the 'SDG 16 Business Framework: Inspiring Transformational Governance' (UN Global Compact 2022).)

Your own corporate peacemaker

As a class, create your own hypothetical international company. Identify its name, sector, products/services, etc. Among its markets, your company operates in a country that suffers violent conflict sporadically between two groups. Divide the classroom into seven areas, titled:

- Products/services

- Marketing and advertising

- Political and external affairs

- Environmental initiatives

- Staff involvement

- Supply chain

- Global initiatives and relations

Individually, using sticky notes or flip chart paper, write down your ideas for how your company could support peace in the country through each of these seven areas. Be as creative as you can! Then you can either:

- As a class, discuss the different ideas suggested.

- Individually, identify which idea is the best in each category (you could draw a star by the idea); as a class, bring together the best ideas (one from each category) and discuss how your company would draw the ideas together as a coherent strategy for the company. You can also do this activity online using a shared online writing space that can be divided into seven areas.

Further readings

Bache, C., and R. Sicina (2021), 'PRME Working Group on Business for Peace, in Principles for Responsible Management Education (PRME)', in *Responsible Management Education* (London: Routledge).

> This chapter overviews the work/topics addressed under 'peace' by the Business for Peace Working Group.

Cook Glen, C., and T. L. Fort (eds.) (2021), *Music, Business and Peacebuilding* (London: Routledge).

> This book argues that music facilitates positive emotions, ethical behaviour, and peace, and business provides a platform for the positive capabilities of music for peace.

LSE Ideas (2022), *Maximising Business Contributions to Sustainable Development and Positive Peace: A Human Security Approach*, UN Business and Human Security Initiative, www.lse.ac.uk/ideas/publications/reports/business-sustainable-development-positive-peace.

> Business can assist societal resilience against shocks, including climate change and pandemics, through local-level strategies, digital technology, and multi-stakeholder partnerships.

Miklian, J., J. E. Katsos, B. Ganson, B. Bull, K. Hoelscher, S. Cechvala, Ø. H. Rolandsen, A. Rettberg, and B. Miller (2021), 'What Covid-19 Taught Us About Doing Business During a Crisis', *Harvard Business Review*, 17 November, https://hbr.org/2021/11/what-covid-19-taught-us-about-doing-business-during-a-crisis.

> A survey of seven cities in the Covid-19 pandemic provides insight on how business faces crises, and benefits from community embeddedness.

Ralph, N. (2021), 'An Introduction to Social Enterprise for Practitioners in Preventing and Countering Violent Extremism', in G. Barton, M. Vergani and Y. Wahid (eds.), *Countering Violent and Hateful Extremism in Indonesia: Islam, Gender and Civil Society* (London: Palgrave Macmillan).

> Focussed on Indonesia but offering insight for other countries, this chapter discusses how social entrepreneurship and businesses may support practitioners working to prevent violent extremism.

References

Arnson, C.J. and T. Whitfield (2005) 'Third Parties and Intractable Conflicts: The Case of Colombia', in C.A. Crocker, F.O. Hampson and P. Aall (eds.), *Grasping the Nettle: Analysing Cases of Intractable Conflict* (Washington, DC: US Institute of Peace Press): 231–68.

Banfield, J., C. Gündüz and N. Killick (2006) *Local Business, Local Peace: The Peacebuilding Potential of the Domestic Private Sector* (London: International Alert), www.internationalalert.org/publications/local-business-local-peace/ accessed 10 October 2022.

BBC (2016) *Colombia-Farc Peace Talks Delayed Over Differences*, 24 March, www.bbc.com/news/world-latin-america-35888464 accessed 10 October 2022.

Braithwaite, J., V. Braithwaite, M. Cookson and L. Dunn (2010) *Anomie and Violence* (Canberra, Australia: Australian National University EPress), https://press.anu.edu.au/publications/series/peacebuilding-compared/anomie-and-violence accessed 10 October 2022.

Business for Peace (2022) *'Business Advancing Peace' – See 'Participants' List*, www.unglobalcompact.org/take-action/action/peace accessed 10 October 2022.

Business for Peace and CDA (CDA Collaborative Learning Projects) (2015) *Advancing the Sustainable Development Goals by Supporting Peace: How Business Can Contribute* (New York: Global Compact).

CDA (2022) *Conflict-Sensitivity and Do No Harm*, www.cdacollaborative.org/what-we-do/conflict-sensitivity/ accessed 10 October 2022.

Christie, D. and M. Wessells (2008) 'Social Psychology of Violence', in L. Kurtz (ed.), *Encyclopaedia of Violence, Peace, & Conflict* (Oxford, UK: Elsevier): 1955–63.

Coca Cola (2021) *2020 Business & Environmental, Social and Governance Report*, www.coca-colacompany.com/reports/business-environmental-social-governance-report-2020 accessed 17 October 2022.

Collin Marks, S. (2001) *Watching the Wind: Conflict Resolution During South Africa's Transition to Democracy* (Washington, DC: US Institute of Peace).

Crane, A., D. Matten and L.J. Spence (eds.) (2013) *Corporate Social Responsibility: Readings and Cases in a Global Context*, 2nd edn (London: Routledge).

The Elders (2022) *Home*, https://theelders.org/ accessed 10 October 2022.

FairWorld Project (2019) *Small-Scale Farmers Stand Up to Nestle Coffee Processing Plant*, 31 January, https://fairworldproject.org/small-scale-coffee-farmers-stand-up-to-nestle/ accessed 10 October 2022.

FIP (2016) *Peace as an Opportunity*, FIP, Bogotá, Colombia, www.academia.edu/26811196/PEACE_AS_AN_OPPORTUNITY_A_PROPOSAL_FOR_TRANSFORMATION_IN_COLOMBIA accessed 10 October 2022.

FIP (Ideas for Peace Foundation) (2022) *About*, https://ideaspaz.org/quienes-somos [use Google Translate for English] accessed 10 October 2022.

Fourie, A. and T. Eloff (2006) 'Exploring the Contributions of the Private Sector to the Social, Economic and Political Transformation Process in South Africa', in J. Banfield, C. Gündüz and N. Killick (eds.), *Local Business, Local Peace: The Peacebuilding Potential of the Domestic Private Sector* (London: International Alert): 508–16.

Freeman, R.E. (2010) *Strategic Management: A Stakeholder Approach* (Cambridge, UK: Cambridge University Press).

Friedman, M. (1962) *Capitalism and Freedom* (Chicago, IL: University of Chicago Press).

Ganson, B. (2017) *Business in the Transition to Democracy in South Africa: Historical and Contemporary Perspectives* (CDA, PRIO, Africa Centre for Dispute Settlement), www.cda collaborative.org/publication/business-transition-democracy-south-africa-historical-contemporary-perspectives/ accessed 10 October 2022.

Ganson, B. (2022) *Conflict Environments Need a Peacebuilding Approach to Business Development* (Institute for Security Studies), 7 March, https://issafrica.org/iss-today/conflict-environments-need-a-peacebuilding-approach-to-business-development accessed 10 October 2022.

Guáqueta, A. (2006) 'Doing Business Amidst Conflict: Emerging Best Practices in Colombia', in J. Banfield, C. Gündüz and N. Killick (eds.), *Local Business, Local Peace: The Peacebuilding Potential of the Domestic Private Sector* (London: International Alert), 273–306.

Harrabin, R. (2021) *Shell: Netherlands Court Orders Oil Giant to Cut Emissions*, 26 May, www.bbc.co.uk/news/world-europe-57257982 accessed 10 October 2022.

Haufler, V. (2001) 'Is There a Role for Business in Conflict Management?', in C. Crocker, F. Hampson and P. Aall (eds.), *Turbulent Peace* (Washington, DC: US Institute of Peace Press): 659–75.

Hlatky, S.V., C. Voillat, A. Bryden, A. Retief, B. Gonsalves and M. Fox (2021) *Conflict Prevention Tool: Developing Multi-Stakeholder Strategies*, www.business-humanrights.org/en/latest-news/conflict-prevention-tool-developing-multi-stakeholder-strategies/ accessed 10 October 2022.

Human Rights Watch (2022) *Colombia Events of 2021*, www.hrw.org/world-report/2022/country-chapters/colombia accessed 10 October 2022.

Hutchings, G. (2017) *The CBM in the Transition to a Democratic South Africa*, Africa Centre for Dispute Settlement Working Paper 2017/4, www.cdacollaborative.org/sdm_downloads/the-cbm-in-a-transition-to-a-democratic-south-africa accessed 10 October 2022.

Ide, T. (2022) *Climate Change, Violent Conflict and Environmental Peacebuilding, Global Trends Analysis* (Germany: Development and Peace Foundation), www.researchgate.net/publication/363285142 accessed 10 October 2022.

Idowu, S. (ed.) (2021) *Current Global Practices of Corporate Social Responsibility: In the Era of Sustainable Development Goals* (Cham: Springer International Publishing).

IEP (Institute for Economics and Peace) (2022a) *Ecological Threat Report 2022: Understanding Ecological Threats, Resilience and Peace, Sydney*, October, http://visionofhumanity.org/resources.

IEP (Institute for Economics and Peace) (2022b) *Home*, www.economicsandpeace.org/about/ accessed 10 October 2022.

Iff, A., D. Sguaitamatti, R.M. Alluri and D. Kohler (2010) *Money Makers as Peace Makers? Business Actors in Mediation Processes*, Working Paper 2 (Bern, Switzerland: Swisspeace).

Killelea, S. (2022) *Why Positive Peace Is Transformational, Peace in an Age of Chaos*, www.peaceintheageofchaos.org/vision/ accessed 10 October 2022.

Killick, N. (2000) 'Adaption of Lederach's Triangle: A Role for People in Business', in J. Nelson (ed.), *The Business of Peace: The Private Sector as a Partner in Conflict Prevention and Resolution* (London: International Alert, Council on Economic Priorities and Prince of Wales Business Leaders Forum): 55.

Kube Energy (2022) *Home*, www.kubeenergy.com/ accessed 10 October 2022.

Lederach, J.P. (1997) *Building Peace: Sustainable Reconciliation in Divided Societies* (Washington, DC: US Institute of Peace Press).

London Mining Network (2019) *Lonmin: Still One of the Unacceptable Faces of British Capitalism*, 26 March, https://londonminingnetwork.org/2019/03/lonmin-still-one-of-the-unacceptable-faces-of-british-capitalism/ accessed 10 October 2022.

Maak, T., N. Pless, M. Orlitzky and S. Sandhu (2022) *The Routledge Companion to Corporate Social Responsibility* (New York: Routledge).

Microsoft (2020) *Corporate Social Responsibility Report*, www.microsoft.com/en-us/corporate-responsibility accessed 10 October 2022.

Miklian, J. (2017) 'Mapping Business-Peace Interactions: Opportunities and Recommendations', *Business Peace and Sustainable Development* 10: 3–27. https://doi.org/10.9774/TandF.8757.2017.de.00002.

Mitchell, R.K., B.R. Agle and D.J. Wood (1997) 'Toward a Theory of Stakeholder Identification and Salience: Defining the Principle of Who and What Really Counts', *Academy of Management Review* 22.4: 853–86.

Nelson, J. (2000) *The Business of Peace: The Private Sector as a Partner in Conflict Prevention and Resolution* (London: International Alert, Council on Economic Priorities and The Prince of Wales Business Leaders Forum).

OHCHR (2022) *The Business, Human Rights and Conflict-Affected Regions Project*, www.ohchr.org/EN/Issues/Business/Pages/ConflictPostConflict.aspx accessed 10 October 2022.

PeaceNexus (2020) *Strengthening Corporate Reporting on Sustainable Development Goal 16, Swisspeace and Engageability*, www.swisspeace.ch/publications/other-publications/strengthening-corporate-reporting-on-sdg-16-on-peace-justice-and-strong-institutions accessed 10 October 2022.

PRME (Principles for Responsible Management Education) (2022a) *Business for Peace Working Group*, http://unprmeb4p.org/ accessed 10 October 2022.

PRME (Principles for Responsible Management Education) (2022b) *Best 10 List Business and Human Rights*, www.unprme.org/resources/prme-best-10 accessed 10 October 2022.

PRME (Principles for Responsible Management Education) (2022c) *PRME Business for Peace Working Group*, www.unprme.org/working-group/prme-working-group-on-business-for-peace.

Ralph, N. (2015) *Peacemaking and the Extractive Industries: Towards a Framework for Corporate Peace* (Sheffield, UK: Greenleaf Publishing).

Ralph, N. and M. Conley-Tyler (2006) *Companies as Peacebuilders: Engaging Communities Through Conflict Resolution*, University of Melbourne Legal Studies Research Paper 196, https://papers.ssrn.com/sol3/papers.cfm?abstract_id=946849 accessed 10 October 2022.

Ralph, N. and E. Kennedy (2014) 'Stakeholder Engagement and Corporate Peacemaking', in P. Molthan-Hill (ed.), *Business Student's Guide to Sustainable Management: Principles and Practice*, 1st edn (Sheffield, UK: Greenleaf Publishing): 321–59.

Rettberg, A. (2007) 'The Private Sector and Peace in El Salvador, Guatemala, and Colombia', *Journal of Latin American Studies* 39.3: 463–94.

Rettberg, A. (n.d.) *Business Led Peacebuilding in Colombia: Fad or Future of a Country in Crisis?* (London: Crisis States Programme, Development Research Centre, London School of Economics and Political Science).

Reuters (2017) *Nespresso Expands Coffee Purchases in Post-Conflict Colombia*, 28 November, www.reuters.com/article/us-nestle-coffee-colombia-idUSKBN1DS2PT accessed 10 October 2022.

Shankleman, J. (2007) *Oil, Profits, and Peace: Does Business Have a Role in Peacemaking?* (Washington, DC: US Institute of Peace Press).

Sweetman, D. (2009) *Business, Conflict Resolution and Peacebuilding: Contributions from the Private Sector to Address Violent Conflict* (Oxford, UK: Routledge).

teleSUR (2016) *Coca-Cola Accused of Funding Colombian Death Squad*, www.telesurenglish.net/news/Colombia-Coca-Cola-Accused-of-Funding-Terrorist-Paramilitaries-20160901-0005.html accessed 10 October 2022.

Tripathi, S. and C. Gündüz (2008) *A Role for the Private Sector in Peace Processes? Examples and Implications for Third-Party Mediation* (Oslo, Norway: OSLO Forum Network of Mediators).

UN Global Compact (2013) *Business for Peace Kicks Off Local Network Event Series in Colombia*, 30 October, www.unglobalcompact.org/news/591-10-30-2013 accessed 10 October 2022.

UN Global Compact (2020) *Advancing Business Understanding of Peace, Justice and Strong Institutions (SDG 16) Country Consultation Reports – See Colombia Report*, https://unglobalcompact.org/library/5889 accessed 10 October 2022.

UN Global Compact (2022) *SDG 16 Business Framework*, https://sdg16.unglobalcompact.org/ accessed 10 October 2022.

van Dorp, M. and C. Bwenda (2021) 'A Tale of Patience and Perseverance', *FriEnt*, 14 December, www.frient.de/artikel/a-tale-of-patience-and-perseverance accessed 10 October 2022.

Vines, A. (1998) 'The Business of Peace: "Tiny" Rowland, Financial Incentives and the Mozambican Settlement', in A. Vines and D. Hendrickson (eds.), ACCORD 3: *The Mozambican Peace Process in Perspective* (London: Conciliation Resources): 66–74.

Wenger, A. and D. Möckli (2003) *Conflict Prevention: The Untapped Potential of the Business Sector* (Boulder, CO: Lynne Rienner).

BRINGING IT
ALL TOGETHER

17
Systems thinking and sustainable management

Néstor Valero-Silva

Overview
Learning objectives
These will:

- Introduce the notion of systems (holistic) thinking in relation to other ways of thinking, such as reductionism.

- Lead to an understanding of the notion of system as a creation of the observer, that is, as a personal and social construct rather than as an objective entity that exists 'out there' and yet to be discovered.

- Introduce the main types of diagram commonly used in systems thinking and practice.

- Appreciate how diagrams (including system diagrams) could contribute to thinking and acting in relation to managerial problems that have a dimension of sustainability.

- Introduce the notion of 'long-lasting products' as a particular application of systems thinking in management.

DOI: 10.4324/9781003294665-22

Introduction

Systems thinking challenged the long-held view that humans were intrinsically superior to other biological entities and were thus the 'masters' of nature. It also contributed to discrediting the assumption that the planet's natural resources were unlimited. Furthermore, it has been at the centre of recent attempts to understand and express the interconnectedness that exists between the natural and the social worlds (Meadows *et al.* 2006). In this sense, systems thinking has helped contemporary societies to improve their appreciation of the complex web of interactions between nature and human activities – and between different social groups. These range from the forecast of weather patterns and their impact on communities, the impact of deforestation on animals and air quality, the evolution and extinction of species, and the spread of viruses and disease to helping governments design and implement meaningful policies in relation to the conservation of natural resources, including attempts to eradicate disease and alleviate poverty.

Other specific areas of application include economic modelling (Lietaer *et al.* 2012); international development and politics; negotiation; public sector management (Eker *et al.* 2018; Seddon 2010; Trochim *et al.* 2006); tourism (Kapmeier and Gonçalves 2018); agriculture (Akhavan *et al.* 2021); science, industrialisation, and ecology (Capra 1997; Carson 2000; BBC News Online 2014); ethics and sustainability (Fisher *et al.* 2013); business management and operational research (Jackson 2019; Mingers and White 2010); and more recently, the development of information systems (Checkland 2002), and of the computer games and internet-based industries. Previous chapters of this book also provide some useful areas of application specifically related to the business world.

It would be impossible to find a simple definition of the concept of 'systems thinking' that would fully address all these areas of application. Perhaps the achievement of a useful approximation could start by considering the relationship between systems thinking and reductionism.

Systems thinking and reductionism

Systems thinking focuses on 'totalities' (wholes) when trying to understand and address the challenges faced by every organisation – see, for example, Churchman (1968), Jackson (2019), and Senge (2010). Instead of trying to solve problems – and problematic situations – in isolation, it assumes them as being embedded in particular organisational structures, cultures, and business environments. Furthermore, some of these challenges could even be the unintended consequences of previous organisational policies.

> ACME, a company that operates in a very competitive and cost-cutting environment, decided to reduce its costs by outsourcing production to developing countries. This was perceived as a very good 'tried and tested', textbook strategy. However, the decision had disastrous consequences for the company's reputation, sales, and its overall competitiveness – when it was reported that overseas workers were grossly underpaid and overworked, that female employees earned considerably less than their male colleagues doing the same job, and that pristine natural environments were being polluted with industrial waste generated by the company's production. The situation was tackled as a 'public relations' issue, in isolation, with a glossy, new marketing strategy that soon backfired when a worker committed suicide by jumping from the roof of the factory. The company then decided to frame the situation as a legal and HR problem that needed 'decisive action', announcing that the facility would be closed. A long strike by the workers and painful redundancy negotiations with the foreign government followed, in the full glare of the press. In response, the company then decided to hire some PR consultants to manage the negative press reports. An international boycott resulted, promoted by angry consumers using social media.

The previous example highlights the need for ACME to use a systems approach towards addressing the company's competitiveness. This way of thinking, which is also often called **holistic** or **systemic** thinking (von Bertalanffy 2015), could have helped ACME to include all its operations and its environment (including the communities in which it operates) as part of their decision-making process. In this sense, adapting the organisation to its environment is at the centre of the 'contingency' and 'organic' approaches to management (Morgan 2006). Perhaps ACME could have followed a more successful long-term strategy involving a mixture of investing in product design, staff training, and dealing with distribution and waste problems, rather than opting for a single 'textbook' solution in isolation. The role of ACME's HRM department needs to be explored in relation to promoting an inclusive and sustainable organisational culture/mindset and human rights; lessons could be learnt in relation to the PRME working groups on 'gender equality' and on 'developing a sustainability mindset', following the discussion in Chapter 9.

> The Foxconn scandal in China that engulfed several Western technology companies in 2012 (*The Economist*, 23 January 2012) and also BP's initial response to the Deepwater Horizon oil spill in the Gulf of Mexico in 2010 (BBC News Online 2010) provide further case studies for analysis.

Conversely, an approach that compartmentalises the complexity and allows managers to focus on certain sections of the organisation (e.g. production), including some immediate interactions (e.g. levels of pollution on the immediate natural environment), is sometimes useful. The type of approach that focuses on a 'slice' of the whole organisation (or problem) is called **reductionism**. The importance of reductionism cannot be underestimated, as it has been successfully used to increase productivity (Taylor 1998) and to solve engineering and scientific problems. Many solutions, especially in science and engineering, can be found by following very well-established problem-solving methods that must be rigorously followed, step by step, in a very orderly and **systematic** manner (Descartes 1998; Kuhn 2012).

Reductionism must be used with caution as, on the one hand, it promotes specialisation; however, on the other, it may reinforce a 'silo mentality' – a criticism that has been levelled against business education! It may also render complex problems down to simple 'cause and effect' mechanisms, as it focuses on very small aspects of the overall situation. Sometimes, steps such as researching the best technological solution, conducting a robust analysis of the competition, commissioning a glossy sustainability report from a consultant, or developing the most advanced product do not, in isolation, guarantee success if there were a failure in considering other factors.

However, as managers are eager to find immediate answers to the challenges they face, it is sometimes very difficult for them to take a **systemic** approach to understanding, firstly, where and how the chosen 'slice' fits within the overall picture. Instead, on many occasions, managers opt for a quick solution, moving on to the next important issue and hoping for the best long-term outcome; time pressures, the unavailability of data, information processing limitations, and lack of experience could hinder the success of a holistic approach.

At this point, it could reasonably be asked: How can managers take decisions and design policies if they should, ideally, begin by considering every element and every relationship inside and outside their organisations, including the natural, social, and business environments? In the search for 'the whole', where do you stop? Where do you draw the line?

Boundary

An important tool in facilitating a systemic (holistic) approach to organisational challenges involves the use of boundaries in order to encapsulate the most important elements and their interactions, thus separating them from others considered less pressing.

A *boundary* is a differentiating device, an **artificial construct** that is not fixed, obvious, or natural. Boundaries may be useful, and they certainly facilitate understanding, debate, and purposeful action; nevertheless, they are, as products of human perception, arbitrary. In other words, boundaries reflect particular interests and social (**power**) relations (Cooper 1986, 1992; Morgan 2006). Consequently, different stakeholders will define different boundaries in relation to the same set of issues or problems. Boundaries also operate as control mechanisms that simultaneously highlight, include, discriminate, and exclude. To **define** what the boundary aims at representing, perhaps in words, could be very useful when trying to explore its rationale. Finally, boundaries are endlessly created and transformed by individuals in organisations.

> A CEO decides to call a meeting to discuss a pressing problem. He/she must choose which manager to invite, the agenda for the meeting, and what information is needed. This involves the creation of a mental boundary around the problem. If one of the participants cannot attend the meeting, the CEO must again make a decision as to whether the meeting should go ahead without this person or if the meeting should be rescheduled. It could be that meeting was scheduled on that particular date in the full knowledge that some managers could *not* attend! The relative importance of the presence of a particular manager (including the information and experience they could bring) at this meeting depends on the CEO's mental boundary – which is, in turn, related to the CEO's interests and objectives.

Boundaries are sometimes perceived as '**closed**', with little or no interaction with elements outside (e.g. when a boundary is drawn around the components of a small machine to understand how it works). However, in most managerial situations, boundaries tend to be '**open**', as the interactions between the inside and the outside are considered important (von Bertalanffy 2015). For example, changes in legislation, the competition, people joining and leaving the organisation, new information, and the social and natural environments may be contributing factors (Checkland 2000).

As we have illustrated, perhaps the most important challenge for a senior manager is to use an appropriate boundary that would help him/her and his/her organisation to understand and address the challenges they face. This is particularly critical, as every middle manager, every department, and every subsidiary has its own agendas and interests. Some of these interests, although entirely legitimate, could be at odds with each other; also, if followed without appropriate checks, they could damage the whole organisation – as recent banking and stock market scandals have demonstrated only too well.

Furthermore, the same senior manager may need to use different boundaries when considering such factors as short- and long-term perspectives; local, regional, or international issues; marketing, financial, operational, and human resources initiatives. Finally, appropriate boundaries are also important when a business professional is considering his/her own career and work–life balance from the short-, medium-, and long-term perspectives.

The environment

As we said earlier, although boundaries are very useful (and necessary) human constructs that allow us to focus on certain elements and interactions and to differentiate these from what lies in the 'background', they also reflect particular interests and social (power) relations. Furthermore, assuming these interests and power relations were absent, as everything has an effect on everything else – as Lorenz's (1972) *Butterfly Effect* metaphor beautifully illustrated – it could be argued that we could talk only about one 'whole': the universe!

In this context, some scientists and business leaders think that the most important boundary worth considering must be placed around the planet Earth. This is also known as the **Gaia theory** (Lovelock 2000, 2007); this theory assumes the planet as a dynamic collection of living and non-living elements that continuously interact with each other. The Gaia theory highlights how the planet has a series of highly complex self-regulatory mechanisms that, within certain parameters, support life. The mechanisms, which include evolution and natural selection (organisms **co-evolve** with their environment), weather patterns, extinction patterns, and changes in composition of the planet's water, air, and land, are found at the centre of contemporary understandings of sustainability, ecology, and science.

By locating the boundary around the planet, the Gaia theory demonstrates how human activity could destroy the planet's self-regulatory mechanisms, thus threatening the possibility of life. Examples include uncontrolled pollution, nuclear waste, global warming emissions, misuse of pesticides (Carson 2000), overuse of antibiotics, deforestation, over-fishing, and population growth (Fisher *et al.* 2013).

The main point to highlight is that these threats do not, in the main, come from isolated actions – although a potential nuclear accident could create irreparable damage. Instead, they could be directly linked to routine **activities** found in families, communities, charities, commercial organisations, and even schools and universities. Each of these activities contributes, to a degree and on a different scale, to the same overall and dangerous outcome. The acknowledgement of such risk has particularly been highlighted by initiatives to reduce household and industrial waste and increase recycling levels, to improve packaging design and transport logistics, and to reduce consumerism and 'planned obsolescence' (London 1932). The notion of the individual and organisational 'carbon footprint' could be considered as an expression of these ideas (Berners-Lee 2020).

Consequently, when **companies and individuals** choose to focus exclusively on the elements and interactions more closely linked to their operations (either **spatially** or **temporarily**), without properly considering their natural, business, and social environment, the long-term survival of their organisations could be at risk. Examples include:

> Pharmaceutical companies aggressively promoting the indiscriminate use of antibiotics to increase sales in the short-term (after spending billions on their development) then these become ineffective as bacteria develop resistance – same companies now blamed for failing to invest in new antibiotics, as they are less profitable than other medicines Financial Times Online (2015); poor farmers destroying their land through small-scale yet relentless deforestation from collecting wood for cooking; large fishing fleets routinely using 'bottom trawling' methods only to collect a particular species

of fish, and destroying the environment it needs to reproduce (*See* Meadow's 2001, *Fish Banks, Ltd.* game, mentioned in Chapter 2). Multinationals facing enormous fines that threaten their survival due to the accumulation of small 'savings' on health and safety measures that later cause deadly chemical and nuclear accidents (BP's Deepwater Horizon in 2010; the Fukushima nuclear disaster in 2011). The promotion of an uncontrolled risk-taking culture (reinforced by the payment of generous short-term bonuses) that produces great financial returns in the short term, and large-scale bankruptcies in the long term. (Barings Bank in 1995; Enron in 2001; Lehman Brothers in 2008)

Having considered the notions of boundaries and of the environment (which has social, business, natural, and temporal dimensions), we can now explore the notion of 'system'.

The system

The word 'system' means different things to different people. People often use expressions such as political systems, religious systems, payment systems, and information systems. Even criminals, compulsive gamblers, and stock market risk-takers talk about 'having a system'. The modern idea of system was first presented by Churchman (1968) and von Bertalanffy (2015) and further developed and applied by several philosophers, scientists, and writers such as Bradbury (2005), Capra (1988, 1997), Carson (2000), and Jackson (2019).

- *Systems* are **dynamic** mental constructs that behave as if they had some **purpose**. For example, when we talk about organisations as systems, we sometimes indicate that they are created to serve a particular moneymaking, social, or charitable purpose; we could say that mission statements reflect, to some extent, the organisation's purpose. However, some organisations could have different purposes, as perceived by different stakeholders, or decide to change their overall purpose as they re-brand themselves.

A university can be understood as a system to provide education; a system that produces knowledge and original research; an entertainment and socialising system for young people; a system that provides employment to academics, administrators, and support staff; a system that provides income for local businesses, employment to residents, and tax revenue to local government; or as a system that promotes teaching, research, and development opportunities towards promoting and achieving the SDGs.

- A system has an **owner**; in other words, every system reflects the views of its creator(s). Systems make sense to someone or to a particular group of people. In the previous example, we can easily see that perhaps the system owners were students and their sponsors are academics, HR managers, and local businesses. Furthermore, multiple systems may have the same owner, as individuals and groups have multiple – and sometimes contradictory – interests.

The development of the high-speed rail system (HS2) between London and the north of England may be seen as a system to move a large number of people from A to B in a cost-efficient and timely manner (train operator); a system that promotes economic growth, employment, and taxes (the treasury); a system that threatens the ecology, scars beautiful landscapes, and pollutes the countryside with emissions/noise and concrete/steel that promote climate change (certain environmentalists and landowners); a system that will provide employment and lucrative contracts (civil engineers, builders, and train manufacturers); a complete misuse of financial resources that could be used for health and education (people located in areas not covered by the planned service and/or worried about at the levels of government debt); and finally, a very inefficient way to improve the country's infrastructure when other options could be cheaper (motorway builders and car manufacturers).

- As human constructs, either individual or social, systems reflect the **ethical values** of their owner(s). To suggest that boundaries are mechanisms that include and highlight also implies that they simultaneously exclude and send into the background. As it is impossible to consider every single actual or potential factor, the selection process required cannot be taken lightly.

Is it necessary to consider natural resources, such as the quality of air or the availability of natural landscapes, in the system that guides planning and decision-making? Should managers consider future generations, climate change, beauty, and happiness? Is it the organisation's responsibility to consider these issues, or someone else's? Is it useful to express the relationships between different issues solely/mainly in financial terms, and if so, for what purpose? Shall we ignore or exclude anything that cannot easily be expressed in financial terms, or shall we create 'convenient' financial proxies? Is it acceptable for an organisation to relate to its environment mainly in terms of threats and opportunities?

Which stakeholders shall I consider or consult in my decision-making process?

Are local workers more important than those in faraway countries? Shall we equate following the law with being ethical and responsible? (See Chapter 9 for an exploration of HRM-related issues.)

Shall I focus my department on short-term financial gains, increasing my annual bonus, rather than on stability and surplus in the long-term (e.g., climate change) as I am planning to leave the company in a couple of years?

- A *system* is a group of **components** (including elements and relationships) linked **in an organised manner**.

The **interaction** between bricks, mortar, steel, and other materials constitutes a particular building – and not these elements by themselves, stored in a warehouse. Furthermore, the same elements may be used to build an office building or a bridge, if organised differently. Conversely, if the materials are not of a certain quality or are not available in sufficient quantities, the construction could either not be completed or would collapse.

Many business organisations have the same functional areas, operate in similar buildings, and have a comparable workforce; however, it is the interaction between these elements that makes them unique to each organisation.

- The **components are affected** by being included in the system and are changed if they leave it.

Taking a fish out of the sea, interrupting its interaction with the seawater and with other creatures that give it sustenance, would cause its death. A very successful manager could become less successful in a different organisational culture, and *vice versa*. A medication (e.g. a pill) that has been unsuccessful in medical trials for its intended purpose or that has been superseded by newer medications may become a big earner when used for a different purpose or in a different market. A life-saving medication for some individuals can constitute a poison for others.

- Systems exhibit **feedback** mechanisms (Ashby 2015; Beer 1985; Wiener 2019). This is to say the information about the outcome of a process is fed back to the beginning of the process to reinforce its action or to slow it down. Examples of **positive** feedback, which could spiral out of control and even threaten the entire system, include the *snowball effect* (i.e. the reinforcing/amplifying effect that creates a snow avalanche) and the *vicious/virtuous circle* (Senge 2010: 81).

The arms race between the West and the former Soviet Union, the use of credit cards and payday loans to cover daily expenses (or to cover previous loans) that

Figure 17.1: A system.

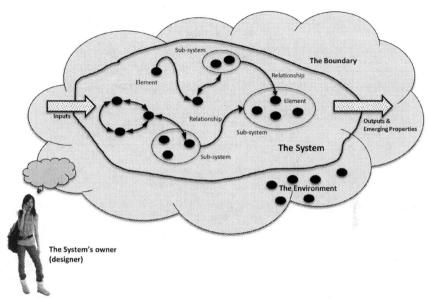

suck people into greater debt, the process of global warming, the link between customer satisfaction and future sales, and addictive behaviours to shopping and consumerism are particular examples of positive feedback mechanisms.

There are other feedback mechanisms that tend to control, or dampen down, the overall process. Examples of this **negative** feedback include:

The biological processes used by the human body to keep its temperature constant; the use of electronic thermostats to start/stop central heating systems, cooling fans, and fridge/freezers; the increase in interest rates to reduce borrowing; policies to reduce complaints to a certain manageable level; and efforts to reduce carbon emissions to internationally agreed levels.

- Systems have **inputs** and **outputs** (involving transformation processes) and may also exhibit **emerging properties**. Most systems interact with their surrounding environment, as energy, information, money, raw materials, products, and waste are transformed and exchanged. People also move across organisational boundaries as they join and leave an organisation. Contractors and consultants belong to more than one organisational system. Finally, systems exhibit properties that cannot be explained by analysing individual components, **emerging** instead from their interaction. This is what is meant by the famous expression attributed to the Greek philosopher Aristotle: '**the whole is greater than the sum of its parts.**'

Life is one of the most interesting emerging properties on the planet, which cannot be explained by analysing the functioning of a single organ or a few organs in isolation – even though not all organs are required to keep a body alive! Happiness is another emerging property that governments around the world are trying to understand, measure, and include in their long-term planning and investment.

Motivation, satisfaction, leadership, loyalty, reputation, culture, work–life balance, and sustainability are also emerging properties routinely used in business studies.

Diagrams

Diagrams constitute effective tools to help managers understand, frame, and communicate organisational problems and issues (as you see in the 'system diagram' earlier). In this sense, diagrams are often selected through personal preference, familiarity, and previous training. For example, flow chart diagrams (*see* Figure 17.5) are routinely used to explain how to operate household appliances and usually accompany self-assembly furniture. Managers who originally trained in finance and engineering may prefer flow charts, while those trained in social sciences may prefer rich pictures. As it is very easy to find examples and explanations of modelling diagrams on the internet and in books (e.g. Waring 2010), the following list is intended to provide a general framework to use as a basis for further research. Please note that sometimes these diagrams are simply classified within what is known as 'soft systems' (qualitative; exploring) and 'hard systems' (quantitative; prediction), for example, Checkland (2000).

Diagrams for exploration, understanding, and brainstorming

Most of these diagrams begin at the centre of the sheet of paper and expand outwards. For example, Buzan's (2014) *spray diagram* expands from an initial element in a branch/tree manner; it is often used for note taking as it can easily represent the structure of an argument. He also developed the *mind maps* used in brainstorming (Buzan 2014). *Fishbone* diagrams (Ishikawa 1986) are commonly used in quality and lean management. There are several free and paid *mind-mapping* software applications available (e.g. FreeMind, WikkaWiki, iMindMap, Prezi).

Checkland (2000) developed *rich pictures*: cartoon-like diagrams that show a great deal of information; they are excellent in addressing complex situations, as

Figure 17.2: Spray diagram.

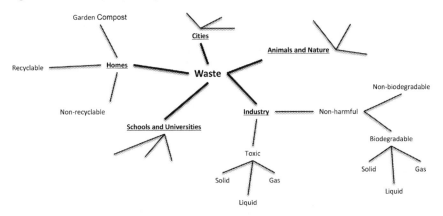

Figure 17.3: Rich picture.

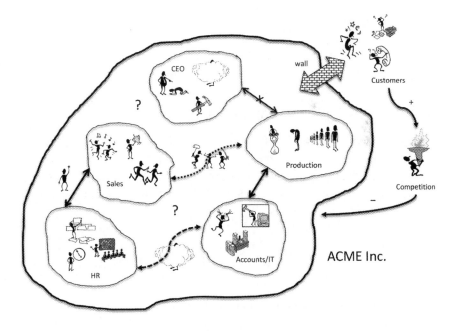

they can display numerical information (hard data) together with people's feelings and emotions (soft data). They promote the sharing of opinions and perceptions in group activities where participants are asked to talk to each other than to modify and enrich the diagram.

Figure 17.4: Sign diagram.

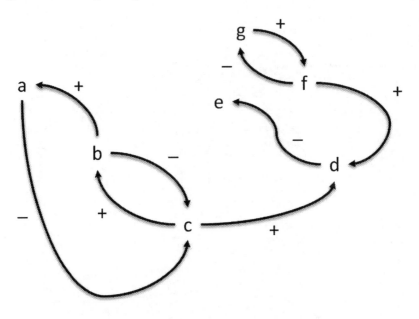

Diagrams that highlight connections

Such diagrams (*see* Figure 17.4) focus on the structure of the situation by high-lighting connections between elements with circles and lines; some show how certain elements influence others by including arrows, highlighting cause and effect, and feedback processes. Examples include **system**, relationship, influence, casual loop, and 'organisational chart' diagrams.

Diagrams for detailed analysis and quantitative model building

Some of these diagrams go beyond showing connectivity to include information such as whether an element influences positively or negatively another element (using plus and minus signs), as in *sign* diagrams. Others focus on processes, such as *input–output* (black box) diagrams; *decision sequence diagrams, structure diagrams*, and *flow charts* are also used to give instructions and, in the early stages of computer games, engineering design (BBC Online 2016; Lee *et al.* 2018) and in the field of *systems dynamics* (Antunes *et al.* 2015; Sterman 2014).

Figure 17.5: Flow chart.

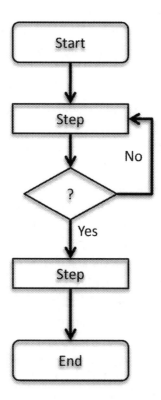

The future of systems thinking and management

Systems thinking has had a profound impact in the management sciences since the 1940s. During WWII, it was used to prevent U-boat attacks on the shipping of supplies and movement of troops from the United States and Canada to the UK, to coordinate the logistic efforts involved in the movement of personnel, ammunition, and supplies, and in the planning of the air defences and air raids. Immediately after the war, it played an important role in the post-war reconstruction of Europe and in Japan (Deming 2018; Ishikawa 1986), the development of welfare institutions such as the National Health System (UK), and in the socio-technical approaches pioneered by the UK's Tavistock Institute of Human Relations in the 1950s. Examples of Tavistock's approach include the study of technological change in mining companies in the UK (Trist and Bamforth 1951) and at Volvo in Sweden (Gyllenhammer 1977). The socio-technical approach aimed at reconciling human (individual/group) needs with technical efficiency. Systems thinking was also applied, although with different degrees of success, in the centralised economies of socialist and communist countries (Myant and Drahokoupil 2010). A very interesting example that highlights the application of dynamic/evolving systems in relation to sustainable development is provided by Hjorth and Bagheri (2006).

Other important areas of application include the development of the total quality management, just-in-time, and lean management movements (Deming 2018; Juran 2008; Ishikawa 1986). Management writers such as Beer (1985), Checkland (2000), and Jackson (2019) developed practical methodologies, such as the viable system model (VSM), systems dynamics, soft systems methodology (SSM), and critical systems thinking (CST), respectively. Finally, Senge's (2010) *The Fifth Discipline* popularised the systems ideas within an even wider audience.

More recently, these concepts have played a role in the development of fair trade and in the controversial 'carbon market mechanisms' (Fisher *et al.* 2013). Finally, it lies at core of current understandings regarding the impact of product design, packaging, transport, waste, and consumption on the environment (Cooper 2016). Issues surrounding sustainable marketing and sustainable consumption, in relation to meeting SDG 12, were discussed in Chapter 8.

In this last area, and in relation to the notion of consumerism and *affluenza*, that is, the compulsive acquisition of products and the discarding of still-functioning products in search for new models that offer the same or similar function, is that systems thinking is at its most promising (the 'goods and services life cycle' was introduced in Chapter 9, towards achieving SDG 12). It has become clear that any improvements in the manufacturing of 'greener' products would have no overall positive impact on the environment even if current levels of consumption were maintained. In fact, not only *per capita* consumption but also the number of consumers is continuously increasing worldwide. This is to say, 'green shopping/consumerism' and 'sustainable consumerism' are still consumerism! However, as the whole economic and social systems are dependent on current production levels, it is neither practical nor socially desirable to terminate all the jobs and the economies built on the premise of unlimited growth and development.

Cooper (2016) advocates instead a circular 'systems thinking' economic model, which

requires that the throughput of materials and energy be mini-
mized by optimising product longevity, reusing or reconditioning
products and their components, and recycling – alongside other
measures such as energy efficiency.

(Cooper 2016: 12)

This economic model would be combined with the concept of 'slow consumption'
(Cooper 2005).

This approach is supported by increasing 'product life-span', which
involves improving production processes, creating skilled jobs in repair
and maintenance work, consumer satisfaction, and second-hand markets. In sum, Cooper believes that the combination of 'longer life –
spans' and 'slow consumption' (within a 'systems thinking' economic
model) would provide an antidote to the notion of 'obsolescence' and
should allow the economy to absorb lower levels of production.

(Fisher *et al.* 2013: 384)

Cooper's ideas provide an excellent example of the relevance of systems thinking in helping individuals, organisations, and communities understand, discuss,
devise, and implement new ways of living and of working that are 'sustainable'
in the long term. In this sense, systemic thinking, with all its tools and diagrams,
provides no definite answers; instead, it provides a starting point in the building of
a more holistic and sustainable future.

Systems thinking and the Sustainable Development Goals

This chapter has provided an overview of the importance of adopting a 'systems
thinking' mindset to address managerial and social situations in relation to achieving the SDGs (e.g. Allen *et al.* 2019; Antunes *et al.* 2015). It also illustrates its
potential contribution to certain PRME working groups, such as on 'developing a
sustainability mindset' – already addressed in Chapter 9 in the context of human
resources management.

The notion of 'system' and its different elements (*see* Figure 17.1) could contribute to all 17 SDGs, for example: sub-systems, outputs, and emerging properties

can easily be linked to goal 13 (climate action), as explored in Chapters 10, 12, and 14 (i.e. 'climate' is an emerging property from the interaction between human and natural sub-systems over time). Expressing and negotiating stakeholders' perceptions, feelings, and emotions (see 'rich pictures') could contribute to goal 16 (peace, justice, and strong institutions), explored in Chapters 4 and 15. Highlighting links between different elements and cause-and-effect relationships (see 'spray diagrams') could be effectively used in the context of goal 11 (sustainable cities and communities) and goal 6 (clean water and sanitation), discussed in Chapters 7, 11, and 14. Emphasising the positive or negative effect of one element or sub-system on another (see 'sign diagrams') could be used in the context of goal 3 (good health and well-being), goal 12 (responsible consumption and production), and goal 9 (industry, innovation, and infrastructure).

To close the 'learning loop', please revisit Chapter 5 to review the link between the 'UN Global Compact, PRME, and the SDGs' (Figure 17.1), and Chapter 1 to review the 'SDGs in relation to the content of this book' (Figure 17.1).

Suggested sessions

Session 1

Video on diagrams

The following Open University (Free Open Learning) video, 'A guide to using diagrams', provides examples of various diagrams: http://youtu.be/TQwA9krV8EA.

Duration: 17 minutes, 20 secconds. The video will be presented in class.

The diagrams follow the analysis of a case study based on certain social and environmental issues (such as population growth and urbanisation) as experienced by the inhabitants of an island in the Mediterranean (0:00–2 minutes, 30 seconds).

The video starts with a rich picture (2 minutes, 33 seconds) produced by the island's inhabitants that is then translated into a spray diagram (6 minutes, 30 seconds), system diagram (9 minutes, 45 seconds), influence diagram (11 minutes, 48 seconds), and a multiple-cause diagram (11 minutes, 50 seconds).

You are asked to produce each of these diagrams following the examples provided in the chapter. Next, you can compare your results with those offered by the video. Please note that there is not a perfect diagram. You will be able to produce more complex diagrams with some practice. Finally, you could improve each diagram after watching the video.

This video can also be watched prior to attending the session, then played and discussed in class.

Session 2

Flow charts

Flow charts are one of the most commonly used diagrams in business and engineering. Their ability to convey information in a highly systematic manner and with very few elements makes flow charts especially useful in explaining processes and to convey instructions. They are also frequently used in the design of websites embedded in the menu options offered to customers (usually on menus on the left-hand side of web pages), to design user manuals, and to explain procedures. It is very easy to produce professional flow charts, as their building blocks are now included as 'autoshapes' in the drawing toolbars in Office-style software packages.

Task

Using the previous basic four elements, select two processes from the following list (including at least ten steps and five yes/no questions) and create a flow chart; do not forget to include 'sustainable management' issues/considerations! Test your chart with the other members of a small group to see if it is clear. Select the best flow chart to present to class. This task can also be completed during independent study and include doing some basic research on flow charts and including more types of elements (e.g. www.rff.com/flowchart_shapes.htm).

- Designing and implementing a policy to encourage employees to cycle to work.

- Reducing the amount of printing at a university, including training, storage, and IT support considerations.

- Job hunting: from the initial decision to seek work to finding a permanent or temporary job.

Figure 17.6: 'Autoshapes.'

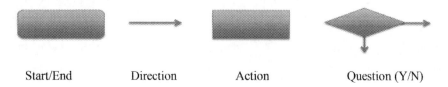

| Start/End | Direction | Action | Question (Y/N) |

Session 3

Sales targets and their impact on corporate reputation: when does an incentive become a bribe?

The aim of this session is to illustrate the interaction between different elements and stakeholders in relation to a particular complex situation, to highlight how porous organisational boundaries are, the usefulness of the concept of emerging properties, the unintended consequences of well-intended organisational policies (e.g. sales targets and bonuses), and to discuss the 'usefulness' of the diagrams.

The final presentation will also illustrate how different individuals and groups will produce different diagrams and recommendations, highlighting the necessarily subjective nature of systemic thinking and practice. This session could be split into two sessions, if considered appropriate.

General group task

GlaxoSmithKline's (GSK) top management has asked your group to provide an outline of the situation described here, followed by some basic suggestions towards addressing this crisis.

Part 1

In groups of four or five students, read the following case study and conduct some general research using the links provided and a general internet search (this research could be done in advance of the class).

- Identify the different stakeholders in this case study.

- Each student must choose one of these stakeholders.

- Each student will sketch a couple of diagrams to express the view of the chosen stakeholder.
  - All students in the group must agree on what type of diagrams to use, for example, a system and an influence diagram, or a system and a rich picture.

Present the diagrams to the other members of the group; create two final diagrams combining the individual contributions.

- What would be the general advice to GSK's top management that emerges from your two group diagrams?

Part 2

- Present to the class and general discussion.

Case study: GlaxoSmithKline (GSK) in China

GSK is a British pharmaceutical company with its headquarters in London. It is currently one of the largest prescription drug companies in the world. Its importance is related to its size, to its financial muscle, to the tax revenues it provides, and to producing medications to alleviate the suffering of millions of individuals from common conditions such as asthma, cancer, and diabetes worldwide.

According to the BBC and other media (*see* 'more information' in the following text), GSK has been recently investigated by the Chinese government over allegedly bribing Chinese doctors to prescribe the firm's drugs. Other practices under the spotlight include paying doctors to give lectures at international conferences (including very generous hospitality and other incentives) and the perceived aggressive marketing techniques by company's sales representatives at doctors' surgeries. It is said that these 'sales and information' visits could make it difficult for health professionals to distinguish between marketing information and scientific information. Furthermore, GSK's use of individual sales targets and performance-related bonuses for its employees has also been criticised (these are human resource management techniques commonly used as an incentive to reward individual or group performance). Please note that other pharmaceutical companies have also faced similar and other criticisms, such as the use of live animals on drug development and testing and the availability and quality of experimentation data (e.g. Goldacre 2013).

A selection of relevant stakeholders invited by the BBC and other media (e.g. *The Guardian*) to give their opinions on these issues include:

- Editor of the British Medical Journal: 'Doctors need independent, unbiased information about drugs.'

- Ben Goldacre (author of the book Bad Pharma): 'Doctors get a lot of their education about which treatment works best from the pharmaceutical industry itself – from doctors who have been paid to give lectures about which drug is best. This free education has been shown to be biased in research and it's non-trivial.'

- The British Medical Association (BMA) Head of Science and Ethics: 'Whilst we agree that GSK should not directly sponsor doctors' going to meetings, we are satisfied that they will continue to financially support education.'

More information:

www.bbc.co.uk/news/business-25415485
www.bbc.co.uk/news/business-23402154
www.theguardian.com/business/2013/jul/24/gsk-china-crisis-questions

Additional background information

The UK government introduced the Bribery Act 2010, aiming at improving corporate transparency and to fight corruption. One of the key elements of this act is its near-universal jurisdiction, that is, it allows for the prosecution of an individual or a company *with links to the UK*, regardless of where the crime was committed (www.gov.uk/government/publications/bribery-act-2010-guidance).

Transparency International (UK) is an NGO that challenges corruption worldwide. Its activities include producing research reports, campaigning, and lobbying. Important reports include *How to Bribe: A Typology of Bribe and How to Stop It, Corruption in the UK, Bribery in China – 10 Lessons from Recent Cases*, and *Global Corruption Report: Climate Change* (www.transparency.org.uk).

Additional teaching material and ideas

1. Films

Several films on environmental and sustainability issues with a systems orientation could be used for class discussion and to provide examples of the relevance of the systems approach to management. A filmography chapter in Fisher *et al.* (2013) is worth consulting for further material (pages 549–63).

Students could be asked to use diagrams to illustrate and discuss each film's main topics, different viewpoints, sub-plots, and how relevant the stories are to their future professional practice, using systems concepts, such as boundaries, feedback, and emerging properties. A few examples are as follows.

Rotten (TV series – Netflix)

A series of investigative documentaries providing a systemic view of the food global supply chain and its unintended consequences. The episodes also highlight the relationship between **climate change**, local crime, and international corruption. Students can produce and compare/discuss diagrams to illustrate the issues presented.

Mindwalk

Director: Bernt Capra, United States, 1990. This film is based on the book *Turning Point* written by Fritjof Capra. The first half of the film provides a very interesting and comprehensive story of the evolution of science *vis-á-vis* developments in Western society since medieval times. The second half is devoted to the evolution of systems thinking, highlighting its possible application in the fields of politics, conservation, science, technology, and business ethics. The main characters, a nuclear scientist, a US presidential candidate, and a poet, provide a very interesting debate on the pros and cons of this approach at the theoretical and at a practical level. Music by Philip Glass. The film is available on VHS and on the internet. (Duration: 1 hour, 52 minutes.)

The Fight for True Farming

Director: Eve Lamont, Canada, 2005. A most interesting film, it provides an opportunity for farmers in Canada, the USA, and France to provide solutions acceptable to the social and environmental *Scrooges* of factory farming. The roles of globalisation and agribusiness in the demise of traditional farms are discussed. GM crops and biodiversity also feature prominently. (Duration: 1 hour, 30 minutes.)

Up the Yangtze

Director: Yung Chang, China, 2007. This film is based on the largest hydroelectric dam in the world, built in China. As entire cities are being submerged and 2 million people displaced, luxury cruise ships take tourists on 'farewell' tours to see the legendary landscape before it is flooded. The film contrasts the experience of naïve and well-intentioned Western tourists with those of crew members native to the region. (Duration: 1 hour, 33 minutes.)

An Inconvenient Truth

Director: Davis Guggenheim, United States, 2006. Al Gore, former US Vice President and presidential nominee, presents an informative documentary on the dangers of global warming. It is taut, intelligent, and darkly humorous. (Duration: 1 hour, 37 minutes.)

Blood in the Mobile

Director: Frank Piasecki Poulsen, Denmark, 2010. We cannot live without our mobile phones, but their production has a dark and bloody side. Minerals used to make our mobiles come from mines in the Eastern DR Congo, funding a brutal civil war responsible for around 5 million deaths, atrocious child labour, and some 300,000 rapes in the last 15 years. It is a war that will continue as long as armed groups can trade the minerals. Director Frank Poulsen travels to Congo and gets access to its largest illegal tin mine, where enslaved children dig for days in narrow tunnels. He then tries to confront Nokia, the world's largest phone company. Are they and other mobile companies implicated in trading 'conflict minerals'? What do you think of Poulsen asking a small child to be his guide into the mines? The issue of 'conflict minerals' is also mentioned in Chapter 13. (Duration: 1 hour, 25 minutes.)

2. RSA Animate

(www.thersa.org/events/rsaanimate)

Short animations from the Royal Society for the Encouragement of Arts, Manufacturers, and Commerce (RSA), based in London. Lectures and other material are also available at this site. The animations are excellent examples of the power of rich pictures and cartoons to convey complex information.

RSA Animate – *Climate change and the future of humanity*

Climate change and the future of humanity | David Wallace-Wells – RSA (thersa.org)

The fate of humanity is in our hands, and the time to act is now. The choices we make today will write the climate future of the next decade. Are we ready for a new chapter?

RSA Animate – *Crisis of capitalism*

www.thersa.org/video/animates/2010/06/rsa-animate---crisis-of-capitalism

Students could be asked to spot the section when the notion of 'systemic risk' is mentioned, then summarise the issues addressed up to that point.

RSA Animate – *Choice*

www.thersa.org/video/animates/2011/06/rsa-animate---choice

Explores the paralysing anxiety and dissatisfaction surrounding limitless choice. This short animation could also be linked to the concepts of consumerism, '*affluenza*', and obsolescence.

3. Gaia theory

There are several resources on 'Gaia theory' available online (including James Lovelock's website). A special edition of the *New Scientist* magazine devoted to this concept, including the views of its critics, can be found at: www.newscientist.com/special/gaia.

4. Systems thinking diagrams

Examples of systems thinking diagrams can be found online. A web search with the words 'systems thinking diagrams' would provide many images to explore and discuss.

5. Sea wall 'eco-engineering' can help boost biodiversity

Visit the following website:

www.bbc.co.uk/news/science-environment-26034196

This piece of news from the BBC News Online could be used to illustrate and discuss issues regarding the interaction between man-made structures and the natural environment. Emphasis could be placed on the fact that the scientists' proposals would not increase the cost of building these sea walls; also, consider the advantages of forming multidisciplinary teams to design and build these structures, as opposed to *managing* these projects as purely engineering jobs. System and influence diagrams could be produced to aid the discussion.

Further readings

Checkland, P. (2000), *Systems Thinking, Systems Practice* (London: Wiley).
> Peter Checkland's main contribution to systems thinking was the development of his soft systems methodology (SSM). As a former chemical engineer, he has an approach that is both very clear and practical. These books provide many examples of how to develop rich pictures and how to progress from achieving a general understanding of a problematic situation to the development and implementation of recommendations for improvement.

Checkland, P., and Poulter, J. (2007), *Learning for Action: A Short Definitive Account of Soft Systems Methodology, and Its Use for Practitioners, Teachers and Students* (London: Wiley).

Fisher, C., Lovell, A., and Valero-Silva, N. (2013), *Business Ethics and Values*, 4th Edition (London: Pearson-Financial Times).
> This is a very popular book on business ethics written with a *systemic* orientation. It has a chapter devoted to corporate social responsibility and another on sustainability. It also contains a filmography chapter with over 100 films (each with a short synopsis) that could be chosen as case studies for class discussions and essays and personal/group independent study.

Jackson, M. C. (2019), *Critical Systems Thinking and the Management of Complexity* (Chichester, UK: Wiley).
> This classic text provides a comprehensive summary of systems thinking in the management sciences. The main sections on functionalist, interpretive, and emancipatory systems approaches include reviews of the main systems methodologies. Jackson provides not only a summary of the methodologies but also an analysis of their strengths and weaknesses. It is written in a very clear and accessible style and is a good source of references for further study.

Morgan, G. (2006), *Images of Organization* (London: Sage).
> This book has become a classic on the study of organisations since its first edition in 1986. The idea of managers using metaphors in 'the art of reading' problematic situations is very powerful indeed. The first four metaphors – organisations as *machines*, *organisms*, *brains*, and *cultures* – are central to the understanding of how systems thinking is interwoven into the different management disciplines. The strengths and weaknesses of each metaphor are particularly important, as are the bibliographical notes provided at the end of each chapter.

References

Akhavan, A., Gonçalves, P. (2021) 'Managing the trade-off between groundwater resources and large-scale agriculture: The case of pistachio production in Iran', *System Dynamics Review* 37.2–3: 155–96.

Allen, C., Metternicht, G., Wiedmann, T., Pedercini, M. (2019) 'Greater gains for Australia by tackling all SDGs but the last steps will be the most challenging', *Nature Sustainability* 2: 1041–50.

Antunes, M.P., Stave, K.A., Videira, N., Santos, R. (2015) 'Using participatory system dynamics in environmental and sustainability dialogues', in Ruth, M. (ed.), *Handbook of Research Methods and Applications in Environmental Studies* (Cheltenham, UK: Edward Elgar Publishing).

Ashby, W.R. (2015) *An Introduction to Cybernetics* (London: Martino).

BBC News Online (2010) 'BP Boss Tony Hayward's Gaffes', *BBC News*, 20 June (www.bbc. co.uk/news/10360084, accessed 6 April 2022).

BBC News Online (2014) 'Sea Walls tweaks boost biodiversity', *BBC News*, 6 February (www. bbc.co.uk/news/science-environment-26034196, accessed 6 April 2022).

BBC Online (2016) 'Designing an algorithm', *BBC News* (www.bbc.co.uk/education/guides/z3bq7ty/revision/3, accessed 6 April 2022).

Beer, S. (1985) *Diagnosing the System for Organizations* (Chichester: Wiley).

Berners-Lee, M. (2020) *How Bad Are Bananas? The Carbon Footprint of Everything* (London: Profile Books).

Bradbury, R. (2005) *A Sound of Thunder and Other Stories* (New York: Harper Perennial).

Buzan, T. (2014) *Mind Maps for Business: Using the Ultimate Thinking Tool to Revolutionise How You Work*, 2nd Edition (Harlow: Pearson Education Limited).

Capra, F. (1988) *The Turning Point: Science, Society, and the Rising Culture* (New York: Bantam).

Capra, F. (1997) *The Web of Life: A New Synthesis of Mind and Matter* (New York: Flamingo, HarperCollins).

Carson, R. (2000) *Silent Spring* (London, UK: Penguin Modern Classics).

Checkland, P. (2000) *Systems Thinking, Systems Practice* (London: Wiley).

Checkland, P. (2002) 'Information systems and systems thinking: Time to unite?' *International Journal of Information Management* 8.4: 239–48.

Churchman, C.W. (1968) *The Systems Approach* (New York: Delacorte Press).

Cooper, R. (1986) 'Organization/disorganization', *Social Science Information* 25.2: 299–335.

Cooper, R. (1992) 'Formal organization as representation; Remote control, displacement and abbreviation', in M. Reed, M. Hughes (eds.), *Rethinking Organization* (London: Sage): 254–72.

Cooper, T. (2005) 'Slower consumption: Reflections on product life cycles and the "throwaway society"', *Journal of Industrial Ecology* 9.1–2: 51–76.

Cooper, T. (2016) *Longer Lasting Products: Alternatives to the Throwaway Society* (Surrey, England: Gower Publishing Limited).

Deming, W.E. (2018) *Out of the Crisis: Reissue* (Cambridge, MA: MIT Press).

Descartes, R. (1998) *A Discourse on Method and the Meditations* (London: Penguin Books).

The Economist (2012) 'Apple and the American economy', *The Economist*, 23 January, 13:46 by R.A. (www.economist.com/blogs/freeexchange/2012/01/supply-chains, accessed 6 April 2022).

Eker, S., Zimmermann, N., Carnohan, S., Davies, M. (2018) 'Participatory system dynamics modelling for housing, energy, and wellbeing interactions', *Building Research & Information* 46.7: 738–54.

Financial Times Online (2015) *Big Pharma Risks Public Backlash on Antibiotics, Says Jim O'Neill*, 14 May (www.ft.com/content/8a6f6cf6-f95e-11e4-ae65-00144feab7de, accessed 6 April 2022).

Fisher, C., Lovell, A., Valero-Silva, N. (2013) *Business Ethics and Values*, 4th Edition (London: Pearson Financial-Times).

Goldacre, B. (2013) *Bad Pharma: How Medicine Is Broken, and How We Can Fix It* (London: Fourth Estate).

Gyllenhammer, P. (1977) *People at Work* (Reading, MA: Addison-Wesley).

Hjorth, P., Bagheri, A. (2006) 'Navigating towards sustainable development: A systems dynamics approach', *Futures* 38: 74–92.

Ishikawa, K. (1986) *Guide to Quality Control* (Tokio: JUSE).

Jackson, M.C. (2019) *Critical Systems Thinking and the Management of Complexity* (Chichester, UK: Wiley).

Juran, J.M. (2008) *Juran on Quality by Design: The New Steps for Planning Quality Into Goods and Services* (New York: Free Press).

Kapmeier, F., Gonçalves, P. (2018) 'Wasted paradise? Policies for small island states to manage tourism-driven growth while controlling waste generation: The case of the Maldives', *System Dynamics Review* 34.1–2: 172–221.

Kuhn, T. (2012) *The Structure of Scientific Revolutions: 50th Anniversary Edition* (Chicago: University of Chicago Press).

Lee, B.H., Struben, J., Bingham, C.B. (2018) 'Collective action and market formation: An integrative framework', *Strategic Management Journal* 39.1: 242–66.

Lietaer, B., Amsperger, C., Brunnhuber, S., Goemer, S. (2012) *Money and Sustainability: The Missing Link* (Axminster, UK: Triarchy Press).

London, B. (1932) *Ending the Depression Through Planned Obsolescence* (http://upload.wikimedia.org/wikipedia/commons/2/27/London_(1932)_Ending_the_depression_through_planned_obsolescence.pdf, accessed 6 April 2022).

Lorenz, E.N. (1972) *Predictability; Does the Flap of a Butterfly's Wings in Brazil Set Off a Tornado in Texas?*, American Association for the Advancement of Science 139th Meeting, MIT (https://static.gymportalen.dk/sites/lru.dk/files/lru/132_kap6_lorenz_artikel_the_butterfly_effect.pdf, accessed 6 April 2022).

Lovelock, J. (2000) *Gaia: A New Look at Life on Earth* (Oxford, England: Oxford University Press).

Lovelock, J. (2007) *The Revenge of Gaia: Earth's Climate Crisis and the Fate of Humanity* (New York: Basic Books).

Meadows, D.L. (2001) *Fish Banks, Ltd: Game Administrator's Manual* (Durham, NH: University of New Hampshire).

Meadows, D.L., Randers, J., Meadows, D. (2006) *The Limits of Growth: The 30-Year Update* (London: Earthscan).

Mingers, J., White, L. (2010) 'A review of the recent contribution of systems thinking to operational research and management science', *European Journal of Operational Research* 207.3: 1147–61.

Morgan, G. (2006) *Images of Organization* (London: Sage).

Myant, M., Drahokoupil, J. (2010) *Transition Economies: Political Economy in Russia, Eastern Europe, and Central Asia* (Hoboken: Wiley).

Seddon, J. (2010) *Systems Thinking in the Public Sector* (Axminster, UK: Triarchy Press).

Senge, P.M. (2010) *The Fifth Discipline: The Art and Practice of the Learning Organization* (London: Random House).

Sterman, J.D. (2014) 'Interactive web-based simulations for strategy and sustainability: The MIT sloan learning edge management flight simulators, part I', *System Dynamics Review* 30.1–2: 89–121.

Taylor, F.W. (1998) *The Principles of Scientific Management* (New York: Dover Publications).

Trist, E.L., Bamforth, K.W. (1951) 'Some social and psychological consequences of the long-wall method of coal-getting', *Human Relations* 4.1: 3–38.

Trochim, W., Cabrera, D., Milstein, B., Gallagher, R., Leischow, S. (2006) 'Practical challenges of systems thinking and modelling in public health', *American Journal of Public Health* 96.3: 538–46.

von Bertalanffy, L. (2015) *General System Theory: Foundations, Development, Applications* (New York: George Braziler).

Waring, A. (2010) *Practical Systems Thinking* (London: International Thompson Business Press).

Wiener, N. (2019) *Cybernetics or Control and Communication in the Animal and the Machine* (London: The MIT Press).

18

Developing sustainably responsible strategies in business

Mathias Schüz

This chapter provides the reader with a better understanding of how companies can assess their strategic options for business development in order to comply with demands from different environments, respectively, stakeholders. For this, it clarifies the deeper meaning and interrelation of fundamental terms, such as *sustainability*, *responsibility*, and *ethics*. Furthermore, it discloses the significance of sustainably responsible activities for the long-term success of business strategies. Participants of this course can:

- Learn how to gain a competitive advantage by developing sustainable strategies that cope with the different challenges of economic, social, and ecological issues.

- Develop strategies that cope with threats and exploit opportunities by applying strengths and compensating for weaknesses.

- Understand the deeper meaning of responsibility, sustainability, and ethics.

- Check whether a strategic option is in compliance with demands for sustainable corporate responsibility.

DOI: 10.4324/9781003294665-23

- Comprehend the deeper ethical reasoning behind the principles of UN Global Compact and Sustainable Development Goals (SDGs).

- Relate the need for sustainable responsible strategies on climate change, among other issues.

Introduction

All living beings must respond to challenges in order to survive, and human beings cultivate the planet in order to realise a happy life. Technological and scientific advances, as well as economic efficiency, allow nature's power and resources to be exploited strategically. Meanwhile, the risks inherent in this have become highly visible while outweighing the opportunities in many regards.

Climate change is probably one of the world's most publicly discussed problems. The recent increase in average global temperature is likely to be caused by humans, that is, anthropogenic in nature (IPCC, 2022), and thus also falls within the sphere of responsibility of humankind (Schüz, 2021b: 304). In addition to climate change, scientific analyses assume eight other anthropogenic factors: eutrophication, loss of biodiversity, changes in land use, ocean acidification, ozone depletion, freshwater consumption, aerosol pollution of the atmosphere, and the introduction of new substances and life forms in general. By mutually reinforcing each other, they can lead to a domino effect that can destroy the balance of the Earth's biosphere irreversibly (cf. Steffen et al., 2015).

Such a collapse would have incalculable consequences for our established economic system, which itself can be regarded as a major cause of the ecological crisis. This would prove true the old wisdom that the consequences of most activities eventually fall back on the causers. For too long, it has been ignored that short-term gains are often a trade-off for losses on the social and environmental front.

Economic profits that are not gained from fair exchange should be considered as robbery. As such, they are no longer the fruit of economic actions as originally understood by ancient philosophers and even later by Adam Smith. They considered 'just exchange' as the basis not only of economics but also of good community life in general (cf. Aristotle, 2009: 1135b15; Smith, 2016: 83 f; Schüz, 2021b: 42 f.). In his *Philosophy of Money*, Georg Simmel elaborated such conclusions on exchange by situating it between robbery and gift, respectively, charity (cf. Simmel, 1989: 66; Schüz, 2021b: 49). Accordingly, exchange is a balance of give and

Figure 18.1: Idea of fair exchange between charity and robbery.

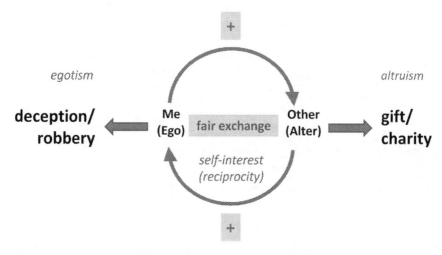

Source: Translated from Schüz (2021a: 8).

take and thus the fundament of economics (see figure 18.1; cf. Aristotle, 2009: 1132b10–20; Cordero, 1988: 682; Smith, 2016: 83; Schüz, 2021b: 40–8).

In the 19th century at the latest, value chains increasingly degenerated into chains of value destruction, in which some of the links were no longer based on exchange relationships but on robberies (cf. Schüz, 2021b: 50 f). With the Industrial Revolution, the centuries-old practice of reciprocity in business and society came to an end.

Countless problems, disasters, and catastrophes caused by the modern corporate world, such as those ascribed to Foxconn in China's supply industry (Chan et al., 2020; Hick, 2012; SACOM, 2012; NN, 2012; Ts and dpa, 2012; cf. ERC, Ethics Research Center, 2016), Monsanto in India's agriculture, Lehman Brothers in the financial industry, BP in the Gulf of Mexico, and Tepco in Fukushima, have broadened the minds of many business leaders, as surveys (Lacy et al., 2010; KPMG, 2011, 2015; PwC, 2010, 2014) and trend research (Ernst and Young, 2013) have proven (Schüz, 2012: 8, 2019: 41–50). Companies have recognised that gaining a long-term competitive advantage is only possible if one has respect for the interests of all the stakeholders involved and for the greater whole of nature. Otherwise, they might lose their stakeholders' trust, an important precondition for successful business and a core purpose of sustainable strategic management. Furthermore, with nature they might destroy the basis of existence in the present and future for their own and future generations (Stead and Stead, 2013: 9ff).

Consequently, companies' understanding of responsibility has undergone a paradigm shift from being purely aligned to the financial interests of shareholders to having a **triple responsibility** encompassing economic, social, and environmental dimensions. Explicitly demanded by Edward Barbier (1987), the idea gained worldwide acceptance with John Elkington's concept of the triple bottom line (1997). Furthermore, the corporate world has learned to respond to the consequences of their activities for **future generations**, that is, acting sustainably, incorporating a time dimension of corporate responsibility, the fourth dimension. The challenge is to do 'business without trade-offs' (Freeman et al., 2020). Sustainably responsible leaders assure fair exchange processes along the whole supply chain, including dealing with nature and all concerned stakeholders (Schüz, 2021b: 50).

Together, the four dimensions of corporate responsibility comprise SCR (**sustainable corporate responsibility**), illustrated by a model developed by Schüz (2012). This model is described in more detail later. It provides a conceptual framework that 'advances our understanding about the role, dynamics, and impact of corporations in the creation of sustainable social, environmental and economic value' complementarily as demanded by one of the *Principles of Responsible Management Education* (PRME, principle 4). How can SCR be applied when developing business strategies?

This book chapter examines such question and outlines a practical approach to integrating SCR into strategic management lessons. First, it addresses why and how strategies and SCR can be integrated into the **open system** of a company. Second, it explains the different key terms, scopes, and degrees of SCR. Third, it links the SCR model to typical models of strategic management, such as PESTEL (political, economic, societal, technological, ecological, and legal) (cf. Farmer and Richman, 1965), Michael Porter's *Five Forces* (Porter, 2008: 3–35), and SWOT/TOWS (strengths, weaknesses, opportunities, and threats) analyses (Weihrich, 1982). Furthermore, it offers three sessions based on a case study. It gives students the opportunity to apply the tools for developing sustainably responsible strategies which are efficient enough for economic survival while, at the same time, being acceptable to different stakeholders and consistent with an environmental agenda. Each session can be completed by undergraduate students in an hour after having been introduced to the topic, based on experiences at the School of Management and Law at Zurich University of Applied Sciences, Switzerland. Finally, further teaching resources are given, and key articles and books for a deeper understanding recommended.

Strategic planning and SCR in the corporate world

The purpose of business strategies is to gain a **competitive advantage** and to support the **survival** of the company. How can one develop those strategies? There are many different approaches, concepts, frameworks, and methods that advise on how to develop business strategies and how to make decisions.

For the reasons set out previously, whatever top managers decide on as their business strategy, it should be sustainably responsible towards the justifiable demands of nature and of **stakeholders**. This increases the opportunities for profitability, stakeholder **trust,** and the needs of the greater whole. They are interdependent. The following **systemic view of companies** reveals the inner link between strategic management and corporate responsibility, since both are exploratory **heuristic research models for reasonable courses of action** in complex and dynamic environments.

Systemic view of companies

Like ecological systems, companies are **viable** when they (a) maintain their identity for generations (**self-preservation**), (b) cooperate with other systems (**co-preservation**), and (c) adapt to their changing environments (**preservation of the whole**). They preserve themselves by exchanging **matter, energy**, and **information**. They use limited resources, such as materials, people, and skills (input), in order to create valuable products or services (output), which external systems are willing to pay for. This transformation process is profitable so long as income exceeds costs (Schüz, 1999: 116ff; Stead and Stead, 2013: 21; Blackmore et al., 2012).

However, there are many areas where the **risk of failure** needs to be considered. All activities are aimed at creating a particular outcome but often have unforeseen consequences too. To what extent can an organisation take these into account? It depends on its intrinsic culture, which functions similarly to a sensory system in natural organisms. Due to its members' respective **virtues** or **vices**, it might filter out environmental information. For instance, the vice of **greed** ignores the needs of customers and other stakeholders and consequently provokes their resistance. Thus, profit-driven companies often have a one-sided view of their environment and correspondingly adopt narrow-minded strategies, such as maximising profits by exploiting their customers or suppliers. In contrast, the virtues of **trustworthiness** and **openness** gain stakeholders' **trust** and lead to better relationships with them based on fair exchange. Companies with **integrity** create and share value for all involved stakeholders (cf. Porter and Kramer, 2006). Profit-driven companies only care about economic performance indicators, such as share prices or credit ratings, while those with integrity also take social and ecological indicators into account, such as consumer complaints or dwindling natural resources. Thus, strategies based on virtues involve corporate structures, processes, and behaviour that respond more adequately to the demands of diverse stakeholders.

Kotter and Heskett (1992), who empirically researched and compared **corporate cultures**, found that they were either '**adaptive**' or '**non-adaptive**' to environmental needs and changes. The former react sensibly and fit in well within the business context: their strategies and practices respond sustainably to changing markets and new business opportunities and threats. The latter ignore all the signals and are just focused on protecting their status: if anything, they are confused by complaints about socially or environmentally insensitive behaviour. For the most part, their **input filters** accept only self-affirming and economic feedback, and so they tend to be seen as 'reactive', 'risk averse', inwardly focused, and 'bureaucratic' (Kotter and Heskett, 1992: 44). Over long periods, they might fail to deliver excellent performance, unless their competitive advantage is based on fraudulent activities or on monopolistic or oligopolistic cartels.

An example of the latter might be the commodity provider Glencore. Economically, it is very successful due to its strong position in the market, but it is still faced with complaints, be they unjustified or legitimate, about its negative impact on the working conditions of its suppliers or its irreversible exploitation of nature (Harvey and Pidd, 2011). According to Glencore's newest sustainability report, it is committed to 'improve our commercial, social, and environmental performance' (Glencore, 2021: 2). Obviously, the company has recognised the need for a change towards an adaptive corporate culture.

One could say that corporate virtues or vices respectively open up or close down a company's filter system for interacting with its environment. In either case, they are the company's responsibility. If it chooses to ignore or suppress this responsibility, it might face expensive (even life-threatening) **feedbacks from authorities** or other stakeholders. In order to minimise such risks and to increase the chances of success, business managers are therefore advised to use **sustainably responsible strategies** when planning their businesses. These strategies should encourage all employees to act more responsibly and, consequently, overcome the company's negative aspects. It may develop more virtuous behaviour in its culture, which, in turn, will increase the acceptance of the stakeholders involved. Actions with negative consequences are viewed as breaches of duty and usually provoke resistance in those affected, who might charge the company for compensation as a result. Such reactions should be kept in mind when planning strategically to secure a company's income in the long term.

Figure 18.2 depicts the company as an open system **creating value** step by step from input to output. A well-formulated vision or mission statement might focus all employees' efforts in one particular direction, while the strategy defines the milestones by which the vision could become reality and reshapes the structure and

Figure 18.2: The company as an open social system.

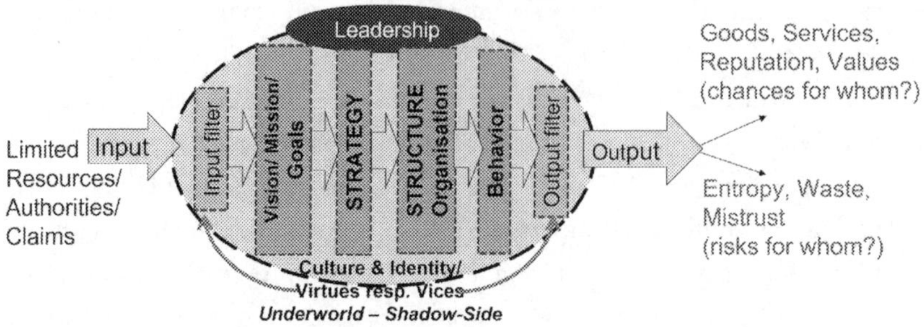

Source: Derived from Rieckmann (2000: 76).

processes of the organisation, which in turn influences organisational behaviour and results in more efficient and effective output.

From a systemic perspective, the success of a company depends on how it responds to environmental demands. Thereby, its strategy becomes a rational concept of how to prevail in the market. Before we discuss how a company can be sustainably responsible, the next section describes the typical stages in the development of a systemic strategy.

Stages of systemic strategy development

In order to meet environmental challenges successfully, a structured approach to the strategy of all organisations is recommended. One convincing 'formula' for identifying '**strategic options**' is to choose a particular **direction** and then select an appropriate strategy **method** (Johnson et al., 2005: 340; cf. Hill and Gareth, 2012). The direction can initially be derived from **Ansoff's matrix** for product and/or market development (ibid.: 354ff; Ansoff, 1988: 109), and then from strategic recommendations proposed by a **SWOT/TOWS analysis**. The methods that a company can follow range from 'organic growth' to 'mergers and acquisitions' and 'strategic alliances' (ibid.: 359).

Although the choice of Ansoff matrix and methods encompasses sustainable responsibility issues, for reasons of space, this chapter will concentrate on strategic development using a SWOT/TOWS analysis (Weihrich, 1982). The following steps in the strategic management process can be taken:

1. The organisation's **vision and mission** have to be defined. They depict the desired future and provide the main purpose and focus for the strategy (Crawford, 2005), something that applies to all activities within the organisation. In addition to principal business activities, they might consist

of key objectives, beliefs, values, and stakeholders (Dobson et al., 2004). However, they will only provide a focus for organisational behaviour if senior leaders act as role models and **'walk the talk'**. Otherwise, such declarations can easily backfire, as demonstrated by the example of **Tepco**, the Japanese energy provider. In September 2010, the firm released its new *Vision 2020*, which made a commitment to 'value social trust', 'open the way to the future', and 'maximize human and technological potential' as three '[m]anagement [p]olicies for the direction of [their] business'. Furthermore, it promised 'to ensure energy security, [and] deliver stable supplies of low-cost, eco-friendly electricity' (Tepco, 2010). Six months later, a nuclear catastrophe took place at Tepco's Fukushima power plant.

2. The company's **external environment (or context)** has to be analysed, and what responses are provoked by **threats** and **opportunities** (Boddy, 2008: 84, 245f). It can be analysed (a) in the industry-specific micro-environment or (b) in the general macro-environment. Porter's 'five forces' – substitutes, barriers to entry, bargaining power of customers, and suppliers, as well as that of competitors (ibid.: 93ff) – characterise the former, while the PESTEL frameworks differentiate between six macro-environmental spheres: the political, economic, societal, technological, ecological, and legal (ibid.: 96ff). Tepco ignored many of the external threats and opportunities, such as the environmentalists' recommendations that it should build at least 15-meter tsunami protection walls along the shore. Instead, to save money, it only built the wall 6 meters high (Kogure, 2012).

3. The **internal environment (or context)** has to be analysed as to whether its elements reveal, in comparison with its competitors, strengths and weaknesses along Michael Porter's **'value chain'** (Porter, 1985: 36–47). These represent the company's ability to run its business profitably and the related consequences responsibly (Boddy, 2008: 248f). After the explosion at Tepco's nuclear plant in Fukushima, many weaknesses (compared to its competitors) came to light (cf. Redaktion, 2012): the company had adopted a strict focus on shareholder value and low safety standards, engaged in corrupt practices with officials, and ignored individual, social, and environmental integrity.

4. The entrepreneurial risk, the opportunity to either lose or secure income, has to be identified by combining the external and internal environments with the following question: How far do the internal strengths and weaknesses allow the company to deal with threats and exploit opportunities? The

answers can be derived from (a) a SWOT analysis and (b) the **TOWS framework** for developing strategic recommendations. The latter considers the different combinations of identified threats ($T_{1, 2,} \ldots$) and opportunities ($O_{1, 2,} \ldots$), weaknesses ($W_{1, 2,} \ldots$), and strengths ($S_{1, 2,} \ldots$), resulting in a list of recommendations (Weihrich, 1982, see Figure 18.3). Tepco could have addressed its low safety standards (W) and the threat from the global anti-nuclear movement (T) by upgrading its safety installations to the standard used by a competitor engaging in best practice (WT strategy).

Figure 18.4 depicts the open system of a company within its different external and internal environments. It clarifies the interdependencies between internal capabilities and external influences. At this point, it should be noted that the term '**environment**' encompasses all the external or internal surroundings of a company with which it exchanges material, energy, or information. For example, in the case of the 'ecological environment', such resources are provided by nature. Internal environments are built by employees who may, for example, put all their efforts into realising the company's goals or who may, on the other hand, withdraw their goodwill for certain possibly vindictive reasons.

5. However, each of the strategic recommendations derived from the TOWS framework has to be checked in terms of whether it is acceptable according to the checklist of the SCR model. Only then, strategists can select and prioritise suitable recommendations. The final decision depends on the company's capabilities and the resources at its disposal.

Figure 18.3: Strategic recommendations through TOWS analysis.

Internal Environment \ External Environment	Opportunities (O)	Threats (T)
Strengths (S)	**SO Strategic Options** *Offensive Strategies:* Generate options here that use strengths to take advantage of opportunities	**ST Strategic Options** *Preventive Strategies:* Generate options here that use strengths to avoid threats
Weaknesses (W)	**WO Strategic Options** *Development Strategies:* Generate options here that take advantage of opportunities by overcoming weaknesses	**WT Strategic Options** *Defensive Strategies:* Generate options here that minimise weaknesses and avoid threats

Source: Adapted from Weihrich (1982); Johnson et al. (2005); Büchler (2014: 81).

Figure 18.4: The company systemically embedded in its different environments.

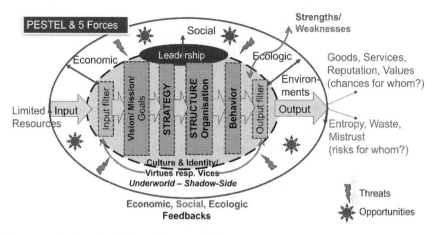

Source: Further developed from Rieckmann (2000: 76).

Since steps 1 to 4 are established tools of strategic management practice, they are not discussed in detail here, but they are applied directly in the Frog case study sessions that follow, together with sustainable responsibility issues. The SCR model and related checklist mentioned in step 5 will be introduced in the following section.

A holistic model for sustainable corporate responsibility

The checklist is based on the SCR model (see Figure 18.11) published in Schüz (2012) and further developed (Schüz, 2021b: 295f). This model outlines in depth what sustainable responsibility means and how far it can be adopted in the business world. It requires a deeper understanding of what responsibility actually means.

The structure of responsibility

The term '**responsibility**' describes the relationship between an acting subject S causing **consequences** $C_{1, 2 \ldots m}$, which are assessed by **authorities** $A_{1,2 \ldots n}$ as positive or negative (cf. Picht, 1969: 319). The structure of any responsibility is depicted graphically in Figure 18.5. A subject, be it an individual or a company, is

Figure 18.5: The structure of responsibility.

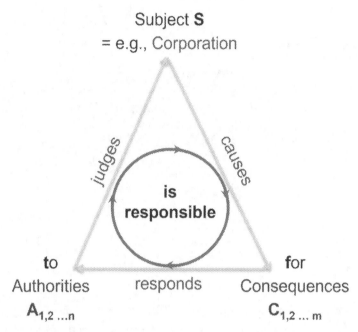

Source: Schüz (2012: 9).

responsible for the intended and unintended consequences of its activities towards different authorities.

Authorities such as stakeholders evaluate a company's activity as responsible or irresponsible, praising or condemning it. Their verdicts differ due to their **different value systems** and their view of the consequences. A magistrate in court might decide to let someone off for a crime, while people with a vested interest, or even the wrongdoer's own conscience, might deem their actions to have been irresponsible. Shareholders usually evaluate disasters differently from other stakeholders, so one can therefore consider responsibility as a **construction** with different solutions (Bayertz, 1995: 4).

For instance, the explosion at Tepco's nuclear power plant in Fukushima can be seen as an act of nature beyond human control, because it was caused by a tsunami. Consequently, the operating company can be absolved from blame. But further investigations showed that Tepco had neglected cracks in the cooling system for economic reasons. Instead, it had bribed safety officials to ignore the faults. Neglected duties of care, mismanagement, and corrupt practices for the sake of maximising profit were therefore jointly responsible for the catastrophe, with tremendous social and environmental implications. As a result, 'the public has targeted Tepco, Japanese politicians, nuclear experts and the media, which has promoted the myth of safe nuclear plants for the past 50 years', as Satoko Kogure, a freelance journalist based in Japan, stated. From his point of view, Tepco and its executives should be held responsible for the disaster, while the Japanese government still tries to exculpate them (Kogure, 2012; cf. Satoko, 2011). This example shows how *responsibility* is a variable term, depending on how one assesses consequences and which authority is accepted. Thus, the (corporate) responsibility Tepco bears changes depending on whether its own government, environmentalists, or the United Nations are recognised as the judging authority.

The triple corporate responsibility

But what should corporate responsibility comprise? It is important to distinguish three dimensions of responsibility, each ranging from narrow to broad.

As mentioned previously, companies are open systems embedded in their economic and social spheres as well as within their own ecological environment. With all of them, they exchange resources. In the long run, they can only survive when they cooperate with other systems (such as those represented by stakeholders) to fit into the greater whole of their different environments: in other words, when they find their ecological niche or the fundamental meaning of their existence.

Figure 18.6: Corporate responsibility as a feedback loop with its environments.

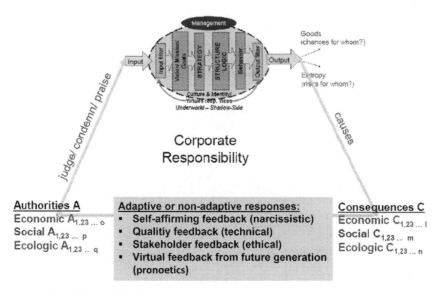

Source: Adapted from Schüz (2019: 238).

Thus, **corporate health** can only be sustained when physical, social, and mental resources are exchanged fairly (Schüz, 1999: 116 ff).

Instead of acting in a purely selfish manner, a company should pursue '**enlightened self-interest**' (Ikerd, 1999) and take on responsibilities that gain the trust of stakeholders, ensuring low **transaction costs**, creating willingness to cooperate in the long term, and protecting its own conditions for existence. Hence, besides economic responsibility, the dimensions of social and ecological responsibilities are fundamental for sustaining long-term survival.

The three dimensions have to be balanced, because at first glance they often appear to be conflicting. Social and ecological engagement seems to harm economic results. But this is an investment which yields returns through stakeholder cooperation in general, especially in terms of customer loyalty. If they are not integrated, the neglected environments **have a negative impact on stakeholder confidence** in the company, thus causing high economic losses.

Consequently, one can **define** (see Figure 18.7) **corporate responsibility** as the following: a manager or a company acts responsibly when they are **responding** (a) to the consequences of their actions, (b) to the authorities **economically** by being profitable to shareholders, **socially** by getting along well with all stakeholders, and **ecologically** by acting responsibly towards the natural world. By responding to shareholders self-preservation is attained; by responding to ethical demands, co-preservation with stakeholders is enabled; and by responding to 'nature' or 'being', preservation of the whole is achieved (Schüz, 1999: 76 f). Figure 18.6 outlines the triple corporate responsibility with its different consequences and authorities.

Figure 18.7: Triple corporate responsibility.

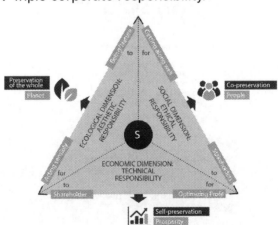

Source: Adapted from Schüz (2017: 34).

The triple responsibility can be reasoned in terms of systems theory as well as philosophy. Sustainable development can only be seen as 'interaction among three systems: the biological (and other resource) system (BS), the economic systems (ES), and the social system (SS)' (Barbier, 1987: 104). Philosophically, businesses do not survive solely by pursuing self-preservation (economic dimension to secure prosperity) but – like all other forms of life – also need to co-preserve the social dimension (to protect all the people they are depending on) as well as to preserve the ecological dimension (to preserve our planet, which nurtures all life forms) (cf. Schüz, 1999: 40 f, 71–81). In other words: 'Business is embedded in society and in a physical world' (Freeman et al., 2020: 21).

The triple corporate responsibility model also resembles John Elkington's concept of the **triple bottom line** (1997). The latter values the output of a company as, for example, worked out in the standards of Global Reporting Initiative (GRI, 2022) or in ratings provided by RobecoSAM (2022). The former also tackles the root causes in order to improve corporate behaviour. For example, Shell and other companies have defined their corporate responsibility according to the **'three Ps'** of people, planet, and profit. They emphasise that these three responsibilities have to be balanced to a large extent in order to achieve sustainable development (Aragón-Correa et al., 2017, cf. Shell, 2015).

However, one can argue that these public statements, as numerous as they might be, could be misleading, because they do not walk the talk in all the three dimensions. The accusation of *greenwashing* can be made. In response, the attacked parties often use the trade-off argument as justification. In this way, they suggest that the perception of one dimension of responsibility is always at the expense of the other (for example, investing in environmental protection at the cost of the economic or social dimension). However, they then ignore that the profits gained are still the result of robbery in one or two dimensions. (cf. Schüz, 2021b: 86). In their book of the same name, Edward Freeman et al. have therefore pleaded for a *Power of And – Responsible Business Without Trade-Offs* (2020) and substantiated the possibilities for this with numerous examples.

The aims, the applied methods of the three dimensions of corporate responsibility, can be characterised in more detail as follows and each illustrated by the example of climate change.

1. The economic dimension and its functional approaches

The economic dimension of sustainable corporate responsibility assures the **profitability** of a company. It delivers the right means to an end in order to ensure survival. Through **technical responsibility**, all existing business administration techniques enable the organisation to **function** and to secure the necessary income to allow all costs to be covered **efficiently**. The aim is to minimise losses and to gain profits through efficient and **effective** products and services based on fair exchange, that respect **reciprocal** benefit of the involved business partners. In this case, the company functions profitably and is able to preserve itself over the long term. However, if their success is measured only in terms of short-term profit maximisation, economic responsibility too often ignores the social and ecological costs. These then take the form of reputational damages or, for example, climate change with the related energy crisis. The ignored costs then threaten the survival of the originators.

2. Corporate social responsibility and ethics

Corporate social responsibility (Mey et al., 2007) is related to *ethics*, which can be defined as the art of 'getting along well with each other' (Schüz, 2019: 99), especially with all internal and external stakeholders. As exchange partners, each of these requires fair treatment, but with different expectations and claims (cf. Sandel, 2009: 27). To cope with their different needs, companies are advised to first weigh the **impact** of their activities on them with the **utilitarian (teleological) ethics**. Then, they should consider whether or not they have respected their fundamental rights according to the **duty (deontological) ethics**. Finally, they can practice **virtue (aretological) ethics** to avoid risky backlashes of predatory behaviour. It inspires how to behave in the most appropriate way according to one's capabilities in a specific situation. This means the company should develop corporate virtues and, with them, an ethical culture in which the employees are able to act ethically with integrity.

The three ethics approaches complement each other, as all have their strengths and limitations (Schüz, 2019: 227 f). They can be applied for solving dilemmas in business and organisations (cf. e.g. Collins and Kanashiro, 2021). The following three exemplary test questions serve as a first orientation for practical applications in ethical business.

The **reciprocity test** asks: 'Does my intended activity treat all affected parties (stakeholders) along the value chain fairly?' (Schüz, 2021b: 261). The exploitative use of natural resources does not pass this test. In turn, the reactions of nature in the form of climate change, species extinction, and pandemics fall back on the polluters. For this reason, the challenge of a '**circular economy**' should be taken up to ensure fair exchange relationships in nature and society (cf. Kirchherr et al., 2017; Ritzen and Sandström, 2017; Michelini et al., 2017; Braungart and McDonough, 2002).

The **'daylight test'** (Pagano, 1987: 8ff) indicates whether an ethical duty is violated with a planned activity: 'How would I feel if my decision became known to my acquaintances or even to the public (media)?' If it does not conform to the rules established in society, it would be criticised accordingly or even denounced. What is not suitable for daylight is then carried out secretly underground (Schüz, 2021b: 261). In the fight against climate change, the forces in society are currently shifting as to which energy sources are still accepted or outlawed. Movements like *Friday for Future* or *Last Generation* are currently trying to influence the public's consciousness so that the use of fossil energy is no longer seen as fit for daylight.

The **empathy test** gives a first hint, whether an activity can be seen as virtue ethically acceptable: 'How would I feel if I myself were affected by my action?' (Schüz, 2021b: 262). When I put myself in the emotional shoes of Pacific Islanders whose land is being successively lost to climate change, I can better understand the urgency of fighting it.

All three ethics approaches, with their corresponding test questions, thus provide clear evidence that the struggle against climate change with the demand for renewable energies is ethically justified. The result is not always so explicit. In any way, they can be related to the triangle of responsibility, as the following Figure 18.8 shows.

Figure 18.8: Corporate social responsibility and ethical approaches.

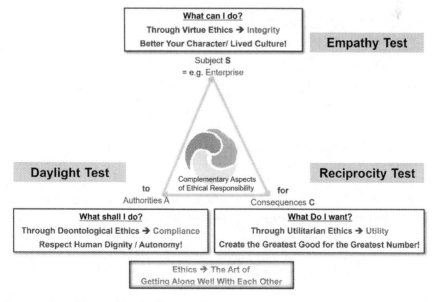

Source: Adapted from Schüz (2021b: 300).

3. Corporate ecological responsibility and aesthetics

The *ecological dimension* refers to aesthetic responsibility. Aesthetics examines how we perceive the environment sensually. Through our sensory organs we perceive what is useful or harmful for our survival. Most negative influences from the environment can be directly tasted, smelled, touched, or heard. The senses normally show us which actions are ecologically sensible and which are not. However, our civilised way of life has alienated us more and more from nature and dulled our senses for it. We have become accustomed to noise, unhealthy air, polluted soil or water. In addition, the technical exploitation of nature has limited its self-healing powers. Aesthetic responsibility appeals to us to act wisely with all our senses, reason, and intuition. It inspires us as to what we should strive for and what we should avoid. As our sensibility and mindfulness grow, so does our creativity. It helps us find meaningful, creative ways to adapt to changed circumstances using new insights, ideas, and strategies.

Thus, the ecological dimension of responsibility is a wake-up call for humanity to organise its activities for the benefit of nature instead of harming it. One example is, the drought and heat of the past summer (IPCC, 2022: 10, 14) have challenged our senses worldwide to no longer ignore the issue of climate change. Dried-up rivers and lakes, melting polar ice caps, forest fires, and devastation of large areas of land are obvious and caused great economic damage.

Scopes of triple responsibility

Each dimension of the triple corporate responsibility model has a different **scope** in terms of how far responsibility is concretely taken. Three steps for each are proposed following Jean Piaget (1932) and Lawrence Kohlberg (1971):[1] (a) the narrow scope of responsibility, striving for **selfish** benefit; (b) the medium or mid-scope,

---

1   Jean Piaget discovered that as children grow, they show different stages of moral development (1932). Lawrence Kohlberg continued Piaget's research with adults. Both defined three main stages of ethical behaviour: the 'preconventional', 'conventional', and 'postconventional' (Kohlberg 1971: 163ff). While preconventional moral behaviour is more egoistically responsive to sanctions and appraisals, conventional morality is based on social convention and reciprocity, thus fair exchange. Only at the postconventional level is the actor oriented to universal principles based on reasonable autonomy, for example, in the sense of Kant's categorical imperative (Schüz, 2019: 151–153), as opposed to law and order, which might represent only particular interests.

Figure 18.9: Different scopes of responsibility.

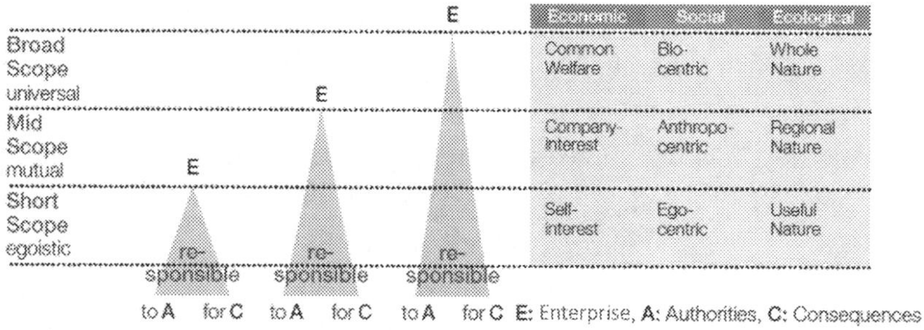

				Economic	Social	Ecological
Broad Scope universal			E	Common Welfare	Bio-centric	Whole Nature
		E				
Mid Scope mutual				Company-interest	Anthropo-centric	Regional Nature
	E					
Short Scope egoistic				Self-interest	Ego-centric	Useful Nature
	re-sponsible	re-sponsible	re-sponsible			

to A   for C   to A   for C   to A   for C   E: Enterprise, A: Authorities, C: Consequences

Source: Schüz (2017: 37).

striving for mutual or **reciprocal** benefit (fair exchange); and (c) the broad scope, striving for altruistic or **universal** benefit – regardless of selfish interests. The second scope represents then fair exchange as the reciprocal middle between egoistic robbery and altruistic charity.

According to Figure 18.9, the scope of responsibility of each dimension can be expressed differently: economic responsibility can range from self-interest and company interest through to the common good; social responsibility can range from egocentric and anthropocentric through to a biocentric orientation; and environmental responsibility can focus from the useful, through the regional, right up to a global scale. Detailed explanations of these categories can be found in Schüz (2012: 12f, 2019: 77ff).

The concept of sustainable corporate responsibility

The triple corporate responsibility model described so far still excludes the whole issue of **sustainability** (cf. Cannon, 2012). While the different scopes of the former are more related to space (e.g. How far does responsibility reach on this planet?), the latter introduces the dimension of **time**. Time becomes a factor when one starts to consider how long responsible actions should last or be sustained.

Because of its worldwide dissemination, we can refer to the term 'sustainability' as it was defined in 1987 by the **Brundtland Commission**: 'Sustainable development is development that meets the needs of the present without compromising the ability of future generations to meet their own needs' (Brundtland Commission, 1987). In short, it declares that we should not create a disadvantage for **future generations** without explaining whether this includes future generations of non-human species, such as animals and plants (the **biocentric** approach), or whether this only takes the future of human beings into account (the **anthropo- centric** approach). Moreover, it does not define what *disadvantage* means. Does it mean securing their survival or – more strongly – that they should have the same life chances as us?

In 2015, the United Nations concretised the idea of sustainability with its 17 Sustainable Development Goals (SDGs) and 169 subgoals. By 2030, goals such as no poverty, zero hunger, clean water and sanitation, climate action, life below water, life on land, etc. are to be achieved (SDG, 2022). The SDGs can be associated with the three dimensions of triple responsibility (see Figure 18.10).

Combined with our model of responsibility, it is now quite easy to illustrate all the different ranges and scopes. The **model** of sustainable corporate responsibility (Figure 18.11) is shown as a **clock** with three different **clock faces** representing the triple corporate responsibility. The three **clock hands** are used to indicate the time period as well as the scope of responsibility achieved: the longer they are, the

Figure 18.10: The UN SDGs related to the triple responsibility model.

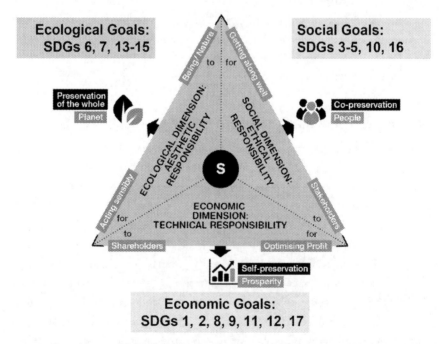

Source: Adapted from Schüz (2021b: 337).

Figure 18.11: Model of sustainable corporate responsibility.

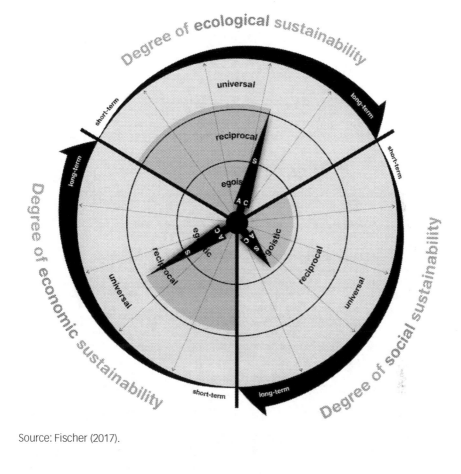

Source: Fischer (2017).

larger scope they represent. The further the hands move round the clock, the more sustainable the responsibility is – in other words, the more the impact on future generations is considered. Like the different scopes, the range of the respective **degrees of sustainability** is divided into three steps: short-term, mid-term, and long-term.

The SCR model can be applied online (Fischer, 2017). There, responsibility profiles as in Figure 18.12 can be obtained by entering percentages of scope and sustainability grades in the input mask (Figure 18.12).

The assessment of the percentages can be carried out via audits, for example, by rating agencies, or with the help of an SCR checklist (Figure 18.13, available and explained in the companion website).

Figure 18.12: Online input mask for percentages of SCR profile in Figure 18.11.

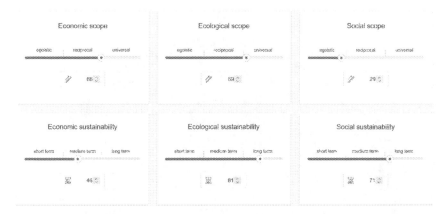

Source: Fischer (2017).

Case A: **Economistic family enterprise**	Case B: **Fundamentalist nature protection organisation**	Case C: **Pragmatic-idealistic pharmaceutical company**
Takes into account social and ecological responsibility and future generations only when it serves its own offspring and long-term profitability.	Privately sponsored and relying on volunteers for its activities, neglecting social needs.	Dedicated primarily to 'improve and preserve human life': when this is fulfilled, profits follow automatically.

Figure 18.13: Examples of organisations' responsibility profiles.

 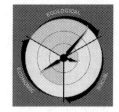 

Source: Schüz (2017: 31).

The strategic importance of SCR

In all scenarios, the SCR model sets the **benchmark** for sustainably responsible strategies. It alerts managers and employees to the essential dimensions of their responsibility with its possible scopes and ranges and allows us to outline the typical **responsibility profiles** of planned actions, individuals, or even entire companies.

Table 18.1: SCR checklist.

Sustainable Corporate Responsibility: SCR Checklist Criteria for acceptance/rejection of a strategic option		
universal: Scope resp. Sustainability Degree: 66.6-99.9%: *altruistic* charity *reciprocal*: Scope resp. Sustainability Degree: 33.3-66.6%: *fair* exchange *egoistic*: Scope resp. Sustainability Degree: 0-33.3%: *unfair/ exploitative* Note: The attainment of the SDGs can also be a criterion for the sustainability degree.	Scope [small: 0-33.3 %] [medium: 33.3-66.6%] [large: 66.6-100%]	Sustainability Degree [shortterm: 0-33.3 %] [midterm: 33.3-66.6%] [longterm: 66.6-100%]
I. Economic dimension: Technical/ Economic responsibility	1	1
I.1 Efficiency: What values/resources are available to realize the option efficiently?	1	1
I.2 Reciprocity: To what extent are the exchange relationships along the option's value chain fair, i. e. in a balance of give and take?	1	1
I.3 Effectiveness: How effectively does the option promote the investor's vision?	1	1
II Social Dimension: Ethical Responsibility	1	1
II.1 Utility ethics (average of II1.a. + II1.b.)	1	1
a. Reciprocity test: Does option treat all affected parties (stakeholders) along the value chain fairly?	1	1
b. Stakeholder discourse (ventilation) test: Has there been a (fictitious or real) discourse with key stakeholders about the option and was this discourse fair and transparent?	1	1
II.2 Duty ethics (average of II.2a. + II.2b.)	1	1
a. Daylight test: How would I feel if the option became known to the public (e. g. media)?	1	1
b. Universalizability/autonomy test (Categorical Imperative): To what extent can the option be elevated to a universal principle or does it violate the dignity/ autonomy of those affected?	1	1
II.3 Virtue ethics (average of II.3a. + II.3b.)	1	1
a. Empathy test: How would I feel if I myself were affected by the option?	1	1
b. Golden mean test: To what extent is the option virtuous, i.e., does it meet the middle ground between two vices and can it be taken as a good example or even as best practice?	1	1
III. Ecological dimension: Aesthetic responsibility	1	1
III.1 Self-reflection: How much does the option serve self-preservation, co-preservation, and preservation of the whole?	1	1
III.2 Reflection on purpose: To what extent are the side effects (e.g. waste) of the option meaningfully integrated back into the natural cycle (e.g. according to the cradle-to-cradle approach)?	1	1
III.3 Holistic reflection: How does the option fit into the larger whole of nature?	1	1

*) Black Knight: Investor who seeks maximum return on investment (RoI) for himself, e.g. by buying companies with lower stock market value than liquidation value in order to break them up and sell the individual parts (e.g. land, machine parks, etc.) at higher prices than they themselves paid for the whole company. They can be invested in the short term (such as Daytrayder), in the mid term and certainly in the long term, if the invested company delivers the profit accordingly.
**) White Knight: Investor who seeks to add value to the company and thereby to themselves through their investment. They tend to be invested for the mid term (such as hedge funds). They can also be invested for the short term (as, for example, a reorganizer), for the mid term, and certainly for the long term.
***) Red Knight: Investor who invests primarily to provide a service to humanity or nature, but also pays attention to profitability. Often foundations, social enterprises, which perform a life-serving mission with great heart and soul (= red). They tend to be invested for the long term (like family businesses). They are rarely invested in the short term (if strategically required), otherwise rather in the mid, mostly in the long term.

Source: Further developed from Schüz (2021b: 291 ff).

They indicate strengths and weaknesses regarding the perceived dimensions of responsibility. They can provide evidence as to whether cars with internal combustion engines or electric motors are more sustainably responsible in the fight against climate change (comparison available at companion website). Furthermore, they allow comparisons with best-practice companies or illustrate gaps between actual and intended profiles. They are particularly useful in selecting the most sustainable strategic options, as we will show in the following case study.

Suggested sessions

General introduction

The following three sessions are an example of how to apply the UN's Principles of Responsible Management Education (PRME). They 'develop the capabilities of students to be future generators of sustainable value for business and society' (principle 1) and follow an 'educational framework' which provides a 'learning experience for responsible leadership' (principle 3).

The sessions use a case study to assist in the development of a sustainably responsible strategy and to apply many of the concepts introduced here as part of sustainable corporate responsibility.

Step by step, the reader has the opportunity to review and select strategic options for their sustainable responsibility in three sessions well-tested at universities.

Case study

The narrative is based on a real case[2] but has been anonymised and modified for teaching purposes in order to focus on sustainable corporate responsibility issues. The aim of the case is to develop **sustainably responsible strategies** for Frog AG in order to resolve its difficult situation. Students should read it carefully and apply their understanding in a series of three sessions, which help progressively to develop strategic options which fulfil sustainably responsible demands from both social and environmental perspectives.

---

2   The German Mainz–based company Werner & Mertz was prosecuted for more than ten years under civil and criminal law for its shoe spray. 224 consumers complained of severe health problems, such as choking and circulatory problems, after using the spray indoors. Finally in 1990, several top managers were sentenced to heavy fines and even imprisonment for negligent bodily injury. With its new product line "Green Frog" (original: 'Grüner Frosch'), the company has been playing a pioneering role and is regarded as a trailblazer for environmentally friendly products (Schüz, 2021b: 302).

The Frog AG case study

The German company Frog AG has been successfully producing shoe polish, leather-care products, and cleansing agents for more than 80 years. Although highly reputable, Frog has recently run into a crisis. For some years, Frog has been selling shoe sprays which probably cause serious health problems. Especially after using it in confined spaces, customers have complained of respiratory problems, dizziness, skin rashes, serious headaches, and nausea, symptoms which sometimes persist for several days.

Dr Sprayman, Frog's CEO, admits to his personal strategic consultant, the freelancer Dr Pestel, that until now the board and the management have not been paying much attention to the customers' complaints. They have discussed the situation in board meetings but not introduced any measures to address the problem. They did not even take any action when the company doctor reported some cases in which employees in the production unit had noticed various health problems in connection with the shoe spray. The executives simply did not want to compromise the sales of this successful and profitable product.

Meanwhile, the editor of a prominent business newspaper has obviously received some insider information about the senior management's attempts to keep the issue quiet. The journalist concerned has started his own research into the case. Police reports have been compiled, and the state attorney has started an investigation. Consumer organisations, health authorities, and medical doctors have begun to warn the public about using the spray in confined spaces. Environmentalists have started a campaign against sprays in general due to their effect on the ozone layer. As a result, even the biggest discounter in the German-speaking market has just announced a product recall.

Frog employees are now regularly receiving enquiries from worried customers without being able to answer them. They therefore pass these questions onto the board, demanding transparency about the real risks of the leather spray. Moreover, after Frog AG's shares slumped sharply, the rumour of an imminent takeover by an American company (a so-called 'black knight') shatters Frog's management and the market. In return, some major shareholders have announced their intention to defend the company against the hostile takeover bid.

During preliminary meetings, Dr Sprayman has mentioned Frog's Ecoclean department, led by Dr Vinegar, which researches and develops new product lines made from pure plant extracts. But Dr Vinegar is regarded as an introvert and is unpopular with his colleagues because of his distant and peculiar behaviour. Dr Sprayman himself considered Dr Vinegar's ideas to be impractical and not marketable. Consequently, he cut Ecoclean's budget considerably, and the board has even been considering closing the department down.

Coincidentally, Dr Pestel has heard one of Ecoclean's market researchers complaining about the bad image that Dr Vinegar's product ideas have inside the company, despite their huge market potential.

Dr Pestel is asked by Dr Sprayman whether he is willing and able to develop restructuring proposals for Frog AG. He is supposed to develop strategic options for coping with the present crisis and for leading the company to a sustainable future. Now it is up to you to support Dr Pestel by carrying out the following tasks, using the online provided worksheets, in order to develop strategic options for Frog AG.

Suggested sessions

Session 1: External and internal influences (60 minutes)

Please note: The indicated worksheets can be downloaded from the companion website.

This session will guide you through the different steps needed to lead Frog AG in the direction of a more sustainably responsible business. Please read the aforementioned case study carefully.

1. Activity: Formulate a brief vision/mission statement for the new Frog AG (use worksheet 1; approximately 10 minutes).

2. Activity: In the next step, analyse Porter's five forces and the relevant environmental spheres according to the PESTEL scheme. Focus on the related threats and opportunities for Frog AG with regard to SCR issues (use worksheet 2; approximately 30 minutes).

3. Activity: Work out Frog's strengths and weaknesses with regard to SCR issues by using Porter's value chain (use worksheet 3; approximately 20 minutes).

Session 2: SWOT/TOWS analysis (60 minutes)

1. Activity: Use the results of session 1 to identify the most challenging threats and opportunities (derived from the Porter's 'five forces' analysis and the PESTEL analysis) and most important strengths and weaknesses (derived from Porter's value chain analysis and the case study). From this, develop strategic options and recommendations with the help of a SWOT/TOWS analysis (use worksheet 4a; approximately 50 minutes).

2. <u>Activity</u>: Prioritise the recommendations according to Frog's capabilities with regard to its culture, available resources, and market situation as described in the previous case study. Select the two most important and feasible strategic options regarding Frog's available resources and capabilities (use worksheet 4b; approximately 10 minutes).

Session 3: SCR compliance (60 minutes)

1. <u>Activity</u>: Select the two prioritised strategic options from session 2, and check their acceptability regarding the SCR model. It might be formulated like: 'Should I invest in more sustainable products such as . . . ?' Go through the questions of the SCR checklist (worksheet 5). The assessment of the respective scopes and sustainability degrees is made in percentages according to the following scheme: values between 0 and 33.3% can be classified as selfish in the sense that more is taken than given in the exchange relationships involved, that is, it is more a case of robbery than fair exchange; values between 33.3 and 66.6% are in the range of fair exchange; values 66.6–100% represent universal/altruistic action that gives more than it takes. In regard with the sustainability degree, you can also check how far the SDGs (as additional material online available at the companion website) are attained.

Additional teaching material and ideas

Developing virtues

Virtues characterise an ethically good person or company. Thus, corporate virtues constitute the character of a good corporate culture. Once developed, they enable individuals or organisations to take on ethical responsibility more effectively according to their capabilities. Virtues can be developed and trained like muscles in a physical body. They shape one's behaviour towards others.

To develop a corporate culture that seeks to achieve as many SDGs as possible requires a corresponding mindset of the employees and should have appropriate resources available. Which of Silvia Schlager's virtues (2009; see also online material at companion website) should be particularly promoted for this purpose?

Getting an overview of consequences

Taking on responsibility means getting an overview of the intended and unintended consequences of one's activity. Only when the consequences for all concerned have been weighed up, to see whether they are more beneficial or harmful, one can accept or refuse the activity as good or bad according to utilitarian ethics. A rough utilitarian assessment of all consequences of an action can be conducted by using the following table with the following example: Shall we bribe an official who has gambling debts in order to be awarded a state contract or not? Or who of the stakeholders (including nature) will profit from CO_2-neutral products and production processes? Who will suffer?

This further activity supports the answer to questions 2.1 in the SCR checklist (worksheet 5). The following example demonstrates a utilitarian ethical stakeholder analysis for bribery: To what extent is the payment of bribes to a politician in debt beneficial and/or harmful for involved stakeholders? Try to weigh the overall results:

List of all affected stakeholders	Beneficial consequences (e.g. bribing an official)	Harmful consequences (e.g. bribing an official)
Politician	Can pay back his/her debts	Risk of being caught
Company	New contract	Penalty in case of discovery
Employee	Job security	
Customer		Receives lower quality because bribe must be refinanced
Competitor		Loses out despite possibly better product range

Competitor's employees		Risk of losing their job security
. . .	. . .	. . .
. . .	. . .	. . .
. . .	. . .	. . .
First result: **Based on utilitarian ethics, bribing an official causes more harm than benefit.**	**Bribing an official is generally beneficial:** **3 × (+).**	**Bribing an official is generally harmful:** **5 × (−).**

Understanding ethical duties

Besides defining consequences, ethical responsibility is an important authority regarding duties to be followed, such as what one should do or what one should desist from doing. By saying that one has to treat every human being not only as a means but also as an end, Immanuel Kant's categorical imperative laid the foundations for such an ethical duty (Kant, 2008). This imperative also postulates that one must respect the dignity of all human beings; this means concretely their autonomy – the fundament of human rights. In this respect, it represents an 'anthropocentric' ethics (centred on human beings).

The UN Global Compact (www.unglobalcompact.org) is the most widespread and accepted catalogue of duties, including human rights, that corporate responsibility should comply with, according to several surveys. Discuss with your colleagues the ten principles of the UN Global Compact and how far they apply Kant's categorical imperative. Which principles do not comply with it? Which principles go beyond anthropocentric duty? How could one formulate a 'biocentric' (centred on all living beings) categorical imperative? Which of the human rights (online available at companion website) indicate how much workers should be paid along the supply chain?

Sustainable responsibility at your university

Use the SCR model to check how far your university's courses and activities – teaching, research, further education, facilities, food, etc. – respect and apply sustainable responsibility. Which responsibility profile would you suggest for your university? Use the SCR checklist to get a deeper insight into sustainable responsibility activities. Try to develop recommendations as to how your university could improve its SCR profile.

Strategic management project

To provide practical experience of sustainably responsible activities, the study programme could give students social and/or environmental assignments which have real impact. Such fieldwork programmes were successfully executed by students from the international management study programme at the School of Management and Law at Zurich University of Applied Sciences, Switzerland.

In groups of four to six, they took on a predefined assignment, contracted by the supervisors with NGOs, companies, or start-ups, or they selected their own project. For example, the students:

- Introduced and organised a new waste recycling system in Ghana together with a local university.

- Raised funds for Syrian refugees and collected and prepared medical equipment and clothes to be transported to relevant areas.

- Organised fundraising events for an orphanage in Nigeria.

- Investigated the shadowy side of the supply chain for leather production and proposed a socially and environmentally clean supply chain to a luxury leather bag producer. The company was then able to use its environmentally friendly track record in subsequent marketing campaigns.

- Developed a strategy for transferring Swiss experience in organic agriculture to China.

Students were not only tasked with doing the practical work to complete these assignments but also had to strategically plan and execute their projects, integrating the economic, social, and ecological impact and working out how to address this impact. Furthermore, they also had to write reports (around 50 pages), where they described the efficiency and effectiveness of their sustainably responsible activities. These projects contribute to the Sustainable Development Goals. As part of their assignment, the students could reflect on how they contribute to one or more of the SDGs.

Further information can be obtained from mathias.schuez@zhaw.ch.

Further readings

Braungart, M., and W. McDonough (2002), *Cradle to Cradle: Remaking the Way We Make Things*, New York: North Point Press; Mulhall, D., and M. Braungart (2010), *Cradle to Cradle: Criteria for the Built Environment*, Nunspeet: Duurzaam Gebouwd/MBDC (2013): *Cradle to Cradle Certified – Product Standard Version 3.0*, ed. by Cradle to Cradle Products

Innovation Institute, www.c2ccertified.org/images/uploads/C2CCertified_Product_Standard_V3.pdf, accessed 14 September 2016.

> The first reference is for the classic in new ecological thinking and acting in business, highlighting how mankind could ideally develop an economy without any waste. Instead, all waste generated by one product should be used as a resource for other products, inspired by the way nature produces no waste but rather has closed cycles of life where one living being uses the output of other living beings as an important resource for survival (i.e. cradle to cradle). The other references give more practical hints on how to implement the cradle-to-cradle approach through technical designs.

Freeman, E. R., K. E. Martin, and B. L. Parmar (2020), *The Power of And – Responsible Business Without Trade-Offs*, New York, NY: Columbia University Press.

> This book discusses the need for a new entrepreneurship that is able to balance the three dimensions of responsibility and the demands of sustainability in a way that avoids trade-offs. As long as trade-offs on the part of decision-makers are noted in their actions, the profits gained are based somewhere in the value chain on unfair exchanges.

Porter, M. E., and M. R. Kramer (2008), 'Strategy and Society: The Link Between Competitive Advantage and Corporate Social Responsibility', in M. Porter (ed.), *On Competition*, Updated and expanded edn, Boston, MA: Harvard Business School Publishing, 479–503.

> This article thoroughly eliminates the prejudice that social responsibility is an obstacle for profitability in business. Moreover, it includes many business opportunities which have yet to be exploited. The authors show how to use strategic planning in order to gain a competitive advantage.

Schüz, M. (2019), *Applied Business Ethics – Foundations of Study and Practice*, Singapore and London: World Scientific Publishing.

> The textbook introduces the foundation and application of business ethics and sustainable corporate responsibility (SCR) in the business world. The provided reasons for business ethics are complemented with practical examples of real-life situations and provide numerous exercises to help reader grasp complex issues, moral dilemmas, and business risks better. It demonstrates how satisfactory solutions can be found in a systematic and strategic way, referring to interdisciplinary research and philosophical reflections.

Verbin, I. (2020), *Corporate Responsibility in the Digital Age*, London and New York: Routledge.

> The book provides a roadmap to help organisations adopt corporate responsibility and sustainability practices in a digital era. It is a step-by-step guide to putting principles into business practice. Each chapter is linked to relevant UN Sustainable Development Goals (SDGs) with relevant real-world examples.

Wettstein, F. (2022), *Business and Human Rights – Ethical, Legal, and Managerial Perspectives*, Cambridge: Cambridge University Press.

> Compliance with human rights along supply chains is increasingly demanded by international legal systems (e.g. EU-Greendeal). This is the first textbook that comprehensively combines business and human rights. It covers legal and non-legal perspectives and provides a solid foundation for cross-disciplinary conversations. It consolidates and synthesises all debates on how human rights can be integrated in business practice.

References

Ansoff, H.I. (1988): *The New Corporate Strategy*, New York: Wiley.

Aragón-Correa, A.J. et al. (2017): 'Sustainability Management Teaching Resources and the Challenge of Balancing Planet, People, and Profits', *Academy of Management Learning and Education*, Vol. 16(3): 469–83, https://journals.aom.org/doi/10.5465/amle.2017.0180.

Aristotle (2009): *The Nicomachean Ethics*, Oxford: Oxford University Press.

Barbier, E.B. (1987): 'The Concept of Sustainable Economic Development', *Environmental Conservation*, Vol. 14(2): 101–10.

Bayertz, K. (1995): 'Eine kurze Geschichte der Herkunft der Verantwortung', in K. Bayertz (ed.), *Verantwortung: Prinzip oder Problem*, Darmstadt, Germany: Wissenschaftliche Buchgesellschaft, 3–71.

Blackmore, C., J. Chapman, and R. Ison (2012): *Systems Thinking: Understanding Sustainability*, The Open University, http://openlearn.open.ac.uk/mod/oucontent/view.php?id=405678, accessed 26 September 2012.

Boddy, D. (2008): *Management: An Introduction*, 4th edn, Harlow, UK: Pearson.

Braungart, M., and W. McDonough (2002): *Cradle to Cradle: Remaking the Way We Make Things*, New York: North Point Press.

Brundtland Commission (1987): *Our Common Future: Towards Sustainable Development*, Chapter 2, World Commission on Economic Development (WCED), www.un-documents.net/ocf-02.htm, accessed 24 September 2012.

Büchler, J.-P. (2014): *Strategie entwickeln, umsetzen, optimieren*, München: Pearson.

Cannon, T. (2012): *Corporate Responsibility: Governance, Compliance and Ethics in a Sustainable Environment*, 2nd edn, Harlow, UK: Pearson.

Chan, J., M. Selden, and P. Ngai (2020): *Dying for an iPhone – Apple, Foxconn, and the Lives of China's Workers*, London: Pluto Press.

Collins, D., and P. Kanashiro (2021): *Business Ethics: Best Practices for Designing and Managing Ethical Organizations*, 3rd edn, Thousand Oaks, CA: Sage Publications.

Cordero, R.A. (1988): 'Aristotle and Fair Deals', *Journal of Business Ethics*, September, Vol. 7(9), 681–90.

Crawford, D. (2005): *The Balanced Scorecard and Corporate Social Responsibility: Aligning Values for Profit*, www.greenbiz.com/news/2005/10/23/balanced-scorecard-and-corporate-social-responsibility-aligning-values-profit, accessed 25 September 2012.

Dobson, P., K. Starkey, and J. Richards (2004): *Strategic Management: Issues and Cases*, Oxford, UK: Blackwell.

Elkington, J. (1997): *Cannibals with Forks: The Triple Bottom Line of 21st Century Business*, Oxford, UK: Capstone Publishing.

ERC, Ethics Research Center (2016): *Global Business Ethics Survey – Measuring Risk and Promoting Workplace Integrity*, Arlington, VA: ECI, https://higherlogicdownload.s3.amazonaws.com/THEECOA/1651fdd3-e31c-4ac8-a93d-9b99f9e75727/UploadedImages/research/GBESFinal.pdf, accessed 12 September 2016.

Ernst & Young (2013): *Six Growing Trends in Corporate Sustainability: An Ernst & Young Survey in Cooperation with GreenBiz Group*, www.ey.com/Publication/vwLUAssets/Six_growing_trends_in_corporate_sustainability_2013/$FILE/Six_growing_trends_in_corporate_sustainability_2013.pdf, accessed 14 September 2016.

Farmer, R.N., and B.M. Richman (1965): *Comparative Management and Economic Progress*, Homewood, IL: Irwin.

Fischer, M. (2017): *Online-Tool for Winterthur SCR-Model*, https://scr-schuez.maecefischer.ch/home, accessed 18 June 2022.

Freeman, E.R., K.E. Martin, and B.L. Parmar (2020): *The Power of And – Responsible Business Without Trade-Offs*, New York, NY: Columbia University Press.

Glencore (2021): *Strengthening our Performance – Sustainability Report 2021*, www.glencore.com/.rest/api/v1/documents/59122a94d9c86731923614217b1ce1dc/GLEN_2021_sustainability_report.pdf, accessed 23 September 2022.

GRI (Global Reporting Initiative) (2022): *Global Reporting Standards*, www.globalreporting.org/how-to-use-the-gri-standards/gri-standards-english-language/, accessed 24 September 2022.

Harvey, F., and H. Pidd (2011): 'Glencore is in Dark Ages Compared with Rivals, Says NGO Boss', *The Guardian*, 19 July, www.theguardian.com/business/2011/may/19/glencore-in-dark-ages-says-ngo-boss, accessed 22 January 2014.

Hick, M. (2012): 'Children Found Working in Foxconn iPhone Factory', *Huffington Post*, www.huffingtonpost.co.uk/2012/01/17/children-found-working-in-iphone-foxconn-factory_n_1209953.html, accessed 25 September 2012.

Hill, C.W.L., and R.J. Gareth (2012): *Strategic Management: An Integrated Approach*, 10th revised edn, Mason, OH: South Western Educational Publishing.

Ikerd, J. (1999): *Rethinking the Economics of Self-Interests*, http://web.missouri.edu/ikerdj/papers/Rethinking.html, accessed 27 September 2012.

IPCC (2022): *Climate Change 2022*, Impacts, Adaptation and Vulnerability – Summary for Policy Makers, https://report.ipcc.ch/ar6wg2/pdf/ IPCC_AR6_WGII_SummaryForPolicymakers.pdf.

Johnson, G., K. Scholes, and R. Whittington (2005): *Exploring Corporate Strategy*, 7th revised edn, Harlow, UK: Pearson Education.

Kant, I. (2008): *Groundwork of the Metaphysics of Morals*, Radford, VA: Wilder Publications.

Kirchherr, J., D. Reike, and M. Hekkert (2017): 'Conceptualizing the Circular Economy: An Analysis of 114 Definitions', *Resources, Conservation and Recycling*, vol. 127, 221–32.

Kogure, S. (2012): *A Lesson Not Yet Learned*, www.ibanet.org/Article/Detail.aspx?ArticleUid=6c2935ff-c51d-4254-a334-4f5fbc5667d4, accessed 26 September 2012.

Kohlberg, L. (1971): 'From Is to Ought', in T. Mischel (ed.), *Cognitive Development and Epistemology*, New York: Academic Press, 151–235.

Kotter, J.P., and J.L. Heskett (1992): *Corporate Culture and Performance*, New York: The Free Press.

KPMG (2011): *KPMG International Survey of Corporate Responsibility Reporting 2011*, www.kpmg.com/Global/en/IssuesAndInsights/ArticlesPublications/corporate-responsibility/Documents/2011-survey.pdf, accessed 16 June 2014.

KPMG (2015): *Currents of Change – The KPMG Survey of Corporate Responsibility Reporting 2015*, https://assets.kpmg.com/content/dam/kpmg/pdf/2016/02/kpmg-international-survey-of-corporate-responsibility-reporting-2015.pdf, accessed 15 January 2016.

Lacy, P., T. Cooper, R. Hayward, and L. Neuberger (2010): *A New Era of Sustainability: UN Global Compact – Accenture CEO Study 2010*, www.accenture.com/SiteCollection Documents/PDF/Accenture_A_New_Era_of_Sustainability_CEO_Study.pdf, accessed 31 March 2014.

Mey, S., G. Cheney, and J. Roper (eds.) (2007): *The Debate Over Corporate Social Responsibility*, Oxford, UK: Oxford University Press.

Michelini, G. et al. (2017): 'From Linear to Circular Economy: PSS Conducting the Transition', *ScienceDirect, Procedia CIRP*, Vol. 64, 2–6, www.Sciencedirect.com.

NN (2012): 'Foxconn: Suizide bei Mitarbeitern', *Die Welt kompakt*, www.welt.de/print/welt_kompakt/print_wirtschaft/article109439140/Foxconn-Suizide-bei-Mitarbeitern.html, accessed 25 September 2012.

Pagano, A.M. (1987): *Criteria for Ethical Decision Making*, UIC – College of Business Administration Research Paper Series, No. 10–05, https://papers.ssrn.com/sol3/papers.cfm?abstract_id=1708237, accessed 22 April 2021.

Piaget, J. (1932): *Le jugement moral chez l'enfant*, Paris: Presses Universitaires de France.

Picht, G. (1969): 'Der Begriff der Verantwortung', in *Wahrheit – Vernunft – Verantwortung: Philosophische Studien*, Stuttgart, Germany: Klett, 318–42.

Porter, M.E. (1985): *Competitive Advantage: Creating and Sustaining Superior Performance*, New York: The Free Press.

Porter, M.E. (2008): 'The Five Competitive Forces That Shape Strategy', in M. Porter (ed.), *On Competition*, updated and expanded edn, Boston, MA: Harvard Business School Publishing, 3–35.

Porter, M.E., and M.R. Kramer (2006): 'Strategy and Society: The Link between Competitive Advantage and Corporate Social Responsibility', *Harvard Business Review* (December): 78–91, http://efnorthamerica.com/documents/events/ccc2008/Mark-Kramer-Keynote/Strategy-Society.pdf, accessed 15 March 2014.

PwC (2010): *CSR Trends 2010*, www.pwc.com/ca/en/sustainability/publications/csr-trends-2010-09.pdf, accessed 25 May 2012.

PwC (2014): *Business Success Beyond the Short Term: CEO Perspectives on Sustainability*, www.pwc.com/gx/en/sustainability/ceo-views/assets/pwc-ceo-summary-sustainability.pdf, accessed 14 September 2016.

Redaktion (2012): *Wie oft muss Tepco in Fukushima die eigene Inkompetenz beweisen bevor eingeschritten wird?*, www.planet-burgenland.at/2012/06/08, accessed 2 October 2012.

Rieckmann, H. (2000): *Managen und Führen am Rande des 3. Jahrtausends*, 2nd edn, Frankfurt, Germany: Peter-Lang.

Ritzen, S., and G.Ö. Sandström (2017): 'Barriers to the Circular Economy – Integration of Perspectives and Domains', *ScienceDirect, Procedia CIRP*, Vol. 64, 7–12, www.sciencedirect.com.

RobecoSAM (2022): *Measuring ESG's Impact on Stock Performance*, www.robeco.com/en/insights/2021/03/measuring-esgs-impact-on-stock-performance.html, accessed 25 September 2022.

SACOM (2012): *New iPhone, Old Abuses: Have Working Conditions at Foxconn in China Improved?*, 20 September, http://sacom.hk/reportnew-iphone-old-abuses-have-working-conditions-at-foxconn-in-china-improved/, accessed 17 June 2014.

Sandel, M.J. (2009): *Justice: What's the Right Thing to Do?* New York: Farrar, Straus and Giroux.

Satoko, O. (2011): 'Former Fukushima Governer Sato Eisaku Blasts METI-TEPCO Alliance: 'Government Must Accept Responsibility for Defrauding the People',' *The Asia-Pacific Journal*, Vol. 9(15), https://apjjf.org/2011/9/15/Onuki-Satoko/3514/article.html, accessed 19 June 2021.

Schlager, S. (2009): *The Power of Action Values: 80 Values as a Foundation for a Constructive Change*, Vienna, Austria: Eutonia.

Schüz, M. (1999): *Werte – Risiko – Verantwortung: Dimensionen des Value Managements*, Munich, Germany: Gerling Akademie Verlag.

Schüz, M. (2012): 'Sustainable Corporate Responsibility: The Foundation of Successful Business in the New Millennium', *Central European Business Review*, Vol. 2, 7–15, http://cebr.vse.cz/cebr/article/view/34, accessed 14 January 2014.

Schüz, M. (2017): *Foundations of Ethical Corporate Responsibility*, Winterthur: ZHAW.

Schüz, M. (2019): *Applied Business Ethics – Foundations for Study and Practice*. Singapore and London: World Scientific Publication.

Schüz, M. (2021a): *Grundlagen der ethischen Unternehmensverantwortung*, 2nd extended edn, SML Essentials No. 1, Zurich, Switzerland: vdf-Hochschulverlag der ETH.

Schüz, M. (2021b): *Angewandte Unternehmensethik – Grundlagen für Studium und Praxis*, 2nd extended edn, München: Pearson Studium.

SDG (2022): *United Nations' Sustainable Development Goals*, www.un.org/fr/sustainable-development-goals

Shell (2015): *Elements of Sustainable Development: Environment, Society and Economy*, http://.shell-livewire.org/business-library/employing-people/management/sustainable-development/Sustainable-development, accessed 16 February 2017.

Simmel, G. (1989): *Philosophie des Geldes* [1900], Frankfurt a. M.: Suhrkamp.

Smith, A. (2016): *The Theory of Moral Sentiments*, Los Angeles, CA: Enhanced Media.

Stead, J.G., and W.E. Stead (2013): *Sustainable Strategic Management*, 2nd edn, Sheffield, UK: Greenleaf Publishing.

Steffen et al. (2015): 'Planetary Boundaries: Guiding Human Development on a Changing Planet with Supplementary Materials', *Science*, Vol. 347(6223), 1259855, https://science.sciencemag.org/content/347/6223/1259855, accessed 16 May 2021.

Tepco (2010): *Vision 2020: Medium to Long-term Growth Declaration*, Press Release, 13 September, www.tepco.co.jp/en/press/corp-com/release/10091301-e.html, accessed 25 January 2014.

Ts and dpa (2012): *Foxconn-Arbeiter sterben fürs iPad*, www.manager-magazin.de/unternehmen/it/0,2828,druck-824713,00.html, accessed 25 September 2012.

Weihrich, H. (1982): 'The TOWS Matrix: A Tool for Situational Analysis', *Long Range Planning* (April): 54–66, www.usfca.edu/fac-staff/weihrich/docs/tows.pdf, accessed 15 December 2013.

Acknowledgements

First of all, I would like to thank the authors of the different chapters again for contributing to the book, for their enthusiasm, and for their hard work on this in addition to their 'normal' workload! A big thanks goes to Ella McFarlane from Routledge for answering *every* question I had!

Thanks to the following colleagues for peer-reviewing the chapters and for their very useful comments and suggestions: Alison Allen, Christina Bache, Barbara Beeby, Craig Bickerton, Serena Brown, Kelly Coate, Doug Cole, Andy Cooke, Alison Edmonds, Barbara Henchey, Lavinia-Cristina Iosif-Lazar, Jennifer Leigh, Florian Kapmeier, Anne Keegan, Caroline Aggestam Pontopiddan, Julie Rosborough, Alfred Rosenbloom, Rajul Singh, David Smith, Roy Smith, and last but definitely not the least, Fiona Winfield. Sincere apologies if we missed anyone – so many people have been so generous with their time.

A big 'thank-you' also to our students who tried and tested many of the ideas in this book!

It was a pleasure to work with Rebecca Marsh (first and second edition) and Ella McFarlane (third edition) and her teams from Routledge – thanks for the countless emails you answered patiently and with great expertise! I would also like to thank John Stuart again for supporting the idea of this book wholeheartedly in 2014 and making it happen. And to Zoe Robinson, Jonas Haertle, and Mette Morsing for writing the forewords for each edition, and to Jerome Baddley and all the others who answered to my 'poem competition'.

A special thanks belongs to my husband, Eric Molthan-Hill, again, and our children, Ansgar and Kiera Molthan-Hill, who stepped in to do many tasks so that I could work on the third edition of this book.

And finally, to the founder of my church, Martin Luther, who taught me about trust and hope in God by writing the following:

> Und wenn morgen die Welt unterginge, so wuerde ich heute noch
> ein Apfelbaeumchen pflanzen!
> (And if the world would end tomorrow, I would still plant an
> apple tree today.)

Although my sincere hope is that humankind will come to reason in time, in this hope I have written some of the chapters, especially the new one, climate change mitigation education, and edited the third edition.

Biographies

Dr Talal Alsharief completed his PhD in 2021, titled 'Improving Patient Flow: Examining the Application of Lean Management and Theory of Constraints Across Different Healthcare Settings', in Operations and Supply Chain Management from Nottingham Trent University. Alsharief also holds two master's degrees, one in Information Technology Management from Valparaiso University, USA, and the second in Global Supply Chain Management from Nottingham Trent University. He has presented several papers across the UK and Europe and has most recently been awarded a certificate in Circular Economy and Sustainability Strategies from the Judge Business School at the University of Cambridge.

Dr Angelo Pietro Bisignano is Director of the International BBA – Global Business at EDHEC Business School. After completing a Laurea Magistrale at the University of Calabria in Italy, he was awarded a PhD in Entrepreneurship at Nottingham Trent University. He owned Dual Blaze, a consultancy firm that supported companies in embedding sustainable practices in their strategies. He mentors start-ups aiming at improving the lives of marginalised people across Europe and in 'base of the pyramid' markets.

Dr Lia Blaj-Ward is Associate Professor (Teaching and Scholarship) at Nottingham Trent University. Her pedagogic practice and scholarship focus on the role that university curricula and experiences play in developing students' future-oriented aspirations (e.g. through projects involving student–staff co-creation or through exploring various aspects of climate change education at university). She is Associate Editor for the *Higher Education Research and Development* journal and, in 2022, she was a joint winner of the journal's inaugural Associate Editor of the Year award. Lia is an Advance HE Aurora Mentor and, since 2019, she has also designed and facilitated bespoke week-long work experience programmes for pre-18 students from a local girls-only school.

Seraphina Brown is Environmental Officer at the University of Nottingham, where she is responsible for a variety of sustainability initiatives targeting the staff and students, spanning the areas of transport, behaviour change and communication, biodiversity, and environmental reporting. Seraphina previously worked for Nottingham Trent University as Education for Sustainable Development Officer, embedding sustainability within the curriculum in the schools of business, law, and social sciences, as well as having a key role in sustainability events at the university. She received her MSc in Environmental Management from the University of Nottingham after having studied at undergraduate level for a BA in Archaeology and Geography.

Elaine Cohen is an expert and influential voice in the field of CSR (corporate social responsibility) and sustainability strategy, reporting, and the CSR interface with HR (human resources) management. She is the author of three books on sustainable practice and reporting, including the first-ever book on CSR and HR (*CSR for HR: A Necessary Partnership for Advancing Responsible Business Practices*, Greenleaf Publishing, 2010). Elaine writes regularly for her *CSR Reporting* blog and other publications and is a frequent chair and speaker at sustainability conferences. As the founder manager of Beyond Business Ltd (www.b-yond.biz), Elaine works with many clients around the globe. Elaine gained over 20 years of business experience in executive positions with Procter & Gamble and Unilever prior to founding Beyond Business Ltd in 2005. Elaine was selected as one of the 100 Top Thought Leaders in Trustworthy Business Behaviour in 2014 and tweets as @elainecohen.

Al Dharmasasmita is Consultant Facilitator for the Carbon Management Programme for Businesses in Nottingham and the East Midlands via Nottingham Business School (NBS), Nottingham Trent University (NTU). Al specialises in Sustainability, the UN Sustainable Development Goals (SDGs), and Education for Sustainable Development (ESD) competencies in business leaders. One who believes that we are all change agents, Al has been involved in educating NBS students and training SMEs in building back better (or building back forward) through the SDGs, decarbonisation strategy, and leadership skills apt for the 21st Century since 2010. Al worked for NTU's Green Academy from 2013 to 2021, embedding the SDGs in all faculties and co-designing and co-leading the Sustainability in Practice online certificate for all NTU students and staff, which was one of the first courses of its kind and shortlisted twice for a Green Gown Award.

Dr Michael Ehret is Professor of Marketing and Digitalisation at the University of Graz. His research focus is on service governance and contract innovation, business model innovation, in particular in business markets and service systems. A particular research focus is on the role of service business models and service institutions in economic development. Previously, he held positions as Reader in Technology Management in the Division of Marketing at Nottingham Business School, Assistant Professor at Freie Universität Berlin, and Visiting Professor at Technical University Munich and Universität Rostock, Germany. Michael publishes regularly in international leading journals, such as the *Journal of Marketing*, *Industrial Marketing Management* and the *Journal of Business Research*. He serves as Senior Associate Editor in the *Journal of Business and Industrial Marketing*, with special responsibilities for the role of business-to-business ecosystems in emerging economies. He is a member in editorial review boards of internationally leading journals, such as the *Journal of Business Research*, *Industrial Marketing Management*, and *Service Science*. Michael also has experience in applied research and consultancy work with companies such as Mercedes Benz, BioCity Nottingham, Roland Berger Strategy Consultants, and Springer Publishing.

Dr Rosa Maria Fernandez Martin is, since June 2023, Senior Lecturer in Economics and Finance at Keele Business School. She previously worked as Associate Professor in Global Sustainable Development at the University of Warwick, where she led the provision on Carbon Literacy and Corporate Social Responsibility (as critical business engagement in sustainability transitions). She also taught modules related to the connection between money, debt, and sustainable development. Before that she worked at the University of Chester for seven years, where she was Programme Leader of Economics and Deputy Head of the Department of Social and Political Science. Previous appointments include the University of Birmingham, as Teaching Fellow responsible for Environmental Economics, and UNED (National Distance Education University – Spain). She was also Associate Tutor in business ethics and sustainability for the University of Bradford and held Visiting Researcher positions at the University of Exeter, York (Canada) and Bradford. Her main research interests relate to renewable energy, energy and food poverty, climate change, corporate social responsibility, and education for sustainable development. She has published numerous articles and book chapters on those topics. She is the convenor of the UACES (Academic Association for Contemporary European Studies) Research Network on the Role of Europe in Global Challenges: Climate Change and Sustainable Development, and she has recently become UACES Treasurer and Trustee. She regularly evaluates research projects for the COST initiative of the European Commission and the ESRC on sustainability-related themes.

Dr Biswaraj Ghosh, PhD, is currently serving as Assistant Manager at Uniqus Consultech (formerly SustainPlus), India, advising clients across industries on their sustainability reporting practice, including integrated reporting, ESG reporting, TCFD, CDP, SASB and GRI compliance, ESG strategy, as well as decarbonisation strategies. Other than this, he is also involved in developing and delivering client workshops on different aspects of sustainability. Additionally, Dr Ghosh serves as Program Director at Quantum Holistic Advisory Services, a niche family-owned management consultancy based in India. In 2022, he has been recognised as a winner under the Emerging Sustainability Professional category. Previously, he has served as Lecturer on Sustainability and Accounting at Nottingham Trent University, UK, and as Visiting Scholar in Germany. Besides this, he has been involved in a number of research projects at the University of Nottingham, University of Derby, as well as Nottingham Trent University. Previously, Biswaraj completed his PhD from Nottingham Trent University, focusing on Management Controls for Sustainability in the UK context. He is well-published in journals, conferences, and book chapter projects. His interests include sustainability accounting and controls, environmental management accounting, transformational leadership, stakeholder management, extra-financial reporting, as well as sustainability strategy. He has been a recipient of several academic awards and scholarships. Dr Ghosh completed an MSc in Corporate Social Responsibility from the University of Nottingham and holds a first-class BA (Hons) degree in Finance, Accounting, and Management from the same university. He has also graduated from a UN award–winning leadership programme and is a recipient of the prestigious Active Citizen and ParliaMentor award.

Dr Helen Goworek is Associate Professor in Marketing at Durham University Business School. She is Co-Lead for Teaching and Research in the UN PRME

Working Group on Climate Change and Environment. She is a Fashion Marketing graduate and gained her master's degree while working in the industry in buying and design management roles. She is the author of three books about the fashion business and retailing that have been translated into Spanish, Russian, and Chinese. She has written book chapters and articles on retail buying, product development, and sustainability and a PhD comprising these topics. Helen has also co-edited journal special issues and participated in funded research projects into sustainable clothing.

Angela Green is Associate Professor in Marketing at Durham University. She is currently leading a module in social marketing, and her primary interests are in sport and digital marketing. She is keen to explore the ways in which digital marketing technologies can influence sustainable practice. Her doctoral research focuses on mobile apps and their potential for brand engagement. Prior to joining Durham, Angela worked at Leeds Beckett University, where she developed the first Sport Marketing degree in British Higher Education. She has also developed digital marketing programmes of study for several developing nations. She has been Co-Chair for the Academy of Marketing Sport Marketing SIG and is Senior Fellow of the Higher Education Academy.

Dr Christian Herzig is Full Professor at the Justus Liebig University (JLU) Giessen, Germany, Chairman of the Board of Directors of JLU's Centre for Sustainable Food Systems, and Programme Director of the MSc programme 'Sustainable Food Economics' at the University's Faculty of Agricultural Sciences, Nutritional Sciences, and Environmental Management. His research revolves around food businesses' role in society, with a particular focus on sustainability management, assessment, and reporting. Christian has held full professorial positions at the University of Kassel, Germany, and Nottingham Trent University, UK. Prior to that, he was Assistant Professor in Sustainability Accounting and Reporting at the University of Nottingham, and Visiting Research Fellow at the Centre for Accounting, Governance, and Sustainability, University of South Australia. He stayed for over a year in South-East Asia (Indonesia, Thailand, the Philippines, and Vietnam), where he carried out an international capacity development and research project on environmental accounting and resource efficiency. During his stay in the Emilia Romagna region of Italy, he carried out a management project on the implementation of an ISO14001 environmental management system. Short-term academic appointments include visiting lectureships at the Free University, Berlin, Germany; the University of Basel, Switzerland; the Grand École in Agricultural, Food, and Environmental Sciences, France; and the Marmara University, Turkey. Christian holds a PhD in Economic and Social Sciences, an MA in Business Administration, and an MSc in Environmental Sciences.

Richard Holmes is a low-carbon consultant for the design and operation of buildings via the CIBSE Chartered Institute of Building Service Engineers, an MEI (Member of the Energy Institute), and a chartered environmentalist. After ten years working for the UK Energy Saving Trust's advice network, the European Energy Agency network, and a local authority carbon management team, Richard set up his own consultancy business (Third Stone Ltd) in 2005. He provides an advisory service to all users of energy, from the construction industry to businesses and public sector organisations. He has delivered training presentations for the Building Research Establishment and is a lecturer in Nottingham Business School and Nottingham Trent University's School of Architecture.

Dr Richard Howarth is Senior Lecturer in Marketing at Nottingham Business School, Nottingham Trent University. He is Assistant Course Leader for BA (Hons) Marketing and works closely with organisations and professional bodies (such as the CIM and MRS) to enhance the employability and workplace impacts of students and graduates. He is Sustainability Coordinator for the Marketing Department. His research interests are related to marketer competences, education for sustainable development, responsible marketer behaviour, sustainability and employability, and related learning and teaching interventions.

Dr Florian Kapmeier is Professor of Strategy at ESB Business School of Reutlingen University in Germany, Research Affiliate of the MIT Climate Pathways Project, and Partner of the US-based NGO Climate Interactive. For his research and teaching, he links system dynamics with empirical research on theory development and testing, focusing on organisational aspects of the managing complex problems, increasingly addressing environmental sustainability issues. Florian is Co-Developer of the interactive En-ROADS Climate Workshop and the role-playing game Climate Action Simulation with En-ROADS and co-author of scientific publications on En-ROADS. His engagement of bringing the Climate Action Simulation to Germany has been recognised by the renowned business school accreditation group AACSB as an 'Innovation that inspires'.

Dr Ellie Kennedy is Senior Educational Developer on the Curriculum Transformation Programme at the University of Nottingham. From 2012 to 2022, she worked as Senior Educational Developer at Nottingham Trent University. During that time, she made instrumental contributions to institution-wide strategic initiatives to embed inclusive practice into learning, teaching and assessment across all subject areas. She has also taught and researched in the fields of English for Academic Purposes, German Studies, and Gender Studies.

Dr Daniel King is Professor of Organisation Studies at Nottingham Trent University, UK, and Co-Director of the Centre for People, Work, and Organisational Practice. Dr King's research focuses on three main, interconnected areas: the contribution critical perspectives of management can make to transforming organisational practice; alternative organisations and alternative ways of organising; and critical perspectives of managing in the third sector. He has published in *Organization Research Methods*, *Organization Studies*, *Human Relations*, *Management Learning*, and *Nonprofit Voluntary Sector Quarterly*. Daniel reviews for a number of leading journals and is Editorial Board Member and Deputy Chair for *Work Employment and Society* and Co-Series Editor of Organizations and Activism, Bristol University Press. He has recently written an undergraduate textbook, *Organizational Behaviour* 4th Edition, with Scott Lawley (Oxford University Press) Email: daniel.king@ ntu.ac.uk.

Dr Jennifer S. A. Leigh is Professor of Management at Nazareth College in Rochester, NY, USA. Her scholarship addresses responsible management education, grand challenges, cross-sector social partnerships, humanistic management, and social innovation. In her area, she works with non-profit and social enterprise agencies focused on refugee resettlement and social impact through service-learning and project-based learning partnerships with her students and as a consultant. Over the past 15 years, Jennifer's editorial roles have spanned open-access publications, traditional peer-reviewed journals, edited books, and a book series. Currently, she is Co-Editor of the *Journal of Management Education* (JME), the 9-book Teaching Methods in Business Education series (Edgar Elgar), and is recent past Co-Editor for *Business Ethics, Environment and Responsibility* (BEER).

Dr Petra Molthan-Hill, PhD, is Professor of Sustainable Management and Education for Sustainable Development at Nottingham Business School, Nottingham Trent University (NTU), UK, and Co-Chair of the United Nations Principles for

Responsible Management Education (PRME) working group on climate change and environment. Molthan-Hill is an international multi-award-winning expert for climate change mitigation tools and education and leads the 'Climate Literacy Training for Educators, Communities, Organisations and Students' (CLT-ECOS) distributed worldwide. She is the editor of *The Business Student's Guide to Sustainable Management* and of *Storytelling for Sustainability in Higher Education: An Educator's Handbook* and the lead author of *The Handbook of Carbon Management: A step-by-step guide to high-impact climate solutions for every manager in every function*. She co-created NTU's 'Future Thinking' framework in 2016, which includes reference to the global Sustainable Development Goals (SDGs), and supported colleagues in all faculties to integrate the SDGs as Lead of NTU's Green Academy until 2021. Among others, she won Gold in the QS Reimagine Education Awards in Sustainability (CLT-ECOS) in 2021, 'The Guardian University Award 2015 for Business Partnership' (Greenhouse Gas Management Project), together with NetPositive, and the Green Gown Award in the Sustainability Professional Award Category in 2016.

Dr Sihle Ndlovu, Higher Colleges of Technology, UAE (GARD Division), is a linguist and sustainability enthusiast currently teaching the Sustainability courses at HCT. Sihle is interested in how language helps the framing of sustainability and how this is manifested in people's day-to-day lives. Sihle has worked with various higher and further education institutions in the UK, including Nottingham Business School, University of Leicester, Sheffield University, Nottingham College, among others.

Dr Tabani Ndlovu is Academic Programme Chair of Marketing at the Higher Colleges of Technology (HCT) in the United Arab Emirates. Prior to his current position, Tabani worked as Senior Lecturer in the Division of Marketing at Nottingham Business School, where he led a suite of postgraduate marketing courses. Outside academia, Tabani worked for a number of international organisations focusing on embedding sustainability into business operations. He holds a PhD in Corporate Governance, an MBA in Corporate Social Responsibility, as well as a BCom Honours degree in Marketing. His current research investigates the appetite for sustainable business practices in different international contexts; social and financial inclusion; cascading of responsible business values between boards and other sections of businesses; as well as corporate governance. Outside academia, Tabani sits on the boards of a number of East Midlands–based organisations and charities and works closely with the Institute of Directors (IoD), where he is a fellow, and explores closer links between the IoD and business schools.

Dr Lynn Oxborrow, DBA, is Professor of Sustainable Small Business Growth at Nottingham Trent University. Lynn's research interests focus on the textiles and clothing industry supply chain. She has been involved in research funded by Defra (UK Department for the Environment, Fisheries, and Rural Affairs) and WRAP (Waste and Resources Action Programme) to understand the environmental and commercial implications of producing clothing that circles for longer, and uncovering the consequences of asymmetrical buyer–supplier relationships in the sustainable clothing supply chain. Lynn's most recent research is exploring sustainable business models with small fashion businesses. Lynn has been instrumental in developing a suite of modules on global supply chain management, each incorporating aspects of ethics and sustainability, for undergraduate and postgraduate students. More generally, Lynn directs a suite of projects to help small businesses become more resilient, innovative, and productive, again considering sustainability as a cross-cutting theme. After she studied Social and Political Science at the University of Cambridge, Lynn's interest in supply chain management was generated through her extensive experience of working in fashion retail management.

Professor Carole Parkes is Emeritus Professor of Responsible Management and Leadership at the University of Winchester and has both a business and an academic background. Carole has been a champion for the UN-backed Principles for Responsible Management Education (PRME) since its inception in 2007 (whilst at Aston Business School). She is Former Chair of the PRME Chapter UK and Ireland, has been Member of the PRME Global Advisory Committee, and worked at the PRME Secretariat in New York as Researcher in Residence. At the PRME 10th Anniversary Global Forum in 2017, Carole was presented with a PRME Pioneer Award 'for her leadership and commitment to the development of PRME' and appointed UN PRME Special Advisor. Carole is Board Member of the Princes Trust – Business in the Community, and Trustee of Students Organising for Sustainability (SOS) and Fircroft College. She is also a journal and book editor and publishes on issues related to sustainability and social justice, including poverty as a challenge to business and management.

Helen Puntha leads the Nottingham Trent University (NTU) Green Academy department at NTU in the UK. The department works with colleagues across the academic disciplines to combine sustainability literacy with subject knowledge. A Senior Fellow of the Higher Education Academy, Helen has more than 15 years of experience in academic development, specialising in active, collaborative learning pedagogies; assessment and feedback; inclusive curriculum; decolonising education; sustainability education; and research-based learning. She co-founded the TILT SPUR scheme, which continues to provide undergraduate students with opportunities to undertake cutting-edge research in collaboration with academic staff, and she co-created the Sustainability in Practice online certificate for all NTU students and staff, which was one of the first courses of its kind and shortlisted for a Green Gown Award. She led the development of the NTU 'Future Thinking and the Sustainable Development Goals' module, which provides academic colleagues with a foundational knowledge of the UN Sustainable Development Goals to facilitate integration of sustainability across the academic disciplines.

Dr Natalie Ralph is a Research Fellow in Geopolitics of Energy at the University of Warwick, UK. As a Political Scientist, with much of her work being interdisciplinary, she researches, publishes, and teaches on renewable and low-carbon energy and technology, ethical business, policy and global governance, sustainability and circular economy, peacebuilding, and community approaches to sustainability/regeneration. She is currently an Honorary Fellow with the Alfred Deakin Institute for Citizenship and Globalisation, Deakin University, Australia; and Associate Investigator with the Australian Research Council Centre of Excellence in Electromaterials Science. Natalie has previously held policy or project management roles in Australian state governments, and to a lesser extent, business and consulting, NGOs, and in eco-communities, providing her with a rich understanding of different sectors and their cultures and needs.

Dr Lorinda Rowledge has 25 years' experience as Co-Founding Partner of a strategic sustainability consultancy, helping clients achieve breakthroughs in performance and impact by integrating ESG/sustainability into core business strategy, brand, product/service design, operations, and reporting. Her most recent book, *CrowdRising: Building a Sustainable World Through Mass Collaboration*, focuses on open innovation applied to business sustainability and social innovation. Lorinda also co-authored the book *Mapping the Journey: Case Studies in Strategy and Action Toward Sustainable Development*. Lorinda served as Founding Provost and Core Faculty for a pioneering MBA in Sustainability Business. Lorinda's passion is finding pathways to catalyse our collective wisdom to co-create a more socially just and environmentally regenerative future.

Dr phil. Mathias Schüz is Professor Emeritus for International Business and Responsible Leadership with exploratory focus on corporate responsibility and business ethics at the School of Management and Law at ZHAW (Zurich University of Applied Sciences), Switzerland. He studied physics, philosophy, and pedagogics and did his doctorate on philosophical consequences of quantum physics. He started his career in business as a trainee and key account manager at IBM. Together with the insurance entrepreneur Dr Rolf Gerling, he co-founded the Gerling Academy for Risk Research in Zurich and ran it for 14 years before becoming a senior lecturer at various universities, and finally professor at ZHAW. He has published numerous articles and books, such as one outlining a new philosophy of economy in German: *Werte – Risiko – Verantwortung. Dimensionen des Value Managements* [Values, Risk, Responsibility: Dimensions of the Value Management] (Munich, Germany: Gerling Akademie Verlag, 1999); another, published with two co-authors, deals with lies in management: *Lügen in der Chefetage* [Lies on the Executive Floor] (Weinheim, Germany: Wiley, 2007). His textbook *Applied Business Ethics – Foundations for Study and Practice* was published in 2019 (Singapore/London/New Jersey: World Scientific Publishing), while the German original appeared in a second, expanded edition at Pearson 2021 under the title *Angewandte Unternehmensethik – Grundlagen für Studium und Praxis*. As an emeritus professor, he is still a visiting faculty at the ZHAW and gives guest lectures and sessions at numerous universities internationally. Being a transdisciplinary researcher, he is co-editor of a new book series published by Springer-Nature titled *Transdisciplinary Management of Social and Ecological Crises* (also editor of first volume to be published 2023).

Dr Rajul Singh is Professor of Sustainable Business Management at Conestoga College in Ontario, Canada. Her teaching and research interests focus on global frameworks for sustainable development, sustainable business models, and the circular economy. As an educator, she teaches and develops curriculum for the Sustainable Business Management certificate and International Business Management degree programs. Her curricular interests include exploring best practices for responsible management education (RME). As a practitioner, she consults the Circular Opportunity Innovation Launchpad (COIL) for supporting organizations in embedding sustainability and circular economy principles in business practices in Canada. Rajul is the co-founder of the PRME at Conestoga initiative in the Conestoga School of Business and has been leading the school's sustainability strategy as a PRME signatory since 2020. As an active member of the UN PRME working group on climate change and environment, she is a certified trainer for the Carbon Literacy Training and an En-ROADS climate ambassador.

Dr Roy Stratton is Associate Professor in Operations and Supply Chain Management at Nottingham Business School, Nottingham Trent University, where he is actively involved in postgraduate teaching, research, and consultancy. His specialisation is in the management of complex delivery systems, including healthcare and project management. Previously, Roy worked for Rolls-Royce Aero Engines in an internal consultancy role and has since been actively involved in a wide range of industry-based and government-funded knowledge transfer research projects. He has published widely in both professional and academic journals and has co-authored two books. Roy has been awarded a BSc in Mechanical Engineering (Nottingham), an MSc in Manufacturing System Engineering (Warwick), and a PhD in Supply Chain Management (Nottingham Trent). Roy is a fellow of the Institute of Mechanical Engineers and currently on the board of directors of the Theory of Constraints International Certification Organization.

Dr Néstor Valero-Silva, PhD, worked in the petrochemical and ceramics industries after graduating as a chemical engineer. Néstor then read for a postgraduate degree in HRM, followed by an MA (Distinction) and a PhD in Management Systems at the University of Hull, UK. He held academic posts at the Universities of Hull and Lincoln before joining the Nottingham Business School. Néstor is a Chartered Member of the Chartered Institute of Personnel and Development and a Senior Fellow of the Higher Education Academy. His research interests emerged from his doctoral studies on systems thinking and management. He has explored and applied systematic thinking in the fields of business ethics, systems thinking and practice, social housing, and information systems, achieving numerous publications and over 16 doctoral completions. Néstor is currently a co-investigator and the chair of the Ethics Board Committee in the Horizon2020 Smart-BEEjS project on Positive Energy Districts, sustainability, and systemic thinking. This £4.5 million project is financed by the Marie Skłodowska-Curie Actions, Innovative Training Networks.

Dr Sigrun M. Wagner is Professor of Sustainability and International Business in the School of Business and Management at Royal Holloway, University of London,

UK. From 2019 to 2023, she was Head of the Department for Strategy, International Business, and Entrepreneurship. A multiple-teaching-award-winning academic, she led the introduction of a sustainability (now corporate responsibility) pathway for undergraduate students and took a lead role in the development of her institution's environmental strategy, working together with senior academic and professional services staff. In 2020, she published a textbook on environmental sustainability for businesses with Routledge and is co-authoring a book on sustainable engineering with colleagues from Royal Holloway, Leeds, and Suffolk. In 2021, she introduced Carbon Literacy Training to Royal Holloway. She is a senior fellow of the Higher Education Academy and a chartered management and business educator. Following her undergraduate degree in Germany, Sigrun completed her master's and PhD at Loughborough University.

Professor Patricia Werhane is Wicklander Chair of Business Ethics, Emerita, at DePaul University, and Ruffin Professor Emerita at the Darden School of Business, University of Virginia. Previously, she was Wirtenberger Professor of Business Ethics at Loyola University Chicago. She has been a Rockefeller fellow at Dartmouth College and a visiting fellow at Cambridge University. In 2014, she was Visiting Fulbright Specialist at All Hallows College in Dublin and a TEDx speaker there. In 2008, she was listed as one of the 100 most influential people in business ethics by *Ethisphere Magazine*. Professor Werhane is the author or over 100 articles and book chapters and the author or editor of 27 books, including *Adam Smith and His Legacy for Modern Capitalism*, *Moral Imagination and Management Decision-Making*, *Alleviating Poverty Through Profitable Partnerships* (with Kelley, Hartman, and Moberg), and *Obstacles to Ethical Decision-Making* (with Hartman, Archer, Englehardt, and Pritchard). Professor Werhane served on the board of Wanger Asset Trust from 1998 to 2006 and on the board of Wanger Asset Management from 2006 to 2007. She is a retired member of Chicago Network. She also serves on the Academic Advisory Board for the Business Roundtable Institute for Corporate Ethics. Professor Werhane is a founding member and past president of the Society of Business Ethics, past president of the American Society for Value Inquiry, and past president of the International Society for Business, Economics, and Ethics. She is the founding editor of *Business Ethics Quarterly*. Today she is the co-producer of an Emmy Award–winning television documentary series, *The Big Questions*, aired on Chicago Public Television PRIME.

Fiona Winfield was Nottingham Business School's Employability Manager until late 2022, having been a Course Leader and Principal Lecturer in Marketing for many years. She is a Senior Fellow HEA and a member of the CMI. She is now a Climate Literacy Trainer and one of the co-creators of NBS's online Climate Literacy and Net Zero courses. Fiona is also one of the authors of the *Handbook of Carbon Management* (2023), and her 'Future-proof your career' project won the EAUC's Green Gown Award 2017 in the Employability category. She also represented NTU in the finals of the 2022 awards in 'Tomorrow's Employees' category. As NBS Employability Manager, Fiona's role was to ensure that employability and NTU's employability taxonomy were firmly embedded within the curriculum, working with fellow academics. Encouraging links between sustainability and employability has been a particular interest for many years, as she firmly believes this will not only benefit the planet and society, it should also help students become more employable. She has been a member of NTU's Sustainable Development Academic Forum and the Employability Team's Sustainability Task Group. Prior to joining NTU, she worked in sales and marketing in the construction industry for nearly a decade.

Dr Aquila Yeong is Senior Lecturer in Operations Management at Nottingham Business School, Nottingham Trent University. His research interest centres on Productivity Improvement through Process Innovation via the alignment of Management Philosophy (such as Theory of Constraints), Technology, and People using Action Research. He contributes towards teaching in all levels: undergraduate, postgraduate, corporate/executive, and online MBA. He is also module leader for Operations Management–related modules, Project and Programme Strategies, and Data Analytics for Managerial Decision-Making. He was previously a research and development engineer with a telco company. His interest in developing solution-based products and services had driven him into managerial roles in engineering, sales and marketing, and customer service. Since joining the academia, he continues to collaborate actively with businesses through Knowledge Transfer Partnership, Productivity Through Innovation (PTI), and direct funding through the Authorised University Consultant platform. His recent work includes the development and deployment of S-DBR (Simplified Drum Buffer Rope) based Decision Support System for SME manufacturing companies. Impact includes more than doubled productivity, empowerment of shop floor personnel, and culture change. He is also a member of Theory of Constraints International Certification Organisation (TOCICO), Institution of Engineering and Technology (IET), and the Association for Project Management (APM).

Dr Maggie (Jing) Zeng is Associate Professor at the University of Kent. Her research interests focus on business ecosystems and strategic management of digital platforms and digital transformation by exploring the emergence, governance, and dynamic interaction between ecosystem players, and strategy in changing environments. She has published in a range of top-quality journals, such as *Journal of Management Studies, Journal of World Business, Strategic Organization, Industrial and Corporate Change, Management and Organization Review, British Journal of Management, Journal of Business Research, European Management Review,* and *International Business Review.*

Index

Printed in the United States
by Baker & Taylor Publisher Services